Ancient History for Beginners

The Ultimate 3-in-1 Guide to Egypt, Greece, and Rome, Major Events, and Key Figures That Shaped the Classical World

Free Bonus from Captivating History (Available for a Limited time)

Hi History Lovers!

Now you have a chance to join our exclusive history list so you can get your first history ebook for free as well as discounts and a potential to get more history books for free!

Simply visit the link below to join.

Or, Scan the QR code!

captivatinghistory.com/ebook

Also, make sure to follow us on Facebook, X, and YouTube by searching for Captivating History.

Table of Contents

Part 1: Ancient Egypt for Beginners

The Story of the Land of the Pharaohs Simplified for People Who Slept Through History Class

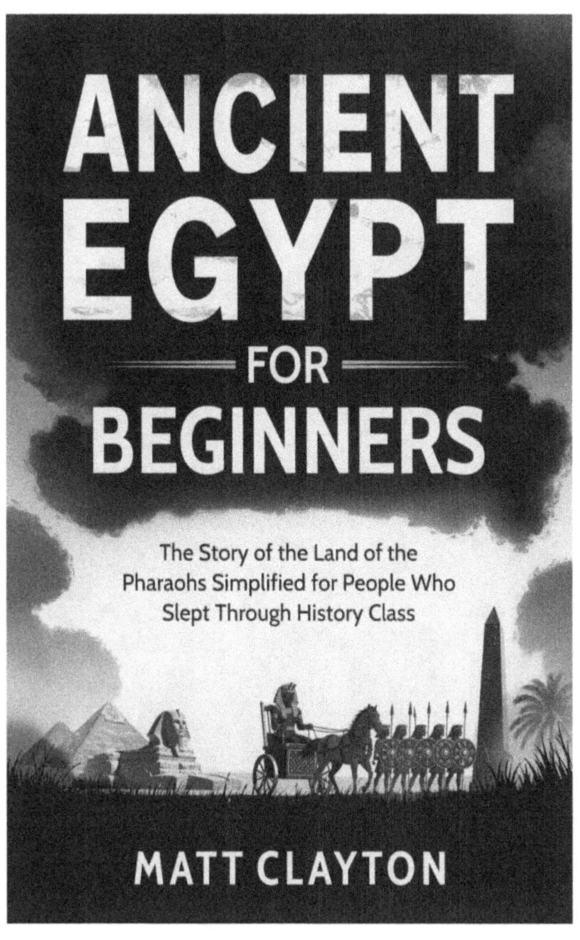

Introduction:
Why Ancient Egypt Still Matters

Picture this: while some people's ancestors were huddling in caves and figuring out which berries wouldn't kill them, the ancient Egyptians were building structures so massive and precise that people today still argue about how they pulled it off. They invented a writing system that began with over seven hundred symbols and expanded to thousands over time. They practiced early forms of cranial surgery to treat head injuries. They created a civilization that lasted three thousand years—that's longer than the time between the fall of Rome and today.

To put that in perspective, Cleopatra lived over two thousand years after the Great Pyramid was built, making her temporally closer to us than to its construction. When travelers visited Egypt during the Roman Empire, the pyramids were already ancient monuments that the Romans had inscribed with their own graffiti.

So why does ancient Egypt still grab our attention? Why do museums pack exhibitions of Egyptian artifacts with crowds? Why does a boy king who died young and had a relatively unremarkable political career remain one of the most famous people in history?

It's because ancient Egypt had it all. It had drama worthy of any modern soap opera—family betrayals, religious revolutions, mysterious deaths. There were military campaigns and empire-building that would make any strategy game player jealous. And we can't forget the engineering feats that baffle experts, even with our modern technology.

Perhaps most fascinating of all, the ancient Egyptians' obsession with death and the afterlife produced some of the most elaborate burial practices humanity has ever devised.

But ancient Egypt wasn't just flash and spectacle. It was a functional, sophisticated society that fed millions of people, maintained law and order, conducted international diplomacy, and created art and literature that still move us today. They did all of this without computers, electricity, or any of the technology we consider essential. They had the Nile River, human ingenuity, and an impressive ability to organize large numbers of people toward common goals.

This book will take you through the entire sweep of ancient Egyptian civilization, from around 3100 BCE when the land was first unified under a single ruler all the way to 30 BCE when Cleopatra died and Egypt became a province of the Roman Empire. That's roughly three millennia of history—longer than most civilizations have existed.

You don't need any prior knowledge about Egypt or ancient history. This book assumes you're starting from scratch, maybe with a few images of pyramids in your head and a vague memory of hearing about King Tut. That's perfect. We'll build up your understanding piece by piece, explaining everything as we go. This won't be a long, boring list of ruler after ruler either. We want to make sure you leave this book with the understanding of how people lived back then and the most important figures who impacted the land.

So let's journey back three thousand years and discover the land of the pharaohs. Welcome to ancient Egypt.

Chapter 1: Before the Pharaohs — The Gift of the Nile

Geography Is Destiny

If you want to understand ancient Egypt, you need to understand one simple fact: the Nile River made everything possible.

Without the Nile, Egypt would be nothing but an empty desert stretching from the Mediterranean Sea to central Africa. With the Nile, Egypt became one of the most powerful civilizations in history. The river didn't just provide water. It also provided life itself, and it shaped every aspect of Egyptian culture, religion, economy, and politics for thousands of years.

The Nile is the longest river in Africa, flowing roughly 4,160 miles from its sources in the heart of the continent northward to the Mediterranean. However, ancient Egyptians only controlled and cared about the final stretch, roughly 750 miles of valleys and deltas.

Unlike most rivers that flood unpredictably and destructively, the Nile's annual inundation usually followed a reliable pattern, though occasionally the floods failed or came too strong. Every summer, heavy rains in the Ethiopian Highlands would swell the river. By late July or early August, the floodwaters would reach Egypt, slowly rising over the riverbanks and spreading across the floodplain. The water would sit there for months, depositing rich, dark silt—essentially free fertilizer—across the fields. Then, just as predictably, the waters would recede in October, leaving behind moist, nutrient-rich soil perfect for planting.

This gave the ancient Egyptians a tremendous advantage. While the Nile's silt provided rich baseline nutrients, Egyptian farmers supplemented the soil with manure and ashes, and they practiced basic field management. Still, they didn't need to pray for rain or worry about droughts the way farmers in Mesopotamia did. They just needed to wait for the Nile to do its thing and then plant their seeds in the fresh mud. The system was so reliable that Egyptians divided their entire calendar around it: Akhet (inundation), Peret (growing season), and Shemu (harvest).

The result was an abundance of crops that could support a large population without everyone needing to farm. That freed people up to become craftsmen, priests, soldiers, scribes, and builders. In other words, the Nile's predictable flooding made civilization possible.

But here's where geography gets confusing for modern readers: Upper Egypt is in the south, and Lower Egypt is in the north.

Yes, you read that correctly. Upper Egypt is downstream from Lower Egypt. This seems backward until you remember that ancient Egyptians were thinking about elevation and the river's flow, not compass directions. The Nile flows from south to north, from the highlands down to the sea. Upper Egypt, in the south, is upriver and at a higher elevation. Lower Egypt, in the north, is downriver and at a lower elevation where the river spreads into the delta before reaching the Mediterranean.

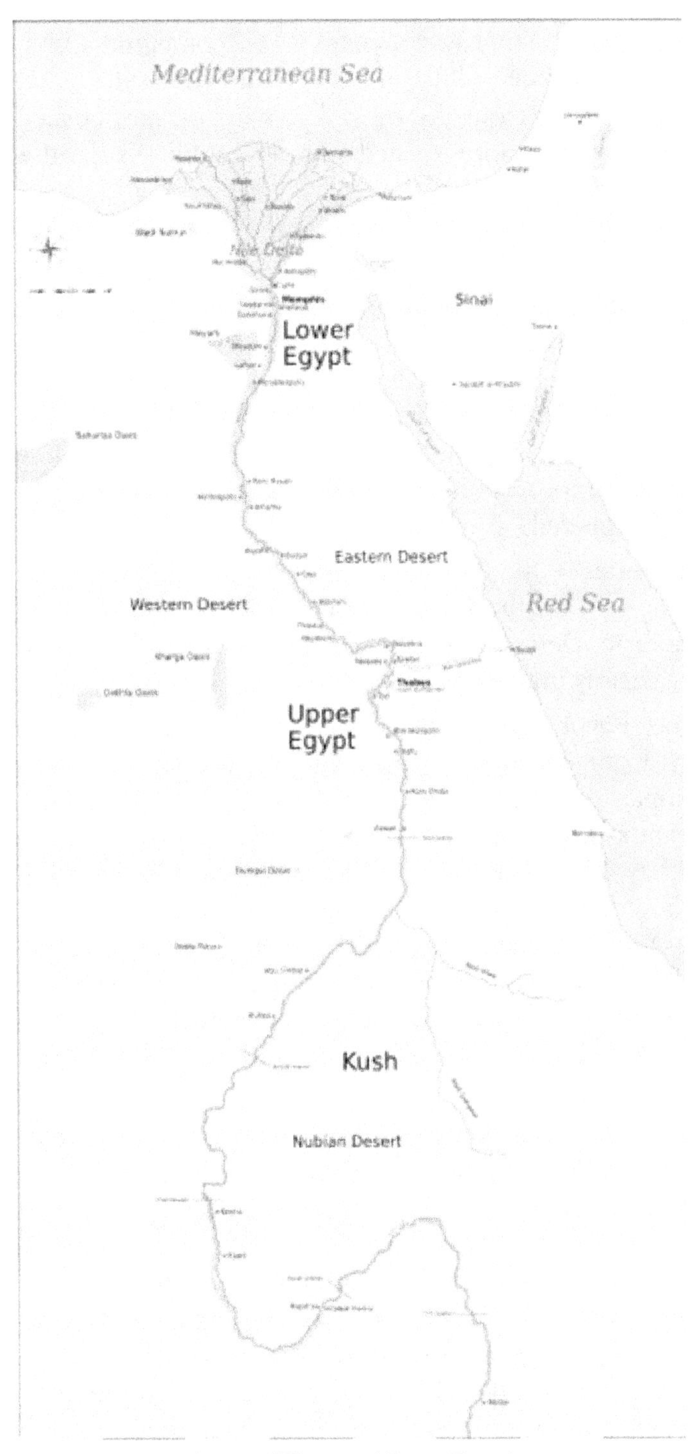

A map of Upper and Lower Egypt.[1]

Upper Egypt was a narrow ribbon of green, sometimes just a few miles wide, squeezed between cliffs and desert on both sides. Communities there were strung out along the river. The narrow valley created a certain kind of culture; it was more isolated and more traditional, with each town having a strong local identity.

Lower Egypt was completely different. Here, the Nile split into multiple branches and spread across a broad delta roughly 150 miles wide. The delta was a patchwork of marshes, channels, and fertile islands. It was lush, green, and soggy. This region could produce even more food than the narrow valley, but it was also more vulnerable to invasion from the Mediterranean or from neighboring regions in the Near East. The delta's culture reflected this openness. It was more cosmopolitan, more influenced by foreign contact, and more commercially minded.

On both sides of the Nile Valley stretched vast expanses of sand and rock. To the west lay the Libyan Desert, part of the Sahara. To the east lay the Arabian Desert, rising to mountains along the Red Sea coast. These were nearly impenetrable barriers.

This was Egypt's great advantage. The deserts provided significant protection from invasion that few other ancient cultures enjoyed. Mesopotamia, for instance, sat on a flat plain with no natural barriers, which meant it faced constant invasions and conquests. Any army trying to invade Egypt from the west or east would have to cross hundreds of miles of desert that could devastate an entire force through thirst and heat. The Mediterranean protected the north, and a series of cataracts (rapids) on the Nile made invasion from the south difficult. While these barriers weren't impenetrable—Egypt eventually faced successful invasions from the Levant, Nubia, and elsewhere—they made conquest far more challenging.

However, this protection came with increased isolation compared to other regions. While Egypt maintained important trade routes to the Levant, Nubia, Sinai, Punt, and across the Mediterranean, the desert barriers reduced casual contact with neighboring peoples. This geographical situation, combined with deliberate cultural policy, led to a kind of conservatism in Egyptian culture. Egyptians developed a certain worldview that their land was the center of creation, the only truly civilized place. They called their country "Kemet," meaning "the Black Land," referring to the rich, dark soil. Everything beyond the fertile strip was "Deshret," the "Red Land"—the lifeless desert.

Of course, the deserts provided some benefits beyond defense. They contained valuable resources, like gold mines, copper deposits, and various types of stone for building and sculpture. The eastern desert offered access routes to the Red Sea, enabling trade with Punt (likely modern Somalia or Eritrea) and other distant lands. The western desert had a string of oases that could support small populations and serve as waypoints for trade routes reaching into Africa.

Even so, over 95 percent of the ancient Egyptian population lived within a few miles of the Nile. Step away from the Nile in most places, and you'd be in a barren wasteland. This created a particular mindset. Egyptians saw their world as an island of order and abundance surrounded by chaos and death. The Nile was the source of life, the gift of the gods, and the reason Egypt existed at all. This reverence for the river would shape Egyptian religion, with the Nile itself deified and its annual flood celebrated as a divine blessing.

Geography also influenced Egyptians in ways that wouldn't become clear until later. The narrow river valley naturally connected communities. Boats could travel the entire length of Egypt, moving goods and people efficiently. The current flowed north, but the prevailing winds blew south, meaning one could sail upriver and float downriver. This made the Nile a natural highway. When Egypt eventually unified under a single ruler, the river would serve as the literal and metaphorical spine of the kingdom.

So, before there were pharaohs or pyramids, before there was any such thing as "Egypt," there was the Nile, flooding faithfully every year, creating a green corridor through the desert, and making life possible in one of the most inhospitable regions on Earth. Everything that followed stemmed from this one geographical fact.

From Hunters to Farmers

Ten thousand years ago, Egypt looked nothing like the Egypt of the pharaohs. There were no pyramids, no temples, and no cities. There wasn't even much of a desert yet.

After the Last Ice Age, North Africa experienced what scientists call the African Humid Period, roughly 9000 to 5500 BCE. During this time, the Sahara wasn't a desert but a savanna, with grasslands, lakes, and seasonal rivers. Early humans hunted wild cattle and gazelle across landscapes that would later become barren sand. They gathered wild plants, fished in lakes that no longer exist, and lived as mobile hunter-gatherers following seasonal resources.

Around 5500 BCE, the climate began to change. North Africa started drying out. The humid period ended, and the Sahara began its gradual transformation into the desert we know today. This process took thousands of years, but by around 3500 BCE, as the land became more arid, people and animals had been pushed toward the few remaining water sources. The most reliable water source in the entire region was the Nile.

This was the time when agriculture came to Egypt, though Egyptians didn't invent it. Farming was first developed in the Fertile Crescent, the region stretching from modern Iraq through Syria to Israel, around 10,000 BCE. The knowledge of growing crops gradually spread to Egypt over thousands of years. By around 5000 BCE, communities along the Nile were growing wheat and barley, raising cattle, sheep, and goats, and living in permanent villages.

This shift from hunting and gathering to farming—what historians call the Neolithic Revolution—changed everything. When people settle down and farm, they can support larger populations. They accumulate possessions and develop crafts and specializations. Social hierarchies emerge. In short, they start building civilizations.

The archaeological evidence for this period comes from sites scattered along the Nile Valley. At places like Merimde Beni Salama in the western delta and El-Omari near modern Cairo, archaeologists found the remains of early farming villages dating to between 5000 and 4000 BCE. These weren't sophisticated settlements. Their homes were simple oval huts, sometimes partially dug into the ground. People stored grain in baskets and pots. They buried their dead in simple graves, sometimes right within the village.

But even in these early communities, we see signs of what would become characteristic Egyptian practices. The dead were buried with grave goods, like pots, tools, and jewelry, suggesting beliefs about an afterlife in which the deceased would need these items. Bodies were typically placed on their sides in a flexed position, often facing west, toward the setting sun. These burial customs would evolve but never fundamentally change throughout Egyptian history.

By around 4000 BCE, Egypt entered what archaeologists call the Predynastic Period. This was when things started getting interesting. Communities were growing larger and more complex. Villages were turning into towns. Trade networks were expanding, and distinct regional cultures were emerging.

The most important of these cultures was the Naqada culture, named after the site where archaeologists first identified it. The Naqada culture developed in Upper Egypt and went through three main phases, which archaeologists creatively named Naqada I, II, and III (dating roughly 4000–3000 BCE).

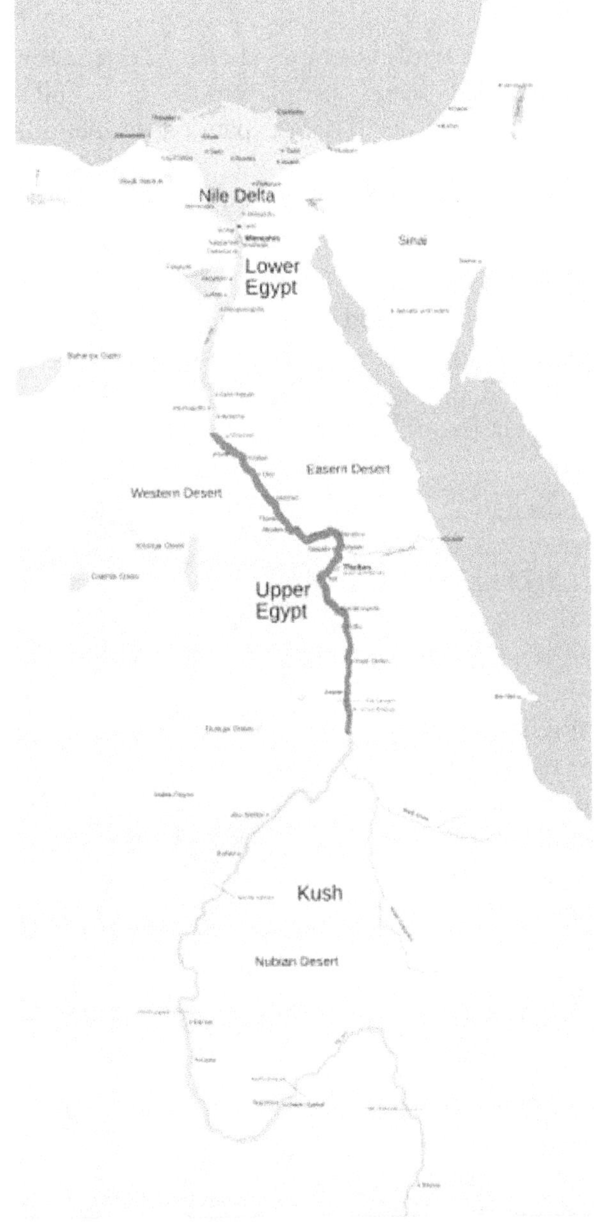

The extent of the Naqada culture.[2]

The Naqada I society was relatively simple. People lived in small agricultural communities, made distinctive pottery with geometric decorations, and created stone tools and weapons. However, there's evidence of growing social differentiation. Some burials are larger and contain more goods than others, suggesting that certain individuals had more wealth and status.

Naqada II marks the period of rapid change. Towns grew larger. Craft specialization increased—some people were now full-time potters, metalworkers, or stone carvers. Trade expanded dramatically, with goods moving long distances up and down the Nile. Egyptian-made objects started appearing in southern Palestine, and foreign goods showed up in Egypt. Copper became more common, and Egyptians were learning to work with it effectively.

The pottery from this period also changed dramatically. Instead of geometric patterns, Naqada II pottery featured painted scenes of boats, animals, humans, and mysterious symbols. Some of these images show boats carrying standards or banners that might represent early gods or tribal symbols.

Most importantly, the Naqada II society was clearly becoming hierarchical. Large tombs appeared that were far more elaborate than anything before. Some burials contained hundreds of pottery vessels, stone tools, jewelry, and other luxury goods. A few individuals were buried like chiefs or kings, suggesting that political leadership was becoming formalized.

During Naqada III (roughly 3200–3000 BCE), writing appeared in Egypt. There is debate over whether Egyptians invented writing independently or were inspired by early Mesopotamian writing systems—the concept of

A jar from the late Naqada II period.[3]

writing might have come from Mesopotamia, but the Egyptian system's form and symbols developed distinctly. The earliest Egyptian writing takes the form of simple labels and tags identifying the contents of storage jars or the ownership of goods. It was not literature yet—just basic record-keeping. But it was the beginning of the hieroglyphic system.

The archaeological record shows the emergence of powerful regional centers—basically proto-kingdoms—competing for control of the Nile Valley in the Naqada III period. Some towns were fortified with massive walls. Artistic depictions show warfare and conquest. Ceremonial objects show rulers smiting enemies and subduing towns.

One of these competing centers was Hierakonpolis (Egyptian name: Nekhen) in Upper Egypt. This was a major city for its time, with population estimates reaching as high as ten thousand people, though such figures are difficult to confirm. Excavations have revealed massive mudbrick walls, elite tombs, a temple complex, and a variety of ceremonial objects. Hierakonpolis was clearly one of the most powerful centers in late Predynastic Egypt.

Another important center was This (or Thinis), farther north in Upper Egypt. Less is known about This because the site hasn't been definitively located, but historical texts identify it as the home city of Egypt's first kings. It was probably the rival to Hierakonpolis for dominance in Upper Egypt.

Meanwhile, Lower Egypt had its own distinct culture and probably its own powerful chiefdoms, though we know less about them. The delta is harder for archaeologists to study because thousands of years of Nile flooding have buried or destroyed most early sites. However, texts and imagery from the Early Dynastic Period reference Lower Egyptian kingdoms that had to be conquered during Egypt's unification.

The archaeological evidence for this period is frustratingly incomplete, but what we have paints a picture of an increasingly sophisticated political organization. Large ceremonial buildings appear at sites like Hierakonpolis and Abydos. Massive tombs were constructed for elite individuals, some with multiple chambers and large quantities of luxury goods. We also start seeing standardized symbols, particularly the serekh, a rectangular frame topped with a falcon that represented royal authority. These weren't just decorative. They were political statements and markers of kingship.

The rulers of these early kingdoms weren't called pharaohs yet—that title came later. But they wielded real power. They commanded labor for building projects, controlled trade routes, and led military forces. Some of them were wealthy enough to be buried with hundreds of pottery vessels, stone tools, copper implements, and jewelry made from exotic materials like lapis lazuli from Afghanistan or obsidian from Ethiopia.

One site that gives us a particularly clear picture of this period is Cemetery U at Abydos in Upper Egypt. Here, archaeologists discovered a series of large tombs dating to around 3200 to 3100 BCE. The most impressive belonged to a ruler designated "Scorpion I" (named after the scorpion symbol found in his tomb). This wasn't a simple grave. It was a complex of multiple rooms covering over forty square meters, filled with hundreds of imported jars from southern Palestine that probably contained wine and other valuable liquids. The wine alone—expensive imported luxury goods—represented enormous wealth. The tomb also contained ivory artifacts, stone vessels, and remnants of what might have been an early form of hieroglyphic writing.

The existence of such elaborate tombs tells us several things. First, these rulers controlled enough resources and labor to construct substantial burial monuments. Second, they were engaged in long-distance trade networks stretching to Palestine and beyond. Third, they believed in an afterlife that would require furnishings and provisions—a belief that would become central to Egyptian culture. And fourth, they felt secure enough in their power to advertise it through conspicuous consumption and display.

But the most telling evidence comes from the imagery that appears on objects from this period. Carved stone palettes, ceremonial maceheads, and decorated pottery show scenes of warfare and domination, including bound captives and walled towns being attacked.

Two crowns became important symbols. The White Crown was associated with Upper Egypt—a tall, bowling-pin-shaped hat. The Red Crown represented Lower Egypt. It had a more complex design, with a tall back and a protruding spiral in front. Later, when Egypt was unified, pharaohs would wear both crowns, either separately or combined into the Double Crown, to emphasize their rule over both regions.

But in the late Predynastic Period, these crowns represented rival kingdoms. Upper Egypt, stretching from roughly modern Aswan to the area around Memphis, was probably the more unified and powerful region by 3200 BCE. Lower Egypt in the delta was likely divided among multiple competing centers, though evidence is limited due to poor preservation in the marshy delta. The historical tradition, recorded much later, claims that there were separate kings of Upper and Lower Egypt before unification, though we can't be certain of the details.

What's crucial to understand about the Predynastic Period is that Egypt wasn't marching inevitably toward unification. Multiple powerful centers were competing with each other. There were probably periods of warfare, alliances, trade relations, and cultural exchange. Different regions had somewhat different pottery styles, burial customs, and artistic traditions.

What we can say is that by around 3100 BCE, one of the Upper Egyptian kingdoms had emerged as dominant. This kingdom, based at either Hierakonpolis or This, had conquered or absorbed its neighbors and controlled the entire southern region. Its rulers had wealth, military power, and ambition. And they were looking north toward the delta.

Why did unification happen when it did? Several factors likely played a role.

Population growth and agricultural expansion might have created pressure for territorial control. More people meant more competition for prime farmland along the Nile. Kingdoms that could control longer stretches of the river had access to more resources and could support larger populations and armies.

Control of trade routes also mattered. The delta was the gateway to the Mediterranean and to trade with the Near East. Access to imported goods—cedar wood from Lebanon, silver from Anatolia, wine and oil from Palestine—was both economically valuable and politically significant, as luxury goods reinforced a ruler's status.

Military technology was improving as well. Copper weapons were becoming more common, giving armies that could afford to equip their soldiers with metal blades an advantage over those still using stone. Organizational sophistication was also increasing, as rulers could mobilize larger forces and sustain longer campaigns.

Another factor was that the concept of kingship was becoming more developed. Rulers claimed divine sanction, presenting themselves as necessary for maintaining cosmic order. A kingdom that could project this image of divinely sanctioned authority more effectively might find it easier to legitimize its expansion.

Finally, there was probably an element of historical accident and individual ambition. Unification required a ruler capable of imagining and executing a conquest of the entire Nile Valley. Not every generation produces such a person.

By 3200 BCE, Egypt was like a pot of water just about to boil. All the necessary ingredients for civilization were present: agricultural surplus, urban centers, social hierarchy, craft specialization, long-distance trade, writing, organized religion, and political leadership. By 3100 BCE, all the pieces were in place. Upper Egypt had a powerful king with military resources and territorial ambitions. Lower Egypt was probably divided and vulnerable. The technological, economic, and ideological tools for state-building had been developed. What happened next would transform this collection of competing chiefdoms into a unified kingdom.

But that unification wasn't inevitable, and it didn't happen peacefully. It would take conquest and a powerful king.

Chapter 2: The Birth of a Civilization—Unification and the Early Dynastic Period

Narmer/Menes: The First Pharaoh

Around 3100 BCE, something remarkable happened along the Nile. For the first time, the entire stretch of river from the Mediterranean delta to the First Cataract came under the control of a single ruler. Egypt became one kingdom, and the age of the pharaohs began. (An interesting side note: Early rulers of Egypt were not known as pharaohs. This term was later used by rulers in the New Kingdom. The label was retroactively applied to previous Egyptian kings.)

The man credited with this achievement is known by two names: Narmer and Menes. Egyptian tradition, recorded thousands of years later by the priest Manetho, identified Menes as the founder of the First Dynasty and the unifier of Egypt. However, the archaeological evidence points to a king named Narmer, whose name appears on monuments dating to this period. Many scholars today believe Narmer and Menes are the same person, though this remains debated. Some suggest Menes might have been Narmer's successor, Hor-Aha, or that "Menes" was a throne name, title, or even a purely symbolic figure representing the unification itself rather than a specific individual.

What we can say with confidence is that a powerful Upper Egyptian king unified Egypt around 3100 BCE. The most important evidence for this unification comes from one of ancient Egypt's most famous artifacts: the Narmer Palette.

The Narmer Palette is a ceremonial stone slab, just over two feet tall, carved from a single piece of siltstone. It was discovered at Hierakonpolis in 1898. Both sides are covered with carved relief scenes.

On one side, Narmer wears the White Crown of Upper Egypt. He's shown in the classic pose that would be repeated thousands of times throughout Egyptian history: the king, larger than anyone else, raises a mace to strike a kneeling enemy he grabs by the hair. Behind Narmer stands a servant carrying his sandals. Above the captive, a falcon (representing the god Horus) perches on papyrus plants (symbolizing Lower Egypt) and holds a rope attached to a man's head (a symbolic representation of Upper Egypt's conquest of the north). Below Narmer's feet, two more enemies lie defeated.

The other side shows Narmer wearing the Red Crown of Lower Egypt, suggesting he now rules both regions. He's shown in a procession with standard bearers, inspecting rows of decapitated enemies, their severed heads placed between their legs. These violent scenes likely represent ritual motifs and symbolic royal power—the king as a victorious warrior—rather than documenting historical events. At the bottom of this side, a bull (representing the king's strength) breaks through the walls of a fortified town.

The palette shows us propaganda, not a detailed historical account. So, how did this unification actually happen? The process probably involved both military conquest and political maneuvering. By 3100 BCE, Upper Egypt had already consolidated into a single powerful kingdom, probably centered at This or Hierakonpolis. Lower Egypt seems to have been divided among multiple competing centers, though poor archaeological preservation in the marshy delta makes this difficult to confirm definitively. An Upper Egyptian king with sufficient military force and organizational skill could conquer the delta piece by piece, absorbing or destroying rival kingdoms one at a time.

The conquest wasn't necessarily quick. Based on the scale of the task, it might have taken years or even decades. Some delta rulers might have submitted without major battles, accepting vassal status under the Upper Egyptian king. Others were probably conquered by force, which would explain the violent imagery on the Narmer Palette and other objects from this period.

Once conquered, Lower Egypt had to be held. This required establishing new administrative centers, installing loyal officials, and projecting royal power throughout the delta. It meant demonstrating that resistance was futile and submission was rewarded. It also required creating powerful symbols of unity that legitimized the new political order.

This was where the symbolism of the Two Lands became crucial. Egypt would forever after be defined as the union of Upper and Lower Egypt—two distinct regions brought together under one pharaoh. The king wore both crowns, carried both sets of royal regalia, and was called "Lord of the Two Lands." Even the hieroglyphic writing of the word "Egypt" showed this duality, depicting both the papyrus plant of the north and the sedge plant of the south bound together.

Memphis, situated at the junction where the Nile Valley meets the delta, became Egypt's administrative center. It was neutral ground in a sense; it was not the old capital of either Upper or Lower Egypt, but a new city positioned to control both regions. From Memphis, a pharaoh could send messages and officials north into the delta or south into the valley with equal ease. The city would remain one of Egypt's most important administrative centers throughout most of Egyptian history, though other cities like Thebes and Amarna would sometimes serve as capitals or royal residences.

The establishment of Memphis marked the beginning of what Egyptologists call the Early Dynastic Period (approximately 3100–2686 BCE), which encompasses the First and Second Dynasties. This was the formative period of Egyptian civilization.

The Early Dynastic Period (3100–2686 BCE)

The Early Dynastic Period saw the basic structures of Egyptian civilization take shape: the institutions of government, the ideology of kingship, the development of writing, the establishment of trade networks, and the creation of a distinctive Egyptian artistic style.

It's frustrating that we don't know as much about this period as we'd like. The Early Dynastic Period left fewer monuments and inscriptions than later eras. Many royal tombs were plundered in antiquity. The written sources from this time are limited, mostly consisting of labels, seal impressions, and short inscriptions rather than detailed historical texts. What we know comes primarily from archaeology, and archaeology can answer only so many questions.

The First Dynasty included around eight to ten kings, though the exact number and sequence are debated because some names appear in some king lists but not others. After Narmer/Menes came kings like Aha (whom some scholars identify as Menes), Djer, Djet, Den, and Qa'a. These names don't mean much to most people today, but these rulers transformed Egypt from a conquered territory into a functioning unified state.

What did these early pharaohs actually do? First off, they established the administration needed to run a unified kingdom. Egypt couldn't be governed by the pharaoh alone; it was too large. Running a unified kingdom stretching 750 miles required organization. The pharaoh couldn't personally oversee every field, every granary, and every workshop. He needed representatives throughout Egypt who could act with royal authority.

The most important official was the tjaty (often called "vizier" in English). He was essentially the prime minister. The vizier oversaw the administration, heard legal cases, managed the treasury, directed public works, and reported directly to the pharaoh. It was one of the most powerful positions in Egypt. Viziers came from the highest ranks of the nobility.

Below the vizier were numerous specialized officials: regional governors controlling Egypt's provinces (nomes), overseers managing royal estates and workshops, treasurers tracking resources, scribes recording everything, military commanders, and high priests managing major temples. Officials were needed to collect taxes, record grain supplies, organize labor, manage irrigation systems, oversee trade, and enforce royal authority. The First Dynasty saw the development of this bureaucracy. Some positions were hereditary, passed from father to son, creating powerful families with generations of administrative experience. Others were appointed based on merit or royal favor.

Ancient Egyptians also developed writing during this period. The early hieroglyphic script that appeared at the end of the Predynastic Period was refined and expanded during the Early Dynastic Period. Writing was initially used for administrative purposes, but it was also used to record royal names and titles, helping to project royal authority and preserve their deeds.

The hieroglyphic writing system became increasingly sophisticated during this period. It used hundreds of signs. Some hieroglyphs were phonetic (representing sounds), some were logograms (representing whole words), and some were determinatives (indicating what category something belonged to). This made the system flexible but complex. It required years of training to master.

Alongside hieroglyphics, Egyptians began developing hieratic script, a more cursive form of writing better suited to being written quickly with a reed pen on papyrus. The earliest examples of hieratic appear late in the Early Dynastic Period. Hieratic would eventually be used for everyday administrative documents, while hieroglyphics remained reserved for formal inscriptions on stone monuments.

The administration ran on documentation. Scribes recorded crop yields, tax receipts, labor assignments, grain storage, and countless other details. This wasn't just bureaucratic fussiness; it was essential for managing resources in a pre-industrial economy. The government needed to know how much grain was in storage to survive low flood years, how much labor was available for construction projects, and how much revenue each province generated. Writing made this possible.

The economy was not monetary. Egypt wouldn't use coinage until the Late Period. Instead, transactions used barter, with values calculated in standard units like the deben (about 91 grams of copper). Workers were generally paid in rations—bread, beer, grain, and oil—though wages varied significantly by class and era. Taxes were collected in kind, which means farmers paid a portion of their harvest, and craftsmen paid in goods they produced. The government redistributed these resources to feed officials, priests, soldiers, and workers on royal projects.

The early pharaohs also developed royal ideology. The king wasn't just a powerful man. He was increasingly understood as divine, the living embodiment of the god Horus. Let's start with ma'at because nothing is more central to understanding how ancient Egyptians saw their world and why the pharaoh was so essential.

Ma'at is difficult to translate into English. It means truth, justice, order, balance, and harmony. It means the proper way things should be. Ma'at was simultaneously a concept, a goddess, and the fundamental principle underlying reality itself. While the principle of ma'at existed since the Early Dynastic Period, the philosophical articulations of the concept would come later, primarily in the Middle Kingdom.

In the Egyptian worldview, the universe existed in a delicate balance between ma'at (order) and isfet (chaos). Before creation, only isfet existed—a formless, chaotic, dark void. The creator god brought forth the ordered world from this chaos, establishing ma'at. But isfet didn't disappear. It constantly threatened to overwhelm creation and return everything to primordial chaos. Ma'at had to be actively maintained through proper behavior, ritual observance, and—most importantly—the actions of the pharaoh.

The king maintained ma'at through his very existence and through his actions. He was the legitimate ruler who maintained the cosmic order and stood between civilization and chaos. When the pharaoh ruled justly, performed the proper rituals, built temples for the gods, and defended Egypt's borders, he was literally holding the universe together. A weak or absent king didn't just create political problems; he also threatened cosmic disaster.

This concept had practical implications. It meant that proper order required a hierarchy. Everyone had their place, from the pharaoh at the top to farmers at the bottom. Social mobility existed, but it was limited. It meant that tradition and precedent were valued over innovation. Egyptians saw their civilization as special, as the one place where ma'at truly prevailed.

Ma'at also had ethical dimensions. Truth-telling, honesty, fairness in judgment, and proper treatment of subordinates weren't just nice ideas but also essential components of maintaining cosmic order. Officials were expected to uphold ma'at in their judgments. The dead would be judged based on whether they had lived according to ma'at. The concept provided something approaching a moral code, though one embedded in ideas about cosmic order rather than ethics.

Now, about the pharaoh himself. What did it mean to be a pharaoh in the Early Dynastic Period?

As we have established, the pharaoh was divine. He wasn't just a ruler chosen by gods; he was a god in human form. Specifically, he was the living Horus, the falcon god who was the legitimate king of Egypt. When a pharaoh died, he became identified with Osiris, the god of the dead, and his successor became the new Horus.

Royal names and titles became increasingly elaborate, emphasizing the king's divine nature and his role as intermediary between gods and humans. The pharaoh's title would eventually expand to five names. The most important was the Horus name, showing the king as the earthly manifestation of Horus. Later came the Two Ladies name (representing the protective goddesses of Upper and Lower Egypt), the Golden Horus name, the prenomen (throne name introduced by the phrase "King of Upper and Lower Egypt"), and the nomen (birth name introduced by "Son of Re").

Only a pharaoh and high-ranking priests could enter the innermost sanctuaries of temples where divine statues resided. The pharaoh performed rituals that ensured the gods' favor, the Nile's flooding, and the sun's daily journey across the sky. In temple reliefs, the pharaoh is always shown making offerings to the gods. In reality, priests performed most daily rituals, but they did so as the king's representatives, acting in his name.

The pharaoh owned all the land in Egypt. All officials served at his pleasure, and all resources were his to command. Any major decision required his approval or was made in his name. This doesn't mean a pharaoh micromanaged everything—the kingdom was too large for that— but theoretically, all power flowed from the king.

The pharaoh's image was carefully controlled. Royal statues and reliefs didn't show the king as he actually looked. They showed an idealized version emphasizing eternal, divine qualities. The pharaoh was always depicted as young and vigorous, with perfect proportions, a serene expression, and a commanding presence. This wasn't personal vanity; it was a theological necessity. The image had to reflect the king's divine nature and eternal role, not his mortal appearance.

This didn't mean pharaohs were puppet figures existing purely for ritual. Many were active rulers who made important decisions, led armies, directed building projects, and shaped policy. However, they operated within an ideological framework that defined them as divine beings maintaining cosmic order.

The early pharaohs built a lot of structures. The royal tombs at Abydos and Saqqara show increasingly sophisticated architecture. These weren't pyramids yet; that came later. Early royal tombs were elaborate mudbrick structures called mastabas (Arabic for "bench," describing their shape). These rectangular structures had underground burial chambers and above-ground chapels where offerings could be presented to the deceased king.

Some of these tombs were enormous. The tomb of King Den at Abydos featured a burial chamber accessed by a stone staircase—the first use of a staircase in Egyptian architecture. The tomb of Qa'a, the last king of the First Dynasty, had over thirty subsidiary chambers surrounding the main burial chamber, possibly used for storing grave goods.

But here's something disturbing about these early tombs: they were surrounded by subsidiary burials—graves of servants and officials buried at the same time as the king. It is widely believed that these individuals died when the king died. Either they were killed as part of the burial ritual, or they committed suicide to serve the king in the afterlife, though some scholars argue that some attendants might have been buried later or symbolically. This practice, called retainer sacrifice, appears in the First Dynasty but seems to have been abandoned by the Second Dynasty, possibly indicating changing religious beliefs or evolving attitudes about the afterlife.

Egypt had to expand its trade networks to support the state. Egyptian objects have been found in Palestine and Lebanon, while imported goods, like cedar wood, wine, and oil, appear in Egypt. Trade expeditions reached the Sinai Peninsula for copper and turquoise. Ships traveled to Byblos on the Lebanese coast to acquire cedar, which Egypt lacked but needed for large construction projects. Trade routes also extended south into Nubia for ivory, ebony, and gold. While some of these connections predated the dynasties, they developed significantly during the Early Dynastic Period.

The early pharaohs also conducted military campaigns. Egypt wasn't just consolidating internally; it was also projecting power beyond its borders. Rock inscriptions in Nubia suggest Egyptian military expeditions extended southward. The Sinai Peninsula, a source of copper and turquoise, came under Egyptian control. These campaigns secured resources, eliminated threats, demonstrated royal power, and provided opportunities for kings to fulfill their ideological role as mighty warriors who defended Egypt and expanded its borders.

The transition from the First to Second Dynasty around 2890 BCE seems to have involved some kind of political crisis, though the details are murky. The last king of the First Dynasty, Qa'a, was followed by kings who might have come from a different family line. There are hints in the archaeological record of instability. Some royal names were later erased, suggesting political conflict or a regime change.

The Second Dynasty continued the trends of the First Dynasty but seems to have been more troubled. Several kings left few traces, suggesting short or unsuccessful reigns. One king, Peribsen, did something unprecedented. Instead of using Horus as his patron deity, he chose Seth, Horus's rival in Egyptian mythology. Later, King Khasekhemwy used both Horus and Seth in his royal name, possibly indicating a reconciliation between competing factions that had divided Egypt.

The fact that Khasekhemwy's name means "The Two Powerful Ones Appear" suggests he was reunifying a divided Egypt. Whatever conflicts occurred during the Second Dynasty—and we can only guess at the details—they seem to have been resolved by the dynasty's end, setting the stage for the Old Kingdom and the age of pyramid building.

By the end of the Early Dynastic Period around 2686 BCE, Egypt had been transformed. The administrative apparatus could manage the kingdom's resources and mobilize large labor forces. Writing was used throughout the government. Trade networks extended throughout the eastern Mediterranean and into Africa. Royal ideology had developed to the point where the pharaoh was understood as a living god, the essential link between the divine and human realms. And Egyptian art had developed its distinctive style, focused on eternal order rather than fleeting moments.

All the pieces were in place. Egypt was ready for its first golden age, the Old Kingdom, when royal power and resources would be concentrated on the most ambitious building projects in human history: the pyramids.

Chapter 3: The Old Kingdom— When Egypt Built for Forever

Around 2686 BCE, Egypt entered what historians call the Old Kingdom, also known as the Pyramid Age. The Old Kingdom encompasses the Third Dynasty to the Sixth Dynasty. By the start of the Third Dynasty, Egypt had been unified for over four hundred years. The administrative systems were functioning smoothly. The ideology of divine kingship was firmly established. The economy was productive. Egypt was ready for something spectacular—monumental building on an unprecedented scale.

That something arrived in the form of King Djoser, the second ruler of the Third Dynasty, who reigned approximately 2667 to 2648 BCE. Djoser was probably a capable king who consolidated royal power and conducted military campaigns in the Sinai, but he would be remembered for building the world's first large-scale stone structure.

Before Djoser, Egyptian monuments were built from mudbrick and wood. These materials were practical. Mud from the Nile was abundant and easy to work with, and mudbrick structures could be quite impressive. But mudbrick crumbled over time. It couldn't achieve the heights or the permanence that stone offered. Stone had been used for certain elements, like doorframes and paving stones, but never for an entire monumental structure in Egypt on this scale.

Djoser's architect, a man named Imhotep, changed that. Imhotep is one of the most remarkable figures in ancient Egyptian history, and he is one of the few non-royal individuals to be remembered thousands of years later. He served as Djoser's chancellor and high priest, but his fame rests on his architectural achievement. Later Egyptian tradition revered Imhotep so much that he was eventually deified, worshiped as a god of wisdom and medicine. The Greeks would identify him with their god of healing, Asclepius. Two thousand years after his death, Egyptians still made pilgrimages to his supposed burial place.

What did Imhotep create that earned such lasting fame? He designed the Step Pyramid at Saqqara, just outside Memphis.

The Step Pyramid began as a traditional mastaba tomb, a rectangular mudbrick structure. However, Imhotep had a different vision. He expanded the mastaba, making it larger. Then he built another, smaller mastaba on top of it. Then another. And another. Eventually, he created a structure rising in six massive steps to a height of about 204 feet. It was the world's first pyramid, even if it didn't have the smooth sides we associate with later pyramids.

Djoser's Step Pyramid.'

The revolutionary aspect wasn't just the stepped design; it was also the material. Imhotep built in stone, specifically limestone quarried nearby and brought to the site. The Step Pyramid used an estimated 330,000 cubic meters of stone and clay—a monumental achievement.

The pyramid sat within a vast complex covering thirty-seven acres, surrounded by a limestone wall over thirty feet high. The complex included courtyards, chapels, ceremonial buildings, and storage rooms. Many of these structures served ritual purposes related to the king's afterlife or to ceremonies associated with royal power.

The Step Pyramid wasn't perfect. Some of the techniques were experimental, and parts of the structure were unstable. Some sections actually collapsed during construction and had to be rebuilt with buttressing walls. But as a first attempt at monumental stone architecture, it was astonishing.

Other Third Dynasty pharaohs attempted their own pyramids, with varying success. Sekhemkhet started a step pyramid but died before completing it. Khaba might have begun another. These projects show that kings learned from Djoser's example, though none matched his achievement during the Third Dynasty.

But these were just the beginning. The next dynasty would take Imhotep's innovation and perfect it, creating structures so iconic that they have become symbols of ancient Egypt itself. The Fourth Dynasty was approaching, and with it, the true Pyramid Age would arrive.

The Great Pyramids of Giza

The Fourth Dynasty (approximately 2613-2494 BCE) was ancient Egypt's architectural apex. Three kings of this dynasty—Khufu, Khafre, and Menkaure—built the pyramids at Giza that still dominate the landscape today. These structures are so massive and precise that they've become among the most recognizable monuments in the world.

The Fourth Dynasty didn't start at Giza. The dynasty's founder, Sneferu (approximately 2613-2589 BCE), was a prodigious builder who experimented with pyramid design and, in the process, built more total stone volume than any other pharaoh. Sneferu constructed at least three pyramids: the Pyramid at Meidum, the Bent Pyramid at Dahshur, and the Red Pyramid at Dahshur.

The Bent Pyramid is particularly significant because it shows Egyptian architects learning in real time. The pyramid starts at a steep angle—about fifty-four degrees—but about halfway up, the angle suddenly changes to a gentler forty-three degrees, creating the distinctive "bent" appearance. Why? Most likely, the steep angle created structural problems, and the architects decided mid-construction to reduce the angle to prevent collapse. The Bent Pyramid marks the transition from step pyramids to true smooth-sided pyramids.

The Bent Pyramid.[5]

Sneferu's Red Pyramid, built after the Bent Pyramid, achieved what earlier attempts had struggled to do: a true pyramid with smooth sides at a consistent angle from base to peak. At about 341 feet high, it was the world's tallest structure when completed. Sneferu had finally perfected the form.

The Red Pyramid.[6]

His son Khufu took this perfection and scaled it up dramatically. Khufu's Great Pyramid at Giza, built around 2560 BCE, is a structure almost beyond comprehension. Originally standing approximately 481 feet tall (now about 455 feet due to loss of the outer casing), it remained the world's tallest human-made structure for almost four thousand years. Its base covers approximately thirteen acres. It contains an estimated 2.3 million stone blocks, each weighing an average of 2.5 tons, though some blocks in the King's Chamber weigh up to 80 tons.

The precision is staggering. The base is level to within approximately 2.1 centimeters across its entire expanse. The sides are aligned almost perfectly to the cardinal directions with an error of only about 3.4 arc minutes (an arc minute is 1/60 of a degree). The blocks fit together so well that you often can't slip a knife blade between them. All of this was accomplished without iron tools (Egypt was still in the Copper Age), without the wheel for transportation, and without pulleys or cranes as we understand them.

So, how was it built? This question has fascinated people for millennia and has generated countless theories, from the plausible to the absurd. Let's focus on what archaeologists and engineers actually know.

The Greek historian Herodotus, who wrote 2,000 years after the pyramid's construction, claimed 100,000 slaves built it over 20 years. This is almost certainly wrong on both counts. According to recent archaeological evidence found in workers' villages and cemeteries, a permanent workforce of around five thousand skilled workers—quarrymen, masons, surveyors, and engineers—was supplemented during the annual flood season (when farm work was impossible) by a rotating labor force of perhaps twenty thousand to thirty thousand workers who hauled blocks and built ramps.

These weren't slaves in the sense Herodotus imagined. Archaeological evidence from workers' villages near the pyramids shows laborers were paid in food rations, received medical care, and had access to meat, which was a luxury for common Egyptians. Graffiti on blocks names work crews with designations like "Friends of Khufu" or "Drunkards of Menkaure," suggesting team pride rather than misery. The workers were organized into rotating crews from different regions, serving what was essentially a labor tax obligation.

Most of the limestone came from quarries near the pyramid site. Workers used copper tools and wooden wedges to split stone along natural bedding planes in the rock. Current evidence suggests blocks were then transported on wooden sledges pulled by teams of workers. Research and experimental archaeology show that wetting the sand ahead of sledges can reduce friction by up to 50 percent—a technique also depicted in Egyptian tomb paintings.

The granite blocks used for internal chambers came from Aswan, nearly six hundred miles south. These were transported by boat during the flood season when the Nile was high enough to bring the boats close to the pyramid site.

The lifting of the stones remains the most debated aspect. The most widely accepted theory involves ramps—probably a combination of a long external ramp for most of the construction and internal ramps or a spiral ramp for the upper levels. As the pyramid grew, the ramp was extended and raised. The ramp would have required almost as much material as the pyramid, but it could be dismantled, and the material could be reused afterward. Alternative theories have been proposed, including levers and cranes, but ramps remain the most practical explanation.

Building the Great Pyramid required extraordinary logistics. Stone had to be quarried, moved, and set in place at a rate of about one block every two minutes if the project took twenty years. This required precise planning, rotating work crews, a constant supply of food and water, tool maintenance, and oversight at every level. The project was likely divided into smaller units with a hierarchy of overseers coordinating everything.

The pyramid wasn't just the triangular structure we see today. It was part of a larger complex, including a mortuary temple where offerings were made to the deceased king, a causeway leading down to a valley temple at the Nile's edge, and smaller pyramids for queens. The entire complex served both the king's burial and his ongoing cult after death.

Khufu's son Khafre built the second pyramid at Giza. It was slightly smaller than his father's, but it appears to be taller because it was built on higher ground. Khafre also built, or at least completed, the Great Sphinx—that enormous limestone statue with a lion's body and a human head, probably representing the king himself. At 240 feet long and 66 feet high, the Sphinx is the world's largest monolithic statue carved from a single piece of bedrock.

Menkaure, Khafre's successor, built the third and smallest of the Giza pyramids, standing about 215 feet tall. While significantly smaller than his predecessors', it's still an enormous structure and features extensive use of granite from Aswan in its lower courses.

The Giza pyramids represent the peak of ancient Egyptian pyramid construction in terms of size and precision. Later pyramids would be built, but none would match these for sheer scale and accuracy. After the Fourth Dynasty, pyramid building continued, but with smaller structures and often shoddier construction.

The pyramids of Giza.[7]

Why did the Fourth Dynasty kings build on such a scale? These pharaohs had enormous resources at their disposal—a wealthy kingdom, productive agriculture, control of trade routes, and an effective administration. They believed profoundly in the afterlife and saw the pyramid as essential for their eternal existence. The pyramid was the pharaoh's stairway to the heavens, his permanent connection between earth and sky. Building such structures also demonstrated royal power, both to subjects and to the gods. A pharaoh who could move millions of tons of stone was clearly capable of maintaining ma'at and defending Egypt.

However, there may have been another factor: prestige and competition. Each king wanted to match or exceed his predecessors. Khufu built bigger than Sneferu. Khafre matched Khufu. This created an escalating cycle of monumental construction that consumed enormous resources, drove architectural innovation, and demonstrated Egypt's capabilities.

The pyramids have endured for over 4,500 years, weathering sandstorms, earthquakes, and attempts at dismantling (many later builders used pyramids as convenient quarries for pre-cut stone). They have inspired awe, wonder, and wild speculation. And they stand as testaments to what humans can achieve when vision, resources, organization, and determination align—even with Stone Age technology.

Life in the Pyramid Age

The pyramids dominate our view of the Old Kingdom, but they were built by a society, not by pharaohs alone. What was life actually like in Egypt during the Pyramid Age? How did ordinary people live while their kings built monuments that would last for eternity?

The Old Kingdom was a time of prosperity and stability for Egypt. The Nile flooded reliably, harvests were good, and the kingdom's borders were secure.

Egyptian society was hierarchical, organized in a clear pyramid itself. At the very top stood the pharaoh, the living god who, in theory, owned all of Egypt. Below him came the royal family and highest officials, such as viziers, high priests, and regional governors who wielded power and lived in luxury.

The next tier consisted of the professional classes: scribes, mid-level priests, skilled craftsmen, merchants, and military officers. These people lived comfortably, though not luxuriously. They had secure positions, steady food supplies, and the respect that came with specialized knowledge or skills.

Below them came the largest group: farmers, laborers, and unskilled workers. These people worked hard, often doing physical labor in harsh conditions, but they weren't slaves in the sense of being property. They had legal rights, could own property, and could seek justice in courts. Their lives were constrained by their position in the social hierarchy, but they were recognized as people with certain protections.

At the bottom of free society came various categories of dependent workers and servants, whose status was somewhere between free and enslaved. Slavery did exist in the Old Kingdom. They could be prisoners of war, criminals, or people who had fallen into debt slavery, though the scale of slavery was smaller than in some later periods or other ancient civilizations. However, it is important to emphasize that the massive building projects weren't built by slave labor; they were built by free workers fulfilling labor obligations to the state, a form of taxation paid in work rather than goods.

Social mobility was limited but not impossible. A talented scribe could rise to become a high official. A skilled craftsman might become overseer of a royal workshop. Merit could sometimes overcome birth, especially in the growing bureaucracy, which needed capable administrators.

Daily life for most Egyptians revolved around agriculture. The Nile's annual cycle dictated everything. During the inundation season (Akhet), when fields were flooded, farmers might be called up for state projects, like pyramid building. During the growing season (Peret), they planted and tended crops. They primarily grew wheat and barley, but they also raised flax for linen, vegetables, and fruits. During the harvest season (Shemu), they worked to bring in the crops before the next flood.

A typical farmer's day began at dawn. He'd eat a breakfast of bread and beer (both staples of the Egyptian diet) and then head to the fields with basic tools—hoes, sickles, and plows pulled by cattle. He'd work through the hot day, returning home at sunset to a simple house made of mudbrick.

Houses varied by social class. A wealthy official might have a large house with multiple rooms, a central courtyard, and even a garden with a pool. The walls would be plastered and painted. Furniture might include chairs, beds, and storage chests. A farmer's house might have just one or two rooms, minimal furniture (perhaps a sleeping platform and some baskets for storage), and a roof used for sleeping during hot nights.

The Egyptian diet was based on bread and beer. Bread wasn't like modern bread. It was coarse and often gritty with sand from the grinding stones, which explains why ancient Egyptian teeth show severe wear. Beer was thick, nutritious, and drunk by everyone, including children (it was safer than water). Those who could afford it supplemented this basic diet with vegetables (onions, garlic, lettuce, and cucumbers), fruits (dates, figs, and grapes), fish from the Nile, and occasionally meat (beef, pork, poultry, or wild game).

The wealthy ate much better, with more meat, elaborate preparations, honey for sweetening, and imported delicacies. Banquets depicted in tomb paintings show elaborate spreads with dozens of dishes, though these scenes likely represent idealized versions of the afterlife rather than everyday meals.

Clothing was simple. Men typically wore kilt-like garments made from linen, sometimes just a loincloth for laborers. Women wore straight linen dresses. The wealthy had finer linen, sometimes semi-transparent, and might wear jewelry made of gold, semi-precious stones, or faience beads. Children often went naked until puberty. Everyone went barefoot most of the time, though sandals made from papyrus or leather were worn when needed.

Family life was central. Marriages were arranged, but they seem to have generally been affectionate partnerships. Marriage required no official ceremony. A couple simply started living together, often with an agreement about property. Women had significant rights for the ancient world. They could own property, conduct business, initiate divorce, and inherit equally with men. A woman's primary role was managing the household and raising children, but she wasn't legally subordinate to her husband in the way women were in many ancient societies.

Children were valued and desired. Infant mortality was high, so families had multiple children, hoping several would survive to adulthood. Children helped with work from an early age, tending animals, helping in fields, or learning trades. Most children didn't receive a formal education, but boys from elite families would be sent to scribal schools around age nine to learn reading, writing, mathematics, and proper behavior. These schools were demanding, and corporal punishment was used freely. A saying from the time claims, "A boy's ear is on his back; he listens when he is beaten."

Recreation existed even in this work-focused society. Tomb paintings show people playing board games like senet and mehen, wrestling, dancing, and watching or participating in athletic competitions. Children played with toys, like dolls, balls, spinning tops, and toy animals. The wealthy enjoyed hunting in the desert or fowling in the marshes. Music was popular, featuring instruments such as harps, lutes, flutes, and drums.

Religion was a part of daily life. Egyptians believed in dozens of gods, each with specific domains and powers. Most people never entered the inner sanctuaries—those were for priests and the pharaoh—but they could pray at temple entrances, participate in festival processions, and worship at local shrines. Household worship was common, with small altars or shrines dedicated to protective deities.

Medical care existed, though it was limited by the era's understanding. Egyptian physicians could set broken bones, stitch wounds, and prescribe medicines made from plants, minerals, and animal products. Medical texts show they recognized different diseases and had specific treatments, though many remedies were more magical than practical. Still, Egyptian medicine was sophisticated for its time, and Egyptian doctors were renowned throughout the ancient world.

Trade connected Egypt to the wider world. Egyptian grain, linen, and papyrus were exported throughout the eastern Mediterranean. In return came cedar wood from Lebanon, olive oil and wine from the Levant, copper from Cyprus and Sinai, and luxury goods from farther afield, including lapis lazuli from Afghanistan, obsidian from Ethiopia, and ivory from Africa. This trade enriched the kingdom and exposed Egyptians to foreign ideas and goods.

The Old Kingdom was also a period of cultural flowering. This era produced some of ancient Egypt's finest art. Statues achieved remarkable naturalism within the conventions of the Egyptian style, reliefs were carved with exquisite detail, and tomb paintings depicted vivid scenes of daily life. The Pyramid Texts, the oldest known religious texts from ancient Egypt, were first inscribed on pyramid walls during the late Old Kingdom, preserving spells and sayings meant to guide the deceased king through the afterlife.

Literature began to develop, though most Old Kingdom texts were practical—administrative records, letters, or instructions. The great literary works would come later, but the foundations were being laid.

For most Egyptians, particularly those in the elite and professional classes, the Old Kingdom was likely a relatively good time to be alive compared to what came before or what they might have experienced in other ancient societies. The kingdom was stable during its peak, harvests were generally good in successful years, and the social order seemed secure. For farmers and laborers, life remained hard with the constant pressure of fulfilling obligations to landlords and the state, and local famines could still occur during poor flood years. If you were born a farmer, you'd die a farmer, but you'd live under a system that, for all its inequalities, provided order, justice (at least in theory), and the assurance that ma'at prevailed in Egypt while chaos ruled beyond the borders.

The pyramids rising on the western horizon weren't just monuments to dead kings. They were visible proof that Egypt was special, that the pharaoh maintained the cosmic order, and that the kingdom had the strength and organization to achieve the impossible. For the people who built them, hauling stones under the desert sun, the pyramids represented more than just a job. They were participating in something eternal, ensuring their king's successful journey to the afterlife, and contributing to Egypt's glory.

The Old Kingdom wouldn't last forever. By the late Sixth Dynasty, cracks were appearing in the seemingly eternal order. But at the time, Egypt was strong, prosperous, and confident. The pyramids would stand forever, and surely, the kingdom would too.

Chapter 4: Collapse and Chaos—The First Intermediate Period

When Central Power Failed

The Old Kingdom didn't end with a bang. There was no major foreign invasion, no dramatic rebellion that toppled the state, no sudden catastrophe. Instead, Egypt's first golden age faded gradually. One day, people looked around and realized the world had changed. The powerful centralized state that had built the pyramids was gone, replaced by fragmented regional powers and weakened kings. Egypt had entered what historians call the First Intermediate Period (approximately 2181–2055 BCE).

The collapse began during the Sixth Dynasty, which had started strongly but grew progressively weaker. The reign of Pepi II, who came to the throne as a child and ruled for an extraordinarily long time—possibly over sixty years, making him one of the longest-reigning monarchs in history—saw royal authority steadily erode. By the time Pepi II died, probably in his nineties, the centralized system his ancestors had built was crumbling.

What went wrong? Why did the seemingly eternal Old Kingdom fall apart?

The answer involves multiple factors, and historians debate which were most important. But several key problems converged to undermine the unified state.

First, there was an environmental crisis. Evidence from multiple sources, including Nile flood records, archaeological data, and climate studies, suggests that Egypt experienced a period of low Nile floods during the late Old Kingdom and early First Intermediate Period. When the Nile didn't flood properly, crops failed. When crops failed, people went hungry. When people went hungry, they couldn't pay taxes. When taxes weren't paid, the government couldn't function. And when the government couldn't function, the entire system started to break down. While the correlation between low floods and political collapse is strong, we should recognize this as a significant contributing factor rather than the sole cause.

There wasn't a single bad year, but there were inadequate floods over an extended period, possibly linked to broader climate changes affecting northeastern Africa. Some years were probably fine, but others were disastrous, and the uncertainty itself was destabilizing. The Old Kingdom had been built on the assumption of a reliable agricultural surplus. When that surplus became unreliable, everything else became vulnerable.

Second, there was a political problem. The central government had become weaker while regional governors had grown stronger. Throughout the Old Kingdom, pharaohs had appointed governors to manage Egypt's provinces (nomes). These governors, called nomarchs, were initially royal appointees who served at the king's pleasure. But over time, particularly during the long reign of Pepi II, these positions increasingly became hereditary in many regions. Nomarchs passed their offices to their sons, creating regional dynasties with their own power bases.

These hereditary nomarchs built their own tombs in their home provinces rather than near the royal pyramid, suggesting they identified more with their region than with the king. They maintained their own courts, officials, and military forces. Gradually, they became semi-independent rulers who happened to acknowledge the distant pharaoh's authority—when it was convenient.

Third, there was an economic crisis tied to how the Old Kingdom government had operated. The pharaohs had granted extensive lands and resources to temples and to support the mortuary cults of deceased kings. These grants were permanent; once they were given, they couldn't easily be taken back. Over generations, more and more of Egypt's productive capacity became locked into these religious endowments, reducing the resources available to the reigning king. While exact figures are debated and difficult to confirm with existing records, scholars suggest that by the late Old Kingdom, a substantial portion of Egypt's agricultural land might have been committed to supporting temples and deceased kings' cults, leaving current pharaohs with shrinking revenue bases.

Fourth, there might have been a succession crisis. After Pepi II's incredibly long reign, the succession became murky. Several short reigns followed, suggesting instability in the royal family. When multiple claimants compete for the throne or when kings die quickly one after another, it undermines the entire system. Regional officials don't know who to support. The administration becomes paralyzed, and authority fragments.

The Seventh and Eighth Dynasties, which followed immediately after the Sixth, are not well known. Later Egyptian tradition claimed the Seventh Dynasty consisted of "seventy kings in seventy days." That is obviously not literally true, but it does indicate chaos and rapid turnover. The Eighth Dynasty kings seem to have been legitimate heirs to the Sixth Dynasty throne, ruling from Memphis, but their authority was limited, and their reigns were short.

By around 2160 BCE, Egypt had effectively split into competing power centers. The traditional capital at Memphis maintained some kings who claimed to rule all Egypt, but their actual control probably extended only over the immediate region. Meanwhile, powerful nomarch families in places like Herakleopolis in Middle Egypt and Thebes in Upper Egypt were establishing their own mini-kingdoms, paying lip service to Memphis while acting independently.

The Ninth and Tenth Dynasties, centered at Herakleopolis, represent one of these rival power centers. The Herakleopolitan kings controlled Middle Egypt and parts of the delta, and they claimed to be the legitimate rulers of Egypt. However, their authority was contested, particularly by an emerging power farther south: Thebes.

The Eleventh Dynasty, which would eventually reunify Egypt, started as just another provincial power based in Thebes in Upper Egypt. Initially, these Theban rulers were simply local strongmen controlling a few nomes around Thebes. But unlike many regional rulers who were content with local power, the Thebans had ambitions to control all of Egypt.

The result was civil war or at least prolonged conflict with Herakleopolis. This conflict played out over decades, with neither side strong enough to decisively defeat the other.

Life in a Fractured Land

What was this fragmented Egypt actually like? The sources are frustratingly limited, but we can sketch an outline.

Central authority had collapsed, but Egypt hadn't descended into complete anarchy. Instead, it had fractured into a patchwork of competing regional powers. Each nome or group of nomes was governed by local strongmen—sometimes hereditary nomarchs from Old Kingdom families, sometimes new men who had seized power. These local rulers maintained order in their territories, collected taxes, administered justice, and sometimes fought with their neighbors over borders and resources.

Some nomes prospered under capable local rulers who weren't sending tribute to a distant capital. Others suffered under weak or exploitative leaders, or they became battlegrounds as competing powers fought for control. The experience varied greatly depending on where you lived and who ruled your region.

Trade and communication between regions became more difficult and fragmented. The unified economic system of the Old Kingdom, where goods and resources flowed freely along the Nile under royal authority, had fractured. Now, goods had to pass through multiple territories, each controlled by different rulers who might demand tolls or simply block passage. While some trade continued, particularly at local and regional levels, the barriers created by political fragmentation reduced the ease and volume of long-distance commerce.

Security deteriorated in some areas. Without a strong central authority, banditry increased. Desert nomads, who had been kept in check during the Old Kingdom by Egyptian military power, raided into the Nile Valley. Some texts from this period speak of famine, social disorder, and the breakdown of traditional hierarchies.

However, we need to be careful about how we interpret these sources. Many of the texts describing chaos and disaster were written by scribes lamenting the loss of the old order and its certainties. These weren't necessarily true descriptions of the current conditions; they were often political propaganda designed to justify the need for strong central authority or nostalgic texts idealizing the past. The reality was probably less universally terrible than these texts suggest, even if it was certainly harder for many people than the stable Old Kingdom had been.

In regions with stable local governance, life probably continued much as it had during the Old Kingdom. You worked, paid taxes to your local lord instead of a distant pharaoh, participated in local festivals, and hoped for a good flood. Local markets functioned. Trade still occurred, though perhaps on a more limited scale. Social hierarchies persisted, though with more fluidity than in the rigid Old Kingdom system.

In less stable regions, survival became harder. When fighting broke out between rival powers, crops might be destroyed, irrigation systems damaged, and villages pillaged. When the Nile floods were poor and there was no centralized grain storage system to provide relief, local famines could be devastating. Archaeological evidence of widespread famine remains uneven across regions, suggesting that suffering was likely concentrated in specific regions and times rather than occurring throughout Egypt.

Some texts mention people selling themselves or their children into servitude to avoid starvation. Other texts describe abandoned settlements and empty fields, suggesting population decline in some regions due to death or migration.

Archaeological evidence suggests that many settlements continued functioning throughout the First Intermediate Period. Craft production continued. Local temples were maintained and sometimes expanded. New tombs were built for local elites. None of this would be happening if conditions were uniformly catastrophic.

One interesting development was increased mobility. When the central authority collapsed, people could move more easily between regions to seek better conditions. If one nomarch was oppressive or if harvests failed in one region, people could migrate to areas with better governance or more food. This was harder to do during the Old Kingdom when the state controlled movement more strictly.

The First Intermediate Period also saw changes in military organization. The large-scale royal armies of the Old Kingdom had been disbanded. Instead, local rulers maintained smaller military forces, such as personal retinues, local militias, and hired troops. This created opportunities for military careers that hadn't existed before. A capable fighter could rise in the service of a local nomarch, potentially achieving status that would have been impossible in the rigid Old Kingdom hierarchy.

For the average Egyptian farmer, the collapse of central authority might not have changed daily life as dramatically as we might think. You still worked your fields, paid your taxes (now to a local ruler instead of a distant king), and worried about the harvest. The pharaoh had always been a remote figure; now he was even more remote. As long as your immediate region was stable and well governed, life could go on much as it had before.

But the psychological impact was real. The Old Kingdom had seemed everlasting, built on cosmic principles that the pharaoh maintained through his divine nature. When that system collapsed, it must have shaken people's fundamental understanding of how the world worked. If ma'at could fail, if the eternal order could break down, what did that mean?

Religious life adapted to the changed circumstances. The great royal mortuary temples and pyramid complexes of the Old Kingdom had been supported by permanent endowments of land and resources. When the central authority collapsed, maintaining these temples became difficult. Some were abandoned, while others were maintained with reduced resources.

However, local temples often flourished. Without needing to send resources to support royal cult centers, local communities could invest more in their own temples. Provincial gods gained more importance. This religious decentralization would have lasting effects on the Egyptian religion.

Culture in a Fragmented Age

Historians used to call the First Intermediate Period a "dark age"—a time of chaos, poverty, and cultural decline between two golden ages. Modern scholars have become more skeptical of this characterization. Yes, central authority collapsed, and records became scarcer, but does that necessarily mean the period was uniformly terrible? Or were different things happening, things that don't show up as clearly in the archaeological record?

The term "dark age" suggests a period we know little about because few texts and monuments survived. This is partly true for the First Intermediate Period—we have fewer royal inscriptions, fewer dated monuments, and less certainty about the exact sequence of rulers. The archaeological record becomes harder to interpret when you don't have a strong centralized authority producing standardized records and monuments.

But "dark age" also implies cultural decline and social misery, and that's where modern scholars have started to push back. The First Intermediate Period looks dark compared to the Old Kingdom, partly because we're looking for the wrong things. We're looking for pyramids, royal inscriptions, and evidence of a centralized administration. When we don't find them, we assume everything collapsed. But maybe Egypt was just organized differently, and cultural production was happening at regional levels.

Political organization had clearly changed. Instead of a single strong pharaoh controlling all Egypt from Memphis, power was dispersed among multiple rulers. These competing rulers fought each other, but they also governed. The system was messier and more fragmented than the Old Kingdom, but it wasn't complete chaos.

In fact, in some regions, evidence suggests areas might have benefited from the collapse of central authority. During the Old Kingdom, provincial resources had been extracted to support the king's building projects and the royal court in Memphis. Now, in areas where capable local rulers emerged, those resources could stay local. A capable nomarch could use local wealth to improve irrigation systems, build local temples, support local craftsmen, and generally benefit his region rather than enriching a distant capital.

The archaeological evidence supports this. We see substantial tomb construction continuing throughout the First Intermediate Period, but it happened in the provinces rather than near Memphis. Nomarchs built elaborate rock-cut tombs in their home territories—places like Beni Hasan, Asyut, and Thebes. These tombs were sometimes quite sophisticated, decorated with painted scenes showing local life, religious rituals, and the nomarch's achievements.

Unlike the pyramids and mastabas of the Old Kingdom, these tombs were carved directly into cliff faces. This was partly practical—stone was harder to transport when the central authority had collapsed—but it also created different architectural possibilities.

The tomb of Ankhtifi at el-Mo'alla, for example, contains biographical inscriptions describing how this nomarch maintained order in his region during a time of crisis: "I gave bread to the hungry and clothing to the naked; I brought the cattle of the herdsman to high ground ... There was no one dying of hunger in my time."

Whether Ankhtifi actually did all this is not as important as what the inscription reveals: even local strongmen felt the need to justify their rule by claiming to maintain ma'at and care for their people. The ideology of good governance persisted even when centralized kingship had collapsed.

The art style in these provincial tombs differs from Old Kingdom art. It's less standardized, more varied, and sometimes less technically accomplished but often more lively and creative. Provincial artists weren't following strict royal artistic conventions; they were developing their own regional styles. This produced art that's rougher in execution but sometimes more interesting and experimental. It was less bound by tradition.

Some scholars argue this shows artistic decline since provincial artists lacked the skill of royal workshops. Others argue it represents artistic freedom; without royal standards to follow, artists could innovate. The truth is probably somewhere in between. Technical skills might have declined in some places when royal workshops closed and master craftsmen weren't training apprentices in the old methods. However, regional styles could flourish because artists weren't constrained by the central authority.

Stelae (stone slabs with inscriptions) from this period also show stylistic changes. Many are roughly carved compared to Old Kingdom standards, but they're also more numerous and more widely distributed. Non-elite individuals could afford commemorative stelae that would have been beyond their means or access during the Old Kingdom. This suggests either that costs had decreased with the collapse of royal workshops or that wealth had been redistributed—or both.

Pottery from the First Intermediate Period also shows regional variation. Without standardized royal pottery workshops, local potters developed distinctive regional styles. Archaeologists can identify where pottery was made based on these regional characteristics, which helps us understand trade patterns and regional interactions during this period.

Literature, interestingly, seems to have flourished during the First Intermediate Period. Some of ancient Egypt's most famous literary texts either come from this period or reflect on it. These include texts lamenting social disorder, instructions on how to behave morally, and reflections on mortality and the meaning of life. The literature of this period reflects genuine anxiety about social disorder, reversed hierarchies, and the absence of strong kingship.

The *Admonitions of Ipuwer* describes a world turned upside down: "Indeed, the land turns around as does a potter's wheel. The robber is now a possessor of riches ... Indeed, noble ladies are gleaners, and nobles are in the workhouse." The text depicts complete social inversion—the wealthy are reduced to poverty, the poor are enriched, and traditional hierarchies have collapsed.

Is this description accurate? Probably not literally. It's likely a literary exaggeration designed to emphasize how far Egypt had fallen from the ideal order, and it might reflect retrospective anxieties about the period rather than providing a report of actual conditions. However, it reveals what Egyptians feared most: not just poverty or violence but the collapse of the social order itself.

The *Instructions for Merikare* takes a different approach. This text, supposedly written by a Herakleopolitan king to his son, provides advice on how to rule: be just, reward competent officials, maintain the borders, care for the welfare of your people, and respect the gods. But it also acknowledges hard realities: "A generation of people passes by, and the gods who were aforetime rest in their pyramids ... Be not evil. Patience is good. Make your monument last through love of you."

This text shows a ruler trying to navigate difficult times, acknowledging that even kings are mortal and that good governance requires more than divine authority. It also requires competence, justice, and earning people's loyalty. It's more pragmatic and less triumphant than Old Kingdom royal ideology.

The *Dispute Between a Man and His Ba* is even more philosophical. In this text, a man debates with his ba (his soul or spiritual essence) about whether life is worth living. The man wants to die and enter the afterlife, but his ba argues for staying alive. The text includes beautiful poetry: "Death is before me today like the recovery of a sick man, like going forth into a garden after sickness. Death is before me today like the odor of myrrh, like sitting under the sail on a windy day." This text shows Egyptians grappling with existential questions about meaning, mortality, and the value of life in difficult times.

By around 2055 BCE, after more than a century of fragmentation, Egypt was ready for reunification. The Theban rulers of the Eleventh Dynasty had gradually extended their control northward, conquering or absorbing rival territories. The Herakleopolitan kingdom had weakened. The stage was set for a Theban king to reunify all of Egypt and establish the Middle Kingdom.

The First Intermediate Period showed that Egyptian civilization was resilient—it survived the collapse of central authority, after all—but also that it deeply valued unified kingship. The disorder of this period would make Egyptians appreciate centralized rule even more when it was eventually restored. The Middle Kingdom that followed would be built on lessons learned during the collapse: the importance of strong but just kingship, the value of provincial loyalty, the need for competent administration, and the dangers of letting royal authority erode.

Chapter 5: The Middle Kingdom—Reunification and Renaissance

Egypt Reunited

Around 2055 BCE, a Theban king named Mentuhotep II achieved what had seemed impossible for over a century: he reunified Egypt. (Scholarly estimates for this reunification vary, with some placing it closer to 2040 BCE, but we'll use the commonly cited date of around 2055 BCE throughout this book.) The First Intermediate Period ended not with a peaceful agreement but with conquest, as the Theban rulers of Upper Egypt defeated their rivals in the north and brought the entire Nile Valley back under a single ruler's control.

Mentuhotep II (who reigned approximately 2055 to 2004 BCE) was the second king of the Eleventh Dynasty to bear that name, but he was the first to control all of Egypt. His predecessors had ruled only the Theban region of Upper Egypt, locked in a long conflict with the Herakleopolitan kings who controlled Middle and Lower Egypt. This civil war had dragged on for decades, with neither side able to deliver a decisive blow.

Mentuhotep II seems to have been both a capable military leader and an effective administrator. He extended Theban control northward, conquering or absorbing territories one by one. The details are frustratingly sparse—we don't have detailed battle accounts or campaign records—but the result is clear. By around 2055 BCE, the Herakleopolitan kingdom had fallen, and Mentuhotep II claimed control over Egypt from the First Cataract in the south to the Mediterranean in the north, though full administrative control over the entire territory, particularly in the delta and northern regions, would have taken time to establish completely.

Reunification required more than military victory; it required convincing provincial rulers throughout Egypt to accept Theban authority. Mentuhotep had to rebuild administrative systems that had fragmented and restore confidence in centralized kingship. The king adopted an epithet to mark the reunification: "Sematowy," meaning "Uniter of the Two Lands." This wasn't just propaganda. Mentuhotep II presented himself as restoring ma'at, bringing back the proper order that had been lost during the chaos of the First Intermediate Period. He was, in a sense, Egypt's second founder, completing what Narmer had done hundreds of years earlier.

Thebes now became Egypt's capital. This represented a significant shift. During the Old Kingdom, Memphis had been the undisputed center of power. During the First Intermediate Period, power had been dispersed among multiple centers. Now, Thebes in Upper Egypt became the royal residence and primary administrative center, though Memphis retained importance as a traditional power center and religious site.

The choice of Thebes had lasting consequences. It elevated the city's patron god, Amun, to national prominence. While Amun had existed as a god during the Old Kingdom, he was relatively minor compared to major state deities. Now, as the god of Egypt's new ruling dynasty, Amun's cult would grow dramatically in wealth and influence, eventually making him the king of the Egyptian gods. The priests of Amun at Thebes would become some of the most powerful people in Egypt.

Mentuhotep II ruled for over fifty years, giving Egypt the stability it desperately needed. However, the Eleventh Dynasty would be short-lived. His successors—Mentuhotep III and Mentuhotep IV—ruled for relatively brief periods. Then, around 1985 BCE, power passed to a new dynasty, the Twelfth, though the transition seems to have been peaceful.

The first king of the Twelfth Dynasty, Amenemhat I (approximately 1985-1956 BCE), might have been Mentuhotep IV's vizier, who took the throne possibly through a coup. Ancient sources hint at irregularities in the succession, and later literature would justify Amenemhat I's rule by emphasizing the need for strong leadership. A text called the *Prophecy of Neferti* (written after the fact, despite its supposed predictive nature) described the chaos of the First Intermediate Period and prophesied the coming of a king named Ameny (short for Amenemhat) who would restore order. This was propaganda designed to legitimize the new dynasty.

Amenemhat I made the crucial decision to move the capital north from Thebes to a new city called Itjtawy, located near the Faiyum region in Middle Egypt. This was strategic. While Thebes was important as the dynasty's ancestral home and as a religious center for Amun, it was far south, making the administration of Lower Egypt difficult. Itjtawy, positioned between Upper and Lower Egypt, could serve as a better administrative center for the kingdom.

This didn't diminish Thebes—the city remained extremely important, and Amun remained the state god—but it showed pragmatic thinking about governance. The Twelfth Dynasty kings would be buried near their new capital, not at Thebes, though they continued to build temples and monuments at Thebes.

Amenemhat I also established a practice that would become characteristic of the Middle Kingdom: co-regency. Near the end of his reign, he elevated his son Senusret I as co-ruler, allowing for a smooth transition of power. When Amenemhat I died—according to later literature, specifically the *Teaching of Amenemhat*, he was assassinated in a palace conspiracy—Senusret I was already established as king and could take full power immediately.

The *Teaching of Amenemhat* is a remarkable text. It was supposedly written by the dead king to his son, warning him about the dangers of court life: "Trust not a brother, know not a friend, make not for yourself intimates—there is no fulfilling of the heart in them." Whether this literary text reflects an actual assassination or was composed to explain a succession crisis and justify Senusret I's rule is uncertain, but either way, it shows the political dangers that even powerful kings faced or that later propagandists wanted people to believe they faced.

Senusret I (approximately 1956–1911 BCE) inherited a stable Egypt and spent his long reign strengthening it further. The Twelfth Dynasty continued with a succession of capable rulers: Amenemhat II, Senusret II, Senusret III, and Amenemhat III. Each contributed to Egypt's prosperity and power, though Senusret III and Amenemhat III particularly stand out.

Senusret III (approximately 1870–1831 BCE) was one of the Middle Kingdom's greatest military leaders. Perhaps more importantly, he undertook significant administrative reforms. Evidence suggests he substantially weakened or reorganized the system of hereditary nomarchs who had become so powerful during the First Intermediate Period. By the end of his reign, the old nome system had been reorganized, with many nomarchs apparently replaced by royal appointees who could be transferred and dismissed. This centralized royal power in a way that hadn't existed since the Old Kingdom.

Amenemhat III (approximately 1831–1786 BCE) presided over what was probably the Middle Kingdom's economic peak. His long reign was peaceful and prosperous. He focused on internal development, particularly large-scale irrigation and reclamation projects in the Faiyum region, turning marshland into productive agricultural land. He exploited the mineral resources of the Sinai and the eastern desert. His reign represents the Middle Kingdom at its most successful—a stable, wealthy, well-administered kingdom under a strong pharaoh.

But the dynasty's end was messy. Amenemhat III was succeeded by Amenemhat IV and then by Queen Sobekneferu, Egypt's first clearly attested female ruler. Sobekneferu's reign was brief—only about four years—and ended without an obvious heir, leading to the end of the Twelfth Dynasty around 1802 BCE.

The Thirteenth Dynasty followed, but it never achieved the stability of the Twelfth. Kings succeeded each other rapidly, suggesting political instability or short reigns for unknown reasons. Egypt remained unified and relatively prosperous during the early Thirteenth Dynasty, but the rapid turnover of rulers indicated underlying problems. The strong centralized state that Mentuhotep II had rebuilt and that the Twelfth Dynasty had perfected was beginning to weaken again.

The Golden Age of Literature and Art

The Middle Kingdom produced some of ancient Egypt's greatest literary works and most beautiful art. Modern scholars often call the Middle Kingdom the "classical age" of Egyptian culture, when the Egyptian language and artistic traditions reached a level of sophistication that later periods would try to imitate.

The language itself is telling. Middle Egyptian, the form of the language used during this period, became the standard "classical" Egyptian that scribes would continue to use for formal inscriptions for over a thousand years, even after the spoken language had evolved into later forms. When you see hieroglyphic inscriptions from the New Kingdom or even the Late Period, they're often written in Middle Egyptian rather than the contemporary language, much like Latin continued to be used for formal documents in medieval Europe long after people stopped speaking it daily.

The Old Kingdom had produced practical texts, like administrative records, royal inscriptions, and religious spells, but relatively little that we'd recognize as literature. The First Intermediate Period had produced some notable works, but they were mostly focused on the crisis of the time. The Middle Kingdom produced a diverse range of literary genres: adventure stories, moral instructions, religious hymns, love poetry, and philosophical dialogues.

The *Tale of Sinuhe* is perhaps the Middle Kingdom's most famous literary work, and it's genuinely good literature by any standard. The story follows Sinuhe, a royal courtier who overhears news of King Amenemhat I's assassination. Fearing he might be implicated, Sinuhe flees Egypt in a panic. He becomes a refugee in Syria, where he rises to become a powerful chief, marries, has children, and leads a successful life. But he never stops longing for Egypt. In his old age, the new pharaoh (Senusret I) invites him home, and Sinuhe returns to Egypt, where he's welcomed and given a proper tomb so he can be buried in his homeland.

The story explores themes of identity, belonging, fear, exile, and redemption. Sinuhe's internal conflict—his success abroad versus his desperate longing for home—feels real. The story doesn't have simple heroes or villains; it has complex characters making understandable choices. The prose is elegant, with vivid descriptions and emotional depth.

The *Eloquent Peasant* is another masterpiece, telling the story of a peasant named Khun-Anup whose goods are stolen by a corrupt official. Seeking justice, the peasant appeals to the local magistrate with a series of elaborate, eloquent speeches about justice, righteousness, and the duties of officials. The magistrate is so impressed by the peasant's eloquence that he keeps delaying judgment just to hear more speeches. Eventually, justice is done—the peasant gets his goods back, and the corrupt official is punished.

The story works on multiple levels. It's entertaining; the peasant's increasingly frustrated eloquence is genuinely witty. It's also a meditation on justice and the moral obligations of those in power. The speeches are beautiful examples of Egyptian rhetoric, filled with metaphors and wordplay. And there's an underlying tension. The magistrate's delay means justice is slow, even when the powerful find the petitioner amusing. Is this really how justice should work?

The "Instructions" genre continued from earlier periods but reached new heights. The *Instructions of Ptahhotep* (possibly from the Old Kingdom but preserved in Middle Kingdom copies) offered advice on proper behavior and wisdom. These texts weren't just lists of rules; they were also thoughtful explorations of how to live well and govern justly.

Religious literature also flourished. Hymns to various gods were composed with poetic beauty. The "Hymn to the Nile" celebrated the river that made Egypt possible: "Hail to you, O Nile, who manifest yourself over this land and come in peace to give life to Egypt." The "Hymn to Senusret III" praised the king but in ways that revealed what Egyptians valued in their rulers: "How the gods rejoice—you have strengthened their offerings. How the people rejoice—you have established their frontiers. How your forebears rejoice—you have increased their portions."

The Coffin Texts, religious spells that had democratized in the First Intermediate Period, were further developed and standardized in the Middle Kingdom. These spells, painted on coffins, were meant to help the deceased navigate the afterlife. They show complex religious thinking about death, the soul, and eternal life.

Art during the Middle Kingdom showed distinctive characteristics. Sculpture achieved a level of realism and psychological depth that was new. The famous statues of Senusret III don't show a generic divine king. They show a specific individual with prominent ears and a serious, almost brooding expression. Some scholars interpret these portraits as showing realistic age and personality. Others argue they're still idealized but representing a new ideal: the king as experienced, serious, burdened by responsibility rather than eternally youthful and triumphant. Either way, they're psychologically complex in a way Old Kingdom royal sculpture rarely was.

Statues of Senusret III.[8]

Private sculptures—statues of non-royal individuals—also flourished. These ranged from traditional standing or seated figures to "block statues," showing a man squatting with his knees drawn up and his body wrapped in a cloak, creating a compact block shape. These block statues would remain popular throughout Egyptian history.

Jewelry from the Middle Kingdom is spectacular. Egyptian craftsmen had always been skilled in metalwork, but Middle Kingdom jewelry shows great refinement. The treasures found in the tombs of Middle Kingdom princesses—intricately designed pectorals inlaid with semi-precious stones, delicate beadwork, and elaborate diadems—demonstrate extraordinary technical skill and artistic sophistication.

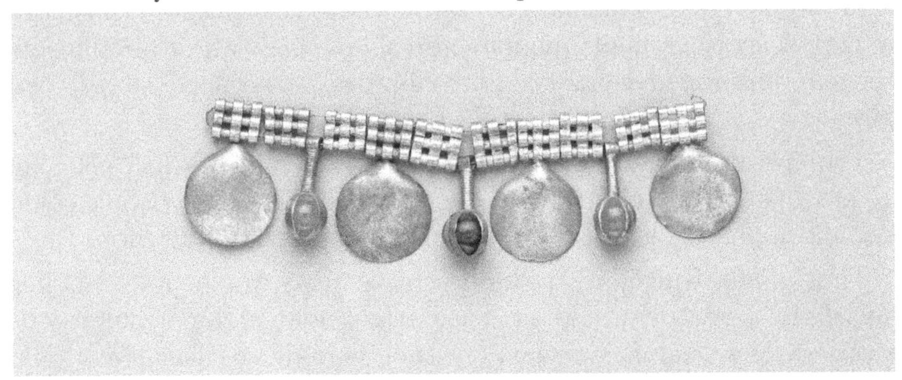

Jewelry from the Middle Kingdom[9]

Architecture during the Middle Kingdom shifted away from the massive pyramids of the Old Kingdom. Kings still built pyramids, but they were smaller and often built with a mudbrick core rather than solid stone. The Middle Kingdom pyramids also don't match their Old Kingdom predecessors in scale or durability (many have collapsed or are poorly eroded), but the pyramid complexes included elaborate temples and tombs.

The mortuary temple of Mentuhotep II at Deir el-Bahri is particularly notable. It is a terraced structure built against the cliff face. This temple inspired one of ancient Egypt's most famous buildings: Queen Hatshepsut's mortuary temple, built right next to it about five hundred years later.

Rock-cut tombs became more elaborate. At Beni Hasan in Middle Egypt, provincial officials carved tombs into the cliffs with painted columns, decorated chapels, and vivid scenes of daily life. These tombs show the wealth and power of even provincial elites during the Middle Kingdom's prosperous years.

Why did the Middle Kingdom produce such a remarkable culture? Stability and prosperity provided the resources and leisure for cultural production. When society is stable and wealthy, it can support artists, poets, and scribes who have time to refine their crafts.

The experience of the First Intermediate Period also forced Egyptians to think deeply about their society, values, and system of government. Literature from this period shows more questioning, more philosophical reflection, and more interest in individual psychology and moral complexity than earlier periods. The breakdown and restoration of order had made Egyptians more conscious of what they valued and why.

Royal patronage encouraged culture. Middle Kingdom pharaohs supported scribal schools, temple workshops, and artistic production. They commissioned literature, built libraries, and valued literacy and learning.

The spread of literacy, which was still limited to a small elite but broader than before, created audiences for literature. More people could read and appreciate texts, creating a market for literary production.

The Middle Kingdom's cultural achievements would have a lasting impact. Its literature would be copied and studied for centuries. Its artistic styles would be imitated by later periods. Its language would become the classical standard. When New Kingdom Egyptians wanted to connect with their glorious past, they looked back to the Middle Kingdom as a golden age of culture and wisdom.

Expansion and Fortification

The Middle Kingdom wasn't just an age of cultural achievement. It was also an age of military expansion and strategic defense. The Twelfth Dynasty pharaohs, particularly Senusret I, Senusret III, and Amenemhat III, pushed Egypt's borders farther than they'd been since the Old Kingdom, established firm control over Nubia to the south, and created defensive systems to protect Egyptian interests.

Nubia was the primary target of Middle Kingdom expansion. This region, stretching south from Egypt's traditional border at the First Cataract, was rich in resources that Egypt desperately wanted: gold, copper, semi-precious stones, exotic wood, ivory, and access to trade routes reaching deep into Africa. During the Old Kingdom, Egypt conducted expeditions into Nubia and maintained trading relationships with the Nubians. During the First Intermediate Period, Egyptian control collapsed, and Nubia became independent.

The Middle Kingdom pharaohs were determined to reassert Egyptian dominance. Senusret I conducted military campaigns into Lower Nubia, the region immediately south of Egypt. He erected a stela at Buhen near the Second Cataract claiming to have established Egypt's border there. However, claiming territory and actually controlling it are different things.

Senusret III took the Nubian conquest to a new level. He conducted at least three major campaigns into Nubia during his reign, pushing Egyptian control firmly to the Second Cataract and beyond. His inscriptions describe these campaigns with unusual frankness about the difficulties involved. One boundary stela erected during his eighth regnal year states: "Southern boundary, made in year 8, under the majesty of the King ... in order to prevent any Nubian from crossing it, by water or by land, with a ship or any herds of the Nubians; except a Nubian who shall come to do trading ... or with a commission. Every good thing shall be done with them, but without allowing a ship of the Nubians to pass ... downstream, forever."

This was a controlled occupation with regulations about trade and movement. Nubians weren't banned entirely; they could trade at Egyptian outposts and pass with permission. However, unauthorized movement across the border was forbidden.

To maintain control, the Middle Kingdom established an elaborate system of fortifications in Nubia. Between the First and Second Cataracts, at least thirteen major forts were built, mostly during the reign of Senusret III. These were substantial military installations with massive mudbrick walls, ditches, bastions, and sophisticated defensive features.

Some of these forts were enormous. The fort at Buhen had walls over thirty feet high and sixteen feet thick, with towers projecting from the walls to allow defenders to fire on attackers from multiple angles. The fort at Semna controlled a narrow passage in the Nile where all boat traffic had to pass. The fort at Mirgissa included not just fortifications but also workshops, granaries, administrative buildings, and housing for the garrison and their families.

These forts served multiple purposes. Militarily, they protected Egypt from Nubian raids and provided bases for Egyptian expeditions farther south. Economically, they controlled trade routes and access to gold mines. Administratively, they extended Egyptian governance into Nubia, with Egyptian officials collecting taxes and enforcing Egyptian law. The forts also served as centers for trade, where Nubians could exchange goods under Egyptian supervision.

The extent and sophistication of these fortifications are remarkable. They show advanced military engineering, with walls designed to resist both direct assaults and siege warfare. They had features like glacis (sloped walls) to prevent mining, dry moats, and carefully planned fields of fire. They also show the Middle Kingdom's administrative capacity. Building and maintaining these forts required organizing labor, transporting supplies, maintaining garrisons, and creating supply chains stretching hundreds of miles from Egypt.

The Middle Kingdom also conducted military operations in the Levant (modern Israel, Palestine, Lebanon, and Syria), though on a smaller scale than in Nubia. Egyptian interest in this region was partly economic—the Levant produced cedar wood, wine, olive oil, and other goods Egypt wanted—and partly strategic, as controlling trade routes through the Levant provided wealth and prevented threats from western Asia.

Evidence for Middle Kingdom activity in the Levant includes Egyptian artifacts found at sites in the region, Egyptian inscriptions mentioning campaigns or expeditions, and references in Egyptian texts to Asian prisoners or tribute. The famous "Execration Texts"—pottery bowls or clay figurines inscribed with the names of Egypt's enemies and then ritually broken—include names of Levantine cities and rulers, showing Egyptian interest in this region.

However, there were no permanent forts or major Egyptian settlements. Instead, Egypt maintained commercial relationships, sometimes backed by military expeditions or threats, with the various city-states of the region. The pharaoh claimed dominance, but actual control was limited.

Trade networks expanded dramatically during the Middle Kingdom. Egyptian expeditions reached Punt (probably somewhere on the Red Sea coast of modern Sudan, Eritrea, or Somalia), bringing back incense, myrrh, ebony, ivory, and exotic animals. Ships traveled to Byblos on the Lebanese coast for cedar. Trade routes connected Egypt with the Aegean world, western Asia, and deep into Africa.

Internally, the Middle Kingdom invested in infrastructure. Irrigation systems were expanded and improved. The Faiyum region, a natural depression west of the Nile, was developed through water management projects that increased agricultural productivity. Canals and water control systems allowed more land to be cultivated.

The Middle Kingdom's expansion and fortification showed Egypt at the height of its power during this period. The kingdom was culturally sophisticated, militarily strong, administratively capable, and economically prosperous. The pharaohs could project power hundreds of miles from Egypt's traditional borders, maintain permanent military installations in conquered territories, and organize complex logistical systems to support expansion.

But this system required a strong central authority. The forts needed to be manned, supplied, and maintained. The administration needed to function smoothly. The pharaoh needed to be effective and respected. When these conditions held, the Middle Kingdom flourished. When they began to break down in the late Thirteenth Dynasty, the entire system became vulnerable.

Chapter 6:
The Second Intermediate Period and the Hyksos

Foreign Rulers on Egyptian Soil

The Second Intermediate Period (approximately 1802–1550 BCE, though scholarly chronologies vary, with some placing the start closer to 1782 or 1750 BCE) was one of ancient Egypt's most dramatic and controversial chapters. For the first time in Egyptian history, Lower Egypt and parts of Middle Egypt fell under the control of foreign rulers—people Egyptians called the Hyksos. This wasn't a brief raid or a temporary occupation. For a period of time (the exact duration is debated among scholars), foreign kings ruled northern Egypt from their capital in the delta, while native Egyptian rulers controlled Upper Egypt from Thebes. Egypt was divided again, but this time, the division wasn't just between competing Egyptian factions. It was between Egyptians and outsiders. The political landscape was complex, with overlapping dynasties, vassal states, and contested buffer regions making the reality more intricate than a simple north–south divide.

Who were the Hyksos? The name comes from the Egyptian phrase *hekau khasut,* which means "rulers of foreign lands" or "foreign chiefs." Later Egyptian propaganda would demonize them as barbaric invaders who conquered Egypt through military force and ruled with cruelty. The reality was more complex.

The Hyksos weren't a single unified people or ethnic group. They were primarily Semitic-speaking peoples from the Levant (the region covering modern Syria, Lebanon, Israel, and Palestine) who had been migrating into the Egyptian delta for generations. During the late Middle Kingdom, particularly during the Thirteenth Dynasty, these migrations increased. Some came as traders, some as laborers, some as mercenaries, and some as refugees fleeing conflicts or famines in their homelands.

This wasn't unusual or alarming at first. Egypt had long maintained contact with neighboring peoples, and foreigners had long settled in Egypt, particularly in the cosmopolitan delta region bordering Asia. Egyptian texts from the Middle Kingdom mention Asian peoples living in Egypt, working in various occupations, and even serving in the Egyptian military.

What changed during the late Thirteenth Dynasty was the weakening of central Egyptian authority. The Thirteenth Dynasty suffered from political instability, with kings succeeding each other rapidly. This created a power vacuum, particularly in the delta, which was far from the Thirteenth Dynasty capital.

Into this vacuum stepped ambitious leaders from the Asiatic communities in the delta. Rather than a single dramatic invasion, the Hyksos takeover was probably gradual. Local strongmen with Asian backgrounds gained control of the delta towns. They established their own power bases, collected taxes, and maintained armies. Eventually, these local rulers united into a kingdom centered at Avaris in the eastern delta. Their leaders declared themselves pharaohs—the Fifteenth Dynasty, ruling approximately 1650 to 1550 BCE.

The Hyksos adopted Egyptian royal titles, used Egyptian administrative systems, wrote their names in hieroglyphs, and presented themselves as legitimate pharaohs. They weren't trying to destroy Egyptian civilization; they were trying to become Egyptian kings. But they still maintained distinctive cultural elements, creating a syncretic hybrid culture at Avaris. They worshiped the Egyptian god Seth (associated with foreign lands and chaos in Egyptian mythology—perhaps an ironic choice, or perhaps they identified with Seth's power and foreignness). They also continued to worship Levantine deities. Archaeological evidence shows substantial Asian cultural elements, including distinctive house styles, burial customs, and pottery types alongside Egyptian forms, demonstrating cultural fusion rather than simple adoption of Egyptian traditions.

Avaris was strategically located in the eastern delta, close to the routes leading to and from the Levant. Archaeological evidence shows that the Hyksos capital was a wealthy, cosmopolitan city. Pottery from Cyprus, the Levant, and Nubia has been found there, indicating extensive trade networks. The city included temples, palaces, and substantial residential areas. This wasn't a military camp or a temporary stronghold; it was the capital of a kingdom that expected to endure.

The extent of Hyksos control is debated. They definitely controlled the delta and possibly parts of Middle Egypt. Upper Egypt, however, remained under the control of native Egyptian rulers based at Thebes— the Sixteenth and Seventeenth Dynasties. Between the Hyksos kingdom in the north and the Theban kingdom in the south lay a buffer zone of smaller kingdoms and local rulers. Some were more aligned with the Hyksos, while others aligned more with Thebes.

The Fourteenth Dynasty, contemporary with and perhaps a vassal of the Fifteenth Dynasty (the Hyksos), controlled parts of the western delta. The Sixteenth Dynasty is less clearly defined. Scholars debate whether this means they were also Hyksos vassals, highly fragmented local rulers in the buffer regions, or native Egyptian rulers in areas between the Hyksos and Theban territories.

These intermediate territories served as buffer zones between the Hyksos and the Thebans, but they also represented opportunities. Both the Hyksos and the Thebans competed for influence over these regions, trying to extend their control or at least ensure these areas didn't support their rivals.

In Upper Egypt, the Seventeenth Dynasty ruled from Thebes, maintaining the traditions of pharaonic kingship and claiming to be the legitimate rulers of all Egypt, even though they controlled only the south. The early Seventeenth Dynasty kings seem to have coexisted with the Hyksos, perhaps acknowledging Hyksos dominance in exchange for being left alone. This was pragmatic but humiliating, and it couldn't last forever.

The Theban kingdom was smaller and probably less wealthy than the Hyksos kingdom. The delta was richer agricultural land and controlled the Mediterranean trade. Thebes, far to the south, had less economic power. However, Thebes had advantages: a strong sense of Egyptian identity and legitimacy, control of the southern trade routes to Nubia (though these were contested), and military traditions. Most importantly,

Thebes had the burning desire to expel the foreigners and reunify Egypt under native rule.

This situation was complicated by yet another group: the Nubians to the south. The Kingdom of Kush, centered at Kerma in Nubia, had grown powerful as Egyptian control weakened. During the Middle Kingdom, this region had been under Egyptian control, with Egyptian fortresses dominating the landscape. Now, those fortresses were in Kushite hands. Kush was a powerful kingdom with its own distinct culture, though it was heavily influenced by centuries of contact with Egypt. Kushite rulers built substantial tombs, controlled valuable trade routes to inner Africa, and fielded armies that could threaten Egyptian territory.

The relationship between the Kushites and Hyksos is murky. Egyptian texts, including the Kamose Stela, mention communication between the two kingdoms. That stela describes intercepting a message from a Hyksos king to the king of Kush, which may represent an actual relationship, or it may be Theban propaganda designed to emphasize the threats they faced. Whether or not there was a formal alliance, the Thebans certainly faced pressures from both directions. The exact nature and extent of any Hyksos–Kushite cooperation is speculative, though.

So, what did the Hyksos bring to Egypt? This is where the story gets interesting. Despite later Egyptian propaganda portraying them as destructive invaders, the Hyksos are widely believed to have introduced important military innovations.

Most significantly, the leading hypothesis among scholars is that they popularized and weaponized the horse and chariot in Egypt, though Egypt might have had limited exposure to these technologies prior to or during the early Hyksos period. Horses weren't native to Egypt and weren't clearly used for military purposes during the Old or Middle Kingdoms. The Hyksos, coming from regions where horses had been domesticated and had chariots developed for warfare, very likely brought this military technology to Egypt. The war chariot—a light, fast, two-wheeled vehicle pulled by horses—revolutionized ancient warfare. It provided mobility, speed, and a stable platform for archers.

The Hyksos also introduced or popularized new types of weapons, like the composite bow (made from multiple materials and more powerful than the simple bows Egyptians had used), new bronze-working techniques, and improved body armor. They brought new musical instruments, new pottery styles, and cultural influences from western Asia.

Ironically, when the Egyptians eventually expelled the Hyksos and reunified Egypt, they adopted all of these innovations themselves. The New Kingdom Egyptian military, which would build an empire larger than anything Egypt had achieved before, would do so using horses, chariots, composite bows, and military tactics learned from or inspired by the Hyksos.

But Egyptians—at least in Thebes—were humiliated by foreign rule over part of their country. Egyptian ideology held that Egypt was the center of creation, the only truly civilized land. Having foreigners rule any part of Egypt violated this worldview.

The Hyksos period would be remembered by later Egyptians as a time of shame and disaster, even though the actual period seems to have been less catastrophic than propaganda suggested.

Life and Culture in a Divided Land

In the Hyksos-controlled delta, life probably continued much as it had during the Middle Kingdom. Farmers farmed, craftsmen worked, and trade flourished. The main difference was that the rulers had foreign origins and foreign names, and the god Seth received more prominence. For most ordinary Egyptians in the delta, the difference between a native Egyptian pharaoh and a Hyksos pharaoh might not have been enormous. Trade continued. Culture developed. Life went on for most Egyptians.

In the Theban kingdom, there was probably more awareness of and resentment toward the division. The Theban rulers maintained a strong Egyptian identity and claimed to be the legitimate rulers of all Egypt. Royal propaganda emphasized the need to restore ma'at and expel the foreigners. This created a militarized society with a mission.

In the buffer zones of Middle Egypt, life was probably less stable. These regions were contested territory, where power could shift between Hyksos influence, Theban influence, and local autonomy. This created opportunities for ambitious local leaders and dangers, from shifting political allegiances and possible conflict.

Cultural production during the Second Intermediate Period continued, though on a smaller scale than during the unified Middle Kingdom. The Hyksos patronized Egyptian artistic traditions while also introducing Asian elements. Scarabs (seal amulets) from the Hyksos period show both Egyptian and Asian motifs. Pottery styles show mixing of Egyptian and Levantine traditions.

A scarab with the cartouche (an oval frame with the name of an Egyptian pharaoh inside) of a Hyksos king.[10]

In Thebes, artistic production maintained conservative Egyptian traditions, emphasizing continuity with the Middle Kingdom and rejecting foreign influences. Theban art from this period looks deliberately old-fashioned, as if asserting, "We are the true Egyptians, maintaining our traditions, while the north has been corrupted by foreigners."

The religious landscape also shifted. In the Hyksos kingdom, Seth became prominent as the patron deity of the ruling dynasty. In Thebes, Amun continued his rise to supreme importance. The religious division reinforced the political division, as there were different gods for different kingdoms.

Military technology evolved during this period, driven by competition between the kingdoms. The Hyksos' superior military technology—horses, chariots, and composite bows—gave them significant advantages. However, the Thebans were learning and adapting. By the late Second Intermediate Period, the Theban kings had begun acquiring horses and chariots, learning to use these new weapons, and developing tactics to counter them.

By the mid-16th century BCE, the situation was becoming untenable from the Theban perspective. The Seventeenth Dynasty kings, particularly Seqenenre Tao and his sons Kamose and Ahmose, would decide that coexistence with the Hyksos was no longer acceptable. They launched a war to expel the foreigners and reunify Egypt.

This wasn't just about reclaiming territory—it was about restoring Egyptian pride, reasserting the proper cosmic order, and proving that native Egyptian rulers could triumph over foreign invaders. The struggle would be difficult, spanning multiple reigns and requiring fundamental changes in Egyptian military organization and tactics.

But when the war finally succeeded, Egypt wouldn't just return to what it had been during the Middle Kingdom. The experience of fighting the Hyksos, the adoption of new military technologies, the militarization of Egyptian society, renewed economic prosperity, religious developments centered on Amun, and the consolidation of the Theban state would all come together to transform Egypt into something new. It would become an aggressive, expansionist empire that would dominate the Near East for centuries. The New Kingdom was about to begin, born from multiple factors, with the struggle against the Hyksos as the catalyst.

Chapter 7: The New Kingdom Begins—Egypt Becomes a Superpower

Throwing Out the Foreigners

The war that would reunify Egypt and establish the New Kingdom began not with careful planning but with frustration and rage. By the mid-16th century BCE, the Theban rulers of the Seventeenth Dynasty had endured Hyksos domination for generations. They paid tribute, acknowledged Hyksos superiority, and kept their ambitions confined to Upper Egypt. But this humiliating arrangement couldn't last forever.

The decisive break came during the reign of Seqenenre Tao (approximately 1560 BCE), one of the last kings of the Seventeenth Dynasty. Egyptian texts tell a story (almost certainly legendary or symbolic rather than factual, but it perhaps contains a kernel of historical accuracy) about what sparked the conflict. The Hyksos king, Apepi, sent a message to Seqenenre complaining that the hippopotamuses in the sacred pool at Thebes were making so much noise that he couldn't sleep—he lived in Avaris, hundreds of miles to the north. This was obviously a deliberate provocation designed to humiliate the Theban king.

Whether this particular story reflects actual events or not, something triggered open warfare. Seqenenre Tao went to war against the Hyksos. We know this because we have his mummy, and it tells a brutal story.

Seqenenre's skull shows multiple severe head wounds from axes and maces, wounds consistent with battlefield trauma. He died violently, probably in battle against the Hyksos or their allies. The war had begun, but the Theban king had paid the ultimate price.

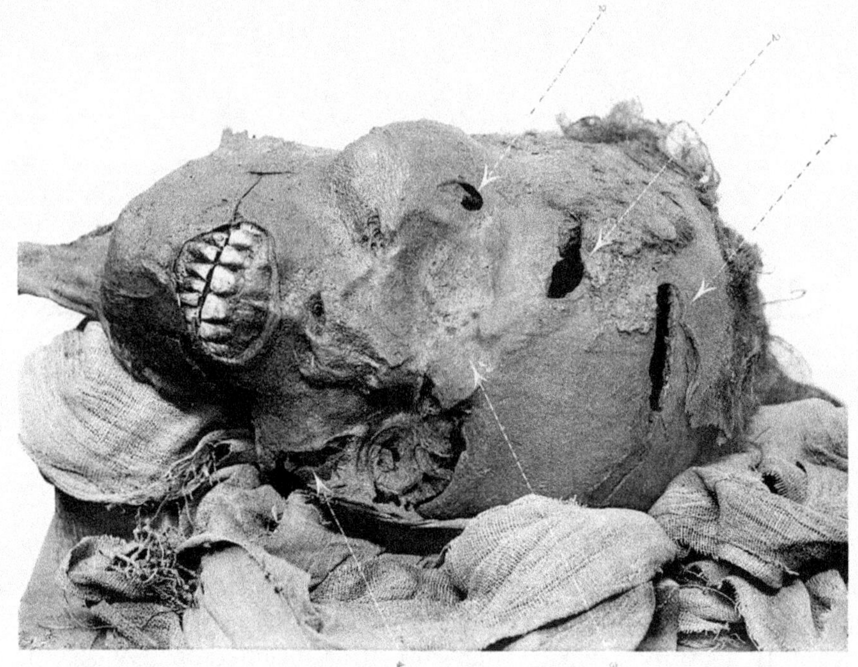

The mummified head of Seqenenre Tao.[11]

Seqenenre's sons continued the struggle. Kamose, who succeeded his father, was determined to complete what Seqenenre had started. We have two stelae that Kamose erected at Karnak Temple in Thebes, describing his campaigns against the Hyksos.

Kamose's stelae describe his frustration at the divided state of Egypt: "I should like to know what use is my strength, when one ruler is in Avaris and another is in Kush, and I sit united with an Asiatic and a Nubian, each man in possession of his slice of Egypt." He saw himself trapped between enemies, controlling only the middle portion of the Nile Valley, while foreigners ruled both the north and the south.

Kamose describes attacking Hyksos territory, capturing towns, and destroying fields. One dramatic passage describes finding and capturing a Hyksos messenger traveling south with a letter from the Hyksos king to the king of Kush, proposing they coordinate their attacks on Thebes. However, this could have been Theban propaganda to justify the war.

Kamose pushed north, reaching the outskirts of Avaris itself. He describes besieging Hyksos strongholds and celebrating victories. But he didn't complete the conquest. Kamose's reign appears to have been relatively brief. He died before the full expulsion of the Hyksos. The war would fall to the next ruler to finish.

That successor was Ahmose I (approximately 1550-1525 BCE), who might have been Kamose's brother or possibly his son. Ahmose would become the founder of the Eighteenth Dynasty and the New Kingdom, though whether he thought of himself as starting a new era, we cannot know. From his perspective, he was likely continuing his family's war to reunify Egypt and expel the foreigners.

Ahmose spent years fighting the Hyksos. The details are frustratingly sparse. We have fragments of information from various sources but no comprehensive account of the war. What we do know comes from biographical inscriptions of soldiers who served under Ahmose, most notably a soldier also named Ahmose, son of Ebana, whose tomb inscription describes his military career.

Ahmose, son of Ebana, describes multiple campaigns. He fought in battles for control of cities in Middle Egypt. He participated in the siege of Avaris, describing at least three separate assaults on the Hyksos capital. He fought in battles in southern Palestine, pursuing Hyksos forces or allies who had fled Egypt.

Eventually, through persistence, military skill, and probably growing advantages in military technology as the Egyptians learned to use horses and chariots effectively, Ahmose succeeded. Avaris fell, and the Hyksos were expelled from Egypt. Ahmose pursued them into southern Palestine, besieging the town of Sharuhen for three years to eliminate the Hyksos as a military threat even beyond Egypt's borders.

However, the war wasn't finished even after the Hyksos were defeated. Ahmose also had to deal with Kush to the south. He campaigned in Nubia, reasserting Egyptian control over territories that had been lost during the Second Intermediate Period. He had to suppress rebellions within Egypt itself as well; there are references to uprisings that he had to crush, suggesting not everyone was enthusiastic about Theban rule.

By the end of Ahmose's reign around 1525 BCE, Egypt was reunified under a single ruler for the first time in over two hundred years. The Second Intermediate Period was over, and the New Kingdom had begun.

Building an Empire

The New Kingdom would be fundamentally different from the Middle Kingdom that had preceded it. The experience of fighting the Hyksos, combined with new military technologies, evolving ideology, economic opportunities, and institutional changes, had transformed Egyptian attitudes about the outside world and militarized Egyptian society. During the Old and Middle Kingdoms, Egypt had generally been content to defend its borders and conduct limited military operations to secure resources. Egypt saw itself as the center of civilization; there was no need to expand beyond its natural borders.

The Hyksos occupation shattered this complacency. Egyptians learned that even their seemingly impregnable homeland could be penetrated and occupied by foreigners. The lesson they took from this was that defense wasn't enough. Egypt needed to project power beyond its borders, create buffer zones of controlled or dominated territories, and ensure that foreign threats never again reached Egyptian soil.

The military that made this expansion possible had been transformed during the struggle against the Hyksos. Egypt now maintained professional military forces made of career soldiers who trained regularly and campaigned frequently. They were supplemented by conscripts and foreign mercenaries, particularly Nubians who were valued as warriors. This was a significant shift from the Egyptians' earlier reliance on laborers.

Most importantly, chariots became the elite striking force of the Egyptian army. Egyptian charioteers, drawn from the nobility, trained extensively in the skills required to fight from a moving chariot. They learned how to drive, shoot composite bows, and coordinate with other chariots. Egyptian chariots were lighter and faster than those used by most other Near Eastern armies, giving Egypt a tactical advantage.

The composite bow, made from wood, horn, and sinew, was far more powerful than the simple bows Egyptians had used previously. It could penetrate armor at greater range, making Egyptian archers devastating on the battlefield. Combined with chariots, which provided mobility and allowed archers to shoot while moving, this created a formidable military force.

The Egyptian military also developed sophisticated logistics and organizational systems. Campaigning in Syria meant marching hundreds of miles from Egypt, supplying armies in foreign territory, maintaining siege equipment, and coordinating operations across vast distances. Egyptian scribes kept detailed records of military organization, supply requirements, and campaign plans. This allowed Egypt to project power far beyond its borders in ways that would have been impossible during earlier periods.

This aggressive, expansionist mentality defined the New Kingdom. Ahmose I had reunified Egypt, but his immediate successors would take the next step. They would expand Egyptian power, creating an empire that would make Egypt the superpower of the ancient Near East.

This expansion began in earnest with Thutmose I (approximately 1504-1492 BCE), the third pharaoh of the Eighteenth Dynasty. Thutmose I campaigned vigorously in both directions. He moved south into Nubia and north into the Levant and Syria. Royal inscriptions credit him with pushing Egyptian control far to the south in Nubia, beyond the Third Cataract of the Nile, and deeper into Sudan than the Middle Kingdom had ever controlled, though the full scope of this control remains debated among scholars. He erected a boundary stela near the Third Cataract, marking the claimed southern extent of Egyptian power. Nubia wasn't just conquered; it was annexed, becoming an Egyptian province administered by an Egyptian official called the "King's Son of Kush" (he usually wasn't actually the king's son—it was an administrative title).

But why was Nubia so important? The same reason it always had been: gold. Nubia was rich in gold deposits, and the New Kingdom pharaohs ruthlessly exploited them. Nubian gold financed Egypt's armies, building projects, and diplomatic efforts. The wealth flowing from Nubia helped make Egypt's imperial expansion possible.

Thutmose I's campaigns in Syria–Palestine (the Levant) were even more significant. According to royal inscriptions, he marched an Egyptian army through Palestine, into Syria, all the way to the Euphrates River. This was farther north than any Egyptian army had gone before. He reportedly erected a victory stela on the banks of the Euphrates, marking what he probably saw as the northern limit of the civilized world.

The Levant was a complex political landscape, dotted with city-states— small kingdoms centered on fortified cities, each with its own ruler. These city-states were wealthy from agriculture and trade, but they were also vulnerable. They constantly competed with each other and were threatened by larger powers. Egyptian conquest offered both threat and opportunity. Submit to Egypt, pay tribute, and you received Egyptian protection and trade access. Resist, and you faced the Egyptian military force.

Thutmose I's campaigns established the pattern that would define Egyptian imperialism for the next several centuries. Egypt didn't directly annex and administer most of the Levant the way it did with Nubia. Instead, it created a system of vassal states. Local rulers remained in power, governing their own territories, but they acknowledged Egyptian suzerainty, paid tribute, and were expected to support Egyptian military operations. Egyptian officials and small garrisons were stationed at key locations to monitor the vassals and intervene if necessary.

This system was relatively efficient from Egypt's perspective. It gave the Egyptians tribute, resources, and security without the full costs of direct administration and occupation. But it also required constant maintenance. Vassal rulers might rebel or stop paying tribute if they thought they could get away with it. Rival powers—particularly Mitanni to the north and later the Hittites—would try to lure Egyptian vassals into their own spheres of influence. Egyptian pharaohs had to be prepared to campaign regularly in the Levant to maintain their dominance.

The wealth flowing into Egypt from its expanding empire was enormous. Tribute came from Nubia, the Levantine vassals, defeated enemies, and trade. This wealth funded massive building projects at home, supported an expanded bureaucracy, enriched the temples (particularly the Temple of Amun at Karnak, which became fantastically wealthy), and created a golden age of prosperity.

The empire also brought cultural exchange. Egyptian art and culture spread throughout the empire, influencing vassal states. Egypt also absorbed influences from its empire, such as foreign goods, foreign artistic motifs, foreign gods, and foreign peoples (prisoners of war, slaves, traders, and diplomats). The New Kingdom would be more cosmopolitan and more internationally engaged than any previous period of Egyptian history.

However, having a large empire brought challenges. As mentioned, managing vassal states required constant attention. Military campaigns were expensive and dangerous. Egyptian sons died fighting in Syria or Nubia. The wealth and power concentrated in the hands of the military elite and the priesthood of Amun could create challenges to royal authority. Egypt also faced rivals who could threaten its empire, particularly Mitanni, a powerful kingdom in northern Syria, which would compete with Egypt for control of the Levant throughout the 15th century BCE.

The Pharaoh Queen

In the midst of this aggressive, militaristic New Kingdom, one of ancient Egypt's most remarkable rulers came to power: Hatshepsut (approximately 1479–1458 BCE), a woman who declared herself pharaoh and ruled Egypt for over two decades.

Hatshepsut's rise to power was unusual, but it was not entirely unprecedented in the complicated world of Egyptian royal succession. She was the daughter of Thutmose I and his principal wife, Ahmose. When Thutmose I died, the throne passed to Thutmose II, who was probably Hatshepsut's half-brother (royal incest was common in New Kingdom Egypt as a way to keep power within the royal family). Hatshepsut married Thutmose II, making her both his half-sister and his wife. She became queen.

Thutmose II's reign was relatively brief and apparently not particularly distinguished. When he died around 1479 BCE, the succession situation was complicated. The designated heir was Thutmose III, a young boy, the son of Thutmose II by a secondary wife named Iset. Thutmose III was legitimate, but he was very young. He was probably only around two to four years old.

In such situations, it was normal for a regent to govern until the young king came of age. Hatshepsut, as the young king's stepmother and the daughter and wife of pharaohs, was the obvious choice for regent. So far, this was all conventional.

What happened next was not. Within a few years of becoming regent, Hatshepsut declared herself pharaoh—not queen regent, not queen consort, but pharaoh, with all the titles, regalia, and authority of a male king. She adopted the full royal titulary, including the names and titles reserved for pharaohs. She wore the traditional pharaonic regalia, including the false beard that symbolized kingship. In artistic representations, she was often depicted with a male body, wearing the traditional king's kilt, though sometimes with feminine features or in some cases clearly as a woman in the king's regalia.

A statue of Hatshepsut.[12]

Why did Hatshepsut take this unprecedented step? The sources don't tell us directly, but we can speculate. Perhaps she believed she was the most qualified person to rule. She was, after all, of the direct royal bloodline and the daughter and wife of kings, while Thutmose III was the son of a secondary wife. Perhaps she had ambitions to rule in her own right, not just as a regent for someone else. Perhaps she saw political challenges that required a pharaoh's full authority to address. Or perhaps it was simply that she could—she had the power, the support, and the will to make it happen.

Hatshepsut's justification for her rule was clever. She claimed that the god Amun himself had decreed she should be king. Elaborate texts and reliefs at her mortuary temple at Deir el-Bahri describe how Amun took the form of Thutmose I and impregnated Ahmose with a divine child—Hatshepsut herself. This "divine birth" narrative, borrowed from traditional royal ideology, presented Hatshepsut as not just legitimate but chosen by the gods.

She also emphasized her royal lineage, presenting herself as Thutmose I's intended heir, the only legitimate child of his principal wife. In her narrative, her rule was the natural continuation of her father's reign, which had been briefly interrupted by the relatively unimportant reign of Thutmose II.

What's remarkable is that Hatshepsut's claim to kingship seems to have been largely accepted. There's no evidence of civil war or significant opposition. The key officials of the kingdom, including Senenmut, her chief steward and probably closest advisor, and other high officials, supported her rule. Thutmose III, the young king she had displaced, remained alive and held some royal status, but he was clearly subordinate. How he felt about this arrangement we can only guess, but he was in no position to challenge Hatshepsut during her lifetime.

Hatshepsut's reign was notable for its focus on building projects and trade expeditions rather than military conquest. This doesn't mean she neglected military affairs—there's evidence of some military campaigns during her reign, particularly in Nubia—but her reign wasn't characterized by the aggressive expansionism of her predecessor and successor.

Her most famous achievement was the trading expedition to Punt, the legendary land far to the south (probably somewhere on the Red Sea coast of modern Sudan, Eritrea, or Somalia). The expedition is commemorated in elaborate reliefs at her mortuary temple, showing ships being loaded with exotic goods like myrrh trees, incense, ebony, ivory, gold, and exotic animals, including baboons. The reliefs even depict the ruler of Punt and his obese wife, a rare example of Egyptian artists depicting foreign rulers with individualized features rather than generic types.

A drawing of the relief of the expedition to Punt.[18]

The Punt expedition wasn't just about acquiring exotic goods; it was also about prestige and demonstrating royal power. A pharaoh who could organize expeditions to distant lands, bring back fabulous wealth, and present incense to the gods was demonstrating the same power and divine favor that earlier pharaohs had shown through military conquest.

Hatshepsut's greatest legacy is in architecture. Her mortuary temple at Deir el-Bahri, on the west bank of the Nile at Thebes, is one of ancient Egypt's most beautiful buildings. Designed by Senenmut, it consists of three terraced colonnades built against the cliff face. The temple's reliefs tell the story of Hatshepsut's reign, including the Punt expedition, her divine birth, her building projects, and her offerings to the gods.

Hatshepsut's mortuary temple at Deir el-Bahri.[14]

She also built extensively at Karnak Temple, adding obelisks, pylons (gateways), and other structures to Amun's great temple complex. These building projects enriched the priesthood of Amun and demonstrated royal piety, reinforcing the connection between the pharaoh and the gods.

Hatshepsut ruled for approximately twenty-two years, dying around 1458 BCE. The circumstances of her death are unknown. We don't know if she died of natural causes, was overthrown, or was assassinated. What we do know is that after her death, Thutmose III, after spending decades as junior partner to his stepmother, took full control of Egypt.

Late in his reign—probably at least twenty years after Hatshepsut's death—Thutmose III ordered Hatshepsut's names and images to be systematically removed from monuments throughout Egypt. Her cartouches (an oval frame with the name of an Egyptian ruler inside) were chiseled out. Her statues were smashed or buried. Her name was erased from the king lists. This was *damnatio memoriae*—the erasure of someone from history.

Why did Thutmose III wait so long to do this? And why did he do it at all? These questions have generated much scholarly debate. Some argue it was personal resentment, a form of revenge for being kept from power for so long. Others suggest it was political. Perhaps late in his reign, Thutmose III faced succession challenges and wanted to ensure his own line succeeded by erasing the precedent of a female pharaoh. Others suggest it was ideological. The concept of a female pharaoh violated ma'at, the proper order, and needed to be erased.

Whatever the reason, Thutmose III's erasure campaign was largely successful. For thousands of years, Hatshepsut was almost completely forgotten, her monuments attributed to other pharaohs. Only in the 19th and 20th centuries did modern archaeologists and historians piece together her story, recognizing her as one of ancient Egypt's most successful and remarkable rulers.

Hatshepsut's reign demonstrated that a woman could successfully exercise power, manage the bureaucracy, conduct foreign policy, and maintain Egypt's position. However, the erasure of her memory also showed the limits of that achievement. Egyptian ideology was fundamentally patriarchal, and a female pharaoh represented a disruption of the proper order that needed to be corrected, even retrospectively.

After Hatshepsut, Egypt would return to aggressive military expansion under Thutmose III, who proved to be one of ancient Egypt's greatest conquerors.

Chapter 8:
Warriors and Conquerors

Thutmose III: The Napoleon of Ancient Egypt

After Hatshepsut's death around 1458 BCE, Thutmose III finally became the sole ruler of Egypt. He had been king in name for many years—sources suggest over twenty years, though this is partly inferred from incomplete records—but he had always been subordinate to his stepmother. Now, approaching middle age, he was finally free to rule on his own terms. And what he chose to do with that freedom would make him one of ancient Egypt's greatest military leaders.

Thutmose III (approximately 1479-1425 BCE, though effectively sole ruler only from around 1458 BCE)

Thutmose III.[15]

conducted numerous military campaigns during his reign—sources suggest at least seventeen, though the exact count and dating are debated among scholars—most of them in Syria-Palestine. He would push Egyptian control farther north than any pharaoh before him, defeat powerful coalitions of enemies, and establish Egyptian dominance over the Levant so thoroughly that it would last for generations. Later historians would compare him to Napoleon Bonaparte. Both were relatively short men (Thutmose's mummy suggests he was about 5'3" tall) who became military geniuses, conducting numerous campaigns, winning decisive battles, and building empires through aggressive warfare, though Thutmose's empire lasted much longer than Napoleon's did.

The first and most famous of Thutmose III's campaigns came early in his sole reign: the Battle of Megiddo in approximately 1457 BCE. This battle would become the most documented military engagement from ancient Egypt, described in detail in inscriptions at Karnak Temple.

A coalition of Canaanite and Syrian city-states, led by the ruler of Kadesh and possibly supported by the kingdom of Mitanni far to the north, had rebelled against Egyptian authority. They assembled their forces at the fortified city of Megiddo, strategically located in northern Palestine and controlling important trade routes. This was a serious challenge to Egyptian dominance in the region, and if successful, could have unraveled Egyptian control throughout Syria-Palestine.

Thutmose III responded with a major military expedition. He marched his army from Egypt through Palestine toward Megiddo. When he reached the vicinity of the city, he faced a strategic choice. There were three possible routes through the Carmel mountain ridge to reach Megiddo: a southern route and a northern route. They were both relatively safe but indirect. A central route through a narrow mountain pass would bring his army out directly in front of Megiddo, but it was potentially dangerous.

His generals advised taking one of the safer routes. However, Thutmose III chose the risky central route, reasoning that the enemy would expect him to take a safer path and would position their forces accordingly. It was a gamble. If the enemy caught his army strung out in the narrow pass, they could be destroyed. But Thutmose was right. His army emerged from the pass to find the enemy unprepared, their forces divided and not positioned to defend against an attack from that direction.

The battle was fought on the plain before Megiddo. The Egyptian inscriptions describe it in detail: the positioning of the forces, Thutmose III fighting from his chariot, the enemy formation breaking and fleeing into the fortified city. The Egyptians pursued, but they couldn't capture the city immediately. The defenders closed the gates, and some soldiers had to be hauled up the walls with ropes and sheets lowered by the people inside.

According to the Egyptian inscriptions, the Egyptians built a fortification wall around the entire city to prevent escape or resupply. The siege of Megiddo lasted approximately seven months before the city finally surrendered. While these details come from Egyptian triumphal accounts—and the lengthy siege has been questioned by some modern scholars as possibly exaggerated—the scale of the victory is clear. Thutmose III captured enormous plunder, including horses, chariots, gold, silver, weapons, armor, and livestock. More importantly, he captured or received the submission of the rulers of numerous city-states that had been part of the rebellion.

The victory at Megiddo was decisive. It broke the coalition against Egypt, reasserted Egyptian dominance in Palestine, and showed that rebellion against Egyptian authority would be met with swift and overwhelming force. And this was only the beginning of Thutmose III's military career.

Over the next two decades, Thutmose III campaigned almost annually in Syria–Palestine. Each campaign had specific objectives. He wanted to punish rebellious vassal states, collect tribute from submissive ones, capture strategic cities, intimidate potential rivals, and gradually extend Egyptian control farther north. Some campaigns were major military expeditions involving battles and sieges. Others were more like royal marches through Egyptian-controlled territory, where the pharaoh's presence reinforced Egyptian authority and vassal rulers came to present tribute and renew their oaths of loyalty.

Thutmose III pushed Egyptian power to its greatest extent. He campaigned as far north as the Euphrates River, which was even farther than his grandfather Thutmose I had gone. He crossed the Euphrates—a feat requiring boats to be built or transported overland—and erected a victory stela on the far bank, next to the stela his grandfather had placed there decades earlier. Egyptian influence extended, at least nominally, from the Fourth Cataract of the Nile in Nubia to the Euphrates in Syria, a distance of over 1,500 miles.

However, maintaining this empire required constant effort. The Levantine city-states were constantly shifting in their loyalties. Local rulers had their own ambitions and would rebel if they thought Egyptian attention was elsewhere. The kingdom of Mitanni to the north was a powerful rival that constantly worked to undermine Egyptian influence and bring Syrian states into its own sphere of influence. This far-flung system required frequent campaigns, and Egyptian influence in distant regions could weaken or collapse quickly when the pharaoh's attention waned.

Thutmose III's solution was a system combining military force, political management, and ideological control. Military force came from regular campaigns; showing up with an army reminded vassals that rebellion had consequences. Political management involved carefully handling the local rulers. Some were left in place if they were loyal, and others were replaced with pro-Egyptian rulers. Sons of local rulers were sometimes taken to Egypt as hostages (or guests, depending on your perspective), where they would be educated in Egyptian ways before being sent back to rule their homelands. Ideological control involved promoting the idea that the Egyptian pharaoh was the supreme ruler ordained by the gods and that serving Egypt brought prosperity while rebelling brought destruction.

The wealth flowing into Egypt from this empire was staggering. The Karnak inscriptions list tribute from Thutmose III's campaigns: gold, silver, copper, lapis lazuli, exotic wood, incense, oil, wine, cattle, horses, chariots, prisoners, and slaves. This wealth enriched the royal treasury, supported the army, funded massive building projects, and benefited the Temple of Amun at Karnak, which received substantial donations from the king and grew incredibly wealthy and powerful.

Thutmose III was also a prolific builder. He constructed extensively at Karnak, adding halls, obelisks, and monuments. His mortuary temple at Thebes (now mostly destroyed) was a major structure. He left inscriptions throughout Egypt and the conquered territories, proclaiming his victories and his devotion to the gods.

When Thutmose III died around 1425 BCE after approximately fifty-four years as king (thirty-two as sole ruler), he left Egypt at the height of its power. The empire was secure, the treasury was full, the military was battle-tested and confident, and Egyptian prestige was at its highest point. His son Amenhotep II would inherit a stable, powerful empire—the fruits of decades of military campaigning and administrative development.

Thutmose III deserves his reputation as one of ancient Egypt's greatest pharaohs. He was a skilled military commander who understood strategy and tactics, a capable administrator who managed a vast empire, and a ruler who combined military force with political intelligence.

The Riches of Empire

The decades following Thutmose III's death saw Egypt at perhaps its wealthiest and most powerful. His son, Amenhotep II (approximately 1427–1400 BCE), and grandson, Thutmose IV (approximately 1400–1390 BCE), maintained the empire, conducting occasional military campaigns but mostly benefiting from the system Thutmose III had established. However, it was Amenhotep III (approximately 1390–1352 BCE), Thutmose IV's son, whose reign represented the absolute peak of New Kingdom wealth, power, and artistic achievement.

Amenhotep III ruled for thirty-eight years over an Egypt that was secure, prosperous, and culturally sophisticated. His reign was largely peaceful. He conducted minimal military campaigns, with perhaps one known major expedition in Nubia during his fifth year. For most of his reign, Egypt was at peace. This wasn't because threats had disappeared but because the empire was so stable and Egyptian dominance so complete that major military expeditions weren't necessary. The system of vassal states functioned smoothly, tribute flowed regularly into Egypt, and potential rivals were either intimidated by Egyptian power or preoccupied with their own problems.

The wealth accumulated from decades of empire was now available for the king to spend on building, arts, and luxury on an unprecedented scale, and spend it he did. Amenhotep III's building program was massive. At Thebes, he constructed a mortuary temple on the west bank that was among the largest religious structures built in Egypt. Reconstructions based on surviving evidence suggest it was over seven hundred feet long and five hundred feet wide. Almost nothing of it survives today except for two massive statues of the king that once flanked the entrance. These statues, known as the Colossi of Memnon, are over sixty feet tall.

Amenhotep III's mortuary temple in 2014. Those two tall statues in the center are the Colossi.[16]

At Luxor, Amenhotep III built most of what is now Luxor Temple, a beautiful structure dedicated to Amun. At Karnak, he added structures including a huge pylon (gateway) and numerous statues. He built palaces, including a sprawling palace complex at Malkata on the west bank of Thebes that served as his primary residence. He constructed temples throughout Egypt and in Nubia. Everywhere he built, he built large, richly decorated structures with the finest materials (granite, sandstone, costly imported wood, and gold).

The artistic quality of work from Amenhotep III's reign was exceptional. Egyptian artists had centuries of tradition to draw on, but during his reign, they achieved a level of elegance that many consider the high point of Egyptian art. Statues show remarkable naturalism within Egyptian artistic conventions. The famous seated statues of Amenhotep III show the king as mature and dignified, with subtle modeling and refined proportions. Reliefs are carved with exquisite delicacy. Painting achieves subtle gradations of color.

Private tombs from this period—tombs of nobles and officials—show similar high quality. Tomb paintings depict banquet scenes, hunting, religious rituals, and daily life, with both technical skill and artistic imagination. These tombs give us our most detailed views of elite life in ancient Egypt, showing clothing, furniture, food, entertainment, and social interaction.

Amenhotep III's court was lavish and cosmopolitan. Foreign ambassadors came to Egypt from throughout the Near East, from the Hittites in Anatolia, to the Mitanni in Syria, to the Babylonians in Mesopotamia. They brought gifts and sought Egyptian favor. The Amarna Letters—diplomatic correspondence from slightly later in the New Kingdom—give us a glimpse of this diplomatic world. Foreign rulers addressed the Egyptian pharaoh as "brother," though with the understanding that Egypt was first among equals. They sent tribute and requested Egyptian gold, which Egypt possessed in abundance from Nubian mines.

The wealth of Amenhotep III's court is evident in the gifts he gave. He sent gold statues, furniture overlaid with gold, jewelry, and luxury goods to foreign rulers. He commissioned hundreds of large stone sculptures for temples. He created a large number of scarabs (seal amulets) commemorating various events of his reign. These commemorative scarabs were distributed widely, serving both as royal propaganda and as gifts that demonstrated the king's wealth.

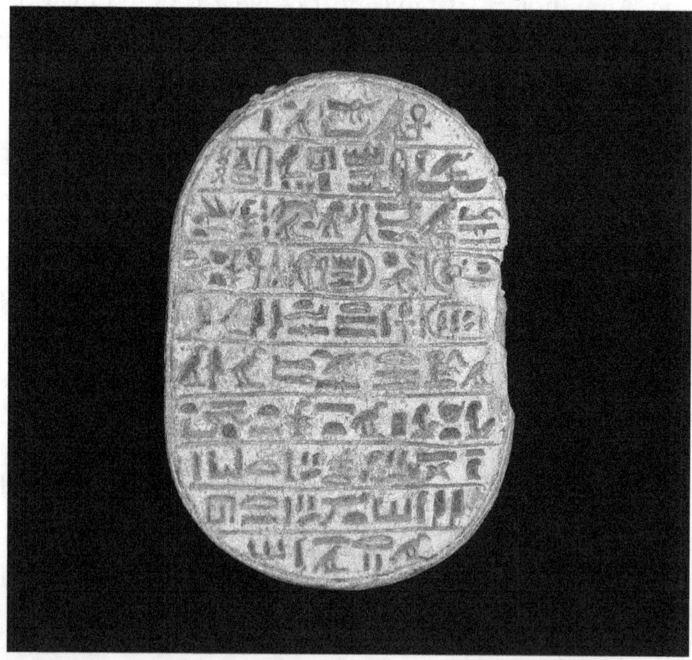

A scarab commemorating Amenhotep III's marriage to one of his wives.[17]

Amenhotep III married many women, as polygamy was standard for pharaohs, but his principal wife was Tiye. She played an unusually prominent role. Tiye was depicted alongside the king in official art more than most queens. She was mentioned in diplomatic correspondence and seems to have wielded real influence. After Amenhotep III's death, she remained influential during their son's reign. Tiye wasn't of royal blood herself—her father is believed to have been a chariot officer and her mother a palace lady-in-waiting—but she rose to become one of ancient Egypt's most powerful queens.

His reign also saw interesting religious developments. While Amenhotep III maintained traditional religious practices and built temples to the traditional gods, there is evidence of growing emphasis on solar deities, particularly the sun disk called the Aten. Some scholars see this as foreshadowing the religious revolution that would take over Egypt during the next reign, though Amenhotep III remained orthodox in his public religious observances.

The king celebrated at least three Sed festivals, traditional jubilee celebrations of royal power that were supposed to occur after thirty years of rule but could be celebrated more frequently. They included the symbolic rejuvenation of the king, religious ceremonies throughout Egypt, and the massive distribution of gifts. The Sed festivals served both religious and political purposes. They demonstrated royal vitality, redistributed wealth, and reinforced the king's relationship with the gods and with his subjects.

Toward the end of his reign, Amenhotep III became ill. Exactly what afflicted him is unclear. His mummy shows signs of various health problems, including severe dental disease and what some scholars interpret as possible obesity, though this is debated due to potential embalming distortion. He might have suffered from painful conditions that made his final years difficult. However, he continued ruling until his death around 1352 BCE; it was one of the longest and most prosperous reigns in Egyptian history.

Amenhotep III's reign represents the high point of New Kingdom Egypt in many ways. The empire was at its most stable. Wealth was at its peak. Art and architecture reached their highest achievements. Egypt dominated the ancient Near East without needing to fight constant wars to maintain that dominance.

But this golden age contained the seeds of crisis. The massive wealth flowing to the Temple of Amun had made the priesthood extremely powerful, potentially rivaling even royal authority. The diplomatic balance that kept peace with Egypt's rivals was delicate and would eventually break down. And the royal succession would bring to the throne one of ancient Egypt's most controversial rulers. His radical religious reforms would nearly tear the Egyptian state apart.

For now, though, Egypt basked in the glory of Amenhotep III's reign. It was Egypt's golden age, and those who lived through it probably believed it would last forever. However, dramatic changes were coming, and they would begin with Amenhotep III's son and successor, who would call himself Akhenaten.

Chapter 9: The Heretic Pharaoh— Akhenaten's Revolution

One God, One City, One Vision

When Amenhotep IV came to the throne around 1352 BCE, nobody could have predicted what was coming. He was the son of Amenhotep III and Queen Tiye, and he inherited an empire at its peak. By all expectations, he would continue his father's policies, maintain the traditional religious practices, conduct the necessary military campaigns to keep vassals in line, and build monuments to the gods while living in luxury. That's what pharaohs did.

Instead, Amenhotep IV would launch the most radical religious revolution in ancient Egyptian history. He would abandon the traditional gods that Egyptians had worshiped for millennia. He would change his own name, build a completely new capital city, and move the entire government there. He would transform Egyptian art into something unrecognizable. And his reforms would severely destabilize the Egyptian state, weakening it both internally and in its international standing.

Early in his reign, Amenhotep IV seemed conventional enough. He was crowned at Thebes, the traditional capital. He married Nefertiti, who would become one of ancient Egypt's most famous queens. He began building projects at Karnak, the great Temple of Amun. Everything appeared normal.

Statue of Akhenaten.[18]

But there were hints of what was coming. The early building projects showed increased emphasis on the sun disk, the Aten. This wasn't entirely unprecedented. Sun worship had always been important in Egypt, and his father, Amenhotep III, had shown interest in solar deities. However, Amenhotep IV took this much further.

By around his fifth year on the throne, the changes accelerated dramatically. Amenhotep IV declared that the Aten was the supreme god. Whether this was true monotheism (the worship of only one god), monolatry (the worship of one god while acknowledging others exist), or henotheism (one supreme god above others) remains debated among scholars. What's clear is that Amenhotep IV rejected the worship of traditional gods and focused his devotion exclusively on the Aten. This was a dramatic break with Egyptian polytheistic tradition that had existed for millennia.

To emphasize this break with tradition, Amenhotep IV changed his name. "Amenhotep" meant "Amun is satisfied," a name that honored the god Amun, whom Amenhotep IV now declared was false. He took a new name, Akhenaten, meaning "effective for the Aten" or "servant of the Aten." From this point on, we'll call him Akhenaten, the name by which he's remembered.

Akhenaten didn't stop with religious reform. He decided to build an entirely new capital city. He couldn't stay in Thebes. That was Amun's city, dominated by the priesthood of Amun and filled with temples to the traditional gods. He needed a clean break, a city devoted solely to the Aten.

Akhenaten chose a site in Middle Egypt that had never been occupied before—a stretch of desert on the east bank of the Nile backed by imposing cliffs. The cliffs formed a natural bay framing the rising sun, creating powerful imagery for a sun-worshiping cult, and the site allowed him to build without associating with traditional religious centers. He named it Akhetaten, "Horizon of the Aten" (modern scholars call the site Amarna). He marked the city's boundaries with a series of stone stelae carved into the cliffs, in which he swore never to move beyond these boundaries, binding both himself and his successors to this site forever.

The construction of Akhetaten began around year five or six of Akhenaten's reign and proceeded with remarkable speed. Within a few years, an entire city had risen from the desert. There were palaces, temples, administrative buildings, workshops, residential neighborhoods, and tombs cut into the cliffs. By year eight or nine, Akhenaten, Nefertiti, their six daughters, and the royal court had relocated to Akhetaten. The government moved. The bureaucracy moved. Elite families built houses there. Akhetaten became Egypt's capital. Thebes, Memphis, and the other traditional cities were abandoned by the royal family and the highest levels of government.

The Great Temple of the Aten at Akhetaten emphasized openness and light, representing a significant departure from traditional Egyptian temples. Traditional temples were dark, mysterious places with enclosed sanctuaries where cult statues of gods resided in dim chambers. Only priests could enter the inner sanctuaries.

The Great Temple of the Aten featured large open courtyards exposed to the sky, with hundreds of altars spread across them. While some traditional temple features remained and archaeological evidence indicates architectural variation within Amarna, the emphasis was clearly on worshiping in sunlight rather than enclosed darkness. Worship of the Aten meant worshiping the sun itself, and that worship happened in full daylight, under the sun's rays. The temple was oriented so the sun would rise directly along its axis, flooding it with light at dawn.

Akhenaten positioned himself as the sole intermediary between the Aten and humanity. In the traditional Egyptian religion, many priests could serve the gods, and laypeople could worship at temples and shrines. In Atenism (as modern scholars call Akhenaten's religion), only Akhenaten could truly worship the Aten, and only through Akhenaten could people access the divine. This made the pharaoh even more central to religious life than before, but it also meant that if you wanted to worship the Aten, you had to go through Akhenaten.

Nefertiti played an unusually prominent role in this religious system. She was depicted in religious scenes alongside Akhenaten, both of them worshiping the Aten and receiving the sun's rays. She appears to have been an active participant in religious rituals, as she was depicted in ways that suggest she had significant religious and possibly political authority, though the full extent of her power remains a subject of scholarly debate. Some reliefs show her in poses and contexts that were typically royal privileges. This level of prominence for a queen was unprecedented in Egyptian royal ideology.

Why did Akhenaten do all of this? What motivated such radical changes? These are questions that have fascinated and frustrated scholars for over a century, and there's no consensus answer.

Some scholars see it as a genuine religious conviction. Perhaps Akhenaten truly believed that the Aten was the only god and that he had a divine mission to convert Egypt to this truth. The hymns to the Aten—particularly the Great Hymn to the Aten, which might have been composed by Akhenaten himself—show real poetic beauty and theological complexity. They describe the Aten as the creator of all life, the source of all light and warmth, and the sustainer of the world. There's a universalism in Atenism that differs from traditional Egyptian religion. The Aten creates and sustains all lands and all peoples, not just Egypt. This could reflect genuine philosophical and theological thinking.

Others see political motivation. The priesthood of Amun at Thebes had become enormously wealthy and powerful. By rejecting Amun and the other traditional gods, Akhenaten broke the power of the old priesthoods. He confiscated their lands and wealth, shut down their temples, and created a new religious system where he was unchallenged as the sole religious authority. From this perspective, Atenism was a power grab disguised as religious reform.

Still others see psychological factors. Some scholars have suggested Akhenaten had physical or mental health issues that affected his behavior. Artistic depictions show him with an unusual body shape. Some medical experts have suggested various conditions, though diagnosing ancient diseases from artistic representations is highly speculative.

Most likely, multiple factors were involved. Akhenaten might have been genuinely religious while also recognizing the political advantages of breaking the old priesthoods. He might have had personal reasons for rejecting the traditional religion while also pursuing his own goals of centralizing power. People are complex, and their motivations often are too.

Modern scholarly interpretations of Akhenaten have varied widely. Early scholars, influenced by their own religious backgrounds, saw him as a proto-monotheist, a visionary who preceded Judaism and Christianity by worshiping one god. Sigmund Freud even wrote a book arguing that Moses was an Egyptian priest who learned monotheism from Akhenaten. This theory is almost universally rejected by scholars, but it shows how fascinated people were by the idea of ancient monotheism. Later scholars took more critical views. Some saw Akhenaten as a failed tyrant who nearly destroyed Egypt by pursuing his obsessions. Others viewed him as mentally ill or physically disabled. More recent scholarship has tried to understand him in his own context, examining the political, religious, and social factors that might have motivated his reforms.

What's clear is that Akhenaten didn't just stop worshiping the old gods himself; he attempted to suppress the traditional religion throughout Egypt. State temples to the traditional gods were closed. Their priesthoods were disbanded. Most dramatically, Akhenaten ordered the names of the old gods, particularly Amun, erased from monuments throughout Egypt. Workers went from temple to tomb, chiseling out the names wherever they appeared. Even his father's name, Amenhotep, was targeted because it contained "Amun."

This was spiritual warfare. By erasing the gods' names, Akhenaten was trying to erase their existence. In Egyptian belief, names had power. To speak a name was to make something real. By removing these names, Akhenaten was attempting to unmake the old gods and render them non-existent.

For devout Egyptians who had worshiped these gods their entire lives, who had been taught that Osiris judged the dead and that Isis protected children and that Horus was the divine king, this must have been profoundly disturbing. Their entire religious worldview was being overturned by royal decree. The gods their ancestors had worshiped for thousands of years were declared false. The temples where they had prayed were closed. The festivals that had marked the rhythm of their year were cancelled.

However, this state-mandated suppression was complex and uneven across Egypt. While the official cults were dismantled, archaeological evidence suggests that household worship of traditional gods continued in private, showing the limits of the revolution's reach into everyday religious life. Evidence from elsewhere in Egypt suggests that many people continued traditional practices in private, keeping small shrines to the old gods in their homes, hidden from official scrutiny. Even at Amarna itself, amulets of Bes (the god who protected households and children), Taweret (the goddess of childbirth), and other household gods have been found. People apparently went through the motions of Aten worship publicly while maintaining traditional practices privately.

Art, Life, and the Weakening Empire

The religious revolution wasn't the only radical change Akhenaten instituted. He also transformed Egyptian art in ways that were just as dramatic and far more visible.

Traditional Egyptian art had been remarkably consistent for over a thousand years. It followed strict conventions: figures shown in profile with the eye viewed from the front, bodies idealized and eternally youthful, and formal compositions emphasizing order and hierarchy. Royal statues showed kings as ageless and perfect, embodying divine power. This style had varied somewhat over time, but the basic conventions remained the same.

Akhenaten's art was radically different. Early in his reign, a new artistic style appeared, the Amarna style. It showed the royal family in ways that broke nearly every convention of traditional Egyptian art.

Akhenaten was depicted with an extremely unusual body. He had an elongated head, a long, thin neck, narrow shoulders, a prominent belly, wide hips, and spindly arms and legs. His face was shown with a long jaw, thick lips, and heavy-lidded eyes. These features were so extreme that early scholars thought they must represent some physical deformity or disease. More recent scholarship suggests it was deliberate stylization. Akhenaten chose to be represented this way.

Nefertiti was shown in this same style, with an elongated skull and distinctive features. Their six daughters were also depicted with the same elongated skulls and unusual proportions. Even courtiers and officials adopted this style in their own depictions.

A relief depicting Akhenaten (his head is lost), Nefertiti, and one of their daughters.[19]

Why? Several theories exist. Some scholars suggest the style was meant to convey religious meaning. Perhaps it was meant to show the royal family as neither fully male nor fully female, transcending normal human categories and purely existing as intermediaries between the divine and the earthly. Others suggest it was meant to emphasize the royal family's divine nature by showing them as different from ordinary humans. Still others think it simply reflected Akhenaten's personal aesthetic preferences or even that he genuinely looked unusual and chose to have everyone depicted in his image.

Whatever the reason, the style was unlike anything in Egyptian art before or after. It appeared suddenly at the start of Akhenaten's reign and disappeared just as suddenly after his death, suggesting it was specifically tied to his rule.

However, the Amarna style wasn't just about unusual body proportions. It also showed unprecedented intimacy and informality in royal imagery. Traditional Egyptian royal art showed pharaohs as distant, formal figures performing religious rituals or smiting enemies. Amarna art showed Akhenaten and Nefertiti in domestic scenes, playing with their daughters, embracing each other, sitting casually, and even kissing. The royal family was shown as a family, with affection and informal interaction.

One famous relief shows Akhenaten and Nefertiti sitting together, their small daughters climbing on them, playing. The sun's rays shine down on them, each ray ending in a little hand, blessing the family. It's charming and completely unlike the formal, distant royal imagery that had dominated Egyptian art for centuries.

Akhenaten, Nefertiti, and their children.[20]

Was this informality genuine? Did Akhenaten and Nefertiti really have an affectionate family life? Or was this political propaganda, presenting the royal family as the perfect family blessed by the Aten? We can't know for sure, but the images are striking.

Life at Amarna was also unusual. The city was built quickly, mostly in mudbrick rather than stone. It was designed to serve as the capital, but it did not have the centuries of accumulated grandeur that places like Thebes or Memphis had. The city stretched along the east bank of the Nile for several miles and was organized into districts.

The central city contained the official buildings: the Great Palace, the Great Temple of the Aten, administrative offices, and military quarters. The royal family lived in the North Palace, which was separated from the main city. Elite officials built large houses in the northern suburb and elsewhere. Ordinary workers lived in a purpose-built workers' village to the south.

The elite houses at Amarna show interesting features. They were large, often over thirty rooms, and organized around central courtyards. They had gardens, chapels, storage magazines, and servant quarters. The houses show clear social stratification. Elite officials lived in comfort, with space and amenities. But even these grand houses were built quickly in mudbrick, without the stone construction that would make them permanent.

The site has been extensively excavated, and it has provided unusually detailed information about daily life in ancient Egypt. Archaeologists have found everything from grand palaces to workers' houses, from royal correspondence to household waste. The Amarna Letters—diplomatic correspondence written on clay tablets in Akkadian (the diplomatic language of the time)—were discovered here, providing invaluable information about international relations during this period.

These letters reveal problems that were developing during Akhenaten's reign. Foreign rulers wrote to the pharaoh complaining about the lack of Egyptian support. Vassal rulers in Syria–Palestine reported attacks from neighboring states or from groups like the Hapiru (possibly related to the Hebrews, though this connection is debated) and begged for Egyptian military assistance. The letters suggest Egyptian control over its empire was weakening.

Akhenaten seems to have neglected foreign policy and military affairs. There's no evidence he ever conducted a military campaign. He didn't campaign in Syria–Palestine to maintain control over vassals, and he didn't lead expeditions to Nubia. He might have been so focused on his religious revolution and on building Amarna that he neglected the practical business of maintaining the empire his ancestors had built.

The consequences were serious. Egyptian influence in Syria–Palestine declined. Vassal states stopped sending tribute or rebelled outright. The Hittites, a powerful kingdom in Anatolia, were expanding southward, threatening Egyptian interests. The kingdom of Mitanni, which had been Egypt's ally, was weakening and would soon collapse. The careful diplomatic balance that had kept the region stable during Amenhotep III's reign was breaking down.

Within Egypt itself, there were signs of strain. The traditional priesthoods had been disbanded, but their wealth had been confiscated by the crown. This meant priests and temple employees had lost their livelihoods. The traditional festivals had ceased, disrupting the social and economic rhythms that had organized community life. The forced worship of the Aten, rather than the gods people had worshiped their entire lives, must have created resentment.

The later years of Akhenaten's reign are murky. Around year twelve or fourteen, something happened. We're not sure what. Nefertiti disappears from the record. Some scholars think she died, while others think she fell from favor. Some have suggested that she became co-regent under a different name. We simply don't know.

A figure named Smenkhkare appears in the records. She or he apparently served as co-regent with Akhenaten. Smenkhkare could have possibly been one of Akhenaten's daughters, but they also might have been a son we don't know about. It could even have been Nefertiti under a different name. Again, the evidence is frustratingly unclear.

By around year seventeen of his reign, Akhenaten died. The circumstances of his death are unknown. He was probably in his early thirties. He was buried at Amarna in a tomb cut into the cliffs east of the city, though his mummy has never been definitively identified.

Akhenaten's death left Egypt in a precarious position. The empire was weakening. The traditional religious establishment had been destroyed, but Atenism had not truly taken root. Egypt needed stability, and Akhenaten's immediate successors would struggle to provide it.

Chapter 10:
The Boy King and the General

Tutankhamun: Famous for Being Forgotten

Of all the pharaohs who ruled Egypt for three thousand years, none is more famous today than Tutankhamun. His golden death mask is one of the most recognizable images in the world. His name is synonymous with ancient Egypt in popular culture. Museums that display his artifacts draw enormous crowds. Movies, documentaries, and books about him appear regularly.

The irony is that Tutankhamun's reign was brief and, particularly in its early years, when he was very young, he served largely as a figurehead. The decisions were made by his advisors. While recent scholarship leaves open the possibility that he might have played a more active role in restoration policies as he grew older, his reign was spent primarily undoing his predecessor's religious revolution and trying to restore stability to Egypt. He never led a major military campaign. He contributed to some temple construction at sites like Karnak and Luxor, though these works were often modest compared to other pharaohs and were frequently usurped by his successors. By ancient Egyptian standards, his accomplishments were limited.

Tutankhamun's fame rests entirely on one fact: his tomb survived largely intact until its discovery in 1922, making it the most complete royal burial ever found from ancient Egypt.

Tutankhamun's famous golden death mask.[21]

When Tutankhamun came to the throne around 1332 BCE (taking the name Tutankhaten initially, later changed to Tutankhamun), he was probably around eight or nine years old, making him far too young to actually rule. Real power lay with his advisors, particularly Ay, an elderly official who had served under Akhenaten, and Horemheb, a powerful military commander who had risen to prominence during the Amarna period.

These men faced a difficult situation. Akhenaten's religious revolution had disrupted Egyptian society, weakened the empire, and created instability. The worship of traditional gods had been suppressed for nearly two decades. Egypt's international standing had declined since Akhenaten had neglected foreign policy and military affairs. The new capital at Amarna lacked the legitimacy and infrastructure of traditional centers like Thebes and Memphis.

The solution was clear: restore the old order. Within the first few years of Tutankhamun's reign, dramatic changes occurred. The court abandoned Amarna and returned to Memphis and Thebes. The traditional gods were restored to prominence. Temples were reopened and repaired. Priesthoods were reinstated, and festivals resumed. The young king's name was changed from Tutankhaten ("living image of the Aten") to Tutankhamun ("living image of Amun"), symbolizing the return to the traditional religion.

A text known as the Restoration Stela, erected at Karnak, describes the situation and the restoration: "Now when his majesty appeared as king, the temples of the gods and goddesses from Elephantine down to the marshes of the Delta had gone to pieces. Their shrines had become desolate, had become mounds overgrown with weeds ... The land was topsy-turvy, and the gods turned their backs upon this land."

The text is propaganda, of course, as it exaggerates the chaos to make the restoration seem more dramatic and necessary. However, it shows how those who came after Akhenaten viewed his reign—as a disaster that had to be corrected.

As Tutankhamun grew into his teens, he might have begun to exercise more personal authority, though we have little evidence of this. Royal inscriptions from his reign are conventional, showing him in traditional pharaonic poses—worshiping gods, smiting enemies, and receiving tribute. These images tell us little about what he actually did or thought.

We do know some personal details about Tutankhamun from his tomb and from analysis of his mummy. He was slightly built, about 5'6" tall. Medical examination has revealed various health issues. He had a clubfoot on his left leg that would have caused him to walk with a limp. He suffered from malaria (DNA evidence of the parasite was found in his remains), and he likely had other genetic issues from generations of royal inbreeding. His parents were likely full siblings. Genetic analysis suggests his father was Akhenaten and that his mother was one of Akhenaten's sisters.

Tutankhamun was married to Ankhesenamun, one of Akhenaten's daughters (and thus probably his half-sister). The couple apparently had two daughters, both stillborn or dying shortly after birth. The mummified fetuses were found in Tutankhamun's tomb. They were placed in small coffins.

Around 1323 BCE, Tutankhamun died. He was approximately eighteen or nineteen years old. The cause of death has been debated extensively, generating numerous theories over the years. Early theories suggested he was murdered. A blow to the back of the head visible in early X-rays suggested violence. However, more recent CT scans have shown this damage was likely caused during the mummification process or by modern handling, not by an ancient blow.

Current medical consensus, based on extensive study of his mummy, suggests he died from a combination of factors. He had a broken leg; the femur of his left leg was fractured shortly before death. The break might have become infected. Combined with his existing health problems (malaria, possible immune issues from genetic disorders, and his clubfoot), an infected wound could have been fatal. While this is the leading theory, other medical hypotheses continue to be discussed, though diagnosing ancient diseases from mummified remains is challenging.

Some scholars suggest he might have fallen from a chariot, though this is speculative. What's clear is that his death was probably not murder but rather the result of health complications in a young man with multiple underlying conditions. In an era before antibiotics, a broken leg leading to infection could easily be fatal, even for a king.

Tutankhamun's death created a succession crisis. He had no surviving children. His widow, Ankhesenamun, was left without an heir. Who would succeed?

A remarkable letter survives in Hittite records, supposedly sent by an Egyptian queen to the Hittite king Suppiluliuma I. The letter writer (probably Ankhesenamun, though not named) asks the Hittite king to send one of his sons to Egypt to marry her and become pharaoh. She writes that her husband has died, that she has no sons, and that she needs a husband.

The Hittite king, suspicious of this unprecedented request, sent an envoy to investigate. Eventually, he agreed and sent a son. However, the Hittite prince never reached Egypt. He was killed, possibly by Egyptian officials opposed to a foreign king.

Whether this story is true or not, what's clear is that the succession was contested. Ay, the elderly advisor, became pharaoh after Tutankhamun. Some artifacts, such as a ring bearing both their names, suggest Ay might have married Ankhesenamun to legitimize his claim to the throne, though there is no definitive evidence of this marriage. Ay's reign was very brief—only about four years—before Horemheb, the military commander, took the throne.

Tutankhamun was buried in a small tomb in the Valley of the Kings, the necropolis where New Kingdom pharaohs were interred. The tomb was probably not originally intended for him. It's unusually small for a royal burial, suggesting it might have been a private tomb that was hastily repurposed when the king died unexpectedly.

The tomb consists of just four rooms: an entrance corridor, an antechamber, a burial chamber, and a small treasury. The burial was rushed. The paint in the burial chamber was still wet when the tomb was sealed, as fingerprints are visible in the paint. Some of the grave goods were recycled from earlier burials, with the names altered. The gold coffins show signs of hasty modification. Everything suggests that Tutankhamun's death was unexpected and that the burial had to be arranged quickly.

But despite the haste and the small tomb, Tutankhamun was buried with incredible wealth. The four small rooms were packed with grave goods: three nested coffins (the innermost of solid gold), a stone sarcophagus, furniture, chariots, weapons, jewelry, clothing, food, wine, oils, cosmetics, and countless other objects—over five thousand items in total.

The relief carving on one of the coffins featuring Tutankhamun and Ankhesenamun.[22]

The tomb was robbed twice in antiquity, shortly after it was sealed. Robbers tunneled through the blocked doorway, ransacked parts of the tomb, and made off with valuable items (particularly oils and unguents (a type of ointment), which were worth their weight in gold). But they were apparently caught or scared away before they could complete the robbery. Officials resealed the tomb, and it disappeared from memory.

Several factors probably contributed to the tomb being forgotten. Tutankhamun's reign was short and occurred during a controversial period that later pharaohs wanted to forget. His tomb entrance was small and unremarkable. Later pharaohs, particularly Ramesses VI, built tombs nearby, and debris from their construction covered Tutankhamun's entrance. Workers building Ramesses VI's tomb even built stone huts directly over Tutankhamun's buried entrance, not realizing there was a tomb beneath.

For over three thousand years, Tutankhamun's tomb lay undisturbed and forgotten, its entrance hidden beneath rubble and huts, while tomb robbers systematically plundered every other royal tomb in the valley.

On November 4th, 1922, British archaeologist Howard Carter, working in the Valley of the Kings under the patronage of Lord Carnarvon, discovered a stone step cut into the bedrock. Over the next few days, his team uncovered a staircase leading to a sealed doorway bearing Tutankhamun's name.

On November 26th, Carter made a small hole in the second sealed doorway and peered inside by candlelight. Lord Carnarvon asked, "Can you see anything?" Carter's reply became famous: "Yes, wonderful things."

The tomb was intact—or at least as intact as it had been after the ancient robberies. The antechamber was packed with objects. The burial chamber contained the king's nested coffins and sarcophagus. The treasury held the canopic shrine with the king's internal organs and countless other precious items.

It took Carter and his team ten years to carefully remove, catalog, and conserve all the objects. The discovery created a worldwide sensation. Newspapers covered it extensively. The public became fascinated with "King Tut." The beautiful objects, especially the golden death mask, captured people's imaginations. There was even talk of a "curse of the pharaohs" when Lord Carnarvon died a few months after the tomb's opening (he died from an infected mosquito bite—nothing supernatural, but the press loved the story).

The treasures from Tutankhamun's tomb have toured the world in various exhibitions, drawing millions of visitors. The golden death mask has become an icon of ancient Egypt and is instantly recognizable around the globe. Tutankhamun, who was virtually unknown before 1922, became the most famous pharaoh in the world.

It's precisely because his reign was brief and relatively insignificant that his tomb was small, easily overlooked, and survived. If Tutankhamun had been a more successful pharaoh—if he'd lived longer, built grand monuments, and conducted great campaigns—his tomb would probably have been larger, more conspicuous, and long since plundered like all the rest.

Tutankhamun is famous for being forgotten.

Horemheb and the Erasure of Amarna

After Ay's brief four-year reign, power passed to Horemheb (approximately 1319–1292 BCE, ruling for about twenty-seven years). He was a general who had served under both Akhenaten and Tutankhamun but who had no royal blood whatsoever. He was a commoner who rose to the throne through military power and political skill. His reign would mark the final end of the Amarna period and the thorough erasure of its memory.

Horemheb's background was in the military. He had served in the Egyptian army, rising through the ranks to become a general. During Tutankhamun's reign, he held the title "Commander of the Army" and was one of the most powerful men in Egypt. When Ay died without a clear heir, Horemheb was positioned to seize power, and he did.

His lack of royal lineage could have been a problem. Egyptian ideology emphasized the divine nature of kingship and the importance of royal bloodlines. But Horemheb handled this cleverly. He legitimized his rule by marrying Mutnedjmet, who was possibly Nefertiti's sister, which gave him a tenuous connection to the royal family. He also presented himself as chosen by the gods. Inscriptions describe how the god Horus selected Horemheb to be king, taking him by the hand and leading him to the throne.

However, legitimacy through divine selection and marriage wasn't enough. Horemheb needed to demonstrate that he could restore ma'at to Egypt. His reign focused on internal reform, the restoration of the traditional religion, and—most dramatically—the erasure of the Amarna period from history.

Horemheb's first priority was administrative reform. Egypt's bureaucracy and legal system had become corrupt and inefficient during the Amarna period. Horemheb issued a long decree, preserved on a stela at Karnak, outlining reforms to address various problems: corrupt officials extorting bribes, soldiers illegally seizing goods from civilians, dishonest tax collectors, and other abuses.

The decree specifies punishments for various crimes, many involving cutting off the nose or ears of offenders or, for serious crimes, execution. It's a harsh document, but it shows how Horemheb tried to restore order and honest administration to a system that had broken down.

He also reorganized the army, strengthening royal control over the military forces. He appointed officials based on merit rather than simply relying on hereditary positions. He worked to rebuild Egypt's international standing. While there's limited evidence of major military campaigns during his reign, some inscriptions suggest military activity in Nubia and Syria, though not on the same scale as earlier warrior pharaohs.

But Horemheb's most lasting impact was his systematic erasure of the Amarna period. He went further than Tutankhamun's restoration of the traditional religion, as he tried to erase all memory of Akhenaten, Smenkhkare, Tutankhamun, and Ay.

Their names were removed from the king lists. In official records, Egyptian history jumped directly from Amenhotep III to Horemheb, as if the intervening reigns had never occurred. Horemheb even dated his own reign from the death of Amenhotep III, claiming all the years back to that point as his own.

Monuments bearing the names of the Amarna pharaohs were defaced. Cartouches were chiseled out. Statues were destroyed or usurped (meaning Horemheb had his own names carved on them). Temples built during the Amarna period were dismantled, their stone blocks reused in new constructions where the blocks would be hidden, literally burying the memory of the heretics.

A statue of Horemheb with the god Amun.[28]

Amarna itself was abandoned. Without royal patronage, the city quickly declined. People moved away, and buildings fell into disrepair. The desert began to reclaim the site. Within a few decades of its founding, Akhenaten's grand capital was a ghost town, slowly disappearing beneath sand and debris.

Why such thorough erasure? The Amarna period represented multiple violations of Egyptian ideological principles. Akhenaten had rejected the traditional gods, threatening the cosmic order. His religious revolution had weakened Egypt internally and internationally. The entire period was seen as a time when Egypt had strayed from ma'at, when the proper order had been violated, and when chaos had threatened to overcome civilization.

By erasing all records of this period, Horemheb was symbolically undoing the damage, pretending it had never happened. In Egyptian belief, if something wasn't recorded or if a name wasn't preserved, it ceased to exist in any meaningful way. By removing the names and records, Horemheb was attempting to unmake the Amarna period, to remove it from history and from cosmic reality.

The erasure was remarkably successful. For centuries, Akhenaten and Tutankhamun were largely forgotten in official records and memory, though some objects bearing their names survived in obscure locations. They appeared in no king lists. Their monuments were destroyed or hidden. Their names survived only in a few obscure references that later generations couldn't interpret.

When Greek and Roman travelers visited Egypt, they saw no record of these pharaohs. It was only in the 19th century CE, when archaeologists began systematically exploring Egypt, that the Amarna period was rediscovered. The ruins of Amarna were excavated, and the Amarna letters were found and translated. Tutankhamun's tomb was discovered intact. The cartouches that Horemheb's workers had chiseled out were still recognizable enough to be read. Slowly, the erased period came back into view, rescued from the oblivion to which ancient Egyptians had consigned it.

Horemheb ruled for approximately twenty-seven years, dying around 1292 BCE. His reign marked the end of the Eighteenth Dynasty. He apparently designated his vizier, Ramesses, as his successor, though this designation is not recorded in contemporary inscriptions and likely occurred near the end of his reign. This Ramesses would become

Ramesses I, founder of the Nineteenth Dynasty.

The Nineteenth Dynasty would see Egypt return to military glory under kings like Seti I and Ramesses II. The Egyptian empire would be restored. Grand monuments would be built. Egypt would once again be a dominant power in the Near East. The disruptions of the Amarna period would become a distant memory, hidden so well that even most ancient Egyptians forgot they had ever happened.

In the modern era, the Amarna period has become one of the most studied periods in all of Egyptian history. Akhenaten is seen as one of history's most fascinating figures. Tutankhamun is the most famous pharaoh in the world. Nefertiti's bust is one of the most recognizable images from ancient Egypt. The period Horemheb tried so hard to erase has become, ironically, one of the most famous periods of Egyptian history. Memory is harder to kill than Horemheb imagined, and the period he tried to forget has refused to stay forgotten.

The famous bust of Nefertiti.[34]

Chapter 11: The Ramessides — Last Gasp of Greatness

Ramesses II: Egypt's Greatest Showman

After the chaos of the Amarna period and Horemheb's restoration, Egypt needed strong leadership to rebuild its power and prestige. That leadership came from the Nineteenth Dynasty, which was founded by Ramesses I around 1292 BCE. Ramesses I's reign was brief—only about two years—but he established a new royal line that would dominate Egypt for over a century.

Real power passed quickly to his son, Seti I (approximately 1290-1279 BCE), who would prove to be one of the New Kingdom's most effective rulers. Seti inherited an Egypt that had survived the Amarna crisis but had lost much of its international standing. The empire in Syria-Palestine had weakened. Seti set about reversing these losses through military campaigns and ambitious building projects.

Seti I was a warrior pharaoh in the traditional sense. He campaigned extensively in Syria-Palestine, reasserting Egyptian control over territories that had slipped away during the Amarna period. He fought against the Hittites for control of strategic cities in Syria. He campaigned in Libya to secure Egypt's western border. His military activities restored Egyptian power and sent a clear message: Egypt was back, and its pharaoh was once again a force to be reckoned with.

However, Seti I wasn't just a warrior; he was also a prolific builder. His greatest monument is his mortuary temple at Abydos, one of the most beautiful temples in Egypt. The temple features some of the finest relief carvings from ancient Egypt, with detailed scenes showing Seti offering tribute to the gods. The reliefs are so precisely carved and so well preserved that they remain breathtaking nearly three thousand years later.

Seti I's mortuary temple.[25]

At Abydos, Seti carved the famous Abydos King List, a chronological list of Egyptian pharaohs from the First Dynasty to his own reign. Notably, the list omits the Amarna pharaohs—Akhenaten, Smenkhkare, Tutankhamun, and Ay—jumping directly from Amenhotep III to Horemheb.

Seti's tomb in the Valley of the Kings is the longest and deepest royal tomb ever constructed there, stretching over four hundred feet into the bedrock. Its walls are covered with religious texts and images guiding the king through the afterlife. The tomb's artistic quality is exceptional, and it remains one of ancient Egypt's most impressive underground monuments.

The interior of Seti I's tomb.[26]

Near the end of his reign, Seti elevated his young son as co-regent, ensuring a smooth succession and allowing the prince to gain experience. When Seti I died around 1279 BCE after ruling for approximately eleven to fifteen years (chronologies vary), his son was ready to take full power. That son would become Ramesses II—and he would rule Egypt for sixty-six years, one of the longest reigns in history.

Ramesses II inherited a stable, prosperous kingdom from his capable father. Egypt's economy was strong. The army was well trained and well equipped. The administration functioned smoothly. International relations were generally good, though there was ongoing tension with the Hittite Empire to the north over control of Syria. Seti I had restored Egypt's power; Ramesses II would take that foundation and build something even more spectacular, at least in terms of visibility and self-promotion.

By the time Ramesses II had died in 1213 BCE, he had fathered over one hundred children with various wives and concubines. He had overseen one of the largest building programs in Egyptian history. His colossal statues stood throughout Egypt. His name appeared everywhere, carved on structures both old and new. He had fought dramatic battles, signed one of the ancient world's most famous peace treaties, and presided over Egypt during decades of prosperity and stability.

Ramesses II wasn't necessarily Egypt's most successful military commander or its most effective administrator, but he was undeniably its most visible ruler. Three thousand years later, when people think of ancient Egypt, they often think of Ramesses, whether it's his massive statues, his grand temples, or his larger-than-life presence.

He's sometimes called Ramesses the Great, and in terms of fame and monument-building, the title fits. But the reality behind the propaganda is more complex. Early in his reign, Ramesses followed his father's example, conducting military campaigns in Syria–Palestine to maintain Egyptian influence. These early campaigns were mostly successful. They were small-scale operations against rebellious vassals or troublesome groups—the normal business of maintaining an empire.

Then came the Battle of Kadesh, the event that Ramesses would commemorate more extensively than any other achievement of his reign.

Ramesses defeating a foe during the Battle of Kadesh.[37]

In his fifth year as pharaoh (around 1274 BCE), Ramesses led a major military expedition north into Syria to confront the Hittite Empire. The Hittites, based in Anatolia (modern Turkey), had been expanding southward and competing with Egypt for control over the wealthy cities of Syria-Palestine. The city of Kadesh, located in what is now Syria near the modern Lebanese border, was a strategic prize. Controlling Kadesh meant controlling important trade routes.

Ramesses marched north with four divisions of the Egyptian army, perhaps sixteen thousand to twenty thousand men in total. The Hittite king Muwatalli II had assembled his own forces, including troops from allied kingdoms throughout Anatolia and Syria. He possibly commanded a similar or even larger number.

What happened at Kadesh is documented in extraordinary detail by the Egyptians. Ramesses had the story carved on temple walls throughout Egypt, accompanied by dramatic images. The account appears at the Ramesseum (Ramesses's mortuary temple), at Abu Simbel, at Karnak, at Luxor, and at Abydos. It's one of the most extensively documented battles in ancient history, at least from one side's perspective.

According to the Egyptian account, Ramesses was tricked by Hittite spies posing as deserters, who told him the Hittite army was far to the north, near Aleppo. Believing this false intelligence, Ramesses advanced quickly with just his first division, the Amun division, leaving his other three divisions strung out behind him along the route.

As Ramesses camped northwest of Kadesh, the Hittite army, which had actually been hiding nearby, launched a surprise attack. They struck the Ra division, the second Egyptian division that was still on the march south of Kadesh, catching it completely unprepared. The Ra division broke and fled in panic toward Ramesses's camp.

The Hittite chariot force then swept into Ramesses's camp itself. The Egyptian soldiers panicked. Officers fled. The situation looked desperate. The pharaoh was surrounded by enemy forces, his army scattered and demoralized, facing defeat and possibly capture or death.

This is where Ramesses's account becomes particularly dramatic. According to the text, Ramesses found himself abandoned by his soldiers. He was alone except for his chariot driver. He prayed to the god Amun, reproaching the god for allowing this to happen after all Ramesses had done for him. Amun responded, promising to give Ramesses the strength of thousands.

Inspired by divine intervention, Ramesses single-handedly charged into the Hittite forces. The texts describe him cutting through enemy ranks like a whirlwind, his arrows never missing, his enemies falling before him. He made six individual charges through the Hittite forces, each time emerging victorious. The enemy was so terrified of his prowess that they threw themselves into the river to escape him.

Eventually, the Ptah division arrived from the south, and then another Egyptian force arrived—possibly the Ne'arin, though the identity of this force remains debated among scholars. The Hittites withdrew across the river. Ramesses had achieved a miraculous victory through his own valor and divine favor.

That's the Egyptian version. It's heroic, dramatic, and makes for great propaganda. However, it's clearly exaggerated, and we can read between the lines to understand what probably actually happened.

The Hittites clearly had a tactical surprise and initially had the upper hand. The Egyptian army was caught unprepared and took heavy losses. Ramesses probably did personally fight—Egyptian pharaohs were expected to lead from the front, and Ramesses seems to have been genuinely brave. But the claim that he single-handedly fought off the entire Hittite army is blatant propaganda.

What likely saved the Egyptians was the arrival of reinforcements—the Ptah division and the additional force—which turned a potential disaster into a chaotic but not catastrophic engagement. The Hittites withdrew, though the reasons for their withdrawal remain unclear. It might have been tactical rather than fear of Egyptian strength.

The next day, according to Egyptian sources, there was more fighting, but it was inconclusive. After this, Ramesses withdrew south, leaving Kadesh in Hittite hands.

Yes, the Hittites kept Kadesh. Egypt didn't achieve its strategic objective of securing the city. Egyptian casualties were significant. By any objective military standard, this wasn't a victory.

However, Ramesses proclaimed it as his greatest triumph. He commissioned texts and reliefs showing his heroic stand. He had poets compose epic accounts of the battle. He made Kadesh the defining moment of his military career, proof of his divine favor and personal courage.

This wasn't unusual for ancient rulers. Spinning military defeats or inconclusive battles as victories was a common practice. But Ramesses took it to an extreme. The sheer volume of inscriptions and reliefs commemorating Kadesh is remarkable. If you visited Egyptian temples in antiquity, you couldn't escape the story of how Ramesses heroically saved Egypt at Kadesh.

An original relief of the Battle of Kadesh in the Ramesseum.[38]

After Kadesh, Ramesses continued campaigning in Syria–Palestine for another decade or so, but without any decisive breakthrough. Neither the Egyptians nor the Hittites could gain a clear advantage. The two powers were roughly equal in strength, and the cost of continued warfare was becoming unsustainable for both.

Around 1259 BCE, about fifteen years after Kadesh, Ramesses and the Hittite king Hattusili III signed a peace treaty. The treaty, recorded in both Egyptian hieroglyphics and Hittite cuneiform, is the first and most comprehensive peace treaty from the ancient world. A copy hangs in the United Nations headquarters in New York as a symbol of early international diplomacy.

The treaty established peace between Egypt and the Hittites, defined their respective spheres of influence in Syria–Palestine, established mutual defense provisions (if either kingdom was attacked by a third party, the other would provide military assistance), and even included extradition provisions for fugitives who fled from one kingdom to the other.

The treaty was sealed by a diplomatic marriage. Ramesses married a Hittite princess, the daughter of Hattusili III. Later, he married another Hittite princess. These marriages helped maintain peace between the two powers for the rest of Ramesses's reign.

The treaty worked remarkably well. Egypt and the Hittite Empire maintained peaceful relations. They corresponded regularly; letters between the Egyptian and Hittite courts survive. They coordinated on diplomatic matters. The costly warfare in Syria came to an end.

This peace allowed Ramesses to focus on what he's most famous for: building.

Ramesses II oversaw one of the largest building programs in Egyptian history. The scale and number of his construction projects were unprecedented, though much of his building projects involved usurping earlier monuments—having his name carved on statues and structures built by previous pharaohs or recycling and re-inscribing monuments from earlier reigns. He built new temples, expanded existing ones, and ensured his name appeared on monuments throughout Egypt.

His most famous monument is Abu Simbel in Nubia, far south of Egypt proper. This temple, carved directly into a cliff face, features four colossal seated statues of Ramesses at its entrance, each about sixty-seven feet tall. Inside, the temple contains halls with more statues and reliefs.

Twice a year, on specific dates aligned with the solar year, sunlight penetrates deep into the temple to illuminate statues in the inner sanctuary—a remarkable feat of ancient engineering and astronomical knowledge.

Abu Simbel also features a smaller temple dedicated to Ramesses's favorite wife, Nefertari, with statues of her standing alongside the king, which is unusual recognition for a queen. The temple's inscriptions proclaim Ramesses's greatness and his divine status.

The Temple of Ramesses II on the left and the Small Temple of Hathor and Nefertari on the right.[29]

In the 1960s, when the construction of the Aswan High Dam threatened to submerge Abu Simbel under Lake Nasser, an international effort organized by UNESCO dismantled the entire temple complex and moved it to higher ground, cutting it into blocks and reassembling it exactly as it had been. It was one of the most ambitious archaeological rescue operations ever undertaken.

Moving the colossal statues.[80]

Ramesses also built the Ramesseum, his massive mortuary temple on the west bank at Thebes. The complex covered an enormous territory and included a temple, palace, storage magazines, and administrative buildings. The Ramesseum once featured a colossal seated statue of Ramesses weighing over one thousand tons, making it one of the largest statues ever carved in ancient Egypt. It now lies in broken pieces. This statue inspired Percy Bysshe Shelley's famous poem "Ozymandias" (Ozymandias being a Greek rendering of one of Ramesses's throne names). The poem's ironic meditation on the impermanence of power and pride is particularly fitting for Ramesses, the king who built so much to ensure his eternal fame.

At Karnak, Ramesses completed the massive hypostyle hall begun by his father Seti I. The hall contains 134 enormous columns, some reaching 70 feet high, their capitals carved in the form of papyrus flowers. The hall is so large that Notre-Dame Cathedral in Paris could fit inside it. While Seti I started this project, Ramesses finished and decorated it, ensuring his name appeared prominently throughout.

The Great Hypostyle Hall.[81]

At Luxor Temple, Ramesses added a new court and pylon entrance, along with six colossal statues of himself and two obelisks (one now stands in the Place de la Concorde in Paris, as it was given to France in the 19th century).

He built temples at Memphis, at Abydos, throughout the Nile Delta, and in Nubia. Everywhere he built, colossal statues of Ramesses dominated the landscape. His cartouches appeared on walls, columns, and doorways. His building program employed thousands of workers, including quarrymen, transporters, sculptors, painters, architects, and administrators.

Why did he build so much? Multiple reasons. Building temples honored the gods and maintained ma'at. It demonstrated the pharaoh's power and wealth. It provided employment and stimulated the economy. It ensured the pharaoh's name would be remembered—and Ramesses was clearly obsessed with ensuring his eternal fame. Building also served as propaganda, impressing Egyptians and foreigners with Egypt's might and the pharaoh's divine status.

Ramesses's family life was equally on a grand scale. He had numerous wives, the most important being Nefertari, whom he married early in his reign and who appears to have been his favorite. She bore several of his children and was honored with her own temple at Abu Simbel and a beautifully decorated tomb in the Valley of the Queens. It is one of the most stunning tombs in ancient Egypt, with vibrant painted reliefs that remain remarkably well preserved.

Horus leading Nefertari by the hand.[53]

After Nefertari's death, Ramesses elevated another wife, Isetnofret, to chief queen. He also married at least one of his own daughters, Bintanath, and possibly a second daughter, Nebettawy. This practice became more common in the later New Kingdom, perhaps influenced by the royal inbreeding of earlier periods or as a way to reinforce royal bloodlines.

Ramesses fathered over one hundred children—some sources say as many as 150, though exact numbers are uncertain. With so many offspring, the succession became complicated. His sons were given ranks, with the eldest being designated crown prince. However, Ramesses lived to around ninety in an era when life expectancy was perhaps thirty-five to forty years, outliving many of his sons. His first dozen sons died before him, and the throne eventually passed to Merneptah, who was the thirteenth son in the official procession lists but the fourth to be designated crown prince due to the deaths of his older brothers. Merneptah was already elderly when he became pharaoh.

Ramesses was an old man when he died. His mummy shows evidence of arthritis, dental problems, and other age-related conditions. However, he remained active, continuing to oversee building projects and administration in his later years.

When he finally died in 1213 BCE, his passing marked the end of an era. He had ruled for so long that most Egyptians had known no other pharaoh. His reign had been prosperous and stable. Egypt had been at peace with major powers like the Hittites, though smaller campaigns continued in Nubia and Libya. The temples were full, the granaries stocked, and the borders secure.

Ramesses II had achieved his goal of eternal fame. His monuments still stand, and his name is known worldwide. He represents ancient Egypt in popular imagination—the powerful pharaoh surrounded by colossal statues and grand temples.

But beneath the propaganda and the monuments, was Ramesses actually a great pharaoh? The evidence is mixed. He signed a treaty that essentially recognized the status quo rather than achieving military dominance. His building projects, while impressive, relied heavily on usurpation and consumed vast resources that would strain Egypt's economy in the decades after his death. His extremely long reign, while stable, meant that an elderly son would inherit, potentially creating succession difficulties.

Ramesses was a master of image management, a pharaoh who understood that appearing powerful could be as important as actually being powerful. He was Egypt's greatest showman. And in ancient Egypt, where the pharaoh was both king and god, where maintaining ma'at required projecting divine authority, showmanship mattered. Whether that makes him "great" depends on how you define greatness.

The Sea Peoples and the Bronze Age Collapse

Around the time of Ramesses II's death and in the decades that followed, the entire eastern Mediterranean world began to collapse. Great kingdoms and civilizations that had existed for centuries suddenly fell. Cities burned, and trade networks disintegrated. Literacy declined or disappeared. Populations decreased dramatically. Archaeologists call this period the Bronze Age Collapse. It was one of the most catastrophic civilizational breakdowns in human history.

Egypt survived this collapse as a unified state, unlike the Hittites or the Mycenaeans, but it lost its entire empire in Syria-Palestine, suffered massive economic disruption, and became significantly weakened. And playing a major role in this chaos were mysterious groups collectively known as the Sea Peoples.

The Bronze Age world of the late 13th and early 12th centuries BCE was highly interconnected. The great powers—Egypt, the Hittites, Mycenaean Greece, Assyria, Babylon, and the kingdoms of Syria-Palestine—traded extensively with each other. Tin from Afghanistan reached the Mediterranean. Copper from Cyprus was worked into bronze throughout the region. Grain from Egypt fed populations far away. Luxury goods, like ivory, incense, precious metals, and dyed textiles, moved along established trade routes.

This world was also interconnected. The great powers communicated diplomatically in Akkadian, the international language. They exchanged gifts and ambassadors. They made treaties and arranged royal marriages. They maintained a balance of power that, while not without conflict, provided relative stability.

Then, starting around 1200 BCE, this world fell apart rather quickly.

The Hittite Empire, which had been Egypt's rival and then its ally, collapsed completely. Its capital, Hattusa, was burned and abandoned. The empire fragmented, and Hittite civilization essentially disappeared from history. The collapse resulted from a combination of factors: severe famines documented in texts, internal political strife, drought, and systemic administrative failure. The groups identified as Sea Peoples might have moved through these already destabilized regions, possibly delivering final blows to territories where Hittite control had already broken down. Where there had been a great power controlling Anatolia and northern Syria, there was suddenly chaos.

The Mycenaean palaces of Greece—centers of the Bronze Age Greek civilization that would later inspire stories of the Trojan War—were destroyed. Most major sites were abandoned or saw only limited later occupation. The elaborate palace-based civilization of Mycenaean Greece vanished, and Greece entered a dark age that would last several centuries.

Cities throughout the eastern Mediterranean were destroyed. Archaeological excavations show dramatic layers of destruction at sites across the region—Ugarit in Syria, Megiddo in Palestine, Hazor in Palestine, and many others. These weren't slow declines but sudden, violent destructions.

Trade networks collapsed. The supply of tin, essential for making bronze, was disrupted. The copper trade from Cyprus ceased. The interconnected economy that had supported the Bronze Age civilizations broke down.

What caused this catastrophe? This question has fascinated and frustrated scholars for decades, and there's still no consensus. The collapse was almost certainly caused by multiple factors working together.

One factor was the groups collectively called the Sea Peoples. Egyptian sources from the reigns of Merneptah (Ramesses II's son and successor) and Ramesses III describe attacks by foreign invaders coming by both sea and land. Egyptian texts list various distinct groups with names like the Peleset, Tjeker, Shekelesh, Denyen, and Weshesh. Modern scholars collectively call these groups the Sea Peoples, though this is a modern term. The ancient sources don't use this exact phrase and instead identify separate groups moving through the region.

Who were the Sea Peoples? We still don't really know. The Egyptian texts don't provide much detail about their origins or society. Some groups might have come from Anatolia, others possibly from the Aegean or Greece, others from Sicily or Sardinia (some of the names have been tentatively connected to later peoples in these regions; for instance, the Peleset are widely believed to be related to the later Philistines, though this connection is not proven). They might have been displaced populations fleeing disasters in their homelands, opportunistic raiders taking advantage of the chaos, or something else entirely.

What we do know is that they appeared in large numbers moving through the eastern Mediterranean. Egyptian reliefs show them with their families, ox-carts loaded with possessions, suggesting they weren't just raiders but displaced peoples looking for new lands.

In Merneptah's fifth year (around 1208 BCE), Egypt faced a major invasion from the west. A Libyan chief named Meryey allied with several Sea Peoples groups and invaded the western Nile Delta with a large force—perhaps tens of thousands of warriors and their families. They apparently hoped to settle in the fertile delta region.

Merneptah, despite being elderly (he had become pharaoh in his fifties after Ramesses II's extremely long reign), responded. He assembled the Egyptian army and met the invaders in battle somewhere in the western delta. The Egyptian account describes a decisive victory. Over six thousand enemies were killed, many more captured, and Meryey fled back to Libya.

An inscription from Merneptah's reign celebrating this victory, known as the Merneptah Stela, is notable for another reason: it contains the earliest known reference to "Israel" outside the Bible. The stela lists various defeated enemies, including a group called Israel located in Canaan, though it tells us nothing else about them.

Merneptah's victory secured Egypt against the immediate threat, but it didn't end the larger crisis. The Sea Peoples continued to move through the eastern Mediterranean, and the collapse of other civilizations continued.

The most detailed Egyptian account of the Sea Peoples comes from the reign of Ramesses III (c. 1186–1155 BCE), who ruled early in the Twentieth Dynasty, about a generation after Merneptah. Ramesses III faced multiple threats during his reign and recorded his victories in detailed reliefs and inscriptions at his mortuary temple at Medinet Habu.

According to these texts and reliefs, in Ramesses III's fifth and eighth years (around 1180 and 1177 BCE), Egypt faced massive invasions by the Sea Peoples. The invaders moved through Syria–Palestine toward Egypt, through regions that had already been destabilized and fragmented following the collapse of major powers. They came by both land (moving down the coast with their families and possessions) and sea (in ships carrying warriors).

Ramesses III describes preparing Egypt's defenses. He fortified the mouths of the Nile and positioned army units along the coast. He also prepared the Egyptian navy to meet the seaborne invasion.

The reliefs at Medinet Habu show two major battles. The first was a land battle in Syria–Palestine or the Sinai, where Egyptian forces met the Sea Peoples' land army. The reliefs show Egyptian troops, including foreign mercenaries, fighting the invaders. The Egyptians claimed victory, with heaps of dead enemies and captives being taken.

The second was a naval battle, probably fought in the Nile Delta. This is depicted in remarkable detail in the reliefs—one of the few ancient Egyptian depictions of naval warfare. Egyptian ships engage Sea Peoples' vessels. Archers shoot from the ships. Men fall into the water. The Egyptian ships appear to be grappling and boarding enemy vessels. The Egyptians claimed a decisive victory, with enemy ships captured or sunk and large numbers of captives taken.

A sketch of the relief of the Battle of the Delta.[35]

Ramesses III's victories were genuine military successes, as they prevented the Sea Peoples from invading and settling in Egypt proper. Since the Sea Peoples didn't settle in Egypt itself, it is believed that the Egyptian defenses held.

However, the wars were costly. The disruption of trade networks hurt Egypt's economy. The collapse of neighboring kingdoms meant fewer trading partners. Egypt became more isolated as a result. Egyptian control over territories in Syria–Palestine was lost entirely. The empire contracted back to Egypt proper and Nubia.

Some of the Sea Peoples groups settled in areas that had been under Egyptian influence. The Peleset settled on the southern coast of Canaan in areas that would become the Philistine cities known in the Bible. Other groups settled elsewhere in the region. Egypt couldn't prevent this—Egyptian power was no longer what it had been.

What caused the Bronze Age Collapse beyond the Sea Peoples themselves? Scholars have proposed multiple contributing factors.

First off, evidence suggests the region experienced severe droughts around this time. Agricultural production would have declined, causing food shortages, economic stress, and population movements. The Sea Peoples themselves might have been climate refugees fleeing failed harvests in their homelands.

Archaeological evidence also shows earthquake damage at many sites during this period. A series of major earthquakes could have damaged cities and disrupted societies already stressed by other problems.

Some destroyed palaces show evidence suggesting internal violence rather than external attack. Popular uprisings against palace elites might have contributed to the collapse.

The Bronze Age civilizations were highly interconnected and dependent on each other for resources. When some parts of the system failed, there was a cascade effect. The collapse of the Hittites disrupted trade routes, which hurt other kingdoms, which affected still others, and so on.

Lastly, even if the Sea Peoples didn't cause the initial collapse, they certainly made it worse. As central authorities weakened, raiding became easier and more profitable. The movement of large groups of displaced peoples put additional stress on societies that were already struggling.

Most likely, the Bronze Age Collapse resulted from all these factors working together. It was a "perfect storm" that overwhelmed the resilience of Bronze Age civilizations.

A dark age descended on much of the eastern Mediterranean. Egypt survived as a unified state, but it was a diminished power in a more dangerous world. The great days of the New Kingdom were ending. Egypt would never again be the dominant power it had been under Thutmose III or even Ramesses II. The next several centuries would see a slow, uneven decline punctuated by occasional recoveries.

The End of an Era

After Ramesses III's victories against the Sea Peoples, Egypt had bought itself time, but the glory days were fading. The Twentieth Dynasty, to which Ramesses III belonged, would continue for several more decades, but each successive pharaoh was weaker than the last.

Ramesses III himself faced serious internal problems. Late in his reign, he survived an assassination plot. Court documents describe a conspiracy involving one of his wives and members of the royal household who plotted to kill him and place a different son on the throne. The conspiracy was discovered, and the plotters were tried and executed. However, the fact that such a conspiracy could occur showed the internal stresses Egypt was experiencing.

Some scholars believe Ramesses III might have actually been killed in the assassination attempt or died shortly after. Medical examination of his mummy revealed that his throat had been cut, possibly during the assassination. Whether he died immediately or survived to see the conspirators punished remains debated, but his death marked the beginning of the end for the Ramesside dynasty.

After Ramesses III, Egypt was ruled by a series of pharaohs, all named Ramesses (Ramesses IV through XI), who reigned in succession over the next century. These later Ramesses pharaohs are often difficult to distinguish from each other. Their reigns were short, their accomplishments limited, and their names chosen perhaps in hope of recapturing the glory of Ramesses II.

During these reigns, the decline of Egypt became increasingly obvious. Egypt's empire in Syria–Palestine was gone. The gold and tribute that had once flowed into Egypt from conquered territories dried up. The economy suffered.

Workers weren't being paid. One of the most remarkable documents from ancient Egypt dates to the reign of Ramesses III—a record of the first recorded labor strike in history. Workers building royal tombs in the Valley of the Kings stopped work and staged a sit-down strike because they hadn't been paid their rations. The fact that royal tomb workers—highly skilled craftsmen working on the most important religious monuments—weren't being paid shows serious economic problems.

The strikes became more frequent under later Ramesses pharaohs. Workers demonstrated, occupied temples, and refused to work until paid. The government struggled to supply basic rations. This wasn't because Egypt had become poor overnight. It was because the administrative system was breaking down. Resources weren't being distributed efficiently. Corruption was increasing. Central authority was weakening.

The power of the priesthood, particularly the priesthood of Amun at Thebes, was growing. As royal authority weakened, the priests of Amun, who controlled vast wealth, extensive lands, and thousands of temple workers, became increasingly independent. The high priest of Amun at Thebes was becoming nearly as powerful as the pharaoh, controlling southern Egypt almost as a separate kingdom.

Tomb robberies became epidemic during the later Twentieth Dynasty. The elaborate tombs in the Valley of the Kings, filled with treasures, were obvious targets. Organized gangs of tomb robbers plundered royal burials over several decades. Court records preserve trials of captured tomb robbers, who described tunneling into tombs, stripping mummies of their gold, and melting down precious objects. Even the tombs of pharaohs who had died just decades earlier were robbed.

The fact that royal tombs could be robbed on such a scale shows the breakdown of authority. These weren't opportunistic thefts but organized criminal enterprises, apparently involving corrupt officials who helped the robbers or looked the other way. The authorities caught some robbers and punished them harshly, but they couldn't stop the wave of robberies.

Military power was also declining. Egypt no longer had the resources or organization to conduct major campaigns. The army increasingly relied on foreign mercenaries, including Libyans and Nubians, who were less loyal to the Egyptian crown. These mercenaries sometimes settled in Egypt, particularly in the Nile Delta, creating foreign communities within Egyptian territory.

By the reign of Ramesses XI (roughly 1099–1069 BCE), the last pharaoh of the Twentieth Dynasty, central authority had effectively collapsed into divided power centers. Egypt was no longer unified under strong central control. In the south, the high priest of Amun at Thebes, a man named Herihor, effectively ruled as an independent king, even taking royal titles. In the north, another official named Smendes controlled the Nile Delta from the city of Tanis. Ramesses XI remained pharaoh in name, but he controlled little actual territory and had minimal authority.

This situation is sometimes called the "Renaissance Era" or the "Wehem Mesut" (meaning "Repeating of Births" or "Renaissance"), a term used in ancient texts suggesting an attempt at reform or renewal. However, it was really a recognition that the old order had collapsed and a new system was emerging.

Chapter 12:
The Third Intermediate Period— Division and Foreign Rule

Egypt Splits in Two

When Ramesses XI died around 1069 BCE, Egypt entered what historians call the Third Intermediate Period—a time of political fragmentation that would last approximately 350 years. The unified kingdom that had existed since the start of the New Kingdom was no more. Instead, Egypt would be divided between competing power centers, ruled by dynasties of Libyan origin, briefly reunified by Nubian conquerors, and eventually invaded by the mighty Assyrian Empire.

This wasn't a sudden catastrophic collapse like the Bronze Age Collapse that had destroyed the Hittites and Mycenaeans. Egypt didn't experience mass destruction of cities or the loss of literacy. Egyptian culture remained vibrant. Temples still functioned, art and religious practices continued to flourish, and daily life for most Egyptians probably didn't change dramatically. However, the centralized political authority that had characterized the New Kingdom was gone. Egypt had fractured politically, even as its cultural traditions continued.

The division was already established before Ramesses XI's death. In the north, a man named Smendes ruled from the city of Tanis in the Nile Delta. When Ramesses XI died, Smendes claimed the title of pharaoh and established what historians call the Twenty-first Dynasty. He controlled Lower Egypt—the delta region and the area around Memphis.

In the south, the high priest of Amun at Thebes controlled Upper Egypt. Herihor, who had been high priest during the final years of Ramesses XI's reign, had already taken royal titles. After Ramesses XI's death, the high priests of Amun continued to rule southern Egypt as a virtual theocracy—a state controlled by religious authorities.

This division between north and south would persist, in various forms, for much of the Third Intermediate Period. Sometimes the division was cooperative, with the northern pharaoh and the southern high priest working together and intermarrying their families. Sometimes it was more hostile, with competition for resources and authority. Regardless, the unified Egypt of the New Kingdom was gone.

Why did Smendes rule from Tanis rather than from Memphis or Thebes, the traditional capitals? It was mostly for practical reasons. Tanis was located in the northeastern Nile Delta, close to the Mediterranean coast and to trade routes to the Levant. It was better positioned for commerce and communication with the outside world. Memphis and Thebes, while still important cities, were less central to the politics of the late 2nd millennium BCE.

Smendes and his successors of the Twenty-first Dynasty weren't particularly powerful. They ruled a diminished kingdom—just Lower Egypt and part of Middle Egypt. They had limited resources. They conducted no major military campaigns and built few monuments. They're known primarily from inscriptions and from finds at Tanis, where archaeologists discovered intact royal tombs in the 1930s and 1940s. These tombs were filled with beautiful objects, including silver coffins and golden masks, showing that the Twenty-first Dynasty pharaohs, while weak politically, still had access to considerable wealth.

The high priests of Amun controlled Upper Egypt. They commanded the wealth of the Amun temple complex at Karnak, one of the richest institutions in Egypt. They married into the royal family of the northern dynasty, maintaining ties. But they ruled independently, conducting their own administration, maintaining their own military forces, and generally acting as kings in all but name.

This situation—two separate power centers in Egypt—might seem strange, but it worked reasonably well for several generations. The Twenty-first Dynasty lasted about 130 years (roughly 1069–945 BCE), during which time Egypt avoided major conflicts and maintained relative stability, even if the kingdom was divided.

Then came the Libyans.

Libyans had been present in Egypt for centuries. They lived west of the Nile Valley in the desert regions. They had raided Egypt periodically, and Egyptian armies had fought against them. However, they had also served as mercenaries in the Egyptian army, and many Libyan families had settled in Egypt, particularly in the delta, over generations.

By the later Twenty-first Dynasty, many Libyans living in Egypt had become thoroughly Egyptianized. They had adopted Egyptian culture, worshiped Egyptian gods, and married into Egyptian families. These were not foreign invaders but assimilated military families whose ancestors had settled in Egypt generations earlier. They were Egyptian in culture, even if they were Libyan in ancestry.

One such family produced a man named Shoshenq, who served as a military commander under the last pharaohs of the Twenty-first Dynasty. Shoshenq was powerful, wealthy, and ambitious. When the last pharaoh of the Twenty-first Dynasty died around 945 BCE, Shoshenq claimed the throne, establishing the Twenty-second Dynasty.

Shoshenq I (ruled approximately 945–924 BCE) was the most powerful pharaoh Egypt had seen since the end of the New Kingdom. He reasserted authority over Egypt, bringing both the north and the south under his influence, though local elites, especially at Thebes, retained considerable autonomy. He placed his own sons in positions of power. One son became high priest of Amun at Thebes, ensuring southern loyalty. Another son governed key cities. Shoshenq was rebuilding centralized royal authority, even if his control wasn't absolute.

He also conducted military campaigns abroad, something Egyptian pharaohs hadn't done effectively for generations. Around 925 BCE, Shoshenq led an army into Palestine. Egyptian inscriptions record that he captured numerous cities in both the northern kingdom of Israel and the southern kingdom of Judah. This campaign appears in the Hebrew Bible—1 Kings 14:25–26 describes how "Shishak king of Egypt" attacked Jerusalem during the reign of King Rehoboam and plundered the Temple and royal palace.

Shoshenq's Palestinian campaign was one of the last significant Egyptian military operations in the Levant. It showed that Egypt could still project power beyond its borders, at least temporarily. However, it didn't restore Egyptian dominance in the region. The campaign was more of a raid than a conquest. Shoshenq took plunder and tribute but didn't establish permanent Egyptian control.

After Shoshenq I's death, the Twenty-second Dynasty continued, but royal authority gradually weakened again. Subsequent pharaohs had less control over the country. Regional strongmen, many of them also of Libyan descent, established local power bases. Governors of major cities became increasingly independent, ruling their territories almost like mini-kingdoms.

By the early 9th century BCE, Egypt was fragmenting again. Multiple rulers claimed royal authority. Historians identify a Twenty-third Dynasty that ruled concurrently with the later Twenty-second Dynasty, based in the delta city of Leontopolis. There was also a Twenty-fourth Dynasty, which briefly ruled from Sais in the western delta. These weren't successive dynasties but overlapping ones. There were different rulers in different cities, all claiming to be pharaoh and all controlling limited territories.

This abundance of pharaohs—sometimes called the "Libyan period" because most of the rulers were of Libyan descent—is confusing even for Egyptologists. The chronology is uncertain, and the relationships between different rulers are unclear. Some pharaohs are known only from a few inscriptions. It's a messy period.

What's clear, though, is that Egypt was weak and divided. No single ruler controlled the entire country. This political fragmentation made Egypt vulnerable. Without a strong central government and a unified military, Egypt couldn't defend itself against external threats. And a major threat was developing to the south—a powerful kingdom that would soon conquer Egypt and briefly reunify the country under foreign rule.

The Nubian Conquest

South of Egypt, in the region called Nubia (roughly corresponding to modern Sudan), a powerful kingdom had emerged. This was the Kingdom of Kush, centered on the city of Napata near the Fourth Cataract of the Nile. The Kushites were culturally connected to Egypt. They worshiped Egyptian gods, particularly Amun, and they saw themselves as inheritors of the Egyptian civilization. However, they were politically independent and becoming increasingly powerful.

Nubia had a long, complex relationship with Egypt. During periods when Egypt was strong, Egypt controlled Nubia, exploiting its gold mines and using it as a source of luxury goods and soldiers. During the New Kingdom, Nubia had been thoroughly Egyptianized, with Egyptian temples, Egyptian administrators, and Egyptian culture imposed on the region.

But when Egypt weakened during the late New Kingdom and the Third Intermediate Period, Nubian independence reasserted itself. A dynasty established itself at Napata. By the 8th century BCE, the Kingdom of Kush had become a major regional power.

The Kushite kings saw themselves as the true upholders of Egyptian tradition and guardians of proper religious practice. While Egypt itself had become fragmented and ruled by Libyan dynasties, the Kushites at Napata maintained Egyptian religious practices with notable devotion. They used Egyptian hieroglyphs and adopted Egyptian royal ideology. In their view, they were preserving authentic Egyptian tradition more faithfully than the rulers in Egypt itself.

Around 760 BCE, a Kushite king named Kashta began expanding northward from Nubia into Upper Egypt. He gained control of Thebes and the surrounding region, establishing Kushite authority over southern Egypt. His daughter Amenirdis became God's Wife of Amun, an important religious position at Thebes.

Kashta's successor, Piye (ruled approximately 747–716 BCE), continued the expansion. Around 728 BCE, Piye launched a major military campaign northward to bring all of Egypt under Kushite control.

An extraordinary document survives from this campaign: the Victory Stela of Piye, a long inscription discovered at Napata. It provides one of the most vivid accounts of ancient Egyptian warfare that has survived from any period.

According to the stela, Piye was motivated by reports that a Delta ruler named Tefnakht, who controlled much of Lower Egypt, was disrespecting the gods and threatening Egyptian tradition. Piye portrayed his campaign as a mission to restore ma'at and proper worship to Egypt.

Piye's army sailed north down the Nile. They encountered resistance from various local rulers (Egypt's political fragmentation meant there were multiple kings and chiefs who had to be defeated individually). The stela describes sieges of cities, naval battles on the Nile, negotiations, and submissions.

When Piye reached Memphis, the city initially resisted. The stela describes how Piye's forces besieged Memphis, attacked its harbor, and eventually captured the city. The victory was celebrated with proper religious rituals. Piye made offerings to the gods and purified the temples that had been "polluted" by improper worship.

The stela lists numerous kings and chiefs who came to bow before the Kushite pharaoh, offering their submission and tribute. Tefnakht himself eventually submitted, though he never personally appeared before Piye. Instead, he sent messages of submission through intermediaries.

Piye's victory stela portrays him as both a mighty warrior and a pious king. He conquered through military force but also through religious authority. He was restoring ma'at and bringing Egypt back to the proper worship of the gods, particularly Amun.

After conquering Egypt, Piye did something unusual—he went home to Nubia. He returned to Napata, leaving Egypt under the control of local rulers who now owed him allegiance. He didn't establish a permanent administrative presence in Egypt or try to rule directly from Memphis or Thebes. He had demonstrated Kushite supremacy and exacted tribute, but he didn't reorganize Egypt's political structure. Perhaps he considered his mission accomplished. After all, Egypt had submitted, proper worship was restored, and his authority was recognized. Perhaps he preferred to rule from Napata, the center of Kushite power. Perhaps he didn't have the resources or interest in permanently occupying Egypt.

Piye's successors took a different approach. His brother Shabaka (ruled approximately 716–702 BCE) actually moved to Egypt and established direct Kushite rule. Shabaka conquered the remaining independent territories in the delta, defeated Tefnakht's successor, and established what historians call the Twenty-fifth Dynasty—the Kushite or Nubian Dynasty.

Shabaka and his successors ruled Egypt from Memphis, presenting themselves as traditional Egyptian pharaohs. They built monuments, restored temples, and patronized Egyptian religion and culture. They commissioned inscriptions in Egyptian hieroglyphs. They also adopted the full Egyptian royal titulary. In many ways, they were model pharaohs, perhaps more devoted to Egyptian tradition than many native Egyptian rulers had been.

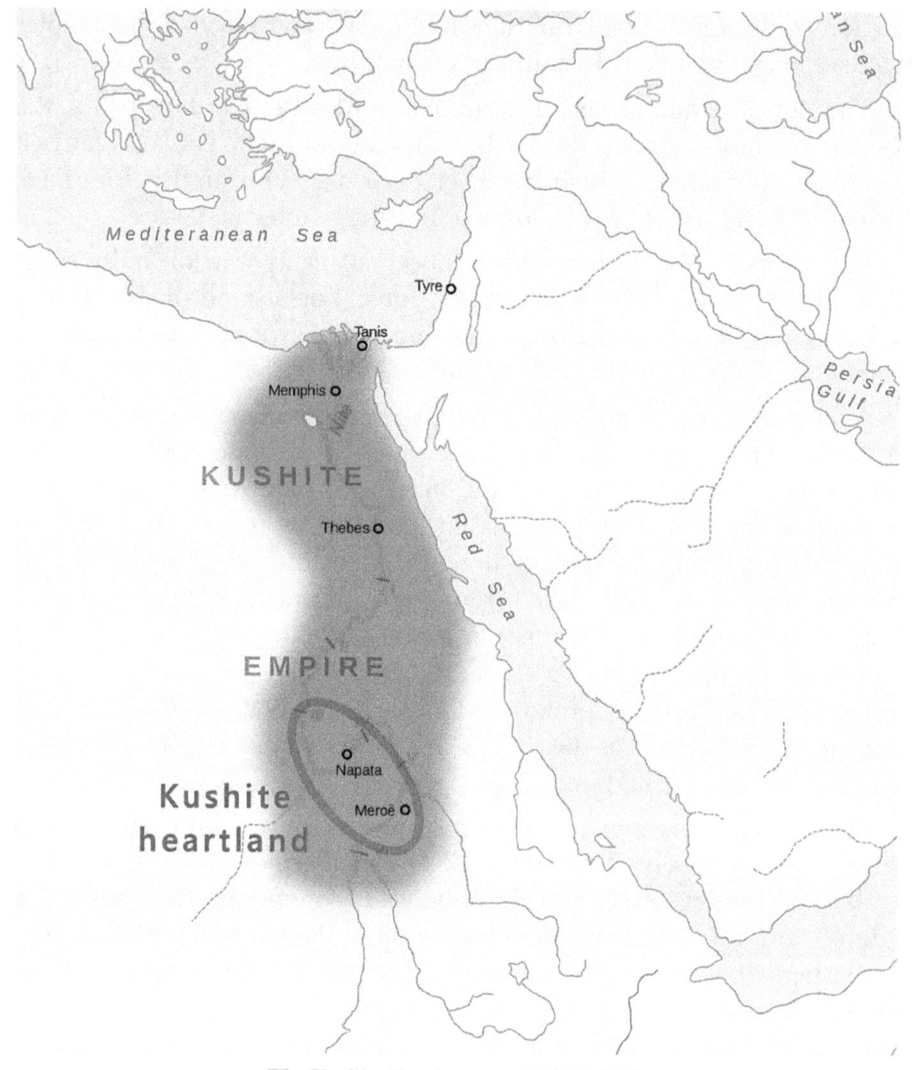

The Kushite Empire around 700 BCE.[34]

The Kushite pharaohs are sometimes called the "Black Pharaohs" in modern literature because they came from a region south of Egypt, which was inhabited by people with darker skin tones than most Egyptians. This is a modern term not used in antiquity, and it's somewhat problematic. Ancient Egyptians didn't categorize people by race in the modern sense, and Nubia had always been part of the Egyptian cultural sphere. But the term reflects the fact that the Twenty-fifth Dynasty represented a period when Egypt was ruled by kings whose base of power was in sub-Saharan Africa.

The most famous Kushite pharaoh was Taharqa (ruled approximately 690-664 BCE), who appears in the Hebrew Bible as King "Tirhakah" of Cush (2 Kings 19:9). Taharqa was an energetic and ambitious ruler. He conducted military campaigns, built extensively throughout Egypt and Nubia, and attempted to restore Egypt to something approaching its former glory.

Taharqa's building program was impressive. He added structures to the Temple of Karnak at Thebes and built temples in Nubia. He restored shrines that had fallen into disrepair during the years of division. Taharqa was trying to rebuild Egypt as a unified, powerful kingdom.

But Taharqa faced a problem that he couldn't overcome—the Assyrian Empire.

The End of Independence

By the 7th century BCE, the Near East was dominated by Assyria, a militaristic empire based in northern Mesopotamia (modern Iraq). The Assyrians had built the most powerful military machine the ancient world had yet seen. They had conquered vast territories, including Mesopotamia, Syria, Palestine, Anatolia, and parts of the Iranian Plateau. They were expanding in all directions, and Egypt was next.

The Assyrian kings wanted to control Egypt for several reasons. Egypt was wealthy. It controlled trade routes

Statue of Tarhaqa.[85]

and had symbolic importance as one of the ancient world's great civilizations. Plus, Egyptian pharaohs had been meddling in the Levant, supporting local rulers who resisted Assyrian domination.

Taharqa, like several Egyptian pharaohs before him, had supported rebellion against Assyria in Palestine. He sent military aid to kingdoms like Judah when they resisted Assyrian conquest. This was traditional Egyptian foreign policy—supporting buffer states to keep hostile powers away from Egypt's borders. However, it put Egypt directly in conflict with the most powerful empire of the age.

The Assyrian king Esarhaddon (ruled 681–669 BCE) decided to deal with the Egyptian problem decisively. In 674 BCE, he launched an invasion of Egypt. The campaign initially failed. The Assyrian army was defeated, perhaps by environmental factors or Egyptian resistance. But Esarhaddon tried again.

In 671 BCE, Esarhaddon invaded Egypt with a large army. This time, the Assyrians were successful. They defeated Taharqa's forces, captured Memphis, and drove Taharqa south to Thebes. Esarhaddon proclaimed himself "king of Egypt, Kush, and Pathos" and claimed to have conquered the entire country.

The conquest wasn't complete, though. Taharqa still controlled Upper Egypt from Thebes. After Esarhaddon withdrew, Taharqa reoccupied Memphis and reasserted his control over Lower Egypt. The Assyrians had won a battle, but they hadn't secured Egypt.

Esarhaddon died in 669 BCE while preparing another campaign against Egypt. His son Ashurbanipal (ruled 669–631 BCE) continued the war. In 667 BCE, Ashurbanipal led another invasion. Again, the Assyrians captured Memphis, and again, Taharqa retreated to Thebes. This time, the Assyrians pursued farther south, pushing into Upper Egypt.

Taharqa died around 664 BCE, probably in Nubia, where he had retreated after the Assyrian invasions. His successor, Tantamani, briefly attempted to reclaim Egypt, marching north and recapturing Memphis. But Ashurbanipal responded with yet another invasion in 663 BCE. The Assyrians drove Tantamani back to Nubia and decisively sacked Thebes.

This sack of Thebes was devastating. The great city, which had been Egypt's religious capital for over a thousand years, was thoroughly plundered. The Assyrians took vast amounts of gold, silver, and precious objects from Thebes' temples. The sack was so traumatic that it was remembered for generations. The Hebrew prophet Nahum, writing decades later, used the fall of Thebes as an example of how even the mightiest cities could be destroyed (Nahum 3:8–10).

The sack of Thebes marked the end of Kushite rule in Egypt. The Twenty-fifth Dynasty was over. The Nubian pharaohs withdrew to their kingdom in Kush, where they would continue to rule for centuries, building pyramids and maintaining Egyptian cultural traditions. But they never again controlled Egypt itself.

Egypt now came under Assyrian dominance, though this control was exercised indirectly. The Assyrians appointed local Egyptian rulers as vassals, requiring them to pay tribute and maintain loyalty to Assyria. The most important of these vassals was Necho I, ruler of Sais in the western delta, who had sided with the Assyrians against the Kushites.

Necho I and his son Psamtik I (ruled 664–610 BCE) would establish what historians call the Twenty-sixth Dynasty, also known as the Saite Dynasty, after their capital at Sais. This dynasty would eventually restore Egyptian independence and usher in the Late Period of Egyptian history.

In the mid-7th century BCE, Egypt had been invaded by a foreign empire for the first time in its long history. The country that had once dominated the Near East, that had built the pyramids and conquered Syria and Nubia, had seen the great temples of Thebes plundered by foreign soldiers. The Third Intermediate Period—those approximately 350 years of political fragmentation—was ending, but not with a restoration of Egyptian power.

Egypt's cultural traditions remained vibrant and distinctly Egyptian. But the days of Egyptian political dominance were over. The future would bring more foreign rule—Persian, Greek, and eventually Roman—until eventually Egypt became a province in other people's empires.

But Egyptians didn't know that yet. In the aftermath of the Assyrian invasions, there was still hope that Egypt could recover, that the ancient kingdom could restore itself one more time. And surprisingly, that hope wouldn't be entirely disappointed.

Chapter 13: The Late Period — Twilight and Foreign Shadows

The Saite Renaissance

After the Assyrian invasions drove out the Kushite pharaohs, Egypt seemed finished as an independent power. The great temples of Thebes had been plundered. Foreign armies had marched through the land. Egypt existed under Assyrian overlordship, its rulers reduced to vassals paying tribute to Mesopotamian kings.

But Egypt wasn't done yet. From the city of Sais in the western Nile Delta, a new dynasty would emerge that would restore Egyptian independence and usher in a remarkable cultural revival. The Twenty-sixth Dynasty, also called the Saite Dynasty, would give Egypt one last period of unity, prosperity, and cultural flowering before the final conquest by foreign empires.

The founder of this revival was Psamtik I (ruled 664–610 BCE), though his father Necho I had laid the groundwork. Necho I had been one of the local rulers the Assyrians installed as vassals after defeating the Kushites. He ruled Sais in the Delta and remained loyal to Assyria, even dying in battle against the Kushite pharaoh Tantamani when Tantamani briefly attempted to reclaim Egypt.

When Necho I died, his son Psamtik inherited control of Sais and the Delta region. Psamtik was still nominally an Assyrian vassal, but he had ambitions beyond simply serving as a puppet ruler.

The key to Psamtik's success was timing. By the 650s BCE, Assyria was becoming overextended. The Assyrian Empire had expanded to an enormous size, stretching from Egypt to Mesopotamia to Iran. Managing such a vast territory required constant military campaigns to suppress revolts and maintain control. Assyria was powerful but strained, fighting a massive civil war between rival claimants to the throne and dealing with rebellions throughout its empire, including a major revolt by Babylon.

Psamtik recognized the opportunity. Gradually, carefully, he began asserting independence through diplomatic maneuvering and building alliances, including with Gyges of Lydia in Asia Minor. He didn't openly rebel—that would have brought Assyrian armies down on him. Instead, he stopped paying tribute, ceased acknowledging Assyrian authority, and started expanding his own power within Egypt. Egypt was far away, difficult to reach, and no longer worth the effort required for Assyria to reconquer it.

To accomplish this, Psamtik needed military force. He couldn't rely solely on Egyptian troops—Egypt's military had weakened during the years of division. So Psamtik did something that would become common in the Late Period: he hired foreign mercenaries.

Greek mercenaries from Ionia and Caria in Asia Minor came to Egypt in large numbers during Psamtik's reign. These Greeks were professional soldiers, well-trained and equipped. Psamtik also employed Carian mercenaries and other foreigners. He established these mercenaries in military colonies in Egypt, particularly in the delta, giving them land in exchange for military service.

With his mercenary army, Psamtik gradually brought all of Egypt under his control, though this required some limited military action against rival Delta rulers and the assertion of authority through military presence in Upper Egypt. He expanded from his base in Sais to control the entire Nile Delta. He moved south, asserting authority over Middle Egypt. The crucial moment came when he gained control of Thebes and Upper Egypt.

The High Priests of Amun at Thebes had ruled southern Egypt independently for generations. To secure their cooperation, Psamtik used a clever strategy. There was a religious position at Thebes called "God's Wife of Amun"—a priestess who held enormous religious and economic power, which carried significant political influence. The position was typically held by a royal princess who remained celibate, and upon her death, another royal princess would be adopted as her successor.

Psamtik arranged for his daughter Nitocris to be adopted by the current God's Wife of Amun as her successor. This gave Psamtik's family control over Thebes' religious establishment and its vast economic resources, and through this religious and economic authority, effective political influence over Upper Egypt. When Nitocris eventually became God's Wife of Amun, she wielded considerable power in southern Egypt on behalf of her father and later her brother.

By around 656 BCE, just eight years after becoming ruler of Sais, Psamtik controlled all of Egypt. He had reunified the country without major warfare, through a combination of military force, political maneuvering, and religious diplomacy. Egypt was independent again, free from Assyrian control.

Psamtik I ruled for 54 years, making his one of the longest reigns in Egyptian history, though not quite matching the extraordinary lengths of Ramesses II (66 years) or Pepi II (possibly 64–94 years). His reign was largely peaceful and prosperous. He didn't conduct major military campaigns abroad—Egypt's days of empire-building were over. But he stabilized Egypt internally, promoted trade, and presided over a cultural renaissance.

This cultural revival is what makes the Saite Period so interesting. Psamtik and his successors deliberately looked backward to Egypt's glorious past, particularly to the Old Kingdom and Middle Kingdom, seeking to recapture the artistic styles and cultural achievements of those earlier periods.

Saite art is characterized by this archaism—the deliberate imitation of earlier styles. Sculptors studied Old Kingdom statues and created new works in the same style. Hieroglyphic inscriptions used archaic forms of language. Religious texts revived ancient spells and rituals that had fallen out of use. Tomb designs imitated earlier periods.

This wasn't simple nostalgia. It was a deliberate political and cultural statement. By connecting themselves to Egypt's ancient past, the Saite pharaohs were asserting continuity with the great pharaohs of old. They were saying: we are the legitimate successors to the pyramid builders, to the great conquerors, to the traditional Egyptian kings. The years of division and foreign rule were an aberration; we have restored the true Egypt.

The Saite Period also saw increased contact with the Greek world. The Greek mercenaries Psamtik had hired remained in Egypt, establishing communities. Greek traders came to Egypt in large numbers, establishing a major trading post at Naucratis in the delta, which became the primary port for Greek commerce with Egypt.

This Greek presence would have enormous long-term consequences. Greeks were fascinated by Egypt—its ancient civilization, its mysterious religion, its monumental architecture. Greek historians like Herodotus would visit Egypt and write about it, spreading knowledge of Egyptian civilization throughout the Mediterranean world. This Greek interest in Egypt would eventually lead to the Greek conquest of Egypt under Alexander the Great, but that was still centuries away.

Psamtik's successors continued his policies. His son Necho II (ruled 610-595 BCE) was more militarily ambitious. He attempted to expand Egyptian power into Palestine. The Assyrian Empire was falling apart in the late 7th century BCE, as it was being destroyed by a coalition of Babylonians, Medes, and others. Necho II saw an opportunity to reclaim some of Egypt's old territories in the Levant.

In 609 BCE, Necho II marched north with an Egyptian army, intending to support what remained of Assyria against the Babylonians. This was not because he liked the Assyrians but because he didn't want Babylon to become too powerful. On his way north, he encountered the army of King Josiah of Judah at Megiddo. Josiah, who was allied with Babylon, tried to stop the Egyptian army. The battle was brief. Josiah was killed, and Necho's army continued north.

Necho briefly controlled parts of Syria-Palestine, but his control didn't last. In 605 BCE, the Babylonian crown prince Nebuchadnezzar (yes, the same Nebuchadnezzar who would later destroy Jerusalem) defeated Necho's army at the Battle of Carchemish in Syria. The Egyptians were driven back, and Babylon, not Egypt, became the dominant power in the Levant.

Necho II is also famous for allegedly attempting to circumnavigate Africa. According to the Greek historian Herodotus, Necho hired Phoenician sailors to sail around Africa, starting from the Red Sea and returning via the Mediterranean. The expedition supposedly took three years and succeeded in completing the journey. Modern historians debate whether this actually happened—Herodotus himself expressed skepticism about some details—but it's possible that such an expedition occurred.

Later Saite pharaohs—Psamtik II, Apries, and Amasis—continued to rule Egypt with varying degrees of success. The Saite Dynasty maintained Egypt's traditional culture while also engaging with the wider Mediterranean world. Greek mercenaries and traders became an increasingly important part of Egyptian society. Egypt was no longer isolated but was becoming integrated into the broader Mediterranean commercial and cultural network.

The last significant Saite pharaoh was Amasis (ruled 570–526 BCE), who came to power through a military coup but proved to be an effective ruler. He maintained good relations with the Greek world, married a Greek woman from Cyrene, and promoted trade with Greece. Under Amasis, Egypt experienced prosperity and stability.

But the Saite revival was about to come to an abrupt end. A new power was rising in the east—Persia—and Egypt was directly in its path. In the mid-6th century BCE, the world's geopolitical landscape changed dramatically. The Persian Empire, under its founder Cyrus the Great, exploded onto the scene, conquering territory at an astonishing rate. Within a few decades, Persia had conquered Media, Lydia, Babylonia, and much of the Near East and central Asia, creating the largest empire the world had yet seen.

Egypt watched nervously. The Persians were clearly building toward a conquest of Egypt. It was the last major independent kingdom in the region, and controlling Egypt would give Persia access to Egypt's wealth and complete Persian domination of the eastern Mediterranean.

Amasis, the Saite pharaoh, tried to prepare. He made alliances with Greek city-states and strengthened Egypt's defenses. He also hired more Greek mercenaries. However, in 526 BCE, before the Persian invasion came, Amasis died. His son Psamtik III became pharaoh, inheriting a kingdom under threat.

In 525 BCE, the Persian king Cambyses II invaded Egypt with a large army. The Egyptians met the Persians at Pelusium, a fortress city in the eastern delta that guarded the approach to Egypt from the Levant. The Battle of Pelusium was decisive. The Persian army, experienced from decades of conquests, defeated the Egyptian forces.

The Persians then marched on Memphis. Psamtik III retreated to the capital, but Memphis quickly fell. Psamtik was captured. According to the Greek historian Herodotus, Cambyses initially spared him but later had him executed when Psamtik allegedly tried to organize a revolt.

Whether this story is true or not, Psamtik disappears from the records. The Saite Dynasty was over. Egypt became part of the Persian Empire.

Cambyses's conquest started the Twenty-seventh Dynasty. Egyptians didn't recognize it as a legitimate dynasty, though. To them, the Persians were foreign conquerors, not true pharaohs.

The Persians ruled Egypt as a satrapy—a province of their empire governed by a Persian-appointed satrap (governor). The satrap collected taxes, maintained order, and ensured Egypt's loyalty to the Persian king. However, the Persians often appointed Egyptians to many high administrative positions within the satrapy, recognizing the importance of local expertise and cooperation.

The Persians were practical. They realized that Egypt had a proud, ancient culture and that ruling Egypt required respecting, or at least accommodating, Egyptian traditions. Persian kings took Egyptian royal titles and presented themselves as pharaohs, at least in official Egyptian documents. They made offerings to Egyptian gods and respected Egyptian temples and priesthoods.

Cambyses's reputation in later Egyptian tradition is terrible. Egyptian sources portray him as a monster who killed the sacred Apis bull, desecrated temples, and mocked Egyptian religion. According to these accounts, he went mad and died as divine punishment for his sacrilege.

How much of this is true? Probably very little. These stories come from sources written much later, during periods when Egypt was trying to resist Persian rule. They're propaganda designed to delegitimize Persian authority. The stories of his madness and sacrilege are likely inventions.

But even if the Persian kings weren't the monsters later tradition made them out to be, Persian rule was unpopular in Egypt. The Egyptians had enjoyed independence under the Saite Dynasty. They didn't like being ruled by foreigners, even relatively respectful ones. Throughout the Persian period, Egyptians would repeatedly revolt, attempting to regain independence.

The second Persian king to rule Egypt, Darius I (ruled 522–486 BCE), was more systematic in his approach. He commissioned the recording and clarification of existing Egyptian laws, completed a canal connecting the Nile to the Red Sea (begun earlier under the Saite pharaohs), and generally tried to integrate Egypt into the Persian administrative system while maintaining the accommodations to Egyptian traditions that had been established. However, he was also extracting significant tribute from Egypt to fund Persian military campaigns elsewhere in the empire.

The Persian period also coincided with major geopolitical changes in the Mediterranean. The Greeks and Persians fought a series of wars, such as the famous Greco-Persian Wars. Egypt, as a Persian province, was drawn into these conflicts. According to Herodotus, Egyptians fought in Persian naval operations against the Greeks, and Egyptian resources supported Persian military campaigns.

In 486 BCE, when Darius I died and his son Xerxes I became king, Egypt revolted. The timing seemed perfect—Xerxes was preoccupied with preparations for his massive invasion of Greece. But Xerxes dealt with the Egyptian revolt swiftly, sending an army that suppressed the rebellion before he launched his Greek campaign.

After the Persian defeat in Greece, Persian control over Egypt weakened. In 460 BCE, a major Egyptian revolt broke out, led by a Libyan prince named Inaros. The rebels controlled much of the delta and even besieged Persian forces in Memphis.

The Athenians, who were at war with Persia, sent a fleet to support the Egyptian rebels. For several years, the Egyptians and their Athenian allies fought Persian forces in Egypt. The rebellion initially succeeded. Inaros defeated a Persian army and controlled significant Egyptian territory.

But Persia was vast and powerful. It assembled a huge army and sent it to Egypt. In 454 BCE, the Persian army crushed the rebellion. Inaros was captured and eventually executed. The Athenian fleet was destroyed. Egypt was firmly under Persian control again.

Another major revolt occurred in 404 BCE, at the very end of Darius II's reign. This time, the revolt succeeded. A native Egyptian named Amyrtaeus, ruling from Sais in the delta, led a successful rebellion and expelled the Persians from Egypt. Egypt was independent again.

Amyrtaeus established the Twenty-eighth Dynasty, but his reign was brief—only about six years. He was overthrown and killed by Nepherites I, who founded the Twenty-ninth Dynasty, ruling from Mendes in the delta.

The Twenty-ninth and Thirtieth Dynasties (collectively 404–343 BCE) represent the last period of native Egyptian rule. These dynasties, ruling from various delta cities, maintained Egyptian independence for about sixty years, successfully resisting several Persian attempts to reconquer Egypt.

These native Egyptian pharaohs were constantly preparing for a Persian invasion. They hired Greek mercenaries in large numbers. They built fortifications and made alliances with Greek city-states, particularly Sparta and Athens, which were happy to support anyone fighting against Persia.

The last native Egyptian dynasty, the Thirtieth, was the most successful. Its pharaohs, particularly Nectanebo I and Nectanebo II, successfully defended Egypt against multiple Persian invasions. They built extensively, including major additions to temples throughout Egypt. They promoted Egyptian culture and religion. For a brief moment, it seemed Egypt might maintain its independence.

But Persia was regrouping. Under Artaxerxes III, a powerful and ruthless king, Persia reconquered much of its lost territory. In 343 BCE, Artaxerxes launched a massive invasion of Egypt with an enormous army—ancient sources claim hundreds of thousands of troops, though these numbers are clearly exaggerated, as was typical in ancient accounts.

Nectanebo II, the last native Egyptian pharaoh, tried to resist. He had fortified the delta. He had hired thousands of Greek mercenaries. He had prepared for years for this invasion.

The head of Nectanebo II.[86]

But the Persian army was too strong. It broke through Egypt's defenses, defeated the Egyptian army, and marched on Memphis. Nectanebo II fled south, eventually escaping to Nubia. Egypt fell to Persia again.

The Thirty-first Dynasty in Egyptian chronology was remembered by later Egyptian sources as particularly harsh. According to these accounts, Artaxerxes III plundered temples, confiscated the temples' wealth, and treated Egypt more as a conquered territory than as a satrapy deserving respect. Archaeological evidence for the severity of this treatment varies by region.

Egypt would remain under Persian control for only about a decade. But for Egyptians, that decade must have seemed hopeless. The last native pharaoh had fled. The temples were plundered. Foreign troops occupied Egypt. The long tradition of native Egyptian pharaonic rule appeared to be ending.

But history had one more surprise in store. A young Macedonian king named Alexander was about to change the world, and Egypt would be transformed yet again.

Chapter 14:
Alexander, Ptolemies, and the End

Alexander the Great

In 332 BCE, a twenty-four-year-old Macedonian king arrived in Egypt and changed its history forever. Alexander III of Macedon—known to history as Alexander the Great—had already accomplished what seemed impossible: he had defeated the mighty Persian Empire in a series of brilliant military campaigns. Now he was bringing his army to Egypt, the richest province in the Persian realm.

After a decade of harsh Persian rule, Egyptians were eager to be free of their conquerors. When Alexander's army approached Egypt from Palestine, the Persian satrap Mazaces surrendered Egypt without a fight. Alexander entered Egypt peacefully, welcomed as a liberator.

Alexander understood the importance of respecting Egyptian culture and religion. He presented himself as a legitimate pharaoh in official Egyptian contexts, not as a foreign invader. He made the proper offerings to Egyptian gods. He adopted Egyptian royal titles and presented himself as the successor to the ancient pharaohs.

This wasn't just political calculation, though it was certainly that. Alexander seemed interested in Egyptian traditions, though how much was genuine curiosity versus political strategy remains debated by historians. He was educated by the philosopher Aristotle and had been raised on Greek culture, which already held Egypt in high regard as an ancient land of wisdom and mystery. The Greeks had been trading with and learning from Egypt for centuries. For Alexander, Egypt represented something ancient, sacred, and worthy of respect.

One of Alexander's first major acts in Egypt was to make a pilgrimage to the oracle of Amun at the Siwa Oasis in the western desert. This was a famous oracle that the Greeks identified with their own god, Zeus. Alexander traveled across hundreds of miles of desert to reach Siwa, where the priests of Amun greeted him.

What happened at Siwa remains unknown. Greek accounts report that the oracle addressed Alexander in a way that was interpreted as recognizing him as the son of Zeus-Amun, confirming his divine status. In Egyptian terms, this meant the god Amun acknowledged Alexander as pharaoh—the god's earthly representative. Whether Alexander actually believed he was divine or whether this was political theater is debated. But the visit to Siwa gave Alexander religious legitimacy in Egyptian eyes and reinforced his position as Egypt's rightful ruler.

Alexander's most lasting contribution to Egypt was the founding of Alexandria. On the Mediterranean coast, on a strip of land between the sea and Lake Mareotis, Alexander chose a site for a new city. According to later tradition, he personally laid out the city's plan, marking the streets with barley meal since chalk wasn't available. The actual architect was likely Dinocrates of Rhodes. He envisioned a great city that would be a center of commerce and culture, connecting Egypt to the Mediterranean world.

Alexandria would become one of the greatest cities of the ancient world, but Alexander wouldn't live to see it. He spent only about six months in Egypt before leaving to continue his conquest of the Persian Empire. He marched east, eventually reaching as far as India. He never returned to Egypt.

In 323 BCE, at the age of thirty-two, Alexander died in Babylon. Modern scholars generally agree that illness—possibly typhoid fever or malaria—was the most likely cause, though ancient sources speculated about poisoning and other theories. His death threw his vast empire into chaos. He had conquered everything from Greece to India, but he had no clear heir. His son would be born after his death, and the child would never rule. Instead, Alexander's generals would fight over his empire for decades.

One of these generals was Ptolemy, who had been one of Alexander's closest companions and most trusted commanders. When Alexander's generals began dividing up the empire, Ptolemy moved quickly to seize Egypt. He understood that Egypt, with its wealth, natural defenses, and ancient prestige, was the most valuable prize.

Ptolemy also did something symbolically important: he diverted Alexander's funeral procession. Alexander's body was being transported from Babylon to Macedonia for burial, but Ptolemy intercepted it and brought it to Egypt instead. By controlling Alexander's body and tomb, Ptolemy was claiming to be Alexander's legitimate successor, at least in Egypt.

The Ptolemaic Dynasty

Ptolemy initially ruled Egypt as satrap, nominally governing on behalf of Alexander's infant son and mentally impaired half-brother, who were the technical heirs to Alexander's empire. But as the wars among Alexander's successors dragged on and it became clear that no one would reunify the empire, Ptolemy declared himself king around 305 BCE. He became Ptolemy I Soter ("Savior"), founder of the Ptolemaic dynasty, which would rule Egypt for nearly three centuries.

The Ptolemaic dynasty was Greek. The Ptolemies spoke Greek, promoted Greek culture, and surrounded themselves with Greek courtiers and officials. Alexandria became a Greek city, the capital of a Greek-ruled kingdom. The Ptolemies brought thousands of Greek and Macedonian settlers to Egypt, establishing Greek colonies and creating a Greek-speaking ruling class.

However, the Ptolemies also understood that to rule Egypt effectively, they needed to accommodate Egyptian traditions. This created a dual system. To the Greeks living in Alexandria and the Greek cities of Egypt, the Ptolemies were Greek kings ruling a Hellenistic kingdom. To the native Egyptians living in the countryside and worshiping in ancient temples, the Ptolemies were pharaohs, the latest in a line stretching back millennia. The same ruler presented two different faces depending on the audience. They commissioned temples built in the traditional Egyptian style, made offerings to Egyptian gods, had themselves depicted in Egyptian art wearing traditional pharaonic regalia, took Egyptian royal titles, and participated in Egyptian religious ceremonies.

The early Ptolemaic period was Egypt's last great age of prosperity. Ptolemy I and his successors rebuilt Alexandria into one of the Mediterranean's most magnificent cities. The city featured wide streets laid out in a grid pattern, impressive public buildings, royal palaces, and harbors. It was the commercial hub of the eastern Mediterranean.

Most famously, the Ptolemies built the Library of Alexandria, which became the ancient world's greatest center of learning. The library aimed to collect all the knowledge in the world, and at its height, it possibly contained hundreds of thousands of scrolls. Scholars from throughout the Mediterranean came to Alexandria to study. The library housed works of literature, philosophy, science, mathematics, and medicine. It was a research center where scholars translated texts, wrote commentaries, and conducted investigations.

The library was part of a larger institution called the Mouseion (Museum)—literally a "temple to the Muses"—which functioned like a modern university and research institute. Scholars at the Mouseion received royal patronage to pursue their studies. They gave lectures, conducted experiments, engaged in philosophical debates, and produced scholarly works.

Some of the ancient world's greatest intellectuals worked in Alexandria during the Ptolemaic period. Euclid wrote his geometry textbook there. Eratosthenes calculated the Earth's circumference with remarkable accuracy. The physician Herophilus conducted anatomical studies. The poet Callimachus catalogued the library's holdings. Alexandria became the intellectual capital of the ancient world, attracting brilliant minds and producing groundbreaking scholarship.

The Ptolemies also built the Pharos of Alexandria, one of the Seven Wonders of the Ancient World. This massive lighthouse, standing over 330 feet tall on an island in Alexandria's harbor, guided ships safely to port with a light that could reportedly be seen for many miles. The Pharos became so famous that its name became the word for lighthouse in several languages (like *faro* in Spanish and Italian).

A 1572 depiction of the Lighthouse of Alexandria—the earliest known representation of it in modern times.[87]

But beneath this cultural brilliance, the Ptolemaic kingdom had serious problems. The dynasty was plagued by internal conflict. Ptolemaic kings and queens fought each other for power in brutal civil wars. Family members murdered each other. Siblings married each other (the Ptolemies adopted the Egyptian royal practice of brother-sister marriage, which they took to extremes).

The Ptolemies also faced resistance from native Egyptians. While they presented themselves as pharaohs and respected the Egyptian religion, they were still foreign rulers whose primary interest was extracting wealth from Egypt to support their wars and lavish lifestyles. The Greek population lived largely separate from native Egyptians, creating social and cultural divisions. Native Egyptians mounted major revolts, particularly in Upper Egypt, where Egyptian culture remained strongest. Some of these rebellions were massive, occasionally leading to periods of de facto native rule in the south.

The dynasty's wealth came largely from agriculture. Egypt's incredibly fertile soil, watered by the Nile's annual floods, produced enormous grain harvests. The Ptolemies exported grain throughout the Mediterranean, making Egypt a major grain supplier for the ancient world. They also controlled trade routes connecting the Mediterranean to the Red Sea, Arabia, and India, profiting from the spice trade and luxury goods.

However, running this economic system required a massive bureaucracy. The Ptolemies created an elaborate administrative apparatus that controlled virtually every aspect of Egyptian economic life. They taxed everything—agricultural production, trade, manufacturing, even activities like fishing and beekeeping. The bureaucracy kept detailed records in Greek, recording taxes, land ownership, production quotas, and administrative decisions. Egypt under the Ptolemies was one of the most thoroughly documented and bureaucratized states in the ancient world.

As the Ptolemaic period continued, the dynasty gradually weakened. Later Ptolemies were less capable than the early kings. Court intrigues intensified. Civil wars became more frequent and destructive. Egypt's economy suffered. Native Egyptian revolts became more serious and harder to suppress.

And a new power was rising in the west—Rome.

Rome had conquered Italy, then defeated Carthage, and then expanded throughout the Mediterranean. By the 2nd century BCE, Rome was the dominant power in the Mediterranean world. The Ptolemies, recognizing Rome's strength, tried to maintain good relations, even declaring Rome as Egypt's protector in their wills. But this made Egypt increasingly dependent on Rome and vulnerable to Roman interference.

By the 1st century BCE, the Ptolemaic dynasty was clearly in decline. Egypt remained wealthy, but the royal family was dysfunctional, the government was corrupt, and Roman influence was growing. The last great Ptolemaic ruler was a woman who became one of history's most famous figures—Cleopatra VII.

Cleopatra: The Last Pharaoh

When most people hear the name Cleopatra, they think of seduction, romance, and beauty. Hollywood movies have depicted her as the ultimate femme fatale, using her charms to manipulate powerful Roman men. This popular image isn't entirely wrong—Cleopatra did have relationships with Julius Caesar and Mark Antony—but it's incomplete and misleading.

Cleopatra and Caesar by Jean-Léon Gérôme (1866).[88]

Cleopatra VII was born in 69 BCE. She was the daughter of Ptolemy XII, a weak and unpopular king who spent much of his reign trying to maintain his throne with Roman support. When Ptolemy XII died in 51 BCE, Cleopatra inherited the throne with her younger brother, Ptolemy XIII, whom she was required to marry under Ptolemaic custom. She was eighteen years old; he was about ten.

Cleopatra quickly showed that she was more capable and ambitious than her brother. She took control of the government and ruled effectively, even dropping her brother's name from official documents—a serious violation of protocol. This created conflict with powerful courtiers who supported Ptolemy XIII. By 48 BCE, Cleopatra had been driven out of Alexandria by her brother's supporters and was raising an army to reclaim her throne.

At this point, Julius Caesar arrived in Egypt.

Caesar was pursuing his rival Pompey, with whom he was fighting a civil war for control of Rome. Pompey fled to Egypt seeking refuge, but Ptolemy XIII's advisors, hoping to curry favor with Caesar, had Pompey murdered. When Caesar arrived in Alexandria, they presented him with Pompey's severed head.

Caesar was reportedly horrified. Pompey had been his enemy, but he was also a fellow high-ranking Roman. Murdering him was dishonorable. Caesar also saw an opportunity. Egypt was wealthy and strategically important. The Ptolemaic civil war gave him an excuse to intervene.

According to Roman tradition, Cleopatra had herself smuggled into Caesar's presence wrapped in a carpet (or possibly a laundry bag). This dramatic entrance caught Caesar's attention. The two quickly formed an alliance. It was certainly political, but it was also apparently romantic and personal.

Caesar supported Cleopatra against her brother. The conflict escalated into the Alexandrian War, during which parts of Alexandria were burned. Some sources state that parts of the Great Library or storage facilities were damaged during this conflict, though the extent of any damage is debated; most scholars believe the main Great Library survived this event. Ptolemy XIII drowned in the Nile while trying to escape. Caesar installed Cleopatra as Egypt's ruler, along with her younger brother Ptolemy XIV (whom she also married as co-ruler, though he was only about twelve years old and had no real power).

Cleopatra and Caesar also had a son, Caesarion ("Little Caesar"), whom Cleopatra claimed was Caesar's heir. Caesar never officially acknowledged him, but he apparently accepted paternity privately. Cleopatra visited Rome with Caesarion and lived in one of Caesar's villas, which scandalized Roman society. A foreign queen living openly in Rome was shocking to Roman sensibilities.

In 44 BCE, Caesar was assassinated in Rome. Cleopatra fled back to Egypt. Her brother-husband Ptolemy XIV died shortly after (possibly poisoned on her orders), and Cleopatra made her son Caesarion co-ruler.

Egypt and Rome were now interconnected. Rome's civil wars would determine Egypt's fate. After Caesar's death, his assassins were defeated by his supporters, primarily Mark Antony and Octavian (Caesar's adopted heir). Antony and Octavian then divided the Roman world between them, with Antony controlling the eastern Mediterranean.

In 41 BCE, Antony summoned Cleopatra to meet him in Tarsus (in modern Turkey). He wanted Egyptian financial support for his planned military campaigns against Parthia. Cleopatra arrived in spectacular fashion, sailing up the river in an elaborate gilded barge, dressed as the goddess Venus/Aphrodite, demonstrating Egypt's wealth and her own elegance.

Antony and Cleopatra formed both a political alliance and a personal relationship. They had three children together. Antony spent extended periods in Alexandria with Cleopatra. They lived lavishly, throwing elaborate parties and enjoying Egypt's wealth. Roman propaganda portrayed Antony as having "gone native," abandoning Roman values for Eastern luxury and being controlled by a foreign queen.

Politically, the alliance made sense for both of them. Cleopatra needed Roman military protection. Antony needed Egyptian wealth to fund his armies. Together, they formed a powerful bloc in the eastern Mediterranean.

But this partnership threatened Octavian, who controlled the western Mediterranean. Octavian portrayed himself as defending traditional Roman values against the corruption of the East. He waged a propaganda campaign against Antony and Cleopatra, depicting Antony as a traitor who had abandoned Rome for Egypt and was planning to make Cleopatra queen of the Roman Empire with Alexandria as the capital.

In 32 BCE, the Roman Senate, dominated by Octavian's supporters, declared war on Cleopatra (not on Antony, though he was their real target). The conflict came to a head at the Battle of Actium in 31 BCE.

Actium was a naval battle fought off the western coast of Greece. Antony and Cleopatra's fleet faced Octavian's fleet. The battle didn't go well for Antony and Cleopatra. Ancient sources disagree on the details, but at some point during the battle, Cleopatra's ships broke away and fled. Antony followed her. Their fleet was defeated, and their army surrendered.

Why did Cleopatra flee? Ancient sources, mostly hostile to her, claim she panicked or betrayed Antony. Modern historians suggest she might have realized the battle was lost and tried to preserve her forces for continued resistance. Whatever the reason, Actium was a decisive defeat.

Antony and Cleopatra retreated to Alexandria. Octavian pursued them, invading Egypt in 30 BCE. As Octavian's forces approached Alexandria, Antony and Cleopatra's situation became hopeless. Their allies deserted them, and their troops surrendered. Egypt was lost.

According to ancient accounts, Cleopatra retreated to her mausoleum (a tomb she had been building). Antony, receiving a false report that Cleopatra had died, attempted suicide by falling on his sword. Mortally wounded, he was brought to Cleopatra's mausoleum, where he died in her arms.

Cleopatra was captured by Octavian's forces. Octavian wanted to take her back to Rome to display in his triumph—a humiliating public parade celebrating his victory. Cleopatra, determined not to be paraded through Rome as a captive, committed suicide. According to tradition, she died from the bite of an asp (an Egyptian cobra), though the exact method is uncertain. She was thirty-nine years old.

Death of Cleopatra by Jean-Baptiste Regnault (1796–1797).[39]

Octavian had Caesarion killed, eliminating any potential rival who could claim to be Caesar's heir. Cleopatra's children with Antony were taken to Rome and raised by Antony's Roman wife.

With Cleopatra's death, the Ptolemaic dynasty ended. Egypt became a Roman province. It would remain under Roman control, and later Byzantine control, for centuries. The age of the pharaohs was over.

Cleopatra was far more than the seductress of popular imagination. She was the only Ptolemaic ruler who learned to speak Egyptian (the other Ptolemies spoke only Greek). Ancient sources report that she spoke multiple languages—perhaps eight or nine—and could converse with diplomats from throughout the known world without translators. She was educated in philosophy, mathematics, astronomy, and literature. She was a capable administrator who managed Egypt's complex economy. Cleopatra was a political strategist who fought desperately to preserve Egyptian independence, pursuing every possible strategy against overwhelming odds.

That she ultimately failed was perhaps inevitable. Rome was too powerful, building an empire that would eventually control the entire Mediterranean world. After Cleopatra, Egyptian culture would continue and evolve, and Roman emperors would even be recognized as pharaohs in Egyptian temple inscriptions for centuries. However, the long tradition of independent Egyptian or Hellenistic pharaonic rule died with her in 30 BCE.

A Roman sculpture of Cleopatra.[40]

Chapter 15:
Religion and the Afterlife

The Egyptian Pantheon

Before we close out the book, let's take a deeper dive into ancient Egyptian culture. We'll start with religion. Ancient Egyptian religion was complex, fluid, and sometimes confusing even to modern scholars who have spent careers studying it. Unlike monotheistic religions with a single god and clear theological doctrines, Egyptian religion featured hundreds of gods and goddesses, no single authoritative scripture, and beliefs that evolved and changed over three thousand years. Gods could merge with each other, take different forms, and be worshiped differently in different places. Yet for all its complexity, Egyptian religion shaped virtually every aspect of Egyptian life.

The Egyptians didn't have a single word equivalent to "religion." Religious practice, ritual, and belief were simply woven into the fabric of existence. The gods were real, present forces that needed to be honored and appeased. Ma'at—the principle of truth, justice, order, and cosmic balance—had to be maintained through proper worship and ritual. The pharaoh served as the intermediary between humans and gods, maintaining ma'at through his performance of religious duties.

The Egyptian pantheon included dozens of major gods and hundreds of minor ones. Some gods were worshiped throughout Egypt, while others were local deities important only in specific regions. Some gods had clear roles and associations, while others had overlapping or contradictory functions. Gods could be depicted in human form, animal form, or hybrid forms combining human and animal features.

Ra (also called Re) was the sun god. He was one of the most important deities in Egyptian religion. He represented the sun's power and its daily journey across the sky. Egyptians believed Ra traveled through the underworld each night, battling the forces of chaos before being reborn each dawn. Ra was often depicted as a man with a falcon head topped by a sun disk. He became so important that many other gods merged with him, creating composite deities like Amun-Ra.

Osiris was the god of the dead and the afterlife, making him one of Egypt's most important and beloved deities. According to Egyptian mythology, Osiris had once been a king of Egypt who taught humans agriculture and civilization. His brother Seth, jealous of Osiris's power, murdered him. In some versions of the myth, particularly those preserved in later Greek retellings, Seth dismembered Osiris's body and scattered the pieces throughout Egypt. Osiris's wife, Isis, searched for the pieces, reassembled his body, and through magic temporarily restored him to life long enough to conceive a son, Horus. Osiris then became the ruler of the underworld, judging the dead and determining who could enter the afterlife. He was typically depicted as a mummified king, painted green or black, holding the symbols of kingship.

Isis was one of the most popular and powerful goddesses. She was associated with magic, motherhood, and protection. Her devotion to Osiris and her role in raising their son Horus made her a model of loyalty and maternal love. She was worshiped throughout Egypt, and her cult eventually spread throughout the Mediterranean world, with temples to Isis built as far away as Britain. She was typically depicted as a woman wearing a throne-shaped headdress or with cow horns and a sun disk.

Horus, the son of Osiris and Isis, was a sky god closely associated with kingship. The reigning pharaoh was considered a living manifestation of Horus. According to mythology, Horus fought his uncle Seth to avenge his father's murder and reclaim the throne of Egypt. After a long conflict, Horus was declared the rightful king. Horus was most commonly depicted as a falcon or as a man with a falcon head. The famous Eye of Horus symbol—representing wholeness, healing, and protection—was one of ancient Egypt's most common protective amulets.

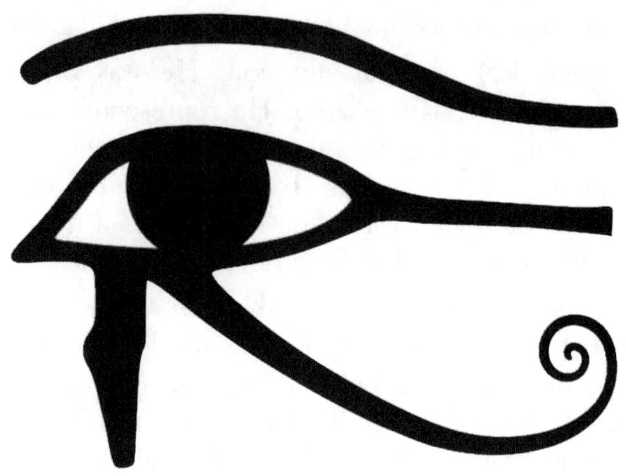

The Eye of Horus.[41]

Anubis was the god of embalming and the protector of the dead. He guided souls through the underworld and oversaw the mummification process. He was typically depicted as a black jackal or as a man with a jackal's head. Black represented both the color of mummified flesh and the fertile black soil of Egypt, symbolizing rebirth.

Thoth was the god of writing, knowledge, magic, and the moon. He was credited with inventing hieroglyphics and served as the scribe of the gods. He was depicted either as an ibis-headed man or as a baboon. Thoth played an important role in the judgment of the dead, recording the results when the deceased's heart was weighed against the feather of ma'at (more on this later).

Seth (also called Set) was the god of chaos, storms, and the desert. He was the murderer of Osiris and the enemy of Horus, yet he also protected Ra's solar boat during its nightly journey through the underworld, fighting off the serpent of chaos, Apophis. Seth represented necessary chaos and wild power. He was dangerous but sometimes useful. He was depicted as a mysterious animal called the "Seth animal," which doesn't correspond to any known creature, with a curved snout, squared ears, and a forked tail.

Hathor was the goddess of love, beauty, music, and joy. She was often depicted as a cow or as a woman with cow ears and horns. She was associated with motherhood, fertility, and celebration. Hathor was also connected to the sky and was sometimes identified as the mother or wife of Horus.

Ptah was the creator god worshiped at Memphis, the patron of craftsmen and architects. Unlike other creator gods who made the world through physical means, Ptah created through thought and speech. He conceived of creation in his heart and brought it into being through his words. He was typically depicted as a mummified man.

Amun was originally a local Theban god who rose to supreme importance during the New Kingdom when Thebes became Egypt's capital. He was associated with air, wind, and hidden power. He merged with Ra to become Amun-Ra, king of the gods. The Amun temple complex at Karnak became the wealthiest and most powerful religious institution in Egypt. Amun was depicted as a man wearing a crown with two tall plumes.

Amun depicted with Seti I.[49]

This is just a small sampling—there were hundreds more gods and goddesses, including Bastet (cat goddess of home and protection), Sekhmet (lioness goddess of war and healing), Sobek (crocodile god of the Nile), Bes (dwarf god who protected households and children), and Taweret (hippopotamus goddess of childbirth).

Each major temple was dedicated to a particular god or group of gods and was considered the god's earthly dwelling place. The temple contained a sanctuary with a statue of the god, which was not merely a representation but a physical focus through which the god's presence manifested on earth. Only priests could enter the sanctuary. Common people couldn't enter the temple's interior but could worship at the temple's outer courts and gates.

Priests served the gods through daily rituals. They woke the god's statue each morning, washed and dressed it, offered it food and drink, and performed ceremonies to maintain ma'at. The priests didn't preach or provide moral instruction. They performed rituals to ensure the proper relationship between gods and humans through the correct performance of ceremonies.

The pharaoh was technically the chief priest of all gods. In temple reliefs and texts, the pharaoh is always shown performing rituals, but usually it was priests acting on his behalf. The pharaoh's divine nature made him the ideal intermediary between the human and divine realms.

Religious festivals brought the gods directly to the people. During festivals, the god's statue would be carried out of the temple on a sacred boat or portable shrine, marched through the streets, and sometimes traveled by river to visit other temples. These processions allowed ordinary Egyptians to see (or at least be near) the god and participate in a religious celebration. Festivals included music, dancing, feasting, and sometimes consultations where people could ask the god questions. The god's response was interpreted through the movements of the sacred barque (boat) carried by the priests.

The Egyptian religion didn't have a rigid doctrine that everyone had to believe. Different cities and regions had different myths about creation and different understandings of the gods. In one region, the world emerged from the primordial waters; in another, it was created by a god's thought and word; in another, it came from a cosmic egg. Egyptians didn't see these contradictions as problems. These different myths could all be true in different ways.

What mattered more was performing the proper rituals, maintaining ma'at, showing respect to the gods, and ensuring the cosmic order continued. At its core, the Egyptian religion was about maintaining the world as it should be, keeping chaos at bay, and ensuring the sun rose, the Nile flooded, and life continued.

Death and the Journey Beyond

Death wasn't the end for ancient Egyptians; it was just a transition to another form of existence. Egyptians devoted enormous resources and attention to preparing for death and guaranteeing a successful afterlife. This preoccupation with death and the afterlife produced some of Egypt's most famous monuments and artifacts, from pyramids to mummies to the *Book of the Dead.*

The Egyptian concept of the person was complex. A person consisted of multiple components, including the physical body, the *ka* (life force or spiritual double), the *ba* (personality or soul that could travel between the living world and the afterlife), the *akh* (transfigured spirit of the successful deceased), the name, and the shadow. All these components needed to be preserved and cared for to ensure a successful existence in the afterlife.

When someone died, their greatest fear was complete oblivion—what Egyptians called the "second death." To avoid this, the dead needed their body preserved, their name remembered, offerings made to sustain them, and successful passage through the dangers of the underworld to reach the realm of Osiris.

Mummification was the process of preserving the body. Egyptians believed the body needed to remain intact for the afterlife. The *ba* needed the body as an anchor to return to, and the deceased would need their body in the afterlife. Initially, natural desiccation in Egypt's hot, dry sand preserved bodies buried in simple graves. However, as elites began building elaborate tombs, artificial preservation became necessary.

The mummification process, as described by the Greek historian Herodotus and confirmed by modern scientific studies, took approximately seventy days and involved several steps.

First, the body was taken to a special workshop, usually located near the tomb or in the desert. Embalmers washed the body with water and wine.

Next, they removed the internal organs, which would decay quickly. Using a hook, they extracted the brain through the nose. The brain wasn't considered important, so it was discarded. They made an incision in the left side of the abdomen and removed the stomach, intestines, liver, and lungs. In earlier periods, these organs were treated, wrapped, and placed in canopic jars, though by the Twenty-first Dynasty and later, practices changed, with organs sometimes placed back in the body and canopic jars serving more of a ceremonial function. The heart was always left in the body; it was considered the seat of intelligence and emotion, and it would be needed for judgment in the afterlife.

The body was then covered and packed with natron, a naturally occurring salt that drew out all moisture. The body remained buried in natron for about forty days, becoming completely desiccated.

After the natron treatment, embalmers washed the body again and rubbed it with oils and resins to keep the skin supple. They sometimes stuffed the body cavity with linen, sawdust, or even sand to maintain the body's shape. They would also pack linen under the skin of the face and limbs to create a more lifelike appearance.

The entire body was then wrapped in hundreds of yards of linen bandages. Between the layers of bandages, embalmers placed protective amulets—small charms of various gods and symbols believed to protect the deceased. A heart scarab was often placed over the heart, inscribed with a spell from the *Book of the Dead* asking the heart not to testify against its owner during judgment.

Finally, the wrapped mummy was placed in one or more coffins. Elite individuals might have multiple nested coffins, with the innermost being human-shaped and decorated with religious texts and images. The mummy was then placed in a tomb along with grave goods—objects the deceased would need in the afterlife.

What objects went into the tomb? It depended on the person's wealth and status, but tombs typically contained the following:

- Food and drink for the deceased's sustenance. These were real provisions, but they were also represented in paintings on tomb walls. The deceased could magically consume the essence of these offerings.

- Clothing, furniture, jewelry, and personal possessions that the deceased had used in life and would need in the afterlife.

- Shabtis (also called ushabtis)—small figurines that would magically come to life and perform labor on behalf of the deceased in the afterlife. The deceased might need to work in the fields of the afterlife, so they brought magical servants to do it for them. Elite tombs might contain hundreds of shabtis.

- Protective amulets and magical texts to help the deceased navigate the dangers of the underworld.

- The *Book of the Dead*—a collection of spells, hymns, and instructions to help the deceased in the afterlife. Despite the name, it wasn't a single book but a compilation of texts that could be selected and customized for each person. These spells were written on papyrus and placed in the tomb or painted on tomb walls or coffins.

However, having a preserved body and grave goods wasn't enough. The deceased still had to successfully navigate the underworld—the Duat—and pass judgment before Osiris.

The journey through the Duat was dangerous. The deceased had to pass through gates guarded by fearsome demons, travel across lakes of fire, avoid monsters and hostile spirits, and speak the correct passwords and spells. The *Book of the Dead* provided guidance for this journey, including illustrations and vignettes, spells for protection, and the secret names of the guardians who had to be appeased.

The culmination of the journey was the judgment before Osiris. This scene is depicted in countless tomb paintings and *Book of the Dead* illustrations. The deceased's heart—the seat of their conscience and moral character—was weighed on a scale against the feather of Ma'at, the symbol of truth and justice. Anubis operated the scales, while Thoth recorded the result.

If the heart was heavy with sin and wrongdoing, it would outweigh the feather. The deceased would then be devoured by Ammit, a monster combining features of a crocodile, lion, and hippopotamus, who waited beside the scales. These people would experience no afterlife.

But if the heart balanced with the feather or was lighter—proving the deceased had lived justly and according to ma'at—they would be declared "justified" or "true of voice." Osiris would welcome them into the afterlife, a paradise called the Field of Reeds, which was imagined as an idealized version of Egypt with abundant harvests, no suffering, and eternal existence in the presence of the gods.

A depiction of the Field of Reeds.[48]

The Field of Reeds was depicted in tomb paintings as a pleasant place resembling the best aspects of earthly Egypt. The deceased would farm, but crops would grow effortlessly. The people would feast but never be hungry. They could enjoy all earthly pleasures without earthly limitations. The blessed dead could also accompany Ra on his solar boat, traveling across the sky each day and through the underworld each night.

Not everyone could afford elaborate mummification and tomb goods. Ordinary Egyptians did their best with simpler burials, but they still sought to preserve the body and provide for the afterlife. Even the poorest Egyptians would try to provide at least a minimal burial, believing that an improper burial condemned the deceased to wander as a restless, suffering ghost.

The living had ongoing obligations to the dead. Family members were supposed to make regular offerings at the tomb—food, drink, and incense—to sustain the deceased's *ka*. The tomb chapel was designed as a place where the living could interact with the dead. Many tombs include a "false door"—a carved representation of a door through which the *ka* could pass between the tomb and the offering chapel, allowing the deceased to receive offerings.

Egyptians could also communicate with the dead through letters. People would write letters on pottery or papyrus, place them in tombs, and ask the deceased for help with problems, like legal issues, illness, or family conflicts. The dead were believed to have power to influence events in the living world, either for good or ill.

This elaborate concern with death and the afterlife wasn't morbid. By preparing for the afterlife, Egyptians were ensuring that life continued forever. Death was just a transition, not an end.

Tombs for Eternity

The evolution of Egyptian tombs reflects changing ideas about the afterlife, available resources, and the problem of tomb robbery. From simple pit graves to massive pyramids to hidden rock-cut chambers, Egyptian tombs were designed to preserve the body, protect it from robbers, and provide for the deceased's eternal needs.

The earliest Egyptian burials were simple graves in the desert sand. The body, wrapped in animal skins or matting, was placed in a shallow pit with a few personal possessions. The hot, dry sand naturally preserved the body through desiccation. These accidental mummies likely inspired later deliberate mummification techniques.

During the Predynastic and Early Dynastic periods, elite burials became more elaborate. Important people were buried in mastabas—rectangular mudbrick structures with flat roofs and sloping sides. The word *mastaba* comes from the Arabic word for "bench" because these tombs resembled the benches outside Egyptian houses.

A mastaba's underground burial chamber contained the body and grave goods, while the aboveground structure contained a chapel where offerings could be made. The burial chamber was sealed after the funeral, but family members could visit the chapel to make offerings and communicate with the deceased. Mastabas could be quite large, with multiple rooms for storing grave goods and elaborate painted or carved decorations.

Example of a mastaba."

The Step Pyramid of Djoser at Saqqara, built around 2670 BCE, revolutionized tomb architecture. The architect Imhotep essentially stacked six mastabas of decreasing size on top of one another, creating a stepped pyramid about two hundred feet high. This was the first large-scale stone building in Egypt and became the prototype for later pyramids.

The true pyramids—with smooth sides meeting at a point—developed shortly after. The great pyramids of Giza, built for the pharaohs Khufu, Khafre, and Menkaure during the Fourth Dynasty (around 2580–2510 BCE), represent the peak of pyramid construction.

But why pyramids? The pyramid shape had a symbolic meaning related to the sun and creation. The pyramid was associated with the *benben* stone, the primordial mound that emerged from the waters of chaos at creation. The pyramid's shape also resembled the rays of the sun descending to earth. Pyramids were essentially elaborate tombs that glorified the pharaoh and ensured his successful journey to the afterlife, where he would join the sun god Ra.

Pyramids were surrounded by complexes, including temples, causeways, and additional structures. The valley temple at the pyramid base conducted funerary rituals. A causeway connected the valley temple to the mortuary temple on the pyramid's east side, where daily offerings were made. There were also smaller pyramids for queens and storage pits for boats.

Pyramids contained burial chambers accessed by narrow passages. These passages were blocked with massive granite blocks after the funeral to prevent tomb robbery. The burial chamber contained the pharaoh's sarcophagus and originally held grave goods, though items might be stored in adjacent rooms or in the temples.

However, pyramids had a flaw: they were obvious targets for tomb robbers. A massive stone structure essentially announced the location of the pharaoh's treasures. Despite elaborate security measures, including false passages, hidden chambers, and massive blocking stones, almost all pyramids were robbed in antiquity, most within a few centuries of their construction.

By the Middle Kingdom, pharaohs experimented with other approaches. Some built smaller, less conspicuous pyramids. Others built elaborate complexes with hidden burial chambers accessible through confusing mazes of passages. But robbers still found the burial chambers, driving New Kingdom pharaohs to try something radically different: complete concealment.

The Valley of the Kings is a remote, narrow valley on the west bank of the Nile across from Thebes (modern Luxor). Here, pharaohs from the Eighteenth through the Twentieth Dynasties (roughly 1550–1070 BCE) were buried in rock-cut tombs carved deep into the valley's limestone cliffs.

A view of the Valley of the Kings.[6]

Instead of advertising the location with a massive pyramid, pharaohs built hidden tombs whose entrances were sealed and camouflaged. The mortuary temples, where offerings were made, were built separately in the valley below. Theoretically, no one would know where the tomb was located except the priests responsible for the burial.

The tombs were elaborate. A corridor descended into the rock, sometimes over two hundred feet down, passing through multiple chambers before reaching the burial chamber. The walls were covered with painted scenes and texts from the *Book of the Dead*, the *Amduat* (a text describing Ra's journey through the night), and other religious texts. The burial chamber contained the pharaoh's stone sarcophagus and nested coffins.

But even concealment failed. The Valley of the Kings was thoroughly plundered in ancient times, probably by the very workmen who built the tombs and lower officials who knew their locations. Court records preserve trials where captured robbers described breaking into tombs, stripping mummies of their gold, and melting down priceless artifacts. By the Third Intermediate Period, priests collected the royal mummies from their plundered tombs and reburied them in hidden locations for protection. Two major groups of royal mummies were discovered in modern times—one in 1881 at Deir el-Bahari, a formal cache containing over fifty royal mummies, and another in 1898 in the tomb of Amenhotep II, which had been reused as a repository for additional royal burials. These discoveries preserved the mummies of some of Egypt's greatest pharaohs, including Ramesses II, Seti I, Thutmose III, and many others. Only one royal tomb in the Valley of the Kings survived largely intact into modern times—Tutankhamun's.

Queens and high officials also had elaborate tombs. The Valley of the Queens, adjacent to the Valley of the Kings, contained tombs for royal wives and children. The tomb of Nefertari, the favorite wife of Ramesses II, features some of the most beautiful tomb paintings in Egypt—vibrant scenes of the queen in the afterlife, meeting gods, playing the board game senet, and journeying through the Duat.

High officials and nobles built tombs appropriate to their status. They were typically smaller than royal tombs but often elaborately decorated. These tombs provide invaluable information about daily life in ancient Egypt. Tomb paintings show farming, hunting, banqueting, and other activities the deceased enjoyed and wanted to continue in the afterlife.

Tomb robbery wasn't just a problem in ancient times. After Egypt fell to foreign powers and the knowledge of hieroglyphics was lost, tombs became treasure troves for antiquity hunters. European collectors in the 18th and 19th centuries acquired thousands of artifacts from plundered tombs. Mummies were ground up for medicine or unwrapped at parties as entertainment. Countless artifacts were destroyed or lost.

Modern archaeology has tried to recover what remains and study tombs scientifically. Archaeological excavations have revealed much about ancient Egyptian funerary practices, religious beliefs, and daily life. Conservation efforts work to preserve tomb paintings and structures damaged by time, humidity, tourists, and ancient vandalism.

Egyptian tombs, whether pyramids at Giza or rock-cut chambers in the Valley of the Kings, demonstrate the Egyptians' conviction that death was not the end. These structures, filled with precious goods and covered with beautiful art and sacred texts, were meant to last forever. They were supposed to be houses for eternity, where the deceased could exist for millions of years. That many have survived for millennia, allowing us to learn about and marvel at ancient Egyptian civilization, would surely please the ancient Egyptians who built them.

Chapter 16:
Daily Life Along the Nile

Society and Social Classes

Egyptian society was hierarchical, with clear distinctions between social classes. Yet compared to many ancient civilizations, Egyptian society offered some degree of social mobility. Even ordinary Egyptians had legal rights and protections, which was unusual for the ancient world.

At the top of the social pyramid stood the pharaoh. He wasn't just a king; he was considered divine. The pharaoh served as the earthly intermediary between humans and the divine realm. The pharaoh owned all of Egypt in theory, though in practice, he delegated authority to administrators. His role was to maintain ma'at through proper rule and religious observance.

The royal family came next—the pharaoh's wives, children, and close relatives. The Great Royal Wife (the pharaoh's principal queen) held considerable status and sometimes wielded real power. Royal children were educated at court and prepared for lives of privilege and responsibility.

Below the royal family were the nobles and high officials. These were the people who actually ran Egypt—viziers who oversaw the government, treasurers who managed finances, generals who commanded armies, and provincial governors who ruled regions on the pharaoh's behalf. These positions were often hereditary, with sons following fathers into office, creating families that maintained power across generations. However, capable commoners could sometimes rise through merit, particularly through military service or scribal training.

Priests formed another important group. Egypt's temples controlled vast lands, wealth, and labor forces. High priests of major temples, particularly the high priest of Amun at Thebes, were among the most powerful people in Egypt. Priests weren't necessarily religious in our modern sense; many were administrators and ritual specialists who served the gods by correctly performing ceremonies. Many priesthood positions were hereditary or appointed, and many were part-time roles, with priests serving in rotating shifts while also pursuing other careers.

Scribes were the educated class who could read and write hieroglyphics, hieratic (the cursive script used for everyday writing), and later demotic (an even more simplified script). Literacy rates in ancient Egypt were probably around 1 to 3 percent of the population, making scribes extremely valuable. They served as administrators, accountants, record-keepers, tax collectors, and bureaucrats. The position of scribe was highly respected and offered a path to advancement.

Soldiers formed a significant class, particularly during the New Kingdom when Egypt maintained a standing army. Egyptian soldiers received land grants and payment in rations. Military service offered opportunities for advancement; successful soldiers could become officers or even high officials. Egypt also employed foreign mercenaries, particularly Nubians and later Greeks, who often settled in Egypt and formed their own communities.

Artisans and craftsmen formed the middle of society. These included sculptors, painters, carpenters, jewelers, potters, metalworkers, weavers, and countless other specialized trades. Skilled craftsmen, particularly those working on royal tombs and monuments, could be quite prosperous and respected. The workers who built the royal tombs in the Valley of the Kings lived in a special village, Deir el-Medina, where they received good wages and enjoyed comfortable lives. Archaeological excavations of this village have provided remarkable detail about the lives of these skilled workers.

The ruins of Deir el-Medina.⁴⁶

At the base of the social pyramid were farmers—the vast majority of Egypt's population. Most farmland was controlled by the pharaoh, temples, or nobles, though some Egyptians, especially in later periods, did hold private land. Farmers who worked state or temple land had hereditary rights to farm it and paid taxes by giving a portion of their harvest. Farming was hard, repetitive work, but farmers generally had enough to eat and lived in stable communities.

Below farmers were laborers—people without land who worked for daily wages on construction projects, in workshops, or wherever temporary labor was needed. And at the very bottom were slaves. Foreign prisoners of war were enslaved and put to work on state projects, in households, or on temple estates, and their treatment could be harsh. Some Egyptians entered servitude because of debt. The status and treatment of enslaved people varied considerably; some had limited rights and could own property, while others lived in conditions closer to chattel slavery. True chattel slavery—people as complete property with no rights—existed but was not the predominant form throughout Egyptian history.

Egyptian society had surprisingly progressive attitudes toward women compared to most ancient civilizations. Egyptian women had extensive legal rights that would have been unusual in Greece or Rome. Women could own property in their own names, inherit wealth, initiate divorce, conduct business, serve as witnesses in court, and make contracts. Documents survive showing women buying and selling property, running businesses, and pursuing legal cases.

Women's primary social role was wife and mother, but this didn't prevent them from having economic independence. Many women worked as weavers, bakers, brewers, musicians, dancers, and in various trades. Upper-class women could own estates and businesses. Women could serve as priestesses, particularly in the cults of female deities. And while extremely rare, women could sometimes become pharaohs.

Children were highly valued in Egyptian society. Having children, especially sons, ensured that someone would care for parents in old age and make offerings to their spirits after death. Daughters were also valued, and Egyptian art frequently shows affection between parents and children. Children of elite families received an education. Boys trained for their future careers as scribes, priests, or officials, while girls learned household management and sometimes received an education in reading and music.

Social mobility existed but was limited. Most people were born into their social class and remained there. Egyptian society valued stability and tradition. Everyone had their place, and maintaining that order was part of maintaining ma'at.

Home, Family, and Food

Most Egyptians lived in houses built of mudbrick—the most practical building material in a land with little timber or stone for construction. Mudbrick was cheap, readily available (made from Nile mud mixed with straw), and well suited to Egypt's climate. It kept homes cool in summer and warm in winter. The downside was that mudbrick deteriorated relatively quickly, which is why relatively few ancient Egyptian houses survived.

Ordinary houses were typically small and simple. A typical farmer's house might have just three or four rooms—a main living area, a storage room, and one or two small bedrooms. The flat roof served as an additional living space, especially in hot weather. Houses were often built close together in villages, with narrow streets winding between them. Archaeological excavations at sites like Deir el-Medina show what workers' villages looked like—rows of similar houses built to a standard plan.

Elite houses were much larger and more elaborate. A wealthy official's house might have dozens of rooms organized around courtyards. These houses included separate areas for men and women, servants' quarters, storage magazines, and workshops. The houses were decorated with painted walls, had multiple stories, and included bathrooms and private shrines. The garden was an important feature. It provided a cool place in Egypt's heat, often with a pool stocked with fish and surrounded by trees and flowers.

Furniture was relatively simple, even in wealthy homes. Egyptians sat on stools, chairs, or cushions on the floor. They slept on beds—wooden frames with woven reed or leather supports, covered with linen sheets and sometimes mosquito netting. Wealthier people had headrests rather than pillows. These curved supports kept the head elevated while protecting elaborate hairstyles. They stored things in wooden chests or large ceramic jars. Oil lamps provided light after dark.

Houses usually had a kitchen area, though it was often outside or in a separate building to keep heat and smoke away from living areas. Cooking was done over open fires or in clay ovens. Most cooking vessels were pottery of various sizes.

The Egyptian diet was based on bread and beer—the two staples that provided most calories for most people. Bread came in many varieties, from coarse loaves for ordinary people to fine white bread for the wealthy. Egyptian bread was made from emmer wheat or barley. It was often quite coarse, containing grit from the grinding stones, which wore down people's teeth.

Beer was the everyday drink for all social classes, including children. Egyptian beer was nutritious and relatively low in alcohol—it was more like liquid bread than modern beer. It was made from barley or emmer wheat, partially baked into loaves, then crumbled into water and allowed to ferment. The result was a thick, sweet, slightly alcoholic beverage that was drunk through straws to filter out the grain particles.

Vegetables were also important. Onions, garlic, leeks, lettuce, cucumbers, and beans were common. Fruits included dates, figs, grapes, melons, and pomegranates.

Meat was a luxury for most people, though elites ate it regularly. Egyptians raised cattle, sheep, goats, and pigs. Poultry—ducks, geese, and domesticated chickens (in later periods)—provided both meat and eggs. Wealthy households might have elaborate farms that raised various animals. Ordinary people ate meat mainly on festival days or special occasions, though they might keep a few chickens or a goat.

Fish from the Nile were an important protein source, especially for ordinary Egyptians. The Nile teemed with fish, and fishing was a common activity. Fish could be eaten fresh, dried, or salted. However, some fish were considered sacred and forbidden to eat in certain regions. Some priesthoods forbade fish consumption due to local religious traditions.

Wild birds, like ducks and geese, could be hunted in the marshes. Wealthy Egyptians enjoyed hunting expeditions in the papyrus marshes, using throwing sticks to bring down birds, though this was as much sport as food gathering.

Food was seasoned with salt, honey, and various herbs and spices. Olive oil (in later periods) and other oils were used for cooking and as condiments. Wine was made from grapes or dates, but it was more expensive than beer and typically drunk by the wealthy.

Egyptians ate two or three meals a day. A simple breakfast might be bread and beer. The main meal, eaten in the afternoon or evening, might include bread, beer, vegetables, and perhaps fish or meat if available. Wealthier people enjoyed more elaborate meals with multiple courses, served on fine pottery or even metal dishes.

Extended families often lived in close proximity, with married sons building houses near their parents. Family ties were strong. Egyptian texts emphasize the importance of respecting parents and repaying them for raising you.

Children worked from an early age, helping with household tasks and learning the skills they would need as adults. But Egyptian children knew how to play. They played with dolls, balls, spinning tops, toy animals, and board games. They also played physical games—wrestling, running, and various ball games.

Life expectancy was short by modern standards—perhaps thirty-five to forty years on average—and childhood mortality was high. But for those who survived childhood, life could be reasonably comfortable, especially in times of prosperity.

Work, Play, and Leisure

The rhythm of Egyptian life followed the agricultural calendar, which in turn followed the Nile's annual cycle. The Egyptian year was divided into three seasons of four months each: Akhet (inundation), Peret (growing), and Shemu (harvest).

During Akhet (roughly July to October), the Nile flooded, covering the fields with water and depositing fresh silt. This was the time when farmers couldn't work their fields, so the state mobilized laborers for construction projects. The great pyramids and temples were built during the inundation season. This wasn't slavery but a form of taxation—able-bodied men served the state with their labor for part of the year and were fed and housed while doing so.

During Peret (roughly November to February), the floodwaters receded, leaving the fields covered with fresh, fertile silt. Farmers plowed the soft ground, often using wooden plows pulled by cattle, and planted seeds. This was the season of hope. If the Nile had flooded properly, crops would grow well, and there would be plenty to eat. If the flooding had been insufficient, there could have been famine.

During Shemu (roughly March to June), the crops matured and were harvested. This was the busiest season for farmers. Grain had to be cut with sickles, threshed to separate grain from chaff, and stored. Tax collectors came to measure the harvest and take the state's share.

Craftsmen worked year-round in workshops. The workshops at Deir el-Medina, where tomb workers lived, show how organized craft work was. Workers received regular rations in exchange for their labor. They worked in teams on specific projects, with foremen supervising and scribes recording everything.

The workweek varied by occupation and period. Evidence from the New Kingdom royal tomb workers suggests a ten-day cycle, with one day off after each ten-day period—a more grueling schedule than our modern five-day workweek. However, religious festivals were frequent and provided additional days off. Between regular days off and festival days, workers probably had roughly sixty to seventy days off per year, though this varied considerably by occupation and period.

Traders traveled up and down the Nile and to foreign lands, exchanging Egyptian grain, linen, and papyrus for luxury goods like incense, ebony, and precious metals. Physicians practiced medicine, using a combination of practical treatments and magic. Teachers educated the children of elites. Servants worked in wealthy households. Fishermen worked the Nile. Builders constructed houses and monuments. Weavers made linen cloth, Egypt's main textile, from flax grown along the Nile. Scribes recorded everything, from tax records to inventory lists. Training to be a scribe took years since they had to learn hundreds of hieroglyphic signs and the cursive hieratic script. Scribal schools used corporal punishment liberally. Texts say teachers threatened to beat lazy students until "their backs listened."

Egyptians still found time for leisure and entertainment. Music and dance were important parts of Egyptian life. Musicians played harps, lutes, lyres, flutes, drums, and other instruments at festivals, banquets, and religious ceremonies. Professional musicians and dancers performed at wealthy households. Music was also important in religious rituals, as priests and priestesses sang hymns to the gods.

Board games were popular. The most famous was senet, a game played on a rectangular board with thirty squares, using stick dice or throwing sticks to determine moves. Senet had religious significance—it was associated with the journey to the afterlife—but it was also played for fun. Other games included mehen (a snake-shaped board game) and a game similar to checkers.

Egyptians enjoyed physical activities and sports. Hunting was popular among the wealthy; pharaohs and nobles hunted dangerous game like lions, wild bulls, and hippopotamuses in the desert and marshes. Fishing and fowling in the marshes were enjoyed by all social classes.

Wrestling was a popular sport, with tournaments and competitions. Swimming was also popular. Running races, stick fighting, and various ball games were played. Children played versions of leapfrog, tug-of-war, and other physical games still played today.

Banquets were important social occasions for the elite. Tomb paintings often depict lavish feasts with guests dressed in fine linen, wearing elaborate wigs and jewelry, and sitting on cushioned chairs while servants bring food and drink. Musicians and dancers entertained. Guests ate, drank wine and beer, conversed, and sometimes got quite drunk. Some banquet scenes show guests vomiting from excess, suggesting Egyptians enjoyed their parties.

Festivals broke the routine of work and provided a community celebration. Major religious festivals could last days or weeks. The Beautiful Feast of the Valley at Thebes involved processions of the gods' statues, offerings at tombs, family gatherings at ancestral graves, and feasting. The Opet Festival at Thebes celebrated the annual flooding of the Nile with processions, music, and celebration. Festivals included food, beer, music, dancing, and opportunities to participate in or witness religious rituals.

Egyptian culture valued joy and celebration, and Egyptian art and texts suggest people found pleasure in family, food, music, festivals, and the beauty of the Nile Valley. The Egyptian concept of the afterlife as an idealized version of earthly life suggests they thought life was good and worth preserving eternally.

Of course, life could be hard. Droughts, poor floods, diseases, accidents, warfare, and oppressive taxation could make life miserable. Not everyone was content with their place in society. Legal documents preserve complaints of corruption, unfair treatment, and other injustices. Life for ordinary Egyptians was often difficult and shaped by forces beyond their control—the Nile's flooding, the demands of the state, and the decisions of distant rulers.

But within these constraints, Egyptians built meaningful lives. They worked, raised families, worshiped their gods, celebrated festivals, enjoyed simple pleasures, and hoped for a good afterlife. They left behind not just monuments and mummies but also traces of everyday existence—letters, shopping lists, work logs, school exercises, love poems, jokes, and complaints. These glimpses of daily life show that ancient Egyptians weren't so different from us. They worried about their jobs, complained about their bosses, loved their families, enjoyed parties, and tried to find meaning and happiness in their brief time on earth.

Chapter 17:
Egyptian Innovations and Legacy

Writing, Science, and Medicine

Ancient Egypt made fundamental contributions to civilization that still influence us today. Egyptian innovations in writing, mathematics, engineering, and medicine laid the groundwork for later developments. While the Egyptians weren't alone in developing these technologies—other ancient civilizations made similar advances—Egyptian achievements were remarkable.

The most visible Egyptian innovation was writing. Egyptian hieroglyphics are among the world's oldest writing systems, developing around 3200 BCE. The word "hieroglyphics" comes from Greek words meaning "sacred carvings," and that's what they were—a writing system used primarily for religious and monumental inscriptions.

Hieroglyphics used hundreds of symbols representing sounds, ideas, or both. Some signs were phonetic, representing sounds like letters or syllables. Others were ideograms, representing whole words or concepts. Still others were determinatives, signs added at the end of words to clarify meaning.

Hieroglyphics were too elaborate for everyday use. For business, letters, and administrative records, Egyptians developed hieratic script—a cursive, simplified form of hieroglyphics that could be written quickly with a reed pen and ink on papyrus. Hieratic developed early in Egyptian history and was used throughout the pharaonic period for practical documents.

Later, around 650 BCE, an even more simplified script called demotic emerged. Demotic was faster to write and became the common script for everyday documents in the Late Period. Egypt primarily used hieroglyphics for religious and monumental texts; hieratic for religious texts (especially funerary papyri), literary manuscripts, and administrative documents for most of Egyptian history; and demotic for daily business and legal documents in later periods. Hieratic continued to be used for religious purposes even after demotic emerged for administrative use.

Egyptian writing was forgotten after Egypt became Christian and adopted Greek and Coptic scripts. The ability to read hieroglyphics was lost by the 4th or 5th century CE. For over 1,400 years, Egyptian hieroglyphics remained indecipherable. They were beautiful but mysterious symbols that no one could read.

The breakthrough came in 1799 when French soldiers in Egypt discovered the Rosetta Stone, a granite slab inscribed with the same text in three scripts: hieroglyphics, demotic, and ancient Greek. Since scholars could read Greek, they had a key to deciphering the other scripts. French scholar Jean-François Champollion finally cracked the code in 1822, using the Rosetta Stone and other bilingual texts to work out how hieroglyphics represented sounds and meanings. This breakthrough opened up Egyptian civilization to modern understanding, allowing scholars to learn about Egyptian history, religion, and culture directly from Egyptian sources.

Egyptian mathematics was practical rather than theoretical. Egyptians needed math for surveying land, calculating taxes, planning construction, measuring grain, and managing resources. They developed a decimal system based on powers of ten, with distinct symbols for one, ten, one hundred, one thousand, and so on.

Egyptian mathematics used addition and multiplication as primary operations. They performed multiplication through repeated doubling—a method that's actually quite efficient. For example, to multiply 13 by 7, they would double 13 repeatedly (13, 26, 52, 104) and then select the appropriate values—in this case 52 + 26 + 13—to reach the correct total of 91. Division worked similarly, as repeated doubling in reverse.

For fractions, Egyptians had an unusual system. They used only unit fractions (fractions with 1 as the numerator, like 1/2, 1/3, 1/4). To express other fractions, they combined unit fractions. So, 3/4 would be written as 1/2 + 1/4. This seems awkward to us, but Egyptian scribes became very skilled at working with them.

Egyptian geometry was also advanced for the time. Surveyors needed to reestablish field boundaries after the annual Nile flood washed away markers. Architects needed to calculate volumes and angles for construction. The Egyptians developed formulas for calculating areas of rectangles, triangles, and circles and volumes of cylinders and pyramids. Their formula for the area of a circle was remarkably accurate. They approximated pi as approximately 3.16, which is close to the true value of 3.14159.

The construction of the pyramids demonstrates sophisticated engineering and mathematical knowledge. The Great Pyramid of Khufu is aligned to true north with remarkable precision; it is just 3/60 of a degree off. The base is nearly perfectly square, with sides differing by less than 2 inches out of over 750 feet. The angles of the faces are precisely calculated to meet at the apex. Achieving this level of accuracy with ancient tools required detailed mathematical planning and surveying.

Egyptian astronomy focused on creating a workable calendar. Egyptians developed a solar calendar of 365 days, which was divided into 12 months of 30 days each, plus 5 extra days. This calendar was remarkably accurate and served as the basis for later calendars, including our modern calendar. Egyptians also observed the stars. They recognized constellations and used stellar observations for timekeeping and to predict the Nile's flooding. The heliacal rising of Sirius (the star's first appearance on the eastern horizon just before dawn) originally coincided with the beginning of the Nile's annual flood, providing a natural marker for the new year. However, because the 365-day calendar lacked a leap year, this coincidence drifted by one day every four years, a discrepancy the Egyptians were aware of.

Egyptian medicine was a mixture of practical treatments and magical spells. Medical papyri survive that describe treatments for various ailments, showing that Egyptian physicians had considerable practical knowledge. Egyptian doctors could set broken bones and immobilize them with splints. They could stitch wounds and perform minor surgery. They extracted teeth and treated wounds with honey (which has natural antibacterial properties, though Egyptians didn't know this; they just used it because it worked). They prescribed various herbal remedies, some of which had genuine medicinal value.

The Edwin Smith Papyrus, dating to around 1600 BCE but copied from older material, is a surgical textbook describing forty-eight cases of injuries and wounds, primarily to the head and torso. For each case, it provides a systematic examination procedure, diagnosis, prognosis, and treatment. The text is remarkably rational, with relatively few magical elements (though some spells are included, particularly for untreatable cases). It distinguishes between injuries that can be treated, injuries that might be treated, and injuries that are untreatable.

The Ebers Papyrus, also from around 1600 BCE, is more comprehensive, covering a wider range of ailments, including internal diseases, skin conditions, eye problems, and gynecological issues. It includes over eight hundred remedies using various plants, minerals, and animal products. Some of these remedies had genuine medicinal properties, such as willow bark (which contains a compound related to aspirin), honey, and various herbs with known therapeutic effects. Others were probably ineffective or even harmful.

Many treatments included spells and incantations along with physical remedies. Egyptians believed that some illnesses were caused by demons or angry spirits, so magical protection was necessary. They wore amulets to protect against disease. They recited spells while applying medicine. This combination of practical treatment and magic seems strange to us, but for Egyptians, the physical and spiritual were interconnected.

Egyptian medical knowledge spread throughout the ancient Mediterranean world primarily through cultural contact rather than direct translation of texts. Greek physicians acknowledged learning from Egyptian medical traditions. The reputation of Egyptian medicine was so high that foreign rulers sometimes requested Egyptian doctors.

The Long Shadow of the Pharaohs

Ancient Egypt has fascinated people for thousands of years, and that fascination has profoundly influenced Western culture and imagination. From ancient Greece and Rome through the Renaissance to modern times, Egypt has served as a source of mystery, wisdom, and inspiration.

The ancient Greeks were fascinated by Egypt. Greek scholars, philosophers, and historians traveled to Egypt and wrote about the Egyptian civilization. Herodotus devoted a substantial portion of his *Histories* to Egypt, describing its geography, customs, religion, and monuments. He got some things wrong, but he preserved valuable information. Greek sources claimed that Plato and other philosophers studied with Egyptian priests, though modern scholars view these claims as possibly legendary. Regardless of whether specific individuals actually studied in Egypt, the Greeks clearly viewed Egypt as an ancient land of wisdom and learning.

The Greeks also influenced how we understand Egypt. They gave us the word "pyramid" (from their word for wheat cake, which had a similar shape). They gave us "hieroglyphics" (sacred carvings). They gave us many of the names we use for Egyptian gods; for instance, we call the god Djehuty "Thoth" because that's what the Greeks called him. The Greeks also engaged in syncretism, equating Egyptian gods with their own deities (such as identifying Amun with Zeus), which sometimes distorted the original Egyptian concept. Greek accounts of Egypt, while sometimes inaccurate, preserved knowledge of the Egyptian civilization during the periods when hieroglyphics couldn't be read.

The Romans, after conquering Egypt in 30 BCE, were also fascinated. Wealthy Romans collected Egyptian antiquities. Egyptian art influenced Roman decorative styles. The Romans transported Egyptian obelisks to Rome; several still stand in Rome today, more than remain in Egypt. Egyptian cults, particularly the worship of Isis, spread throughout the Roman Empire. Isis temples were built from Britain to Mesopotamia.

During the Middle Ages, knowledge of ancient Egypt declined in Europe. Egypt was part of the Islamic world, and direct European contact was limited. But Egypt remained a source of mystery and legend. Biblical accounts of Egypt—the Exodus story, Joseph in Egypt, the Flight into Egypt—kept Egypt in the European consciousness. Egypt was imagined as a land of wonders, magic, and ancient secrets.

The Renaissance brought renewed interest in ancient Egypt as Europeans rediscovered classical learning. Scholars studied Greek and Roman accounts of Egypt, and Egyptian artifacts began appearing in European collections. But without the ability to read hieroglyphics, Europeans still couldn't truly understand Egyptian civilization.

Napoleon's invasion of Egypt in 1798 marked a turning point. Napoleon brought scholars and scientists along with his army. They studied, measured, drew, and described Egyptian monuments, producing the massive *Description de l'Égypte* that introduced Egypt to European audiences in unprecedented detail. This expedition also yielded the Rosetta Stone, which would prove crucial to finally deciphering hieroglyphics. After Champollion's breakthrough in 1822, Egyptology emerged as a serious scholarly discipline. European scholars could finally read Egyptian texts, study Egyptian history from Egyptian sources, and begin to understand Egyptian civilization on its own terms rather than through Greek and Roman filters.

The 19th century saw "Egyptomania," a popular fascination with all things Egyptian. Egyptian motifs appeared in architecture, art, fashion, and design. Museums competed to acquire Egyptian artifacts. European and American tourists flocked to Egypt. Archaeological expeditions—some scholarly, others little better than treasure hunting—excavated sites throughout Egypt. Thousands of artifacts were shipped to European and American museums.

This period was problematic in many ways. Archaeological methods were often crude, destroying information. Mummies were unwrapped as public entertainment. Artifacts were scattered across the world, removed from their cultural context. Local Egyptian interests were often ignored. However, this period also established Egyptology as a discipline and brought the ancient Egyptian civilization to worldwide attention.

The 20th century brought more scientific archaeology. Egyptologists developed better methods, asked better questions, and built more complete pictures of the Egyptian civilization. They discovered royal mummy caches, the workers' village at Deir el-Medina, the city of Amarna, and numerous tombs and temples.

Egypt in popular culture has also been influential. Egyptian themes appear constantly in Western art, literature, film, and design. The Art Deco movement of the 1920s incorporated Egyptian motifs. There are Egyptian-themed buildings in cities worldwide. Egyptian symbols appear in jewelry, fashion, and graphic design.

Movies have shaped how people imagine ancient Egypt. Films, from classic Hollywood epics like *The Ten Commandments* to modern blockbusters like *The Mummy*, have depicted Egypt, though usually with more attention to drama than accuracy. These films have created powerful popular images of Egypt that influence how millions of people envision the ancient world.

Egyptian symbolism even appears in unexpected places. The pyramid on the US dollar bill references Egyptian symbolism adopted by Enlightenment thinkers. Obelisks appear in cities worldwide; some are genuine Egyptian obelisks transported abroad, while others are modern copies.

This cultural influence isn't always positive. Popular culture often reduces Egypt to stereotypes—mummies, curses, pyramids in deserts. Many popular depictions of Egypt are historically inaccurate. The fascination with Egypt can become orientalism—imagining Egypt as exotic, mysterious, and other, rather than as a human civilization with complexity.

Modern Egyptology tries to understand ancient Egypt on its own terms, as a real place inhabited by real people, not as a land of mystery and magic. However, the romantic image of Egypt persists, and for many people, Egypt remains a source of fascination, wonder, and imagination.

What We're Still Learning

Despite over two centuries of Egyptology, we're still learning about ancient Egypt. New discoveries continue to surprise scholars. New technologies reveal information invisible to earlier archaeologists. New questions generate new insights.

In 2017, archaeologists discovered a massive statue of Ramesses II submerged in a Cairo slum. The same year, scientists used cosmic-ray muon detectors (essentially imaging empty space inside pyramids using particles from space) to discover a previously unknown large void in the Great Pyramid of Khufu. What this void represents remains unknown, but this technology shows how new methods can reveal new information about even the most studied monuments. In 2019, dozens of sealed coffins were found at Saqqara; they had been untouched for millennia. In 2020, more than one hundred sealed sarcophagi were discovered at Saqqara, containing well-preserved mummies.

Modern technology has revolutionized Egyptology in recent decades. Satellite imagery reveals hidden structures. Ground-penetrating radar maps underground features without excavation. DNA analysis of mummies has revealed family relationships, diseases, and genetic information. Chemical analysis of mummies can determine ancient diets, trace exposure to pollution, and identify causes of death. 3D scanning creates perfect digital records of artifacts and structures.

Climate studies using ice cores, sediment analysis, and other techniques have revealed information about ancient climate, Nile flooding patterns, and environmental changes. These studies help explain historical events. Periods of instability often correlate with poor Nile floods caused by climate change. Understanding ancient climate helps explain the rise and fall of Egyptian power.

New archaeological approaches focus on questions earlier scholars ignored. Recent work examines the daily life of ordinary Egyptians, not just kings and nobles. Studies investigate ancient Egyptian cities, which were less studied than tombs and temples because urban sites are often covered by modern settlements. Research now explores the Egyptian economy, trade networks, and administrative systems. Gender studies examine women's roles in Egyptian society. All these approaches broaden our understanding of ancient Egypt.

We're also reexamining old assumptions. Earlier scholars often simply accepted Greek and Roman accounts of Egypt. Modern Egyptologists read Egyptian sources directly and recognize that Greek and Roman writers sometimes misunderstood or distorted Egyptian culture. Earlier scholars sometimes imposed their own cultural assumptions. Modern scholars try to understand Egypt on its own terms, recognizing their own biases and limitations.

Fundamental questions remain unanswered or debated. How exactly were the pyramids built? We have a general understanding, but specific details of construction methods remain uncertain. The Great Sphinx remains mysterious. When was it carved? Most scholars date it to the reign of Khafre (around 2500 BCE), but some suggest it's older. Who does it represent? Probably Khafre, but this isn't certain. Why was its nose destroyed? We don't know, though various legends exist.

Many aspects of Egyptian religion remain unclear. Egyptian religious texts are often cryptic and symbolic, so they are difficult to interpret definitively. The relationship between different gods, the nature of Egyptian beliefs in the afterlife, and the details of religious rituals are still debated among scholars.

Egyptian history itself has gaps and uncertainties. Chronology is debated. Different scholars propose different dates for various events, sometimes differing by decades or even centuries. Many pharaohs are known only from fragmentary evidence. Entire periods, like the Second Intermediate Period, remain poorly understood. The causes of major historical events, like the Bronze Age Collapse, the fall of the New Kingdom, and the success of Alexander's conquest, remain subjects of scholarly debate.

Conservation is an ongoing challenge. Egyptian monuments and artifacts are threatened by time, environmental damage, tourism, and urban development. The high water table in the Nile Delta poses a threat to archaeological sites. Air pollution in Cairo damages stone monuments. Tourism, while economically important, brings crowds that stress ancient structures. Rising groundwater threatens the Sphinx and nearby monuments. Climate change may affect preservation. Egyptologists work with conservators, engineers, and Egyptian authorities to preserve monuments for future generations.

Today, Egyptian scholars play leading roles; for decades, Egyptology was dominated by Europeans and Americans. International teams from around the world work in Egypt. The field is slowly becoming more diverse in terms of gender and ethnicity, though it still has work to do.

Ancient Egypt continues to surprise, inspire, and challenge us. Despite centuries of study, Egypt hasn't given up all its secrets. Every excavation season brings new finds. Every new technology reveals new information. Every generation of scholars asks new questions and develops new interpretations.

Conclusion:
Three Thousand Years in Perspective

When we step back and look at ancient Egypt's entire sweep of history—from the first unification around 3100 BCE to Cleopatra's death in 30 BCE—we're looking at roughly three thousand years of continuous civilization. To put that in perspective, the entire span from the fall of Rome to today is less than two thousand years. Ancient Egypt lasted longer than most civilizations have even existed.

What made Egypt last so long? Geography provided natural advantages. An effective organization allowed Egyptians to build monuments, maintain armies, and manage resources. Religion provided ideological unity through the concept of ma'at. Their culture valued tradition and continuity. Yet Egypt also adapted when necessary, adopting new technologies and absorbing useful foreign influences while maintaining its core identity.

Of course, Egypt changed considerably over three millennia. The Egypt of the Old Kingdom pyramid builders was quite different from the New Kingdom or the Ptolemaic period. Egypt was never frozen in time; it was a living, changing civilization that showed remarkable resilience, bouncing back from chaos to reunify and rebuild.

Why does Egypt still fascinate us? The monuments that still stand—the pyramids, temples, and tombs—remain impressive after thousands of years. The art is beautiful and instantly recognizable. But Egypt fascinates us for deeper reasons too. It was one of humanity's first great civilizations, demonstrating what organized societies could achieve. And the more we learn, the more familiar the Egyptians seem.

Egypt's three-thousand-year run eventually ended. No civilization lasts forever. But what Egypt achieved—the monuments they built, the knowledge they developed, and the culture they maintained—continues to inspire us. Ancient Egypt is gone, but it hasn't been forgotten, and its story continues to unfold as new discoveries are made and new questions are asked.

Part 2: Ancient Greece for Beginners

Greek History Simplified for People Who Slept Through History Class

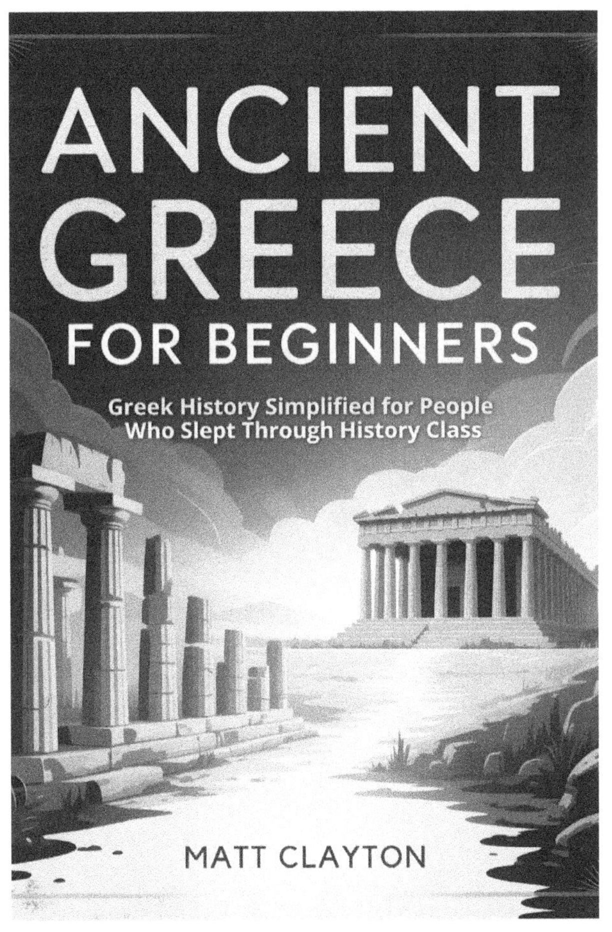

Introduction
Your Ticket to Ancient Greece

If you're reading this, chances are you either slept through history class or your teacher made ancient Greece sound about as exciting as watching paint dry on an old vase. Maybe you vaguely remember something about the Olympics, or you've seen a movie with men in sandals yelling, "This is Sparta!" Either way, you're here now, and that's what matters.

Here's the truth: ancient Greece is one of the most fascinating, influential, and downright wild periods in human history. Athens developed one of the earliest and most impactful forms of democracy. Greeks wrote plays that still make audiences cry, asked questions that philosophers still can't answer, and built temples that still awe visitors thousands of years later. They were brilliant, brutal, creative, and competitive.

And they shaped everything that came after. When you vote in an election, you're following an ideal of citizen participation inspired in part by Athens. When you go to the theater, thank Athens again. When you use words like "philosophy," "democracy," "chaos," and "marathon" (the name of the battle that inspired the modern race), you're speaking Greek. When you study geometry, biology, or physics, you're following in the footsteps of Greek thinkers who developed methods of logic and reasoning crucial to later scientific advances.

What You'll Discover

This book will take you on a journey spanning over a thousand years, from the Bronze Age rise of the Minoans to the Hellenistic Age's final decline. You'll meet the mysterious Minoans of Crete, the Mycenaean warrior-kings who possibly fought the Trojan War, the Spartans who created a society obsessed with military perfection, and the Athenians who invented democracy and then used it to build an empire.

You'll witness Leonidas and his three hundred Spartans resisting the massive Persian army at Thermopylae. You'll see Greek city-states, including Athens and Sparta, repel two major Persian invasions. You'll watch the philosopher Socrates annoy people by asking questions until they sentenced him to death. You'll follow Alexander the Great as he conquers most of the known world by the age of thirty.

You'll see the birth of the Olympic Games, the construction of the Parthenon, the writing of history's first histories, and Greek thinkers laying early foundations for rational inquiry and empirical observation.

A Note on Honesty

This book won't pretend the Greeks were perfect. They practiced slavery on a massive scale. They denied women basic rights. They could be brutal and arrogant. Athenian democracy only applied to adult male citizens, which was maybe 10 to 20 percent of the population.

We're not going to sugarcoat the uncomfortable parts. The Greeks were real people with real flaws. What made them remarkable wasn't moral perfection; it was their willingness to question, experiment, and push boundaries.

This book also won't drown you in academic jargon or assume you already know who Pericles was. We'll introduce people, places, and concepts as we go.

Let's Begin

We're about to travel back to a world of city-states and citizen-soldiers, of gods and heroes, of philosophers and playwrights. We'll start with the mysterious palace civilization of Crete, journey through the chaos of the Dark Age, watch democracy be born, witness the clash between East and West, and follow Alexander the Great as he conquered the known world from Greece to India.

By the time we're done, you'll understand why this small, mountainous peninsula managed to shape the entire Western world and why we're still talking about it more than two thousand years later.

Welcome to ancient Greece. Let's dive in.

Chapter 1 – Welcome to the Cradle of the West

The Mediterranean Stage: Geography and Climate

If you look at a map of Greece, the first thing you'll notice is how broken up everything is. Mountains everywhere. Hundreds of islands scattered across the sea. Coastline that twists and turns for thousands of miles. This wasn't a landscape that encouraged unity.

The Greek mainland is dominated by mountain ranges that divide the land into small valleys and coastal plains. The Pindus Mountains run like a spine down the western side of the peninsula. Mount Olympus in the north rises to nearly ten thousand feet, so high that the Greeks imagined their gods lived at its peak, above the clouds where mortals couldn't reach.

These mountains meant that ancient Greek communities developed in isolation from each other. A valley might be only thirty miles from the next valley, but the mountain pass between them could be treacherous. Travel was difficult and dangerous, so communities stayed local. They developed their own dialects, customs, gods (though with significant overlap), and eventually governments.

The sea, however, was a different story. Greece has one of the longest coastlines in the Mediterranean relative to its size. No point in Greece is more than about eighty-five miles from the sea. The Aegean Sea, dotted with islands, lies to the east. The Ionian Sea stretches to the west. The Mediterranean opens to the south.

For the Greeks, the sea was a highway. It was far easier to sail from Athens to the island of Delos or even to the coast of Asia Minor (modern-day Turkey) than it was to walk to Thebes, which was only thirty miles away but required crossing mountains. Greek ships could hug the coastline, hopping from island to island, connecting communities across the water in ways that mountains prevented on land.

Because mountains kept communities separate, Greece never became a unified empire like Egypt or Persia. Instead, it developed as hundreds of independent city-states, which the Greeks called a *polis* (plural: *poleis*). Each polis was its own country with its own laws, government, and army. Athens was one polis. Sparta was another. Thebes, Corinth, and Megara are other well-known examples.

Geography wasn't the only reason the city-states remained independent. Greek political philosophy emphasized local autonomy and self-governance. Cultural rivalry between cities was fierce, as each *polis* took pride in its own identity and resisted outside control. The Greeks valued their independence and fought to maintain it, even when unification might have made them stronger against external threats.

But because the sea connected these communities, Greeks shared a common culture despite their political divisions. They spoke variations of the same language. They worshiped the same gods. They competed in the same athletic festivals. They recognized each other as Hellenes, or Greeks, even when they were fighting each other.

The climate also played a role. Greece has a Mediterranean climate. It has hot, dry summers and mild, wet winters. This meant the growing season was limited. The rocky soil wasn't particularly fertile. Ancient Greeks could grow olives, grapes, and some grain, but feeding a large population was always a challenge.

This agricultural limitation had two major effects. First, it encouraged trade. Greeks needed to import grain, so they became seafarers and merchants, trading olive oil, wine, and other goods for the food they needed. Second, it encouraged colonization. When a city's population grew beyond what the land could support, the solution was often to send people overseas to found new colonies.

The landscape also shaped Greek military tactics. In the narrow valleys and mountain passes, large cavalry forces were less effective than in the open plains of Persia or Egypt. Greek warfare evolved around heavily armed foot soldiers known as hoplites who fought in tight formations called phalanxes. The terrain favored defenders. An army holding a mountain pass could stop a much larger force, as the Spartans famously proved at Thermopylae.

So when you think about ancient Greece, don't imagine a unified nation. Imagine a fragmented landscape of independent communities, divided by mountains but connected by the sea, competing with each other constantly but also sharing a common identity. The geography didn't just influence Greek history; it determined it.

The Greeks' View of the World (Hellenes vs. Barbarians)

The ancient Greeks didn't call themselves "Greeks." That's a Latin word that came later. They called themselves Hellenes, and they believed they were fundamentally different from everyone else.

To the Greeks, the world was divided into two types of people: Hellenes and *barbaroi* ("barbarians"). And no, "barbarian" didn't necessarily mean savage or uncivilized, though it sometimes carried that implication. The word *barbaroi* was originally just Greek for "those who speak bar-bar," people whose language sounded like meaningless babbling to Greek ears.

What made someone a Hellene? It wasn't about which city-state you belonged to. A person from Athens and a person from Sparta might be bitter enemies, but they were both Hellenes. Greekness was cultural and ethnic, not political.

Being a Hellene meant you spoke Greek. The language had dialects, like Doric, Ionic, and Aeolic, but they were mutually understandable. You would also participate in Greek religious practices. You worshiped the Olympian gods: Zeus, Hera, Athena, Apollo, and the rest. You attended the great religious festivals like the Olympics or the games at Delphi. Hellenes shared a cultural heritage. You knew the stories of Homer (the *Iliad* and the *Odyssey*). You knew the myths and legends that every Greek child learned.

But here's something crucial to understand. Being a Hellene didn't mean you could become a citizen anywhere in the Greek world. Citizenship was different in each polis. In Athens, for example, citizenship required that both your parents were Athenian citizens. Foreigners who lived in Athens for generations, called *metics*, could be culturally Greek, speak the language perfectly, and worship the same gods, but they could never become full citizens, no matter how long they stayed or how much they contributed to the city. Cultural identity and legal citizenship were two separate things.

Non-Greeks (*barbaroi*) included the Persians, who built the largest empire the world had yet seen. It included the Egyptians, whose civilization was already ancient when Greece was just getting started. The distinction wasn't primarily about sophistication or power; it was more about culture and identity.

The Greeks were aware that other peoples had impressive civilizations. They respected Egyptian knowledge, especially in mathematics and medicine. They recognized Persian military might. However, they still saw themselves as different and, in important ways, superior. Free Greeks governed themselves through assemblies and councils. Barbarians, in the Greek view, bowed to kings and emperors. Greeks valued reason and debate. Barbarians simply obeyed.

This distinction became particularly important during the Persian Wars, when the Greeks framed their conflict as a struggle between freedom and slavery, between the Greek way of life and Persian despotism. Whether this was fair to the Persians is debatable, as Persian society was more complex than Greek propaganda suggested, but it's how the Greeks understood their world.

But here's something interesting: Greek culture was remarkably inclusive in one specific way. When Greeks established colonies around the Mediterranean, they brought their culture with them. People in these colonies, even if they had mixed heritage, could be Hellenes if they adopted the Greek language, religion, and customs. Later, after Alexander the Great's conquests, Greek culture spread even farther, and the boundaries of who could be considered "Greek" became more fluid.

The Hellene barbarian distinction shaped how Greeks saw themselves and their place in the world. It gave them a sense of common identity even when they fought each other. It also gave them a sense of mission. They sought to preserve Greek culture and Greek freedom against the massive empires that surrounded them.

This worldview had its problems. It could lead to arrogance and cultural blindness. But it also helped create a civilization that valued questioning, debate, and individual excellence in ways that few ancient cultures did.

A Quick Map of Time: The Major Eras

Ancient Greek history spans roughly 1,500 years, from around 1600 BCE to 146 BCE. That's an enormous stretch of time. To put it in perspective, that's about as long as the period from the fall of Rome to today. So when we talk about "ancient Greece," we're not talking about one static civilization. We're talking about a culture that rose, peaked, transformed, and eventually merged into something else.

Historians break this long period into several major eras. Think of these as chapters in a much longer story.

The Bronze Age (c. 3000–1100 BCE)

Before there was classical Greece—before Athens, before Sparta, before democracy—there were the Bronze Age civilizations of the Aegean. These were the Minoans on Crete and the Mycenaeans on the Greek mainland.

The Minoans built elaborate palaces and dominated the sea trade. The Mycenaeans built fortress cities and fought wars. These people spoke an early form of Greek and created the world that Homer would later write about in his epics. They're important because they laid the foundation for everything that came after.

But around 1200 BCE, this Bronze Age world collapsed. Cities were destroyed, palaces burned, trade networks broke down, and writing disappeared. What caused this collapse is still debated. It was probably a combination of invasions, natural disasters, and internal upheaval. What matters is that the lights went out across the eastern Mediterranean, and Greece entered a dark age.

The Dark Age (c. 1100–800 BCE)

The period after the Bronze Age collapse is called the Greek Dark Age, and the name fits. Archaeological evidence shows that populations declined dramatically. People abandoned large settlements and retreated to small, isolated villages. Writing disappeared. Trade nearly stopped. It was a period of poverty and isolation.

However, the Dark Age wasn't completely dark. Greek-speaking peoples migrated and settled across the Aegean region. Oral traditions kept stories and legends alive. Gradually, communities began to recover and reorganize. By the end of this period, the foundations for the classical Greek world were being laid.

The Archaic Period (c. 800–500 BCE)

This is when Greece truly begins to take the shape we recognize. Writing returned; it was borrowed and adapted from the Phoenicians. The population grew, and trade resumed. The polis (the independent city-state) emerged as the fundamental unit of Greek political organization.

This was an era of innovation and expansion. Greeks colonized the Mediterranean, founding new cities from Spain to the Black Sea. They experimented with different forms of government. Art and architecture flourished. The first Olympic Games were held in 776 BCE. Homer's epics were written down. Philosophy began with thinkers who asked fundamental questions about the nature of reality.

By the end of the Archaic period, Athens was moving toward democracy, and Sparta had developed its unique military society. The stage was set for Greece's moment in the spotlight.

The Classical Period (c. 500–323 BCE)

This is the Greece most people think of. The Persian Wars united the Greeks against a common enemy and launched Athens to preeminence. The city entered its Golden Age under Pericles, building the Parthenon and becoming a center of culture, philosophy, and drama.

Socrates walked the streets of Athens, questioning everything. His student, Plato, founded his Academy. Playwrights like Sophocles and Euripides created tragedies that audiences still perform today. Herodotus and Thucydides invented the writing of history as we know it.

However, this glorious period was also marked by conflict. The Peloponnesian War between Athens and Sparta tore Greece apart for twenty-seven years, ending with Athens's defeat and the beginning of Sparta's brief supremacy. After Sparta came Thebes. After Thebes came Macedon under Philip II, who conquered the Greek city-states and ended their independence.

Philip's son, Alexander the Great, then conquered the Persian Empire and spread Greek culture across the known world. His death in 323 BCE marks the end of the Classical period and the beginning of something new.

The Hellenistic Period (323–146 BCE)

After Alexander died, his generals carved up his empire into kingdoms—the Ptolemies in Egypt, the Seleucids in Asia, the Antigonids in Macedon. These weren't traditional Greek city-states anymore. They were territorial monarchies ruling diverse populations.

But Greek culture (Hellenistic culture) dominated from the Mediterranean to India. Greek became the international language of commerce and learning. Alexandria in Egypt became the intellectual capital of the world, home to the famous Great Library and Mouseion.

Science and mathematics flourished. Philosophy evolved into new schools, like Stoicism and Epicureanism.

The Hellenistic period ended gradually as Rome conquered the Greek east. The final blow to Greek political independence came in 146 BCE when Rome destroyed Corinth and made Greece a province. However, Hellenistic culture itself continued to flourish, especially in Egypt under the Ptolemies, until 30 BCE, when Rome annexed Egypt after the defeat of Cleopatra and Mark Antony. But in a real sense, Greek culture never died. It simply transformed, influencing Rome and, through Rome, all of Western civilization.

Understanding these periods helps make sense of the story we're about to tell. Ancient Greece wasn't one thing. It was a culture that evolved, adapted, achieved greatness, declined, and ultimately survived by transforming itself and influencing everything that came after.

Now let's go back to the beginning and meet the people who started it all.

Chapter 2 – Lost Worlds: The Bronze Foundations and the Dark Age

The Sea Kings of Crete: The Minoan Civilization

Long before there was Athens or Sparta, before Homer sang of heroes, before anyone called themselves Hellenes, there was Crete. On Crete, there was a civilization so sophisticated that when archaeologists first discovered it in the early 1900s, they could hardly believe what they had found.

The Minoans, named after the legendary King Minos, built the first great civilization in Europe. From roughly 2700 to 1450 BCE, they played a dominant role in Aegean maritime trade from their island stronghold. Their palaces were architectural marvels. Their art was vibrant and naturalistic. Their ships connected Mediterranean trade routes. And then, suddenly, they vanished.

The center of Minoan civilization was Knossos, a sprawling palace complex on the northern coast of Crete. Calling it a "palace" doesn't quite capture what it was. Knossos covered about six acres and had hundreds of rooms spread across multiple stories. It had indoor plumbing with running water and sophisticated drainage systems. It had storage rooms that could hold enough food to feed thousands. It had workshops for craftsmen, religious shrines, administrative offices, and residential quarters.

What Knossos didn't have were defensive walls.

This is striking. Most Bronze Age palaces were fortresses. The Mycenaeans on the mainland built massive stone walls around their cities. The Hittites in Anatolia fortified everything. But Knossos and other Minoan palaces on Crete were wide open. There were no walls or obvious military defenses.

The remains of the Palace of Knossos.[47]

This suggests the Minoans felt secure, though the absence of walls doesn't prove they were peaceful. Some scholars argue that their security stemmed from their naval power. Their ships controlled the seas so effectively that no one dared attack the island. Others point to Crete's geographic isolation. The evidence suggests that Minoan ships played a crucial role in Aegean trade, so it is possible they weren't a militant society. Whether through naval strength, isolation, or a genuinely less militaristic culture, the Minoans didn't feel the need to fortify their palaces the way other Bronze Age peoples did.

The palace at Knossos was a maze of corridors, stairways, and rooms. It's easy to see how this place might have inspired the later Greek legend of the Labyrinth—the impossible maze where King Minos imprisoned the Minotaur, a half-man, half-bull monster. The myth says the hero Theseus navigated the Labyrinth, killed the Minotaur, and escaped using a thread given to him by Minos's daughter Ariadne.

Bulls were certainly important to the Minoans. Palace walls were decorated with frescoes showing young athletes performing death-defying acrobatics, vaulting over charging bulls, grabbing their horns, and somersaulting over their backs. Whether this was sport, ritual, or both is unclear. But it was dangerous, and it was central to Minoan culture.

Bull-leaping fresco at the Palace of Knossos.[48]

Minoan art is distinctive. Unlike the rigid, formal art of Egypt or Mesopotamia, Minoan frescoes are fluid and lively. They show dolphins leaping through waves, women in elaborate dresses, flowers and plants, and religious processions. They used bright blues, reds, and yellows. The figures move naturally. There's a joy to Minoan art that you don't often see in the ancient world.

Women appear prominently in Minoan art and might have held significant roles in religious and ritual life, though their actual social and political status remains debated among scholars. Frescoes show women participating in religious ceremonies, overseeing rituals, and engaging in public activities. Some scholars believe Minoans worshiped a mother goddess.

The Minoans were master traders and seafarers. Their pottery has been found throughout the eastern Mediterranean, including in Egypt, on the Greek mainland, in Asia Minor, and on Cyprus. They traded in wine, olive oil, textiles, and luxury goods. They imported tin and copper to make bronze, gold and silver for jewelry, and exotic items from distant lands.

The Minoans were literate and kept detailed records of their palace economies. However, we can't read what they wrote. The earliest Minoan script is called Linear A. It appears on clay tablets found at Knossos and other sites, usually recording inventories and transactions. Scholars have been trying to decipher Linear A for over a century without success. We know it's a syllabic script where each symbol represents a syllable, but we don't know what language it represents. Linguistic analysis suggests it is unrelated to Indo-European languages, meaning it's not Greek or any language family we're familiar with.

Around 1450 BCE, something catastrophic happened to the Minoan civilization. The palaces were destroyed. Some were even burned. Knossos survived, but it came under new management: the Mycenaean Greeks from the mainland. The Minoan culture didn't disappear overnight, but it was never the same.

What caused the collapse? Theories abound. A massive volcanic eruption on the island of Thera (modern Santorini) around 1600 BCE sent tsunamis crashing into Crete and covered parts of the island in volcanic ash. This disaster weakened Minoan power, though the civilization recovered for another century and a half.

Archaeological evidence suggests that around 1450 BCE, Mycenaean Greeks from the mainland established control over Crete. Whether this happened through military conquest, gradual political takeover, or a combination of factors remains debated. What's clear is that after 1450 BCE, Mycenaean Greeks were in charge at Knossos, using Linear B script (an adaptation of Linear A that records Greek) to administer the palace.

The Minoans had created Europe's first great civilization, but they would not be its last. That distinction would belong to the Greeks, who took control of their island.

The Age of Heroes: The Mycenaean Civilization

The Mycenaeans were not like the Minoans. Where the Minoans built unfortified palaces and painted dolphins, the Mycenaeans built fortress cities and buried their kings with weapons. Mycenaean elite culture emphasized warfare and fortifications, suggesting a highly militarized society. These were the Greeks who would become the heroes of legend—Agamemnon, Achilles, and Odysseus. This was the world Homer sang about.

Mycenaean civilization flourished on the Greek mainland from roughly 1600 to 1100 BCE. The name comes from Mycenae, the most powerful of their cities, located in the northeastern Peloponnese. Mycenaean cities dotted the landscape and included Pylos, Tiryns, Athens, Thebes, and Iolkos. Each was an independent kingdom ruled by a *wanax* (similar to a king).

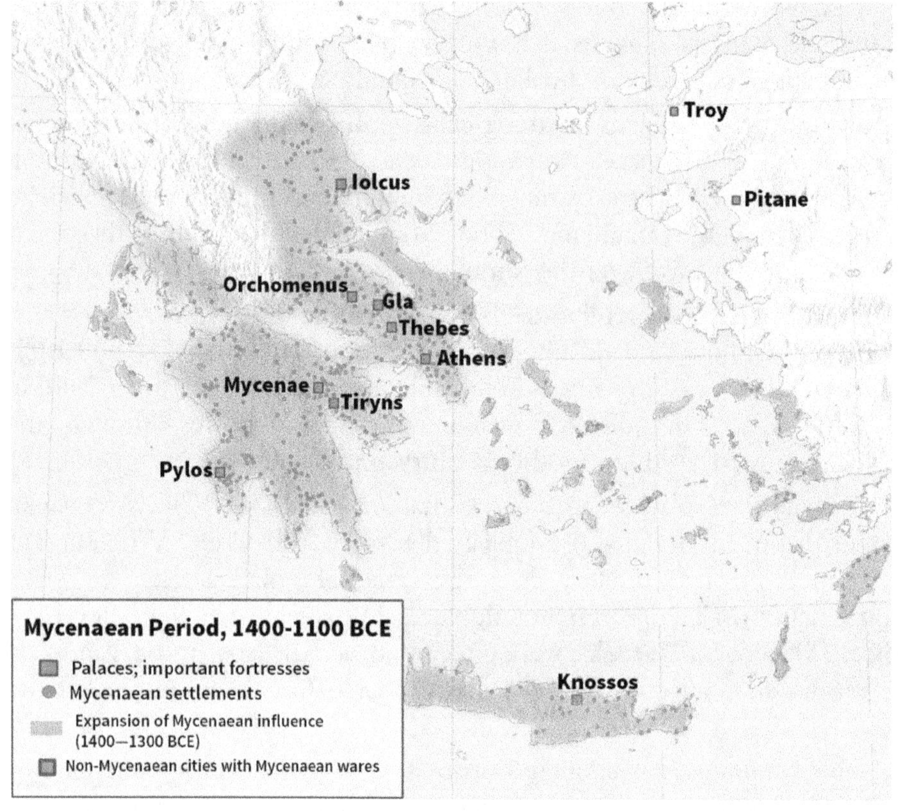

Map of Mycenaean world.[49]

The first thing a person would have noticed about a Mycenaean city was its walls. These weren't simple defensive barriers. They were massive constructions of huge limestone blocks, some weighing several tons, fitted together without mortar. Later Greeks, unable to imagine humans building such things, called them "Cyclopean walls." They imagined they had been built by the mythical one-eyed giants called Cyclopes.

The citadel of Mycenae sits on a hill dominating the Argive Plain. To enter, you pass through the Lion Gate, topped with a relief sculpture of two lions flanking a column. Inside, the citadel contains a palace complex, houses for the elite, storage rooms, workshops, and a secret underground cistern that could provide water during a siege. Everything about Mycenaean architecture suggests they expected an attack and were ready.

The Lion Gate today.[50]

This wasn't paranoia. The Mycenaeans fought each other constantly. Each city-state was independent and competitive. Kings raided each other's territories for cattle, slaves, and glory. War was how Mycenaean elites proved themselves and gained wealth.

According to later Greek tradition preserved in Homer's epics, the Mycenaean kingdoms sometimes united for larger campaigns. The legendary Trojan War would have been such an occasion. Multiple kingdoms supposedly joined under Agamemnon of Mycenae to sail across the Aegean and besiege Troy, a wealthy city on the coast of Asia Minor.

Did the Trojan War really happen? We don't know for certain. There was definitely a city called Troy (or Ilion) where Homer said it was. Archaeologists have found its ruins at Hisarlik in modern Turkey. The site shows evidence of multiple cities built on top of each other, destroyed and rebuilt over centuries. One of these layers, dating to around 1200 BCE, shows signs of destruction by fire and war.

So there was a Troy, and it was destroyed around the right time. But was there really a ten-year siege? Did Agamemnon lead a Greek coalition? Did Achilles kill Hector? Did Odysseus build a wooden horse? We have no evidence of it. What we have is a powerful story that later Greeks believed reflected their ancestral past—a story of heroes, honor, rage, and the terrible costs of war.

What we do know for certain is that Mycenaean Greeks were warriors and sailors. Archaeological evidence shows they engaged in extensive trade throughout the Mediterranean, and they might have conducted raids, though the extent of their military expeditions beyond Greece remains debated. Their pottery has been found as far away as Italy, Egypt, and the Levant. They imported amber from the Baltic, ivory from Syria, and gold from Egypt.

The Mycenaeans also adopted and adapted Minoan practices. After taking control of Crete around 1450 BCE, they assumed control of Minoan trade networks, learned Minoan artistic techniques, and adapted the Minoan Linear A script to write their own language. This adapted script is called Linear B, and unlike Linear A, we can read it.

Linear B was deciphered in 1952 by Michael Ventris, an amateur linguist who proved that the tablets recorded an early form of Greek. The tablets are mostly administrative records, documenting inventories of grain, livestock, textiles, and weapons. They list offerings to the gods, rations for workers, and assignments of land. They're bureaucratic documents, not literature, but they tell us a great deal about how the Mycenaean society functioned.

Mycenaean palaces were administrative centers that controlled the surrounding territory. The king and his bureaucrats tracked everything: how much grain each village produced, how many sheep were raised, how much bronze was available for weapons, how much wool was spun into cloth. This was a literate, organized society with record-keeping and centralized control.

The tablets also reveal aspects of the Mycenaean religion. They mention gods whose names would be familiar to later Greeks, like Zeus, Hera, Poseidon, Hermes, Athena, Artemis, and Dionysus. Some deities known from the later Greek religion appear in Linear B tablets, though their roles and attributes in the Bronze Age might have differed from what we know of the Classical Greek religion. The religious continuity is there, but we shouldn't assume the Bronze Age gods were identical to the Olympians of Homer or later Greek worship.

Mycenaean kings were buried in impressive tombs. At Mycenae, archaeologist Heinrich Schliemann discovered shaft graves containing spectacular grave goods. There were gold masks, bronze weapons inlaid with gold and silver, jewelry, and imported luxury items. One mask, which Schliemann famously (and incorrectly) declared was "the mask of Agamemnon," shows the extraordinary wealth these rulers commanded.

The Mask of Agamemnon.[51]

Later Mycenaean royalty were buried in tholos tombs, massive beehive-shaped chambers dug into hillsides and covered with earth. The Treasury of Atreus at Mycenae has a dome that rises forty-three feet and was the largest unsupported dome in the world until the Romans built the Pantheon over a thousand years later.

But for all their power and sophistication, the Mycenaeans were heading toward catastrophe. Around 1200 BCE, their world would come crashing down.

The Great Collapse: The Bronze Age Mystery

Around 1200 BCE, the eastern Mediterranean world fell apart. It wasn't just Greece. Across the region, great civilizations collapsed almost simultaneously. The Hittite Empire in Anatolia vanished. Egyptian power declined sharply. Cities throughout the Levant were destroyed. Trade networks that had connected the Mediterranean for centuries broke down.

In Greece, the devastation was severe. Mycenaean palaces were burned and abandoned. Pylos was destroyed and never rebuilt. Mycenae itself suffered massive damage. Populations declined dramatically. Archaeological surveys suggest Greece lost up to 90 percent of its population in some regions.

Writing disappeared. The administrative systems that had tracked grain and bronze vanished. The long-distance trade networks collapsed. The specialized craftsmen who made luxury goods were gone. The centralized palace economies that had organized production were finished.

This wasn't just a political collapse. This was a civilizational breakdown.

What caused it? Historians have debated this question for decades and still don't have a definitive answer. The most honest response is probably that several things worked together to create a perfect storm.

One definite factor was warfare. Egyptian records from this period mention invasions by "Sea Peoples"—mysterious raiders from the sea who attacked Egypt, Cyprus, and the Levantine coast. We don't know exactly who these Sea Peoples were. They might have been displaced populations fleeing troubles in their own lands, or they might have been opportunistic raiders taking advantage of growing instability. Either way, they contributed to the chaos.

Climate change likely played a role. Evidence suggests the eastern Mediterranean experienced a prolonged drought during this period. Crops would have failed. Food shortages would have created unrest. Populations would have moved, putting pressure on neighboring regions. Hungry people make desperate decisions.

Earthquakes could have compounded the problems. The Aegean region is seismically active, and archaeological evidence shows that several Mycenaean sites suffered earthquake damage around this time. A major earthquake could destroy a palace and its surrounding town. That means multiple earthquakes over a short period could be catastrophic.

Systems collapse is another possibility. Bronze Age civilizations were interconnected through trade. Making bronze requires copper and tin, which usually came from different regions. If trade routes were disrupted, people couldn't make bronze tools or weapons. If they couldn't make weapons, they couldn't defend themselves. If one civilization collapsed, it could trigger a cascade effect as others lost access to necessary resources.

Internal upheaval probably contributed too. Mycenaean society was hierarchical and controlled from the palace centers. If the king and his bureaucracy lost control, whether through war, natural disaster, or internal rebellion, the whole system could unravel. Without the palace organizing production and redistribution, local economies would collapse.

As we said, the truth is probably all of the above. It was likely a perfect storm of disasters: drought and famine, earthquakes, invasions, trade disruption, and internal breakdown. One problem would have made societies vulnerable to others. The combination was overwhelming.

What's clear is that the world that emerged after 1200 BCE was dramatically different from what came before. The palaces were gone. The kings were gone. The bureaucrats, the scribes, and the specialized craftsmen were all gone. Greece entered a period historians call the Dark Age, and the name is appropriate.

But here's something important to remember. While civilization collapsed at the elite level, people survived. They continued farming, herding, and living in small communities. They told stories about the great heroes of the past, stories that would eventually become the *Iliad* and the *Odyssey*. They remembered the gods, and they spoke Greek.

The Bronze Age world was gone, but Greek culture survived, kept alive in oral traditions through centuries of poverty and isolation. Eventually, slowly, it would begin to rebuild.

The Quiet Centuries: The Greek Dark Age

The period from roughly 1100 to 800 BCE is called the Greek Dark Age, though "quiet centuries" might be more accurate. It wasn't completely dark. People lived, farmed, raised families, and told stories. However, it was a dramatic step backward from the sophistication of the Mycenaean world.

Archaeological evidence from this period is sparse. Settlements were small; they were more like villages than towns. Houses were simple structures of mudbrick and thatch. There were no palaces, no monumental architecture, and no elaborate tombs. Pottery was functional but plain, lacking the artistic sophistication of earlier or later periods.

Most significantly, writing disappeared. The Linear B tablets stop around 1200 BCE, and for the next four hundred years, Greece was illiterate. Knowledge and stories were preserved orally, passed down through generations by memory. Without written records, we know frustratingly little about what happened during these centuries.

The population declined dramatically. Surveys of archaeological sites show that many Mycenaean-era settlements were abandoned. People retreated to defensible hilltop locations or scattered into isolated farmsteads. Greece might have lost 75 to 90 percent of its population in some regions, though exact figures are impossible to determine.

Trade contracted severely. The long-distance maritime networks that had connected Greece to Egypt, the Levant, and Cyprus largely ceased. A few imported items from the Near East still appear in Greek sites, but the flow of goods reduced to a trickle. Greeks became more isolated and more focused on local survival than international commerce.

The political structure changed fundamentally. There were no more palace bureaucracies, no more *wanax* ruling from fortified citadels. Instead, Greece fragmented into small communities led by local chiefs or councils of elders. These were societies where everyone knew everyone else, not the organized kingdoms of the Bronze Age.

But life continued. People grew barley and wheat. They raised sheep and goats. They made pottery for everyday use. They buried their dead, usually in simple graves with few grave goods. They worshiped the gods, though without the elaborate rituals organized by palace priesthoods.

Around 1050 BCE, a new burial practice appeared: cremation. Bodies were burned on funeral pyres, and the ashes were placed in urns. This practice is quite different from earlier inhumation burials and became the standard during much of the Greek Dark Age. Whether this represents a change in religious beliefs or was simply practical is unclear.

During this period, Greeks began migrating across the Aegean to the coast of Asia Minor (modern Turkey). The traditional story, recorded by later Greek historians, says that different Greek tribal groups colonized different regions. Ionians settled the central coast and islands like Samos and Chios. Aeolians moved to the northern coast. Dorians went to the southern coast and islands like Rhodes. These migrations established a Greek presence throughout the Aegean Basin, creating communities that would remain Greek-speaking for thousands of years.

One significant development during the Greek Dark Age was the introduction of iron. Bronze had been the premier metal for tools and weapons throughout the Bronze Age, but iron is more abundant and, once you know how to work it, more practical. Iron ore is much more common than copper and tin. An iron blade can be harder and sharper than bronze.

Iron-working knowledge probably spread to Greece from the Near East or Cyprus around 1050 BCE. By 900 BCE, iron had replaced bronze for most everyday tools and weapons. This democratized access to metal implements. A person no longer needed long-distance trade networks to get the materials for functional tools. This might have contributed to the eventual recovery of Greek society.

Toward the end of the Dark Age, around 900 to 800 BCE, things began to improve. Populations started growing again. Settlements became larger and more prosperous. Pottery grew more sophisticated. Trade connections began to reestablish. The stirrings of recovery were underway.

Songs of Heroes: Homer and the Epic Tradition

Sometime around 750 to 700 BCE, Greek culture produced two poems that would shape Western literature for millennia: the *Iliad* and the *Odyssey*. Attributed to a poet named Homer, these epic poems told stories of heroes, wars, gods, and the human condition with such power that they have never stopped being read.

Whether Homer actually existed as a single person is debated. The poems might have been composed by one brilliant poet, or they might have been the culmination of a

A bust of Homer.[59]

long oral tradition, assembled from songs and stories passed down through generations. Ancient Greeks believed Homer was real. They thought he was a blind bard who sang of the Trojan War and its aftermath. Modern scholars are more cautious. What matters is that these poems appeared, in roughly their current form, during the 8th century BCE.

The *Iliad* doesn't tell the whole story of the Trojan War. It focuses on a few weeks during the tenth and final year of the siege of Troy. The plot centers on the rage of Achilles, the greatest Greek warrior, who withdraws from battle after being dishonored by Agamemnon, the Greek commander. Without Achilles, the Greeks suffer terrible losses. His best friend Patroclus borrows Achilles's armor and enters the battle to save the Greeks, but he is killed by Hector, the greatest Trojan warrior. Achilles, mad with grief and rage, returns to the battle, kills Hector in single combat, and desecrates his body.

The poem ends not with Troy's fall but with Hector's funeral. In a powerful final scene, Hector's father, King Priam, comes alone to Achilles's tent to beg for his son's body. Achilles is reminded of his own father and pities him. He returns Hector's body, and the two enemies share a moment of human connection in the midst of war's brutality.

The *Iliad* is about many things: honor, glory, the cost of rage, and the tragedy of war. It shows heroes who are magnificent, petty, brave, and cruel. It shows gods who are immortal but behave like petulant humans, interfering in mortal affairs for their own amusement. It recognizes war's glory—the *kleos* (glory) that warriors sought—while never flinching from its horror.

The *Odyssey* is a different kind of poem. It's an adventure story following Odysseus's ten-year journey home to Ithaca after the fall of Troy. Odysseus faces monsters and witches, including the Cyclops Polyphemus, the enchantress Circe, the Sirens whose song lures sailors to their deaths, the six-headed monster Scylla, and the whirlpool Charybdis. He visits the underworld and meets the shades of dead heroes. He loses all his men through misfortune and their own foolishness.

Meanwhile, back in Ithaca, his wife Penelope fends off suitors who assume Odysseus is dead and want to marry her and take his kingdom. His son, Telemachus, has grown from boy to man during his father's absence. When Odysseus finally returns, disguised as a beggar, he must prove his identity and reclaim his home by slaughtering the suitors with Telemachus's help.

The *Odyssey* celebrates cleverness over strength. Odysseus is *polytropos* ("of many turns," which means he is versatile and cunning). He survives not by being the best fighter (that was Achilles) but by being smart, adaptable, and relentlessly determined to get home. He lies, he tricks, he endures humiliation—whatever it takes to survive and return to his family.

Together, these poems gave Greeks a shared cultural reference point. Every educated Greek knew Homer's stories. Verses from the epics were quoted constantly. Achilles, Hector, and Odysseus became models of different virtues and warnings of different flaws. The poems raised questions. Is glory worth its cost? What makes a good leader? How should we treat enemies? What does it mean to be civilized?

The poems also preserved memories of the Bronze Age world. Homer describes warriors using bronze weapons and fighting from chariots, which were techniques from the Mycenaean era that were obsolete by his own time. He mentions palaces and kingdoms that had vanished centuries earlier. His geography is sometimes confused, combining real places with legendary ones, which suggests these might be cultural memories filtered through generations of oral retelling.

But Homer's poems did more than preserve the past. They defined Greek values and identity. The heroes were flawed humans, not perfect beings. They struggled with anger, pride, fear, and grief—emotions every Greek (and every human) could recognize. The gods were powerful but unpredictable, helping their favorites and punishing those who offended them. Mortals had to navigate a world where you might do everything right and still suffer because some god decided to make your life difficult.

These poems established the epic tradition in Western literature. Every hero's journey, every quest narrative, every story of war and homecoming echoes Homer. Virgil's *Aeneid*, Dante's *Divine Comedy*, Milton's *Paradise Lost*, and Joyce's *Ulysses* all engage with Homer. The *Iliad* and *Odyssey* set the template.

For the Greeks themselves, Homer was education. Boys memorized long passages. The poems taught Greek virtues, like courage, honor, loyalty, hospitality to strangers (*xenia*), and respect for the gods. They taught the Greek language; Homer's poetic dialect became the literary standard. They taught history and mythology, where the Greeks came from, how their world was ordered, and why things were the way they were.

As Greece emerged from the Dark Age into the Archaic period, Homer's poems provided cultural unity. Greeks across hundreds of independent city-states, speaking different dialects and following different governments, could all claim these heroes as their ancestors, these gods as their pantheon, and these values as their inheritance. The poems helped define what it meant to be Greek.

From these foundations—the Minoan palaces, the Mycenaean fortresses, the survival through dark centuries, and the songs of Homer—classical Greek civilization would arise. The stage was set for the next act: the birth of the polis and the Archaic revolution that would transform Greece forever.

Chapter 3 – The Archaic Revolution: Birth of the City-State

A Community of Citizens: The Birth of the Polis

Around 800 BCE, something new began to emerge from the ruins of the Greek Dark Age. Populations were growing. Trade was returning. And Greeks were creating a new form of political organization that would define their civilization for the next five hundred years: the polis.

The word polis is usually translated as "city-state," but that translation doesn't quite capture what it meant. A polis wasn't just a city with surrounding territory. It was a community of citizens, a political entity where members shared identity, governance, and mutual obligations. The polis was the center of Greek life, loyalty, and identity.

Each polis was typically independent and sovereign. It had its own laws, its own government, its own army, its own coinage, and its own calendar. Athens was a polis. So were Sparta, Thebes, Corinth, Megara, and hundreds of others. Some were large and powerful, controlling substantial territory. Others were tiny, perhaps just a town and a few surrounding villages. But each considered itself an autonomous political community, though in practice some smaller settlements remained subordinate to larger neighbors.

The physical layout of most major poleis followed a similar pattern, though this varied considerably in smaller or earlier settlements. At the center was the acropolis (literally "high city"), a defensible hill that served as a refuge in times of war and as a sacred space for temples. The most famous acropolis is in Athens, crowned by the Parthenon (built in the 5th century BCE, well after the Archaic period), but many poleis had one.

Ruins of the Temple of Apollo in Corinth. The city's acropolis can be seen in the background.[58]

Below the acropolis lay the town itself, and at its heart was the agora, which was the marketplace and public square. The agora was where citizens gathered to buy and sell goods, but it was much more than a market. It was where people met to discuss politics, where orators gave speeches, philosophers taught, and news was shared. The agora was the social and political heart of the polis.

Around the town, farmland stretched out—the chora. Most citizens of a polis were farmers who lived in the surrounding countryside and came to town for festivals, assemblies, and market days.

What made someone a citizen? This varied by polis, but citizenship always meant more than just living somewhere. It was a legal status that brought both rights and responsibilities. Citizens could participate in political assemblies, vote on laws, hold office, and own land. In return, they were expected to fight in the army when called, contribute financially to the state, and participate in religious festivals and civic life.

Citizenship was exclusive. In most poleis, only adult males born to citizen parents could be citizens. Women, foreigners (even those born in the city), and slaves had no political rights. In Athens, citizenship would eventually require that both parents were Athenian citizens. This meant citizenship was hereditary and jealously guarded. A polis wasn't an open community that anyone could join; it was a closed club of citizens who shared common ancestry and identity.

This exclusivity created a strong sense of belonging among citizens. You weren't just living in a polis. You were part of it, invested in it, and responsible for it. The polis belonged to its citizens collectively, and they governed it together through assemblies, councils, and magistrates. The specific form of government varied—some poleis were oligarchies ruled by wealthy elites, others developed democracy, a few retained kings—but the principle remained: citizens governed themselves.

The polis also had religious significance. Each polis had patron gods and goddesses who protected it and received worship at civic festivals. Athens had Athena. Sparta had Artemis and Apollo. Corinth had Aphrodite. These weren't just private religious beliefs. Civic religion was part of what bound citizens together. Participating in religious festivals was a civic duty, and impiety toward the city's gods could be punished.

Why did the polis develop this way? Geography played a role. The mountainous terrain of Greece encouraged small, independent communities rather than large centralized kingdoms. The polis was also a political choice, a way of organizing society that emphasized local control, citizen participation, and communal identity.

The development of the polis marked a significant shift from Bronze Age political structures. The Mycenaean *wanax* and their palace bureaucracies were gone. In their place came communities where citizens, at least those with citizenship status, had a voice in governance. This wasn't democracy yet in most places, but it was a step toward the idea that political power came from the citizen body rather than from hereditary monarchs. That said, important continuities remained, including religious practices, regional identities, and certain elite traditions that connected the polis system to earlier Greek culture.

The emergence of the polis around 800 to 700 BCE set the template for Greek political life. For the next several centuries, the polis would be the fundamental unit of Greek civilization. Greeks didn't think of themselves as subjects of a king or empire; they thought of themselves as citizens of their polis. Your polis was your identity, your loyalty, your home. Greeks would fight and die for their polis. They would also refuse to surrender their independence even when unification might have made them stronger.

This intense local patriotism had consequences. Greece would remain politically fragmented, with hundreds of independent poleis competing and often warring with each other. But this fragmentation also created diversity and experimentation. Different poleis tried different forms of government, different social systems, and different economic strategies. Some succeeded, while some failed. However, the competition and variety generated innovation and energy that propelled Greek culture forward.

The polis wasn't perfect. Its exclusion of women, foreigners, and slaves from citizenship was a huge limitation. Its fierce independence prevented Greek unity and left the poleis vulnerable to external threats. But the polis created communities where citizens participated in their own governance, debated policy, and took collective responsibility for their society. This was the foundation on which classical Greek civilization would be built.

From Kings to Oligarchs: Early Governance

In the early Archaic period, most poleis transitioned away from a monarchy toward rule by aristocratic elites—a system called oligarchy, literally "rule by the few." This transition was gradual and varied by location, but the pattern was common throughout Greece.

The Mycenaean kingdoms had been ruled by *wanax* (kings), who controlled palace economies through extensive bureaucracies. When the Bronze Age collapsed, these centralized kingdoms disappeared. During the Greek Dark Age, local leaders—*basileis* in Greek, often translated as "kings" but really meaning something closer to "chiefs"—held authority in small communities. These *basileis* were primarily war leaders and judges, not absolute monarchs.

As poleis developed, power shifted from individual *basileis* to councils of aristocrats, the *aristoi,* meaning "the best people." These were landholding families who claimed descent from the heroes of old. They owned the best farmland, commanded the most retainers, and formed the social and military elite of the polis's army. Their wealth, military importance, and noble lineage gave them political dominance.

In many poleis, aristocratic councils gradually superseded or eliminated kingship altogether. Athens provides a clear example. According to tradition, Athens had kings in the distant past, but by the 7th century BCE, power had passed to nine annually elected magistrates called archons, all drawn from aristocratic families. These archons handled military, religious, and judicial affairs. After their year in office, they became members of the Areopagus, a council of ex-archons that held a lot of power.

Sparta kept its monarchy, but there was an unusual twist. Two kings from different families ruled at the same time. Their power was limited by a council of elders (the Gerousia) and annually elected magistrates (the ephors). Spartan kingship was hedged with so many restrictions that it was hardly absolute rule.

In other poleis, oligarchies governed through councils restricted to wealthy citizens. In Corinth, the Bacchiad family ruled as an oligarchy for nearly a century, with only family members eligible for office. In Thebes, political power rested with a select group of wealthy landowners.

This oligarchic system created social tensions. The aristocrats held most of the land, most of the wealth, and all the political power. They formed the social and military elite, though in Greek terrain, cavalry forces were limited compared to other regions. Below them were ordinary citizens, like the small farmers, craftsmen, and traders, who had citizenship status and military obligations but limited political voice. Below them were non-citizens and slaves who had no voice at all.

Conflicts arose over several issues. Land ownership was a constant problem. Aristocrats accumulated land while small farmers struggled. When farmers fell into debt, they risked losing their land or even their freedom. In some places, debtors could be enslaved or forced to work as tenant farmers on land they once owned.

Legal disputes also favored the wealthy. In early Archaic Greece, laws were unwritten and administered by aristocratic magistrates who could interpret them however they wished. If you were a poor farmer bringing a case against a wealthy landowner, you had little hope of fair treatment.

Military changes intensified these tensions. In the early Archaic period, aristocratic champions and individual warriors played prominent roles in battles, much as Homeric heroes did. But gradually, a new military formation emerged: the phalanx, made up of heavily armed infantrymen called hoplites.

A hoplite carried a large round shield, a spear, and wore bronze armor. In battle, hoplites fought in tight formation, with their shields overlapping and their spears pointed forward. The phalanx was devastatingly effective. A disciplined formation of hoplites could defeat larger numbers of less organized troops.

A hoplite, c. 500 BCE.[54]

Hoplites weren't exclusively aristocrats. They were citizens wealthy enough to afford armor, which included prosperous farmers, successful craftsmen, and traders. These men now formed the backbone of many poleis' military power. They fought in the phalanx, risked their lives defending the polis, and, some historians argue, increasingly demanded political rights equal to their military importance. However, the direct connection between hoplite warfare and political reform remains debated among scholars. The relationship was likely more complex and varied across different poleis than a simple cause-and-effect.

This created pressure on the oligarchic system. If you're expected to fight and die for the polis, shouldn't you have a say in how it's governed? If the polis depends on hoplites for defense, shouldn't hoplites have political representation?

Different poleis responded differently to these pressures. Some oligarchies resisted change and maintained exclusive rule. Others gradually expanded political participation, allowing more citizens into assemblies and magistracies. Still others experienced violent upheaval as tensions boiled over into conflict.

One response to these social tensions was the written law code. Putting laws in writing and displaying them publicly limited aristocratic judges' ability to manipulate the legal system. Everyone could see what the law said. This didn't create equality, as the rich still had advantages, but it was a step toward transparency and accountability.

These tensions also sometimes led to reform, as in Athens, where leaders like Solon would attempt to address grievances through legislation. Sometimes they would lead to tyranny, as ambitious individuals seized power by championing popular causes against the oligarchs. And sometimes they would lead to revolution, as citizens overthrew exclusive oligarchies and established broader participation.

The transition from kingship to oligarchy wasn't the end of Greece's political evolution; it was just one step in a longer journey toward various forms of citizen governance.

Hungry for Land: The Age of Colonization

Between roughly 750 and 550 BCE, Greeks spread across the Mediterranean and Black Sea in one of the most dramatic expansions in ancient history. They founded hundreds of new colonies from Spain to the coast of modern Ukraine and from southern France to North Africa. This Greek colonization movement transformed the Mediterranean world and spread Greek culture far beyond the Greek homeland.

Why did the Greeks leave home? The motivations were diverse and complex. Population pressure was one significant factor. During the Greek Dark Age, populations had declined dramatically. But by the 8th century BCE, recovery was underway. Populations grew, and Greece's rocky soil couldn't support everyone. Farmland was limited, and the best land was already owned by aristocratic families. Younger sons with no prospect of inheriting land faced grim choices: scrape by as landless laborers or seek opportunities elsewhere.

But the need for farmable land wasn't the only motivation. Political conflict drove many emigrants. When rival factions fought for control of a polis, the losers often left rather than face persecution. Exiles needed somewhere to go. Colonization offered a solution.

Trade opportunities attracted others. As long-distance commerce recovered, merchants identified promising locations for trading posts—places where Greek goods could be exchanged for grain, metals, slaves, and other commodities. Colonies could serve as permanent trading stations, facilitating commerce and generating wealth. Some individuals sought adventure or escape from debt or legal troubles.

Some colonies were founded by official expeditions organized by a mother city (*metropolis* in Greek). The mother city would appoint a founder (*oikist*) to lead colonists to a predetermined location. The colonists would establish a new polis, complete with an agora, temples, and farmland divided among settlers. While new colonies were generally politically independent (*apoikia*), they typically maintained religious and sentimental ties with their mother cities. Some retained closer economic or political connections than others.

Other colonies developed more informally, as traders established settlements that gradually grew into permanent communities. Pirates and adventurers also founded settlements in promising locations. The colonization process differed greatly, reflecting the disunited nature of the Greek world.

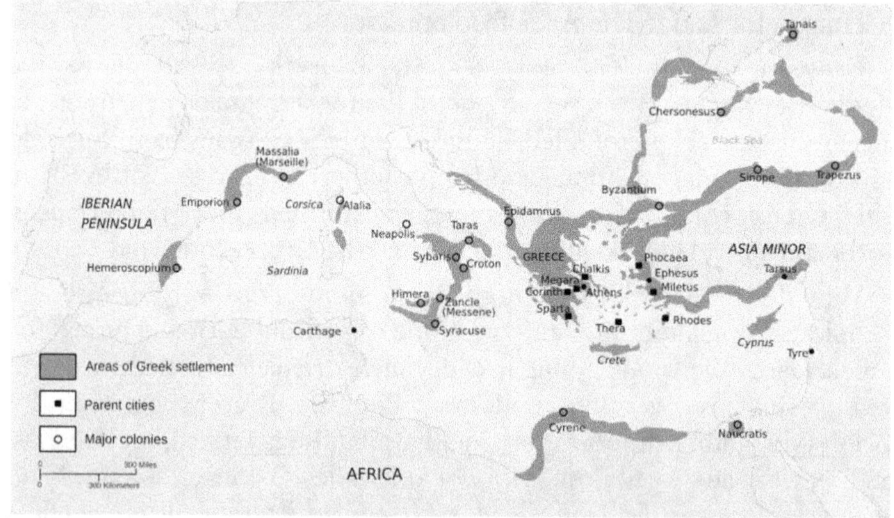

Greek colonies in the Archaic period.[55]

Greek colonies spread in all directions. To the west, Greeks colonized southern Italy and Sicily in such numbers that the region became known as Magna Graecia ("Greater Greece"). Cities like Syracuse, Tarentum, and Neapolis (modern Naples) were founded during this period. Syracuse, founded by the Corinthians around 733 BCE, would become one of the most powerful Greek cities anywhere.

Farther west, Greeks reached southern France, founding Massalia (modern Marseille) around 600 BCE. They even established colonies on the eastern coast of Spain. Greeks were settling the western Mediterranean, competing and trading with Phoenicians who were doing the same from the opposite direction.

To the north and northeast, Greeks colonized the coast of Thrace and the shores of the Black Sea. Cities like Byzantium (later Constantinople, now Istanbul) controlled strategic locations on trade routes. Black Sea colonies could access the grain-rich regions of what is now Ukraine and southern Russia, importing vast quantities of wheat back to Greece.

To the south, Greeks established colonies in North Africa. Cyrene, founded around 630 BCE in what is now Libya, became wealthy from agriculture and the export of silphium, a valuable medicinal plant. Egypt, while not colonized by the Greeks, saw Greek traders establish a permanent trading post at Naucratis in the Nile Delta.

These colonies transformed Greek civilization. They helped ease land pressures by providing farmland for landless Greeks. They generated wealth through trade, accessing resources unavailable in Greece itself, like grain from the Black Sea, timber from Thrace, metals from Spain and Italy, and slaves from various regions.

Colonization spread the Greek language, religion, and culture across the Mediterranean. Even as poleis remained politically independent, a broader Greek cultural world emerged. A merchant from Athens could travel to Syracuse in Sicily or Olbia on the Black Sea and find familiar temples, gods, language, and customs. The Greek world became much larger than Greece itself.

Contact with other cultures influenced Greece's development. In Italy, Greeks encountered Etruscans and Romans. In the eastern Mediterranean, they traded with Phoenicians, Egyptians, and various Near Eastern peoples. These interactions brought new ideas, artistic styles, technologies, and goods into Greek culture. The alphabet that the

Greeks adopted from the Phoenicians enabled the return of literacy. Artistic motifs from Egypt and the Near East influenced Greek art. Military tactics learned from various peoples improved Greek warfare.

Colonization also intensified competition among Greek poleis. Mother cities competed to establish colonies in strategic locations. Colonies competed with each other for territory and trade advantages. This competition drove innovation and ambition, but it also created conflicts. Wars between Greek colonies or between colonies and native populations were common.

The native peoples Greeks encountered had varied experiences with Greek colonization. Sometimes, Greeks established colonies in sparsely populated areas with minimal conflict. Sometimes, they displaced existing populations through force. Often, they engaged in trade and cultural exchange with neighboring peoples, sometimes leading to intermarriage and cultural blending. The Greeks generally considered non-Greeks (*barbaroi*) inferior, but practical considerations often led to cooperation and coexistence.

By 550 BCE, the age of widespread colonization was winding down. The most desirable locations had been settled. Existing colonies consolidated their territories rather than found new settlements. However, the impact was permanent. The Mediterranean had become, in significant ways, a Greek sea, though Phoenicians (and their Carthaginian colonies), Etruscans, and other peoples continued to control substantial regions. Greek culture, trade, and political models influenced areas far from mainland Greece.

The age of colonization was one of the most consequential developments in Greek history. It eased social pressures in mainland Greece, generated wealth through expanded trade, spread Greek culture far and wide, and created a huge network of independent Greek cities connected by language, religion, and culture despite political fragmentation.

The Rise of the Strongman: Tyranny

As social tensions increased in many poleis during the 7th and 6th centuries BCE, a new political phenomenon emerged: the tyrant. In Greek, a *tyrannos* was someone who seized power outside the traditional constitutional framework. This person was not necessarily cruel or oppressive (though some certainly were), but he was a person who ruled without legal authority, often by popular support and military force.

The Greek concept of tyranny is important to understand because it differs from the modern meaning. Today, "tyrant" means a brutal dictator. In ancient Greece, it simply meant someone who took power unconstitutionally. Many Greek tyrants were popular reformers who improved their cities. Others were oppressive. The term described how they gained power, not necessarily how they used it.

Tyrants typically emerged from the aristocracy but positioned themselves as champions of ordinary citizens against the oligarchic establishment. The pattern was common. An ambitious aristocrat would recognize popular grievances, such as land distribution, debt burdens, or exclusion from political power, and use these issues to build support. With backing from discontented citizens and perhaps a personal armed force, he would seize control of the polis, overthrowing or sidelining the oligarchic government.

Once in power, tyrants often enacted popular reforms. They redistributed land seized from political enemies, providing farms to landless citizens. They reduced or canceled debts, easing burdens on poor farmers. They sponsored public works projects, such as temples, fortifications, and water systems, creating employment and enhancing the city's prestige. They promoted trade and manufacturing, which benefited merchants and craftsmen. These policies made tyrants popular with ordinary citizens even as they enraged the dispossessed aristocrats.

Tyranny appeared across the Greek world, but it was particularly common in wealthy commercial poleis. Corinth provides a classic example. Around 657 BCE, Cypselus overthrew the Bacchiad oligarchy that had ruled Corinth for decades. The Bacchiads were an aristocratic clan that monopolized power and wealth. Cypselus, who came from a Bacchiad family himself, positioned himself as a champion of excluded citizens. After seizing power, he ruled for about thirty years and was followed by his son, Periander, who ruled for another forty years. Under the Cypselid tyranny, Corinth became one of Greece's most prosperous and powerful cities, dominating trade and founding colonies.

Sicyon, Megara, Athens, Miletus, and many other poleis experienced tyranny during the Archaic period. Some tyrannies lasted decades, while others collapsed quickly. But the phenomenon was widespread enough to be recognized as a distinct stage in Greek political development. It was a transitional stage between an exclusive oligarchy and broader forms of government.

Tyrants maintained power through various means. Popular support was crucial. As long as the majority of citizens benefited from the tyrant's rule, they would tolerate or support his unconstitutional position. Military force mattered too. Tyrants often maintained bodyguards and controlled the city's armed forces. Building projects and festivals kept people employed and entertained. Alliances with other tyrants or foreign powers provided external support.

However, tyranny had weaknesses. It depended on the individual tyrant's ability and popularity. A capable, popular tyrant could rule successfully for decades, but his sons often lacked his qualities. The second or third generation of a tyrannical dynasty typically proved less competent, more oppressive, or simply less necessary. Once the original grievances that brought the tyrant to power were addressed, citizens questioned why they should tolerate unconstitutional rule.

Opposition came from multiple directions. Dispossessed aristocrats schemed constantly to regain power, sometimes calling on Sparta, which opposed tyranny in principle, for help. Citizens who initially supported the tyrant might turn against him if his rule became oppressive or if his reforms succeeded so well that his continued rule seemed unnecessary. Rival ambitious men might attempt their own coups.

Most tyrannies eventually fell. Some were overthrown by aristocratic factions, others by popular uprisings, and still others by foreign intervention. In Athens, the Peisistratid tyranny (which we'll examine in detail in the next chapter) was overthrown in 510 BCE with Spartan help. In Corinth, the Cypselids were eventually expelled.

What did tyranny accomplish? In the short term, tyrants addressed social tensions that oligarchies couldn't or wouldn't resolve. They broke the stranglehold of exclusive aristocratic rule. They demonstrated that power didn't have to reside solely in hereditary noble families. They also promoted economic development and civic pride through building projects and support for trade.

In the longer term, tyranny helped pave the way for democracy in some poleis. By weakening aristocratic power and demonstrating that non-aristocrats could govern effectively, tyrants showed that political participation could be broadened. Once tyranny ended, some poleis—most famously Athens—established democratic systems that gave political rights to broad classes of citizens. Other poleis returned to an oligarchy or mixed constitutions, but even these were usually less exclusively aristocratic than before.

The age of tyranny was largely over by the end of the 6th century BCE. Later Greek political thought would view tyranny negatively, as an illegitimate seizure of power that destroyed constitutional government. But in the Archaic period, tyranny disrupted rigid oligarchies and allowed for political innovation and social reform that might not have occurred otherwise.

Finding the Voice: The Invention of the Alphabet

One of the most important developments of the Archaic period occurred around 800 to 750 BCE. Greeks adopted and adapted an alphabetic writing system from the Phoenicians. This return of literacy after four centuries would transform Greek civilization, enabling everything from written law codes to philosophy to the recording of epic poetry.

The Mycenaeans had been literate, using Linear B to record palace administration. But when the Bronze Age collapsed around 1200 BCE, writing disappeared. For four hundred years, Greece was illiterate. Knowledge, stories, and traditions were preserved orally, passed down through memory and performance. This worked well enough, but oral culture has limitations. Complex information is difficult to preserve accurately across generations. Administrative organization requiring detailed record-keeping becomes nearly impossible.

The return of writing changed everything. Greeks adapted the alphabetic writing system from the Phoenicians, seafaring traders from the Levantine coast (modern Lebanon) who had developed an efficient consonantal script. The Phoenician alphabet used about twenty-two symbols, each representing a consonant sound. It was simpler and more flexible than earlier writing systems, like Egyptian hieroglyphics or Mesopotamian cuneiform, which used hundreds of symbols.

Greeks made a crucial innovation, though. They added vowel symbols to the Phoenician alphabet. Phoenician writing represented only consonants, so readers had to infer vowel sounds from context. This worked for Phoenician (a Semitic language) but was problematic for Greek (an Indo-European language with a different linguistic structure). Greeks took several Phoenician consonant symbols that represented sounds Greek didn't use and converted them to vowels: alpha, epsilon, iota, omicron, and upsilon.

This adaptation created what we might call the first fully phonetic alphabet, a writing system in which symbols explicitly represent both consonant and vowel sounds. Anyone who learned this alphabet could, in theory, write anything in their language phonetically. This was more accessible and versatile than earlier writing systems. You didn't need years of scribal training to become literate. The Greek alphabet could be learned relatively quickly and used by anyone, not just professional scribes.

The alphabet spread rapidly across the Greek world, though different regions developed variant forms. Eventually, the Ionian version (used in Athens and much of eastern Greece) became standard. The Greek alphabet would later be adapted by the Romans into the Latin alphabet, which is still used across the Western world today. Greek letters are still used in mathematics and science (alpha, beta, gamma, delta, and so on).

Why did literacy matter so much? Written records allowed for new forms of social organization. Laws could be written down and publicly displayed, limiting interpretation by powerful judges. Contracts and commercial agreements could be recorded, helping trade. Government decisions could be documented, creating accountability and transparency.

Writing enabled new forms of cultural expression. Epic poetry could be recorded, preserving works like the *Iliad* and *Odyssey* that might otherwise have been lost or significantly altered over time. Lyric poetry flourished as poets like Sappho and Archilochus composed personal, emotional verses. Historical events could be documented, eventually leading to the birth of history as a discipline with Herodotus and Thucydides.

Philosophy emerged in the 6th and 5th centuries BCE partly because writing allowed complex arguments to be preserved and analyzed. Pre-Socratic philosophers like Thales, Anaximander, and Heraclitus could write down their theories about the nature of reality, allowing others to read, debate, and refine these ideas. Without writing, philosophy as a systematic discipline would have been far more difficult.

Political thought benefited from literacy. Written constitutions and law codes like those attributed to Lycurgus in Sparta or Solon in Athens established legal frameworks that could be referenced and debated. Political proposals could be drafted, circulated, and polished before being presented to assemblies. The later development of democracy in Athens would have been far more difficult without literacy to support its increasingly complex administration.

Science and mathematics advanced with written records. Observations could be documented and compared across time. Mathematical concepts could be worked out in writing and preserved for future study. The geometric proofs developed by later Greek mathematicians depended entirely on written notation.

Literacy was necessary for these developments, but it was not the sole cause. Political, economic, and cultural factors all contributed to the intellectual flowering of Classical Greece.

The rise of literacy also changed education. In oral cultures, education meant memorization and performance under the guidance of elders who held traditional knowledge. With writing, education could include reading texts, studying written works, and engaging with ideas from elsewhere. Libraries could preserve accumulated knowledge. Schools could use written texts to teach standardized curricula.

Not everyone became literate, of course. Literacy rates in ancient Greece are estimated by some scholars at perhaps 10 to 15 percent of the population at most, though precise figures are difficult to determine and likely varied considerably by time and place. Literacy was concentrated primarily among urban elites—the aristocrats, merchants, and scribes—while rural populations remained largely oral in their culture. Most Greeks remained illiterate throughout antiquity. However, even limited literacy transformed society. Literate individuals could read public inscriptions of laws and decrees. Professional scribes could write letters and contracts for illiterate clients. Written texts could be read aloud, making their content accessible to non-readers.

The Greeks recognized writing's importance. They attributed the alphabet's invention to the legendary Phoenician prince Cadmus, acknowledging their debt to Phoenician traders. They understood that writing was a tool that humans created and adapted for their own purposes. This awareness of writing as technology rather than a divine gift reflects the rational, pragmatic approach that would characterize much of Greek thought.

The adoption of the alphabet was one of those technological changes that enabled everything else. Without writing, there would have been no written law codes to limit aristocratic power, no preserved philosophy, no recorded history, no dramatic texts, and no geometry textbooks. Much of what we consider "classical Greek civilization" depended on literacy.

Chapter 4 – The Two Pillars: Athens and Sparta

The Iron Discipline: Spartan Life and Military System

If you had to pick two Greek city-states that represented opposite approaches to nearly everything, you'd pick Athens and Sparta. Athens would become famous for democracy, philosophy, art, and debate. Sparta became famous for one thing: war. Spartan society was dominated by military concerns to an extraordinary degree. Training, discipline, and combat readiness shaped nearly every aspect of citizen life. However, the Spartans weren't machines. They had religious festivals, social customs, and family bonds. Still, no Greek city came close to Sparta's single-minded focus on military excellence.

Sparta was located in the southern Peloponnese in a fertile valley called Lacedaemon (which is why Spartans were sometimes called Lacedaemonians). The city itself had no walls. This wasn't an oversight. Spartans believed their army was their wall. And they were right.

To understand Sparta, you need to understand how it came to be this way. Around 700 BCE, Spartans faced a problem: they needed more land. Their solution was to conquer their neighbors. They invaded Messenia, the region to their west, and after a brutal war, which lasted decades, they succeeded. However, instead of just taking the land and moving on, Spartans turned the conquered Messenians into helots—state-owned agricultural slaves bound to the land.

This created a new problem. Ancient sources claimed the helots outnumbered Spartans by at least seven to one, possibly more, though this figure might reflect Spartan fears more than an actual census; modern scholars debate the true ratio. What's certain is that helots vastly outnumbered Spartan citizens. The Spartans were sitting on top of a massive enslaved population that, understandably, hated them. The helots revolted in the 7th century BCE, and it took Sparta decades to crush the rebellion. This experience transformed Spartan society.

The Spartans realized that to maintain control over the helots, every Spartan male had to be a soldier, ready to suppress revolts at any moment. They couldn't afford weakness, and they couldn't afford distractions. They also couldn't afford to let citizens pursue their own interests. Sparta became a military society dedicated entirely to one purpose: staying strong enough to keep the helots enslaved.

Spartan boys were taken from their families at age seven and entered the *agoge*, the brutal state education and training system. From seven to eighteen, boys lived in barracks, trained constantly, and endured hardships designed to toughen them. According to various sources, they were deliberately underfed so they'd learn to steal food without getting caught. Getting caught meant punishment, not for stealing but for being clumsy enough to get caught. They slept on thin reed mats. They trained in combat, athletics, and endurance. They learned to endure pain without complaint.

Many stories about the agoge come from later sources, so they might be exaggerated or legendary, but the core truth is real. Spartan education was harsh. One famous story tells of a Spartan boy who stole a fox and hid it under his cloak. When questioned by his instructors, the fox began biting and clawing at the boy's stomach. The boy said nothing. He didn't move, letting the fox tear into him rather than admit he'd been caught. According to the story, he died from his wounds without making a sound. Whether this actually happened is questionable, but that Spartans told this story and admired the boy's behavior tells us what they valued.

At age twenty, if a young man passed his final tests, he became a full Spartan citizen-soldier. In theory, he remained a soldier ready for duty until age sixty. However, he still didn't live at home. Spartan men lived communally, eating together in mess groups called *syssitia*. Every night, Spartan citizens gathered with their mess groups to eat the same simple food, most famously a black broth made from boiled pork, vinegar, and salt that other Greeks found disgusting. One foreign visitor supposedly tasted it and said, "Now I understand why Spartans don't fear death."

Marriage existed in Sparta, but it was unlike marriage elsewhere in Greece. A Spartan man could marry, but he continued living in the barracks until age thirty. He would visit his wife secretly at night and return to the barracks before dawn. Only at thirty could a Spartan man finally live in his own household, though he still spent most of his time with his military unit and ate dinner with his mess group.

Why this extreme system? Because the Spartans believed that personal comfort and family ties made men soft. They wanted soldiers who were loyal to Sparta first, to their unit second, and to their family a distant third. They wanted men who would never break in battle because they had been trained since childhood to endure anything.

And it worked. Spartan hoplites were the finest infantry in Greece. In the phalanx formation, where discipline and cohesion mattered more than individual heroics, Spartans were unmatched. They drilled constantly, practicing maneuvers that other Greek armies attempted rarely, if at all. In battle, Spartan phalanxes didn't break. They didn't panic or run. Other Greeks feared facing Spartans on the battlefield because Spartans very rarely lost—at least, that was their fearsome reputation during the Archaic and early Classical periods.

Later sources describe Spartans fighting in perfect silence except for the sound of flutes keeping rhythm for their march. While other Greek armies charged into battle shouting and yelling, Spartans supposedly advanced slowly and steadily in complete formation, their long spears leveled, their shields locked, flutes playing. Whether this specific practice is historical or a literary trope that grew over time, the image captures how other Greeks saw Spartans: disciplined, professional, and terrifying.

Spartan society didn't just control men. It controlled women too, though in unexpected ways. Spartan women had more freedom and rights than women in most other Greek cities, though the extent of their independence is debated among historians and likely varied over time. They couldn't vote or hold office, but they could own property, manage estates, and speak more openly than their Athenian counterparts.

Why? Because Spartan men were always away training or fighting. Someone had to manage the estates, supervise the helots who worked the land, and handle business. That someone was Spartan women. They received physical education. This wasn't military training but rather athletics to make them strong and healthy for childbearing. Women were expected to produce strong sons for Sparta's army.

They were educated as well. Spartan women had a reputation for being outspoken and sharp-tongued. Plutarch recorded several sayings attributed to Spartan mothers. One, handing her son his shield as he left for war, supposedly told him, "Come back with this, or on it." In other words, she wanted him to return victorious or die in battle and be carried home on his shield. Don't come back defeated. This might be a legend, but it captures how Spartans thought about military honor.

The helots made this entire system possible. They worked the land, produced the food, and allowed Spartan citizens to spend all their time training. Without helots, Sparta couldn't function. But the helots were also Sparta's greatest vulnerability. If the helots ever successfully revolted, Spartan power would collapse.

Spartans dealt with this danger through various means of social control. According to some ancient sources, the Spartan state formally declared war on the helots each year. This wasn't an actual war; it was a legal fiction that allegedly allowed young Spartans in an elite unit called the *Krypteia* to hunt and kill any helot they deemed dangerous without legal consequences. Ancient sources describe the Krypteia going into the countryside at night to murder helots, particularly strong or intelligent ones who might lead a revolt. However, our sources on the Krypteia are fragmentary and contradictory, and modern historians debate the extent and nature of this institution. What's clear is that Sparta used terror and violence as tools to keep the helot population subjugated.

Sparta also had another class called *perioikoi*—"those who live around." These were free people living in towns around Sparta who weren't full Spartan citizens. They couldn't participate in Spartan political life, but they weren't enslaved. They worked as craftsmen, traders, and merchants, which were occupations that Spartan citizens considered beneath them. Perioikoi also fought in Sparta's army, though not in the elite front ranks, which were reserved for full citizens.

The Spartan government was complex and unusual. They kept two kings from two different royal families, and both ruled simultaneously. These kings led the army in war but had limited power at home. The real political power rested with five ephors—magistrates elected annually by the citizen assembly. The ephors could prosecute kings, conduct foreign policy, and run daily affairs. There was also the Gerousia, a council of twenty-eight elders over the age of sixty plus the two kings. The Gerousia proposed laws and served as a supreme court.

Spartans believed their system had been established by a legendary lawgiver named Lycurgus. According to tradition, Lycurgus went to the Oracle of Delphi, where he received divine approval for his laws. He made the Spartans swear they wouldn't change anything until he returned. Then he went into exile and never came back, binding Spartans to his system forever. This story is probably fiction, but Spartans believed it, which meant they considered their system divinely ordained and unchangeable.

This resistance to change became Sparta's fatal flaw. The system worked brilliantly for producing soldiers, but it was rigid and couldn't adapt. The Spartan population slowly declined, probably because so many died in warfare and because Spartan citizenship requirements were strict. By the Classical period, there were only a few thousand full Spartan citizens, though they ruled tens of thousands of helots and perioikoi.

However, in the Archaic and early Classical periods, Sparta was the dominant military power in Greece. Other city-states feared and respected the Spartans. When the Persian Empire threatened Greece, everyone looked to Sparta to lead the defense. Spartan soldiers at Thermopylae would become legendary. Spartan warriors at Plataea would help save Greece.

The price of this power was enormous. Spartans gave up art, philosophy, commerce, literature, and individual ambition. They lived under constant discipline, in fear of helot revolt, maintaining a system that required every generation to be as tough as the last. They created a society that was stable, powerful, and utterly foreign to how most Greeks lived.

Athens, as we're about to see, chose a different path entirely.

The Long Road to Self-Rule: Early Athenian Reform

While Sparta was building its military machine, Athens was stumbling toward something unprecedented: a political system where common citizens had real power. But Athens didn't start with democracy. It started with kings, moved to aristocratic oligarchy, experienced tyranny, and only then—through a series of reforms driven by crisis—eventually created democracy.

Athens occupied Attica, a large triangular peninsula in central Greece. Unlike many Greek regions, Attica had been unified under Athenian control early on, giving Athens a larger territory and population than most poleis. This would matter later, as more citizens meant more soldiers, more farmers, and eventually, more political participants.

According to tradition, Athens once had kings, but by the 7th century BCE, power had passed to aristocratic families who ruled through magistrates called archons. Nine archons were elected annually from aristocratic families. After serving, they joined the Areopagus, a council of ex-archons that held significant power. This was an oligarchy, or rule by wealthy landowners who made the laws, judged legal cases, and controlled policy.

For ordinary Athenians (small farmers, craftsmen, and traders), this system was increasingly oppressive. Land ownership was concentrated in fewer hands as wealthy families accumulated property. Poor farmers fell into debt, and Athenian law allowed creditors to enslave debtors who couldn't pay. Families lost their land and their freedom. Social tensions built toward a breaking point.

The first major reformer was Draco around 621 BCE. We know almost nothing about Draco himself, but we know he did something important. He wrote down Athens's laws and displayed them publicly. Before Draco, laws were unwritten and interpreted by aristocratic judges who could twist them however they wished. Even though most Athenians couldn't read them, written laws meant the laws themselves were fixed and couldn't be changed at a judge's whim. This limited manipulation of the justice system.

However, Draco's laws were notoriously harsh. The penalties for almost every offense, from murder to stealing a cabbage, were the same: death. Later Greeks joked that Draco's laws were written in blood, not ink. The word "draconian" still means an excessively severe law, derived from Draco's name. His harsh penalties didn't solve Athens's problems, as debt, land inequality, and social conflict remained.

By 594 BCE, Athens was on the verge of civil war. Rich and poor were ready to fight. The aristocrats needed someone both sides could trust to reform the system before violence erupted. They turned to Solon, an aristocrat who was also a respected poet and wise man. Both sides agreed to give Solon extraordinary powers to reform Athens's laws and constitution. What he did was remarkable.

A bust of Solon.[56]

Solon's first act was to cancel all debts secured by one's freedom. Athenian citizens who had been enslaved for debt were freed. Those who had been sold abroad as slaves were brought back at public expense. The practice of enslaving citizens for debt was abolished. This was the *seisachtheia*—the "shaking off of burdens." For ordinary Athenians drowning in debt, this was liberation.

But Solon didn't redistribute land, which disappointed the poor who wanted the aristocratic estates divided up. Solon believed in moderate reform, not revolution. He wanted to ease tensions without destroying the property rights that gave society stability. The rich weren't thrilled either. They'd lost some of their slaves and couldn't enslave debtors anymore. Solon later wrote that he'd given the people "as much power as they needed, nothing more," and that both rich and poor were unhappy with him, which meant he'd probably found the right balance.

Solon reorganized Athenian society into four classes based on wealth measured in agricultural production. The highest class, the *pentakosiomedimnoi* (those producing five hundred measures of grain or equivalent), could hold the highest offices, including archon. The second class, *hippeis* (cavalry, which referred to men who were wealthy enough to maintain a horse), could hold most offices. The third class, *zeugitai* (those who could afford hoplite armor), could hold minor offices. The fourth class, the *thetes* (wage laborers and the poor), couldn't hold office but could participate in the Assembly and law courts.

This system was still based on wealth, not birth. An aristocrat who lost his fortune dropped in class. A successful merchant or farmer who became wealthy could rise. It wasn't a democracy since the poor still couldn't hold office, but it was more open than a pure oligarchy based on noble bloodlines.

Solon also reformed Athens's government structure. He created a new council, the Boule of 400, with one hundred members from each of Athens's four traditional tribes. This council prepared business for the Assembly. He empowered the Assembly of all citizens to vote on laws and major decisions, though the aristocratic Areopagus still held significant power. He reformed the courts, allowing any citizen to bring prosecutions, not just victims or their families. This meant citizens could hold officials accountable.

Solon wrote new laws to replace most of Draco's harsh code, though he kept Draco's homicide laws. He encouraged trade and craft production, inviting foreign craftsmen to settle in Athens and even granting citizenship to whole families who moved to Athens to practice trades. He standardized weights and measures and promoted olive cultivation; Athens would become famous for exporting olive oil.

After completing his reforms, Solon left Athens for ten years. He'd made the Athenians swear they wouldn't change his laws while he was gone. This was shrewd since it forced the Athenians to live with the new system long enough to see if it worked rather than immediately undoing what they disliked.

Solon's reforms didn't solve everything. Tensions between the rich and poor remained. Different aristocratic factions competed for power. However, Solon had accomplished something important: he'd shown that reform was possible, that Athens's system could change without bloody civil war, and that ordinary citizens could have some voice in their own governance.

After Solon, Athens experienced a period of instability. Factions led by different aristocrats struggled for dominance. Eventually, around 561 BCE, one aristocrat named Pisistratus seized power and made himself tyrant. Remember, "tyrant" didn't necessarily mean brutal dictator; it meant someone who took power unconstitutionally. Pisistratus was actually quite popular.

Pisistratus promoted himself as a champion of the common people against the aristocracy. He was overthrown twice and came back twice, finally securing power around 546 BCE and ruling until his death in 527 BCE. During his rule, he redistributed some land from his aristocratic enemies to landless citizens. He provided loans to small farmers and promoted religious festivals, particularly the Panathenaea and the City Dionysia, which became major Athenian celebrations. Pisistratus commissioned building projects that employed workers and beautified Athens. He supported arts and culture; it's possible that the first written versions of Homer's epics were produced under his patronage.

Pisistratus didn't dismantle Solon's constitution, but he made sure his supporters held the offices. The Assembly still met, and the courts still functioned. However, real power rested with Pisistratus and his armed supporters. For ordinary Athenians, this was probably fine. Pisistratus was competent, relatively benign, and his policies benefited them.

Pisistratus's sons succeeded him. The older son, Hippias, ruled capably at first, but the younger son, Hipparchus, was murdered in 514 BCE by two men, Harmodius and Aristogeiton, in a personal vendetta over a love affair. Athenians later mythologized Harmodius and Aristogeiton as tyrannicides, though. They were seen as heroes who struck a blow for freedom. Statues of them were erected in the agora, and they became symbols of resistance to tyranny.

After Hipparchus's death, Hippias became paranoid and oppressive. His rule grew harsh. Aristocratic families schemed against him. One faction, the Alcmaeonids, was in exile and wanted back into Athens. They enlisted help from Sparta, which opposed tyranny, even though

Sparta itself was hardly free. In 510 BCE, a Spartan army invaded Attica, besieged the tyrants on the Acropolis, and forced Hippias into exile.

The Peisistratid tyranny was over. Athens was free from tyranny. But what would replace it? Different aristocratic factions competed to dominate the new government. One faction, led by Isagoras, represented the traditional aristocracy. The other, led by Cleisthenes of the Alcmaeonid family, took a different approach. Cleisthenes positioned himself as a reformer and won the support of the common people by proposing radical changes that would give them real political power.

What Cleisthenes did next would transform Athens forever.

Inventing Democracy: Cleisthenes and the Citizen Body

In 508 BCE, Cleisthenes did something revolutionary. Facing opposition from aristocratic rivals, he took his case to the *demos*—the common people—and promised them a share of political power if they supported him. They did, and Cleisthenes delivered. What he created wasn't just a reform of the Athenian government. It was a fundamentally new system: *demokratia*, rule by the demos.

The word "democracy" literally means "power of the people." However, what Cleisthenes created was more specific. It was a direct democracy in which citizens participated personally in making laws and decisions, not a representative democracy in which citizens elect others to govern for them. Every male citizen had the right—and the responsibility—to participate directly in governing Athens.

Cleisthenes's reforms were brilliant in their design. His goal was to break the power of traditional aristocratic families and redistribute political influence more broadly. He did this by completely reorganizing how Athens was structured.

Previously, Athens was divided into four traditional tribes based on kinship ties and controlled by aristocratic families. Cleisthenes reorganized the political role of these tribes and created ten new tribes by artificial means. Each new tribe was made up of *demes* (local districts or villages) from three different regions of Attica: the city, the coast, and the inland. These demes were distributed so that each tribe contained a mix of citizens from different regions and different social backgrounds.

This was genius. The new tribes had no historical basis and no traditional aristocratic leadership. Citizens' primary political identity shifted from their family to their tribe and deme. Aristocrats still existed and still had influence, but they could no longer automatically control blocs of voters based on kinship networks. Political competition opened up as a result.

Each tribe contributed fifty men to a new council, the Boule of 500 (which replaced Solon's Boule of 400). The Boule prepared business for the Assembly, managed daily administration, oversaw finances, and handled foreign relations. Members were selected by lot from citizens over thirty, and they served one-year terms. Any citizen could serve, though no one could serve more than twice in a lifetime. Selection by lottery meant every citizen had an equal chance of serving. This rotated political experience throughout the citizen body rather than concentrating it in a small elite.

The Assembly—the Ekklesia—became the supreme governing body of Athens. Any male citizen over eighteen could attend, speak, and vote. The Assembly met on the Pnyx, a hill west of the Acropolis, about forty times a year. Thousands of citizens would gather to debate laws, declare war, approve treaties, vote on taxes, decide whether to ostracize someone, and handle virtually every major decision Athens made.

This was direct democracy in action. When Athens decided to go to war, the decision was made by citizens who would do the fighting. When Athens passed a law, the citizens who would live under that law voted on it. When Athens approved a budget, citizens who would pay taxes or benefit from public spending made the choice.

The courts also became more democratic. Large juries of citizens, sometimes hundreds of people, heard cases. Jurors were selected by lot from volunteers. Both the prosecution and defense were presented by the parties themselves, not by professional lawyers. The jury voted by secret ballot, and the majority ruled. This meant that legal cases were decided by masses of ordinary citizens, not by aristocratic judges.

Cleisthenes introduced one more innovation: ostracism. Once a year, the Assembly could vote to exile any citizen for ten years without trial and without confiscating his property. Citizens wrote a name on a broken piece of pottery—an *ostrakon*—and the person with the most votes (if at least six thousand votes were cast) was exiled. This was meant as a safety valve to remove potential tyrants or politicians who were becoming too powerful, preventing civil war by peacefully removing troublemakers.

Did Cleisthenes's system constitute democracy as we'd recognize it? Yes and no. It was democracy for those who counted as citizens, but that was a minority of Athens's population. Women couldn't participate.

Slaves couldn't participate. Metics (foreign residents) couldn't participate, even if they'd lived in Athens for generations. Only free adult males born to Athenian citizen parents could participate.

Even among citizens, participation wasn't equal. Wealthy citizens had more time to engage in politics because they didn't need to work constantly to survive. They could speak more persuasively because they were better educated. In practice, aristocrats and wealthy citizens still dominated Athenian politics, but they dominated through persuasion and election, not by birthright. Any citizen could challenge them, propose laws, or speak in the Assembly.

The system also had problems. Direct democracy can be chaotic. Popular speakers could sway the Assembly with emotional appeals. The poor majority could vote to seize wealth from the rich. Decisions made in the heat of the moment could prove disastrous. Athens would eventually make some terrible choices through democratic vote, which we'll see during the Peloponnesian War.

But the system also had strengths. It gave ordinary citizens real investment in their polis. Citizens served in government, fought in the military, and participated in courts. They weren't passive subjects; they were active participants. This created loyalty and engagement that Athens's enemies couldn't match. When Athenians fought to defend their city, they were literally defending their own government, laws, and decisions.

The system also rotated political experience. Because offices were filled by lot and because jury service was open to all, thousands of citizens gained practical experience in governance. This wasn't professional politicians ruling over passive masses. This was citizens governing themselves, learning by doing.

The Boule of 500 is a good example. Each tribe's fifty representatives rotated in serving as the executive committee—the *prytaneis*—for one-tenth of the year. During their thirty-six days in charge, one member was selected by lot each day to serve as chairman. This meant that in a given year, five hundred different citizens held some governmental responsibility, and fifty served in top administrative positions. Over a generation, thousands of citizens would have direct experience running Athens.

Democracy developed further over the next decades. Pericles later introduced pay for jury service and attending Assembly meetings, which allowed poorer citizens to participate more fully. The system evolved and adapted. However, the core principle Cleisthenes established remained: citizens governing themselves through direct participation.

Athens's democracy was an experiment. No other major city had tried anything like it. Most Greek cities remained oligarchies or were ruled by tyrants. Sparta, the military powerhouse, had a mixed constitution that was definitely not democratic. Other Greeks looked at Athenian democracy with skepticism or horror. Giving power to the many seemed like a recipe for chaos. How could ignorant farmers and craftsmen make complex policy decisions? How could you prevent rabblerousers from manipulating the mob?

These were fair questions, and Athenian democracy would indeed struggle with these problems. But Athens also showed that democracy could work. The city would become wealthy, powerful, and culturally brilliant while governed by its citizens. Ordinary citizens would help defeat the Persian Empire. Athenian democracy would become Athens's proudest achievement and would inspire political thought for the next 2,500 years.

Cleisthenes didn't create democracy alone. He built on Solon's reforms and learned from tyranny's failures. He responded to the political crisis with creative solutions, and he succeeded because ordinary Athenians supported him and wanted political power. But Cleisthenes designed the system and deserves credit as democracy's founding figure, even if later Athenians sometimes forgot his name while celebrating their democratic achievements.

By 500 BCE, Athens had been transformed. It was now a democracy. Sparta remained a stable military oligarchy focused entirely on war. These two visions of the polis—democratic Athens and militaristic Sparta—would define Greek politics for the next century. They would soon need each other to survive the Persian invasion, and then they would spend decades fighting over which system should dominate Greece.

Cultural Crossroads: Comparing and Contrasting the Two

Athens and Sparta weren't just different; they were opposite in almost every way that mattered. If you dropped an Athenian in Sparta or a Spartan in Athens, they'd be utterly confused by how the other city lived. Let's compare them directly to understand just how different two Greek cities could be.

Government: Athens was a democracy where thousands of citizens participated directly in political decisions. The Assembly made laws. Juries decided court cases. Officials were selected by lot or elected for short terms. Every citizen could speak, vote, and serve. Sparta was an oligarchy with two kings, five ephors, a council of elders, and an assembly that mostly rubber-stamped decisions made by others. Political power rested with a small group of elites. The system was designed for stability, not participation.

Military: Sparta's entire society was organized around producing superior soldiers. Spartan male citizens were expected to serve as warriors from age twenty to sixty, training constantly and fighting in what was widely considered the finest phalanx in Greece. Athens relied on citizen-soldiers who were farmers and craftsmen most of the year and warriors when needed. Athenian hoplites were capable but not an elite fighting force like the Spartans. Athens's military strength came from numbers and especially from its navy, which became the largest in Greece.

Social Structure: Sparta had three classes: Spartan citizens (a small minority), perioikoi (free non-citizens), and helots (enslaved agricultural workers who vastly outnumbered citizens). The entire system depended on helot labor, which meant Spartans lived in constant fear of revolt. Athens had citizens, metics (foreign residents), and slaves. Slavery existed in Athens, but it wasn't as central to the economy. More Athenians worked their own land or practiced trades.

Women: Spartan women had more freedoms than women in most other Greek cities. They could own property, manage estates, and exercise. They were educated and could speak more openly than women elsewhere. They had to run things while men were away training or fighting. Athenian women were restricted to the household. They couldn't own property, participate in politics, or appear in public without a male guardian. Upper-class Athenian women lived secluded lives focused on managing households and raising children. Working-class women had more freedom by necessity, but they still had no political rights.

Economy: Sparta despised trade and commerce. Citizens couldn't engage in business, as it was considered beneath them. They lived off the produce of helot labor on their land. Sparta deliberately discouraged the accumulation of wealth and commercial activity, though exactly how they did this is debated; later sources mention iron bars, but archaeological evidence for such practices is lacking. Athens embraced commerce. It became the busiest port in Greece, trading olive oil, wine, pottery, and silver throughout the Mediterranean. Athenian merchants and craftsmen grew wealthy. The city's prosperity came from trade, not just agriculture.

Education: Spartan education was the agoge, a brutal military training system that started from age seven. It was focused on creating tough, obedient soldiers. Boys learned to fight, endure pain, and obey orders. That's about it. There was no philosophy, literature, or art in Spartan education. Athens valued intellectual development. Boys learned reading, writing, mathematics, music, poetry, and athletics. Wealthy families hired tutors. As Athens grew prosperous, philosophy, rhetoric, and debate became central to education. Athens produced philosophers, while Sparta produced soldiers.

Culture: Sparta produced far less art, architecture, literature, or philosophy than Athens, especially after the full institutionalization of its military system. Early Sparta, in the Archaic period, actually had significant cultural and artistic production, but as the military ethos hardened, this largely ceased. Classical Sparta wrote a few poems, mostly about war and duty. Their buildings were plain. They avoided luxury and beauty, seeing them as corrupting influences. Athens became the cultural capital of Greece. Athenians built the Parthenon and other magnificent temples. They developed drama, both tragedy and comedy. Philosophers like Socrates walked Athenian streets. Historians like Herodotus and Thucydides wrote there. Sculptors, painters, and poets flocked to Athens. Athens cared about beauty, wisdom, and art. Sparta didn't, at least not by the Classical period.

Values: Sparta valued obedience, discipline, endurance, military excellence, and stability. The ideal Spartan was tough, brave, loyal to the state, and willing to die without hesitation. Individual desires didn't matter. Spartans were supposed to be identical, interchangeable parts in a military machine. Athens valued freedom, creativity, ambition, wisdom, and achievement. The ideal Athenian was versatile. He would be good at speaking, thinking, fighting if necessary, and contributing to civic life. Individual excellence was celebrated. Athenians competed with each other constantly to prove their worth.

Foreign Policy: Sparta led the Peloponnesian League, a network of allied cities that followed Sparta's lead in military matters. Sparta generally left allies alone as long as they provided troops when asked. Sparta rarely went far from home and didn't seek to build an empire.

Athens created an empire. It started as the leader of the Delian League, a defensive alliance against Persia, but Athens gradually turned allies into subjects, demanding tribute and interfering in their governments. Athens was aggressive, expansionist, and imperialistic.

Despite these differences, Athens and Sparta had important similarities. Both were Greek. Both spoke Greek (though different dialects). Both worshiped the same gods. Both competed in the Olympic Games. Both valued courage and honored military achievement. Both excluded women, slaves, and foreigners from citizenship. Both believed Greeks were superior to barbarians. Both loved their polis intensely and would fight to defend it.

But the differences mattered more. These two cities represented different answers to questions about how society should be organized, what values should matter most, and what humans should strive for. Sparta chose order, stability, and military excellence at the cost of freedom and culture. Athens chose freedom, creativity, and individual ambition at the cost of stability and order.

Here's the interesting thing: Greeks at the time recognized that both systems had merits. Some admired Sparta's relative stability (though it is important to note that Sparta did face population decline, economic pressures, and the constant threat of helot revolt), its discipline, and its military prowess. The Spartan system changed slowly compared to more volatile cities. Sparta had fewer tyrants and less frequent civil wars than many poleis. Spartans were the best soldiers in Greece. There was something appealing about that consistency and martial excellence.

Others preferred Athens's energy, creativity, and freedom. Athens was dynamic and innovative. It produced art and ideas that influenced all of Greece. Athenian democracy gave citizens a voice in their own governance. There was something appealing about that freedom and intellectual life.

Both cities would soon face their greatest test. When Persia invaded Greece in 492 BCE, Athens and Sparta would need to work together to survive. After the Persian threat ended, they would spend decades fighting each other to determine which system would dominate Greece. The rivalry between Athens and Sparta would shape Greek history throughout the Classical period.

For now, in the early 5th century BCE, both cities had reached their mature forms. Sparta was the dominant land power, its army feared throughout Greece. Athens was a rising democracy, its navy growing. The stage was set for the next great chapter in Greek history: the moment when Greeks would prove themselves against the superpower of their age. The Persians were coming, and everything was about to change.

Chapter 5 – Fire and Freedom: The Persian Wars

Trouble in the East: The Ionian Revolt

By 500 BCE, the Greek world extended far beyond mainland Greece. Greek cities dotted the coast of Asia Minor, the western edge of what is now Turkey. These were wealthy, cultured cities: Miletus, Ephesus, Phocaea, and dozens of others. Miletus was one of the richest cities in the Greek world. It was a center of philosophy and traded with colonies stretching from Egypt to the Black Sea. These cities had marble temples, bustling harbors, and populations that spoke Greek and worshiped Greek gods. The people considered themselves Greek, though after centuries of interaction with non-Greek peoples and the development of distinct local identities, Ionian Greek identity was more complex than simply equating them with mainland Greeks.

But they had a problem. They weren't free.

These cities, collectively called Ionia, had fallen under Persian control decades earlier when the Persian king Cyrus conquered the Lydian kingdom that had previously ruled them. The Persian Empire, which had conquered everything from Egypt to India, was the superpower of the ancient world. Compared to Persia, the Greek cities were tiny, insignificant specks on the edge of the empire. Persian kings barely noticed them; they were just another group of subjects paying tribute.

Persian rule wasn't necessarily brutal by ancient standards. The Persians generally allowed subject peoples to maintain their own customs, worship their own gods, and govern their own local affairs as long as taxes were paid and loyalty was maintained. But Persian rule still chafed. The Persians installed tyrants to govern the Ionian cities, ensuring loyalty to the Persian king. These tyrants were Greeks themselves, but they ruled for Persia's benefit, not their cities'. Taxes flowed to the Persian court at Susa. Persian satraps (provincial governors) interfered in local affairs when it suited them. Young Ionian men were conscripted to fight in Persian wars that weren't their concern.

Meanwhile, across the Aegean, Greeks in cities like Athens were experimenting with democracy and self-governance. The Ionians saw their mainland cousins enjoying freedom while they lived under foreign domination. The contrast grew more painful with each passing year.

In 499 BCE, the situation exploded. The tyrant of Miletus, a man named Aristagoras, had a problem. He had persuaded the Persians to let him lead an expedition to conquer the wealthy island of Naxos, promising it would be easy and profitable. It wasn't. The expedition failed miserably, and Aristagoras had spent Persian money with nothing to show for it. He feared the Persian king would punish him for the failure, possibly removing him from power or worse.

Facing potential removal or execution, Aristagoras made a desperate gamble. He gave up his tyranny, declared Miletus a democracy, and called on the other Ionian cities to revolt against Persian rule. It was a calculated move. Aristagoras needed allies and popular support if he was going to survive Persian retaliation, and positioning himself as a champion of freedom rather than a tyrant served his purposes.

It was also audacious. The Persian Empire had hundreds of thousands of soldiers, vast resources, and a reputation for crushing rebellions with overwhelming force. When the Babylonians had revolted a generation earlier, Darius had besieged their city for nearly two years and then impaled three thousand of their leaders. The Ionians knew what they were risking. Even united, they were no match for Persia militarily.

However, the appeal of freedom proved irresistible. City after city joined the revolt. Persian-appointed tyrants were overthrown or fled. Democratic governments were established in their place. For the first time in decades, the Ionian cities were governing themselves. It felt like liberation.

Aristagoras knew this wouldn't last without external help, which was why he crossed the Aegean to seek support from mainland Greece. He went to Sparta first. Sparta had the best army in Greece, and Aristagoras hoped Spartan soldiers might tip the balance. He met with King Cleomenes and tried to persuade him to help. According to Herodotus, Aristagoras brought a bronze map—possibly the first map Cleomenes had ever seen—showing how rich the Persian Empire was and how much gold and silver awaited any army that could defeat it. He pointed out all the peoples Persia had conquered, emphasizing how easily the Persians might be defeated by superior Greek warriors.

But Cleomenes asked a practical question: how far was it from the Ionian coast to the Persian capital at Susa? When Aristagoras admitted it was a three-month journey inland, Cleomenes refused. Sparta didn't campaign that far from home. The logistics were impossible, the risks were enormous, and Sparta had no interest in foreign adventures. Aristagoras was ordered to leave Sparta before sunset.

Aristagoras had better luck in Athens. Athens had historical ties to Ionia. Athenians considered the Ionians their kinsmen, fellow members of the Ionian ethnic group who had migrated to Asia Minor from Attica centuries earlier. Athens had recently established its democracy under Cleisthenes and perhaps felt sympathy for the Ionians trying to throw off tyranny. Or maybe Athens simply saw an opportunity to strike at Persia, gain influence in Asia Minor, and access the region's wealth. Whatever the reason, the Athenian Assembly voted to send twenty ships to support the revolt. The city of Eretria on the island of Euboea, which also had ties to Ionia, sent five more.

Twenty-five ships weren't much—maybe five thousand soldiers total—but they were enough to encourage the Ionians and raise hopes that mainland support might grow. The revolt spread from city to city. Persian-installed tyrants were overthrown, and democratic governments were established. For a moment, it looked like the Ionians might actually succeed.

In 498 BCE, the Ionian forces, reinforced by the Athenian and Eretrian ships, marched inland to Sardis, the capital of the Persian satrapy of Lydia and one of the richest cities in the empire. They caught the Persians by surprise and captured the lower city, though the citadel remained in Persian hands. A fire broke out, but whether it was intentional or accidental isn't clear. Herodotus suggests it started when a soldier set fire to a reed house, and the flames spread uncontrollably through the city. The fire at Sardis destroyed a temple sacred to the local goddess Cybele, an act that would later be used to justify Persian retaliation against Greek temples.

But the success was short-lived. A Persian counterattack caught the Greek forces retreating from Sardis and defeated them at the Battle of Ephesus. The Athenians and Eretrians, spooked by the defeat and perhaps realizing they'd bitten off more than they could chew, sailed home and refused to send further help. Herodotus notes dryly that these twenty ships were "the beginning of evils for both Greeks and barbarians." They had accomplished little militarily but had given Persia a reason to view mainland Greece as an enemy.

The Ionians were on their own. The revolt continued for five more years, but the outcome was never really in doubt. Persia had unlimited resources and manpower. The Persian king, Darius I, methodically reconquered the rebel cities one by one. Persian armies besieged towns, and the Persian fleets blockaded harbors. City walls were breached. Populations were massacred or enslaved. Refugees fled from city to city as the Persian noose tightened.

By 494 BCE, only Miletus held out. The Persians assembled a massive fleet—reportedly six hundred ships drawn from their Phoenician, Egyptian, and Cypriot subjects—and besieged Miletus by land and sea. The Ionians gathered their own ships for a final naval battle at Lade, an island near Miletus. They had about 350 ships; they were outnumbered, but not impossibly so. If they could win at sea, they could break the blockade and prolong the war.

But their unity crumbled. Some contingents, particularly the Samians, had been bribed or persuaded by Persia to defect. Others lost their nerve. During the battle, much of the Ionian fleet fled or switched sides. The Persians won decisively. With naval superiority secure, they besieged and captured Miletus. The city that had sparked the revolt was destroyed as an example. Most of its population was killed or enslaved. The male survivors were deported to the mouth of the Tigris River deep in the Persian Empire, separated from their homeland forever. Women and children were enslaved.

The destruction was so complete and the suffering so intense that when news reached Athens, a playwright named Phrynichus produced a tragedy called *The Capture of Miletus*. The Athenian audience wept openly in the theater and then fined Phrynichus for reminding them of their own failures and the fate of their kinsmen. The play was banned from ever being performed again.

The Ionian Revolt was over. The cities were punished harshly, though some ancient sources suggest Persia eventually granted certain cities more local autonomy than before, possibly even allowing democratic forms of government in some cases, though the extent of such reforms remains debated, and Persian oversight continued. The empire had learned from the revolt.

So had the Greeks. They'd learned that Persia could be hurt, that Persian armies could be beaten, and that unity among Greek cities was nearly impossible to maintain. They'd also learned that Persia didn't forget insults. King Darius hadn't forgotten that Athens and Eretria had helped burn Sardis. Darius reportedly had a servant remind him three times at every dinner, "Master, remember the Athenians."

The Ionian Revolt had been the opening move in a larger conflict that would determine whether Greeks would remain free or become subjects of the Persian king. The mainland Greeks had just painted a target on themselves, and they had no idea what was about to hit them.

The Shock of Marathon: First Invasion

In 492 BCE, Darius launched his first strike against mainland Greece. He sent an army under his son-in-law Mardonius across the Hellespont, the strait separating Asia from Europe, into Thrace, conquering territory along the northern Aegean coast. However, a storm destroyed much of the Persian fleet off Mount Athos, and the expedition was recalled. It was a setback, not a defeat. Darius was far from finished.

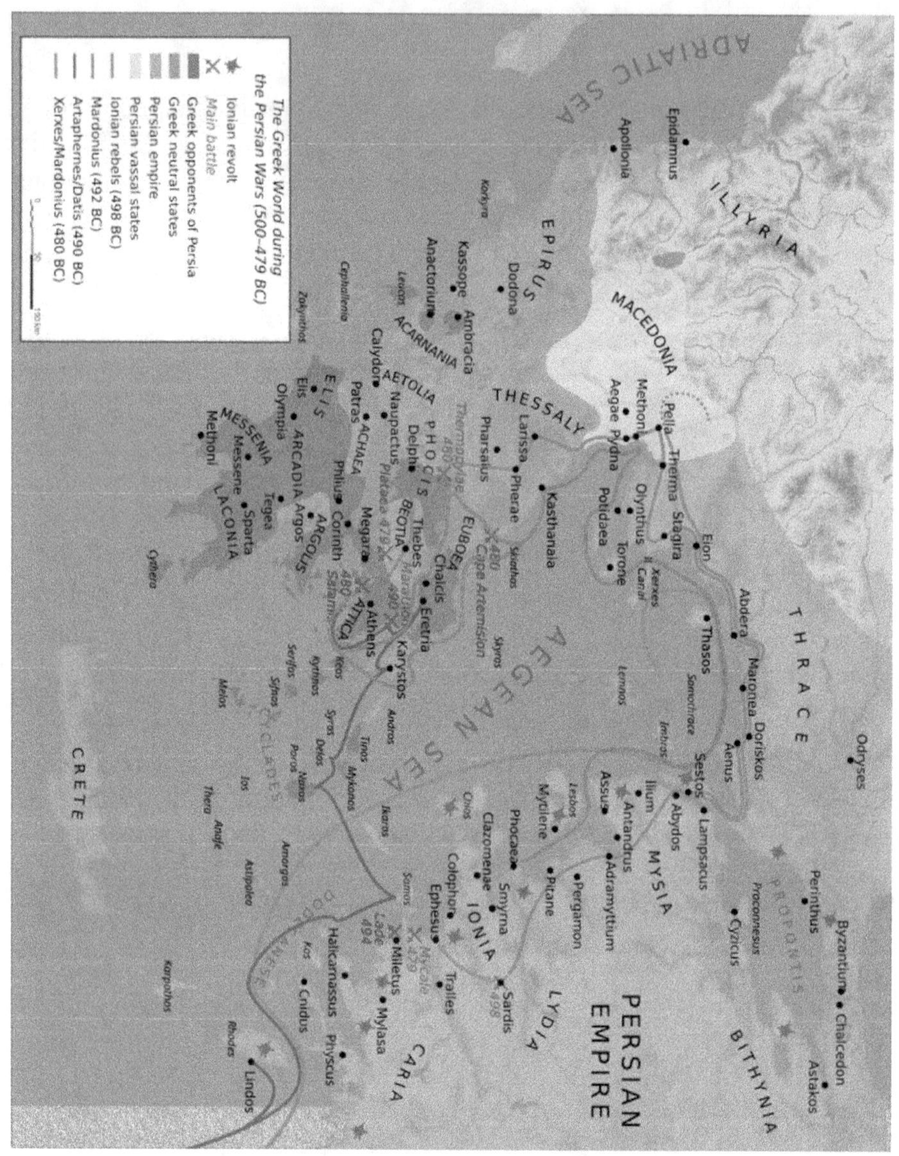

The Greek world during the Greco-Persian Wars.[57]

Two years later, in 490 BCE, Darius tried again with a different strategy. Instead of marching an army overland through difficult terrain, he sent a naval expedition directly across the Aegean. A fleet carrying perhaps twenty-five thousand soldiers—the numbers are disputed, but it was substantial—sailed from island to island, accepting the submission of Greek cities along the way. Most surrendered without fighting. Resistance seemed pointless.

The fleet's first major target was Eretria on Euboea, which had helped the Ionians burn Sardis. After a brief siege, the city fell through betrayal. The Persians enslaved the entire population and burned the city's temples in revenge for Sardis. Then the fleet crossed the narrow strait to mainland Greece and landed at Marathon, a coastal plain about twenty-six miles northeast of Athens.

Marathon was chosen deliberately. It offered a good beach for landing ships, open ground suitable for Persian cavalry, and was near enough to Athens to threaten the city directly. There was also a political dimension. The Persians brought Hippias, the old Athenian tyrant who had been expelled in 510 BCE, with them. The Persians intended to reinstall him as Athens's ruler, making Athens a Persian client state.

Athens faced a desperate situation. A Persian army sat less than a day's march from the city. Most Greek cities had already submitted to Persia. Sparta, the only power that could help, was celebrating a religious festival and claimed its laws forbade the army from marching until the moon was full. Athens was effectively alone.

The Athenians made a courageous decision. Instead of cowering behind the city walls and hoping the Persians would go away, they marched out to meet them. The Athenian army—about ten thousand hoplites plus perhaps one thousand men from the small city of Plataea, which honored its alliance with Athens even when larger cities stayed home—took a position in the hills overlooking the Marathon plain, blocking the roads to Athens.

It was an aggressive move born of necessity. The Athenians couldn't simply wait in Athens for a siege. They didn't have enough food stored for a prolonged blockade, and the Persian fleet could land troops anywhere along the coast. It was better to engage the enemy on the ground of their choosing, where the hills protected their flanks and prevented the Persian cavalry from maneuvering around them.

For several days, the two armies faced each other without fighting. The Athenian generals debated what to do. Athens had ten generals at this time, each commanding in rotation. Some argued they should wait for Spartan reinforcements since Sparta had promised to send its army after the religious festival ended. Others, including a general named Miltiades, who had lived under Persian rule and understood how the Persians fought, argued they should attack immediately. The longer they waited, he argued, the more likely Persian cavalry would overwhelm them, or the Persians would load their troops back on ships and sail directly to an undefended Athens.

Miltiades had another worry. He knew that some Athenians were in contact with the Persians. These sympathizers might betray the city if they thought a Persian victory was inevitable. The longer this standoff continued, the more likely treachery became. Athens needed a decisive victory, and they needed it soon.

The deadlock broke when scouts reported that the Persian cavalry had been sent away from the camp—or so the Greeks believed. The question of where the Persian cavalry was during the battle remains one of history's great debates. Ancient sources suggest they might have been loading back onto ships, possibly preparing to sail around to Athens while the main Persian force kept the Greek army pinned at Marathon, but this is an interpretation rather than a known fact. What's clear is that the Persians fought without cavalry support. This was Athens's moment. Without cavalry to protect their flanks and threaten the Greek formation, the Persian infantry was vulnerable.

Miltiades convinced the other generals to attack. It was his day to command, and he made his move. The Athenian hoplites formed their phalanx, eight ranks deep in the center but possibly deeper on the wings, and began advancing across the plain toward the Persian position about a mile away.

As they drew closer, perhaps when they came within range of Persian arrows, the order was given to charge. The Athenians broke into a run. This was not a mindless sprint that would exhaust them, but a steady jog in formation that covered ground quickly while keeping the phalanx together. This was unprecedented. Greeks didn't charge at a run. However, Miltiades understood that every second his men spent under Persian fire would weaken them before they even reached the enemy line.

The Persians were accustomed to enemies who fled from their arrows or were pinned down by archery before the hand-to-hand fighting even started, so they were astonished to see Greeks charging directly at them in formation. Herodotus says the Persians thought the Athenians were insane "since they were few and yet were charging at a run, having neither cavalry nor archers." The Persians were about to learn that discipline and heavy armor could defeat arrows if the enemy closed the distance fast enough.

The battle that followed was vicious and chaotic. The Persian center, composed of their best troops, pushed back the Athenian center and threatened to break through. The Athenian line bent inward as the Persian center advanced. This was dangerous. If the Persian center broke through completely, they could split the Greek army and attack it from behind.

But the Athenian wings, reinforced by Miltiades's strategic decision to strengthen the flanks at the center's expense, defeated the forces opposite them, which included Greek mercenaries and subject peoples who weren't as motivated or well trained as the Persian core troops. Then, in a move that required remarkable discipline and communication, the Athenian wings didn't pursue their defeated enemies. Instead, they wheeled inward and attacked the Persian center from both sides.

The Persian army, which moments before had been on the verge of victory, suddenly found itself enveloped, being hit from three directions at once. The Persian troops in the center, which were already engaged with the Athenian center to their front, now had Athenian hoplites crashing into their flanks. The formation broke. What had been a disciplined army became a mob of men trying to survive.

The Persian army shattered and ran for their ships beached on the shore. The Athenians pursued, fighting all the way to the water's edge. This was the most dangerous moment for the Persians. The soldiers were weighed down with equipment, exhausted from fighting, and trying to wade through surf and scramble onto ships while Greek hoplites stabbed and hacked at them from behind. Men drowned in their armor. Ships pushed off from shore with soldiers desperately clinging to the sides.

The fighting in the surf was particularly fierce when the Athenians tried to capture the beached ships. They succeeded in taking seven vessels, but it cost lives. One Athenian, Cynegeirus, supposedly grabbed the stern of a Persian ship and had his hand cut off by an axe. His brother, the playwright Aeschylus, who would later write tragedies performed throughout Greece, also fought at Marathon. He was prouder of this service than of any of his theatrical achievements.

According to Herodotus, the Persians lost about 6,400 men killed. The Athenians lost 192, though modern historians suspect this suspiciously specific figure might be a commemorative number rather than an actual casualty count. It possibly represents the number of men buried in the burial mound. Whatever the precise numbers, there's no doubt the Athenian victory was decisive. The Persian army, which had seemed unstoppable, had been beaten in open battle by a smaller Greek force.

Among the Athenian dead was the polemarch Callimachus, who had cast the deciding vote in favor of Miltiades's plan to attack. His body was later recovered and buried with honors. Also killed was Stesilaus, one of the ten generals. But the victory belonged to Miltiades, who had understood Persian tactics, recognized the moment to attack, and led the Athenians to an astonishing triumph.

However, the battle wasn't quite over. The Persian fleet didn't sail away in defeat. It sailed south, rounding Cape Sounion and heading for Athens itself. The city was virtually undefended. If the Persians could land their army at Athens before the Greek soldiers returned from Marathon, they could capture the city unopposed. Some Persians might have hoped that Athenian traitors would open the gates for them.

The Athenian army force-marched back to Athens. According to tradition, they covered the twenty-six miles in full armor—probably fifty to sixty pounds of equipment—in time to man the city's defenses before the Persian fleet arrived. This was an extraordinary feat of endurance. The soldiers had just fought a brutal battle, pursued fleeing enemies for miles, and now had to march home at speed while wearing heavy armor under the hot Greek sun.

When the Persian fleet rounded the point and saw the Athenian army standing ready on the shore, drawn up in battle formation, the Persian commanders decided they'd had enough. They turned their ships around and sailed back to Asia. There would be no victory for Persia this year. The expedition that was supposed to punish Athens for helping the Ionian rebels ended in defeat and humiliation.

The Battle of Marathon became instantly legendary. It was celebrated as the moment Greeks proved their courage, and it showed that a love of freedom could overcome the vast might of a despotic empire. The 192 Athenians who died were buried on the battlefield under a great mound, the Soros, that still stands today. They were honored as heroes who saved not just Athens but also the Greek way of life itself.

One legend connected to Marathon, though it was not recorded until centuries later and is probably not historical, tells of a messenger named Pheidippides. According to the story, he first ran from Athens to Sparta—

roughly 140 miles—in just two days before the battle to request Spartan aid. Then, after the Athenian victory, he ran from Marathon to Athens to announce the triumph, shouting "Nenikēkamen!" ("We have won!") before collapsing dead from exhaustion. This story, whether true or not, inspired the modern marathon race of 26.2 miles, commemorating the legendary run from the battlefield to Athens and an ancient Greek victory that changed history.

The Battle of Marathon also had profound political consequences. It elevated Athens's status among Greek cities. Before Marathon, Athens was important but not dominant. After Marathon, Athens had defeated the Persian Empire virtually alone, with help only from tiny Plataea. This gave the Athenians immense confidence in their democracy, army, and destiny. It showed that free citizens fighting for their own city could match or exceed professional soldiers fighting for an empire. The victory validated the democratic experiment and convinced the Athenians they were special.

For Miltiades, the hero of Marathon, the aftermath was bittersweet. He led an expedition to attack Persian-controlled islands the following year, but it failed, and he was wounded. The Athenians, ungrateful or simply realistic about military failure, prosecuted him for the expedition's costs. He died of his infected wound before the trial ended. Athens honored heroes but didn't tolerate failure, even from those who had saved the city.

Marathon didn't end the Persian threat. If anything, it made it worse. Darius began preparing a much larger expedition to crush Greece once and for all. He died in 486 BCE before he could launch it, but his son Xerxes inherited both the Persian throne and his father's determination to punish Greece. The Persians would return, and next time, they would bring an army so large that all of Greece combined might not be able to stop it.

The Lion at the Gate: Thermopylae

For ten years after Marathon, Greece waited for the Persian revenge that everyone knew was coming. The delay wasn't because Persia had given up; it was because Darius died in 486 BCE, and his son Xerxes first had to secure his throne, then suppress a major revolt in Egypt, and then deal with unrest in Babylon before turning his attention back to Greece. However, Xerxes never forgot his father's obsession with punishing the Greeks.

When Xerxes finally moved in 480 BCE, he did so on an unprecedented scale. This wouldn't be a raid or a punitive expedition. This would be a full-scale invasion intended to conquer Greece entirely and incorporate it permanently into the Persian Empire. Ancient sources claim his army numbered over one million men. Herodotus famously described the army drinking rivers dry as it passed. Modern historians estimate the actual force was probably between 100,000 and 300,000 soldiers, which is still enormous by ancient standards and larger than any army Greece could hope to field.

The Persians spent years preparing for this invasion. They stockpiled supplies at depots along the invasion route. They dug a canal through the Athos peninsula, which is over a mile long, to avoid the storms that had wrecked the previous Persian fleet there. They constructed two boat bridges across the Hellespont by lashing hundreds of ships together side by side. When storms destroyed the first bridges, Xerxes allegedly had the engineers executed and ordered the sea itself whipped three hundred times as punishment, which tells you something about how the Persians viewed obstacles.

The army that crossed into Europe was truly multinational. The Persian Empire's strength came from conscripting soldiers from all its subject peoples. There were Persians and Medes in their elaborate armor, Babylonians and Assyrians with their bronze helmets and linen breastplates, Egyptians with their wooden shields and curved swords, Indians with cotton clothing and bamboo bows, Ethiopians wearing leopard and lion skins, and Thracians with fox-skin caps. There were Phrygians, Armenians, Lydians, Carians, and Ionians—dozens of peoples, each with their own equipment, marching under Persian command. The army must have been an incredible sight.

Xerxes brought his household, court, harem, and throne. He brought everything needed to rule an empire. It is possible that he planned to stay in Greece and govern it personally once it was conquered. The fleet that accompanied the army numbered perhaps six hundred to eight hundred warships plus hundreds of transport vessels. It was the largest military force ever assembled at that point in history.

Greek cities faced an impossible choice: resist and face annihilation, or submit and survive as Persian subjects. Many chose submission. Thebes, one of the largest and most powerful cities in mainland Greece, *medized* (the Greek term for siding with Persia). The Thebans calculated that resistance was futile. Argos, another major city, stayed neutral.

Thessaly and other northern regions submitted as the Persian army approached. Their location made resistance impractical. Even among those who chose to resist, many doubted Greece could win.

Only a coalition of cities, led by Sparta and Athens, was prepared to fight. But even this alliance was shaky. Cities squabbled over strategy and command. Southern cities wanted to defend only the Peloponnese and abandon everything north of the Isthmus of Corinth. Athens insisted on a forward defense. The Greeks were outnumbered, outmatched, and barely united.

The Greek strategy was born of desperation and cleverness in equal measure. They couldn't match Persia in open battle; the numbers were too lopsided. Instead, they would use Greece's geography as a weapon. Narrow mountain passes could negate the Persian numbers. Greek ships, which were heavier and better suited to close-quarters fighting, could contest Persian naval superiority in confined waters. The plan was to hold the Persians at chokepoints, buy time, and hope that Persian logistics would fail or that the invasion would lose momentum.

The first chokepoint was Thermopylae, a narrow coastal pass between the mountains and the sea in central Greece. The name means "Hot Gates," from the hot springs that bubbled up nearby. At its narrowest point, the pass was perhaps fifteen meters wide—just wide enough for a single cart with a little room on each side. An army trying to force the pass would have to attack in a narrow column, unable to deploy its full strength. A small force could hold it against a much larger one, at least for a while.

King Leonidas of Sparta led the Greek defense. The famous three hundred Spartans he brought were his personal guard. According to later tradition, they were all men with living sons who could inherit their family positions, though this detail might be an embellishment emphasizing their sacrifice. Leonidas certainly expected this to be a one-way mission. However, Leonidas also commanded about seven thousand other Greek soldiers from various cities: perhaps seven hundred from Thespiae, four hundred from Thebes, one thousand from Phocis, and contingents from Arcadia, Corinth, Mycenae, and other poleis. Ancient sources often focus on the three hundred Spartans because they make a better story, but the defense of Thermopylae was a panhellenic effort.

Leonidas at Thermopylae by Jacques-Louis David (1748–1825).[58]

The Greeks fortified the middle of the pass, where an old defensive wall already existed, rebuilding it to shoulder height. They positioned themselves to block the road and waited. When the Persian army arrived and spread across the plain south of the pass, it must have been a terrifying sight: thousands upon thousands of tents, campfires stretching to the horizon, and a constant noise of men, horses, and equipment.

Xerxes allegedly sent scouts to observe the Greek position. The scouts reported something baffling: the Spartans were exercising in the open and combing their long hair, seemingly unconcerned by the massive army confronting them. Xerxes consulted with Demaratus, an exiled Spartan king who accompanied the Persian court. Demaratus explained this was how Spartans prepared for battle. When they groomed themselves carefully, it meant they were ready to die. Xerxes still didn't believe a tiny force would actually fight.

Xerxes waited four days, apparently expecting the Greeks to flee once they fully grasped the hopelessness of their position. The Greeks didn't flee. On the fifth day, Xerxes's patience ran out. He ordered the attack.

The first assault was made by Medes and Cissians, troops from the empire's eastern regions. They advanced into the pass and discovered what it meant to fight Spartans in terrain that favored the phalanx. The Persians couldn't deploy their cavalry in the narrow pass. Their archers couldn't shoot effectively because the pass was too confined, and their own men blocked the field of fire. They had to advance in narrow columns directly into overlapping Greek shields and spears.

The Greek phalanx was designed for exactly this kind of fighting. Hoplites stood shoulder to shoulder, shields locked together, creating a bronze wall, spears protruding forward like a hedge of steel. Any Persian who got close enough to engage had to face multiple spear points at once while Greek shields blocked his weapons. The Persians couldn't outflank the phalanx because the mountains and sea hemmed them in. They could only push straight ahead and die on Greek spears.

The Persians attacked repeatedly throughout the day and were driven back with heavy casualties each time. Bodies piled up in the pass. Persian commanders reportedly whipped their men to force them forward into the killing ground. It didn't matter. The Greek position was too strong, their equipment too superior for this kind of fighting, and their discipline too solid to break under pressure.

On the second day, Xerxes sent forward his Immortals—the elite ten-thousand-man guard unit, the best troops in the Persian army. Surely they could break through where lesser troops had failed. They couldn't. The Immortals attacked and were repulsed like everyone else. According to Herodotus, the Spartans sometimes pretended to retreat in disorder, luring the Persians into pursuing them, and then suddenly wheeled around and slaughtered the disordered Persian troops. Whether this actually happened or is an embellishment, it represents the tactical sophistication the Spartans possessed. They didn't just hold their position; they fought intelligently.

By the end of the second day, thousands of Persians were dead, and the Greeks held firm. Xerxes had no solution. He reportedly jumped from his throne three times while watching the battle, terrified that his whole invasion would bog down at this single pass while winter approached.

Then came the betrayal. A local Greek man named Ephialtes came to Xerxes and offered to show the Persians a mountain path—the Anopaia trail—that led around the pass, allowing troops to descend behind the Greek position. Ephialtes was motivated by the promised reward and perhaps resentment at being left out of the fighting. Or maybe he simply calculated that Persia would win and wanted to be on the winning side. Whatever his reasons, his name became synonymous with betrayal in Greek culture. The Greek word *ephialtes* still means "nightmare."

The path was known to the Greeks. They'd posted Phocian soldiers to guard it. But the Phocians were surprised when the Persian forces, led by the Immortals, climbed the trail through the night. When the Persians came upon them at dawn, the Phocians didn't hold their ground and fight to the death. They withdrew to higher positions to defend their own territory rather than maintaining the critical path, and the Persians continued their descent toward the southern end of Thermopylae.

When Leonidas learned at dawn that the Persians were flanking his position, he knew the defensive position was lost. The Greek army was about to be caught between Persian forces in front and behind. He faced a grim choice. He could order a full retreat, saving most of his men but abandoning the pass and likely being harassed or destroyed during the withdrawal. Or he could hold the position as long as possible, buying time with lives.

Leonidas made a calculated decision. He ordered most of the Greek army to retreat and march south to the next defensive position. He and his three hundred Spartans would stay. The seven hundred Thespians, who came from a small city that chose honor over survival, refused to retreat and stayed with Leonidas. The four hundred Thebans were also still present. Their initial participation in the defense suggests some level of commitment, though later sources hostile to Thebes (which sided with Persia after Thermopylae) claim they remained unwillingly and eventually surrendered. The truth about the Thebans' actions is contested, but that is because it is complicated by later political animosity toward Thebes for medizing.

About 1,500 men, perhaps 2,000 at most, prepared for the last stand. They abandoned the defensive wall they'd been holding and moved forward to a wider part of the pass where they would have more room to fight in their final battle. This wasn't about holding a position anymore. This was about killing as many Persians as possible before dying and buying time for the rest of the Greek army to escape.

When the Persians attacked on the third day, the Greeks fought with suicidal fury. They knew they would die. The question was how many Persians they could take with them. They fought until their spears broke and then fought with swords. When their swords broke, Herodotus claims they fought with hands and teeth, though this may be a dramatic embellishment. What's certain is they fought with desperate courage, knowing no help was coming.

Leonidas fell early in the battle, and the fighting devolved into a savage struggle over his body. In Greek culture, recovering a fallen warrior's body for proper burial was a sacred duty. The Spartans fought ferociously to protect their king's corpse while the Persians fought equally hard to capture it as a trophy. Four times, according to Herodotus, the Spartans beat back the Persians and recovered Leonidas's body. Two of Xerxes's brothers died in this fighting.

Eventually, the Persian flanking force emerged from the mountain path behind them, and the last Greeks were surrounded. They retreated to a small hillock in the pass. Tradition says it's the hill that still exists there, though archaeologists debate this. The remaining Greeks climbed this hill and made their final stand.

The Persians surrounded the hill completely. By this point, they'd lost any desire to engage these maniacs in hand-to-hand combat. Persian commanders ordered their archers to simply shoot the Greeks down from a distance. Arrows fell like rain. The Greeks held their shields up and endured the storm as long as they could, but there were too many arrows from too many directions. One by one, the last defenders fell. Every Greek who had stayed with Leonidas died on that hill.

The Persians had won the battle. The pass was open. However, the cost had been enormous. There were thousands of Persian casualties, three days of brutal fighting to dislodge a tiny force, and the main Greek army had escaped intact to fight again. The Persians had lost time, momentum, and morale while learning that Greeks would fight to the death rather than submit.

More importantly, Thermopylae became legendary. The Greeks had lost, but it was a defeat that inspired people rather than demoralized them. The Spartans who stayed with Leonidas became the ultimate example of martial courage and devotion to duty. Soon after, a memorial was erected at Thermopylae with an inscription written by the poet Simonides: "Go tell the Spartans, stranger passing by, that here, obedient to their laws, we lie."

The message wasn't just about bravery. It was about citizenship, duty, and the willingness of free men to die for their polis and their laws. The Spartans at Thermopylae became a symbol of what Greeks were fighting for: the right to live under their own laws, in their own way, free from foreign domination. The battle was a military defeat, but it was a moral and psychological victory that unified Greek resistance.

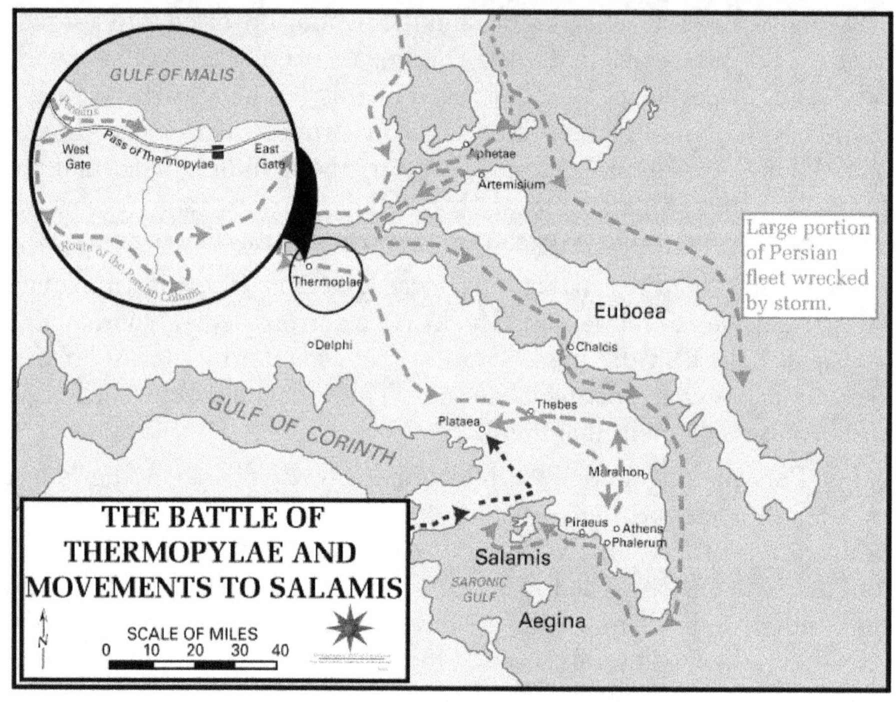

Major events in the second Persian invasion.[59]

While Leonidas and his men fought at Thermopylae, the Greek fleet engaged the Persian navy at Artemisium, a strait on the northern coast of Euboea. The timing was coordinated. The land army at Thermopylae and the fleet at Artemisium worked together to block both Persian routes into Greece.

The Greek fleet, commanded by the Spartan Eurybiades but dominated by Athenian ships under Themistocles, numbered perhaps 270 triremes. The Persian fleet was far larger—maybe six hundred to eight hundred warships initially, though storms had already damaged many. The Greeks chose Artemisium because the narrow waters negated the Persians' numerical advantage, just as the pass at Thermopylae neutralized their massive army.

For three days, the fleets clashed in the strait. The battles were brutal and exhausting. Greek triremes rammed Persian ships, marines fought on decks, and wreckage choked the waters. Neither side won decisively, but the Greeks inflicted significant damage on the Persian fleet and proved they could fight Persian ships effectively. More importantly, Athenian crews gained invaluable experience in naval combat—experience they would desperately need.

When news arrived that Thermopylae had fallen and the Persian army was marching south, the Greek fleet withdrew. There was no point holding Artemisium if the Persians controlled the pass behind them. The Greeks sailed south, shadowing the Persian advance, while Xerxes continued south with his vast army. Athens lay ahead, and behind it, the battles that would determine whether Greece would survive as a collection of free cities or become merely another province in the Persian Empire. But the Greeks had bought time at Thermopylae, and they would use that time well.

Triumph at Sea and Land: Salamis and Plataea

After Thermopylae, the Persian advance seemed unstoppable. The army marched south through Boeotia. Thebes and most other Boeotian cities welcomed them or offered no resistance. Nothing stood between Xerxes and Athens.

The Athenians couldn't defend their city against such an overwhelming force. In an extraordinary act of collective courage and desperation, they evacuated Athens entirely. The decision must have been wrenching. Athenians were abandoning their homes, temples, and ancestral lands—everything that defined them as a community. But they'd had warning and time to prepare.

Most refugees went to the nearby island of Salamis, visible from Athens across a narrow strait. Others went to Troezen in the Peloponnese, whose citizens generously agreed to shelter Athenian families. The Athenian fleet, which had been built up over the previous decade under Themistocles's urging, ferried people to safety. Women clutched children. Elderly citizens took what possessions they could carry. Families said goodbye to homes they'd never see again. Athens became a ghost town; it was eerily silent except for a small group of defenders who barricaded themselves on the Acropolis.

When the Persians arrived, they found the city nearly empty. They occupied Athens, climbed the Acropolis, and slaughtered the small group of defenders who had stayed. Then they burned everything. The temples went up in flames, including the predecessor to the Parthenon. The wooden structures burned quickly. Stone buildings were destroyed. Columns were toppled, and sculptures were smashed. This was revenge for Sardis, Marathon, and the Greeks' stubborn refusal to submit. Smoke from the burning city could be seen from Salamis, where Athenian refugees watched their home die.

But the Athenian fleet—roughly two hundred warships, almost half the total Greek navy, carrying most of Athens's fighting-age men—was intact and waiting in the narrow straits between Salamis and the mainland. The Greek allied fleet gathered at Salamis numbered perhaps 370 to 380 ships total. It was facing a Persian fleet that might have started with six hundred to eight hundred vessels but had been reduced by storms and previous naval skirmishes at Artemisium.

The question now was whether the Greeks would stay and fight or sail away to save what remained of their people and cities. The Athenians wanted to fight at Salamis. The straits were narrow—perfect for negating the Persian numerical advantage. But many other Greek commanders wanted to retreat to the Isthmus of Corinth and defend only the Peloponnese. From their perspective, Athens was already lost. Why risk the entire fleet trying to defend a burned city? Better to protect what could still be saved.

The council of war among Greek commanders grew heated. Themistocles, the Athenian leader who had convinced Athens to build its fleet, argued passionately that Salamis was where they had to make their stand. The narrow straits would work against the Persians just as Thermopylae's pass had worked for the Greeks on land. In confined waters, the heavier Greek triremes (warships with three banks of oars) would have the advantage. They could ram Persian ships and back away before being surrounded. Persian numbers wouldn't help them in tight quarters where they couldn't maneuver.

But Themistocles was losing the argument. The Spartan admiral and representatives from Corinth and other Peloponnesian cities insisted on retreating. The meeting broke up with no decision except to continue the debate the next day. Themistocles knew that if the debate continued, the Greeks would retreat and the Persian fleet would hunt them down in open water, where Persian numbers would be decisive.

So, Themistocles did something brilliantly devious. That night, he sent his slave Sicinnus secretly to the Persian camp with a message for Xerxes. The message claimed Themistocles was secretly a Persian sympathizer who wanted to help Xerxes win. It warned that the Greek fleet was planning to escape during the night and scatter in all directions.

If Xerxes wanted to destroy the Greek navy, he should block the exits from the Salamis straits immediately and trap them.

Xerxes took the bait. He ordered his fleet to move during the night to block both exits from the strait. Egyptian ships blocked the western exit. Other Persian squadrons blocked the eastern exit and patrolled the strait itself. Persian marines landed on the small island of Psyttaleia in the middle of the strait to rescue Persian sailors or kill Greek sailors who ended up there. The Persians rowed all night, exhausting their crews, to spring the trap.

When dawn broke, Greek scouts reported that the Persians had them surrounded. The Greek commanders realized retreat was no longer an option. They would have to fight whether they wanted to or not. Themistocles had forced the battle he knew Greece needed.

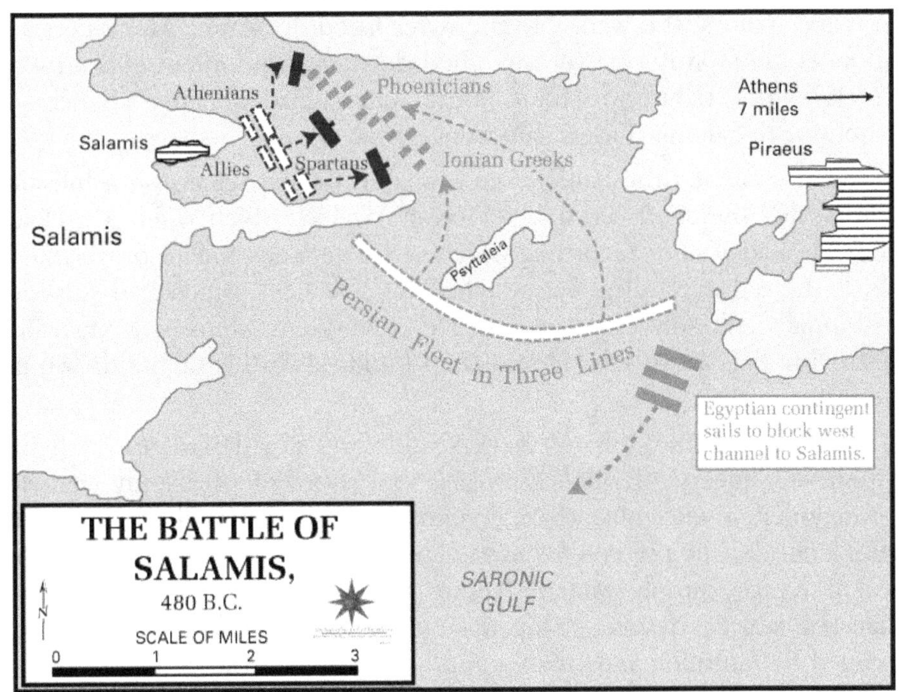

Movements in the Battle of Salamis.[60]

The Battle of Salamis began in the morning. The Persian fleet entered the narrows from the south, ship after ship filing into the confined space. This was precisely what Themistocles had wanted. The Persian ships, designed for fighting in open water where they could maneuver, found themselves crowded together in a space perhaps a mile wide. Ships collided with each other. Formations broke down. The Persian numerical advantage became a liability as hundreds of ships tried to operate in waters too narrow for them.

The Greek ships attacked aggressively. Greek triremes were heavier than most Persian vessels and sat lower in the water, making them more stable in rough seas and tight quarters. They had bronze rams on their prows designed to smash into enemy ships and crack their hulls below the waterline. Greek tactics were simple: row hard at an enemy ship, ram it, back away using oars, then repeat or move to the next target.

The battle quickly became chaotic and brutal. Greek ships drove into the mass of Persian vessels, ramming and then withdrawing before they could be surrounded. Persian ships couldn't deploy properly. They hit each other trying to maneuver. When a Greek trireme smashed into a Persian vessel and cracked its hull, the Persian ship would begin taking on water. Sailors who went into the water faced drowning. Many Persian sailors couldn't swim or were weighed down by equipment and armor. Greek sailors, fighting in their home waters, had a better chance of swimming to Salamis if their ship went down.

Xerxes watched the battle from a golden throne set up on a hillside overlooking the strait—probably Mount Aigaleo, which offered a clear view. He had scribes recording which of his captains fought bravely and which showed cowardice. He watched his vast fleet, which had seemed unstoppable, dissolve into chaos. He saw Greek ships systematically destroying Persian vessels. He watched hundreds of his sailors drown in the strait.

Before the battle, one of Xerxes's advisors urged him not to fight. Artemisia, queen of Halicarnassus and one of the only female commanders in ancient warfare, argued that Xerxes should avoid a naval battle entirely. She predicted that the Greek alliance would fracture on its own if Xerxes simply waited. Xerxes ignored her advice. During the chaos of battle, Artemisia's ship was pursued by Athenian triremes. She escaped by ramming and sinking another ship in Xerxes's fleet. Xerxes, watching from shore, saw the ramming and assumed she had sunk a Greek ship. He reportedly praised her courage, saying, "My men have become women, and my women have become men."

The battle raged for hours. Greek marines boarded damaged Persian ships and killed the crews. The waters of the strait turned red with blood.

By afternoon, the Persian fleet was shattered. Hundreds of ships had been sunk or damaged. Thousands of sailors were dead. The survivors fled back toward Phaleron Bay, where the main Persian fleet was anchored. The Greeks pursued but stopped short of a full-scale chase. They had won decisively and didn't want to risk everything by pursuing a still-dangerous enemy into open water.

The naval defeat changed Xerxes's strategic situation. Without naval supremacy, he couldn't safely supply his massive army through the winter. Every bite of food, every weapon, every piece of equipment had to come by land or sea from Asia. Greek control of the seas meant those supply lines were vulnerable. Winter was approaching. Keeping hundreds of thousands of men fed in hostile territory without secure sea lanes was impossible.

Xerxes made a crucial decision: he would return to Asia with much of his army, leaving his most capable general, Mardonius, with a picked force of perhaps fifty thousand to seventy thousand elite troops to continue the campaign the following spring. Mardonius would winter in friendly Thessaly and then complete the conquest of Greece when the campaigning season resumed.

The Greeks had won time. They'd proven that the Persians could be beaten at sea as decisively as they'd been beaten on land at Marathon. Xerxes's invasion, which had seemed unstoppable after Thermopylae, had been checked. However, the war wasn't over. A Persian army still occupied northern Greece, and Mardonius was one of Persia's best generals.

The following spring, in 479 BCE, the war reached its final climax. Mardonius, commanding the Persian force that had wintered in Thessaly and Boeotia, sent envoys to Athens with an offer. The message was simple and tempting. Athens had fought bravely, but continued resistance was pointless. If Athens were to switch sides and join Persia, it would be rewarded generously. Athens would be given land, autonomy, and favor. Persian money would rebuild the burned city. Athens would become Persia's privileged ally in Greece and would be given authority over other Greek cities.

It was a clever offer. Athens had already sacrificed everything. The city was destroyed, the population scattered, and the economy ruined. Continued fighting meant more suffering with no guarantee of victory. Accepting Persian terms meant peace, reconstruction, and prosperity. Many Athenians must have been tempted.

The Athenians refused. According to Herodotus, they told the Persian envoys that as long as the sun followed its current path in the sky, Athens would never make peace with Xerxes. They'd already lost their city once for freedom. They wouldn't trade that freedom now for Persian gold and empty promises of autonomy.

Mardonius's response was to march on Athens again. His army entered the already ruined city and burned what little remained standing. The Athenians evacuated to Salamis for the second time, watching their homes burn again. However, this time around, Sparta finally mobilized its full strength. The Spartans recognized that if Athens fell or switched sides, they would face Persia alone. So, they led the largest Greek army ever assembled north into Boeotia.

The Spartan regent Pausanias commanded perhaps forty thousand Greek hoplites plus tens of thousands of light troops (slaves and helots who served as skirmishers). The Greek force included contingents from dozens of cities, who were united in defense of their freedom. Against them, Mardonius commanded perhaps fifty thousand to seventy thousand troops, including Persian and Median cavalry and infantry, plus Greek allies like the Thebans who had chosen to support Persia.

The two armies met on the plain near Plataea, a small city at the edge of Theban territory. For more than a week, the armies maneuvered and skirmished without committing to a major battle. Mardonius had learned from Thermopylae. He wanted to fight on open ground where his cavalry could operate and where Persian archers could shower the Greeks with arrows. Pausanias wanted to fight on broken ground where the Greek phalanx would have the advantage and Persian cavalry would be less effective.

The stalemate dragged on. Persian cavalry harassed Greek supply lines and poisoned the Greeks' water source. The Greeks had to reposition during the night to find water and better ground. Mardonius, seeing the Greeks moving in the darkness, thought they were retreating in disorder and ordered an immediate attack. The Greeks were caught while still organizing their positions, their units scattered across the plain and not in proper formation.

A 19th-century illustration of the Battle of Plataea.[61]

What followed was the largest land battle of the Persian Wars and one of the largest battles in Greek history up to that point. The fighting was ferocious and desperate. On the Greek right, Spartan and Tegean hoplites faced the best Persian infantry. Pausanias, commanding the Spartans, held his position and prayed to the goddess Hera for victory while his men died around him. He refused to order the attack until the omens were right. It was either remarkable piety or battlefield psychology, making his men hold their ground under intense pressure while building their discipline and anger.

When Pausanias finally ordered the advance, the Spartans crashed into the Persian lines like a human avalanche. The Persian infantry fought bravely. They formed shield walls and shot arrows. But they weren't equipped or trained for this kind of close-quarters phalanx fighting. Greek hoplites with heavy armor, large shields, and long spears had every advantage in hand-to-hand combat. The Spartans pushed forward relentlessly.

Mardonius led his elite Persian troops from the front, fighting personally. According to Herodotus, a Spartan hoplite named Aristodemus killed Mardonius with a spear thrust, though other sources credit different Greek soldiers. What matters is that Mardonius died in the fighting. With their commander dead, Persian morale collapsed. The elite troops who had been holding against the Spartans broke and fled toward their fortified camp.

On other parts of the battlefield, Athenians and other Greeks were fighting Theban hoplites and other Greek medizers. These were Greeks fighting Greeks, which made it particularly bitter. The Athenians eventually drove the Thebans back, and the Greek phalanx began to converge on the Persian camp.

The Persians had built a wooden-walled fort as their base, and the survivors fled there seeking protection. The walls should have been a strong defensive position. However, walls meant nothing to Greeks who'd fought through the narrow pass at Thermopylae and stood against impossible odds. The Greeks stormed the fortifications, broke through the wooden walls, and poured into the camp. What followed was a massacre. The trapped Persian soldiers were cut down by the thousands. Few escaped. The Persian army that was supposed to conquer Greece was annihilated.

Greek casualties were significant. Herodotus reports that 159 Spartans, 52 Athenians, and 16 Tegeans were killed, though other cities suffered losses too. Persian losses were catastrophic; tens of thousands died in the battle and the subsequent slaughter in the camp.

On the same day—or so later Greeks claimed, and the coincidence was too perfect to be accidental, even if not literally true—the Greek fleet won another decisive victory at Mycale on the coast of Asia Minor. Greek ships, emboldened by Salamis, crossed the Aegean and attacked the beached Persian fleet. The Greeks landed their marines, defeated the Persian force defending the ships, and burned the Persian fleet where it sat. The Ionian cities, seeing Persian power broken, revolted again and this time successfully joined the Greek alliance.

The Persian invasion was over. Xerxes's dream of conquering Greece had died in the waters of Salamis and on the field of Plataea. The Persian army limped back to Asia. Many Greek cities in Asia Minor broke free from Persian control in the immediate aftermath, though this "liberation" would prove temporary and uneven. Persian influence in the region would continue for decades, and complete independence would only come much later. Still, the vast empire that had seemed unstoppable had been checked by a coalition of independent cities that loved their freedom more than they feared death.

The Persian Wars ended in an astonishing, unlikely Greek victory. The Greeks faced a superpower that controlled territory from Egypt to India. They had won through courage, clever tactics, and willingness to sacrifice everything rather than submit to foreign rule. Greeks learned that their way of life, with its squabbling cities, its contentious assemblies, and its emphasis on individual achievement, could triumph over the organized might of eastern despotism.

But victory came at enormous cost. Athens was destroyed twice. Greek casualties across multiple battles numbered in the thousands. The Greek world had been devastated by invasion. Alliances formed during the war created new tensions, and the experience of fighting together had changed the balance of power among Greek cities in ways that would have profound consequences.

Athens emerged from the war as a major power. The Athenian navy had been crucial at Salamis and Mycale. The Athenians' sacrifice earned them respect and influence. Sparta's military reputation was confirmed and enhanced. The coalition had saved Greece, but the alliance was fragile and built on temporary shared interests rather than a lasting friendship.

Seeds of future conflict had been planted. Athens and Sparta had cooperated to defeat Persia, but they had fundamentally different visions for what Greece should become. Athens would use its naval power to build an empire. Sparta would resist Athenian expansion. The Persian Wars were over, but the Greek wars against each other were just beginning.

Chapter 6 – The Golden Age and the Great War

Building an Empire: The Delian League

The Persian Wars ended in 479 BCE with a Greek victory, but the question of what came next divided the Greek world almost immediately. Sparta wanted to go home. The Spartans had done their part; they'd led the defense of Greece, their hoplites had broken the Persian army at Plataea, and now they wanted to return to the Peloponnese and resume their lives. Sparta had no interest in foreign adventures or overseas commitments. The helots back home were restless, and Spartan citizens were needed to maintain control there.

Athens saw things differently. The Persians had been driven from mainland Greece, but the threat wasn't over. Persian forces still controlled or threatened Greek cities in Asia Minor and the Aegean islands. The Persian navy, though badly damaged, still existed. Xerxes still sat on his throne in Persia, and there was no guarantee he wouldn't try again. Athens argued that the Greeks needed to stay on the offensive. They should liberate the Greek cities still under Persian control, protect Greece against future invasions, and make Persia pay for what they'd done. The formal war would continue for decades, with a peace treaty not concluded until around 449 BCE, according to most modern historians.

Athens had another motivation that wasn't purely altruistic. The city had been destroyed twice during the war. The Athenian economy was in ruins. Rebuilding would be expensive, and Athens needed money. Control of the Aegean Sea and the trade routes that crossed it could make Athens wealthy. Leadership of an anti-Persian alliance would give Athens power and influence. The opportunity to transform Athens from a regional power into something much greater was there for the taking.

Sparta initially tried to maintain leadership of the Greek alliance. The Spartan regent Pausanias, the victor of Plataea, led a Greek fleet in 478 BCE to liberate Greek cities in Cyprus and Byzantium. However, Pausanias's leadership was disastrous. He was arrogant and autocratic, allegedly adopting Persian dress and manners. He offended the allied commanders and alienated the cities he was supposed to be liberating. Rumors spread that he was conspiring with Persia. Whether the accusations were true or not—they might have been at least partially Athenian propaganda—Sparta recalled Pausanias and essentially withdrew from overseas leadership.

This created a vacuum that Athens eagerly filled. In 478/477 BCE, Athens organized a new alliance specifically dedicated to continuing the war against Persia. The alliance would be called the Delian League, named after the island of Delos, where the league's treasury was kept and where representatives met. It would become one of the most successful and controversial alliances in Greek history.

The structure of the Delian League seemed fair and reasonable on paper. Member cities would contribute either ships and crews to the allied fleet or money to pay for ships if they couldn't provide them directly. Athens, with the largest navy in Greece, would command the fleet. Aristides, an Athenian statesman known for his fairness and honesty, assessed each member's contribution based on their wealth and resources. No one could accuse Aristides of unfairness; he was so respected that Athenians nicknamed him "the Just."

The league's stated purpose was to liberate Greek cities from Persian control, protect against future Persian aggression, and punish Persia for the invasion by raiding Persian territory. Every member city swore an oath of alliance, and lumps of iron were thrown into the sea, symbolizing that the alliance would last until the iron floated, meaning forever.

Initially, the Delian League worked exactly as advertised. Under Athenian leadership, particularly under the general Cimon (son of Miltiades, the hero of Marathon), the league achieved spectacular successes. Greek cities in Asia Minor and along the Thracian coast were liberated from Persian control. The league's fleet hunted down Persian ships and destroyed them. In the 460s BCE, Cimon led a major expedition to the Eurymedon River in Asia Minor and won a stunning double victory, destroying the Persian fleet and then landing troops to defeat the Persian army on the same day.

These victories were significant. Cities that had lived under Persian rule for decades were freed, and the Persian threat to the Aegean was pushed back. The league was accomplishing its mission. Athens genuinely was the liberator and protector it claimed to be.

But things changed gradually. The nature of the alliance began to shift in ways that benefited Athens at the expense of other members. More and more cities chose to contribute money rather than ships. This made sense for small cities since building and maintaining a trireme warship was expensive, and manning it required 170 rowers. It was easier to pay Athens to provide the ships. However, this meant that Athens controlled an ever-larger fleet while other cities had no ships of their own.

Athens, meanwhile, used the money not just to build warships but also to pay Athenian rowers. This created jobs for thousands of Athenian citizens, particularly the poorer classes who rowed the ships. The fleet became an economic engine for Athens. Athenian power and prosperity depended on the league's continued existence and expansion. Moreover, the empire secured vital grain imports from the Black Sea region; Athens couldn't feed its population from Attic farmland alone. Control of the sea lanes meant survival. The tribute also funded the payments that allowed poorer citizens to serve on juries and attend the Assembly, making Athenian democracy feasible for all citizens, not just the wealthy who could afford to participate in politics without compensation. The empire and Athenian democracy became inseparable—one sustained the other.

The league also began to serve Athenian interests beyond just fighting Persia. When the island of Naxos tried to withdraw from the league around 470 BCE, Athens responded with force. Naxos was besieged, forced back into the league, and punished. Its walls were torn down. The message was clear: you couldn't leave the league. What had been presented as a voluntary alliance was becoming compulsory.

The Athenian historian Thucydides, writing decades later, identified this as the moment when the league's nature fundamentally changed. Naxos was "the first allied city to be enslaved contrary to established usage," he wrote. The word "enslaved" is harsh but telling. Cities that had joined freely to fight Persia were now being forced to stay in an alliance whose purpose was increasingly unclear.

Other cities that tried to leave were similarly crushed. Thasos revolted in 465 BCE over a dispute about trade and mining rights—nothing to do with Persia—and Athens besieged the city for two years until it surrendered. Thasos lost its fleet, had to pay a huge indemnity, and effectively became a subject of Athens. The pattern repeated with other cities. Rebellion meant siege, defeat, punishment, and loss of autonomy.

In 454 BCE, Athens moved the league's treasury from Delos to Athens itself. The official reason was security; keeping the treasury on a small island was risky. However, the real reason was control. With the treasury in Athens, the Athenians could access the money directly. They began using league funds for Athenian purposes. The massive building program that would create the Parthenon and beautify Athens was likely funded in part by league contributions. Direct documentation doesn't survive, but the circumstantial evidence and contemporary political complaints strongly suggest this.

The allies protested, but they were powerless to stop it. Pericles, Athens's dominant political figure by the 440s BCE, dismissed the complaints. As long as Athens protected the allies from Persia, he argued, how Athens spent the money was Athens's business. If the allies didn't like it, they could build their own fleets and defend themselves. Of course, Athens wouldn't let them do that either.

By the mid-century, the Delian League had transformed into something its founders probably hadn't intended: an Athenian empire. Athens controlled the league absolutely. Member cities, which counted well over a hundred at the empire's height, with numbers fluctuating around 150to 200 based on surviving tribute records, had to follow Athenian foreign policy. They had to use Athenian weights, measures, and coinage. Serious legal cases from allied cities were heard in Athenian courts under Athenian law by Athenian jurors. Athens sometimes installed garrisons in allied cities or established colonies of Athenian citizens in allied territory. The allies had to pay tribute; yes, the word changed from "contributions" to "tribute," which tells you everything about how the relationship had evolved.

This imperial system was enormously profitable for Athens. Money flowed into the city from hundreds of allied or subject cities. This wealth funded everything that made 5th-century Athens remarkable: the building programs, the dramatic festivals, the payments to citizens for jury service and attending the Assembly, and the fleet that made Athens the greatest naval power in the Mediterranean.

The Athenians themselves were remarkably honest about this transformation. Pericles, in a famous speech recorded by Thucydides, acknowledged that "your empire is now like a tyranny: it may have been wrong to take it, but it is certainly dangerous to let it go." The Athenians knew they were running an empire. And they knew their allies resented them. Many Athenians accepted these costs as the price of Athenian greatness and security, prioritizing power and prosperity over popularity with their subjects. The empire made Athens great, and for most Athenians, that justified the resentment it created.

However, not all Athenians were comfortable with this. Some worried about the moral implications of ruling other Greeks by force. The playwright Euripides wrote plays that questioned Athenian imperialism. Thucydides himself, though he admired Athenian power, was clearly troubled by what Athens had become. Most Athenians didn't seem to notice or care about the contradiction. They celebrated democracy at home while denying it to their subjects abroad. They praised freedom while forcing other Greeks to obey Athenian commands.

From the perspective of the subject allies, Athens had betrayed the league's founding principles. They'd joined voluntarily to fight Persia and protect Greek freedom. Now they were subjects of an Athenian empire, paying tribute, losing autonomy, and seeing their money spent on Athenian projects while they lacked a voice in how the alliance operated. To be fair, some allies did benefit. Athenian naval power protected trade routes, suppressed piracy, and provided security against Persian resurgence. Smaller cities gained stability they couldn't have achieved alone. However, these benefits came at the cost of independence, and for many Greeks, freedom mattered more than security. The great liberator had become an oppressor, or at least a domineering protector who demanded obedience in exchange for protection.

Other Greek states watched this transformation with alarm. Sparta had stayed largely out of Aegean affairs since withdrawing from overseas leadership, but the growth of Athenian power was impossible to ignore. By the 440s and 430s BCE, Athens had become the richest and most powerful Greek state, commanding hundreds of ships and collecting tribute from hundreds of cities. This was a dramatic shift in the balance of power.

Corinth, a major commercial power and a Spartan ally, was particularly worried. Athenian trade and Athenian colonies were competing with Corinthian interests throughout the Greek world. Thebes, which dominated Boeotia, resented Athenian interference in central Greece. Even states that had fought alongside Athens against Persia began to fear Athenian ambitions.

The irony was profound. Greece had united, however imperfectly, to defend its freedom against Persian imperialism. Now, barely a generation later, an Athenian empire was dominating the Aegean, and Greeks were preparing to fight Greeks over whether Athens should be allowed to continue its imperial expansion. The victory over Persia had saved Greek independence, but it had also created conditions for Greece's self-destruction.

For now, though, in the mid-5th century BCE, Athens stood at its peak. The Persian threat had receded. Tribute flowed in from across the Aegean. The fleet ruled the seas. The city was being rebuilt in marble rather than wood, with monuments that would last millennia. Democracy was flourishing. Culture was exploding in new directions. This was Athens's moment of greatest power and achievement—what later generations would call the golden age.

Democracy's Flowering: Pericles and Athens

If you could visit Athens in the 440s and 430s BCE, you'd find a city unlike anywhere else in the Greek world or anywhere in the world, for that matter. Athens in its golden age was loud, chaotic, argumentative, and gloriously alive with political energy. On Assembly days and when the courts were in session, thousands of citizens gathered in the agora to argue about politics, listen to speeches, serve on juries, or conduct business. The city hummed with debate, gossip, lawsuits, and democratic participation on a scale that would have seemed insane to most ancient peoples, though in practice, many citizens lived in rural Attica and couldn't attend regularly, meaning active political participation was more feasible for those living in or near the city itself.

At the center of this energy, for nearly three decades, stood Pericles. He wasn't a king, tyrant, or dictator. He held no permanent office and could be voted out at any time. But he was elected strategos—one of ten generals—fifteen times over his career continuously from 443 BCE until his death in 429 BCE (with one exception when he was briefly removed from office in 430 BCE). He used this position to guide Athenian policy, champion democracy, and transform Athens into the cultural capital of Greece.

A bust of Pericles.[62]

Pericles came from an aristocratic family. His mother was a member of the Alcmaeonid clan, one of Athens's most powerful families. His father Xanthippus had commanded the Greek fleet at Mycale. According to later ancient sources, Pericles received the best education available, studying with the philosopher Anaxagoras and learning rhetoric from the sophist Protagoras. He was wealthy, well connected, and brilliant—exactly the sort of person who in an earlier era would have competed with other aristocrats for power.

But Pericles chose a different path. He became a champion of democracy and positioned himself as a leader of the demos, or the common people. This wasn't entirely altruistic. Athenian politics had roughly two factions: the aristocratic conservatives, who wanted to limit democracy and maintain traditional elite privileges, and the democratic radicals, who wanted to expand citizen participation and reduce aristocratic power. Pericles allied himself with the democrats, recognizing that his path to power ran through popular support rather than aristocratic backing.

Under Pericles's leadership, Athenian democracy reached its fullest development. Cleisthenes had created the basic democratic structure a generation earlier, but Pericles expanded and deepened it. His reforms made democracy functional for all citizens, not just those wealthy enough to spend time on politics without compensation.

The most important reform attributed to Pericles was the introduction of pay for jury service. Before this, serving on juries meant losing a day's wages. Poor citizens couldn't afford to participate regularly. This meant that in practice, the courts were dominated by the wealthy who had leisure time. Pericles introduced payment for jury service (*misthos*), allowing poor citizens to serve without suffering economic hardship. Payment for attending the Assembly would come later, likely around 400 BCE, after Pericles's death.

Critics, particularly wealthy conservatives, were horrified. They argued that paying citizens for jury service would attract the wrong sort of people: lazy men looking for easy money rather than serious citizens devoted to justice. They worried that poor citizens would become too dependent on state payments and vote for politicians who promised them more benefits. Some conservatives sarcastically called the payments "the sophist's wage," implying that citizens were being bribed to pretend to care about their civic duties.

But Pericles argued that democracy meant rule by all citizens, not just those who could afford time off. If citizens were expected to serve the state by fighting in the army, rowing in the fleet, and serving on juries, then the state should compensate them fairly. The wealthy could afford to serve for free; the poor couldn't. Payment leveled the playing field, at least in the courts.

The Athenian Assembly met on the Pnyx, a hill west of the Acropolis. About forty times a year, thousands of citizens would gather to debate and vote on laws, declarations of war, treaties, budgets, and every other major decision. For certain particularly important matters, such as ostracism or grants of citizenship, a quorum of six thousand citizens was required, though ordinary business could proceed with fewer. Any citizen could speak, though in practice, trained orators dominated the debates. Anyone could propose a law. Every citizen had one vote, and it counted equally whether he was rich or poor, educated or illiterate, aristocrat or laborer.

The Assembly was chaotic and rowdy. Citizens shouted approval or disapproval during speeches. They heckled speakers they disliked. They laughed at jokes and booed bad arguments. Voting was usually by a show of hands, though important decisions might use a secret ballot. The atmosphere was more like a sports event than a modern legislature.

Juries were even more democratic and more unusual by ancient standards. Athenian juries were massive, typically consisting of 201 or 501 citizens, sometimes more for important cases. Jurors were selected by lot each day from volunteers. Any citizen over thirty could volunteer. This meant that a trial might be decided by hundreds of ordinary Athenians with no legal training, chosen at random that morning.

There were no judges in the modern sense, and there were no professional lawyers, prosecutors, or defense attorneys. The plaintiff and defendant represented themselves, delivering timed speeches explaining their case. Each side could call witnesses. After hearing both sides, jurors voted on guilt or innocence. If the defendant was found guilty and the penalty wasn't fixed by law, there would be a second round of voting to determine the punishment, with both sides proposing penalties and the jury choosing between them. There was no appeal. The majority ruled, and the decision was final.

This system seems crazy by modern standards. How could untrained citizens make complex legal decisions? How could justice be served when juries were essentially mobs of random people? But Athenians believed this was exactly the point. The law shouldn't be a mystery understood only by experts. Justice shouldn't be decided by a small elite. The community as a whole should determine guilt or innocence, and punishments should reflect community values.

Athenians were litigation-happy. Thousands of cases came before the courts each year—disputes over property, contracts, inheritances, assault, theft, and especially political prosecutions. Athenian politicians regularly sued each other, using the courts as an arena for political combat. This meant that persuasive rhetoric mattered enormously. If you could convince a jury, you won. If you couldn't, you lost, even if the law and facts were on your side.

This created demand for teachers of rhetoric—the sophists—who charged fees to teach wealthy young men how to argue persuasively. Critics complained that sophists taught students to make the weaker argument appear stronger and to win through verbal trickery rather than truth. The philosopher Socrates was famously suspicious of sophistic rhetoric and the Athenian love of persuasive speaking over genuine wisdom.

Pericles himself was a masterful orator. Ancient sources describe him as dignified, reserved, and extraordinarily persuasive. He didn't shout or gesture wildly like some politicians. He spoke with careful, measured authority that commanded attention. The comic playwright Aristophanes joked that Pericles wielded "the lightning and thunder of Zeus" with his speeches. When Pericles spoke in the Assembly, people listened.

His most famous speech, or at least the most famous speech Thucydides attributes to him, was the Funeral Oration, delivered in 431 BCE to honor Athenians who died in the first year of the Peloponnesian War. Thucydides's version of this speech (we don't have Pericles's actual words, only Thucydides's reconstruction) has become one of the most celebrated statements of democratic values in Western literature.

In the speech, Pericles celebrated Athens as a model for all Greece. "Our constitution is called a democracy because power is in the hands not of a minority but of the whole people," he declared. Athens didn't copy other cities; other cities copied Athens. Athenians were free to live as they pleased and were encouraged to debate and disagree. They valued beauty without extravagance, wisdom without softness, and wealth as an opportunity for action rather than for boasting.

The speech was brilliant propaganda. It defined Athens by its values—freedom, openness, courage, and culture—rather than by its power. It claimed moral superiority for democracy over other systems. It assured grieving families that their loved ones had died for the greatest city in the world, defending principles worth dying for.

But the speech was also honest about what Athens had become. Pericles acknowledged that Athens ruled an empire "like a tyranny," but argued this was necessary and justified. He celebrated Athenian power openly. Athens didn't need Homer to sing its praises; Athens's achievements spoke for themselves. The speech captured the confidence, bordering on arrogance, of Athens at its peak.

Under Pericles, Athens also became physically beautiful. The massive building program that created the Parthenon and other monuments on the Acropolis was Pericles's vision. Before the Persian Wars, the Acropolis had temples and sacred buildings. The Persians destroyed them all. For thirty years, the ruins remained, a deliberate reminder of Persian sacrilege and Athenian sacrifice.

Pericles decided Athens should rebuild but not just restore what was lost. Athens would build monuments worthy of the greatest city in Greece, temples that would last forever, built in marble instead of wood, decorated by the finest sculptors, and designed by the best architects. The Parthenon, dedicated to Athena, would be the centerpiece: thirty feet tall, surrounded by forty-six massive columns, decorated with intricate sculptural friezes showing battles, processions, and mythological scenes. It would be beautiful, awe-inspiring, and a permanent statement of Athenian power and culture.

The Parthenon.[63]

Critics attacked the building program as wasteful vanity. Thucydides (a different Thucydides, not the historian) accused Pericles of "dressing Athens up like a harlot" with expensive jewelry while allied cities suffered. The money came from tribute, so it should be spent on defense, not on making Athens pretty.

Pericles's response was unapologetic. As long as Athens defended the allies, how Athens spent the money was Athens's business. Besides, the building program employed thousands of Athenian artisans, sculptors, laborers, carpenters, and painters. It enriched the city economically and culturally. Centuries from now, people would look at these monuments and know Athens had been great. He was right about that.

The Parthenon was completed in 438 BCE, with the sculptural decorations finished a few years later. It stood—and still stands, though damaged—as the ultimate symbol of Athens's golden age. When ancient travelers listed the wonders of the world, Athens's monuments were celebrated alongside the pyramids of Giza and the Hanging Gardens of Babylon. The Parthenon represented Athenian democracy, culture, imperialism, and confidence all in one massive marble structure.

But Athenian democracy, for all its achievements, had severe limitations that Pericles never addressed and probably never questioned. Democracy was only for citizens, and citizenship was restricted. Women couldn't participate in politics, hold office, or vote. They couldn't own property in their own names or represent themselves in court. Upper-class women lived secluded lives, rarely appearing in public. They managed households but had no public role. Working-class women had more freedom by necessity. They worked as vendors, midwives, and weavers, but they still had no political rights.

Slaves were everywhere in Athens. Perhaps one-third of Athens's population was enslaved. They worked in homes, workshops, mines, and fields. Some were treated relatively well, working alongside free laborers and sometimes earning enough to eventually buy their freedom. Others, particularly those working in the silver mines at Laurium, endured brutal conditions and short lives. Democracy depended on slave labor to function. Citizens had time for politics in part because enslaved people did much of the work.

Metics—foreign residents—could live and work in Athens, sometimes for generations, but could never become citizens, no matter how long they stayed or how much they contributed to the city. They paid taxes, fought in the army, and participated in the economy, but they had no political voice. Citizenship was hereditary and jealously guarded. In 451 BCE, Pericles himself sponsored a law requiring that both parents be

Athenian citizens for their children to be citizens, further restricting who counted as Athenian.

So, when Pericles celebrated "democracy" and "rule by the people," he meant rule by perhaps 40,000 to 60,000 adult male citizens out of a total population of perhaps 300,000 to 400,000 people. The majority of people living in Athens had no political rights at all.

Modern critics point out this hypocrisy, and they're right to do so. Athenian democracy was deeply exclusionary. But we should also recognize that by ancient standards, Athens was radical. No other major city allowed anything like this level of participation, even for its citizens. Most were oligarchies where a few dozen or a few hundred wealthy men controlled everything. Athens gave political power to tens of thousands of ordinary men who would have had no voice anywhere else.

Cultural Explosion: Drama, Philosophy, and Art

While Athenian politicians debated in the Assembly and generals commanded fleets, Athens was experiencing an explosion of cultural creativity that would influence Western civilization for millennia. The same decades that saw the building of the Parthenon also produced revolutionary developments in drama, philosophy, sculpture, and art. Athens in the 5th century BCE wasn't just politically innovative; it was also culturally transformative.

The heart of Athenian cultural life was theater, and theater was deeply connected to democracy and civic religion. Twice a year, during festivals honoring the god Dionysus, Athens held dramatic competitions. The City Dionysia in spring was the major event. For several days, thousands of Athenians gathered in the Theatre of Dionysus on the slope of the Acropolis to watch plays.

These weren't optional entertainment for those who could afford tickets. Theater was a civic duty, a religious observance, and a shared community experience all at once. Productions were funded through a combination of state support and private sponsorship. Wealthy citizens were assigned as *choregos*—sponsors who bore most of the production costs as a form of public service (and competition for prestige), while the state covered certain expenses like actors' pay. Metics likely attended as well, as well as possibly some slaves and foreigners, though evidence for non-citizen attendance is limited.

Greek theater had two main forms: tragedy and comedy. Tragedies dealt with serious themes, like fate, justice, the relationship between humans and gods, and the consequences of hubris and moral choices. They drew heavily on mythology, retelling familiar stories but exploring their deeper meanings and moral complexities. Comedies were satirical, bawdy, politically sharp, and often hilarious, mocking politicians, philosophers, social trends, and Athens itself.

The three great tragedians whose works survive are Aeschylus, Sophocles, and Euripides. Each brought something different to the form and pushed Greek drama in new directions.

Aeschylus, who fought at Marathon and possibly Salamis, was the earliest of the three. His plays explored grand cosmic themes like justice, divine will, and the cycle of revenge and redemption. His masterpiece, the *Oresteia* trilogy, tells the story of Agamemnon's murder by his wife Clytemnestra and the subsequent revenge by their son Orestes. The trilogy ends with the establishment of the Athenian court system, transforming the cycle of blood revenge into civilized justice. It's both a thrilling story and a meditation on how societies move from barbarism to law. Aeschylus died in 456 BCE, but his plays continue to be celebrated today.

Sophocles dominated Athenian theater for much of the 5th century. He won first prize at the City Dionysia approximately twenty times and reportedly never finished lower than second. His plays focused on individual characters facing impossible moral dilemmas. *Oedipus the King* tells the story of a man who unknowingly killed his father and married his mother, then desperately tried to uncover the truth even as everyone warned him to stop asking questions. It's a devastating exploration of fate, knowledge, and the limits of human understanding. *Antigone* examines the conflict between divine law and human law and between family duty and civic obligation through a young woman who defies the king to bury her brother.

Sophocles's characters feel psychologically real in ways that ancient literature rarely achieved. They struggle with doubt, make mistakes, suffer consequences, and endure. His plays don't provide easy moral answers; they present genuinely difficult choices where doing the right thing leads to disaster. This moral complexity reflected the complexities of democratic Athens, where citizens constantly faced difficult decisions about justice, duty, and the common good.

Euripides was the most controversial and psychologically daring of the three. His plays questioned traditional values, explored the darker aspects of human nature, and gave powerful voices to women and slaves—people who had no voice in Athenian politics. *Medea* tells the story of a foreign woman who murders her own children to punish her unfaithful husband. It's horrifying, but Euripides makes you understand Medea's rage and betrayal. *The Trojan Women*, produced in 415 BCE during the Peloponnesian War, depicts the aftermath of the fall of Troy from the perspective of the conquered women. It's a powerful anti-war statement that questioned Athenian imperialism when Athens was at war and conquering other cities.

Euripides wasn't as popular as Sophocles during his lifetime (he only won first prize five times), but his psychological realism and willingness to challenge conventional morality influenced later drama enormously. He died in 406 BCE, and the Athenians, who had often been uncomfortable with his plays, mourned him deeply.

Comedy was different. It was louder, ruder, and more directly political. The greatest comic playwright was Aristophanes. His plays were crude, vulgar, and brutally funny, mocking politicians, philosophers, and generals without mercy. Nothing was off-limits.

In *The Knights*, he portrayed the Athenian demos (the people) as a senile old man being manipulated by a sleazy politician. In *The Clouds*, he savagely satirized Socrates as a sophist who taught students to make bad arguments sound good and to cheat their creditors. In *Lysistrata*, the women of Greece go on a sex strike to force their husbands to end the Peloponnesian War. The play is hilarious, sexually explicit, and also a serious meditation on war's costs.

Aristophanes could get away with this because Athenian democracy tolerated and even encouraged criticism and mockery. You could stand in the Theatre of Dionysus and watch a play that brutally mocked the generals, the Assembly, and the whole democratic system performed at a state-sponsored festival. This was freedom of speech in action. It was messy, uncomfortable, and vital.

While playwrights explored human nature through drama, philosophers were developing new ways of thinking about the world, knowledge, and morality. The intellectual revolution happening in Athens would reshape Western thought.

Earlier Greek philosophers had already been asking radical questions about the nature of reality, and many, including some sophists and pre-Socratic thinkers, had engaged with ethics, human knowledge, and society. But 5th-century Athens saw philosophy become more intensely focused on human concerns, like ethics, politics, knowledge, and how to live a good life. The sophists, professional teachers who charged fees, taught rhetoric, debate, and practical wisdom to wealthy young men. Some sophists seemed to argue that truth was relative and that persuasive speech mattered more than actual virtue; in other words, that might made right. Critics worried they were teaching cynical manipulation rather than genuine wisdom.

Then came Socrates. He didn't write anything down. Everything we know about him comes from his students and contemporaries, particularly Plato and Xenophon, who provide different but complementary perspectives on his life and teachings. Socrates transformed philosophy by making it a matter of constant questioning rather than providing answers. He wandered around Athens engaging anyone who would talk with him in philosophical dialogue, asking seemingly simple questions that revealed how little people actually understood about concepts they took for granted. What is justice? What is courage? What is virtue? When people gave confident answers, Socrates would ask follow-up questions until their certainty crumbled and they realized they didn't really know what they were talking about.

This made him deeply annoying to many Athenians, but Socrates believed this questioning was essential. The unexamined life, he famously said, is not worth living. You couldn't live ethically if you hadn't thought carefully about what ethics meant. Conventional answers weren't good enough. You had to understand why things were right or wrong, not just accept what society told you.

Socrates insisted that virtue was knowledge. If you truly understood what was good, you would do it. People only did wrong because they were confused or ignorant about what was actually good for them. This was a radical idea that suggested moral education was possible and essential.

Socrates also questioned democracy, which didn't make him popular. In Plato's writings, Socrates uses the analogy of governing being like sailing a ship. You wouldn't let just anyone steer, regardless of whether they knew how. Why, then, should anyone be allowed to vote on complex political matters regardless of whether they understood them? Shouldn't governance require expertise? This critique of democracy, as presented by Plato, would influence political philosophy for centuries, though it didn't prevent Socrates from staying in Athens and obeying its laws (mostly).

Socrates would eventually be executed by Athens in 399 BCE on charges of impiety and corrupting the youth. Whether this was a legitimate claim or political persecution remains debated. His student Plato would carry on his philosophical project, founding the Academy and writing dialogues that preserved Socratic questioning while developing a comprehensive philosophical system.

Plato's student Aristotle would study at the Academy and then found his own school, the Lyceum. Between them, Socrates, Plato, and Aristotle would create the foundation of Western philosophy. This all took place in Athens, all within a span of about a century.

While philosophers questioned and playwrights explored, sculptors were revolutionizing how humans depicted the body. Earlier Greek sculpture had been stiff and stylized, with the "archaic smile" and rigid poses of *kouroi* (standing male statues). But 5th-century sculptors achieved something unprecedented: they made marble look alive.

The sculptor Myron created bronze statues like the *Discus Thrower* that captured bodies in motion with perfect anatomical accuracy. Polykleitos wrote a treatise on ideal proportions and created statues like the *Doryphoros* (Spear-Bearer) that embodied his mathematical approach to representing the perfect human form. These weren't just technically skillful; they were also beautiful, capturing both physical perfection and an idealized human dignity.

Phidias is widely considered the greatest sculptor of the age. He served as chief artistic director for the Parthenon's sculptural program. The temple's pediments, metopes, and frieze were

A Roman copy of the Discus Thrower."

filled with sculptures depicting mythological battles, the birth of Athena, and a grand procession of Athenian citizens. These sculptures showed figures in complex poses, with flowing drapery that revealed the body beneath, faces that conveyed emotion, and compositions that made the stone seem to move.

Phidias also created the statue of Athena Parthenos that stood inside the Parthenon. It was nearly forty feet tall, made of gold and ivory, and showed the goddess in full armor. It was one of the most famous statues in the ancient world, though it no longer survives. He later created an even more famous statue of Zeus at Olympia, which was considered one of the Seven Wonders of the Ancient World.

Greek sculpture from this period influenced art for the next 2,500 years. Renaissance artists studied Greek proportions and poses. Neoclassical sculptors tried to recreate Greek ideals. Even today, our ideas about how to represent the human body in art owe an enormous debt to 5th-century Athenian sculptors.

A Roman copy of Phidias's Athena. It is thought to be the most faithful reproduction of this work.[65]

Painting was also flourishing, though almost none of it survives. We know from ancient descriptions that painters like Polygnotus created large-scale narrative paintings that were celebrated throughout Greece. Vase painting reached its artistic peak, with red-figure technique allowing painters to show fine details of anatomy, drapery, and facial expressions on pottery that served both practical and decorative purposes.

Architecture, of course, reached its culmination in the Parthenon. However, the Parthenon wasn't the only new building. The Propylaea, the monumental gateway to the Acropolis, was completed in the 430s BCE. There was the Temple of Athena Nike and the Erechtheion with its famous Porch of the Caryatids. Athens was being rebuilt as a showcase of architectural achievement. The buildings weren't just large; they were also precisely designed with subtle curves and optical refinements to appear perfectly straight and proportioned to the human eye.

The Porch of the Caryatids.[66]

All of this cultural production was interconnected with Athenian democracy and imperialism. The theater reinforced civic identity and allowed the public to explore moral questions. Philosophy questioned the very basis of society and knowledge. Sculpture and architecture made Athens physically beautiful and proclaimed its greatness to the world. Democratic participation made citizens feel invested in Athens's cultural achievements.

But this golden age was also fragile. It depended on continued peace, prosperity, and Athenian power. The empire that funded the Parthenon was creating enemies throughout Greece. The democracy that tolerated Aristophanes's mockery would eventually execute Socrates. The confidence that produced such incredible art would lead Athens into disastrous wars.

However, for a few decades in the mid-5th century BCE, everything seemed to come together in Athens. It was one of those rare historical moments when a single city produced an extraordinary concentration of talent and achievement. Playwrights, philosophers, sculptors, architects, and orators all worked in the same city at the same time, pushing each other to greater achievements and creating works that would be studied and admired for millennia.

But what was daily life actually like for ordinary Athenians living through this golden age? Behind the grand monuments and philosophical debates, people still had to eat, work, raise families, and manage households.

Most Athenians lived simply. Houses were small, built around central courtyards, with plain exteriors facing narrow streets. Wealthy homes might have multiple rooms and decorative elements, but even prosperous citizens lived modestly by modern standards. Furnishings were basic. They had beds, chairs, and storage chests. Windows were small and high up for privacy and security. The focus of the home was the hearth, sacred to the goddess Hestia, where the family cooked and gathered.

The household (*oikos*) was the fundamental unit of Athenian society. A typical household included the male head of household, his wife, children, and possibly elderly parents, along with slaves if the family could afford them, though many poorer citizens owned no slaves at all. The husband managed external affairs. The wife managed the household, supervising slaves if the family had them or doing the labor herself if not, along with organizing food production, weaving cloth, and raising young children. Respectable women rarely left the house except for religious festivals or visits to female relatives.

Food was simple but adequate. Bread was the staple, made from barley or wheat. Olives and olive oil appeared at every meal. Vegetables, such as onions, garlic, lentils, and cabbage, added variety. Fish was common; meat was expensive and usually reserved for religious festivals when sacrificed animals were cooked and shared. Wine, always diluted with water, accompanied meals. Drinking undiluted wine was considered barbaric.

The agora was the heart of daily economic and social life. Every morning, farmers brought produce to sell. Vendors offered fish, bread, pottery, cloth, tools, and everything else Athenians needed. The agora buzzed with commercial activity. Men met friends, discussed business, and heard the latest political news. It was where Socrates famously wandered, engaging passersby in philosophical conversation.

For wealthier citizens, evenings might bring symposia, which were drinking parties that were a central feature of elite male social life. These weren't wild orgies, though they could get rowdy. After dinner, men reclined on couches, drank wine, talked, sang songs, discussed philosophy, played games, and enjoyed entertainment from hired musicians or dancers. Symposia were where friendships were cemented, political alliances were formed, and ideas were exchanged among the upper classes. Women didn't attend except for hired entertainers; respectable wives stayed home.

Physical fitness was valued. Men exercised at *gymnasia*, public spaces with running tracks, wrestling grounds, and baths. Exercise wasn't just about health; it was also about cultivating the ideal body. Young men trained, older men stayed fit, and everyone socialized. The gymnasium was also an intellectual space. Philosophers taught there, conversations happened, and ideas spread.

Religious life pervaded daily existence. Household shrines honored domestic gods. Public festivals punctuated the year with processions, sacrifices, and feasts. Religion wasn't about personal salvation or moral guidance. It was more about maintaining proper relationships with the gods who could help or harm the community. Sacrifices, prayers, and rituals sought to secure divine favor and avoid divine anger.

Childhood in Athens was short. Boys from wealthy families received an education, learning to read, write, play musical instruments, and recite poetry. At age eighteen, they entered military training. Girls received no formal education, instead learning household management from their mothers. Marriage came early for girls. It is commonly believed they married at around fourteen or fifteen, though ages likely varied. Men usually married in their twenties or thirties in arrangements made by their fathers.

For all its cultural brilliance, daily life in Athens was constrained by gender, class, and status. Citizens enjoyed freedom and opportunity. Women, slaves, and metics lived more restricted lives. The golden age was golden for some (adult male citizens) and far less so for others. However, even for those who benefited, life was precarious. War, disease, and political upheaval could destroy that comfort and security in moments.

And the Peloponnesian War was coming. The long struggle between Athens and Sparta would test everything Athens had built. The golden age would not survive the war, but the cultural achievements would endure long after Athens's political power faded. The plays, the philosophy, the sculptures, and the buildings would remain, testifying to what humans could achieve when given the freedom, resources, and drive to create something that lasts.

Greek Fights Greek: The Peloponnesian War (431–404 BCE)

The war that destroyed Athens's golden age began over a minor dispute in a city most Greeks had barely heard of. However, the Peloponnesian War wasn't really about that dispute, just as World War I wasn't really about an assassination in Sarajevo. The war happened because two incompatible power structures—the Athenian naval empire and the Spartan land-based alliance—had been on a collision course for decades.

Thucydides, the Athenian general who wrote the definitive history of the war, understood this. He distinguished between the immediate causes (the specific incidents that triggered the fighting) and the real cause, which he identified as "the growth of Athenian power and the fear this caused in Sparta." Sparta watched Athens transform from an ally against Persia into an imperial power that dominated the Aegean. Spartan leaders worried that Athens's expansion would eventually threaten Sparta itself. Athens, meanwhile, believed Sparta resented Athenian success and would attack eventually anyway, so Athens might as well expand while it could.

This is a classic security dilemma. Each side's efforts to ensure its own safety made the other side feel threatened, leading to an arms race and increasing hostility until war became inevitable.

The immediate trigger came from Epidamnus and Corcyra, cities on the northwestern Greek coast. Epidamnus experienced internal conflict and asked its mother city, Corcyra, for help. Corcyra refused. Epidamnus then asked Corinth, which agreed to help. This angered Corcyra, which attacked Epidamnus. Corinth prepared a large fleet to support Epidamnus, and Corcyra, realizing it needed allies, turned to Athens.

Corcyra had a large navy, second only to Athens. If Corinth defeated Corcyra and absorbed its fleet, the balance of naval power would shift. Athens decided to ally with Corcyra, sending a small fleet to support them. A naval battle followed in 433 BCE, and Athens's presence prevented a Corinthian victory.

Corinth was furious. Corinth was a major member of Sparta's Peloponnesian League, an alliance system Sparta had built over the previous century to maintain its dominance in the Peloponnese and counter Athenian power. Unlike Athens's Delian League, which had become an empire, the Peloponnesian League gave member cities more autonomy while requiring them to follow Sparta in war. Corinthian leaders went to Sparta and demanded action against Athens, arguing that Athens's expansion threatened all of Sparta's allies and would eventually threaten Sparta itself. Other Spartan allies echoed these concerns.

Then Athens made things worse. Potidaea, a city in northern Greece, was a Corinthian colony but also a tribute-paying member of Athens's empire. Athens, worried about Potidaea's loyalty given rising tensions with Corinth, demanded that Potidaea tear down its walls, expel Corinthian magistrates, and send hostages to Athens. Potidaea refused and revolted, so Athens besieged the city. Corinth sent troops to help Potidaea. Athenian and Corinthian soldiers fought each other, though their cities weren't officially at war yet.

Finally, Athens issued the Megarian Decree, banning the city of Megara (another Spartan ally) from trading in any port controlled by Athens or its empire. This was economic warfare. Megara's economy depended on trade, and Athens controlled most major ports. The decree would strangle Megara economically.

Sparta demanded that Athens revoke the Megarian Decree and grant autonomy to its allies. Athens, led by Pericles, refused. Pericles argued that backing down would make Athens look weak and invite further demands. Better to fight now than after more concessions. Sparta's allies pressed for war. In 431 BCE, Sparta declared war on Athens, and the Peloponnesian League invaded Attica.

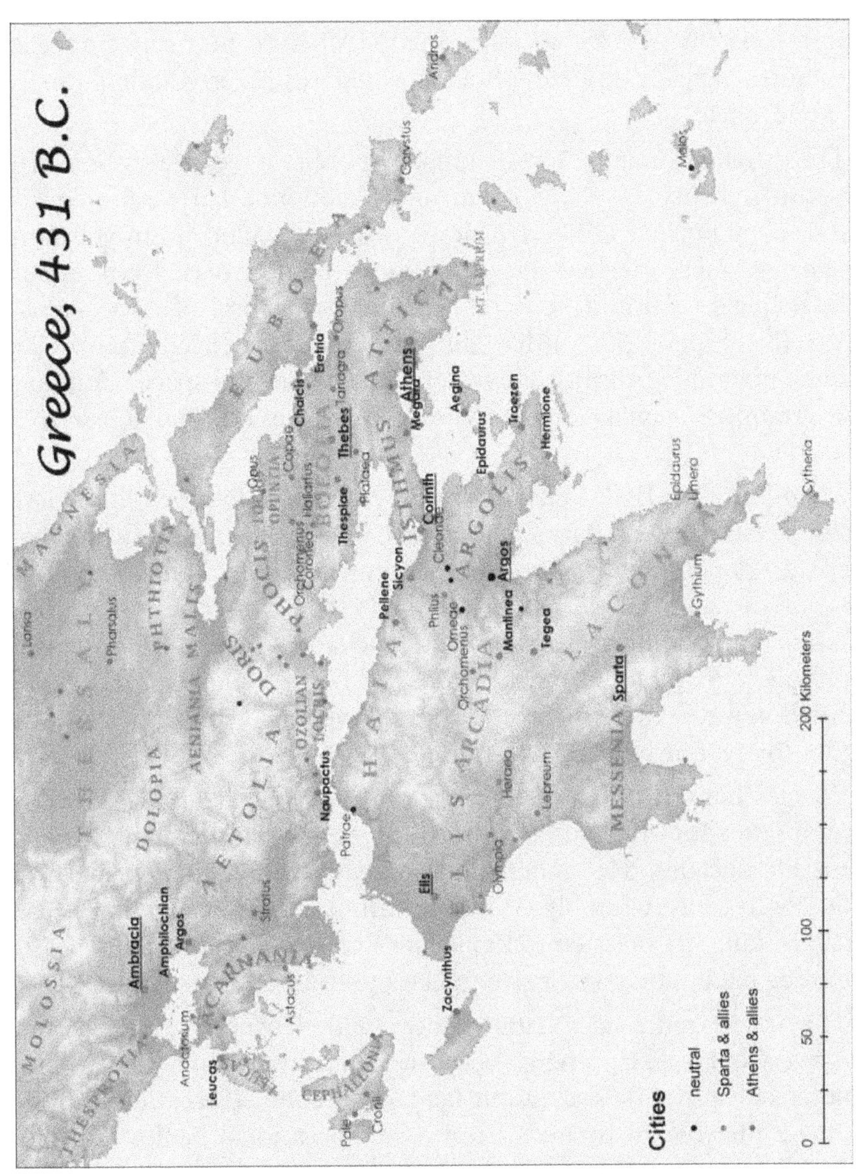

Greek cities at the beginning of the Peloponnesian War.[67]

Pericles had a strategy. Sparta's army was unbeatable on land, but Athens didn't need to fight them there. Athens had the largest navy in Greece, walls connecting the city to its port at Piraeus, and an empire that provided tribute and supplies. Pericles's plan was to avoid land battles, let the Spartans invade Attica and burn farmland if they wanted, bring the rural population inside Athens's walls, use the navy to raid Peloponnesian coasts, and wait for Sparta to exhaust itself. Athens could import food by sea. The walls made Athens effectively an island, immune to siege. Eventually, Sparta would realize it couldn't win and would negotiate.

The strategy made sense militarily, but it was psychologically devastating. Every spring, Spartan and Peloponnesian armies invaded Attica. They burned crops, cut down olive trees, and destroyed farms. Athenian farmers watched their livelihoods be destroyed from Athens's walls, helpless to stop it. The entire rural population of Attica—tens of thousands of people—crowded into Athens. They lived in makeshift shelters, in temple precincts, anywhere they could find space. Conditions were cramped, sanitary facilities were overwhelmed, and tensions ran high.

Then, in 430 BCE, plague struck Athens. We don't know what disease it was. It could have been typhus, typhoid, or a viral hemorrhagic fever. It spread rapidly through the crowded city, killing thousands. Thucydides survived it and described the symptoms: high fever, inflammation, vomiting, diarrhea, unquenchable thirst, and skin covered in pustules. People died quickly, and the bodies piled up. The plague returned in waves over the next few years, eventually killing perhaps one-quarter to one-third of Athens's population.

Pericles himself caught the plague and died in 429 BCE. His death was a disaster for Athens. He'd been the steady hand guiding Athenian policy for decades. He understood strategy, commanded respect, and could control the Assembly. Without him, Athenian leadership became unstable and inconsistent. Politicians competed for influence by proposing increasingly aggressive policies to win popular support.

The war ground on. Neither side could deliver a knockout blow. Sparta couldn't take Athens because of its walls and navy. Athens couldn't defeat Sparta's army on land. The conflict became a grinding stalemate punctuated by raids, sieges, and occasional battles that didn't decisively change anything.

But the war produced moments that revealed the brutality and moral complexity of the conflict. In 428 BCE, the city of Mytilene on the island of Lesbos revolted from Athens's empire. Athens besieged the city and forced its surrender. The question was what to do with the Mytilenians. The Athenian Assembly, angry at the betrayal, voted to execute all adult males and enslave all women and children. A ship was sent with these orders.

The next day, many Athenians felt uneasy about the decision. The Assembly met again to reconsider. Cleon, a politician who had risen to prominence after Pericles's death, argued for carrying out the execution. The Mytilenians had betrayed Athens and deserved death. Mercy would make Athens look weak and encourage other revolts. Another politician, Diodotus, argued against. Mass execution wasn't about justice; it was about whether the policy would benefit Athens. Killing everyone wouldn't stop future revolts. It would just make cities fight to the death rather than surrender. It would be better to punish the leaders and spare the people.

The Assembly reversed its decision. A second ship raced to catch the first. It arrived just in time. The massacre was called off, though the revolt's leaders were executed, and Mytilene lost its fleet and autonomy. The Mytilenian Debate, as Thucydides recorded it, showed Athenian democracy at its most volatile. It was capable of near-genocide one day and mercy the next. Decisions were driven by rhetoric and emotion rather than careful deliberation.

Two years later, in 425 BCE, Athens scored an unexpected victory. An Athenian fleet established a fort at Pylos on the Peloponnesian coast. Sparta sent forces to dislodge them, including troops stationed on the nearby island of Sphacteria. Through a combination of luck and Athenian naval skill, the Spartan forces on Sphacteria were cut off and besieged. After weeks, about 120 Spartiate hoplites, plus perioikoi and helots, surrendered.

This shocked the Greek world. Spartans didn't surrender. They fought to the death. The idea that Spartans could be trapped and forced to capitulate shattered Sparta's aura of invincibility. Athens held the prisoners as hostages, threatening to execute them if Sparta invaded Attica again. Sparta sued for peace, offering significant concessions. However, Athens, emboldened by its success and urged on by Cleon, demanded terms so harsh that Sparta refused. The war continued, but the balance of fear had shifted.

The Peace of Nicias in 421 BCE should have ended the fighting, but it created more problems than it solved. Sparta's allies felt betrayed by the terms, which favored Athens. Athens's aggressive faction wanted to continue expansion. The peace was always fragile.

In 416 BCE, Athens revealed just how ruthlessly imperial it had become. The island of Melos wanted to remain neutral in the war. Melos had historic ties to Sparta but hadn't actively helped either side. Athens demanded that Melos join its empire. The Melians argued they had the right to remain neutral. After all, they'd done nothing to harm Athens.

The discussion between Athenian envoys and Melian leaders, as Thucydides recorded it (whether historically accurate or his literary invention), became one of history's most famous statements of realpolitik. The Athenians stated bluntly, "The strong do what they can and the weak suffer what they must." Justice was irrelevant. Power determined outcomes. Melos should submit because Athens was stronger. Appeals to fairness, neutrality, or the gods were meaningless.

Melos refused to submit, so Athens besieged the island. When Melos finally surrendered, Athens executed all adult males and enslaved the women and children. The Melian massacre wasn't militarily necessary, as Melos posed no threat. It was a demonstration of power and a warning to other cities considering resistance or neutrality. Athens had become what it once fought against: an empire maintaining control through terror.

The following year would see Athens make the decision that would ultimately destroy its power. But that catastrophe was still ahead. For now, Athens seemed invincible. It was ruthless, powerful, and convinced that might made right.

Disaster in Sicily: Athens's Fatal Gamble (415–413 BCE)

In 415 BCE, the Athenian Assembly debated the most consequential decision in the city's history. The question was whether to launch a massive military expedition to conquer Sicily, a large island far to the west of Greece. It was wealthy and mostly uninvolved in the war between Athens and Sparta.

The proposal came from Alcibiades, a young, brilliant, aristocratic, and wildly ambitious man. Alcibiades was everything Athens both admired and feared: charismatic, persuasive, and brave in battle but also arrogant, self-serving, and driven more by personal glory than civic duty. He was Pericles's ward (his mother's cousin) and had learned politics from the master, but where Pericles was measured and strategic, Alcibiades was reckless and opportunistic.

Alcibiades argued that Sicily represented an incredible opportunity. The island was rich, producing grain, timber, and wealth that could fund Athens's war effort. Its major city, Syracuse, was large and powerful but politically divided. If Athens conquered Sicily, it would control the western Mediterranean, gain enormous resources, and become unstoppable. Young Athenians, tired of years of stalemate with Sparta, were seduced by dreams of easy conquest and adventure.

Nicias, the general who had negotiated the peace with Sparta, argued passionately against the expedition. He was older, more cautious, and understood how dangerous this venture was. Athens was still technically at war with Sparta, and the Peace of Nicias was collapsing. Sending Athens's best troops and ships halfway across the Mediterranean while enemies lurked at home was strategically insane. Sicily wasn't a threat to Athens. Syracuse hadn't done anything to justify an invasion. The expedition was unnecessary, expensive, and dangerous.

Nicias tried a different tactic. If the Assembly insisted on the expedition, he argued, it needed to be done properly. He listed the enormous forces that would be required: hundreds of ships, tens of thousands of soldiers, and a massive amount of supplies. He deliberately inflated the numbers, hoping to scare the Assembly into abandoning the plan. It backfired completely. The Assembly, rather than being deterred by the scale, became more excited. If the expedition needed to be that large, it must be truly important! They voted to approve everything Nicias requested and more.

In the summer of 415 BCE, Athens launched the largest military expedition in Greek history. The fleet that gathered at Piraeus numbered perhaps 134 triremes plus dozens of supply ships. It was the largest armada Athens had ever assembled. The force included over five thousand hoplites, hundreds of archers and slingers, and support personnel. Counting sailors, soldiers, and non-combatants, an estimated thirty thousand to forty thousand men were involved. The accumulated power of the empire had been poured into one massive expedition.

Three generals commanded: Alcibiades, who had pushed for the expedition; Nicias, who opposed it but was given command anyway; and Lamachus, an experienced but less politically prominent general. This divided command would prove disastrous. Alcibiades wanted aggressive action. Nicias wanted to be cautious. They couldn't agree on a strategy.

The fleet departed with a lot of fanfare and excitement. Families gathered to watch, cheering as the ships left. Athens had never seemed more powerful. The expedition felt like a celebration of Athenian greatness, a demonstration that Athens could fight Sparta and conquer Sicily at the same time. Hubris dripped from every sail.

Things started going wrong immediately. Just before departure, someone vandalized the Herms, sacred stone pillars with heads of the god Hermes. This was shocking sacrilege. Worse, rumors spread that Alcibiades and his friends were responsible for it as part of a plot against democracy. Alcibiades demanded an immediate trial to clear his name before the fleet left. His enemies refused, saying the expedition was too important to delay. Let him go, they said, and face trial when he returned.

This was a trap. After the fleet reached Sicily, Alcibiades was recalled to Athens to face charges of impiety and conspiracy. He knew what awaited him; his political enemies controlled the prosecution, and the charges carried the death penalty. Rather than return to almost certain execution, Alcibiades fled. He went to Sparta and offered his services to Athens's greatest enemy, advising the Spartans on how to defeat Athens. It was betrayal on a spectacular scale.

Herma Demosthenes.[68]

The expedition now had divided command between Nicias, who still thought the whole thing was a bad idea, and Lamachus, who wanted to attack immediately. They compromised on a cautious approach. They would sail around Sicily, gathering intelligence, trying to find allies, and delaying the actual assault on Syracuse. This gave the Syracusans time to prepare. When Athens finally laid siege to Syracuse, the city was ready.

The siege of Syracuse became a grinding stalemate. Athens built walls around the city to cut it off. Syracuse built counter-walls. Battles were fought. Ground was gained and lost. Lamachus was killed in battle, leaving only Nicias in command. Syracuse received reinforcements from other Sicilian cities and, critically, from Sparta. A Spartan general named Gylippus arrived with troops and took command of Syracuse's defense. He was competent, aggressive, and understood Athenian tactics. The balance shifted.

Athens sent another massive fleet with thousands more soldiers under the general Demosthenes. For a moment, it seemed Athens might still win through sheer weight of numbers. However, the reinforcements couldn't break the deadlock either. The siege dragged into its second year. Athenian soldiers were dying from disease, exhaustion, and combat. Supplies ran low, and morale collapsed.

By 413 BCE, even Nicias recognized the expedition had failed. The generals decided to retreat. It would be a humiliating defeat, but at least the army and fleet would survive to fight another day. But then there was a lunar eclipse. The Athenian soothsayers interpreted this as a bad omen and warned against immediate departure. Nicias, who was deeply religious and superstitious, delayed the retreat for nearly a month to wait for better omens.

That delay was catastrophic. The Syracusans realized the Athenians were planning to escape and moved to prevent it. They attacked the Athenian fleet in Syracuse's harbor. The battle was desperate and chaotic. Ships rammed each other in confined waters, marines fought on decks, and the harbor became choked with wreckage. The Athenian fleet was destroyed. Most of the ships were sunk or captured. Thousands of sailors drowned.

With the fleet gone, the Athenian army was trapped. They tried to retreat overland, marching through Sicily while Syracusan forces constantly harassed them. The retreat became a nightmare. Soldiers died from thirst, exhaustion, and attacks. The army fragmented. Nicias and Demosthenes tried to maintain order, but discipline broke down.

Finally, the Syracusans caught up with the retreating army and surrounded them. The Athenians surrendered. Nicias and Demosthenes were executed despite promises of mercy. The captured soldiers were imprisoned in stone quarries outside Syracuse. The quarries were open to the sun and rain, with no shelter, little food, and less water. Men died by the hundreds from exposure, disease, and starvation. Some were eventually sold as slaves. Most died in the quarries.

Of the massive force Athens sent to Sicily—perhaps forty thousand men total, including reinforcements—only a handful of the captured soldiers ever returned home. Nearly two hundred ships were lost. Thousands of Athens's best soldiers, sailors, and officers were dead or enslaved. It was the worst military disaster Athens ever experienced, and it was one of the worst disasters in all of Greek military history.

The psychological impact was as devastating as the material loss. Athens had seemed invincible. The expedition to Sicily was supposed to prove Athenian greatness. Instead, it demonstrated Athenian hubris, poor leadership, and the limits of Athenian power. The disaster showed every subject city that Athens could be beaten.

The End: Athens's Final Struggle and Surrender (413–404 BCE)

After the Sicilian disaster, most observers expected Athens to surrender within months. The city had lost a devastating number of its military-age male citizens, most of its fleet, and its treasury was nearly empty. Subject cities across the empire saw weakness and revolted. Persia, recognizing an opportunity to weaken Greece and reclaim the Ionian cities, began funding Sparta to build a fleet capable of challenging Athens at sea.

But Athens refused to quit. The city's resilience was extraordinary. Using reserve funds stored on the Acropolis (silver that had been set aside for absolute emergencies), Athens built a new fleet. Democratic institutions continued functioning. The Assembly still met, and citizens still served on juries. Athens maintained control over enough of its empire to collect some tribute. The war continued.

Sparta changed its strategy on the advice of the traitor Alcibiades (who later fled Sparta for Persia after allegedly seducing a Spartan queen). Instead of seasonal invasions, Sparta established a permanent fort at Decelea in northern Attica. This was far more damaging than previous raids. Athenian farmers couldn't work their land. Over twenty thousand slaves fled to the Spartans, including skilled workers from the silver mines at Laurium. Athens's silver production collapsed. The city was under constant pressure and harassment, even though its walls still protected it.

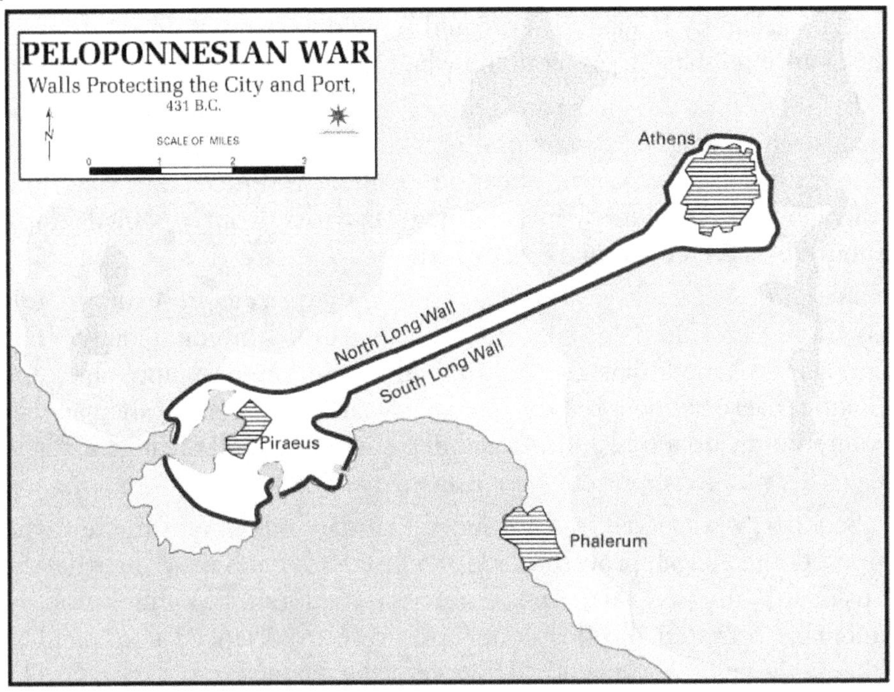

The walls protecting Athens during the war.[69]

Athens also tore itself apart politically. In 411 BCE, a group of oligarchs staged a coup, overthrowing democracy and establishing the rule of the Four Hundred. The oligarchs argued that Persia would only support Athens if it abandoned democracy for oligarchy. The coup was supposed to end the war on favorable terms. Instead, it divided Athens. The Athenian fleet stationed at Samos refused to recognize the oligarchy and remained democratic. The Four Hundred quickly collapsed, replaced by the more moderate regime of the Five Thousand, which eventually restored full democracy. The internal turmoil wasted energy Athens couldn't afford to lose.

The war's final phase was a series of naval battles for control of the Hellespont, the narrow strait connecting the Aegean to the Black Sea. Athens depended on grain imported from the Black Sea region. Without access to the Hellespont, Athens would starve. Sparta, with Persian gold building fleet after fleet, could finally challenge Athens at sea.

Athens won several impressive naval victories in these years. Athenian sailors and admirals proved that even after Sicily, they were superb.

However, the strategic equation had changed fundamentally. Athens couldn't afford to lose ships because it couldn't afford to replace them. Sparta, backed by Persian silver, could rebuild after every defeat. It was a war of attrition that Athens couldn't win.

In 406 BCE, Athens won a major naval victory at the Arginusae Islands, defeating a Spartan fleet and securing the Hellespont temporarily. But a storm after the battle prevented the victorious Athenian commanders from rescuing survivors from disabled ships. Hundreds of Athenian sailors drowned.

When the generals returned to Athens, they faced prosecution. The Assembly, grief-stricken and furious, demanded accountability. The generals explained that the storm had made rescue impossible, but emotion overwhelmed reason. In an illegal single vote (Athenian law required individual trials), the Assembly condemned all eight generals to death. Six who were present were executed.

Socrates, who served in the council that day, was one of the few who opposed the illegal procedure. He refused to participate in what he considered unjust. His opposition was ignored. Within months, Athenians regretted the decision; these were experienced commanders Athens desperately needed. However, the damage was done. The Arginusae trial showed democracy at its worst: emotion overruling law, grief producing injustice, and the mob condemning the men who had just saved them.

In 405 BCE, the war ended at Aegospotami on the Hellespont. The Athenian fleet, numbering about 180 ships, was beached. The Spartan admiral Lysander surprised them at dawn before most crews had even boarded their vessels. It was slaughter, not battle. The Spartans captured or destroyed almost the entire Athenian fleet. Thousands of captured Athenian sailors were reportedly executed. Athens's navy, the source of its power for seventy years, was obliterated in a single morning.

Without ships, Athens couldn't import food. Sparta besieged Athens by land and blockaded Piraeus by sea. Through the winter of 405/404 BCE, Athens starved. Food supplies dwindled and then disappeared. People died in the streets. Desperate Athenians debated what to do. Some wanted to fight to the death. Others argued for surrender. The Assembly, starving and desperate, finally voted to negotiate.

The terms demanded by Sparta were harsh. Athens would lose its entire empire. Every subject city would be freed from Athenian control.

The Long Walls connecting Athens to Piraeus would be torn down, leaving Athens defenseless. All remaining ships except twelve patrol vessels would be surrendered. Athens would become Sparta's ally, following Spartan foreign policy. Democracy would be abolished and replaced with an oligarchy.

Some of Sparta's allies, particularly Corinth and Thebes, demanded harsher terms. They wanted Athens destroyed completely. Sparta refused. The Spartans reportedly said that Athens had saved Greece from Persia, and for that service, Athens deserved to survive. Whether this was genuine gratitude or cold strategic calculation (destroying Athens would make Sparta's allies too powerful), Sparta insisted on terms that preserved Athens as a city, if not as a power.

In spring 404 BCE, Athens surrendered. The walls came down to the sound of flutes. Spartans and their allies celebrated as the fortifications that had made Athens invincible were demolished stone by stone. The remaining ships were handed over. Democracy was abolished. An oligarchy of thirty pro-Spartan Athenians, known as the Thirty Tyrants, took power and ruled through terror, executing or exiling democratic leaders and confiscating property. The Thirty Tyrants' reign lasted eight brutal months before democratic forces overthrew them and restored democracy in 403 BCE.

The Peloponnesian War had lasted twenty-seven years (431–404 BCE, interrupted by the six-year Peace of Nicias). It killed tens of thousands of Greeks, destroyed cities, impoverished regions, and weakened the Greek world. Athens lost everything: its empire, its fleet, its wealth, its power, and its confidence.

Thucydides wrote his history of the Peloponnesian War believing it would be "a possession for all time." It was not just a chronicle of events but a study of human nature, power, and the dynamics of conflict. He was right. The Peloponnesian War demonstrated how fear and ambition drive states into war, how confidence leads to overreach, how democracies can make catastrophic decisions through emotion, and how wars consume everything and last far longer than anyone expects.

The golden age of Athens died with the war. The Parthenon still stood. The plays were still performed. Philosophical inquiry continued. But the confidence, the wealth, and the sense that Athens was destined for greatness were gone. Greece would never again reach the heights it had achieved in 5th-century Athens. The brief moment when a single city combined democracy, imperial power, and cultural brilliance had ended, and it would not come again.

Sparta won the war but proved incapable of managing peace. Sparta's dominance lasted barely thirty years. The Spartans proved as oppressive as Athens had been, installing oligarchies in cities that had hoped for freedom and acting as Greece's new imperial power. Sparta's arrogance and brutality turned former allies into enemies. In 371 BCE, the Theban general Epaminondas shattered Spartan military supremacy at the Battle of Leuctra. Using revolutionary tactics (massing troops in an unprecedented deep formation on one wing), Epaminondas defeated the supposedly invincible Spartan army and killed one of Sparta's two kings. For the first time in two centuries, Sparta had been decisively beaten in open battle.

Thebes became Greece's dominant power, but its supremacy was brief. Epaminondas invaded the Peloponnese, liberated Messenia from Spartan control (freeing the helots who had been enslaved for centuries), and reduced Sparta to a second-rate power. But when Epaminondas died in battle at Mantinea in 362 BCE, Theban power collapsed with him. Greece descended into a chaotic free-for-all with no dominant power. Exhausted city-states constantly fought each other, and there was no end in sight. This was the weakened, divided Greek world that Macedon would conquer a generation later.

Chapter 7 – The Hellenistic Sweep: From Macedonia to World Empire

The Rough North: The Rise of Macedon

For centuries, the Greek city-states barely noticed Macedonia. The kingdom to the north was perceived as a backwater by southern Greeks. It was rural, mountainous, politically unstable, and culturally different in ways that southern Greeks often dismissed as backward. Macedonians spoke a Greek dialect that city Greeks could barely understand. They were ruled by kings rather than assemblies, lived in scattered villages rather than urban centers, and maintained a warrior aristocracy that seemed more barbarian than Hellenic to sophisticated urbanites. Many Athenians and Spartans viewed Macedonians as crude rustics, often dismissing them as barely Greek at all.

This condescension was a fatal mistake. In the mid-4th century BCE, Macedonia would conquer all of Greece, and a Macedonian king would build an empire stretching from Greece to India. The city-states that had dominated Greek politics for centuries would become subjects of a northern kingdom they had dismissed as irrelevant.

The transformation began with Philip II, who became king of Macedonia in 359 BCE. Philip inherited a kingdom in crisis. His predecessor had been killed in battle against the Illyrians. The royal treasury was empty. Multiple pretenders claimed the throne.

Macedonia's neighbors, namely the Illyrians, Paeonians, and Thracians, all saw an opportunity to raid or conquer Macedonian territory. The kingdom seemed likely to fragment or be absorbed by its enemies.

Philip was twenty-three years old, but he'd spent three years as a hostage in Thebes during the city's brief period of dominance in the 360s BCE. Scholars generally hypothesize that during his time in Thebes, Philip observed the military innovations of Epaminondas, the general who had broken Spartan power at the Battle of Leuctra in 371 BCE. Epaminondas had revolutionized Greek warfare by massing troops in deep formations and using coordinated movements rather than simple frontal charges. Philip is thought to have learned these lessons well, though ancient sources don't explicitly confirm this connection.

Philip's first priority was survival. He bought off some enemies with tribute, made alliances with others, and dealt with the most immediate threats through quick, decisive campaigns. Within two years, he'd secured Macedonia's borders and eliminated rival claimants to the throne. Then he began building.

Philip transformed the Macedonian army into the most formidable fighting force in the Greek world. His innovations combined Greek military tactics with Macedonian advantages in cavalry and manpower. The result was an army that proved capable of defeating any Greek city-state and most combinations of city-states in the battles it fought.

The centerpiece of Philip's military revolution was the *sarissa*, a pike between thirteen and twenty-one feet long, roughly twice the length of a standard Greek spear. Macedonian infantry, organized in a phalanx, wielded these enormous pikes with both hands. The front five ranks could all project their sarissas forward, creating a nearly impenetrable forest of spearheads. Enemy hoplites with their shorter spears couldn't reach Macedonian soldiers without first breaking through multiple ranks of pikes.

Macedonian phalanx.[70]

The Macedonian phalanx was devastating but inflexible. It could move forward in formation but struggled with rough terrain, turning, or responding to threats from the flanks or rear. Philip solved this problem by combining the phalanx with elite infantry called *hypaspists*, who fought with shorter weapons and could maneuver more flexibly and, most importantly, with heavy cavalry.

Macedonian cavalry, drawn from the kingdom's aristocracy, was far superior to cavalry in southern Greece. The Macedonian Companions rode larger horses, wielded long lances, and trained constantly for coordinated charges. They were shock troops who could smash through enemy formations or exploit gaps created by the phalanx. Philip used cavalry and infantry together in combined-arms tactics that no Greek city-state could match.

Philip also professionalized his army in ways Greek city-states never had. Macedonian soldiers were paid, trained year-round, and served on long campaigns far from home. Greek city-states relied on citizen-soldiers who served for limited periods and wanted to return to their farms. Philip's professionals could campaign continuously, besiege cities for months, and march hundreds of miles. They were a standing army, not a militia.

With this military machine, Philip began expanding. He didn't immediately attack the major Greek city-states. Instead, he moved methodically through the north, conquering Thrace and gaining control of gold and silver mines, which made Macedonia wealthy. He established or captured cities along the coast, building a fleet and securing trade routes. He intervened in regional conflicts to expand Macedonian influence.

Southern Greeks initially ignored Philip's expansion. They were absorbed in their own conflicts. Thebes and Sparta had exhausted each other. Athens had partially recovered from the Peloponnesian War but was primarily interested in rebuilding its naval power and protecting trade routes, not fighting land wars in the north. The Greek cities saw Philip as a local power, maybe a nuisance, but not a threat to them.

The Athenian orator Demosthenes saw things differently. From the 350s BCE onward, Demosthenes delivered speech after speech warning Athens that Philip was dangerous, that every Macedonian expansion brought Philip closer to controlling all Greece, and that Athens needed to act before it was too late. These speeches, called the Philippics, are masterpieces of rhetoric. They're also case studies in how democracies struggle to respond to distant threats until it's too late.

Demosthenes faced several problems. First, Philip was clever about not provoking Athens directly. He expanded into regions Athens didn't care much about. Philip actually sent diplomatic letters expressing friendship and avoided open conflict with major city-states. Second, Athenians were war-weary and focused on commerce, not military adventures. Third, Philip had allies in Athens, politicians who argued he was reasonable, that accommodation was possible, and that Demosthenes was a warmonger exaggerating the threat.

By the time Athens recognized the danger, Philip controlled most of northern Greece and was moving south. In 346 BCE, Athens made peace with Philip, essentially conceding his conquests in exchange for promises to respect southern Greek independence. Philip used the peace to consolidate his gains and prepare for the next phase.

The final confrontation came in 338 BCE. Philip intervened in a conflict called the Sacred War, positioning himself as a defender of Greek religious sites. Athens and Thebes, finally recognizing that Philip intended to dominate all Greece, formed an alliance to stop him. The two sides met at Chaeronea in central Greece.

The combined Athenian-Theban army outnumbered Philip's forces, and they were fighting on familiar terrain. However, Philip's army was professional, trained, and led by the best general of the age. Philip used his cavalry, commanded by his eighteen-year-old son Alexander, to devastating effect. The Macedonian phalanx broke the Athenian and Theban lines. Thebes's elite Sacred Band—three hundred warriors who'd never been defeated—were destroyed, fighting to the death rather than surrender according to ancient sources, though whether literally every man fell or a handful survived remains uncertain.

Athens and Thebes were defeated. Philip could have destroyed both cities, but he chose a different approach. He made moderate peace terms with Athens. There would be no destruction or occupation, but Athens had to acknowledge Macedonian supremacy. Thebes was treated more harshly, but it was not destroyed either. Philip understood that destroying famous Greek cities would create resentment.

Philip then organized the Greek city-states into the League of Corinth in 337 BCE. Every major Greek city except Sparta joined. The league supposedly guaranteed Greek autonomy and peace, but Philip was elected *hegemon,* or military leader. Macedonia controlled Greek foreign policy. The city-states were autonomous in theory but subjects in practice.

Philip announced that the League of Corinth would invade Persia to avenge the Persian invasions of 490 and 480 BCE. This was brilliant propaganda. Philip cast himself as the champion of Greek civilization, leading a panhellenic crusade against the barbarians who'd once threatened Greece. It united Greeks behind a common cause (or at least gave them a common enemy), and it promised glory and wealth from conquering the richest empire in the world.

However, Philip never led the invasion. In 336 BCE, at his daughter's wedding, Philip was assassinated by one of his bodyguards. The motives remain unclear. It could have been a personal grudge, a political conspiracy, or both. Philip was forty-six years old. He'd transformed Macedonia from an obscure kingdom into the dominant power in Greece in just twenty-three years.

His son, Alexander, was twenty years old. He had been trained by the best general in the world and educated by Aristotle. Alexander would take his father's army and plans and do something even Philip probably hadn't imagined: conquer the Persian Empire and change the ancient world forever.

The rise of Macedonia under Philip marked the end of the classical Greek world of independent city-states. The politically independent, polis-centered civilization that had produced Athens's democracy, Sparta's military excellence, and the cultural achievements of the 5th and 4th centuries was finished. The future belonged to kingdoms and empires, not citizen assemblies. Greek culture would spread across the Mediterranean and into Asia, but it would do so as the culture of conquerors and colonizers, not as the achievement of autonomous city-states.

A World at His Feet: The Conquests of Alexander the Great

Alexander became king of Macedonia in 336 BCE at the age of twenty, inheriting his father's kingdom, army, and plan to invade Persia. What he did with that inheritance would make him the most famous conqueror in ancient history and fundamentally reshape the Mediterranean and Near Eastern world.

Alexander's education had prepared him for greatness, or at least convinced him he was destined for it. Philip had hired Aristotle, the greatest philosopher of the age, to tutor Alexander and a group of young Macedonian nobles. For three years, Aristotle taught Alexander literature, philosophy, science, and ethics. Alexander developed a lifelong love of Homer's *Iliad*, reportedly sleeping with a copy of it under his pillow and seeing himself as a new Achilles. Whether Aristotle's philosophical teachings deeply influenced Alexander's worldview is debated, but the connection between the greatest conqueror and the greatest philosopher became legendary.

Alexander's military education came from his father and from experience. He commanded cavalry units at Chaeronea at age eighteen, proving himself brave and capable. He learned strategy from watching Philip, absorbed the mechanics of siege warfare, and understood combined-arms tactics. When his father was assassinated, Alexander was ready. He was militarily competent, intellectually confident, and burning with ambition.

However, Alexander's succession wasn't automatic. He was young and untested as king. Some Macedonian nobles supported rival claimants. Greek city-states, seeing an opportunity in the chaos following Philip's death, began discussing revolt. Thebes actually did revolt, expecting other cities to join and thinking the young king couldn't control his kingdom and fight Greece at the same time.

Alexander moved with devastating speed. He marched south to Thebes with his army. When Thebes refused to surrender, he destroyed the city. Thebes was razed. Its population was largely enslaved, and others were killed. Only the house of the poet Pindar and the temples were spared. The message was clear: revolt against Alexander meant annihilation. The other Greek cities quickly reaffirmed their membership in the League of Corinth. No one else tried to rebel.

With Greece secured, Alexander turned to Persia. In the spring of 334 BCE, he crossed the Hellespont into Asia Minor with an army of perhaps forty thousand to fifty thousand men—Macedonians, Greeks from the League of Corinth, and various allies. It was a large force by Greek standards, but it was tiny compared to the resources the Persian Empire could mobilize. Persia controlled territory from Egypt to India, commanded millions of subjects, and possessed wealth that dwarfed anything Greece could imagine.

Alexander's invasion was audacious to the point of madness. He was attacking the largest empire in the world with an army that, if destroyed, couldn't be replaced. He had no fleet to speak of, while Persia controlled the seas. He was heading into hostile territory thousands of miles from home, where Persian armies could attack from multiple directions. A sensible strategic analysis suggested that Alexander would be defeated, probably quickly.

Alexander won his first major battle at the Granicus River in May 334 BCE, just days after crossing into Asia. Persian satraps had gathered an army to stop the invasion. They chose to fight at the Granicus, a river with steep banks that would force Alexander's army to fight at a disadvantage while crossing. It was a reasonable defensive plan.

Alexander attacked anyway, personally leading the cavalry charge into the river and up the opposite bank while under fire. It was reckless and nearly got him killed. His helmet was split by a sword blow, and one of his Companions saved his life. But the charge succeeded. The Macedonian cavalry broke the Persian line, the phalanx followed, and the Persian army collapsed. The satraps fled or died. The psychological impact was enormous. The Persians weren't invincible.

Alexander spent the next year conquering western Asia Minor. Cities opened their gates, sometimes welcoming him as a liberator from Persian rule. He "freed" Greek cities from Persian control, though in practice, they became subject to Macedonia. He captured coastal cities that could serve as bases for the Persian fleet, gradually neutralizing Persia's naval advantage by controlling the ports.

The Persian king, Darius III, wasn't taking Alexander seriously enough. Darius assumed Alexander was a minor problem that the satraps could handle. When those satraps kept losing, Darius finally assembled a royal army and marched to confront Alexander personally in 333 BCE. The two armies met at Issus, on the coast of what is now southern Turkey.

Darius had more soldiers. Ancient sources claim he had hundreds of thousands, though modern estimates suggest perhaps 80,000 to 100,000. Alexander had perhaps forty thousand men. However, Darius made a crucial mistake. He chose to fight on narrow coastal ground where he couldn't use his numerical superiority effectively. Numbers mattered less when armies couldn't deploy in broad formations.

Alexander deployed his phalanx in the center, cavalry on the wings, and waited for Darius to attack. When Persian forces engaged the phalanx, Alexander led a cavalry charge aimed directly at Darius's position. This was Alexander's signature tactic: use the phalanx to fix the enemy in place, then smash through with heavy cavalry aimed at the enemy commander. It worked brilliantly. Alexander's Companions broke through the Persian lines and drove toward Darius himself.

Darius panicked and fled. Once the king ran, the Persian army's morale collapsed. The battle became a rout. Thousands of Persians were killed in the retreat. Alexander captured Darius's camp, including his mother, wife, and children. Darius escaped, but his prestige was in tatters. The Persian king had run from battle. Alexander treated the royal family with respect and sent messages to Darius offering peace in exchange for half the Persian Empire.

Darius refused. He was still king of Persia, and he thought he could defeat this Macedonian upstart. Alexander, for his part, wasn't interested in half of Persia. He wanted it all.

Alexander spent the next two years conquering the eastern Mediterranean coast. He besieged Tyre for seven months, eventually building a causeway to the island city and taking it by storm. He conquered Gaza after another difficult siege. He entered Egypt, where he was welcomed as a liberator from Persian rule and crowned pharaoh. While in Egypt, he visited the oracle of Amun at the Siwa Oasis. What the oracle told him is unknown, but Alexander emerged claiming divine parentage. He was the son of Zeus-Amun. Whether he believed this or used it for propaganda, it reinforced his growing sense of destiny.

By 331 BCE, Alexander controlled the entire eastern Mediterranean coast. He'd cut off Persia from the sea, secured his supply lines, and prepared for the final confrontation with Darius. He marched into Mesopotamia, seeking battle. Darius assembled another massive army and chose the battlefield carefully. This time, they would fight on the plains near Gaugamela, where flat, open ground would let him use his numerical advantage and cavalry effectively.

The Battle of Gaugamela in October 331 BCE was the decisive engagement of the war. Darius commanded perhaps 100,000 to 250,000 troops (the numbers are disputed and probably exaggerated by ancient sources, but he significantly outnumbered Alexander). His army included cavalry from across the empire, Greek mercenaries, and scythed chariots designed to break formations. It was the largest army Persia could field, and Darius was personally commanding it.

Alexander had perhaps forty-seven thousand troops. He was outnumbered roughly two-to-one at the minimum, possibly more. Darius's plan was to use his cavalry superiority to envelop Alexander's flanks while the center held. The scythed chariots would disrupt the Macedonian phalanx.

Alexander's response showed his tactical genius. He deployed his phalanx in the center with gaps that allowed the chariots to pass through harmlessly, allowing the light troops to kill the chariot crews. He strengthened his flanks to prevent envelopment. Then he personally led a cavalry charge aimed at a weak point in the Persian line, not straight at Darius this time, but at an angle, targeting the junction between the Persian cavalry and infantry.

The charge broke through. Alexander's Companions drove deep into the Persian formation, wheeling toward Darius's position. Once again, Darius fled. And once again, his army's morale collapsed when the king ran. The battle became a massacre. Thousands of Persians died in the retreat. Alexander pursued, but he couldn't catch Darius.

Gaugamela destroyed the Persian Empire's ability to resist. Darius still lived and still claimed to be king, but his armies were broken. Alexander marched into Persia's heartland unopposed. Babylon opened its gates in welcome. Susa surrendered. Alexander entered Persepolis, the ceremonial capital of Persia, in January 330 BCE.

What happened next is controversial. According to ancient sources, during a drinking party, Alexander and his companions set fire to the royal palace complex at Persepolis. Whether this was deliberate revenge for Xerxes burning Athens 150 years earlier, drunken vandalism, or a symbolic statement that Persian power was finished, the result was the same: the center of Persian royalty went up in flames.

Alexander pursued Darius eastward. In July 330 BCE, Darius's own satraps, recognizing the war was lost and hoping to curry favor with Alexander, murdered Darius and fled. Alexander found Darius's body and gave him a royal funeral. The Persian Empire, which had dominated the Near East for over two centuries, no longer existed. Alexander was now king of Asia.

Mosaic of Alexander fighting Darius III.[71]

Most conquerors would have stopped. Alexander had achieved something unprecedented. A Macedonian king controlled one of the largest empires the world had ever seen. He could consolidate his gains, organize his conquests, and return home in triumph. Instead, Alexander kept going.

He spent the next three years (330–327 BCE) conquering central Asia. This was a brutal, grinding campaign. The satraps who'd killed Darius led a resistance. Local populations rebelled. The terrain was harsh, full of mountains, deserts, and hostile territory. Alexander's army besieged fortresses, fought guerrillas, and endured hardships far from home. The men wanted to go back to Macedonia. Alexander insisted on pushing forward, conquering every region that had once been part of the Persian Empire.

During this period, Alexander's character darkened. Power and constant victory were changing him. He adopted Persian royal customs, wearing Persian dress and attempting to require *proskynesis* (prostration before the king), a custom he tried to impose on his Macedonian and Greek companions with little success, as they found it deeply offensive. Greeks didn't prostrate themselves before anyone. Alexander executed Philotas, one of his commanders, on charges of conspiracy, and killed Philotas's father, Parmenion, one of Philip's most trusted generals. In a drunken rage at Samarkand in 328 BCE, Alexander personally killed

Cleitus, one of his oldest companions, who'd saved his life at the Granicus. Cleitus had criticized Alexander for adopting Persian customs and claiming divine parentage.

Alexander regretted killing Cleitus, but the incident showed how paranoid and autocratic he had become. The young king who'd studied philosophy with Aristotle was becoming increasingly autocratic and tolerated no dissent. The army obeyed out of fear and discipline rather than love.

In 327 BCE, Alexander invaded India. He crossed the Hindu Kush mountains and entered the Punjab region, winning a major battle against King Porus at the Hydaspes River in 326 BCE. Porus commanded war elephants, animals the Macedonians had never fought before. Alexander won anyway, using cavalry to attack the elephants from the flanks and drive them back into Porus's own infantry.

Alexander's army had reached its limit. The soldiers had been campaigning continuously for eight years. They'd marched thousands of miles from home through deserts, mountains, and jungles. They'd fought dozens of battles. They'd seen companions die far from home. Rumors said Alexander wanted to continue east, conquering more of India, perhaps reaching the edge of the world. The army mutinied, not violently, but they refused to go farther.

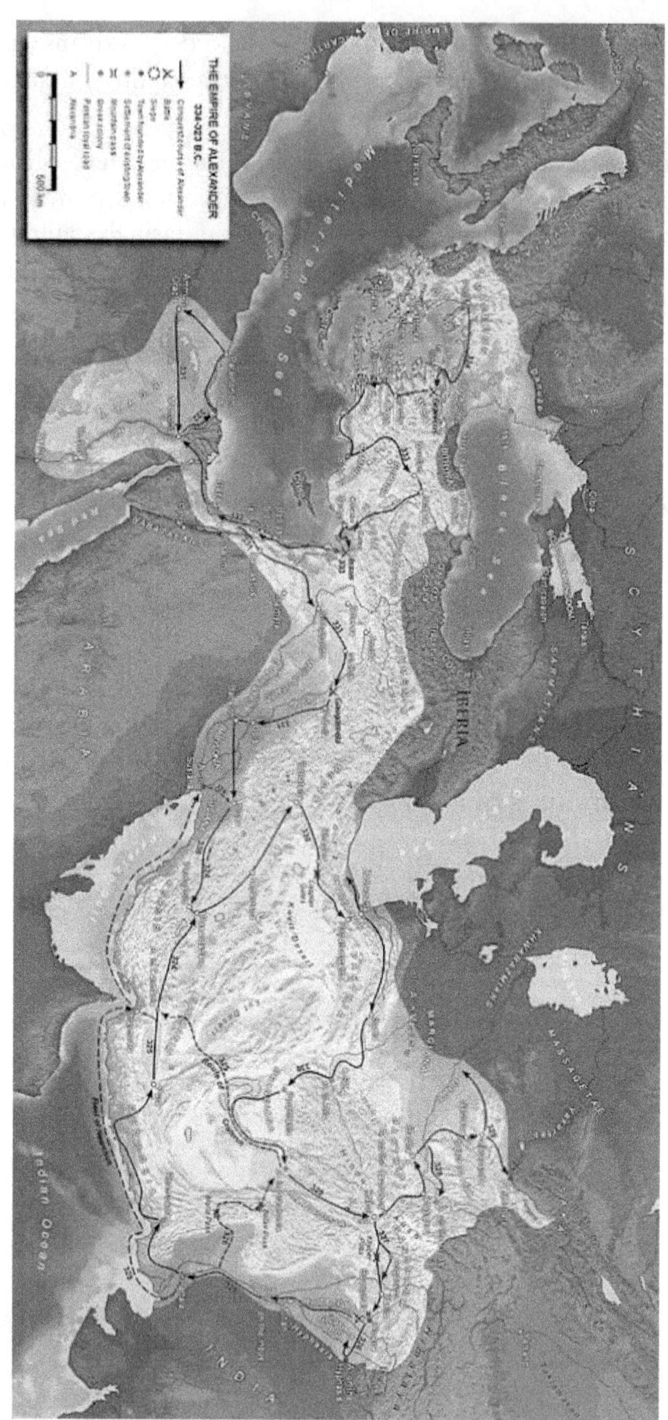

Alexander's empire at its greatest extent.[72]

Alexander tried persuasion, threats, and sulking. None of it worked. The army wouldn't move. Finally, Alexander had to accept reality. He ordered a return, but rather than retracing his route, he marched his army through the Gedrosian Desert in southern Iran—one of the most hostile environments on Earth. It was an extremely costly ordeal that killed thousands of soldiers and support personnel from thirst, heat, and starvation.

Alexander reached Babylon in 323 BCE and began planning new campaigns. He never stopped thinking about conquest. However, in June 323 BCE, after a night of heavy drinking, Alexander fell ill. Over ten days, he grew progressively weaker. On June 10th or 11th, 323 BCE, Alexander died in Babylon. He was thirty-two years old.

The cause of death remains debated. It could have been fever from disease (malaria, typhoid, or something else), complications from wounds and years of hard living, or poison. The ancient sources can't agree. What is clear is that Alexander's death created an immediate crisis. He'd conquered an empire stretching from Greece to India, but he made no provisions for succession.

Alexander's achievements were staggering. In thirteen years, he'd conquered the Persian Empire, invaded central Asia and India, founded over twenty cities (many named Alexandria), and spread Greek culture across the Near East. He'd never lost a pitched battle. He'd personally led cavalry charges in nearly every major engagement. He was brave to the point of recklessness, brilliant tactically, and driven by ambition that bordered on madness.

Alexander the Great was a conqueror, not an administrator. The empire he built was held together by his charisma and military force, not by institutions or sustainable governance. His treatment of conquered peoples varied wildly; he could be generous or brutal. He promoted cultural fusion, marrying a Persian princess and encouraging his men to marry local women, but this was as much about binding the empire together as about genuine cultural appreciation.

Alexander's legacy is complex. He destroyed the Persian Empire and ended Persian domination of the Near East. He spread Greek culture and language across vast territories, creating the Hellenistic world that would last for centuries. He inspired countless later conquerors who saw him as the ultimate warrior-king. However, he also left a trail of destroyed cities, massacred populations, and an empire that immediately fell apart after his death because it depended entirely on him.

The Splintered Kingdom: The Wars of the Diadochi

When Alexander died in June 323 BCE, he left behind an empire stretching from Greece to India and a question that would kill thousands: who would inherit everything?

Alexander's deathbed succession was a disaster. His half-brother Arrhidaeus was mentally disabled and couldn't rule. His wife, Roxana, was pregnant but hadn't given birth yet. According to legend, Alexander's generals gathered around him as he lay dying and asked who should inherit the empire. Alexander supposedly whispered "the strongest," though he may have been trying to say "Krateros," the name of one of his generals. Or maybe he was too weak to speak at all, and someone made up the answer later. Either way, the ambiguity guaranteed civil war.

The generals, known as the Diadochi, or "successors," tried to keep up appearances at first. They declared Arrhidaeus king (renaming him Philip III) and agreed that if Roxana's baby was a boy, he'd be co-king. Roxana did have a son, named Alexander IV. So, the empire officially had two kings: one who was too mentally incompetent to rule and one who couldn't walk yet. The real power belonged to the generals who commanded armies.

They divided the empire like mob bosses carving up territory. Perdiccas, who'd been Alexander's second-in-command, became regent. Ptolemy grabbed Egypt and never let go. Antigonus took much of Asia Minor. Lysimachus got Thrace. Seleucus received Babylonia. Antipater, who had been running Macedonia while Alexander conquered Asia, kept Greece and Macedonia.

This arrangement lasted about two years before everyone started killing each other.

These weren't bureaucrats content with safe administrative posts. They were conquerors who'd followed Alexander across the known world. They had led cavalry charges, besieged cities, and defeated armies. They were ambitious, ruthless, and commanded soldiers who'd follow them anywhere. Asking them to peacefully share power was like asking wolves to share a kill.

The Wars of the Diadochi spanned roughly forty years, with the decisive phase ending around 281 BCE. The fighting was spectacularly brutal. Alliances formed and dissolved overnight. Former friends betrayed each other. Armies marched thousands of miles to fight battles that changed nothing. Both of Alexander's heirs were murdered: Philip

III in 317 BCE, young Alexander IV and his mother Roxana in 310 BCE. With the legitimate heirs dead, the pretense evaporated. The Diadochi stopped claiming to rule for Alexander's family and started building their own kingdoms.

Perdiccas, the regent who tried to hold everything together, made himself everyone's enemy and was murdered by his own officers in 321 BCE while invading Egypt. Eumenes, probably the most talented general of the bunch but handicapped by not being Macedonian, fought brilliantly for years trying to preserve Alexander's empire. He was eventually betrayed by his own troops and executed in 316 BCE. Craterus, one of Alexander's most respected generals, died in battle in 321 BCE. The list of the dead grew longer every year.

The survivor who scared everyone was Antigonus One-Eye (yes, that was actually what they called him). By the 310s BCE, Antigonus controlled most of Asia Minor and parts of Syria. He had the resources and ambition to reunite Alexander's empire under his own rule. This terrified the other Diadochi, who hated each other but feared Antigonus more. They formed a coalition against him.

The final showdown came at Ipsus in 301 BCE. Antigonus was eighty years old—ancient by Greek standards—and, according to estimates, commanded around seventy thousand troops. Against him stood a coalition led by Seleucus and Lysimachus with comparable numbers, supplemented by 480 war elephants reportedly provided by the Indian king Chandragupta Maurya in exchange for territory. The elephants would prove decisive.

Antigonus's son Demetrius, who'd later earn the nickname "Besieger of Cities," led a devastating cavalry charge that broke through the coalition's lines. It was a brilliant move that should have won the battle. However, Seleucus used his elephants to cut off Demetrius's return. The elephants formed a living wall that the cavalry couldn't penetrate. Antigonus, abandoned by his cavalry, watched his infantry collapse. He died fighting, defiant to the end. His death ended any hope of reuniting Alexander's empire.

After Ipsus, the empire was permanently fractured and effectively divided into separate kingdoms. The political map crystallized around three major kingdoms that would dominate the Greek world for the next two centuries.

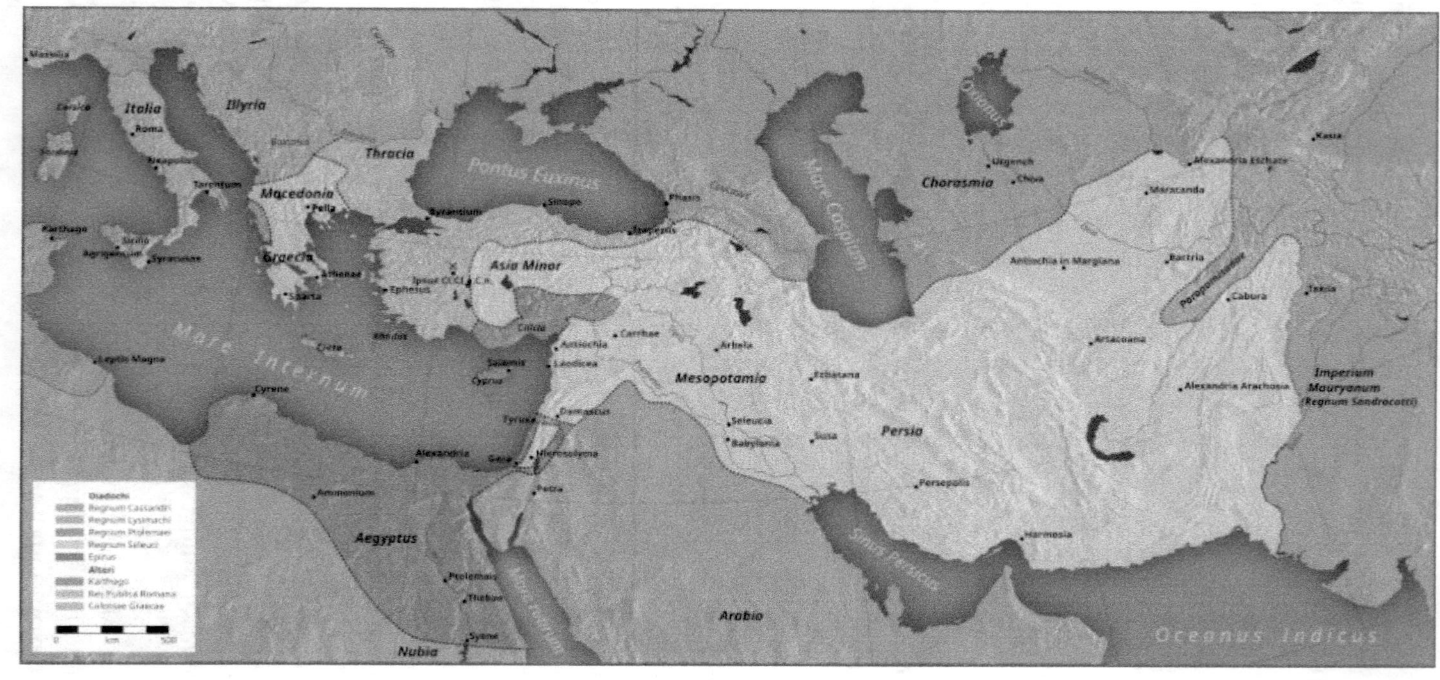

How Alexander's empire was divided.[78]

Egypt went to Ptolemy and his descendants. Ptolemy was the smartest of the Diadochi. He'd grabbed Egypt immediately after Alexander died and successfully secured it from outside attack. Egypt was defensible, incredibly wealthy, and came with Alexandria, the greatest city of the age. The Ptolemies ruled as pharaohs to the Egyptians and Greek kings to the Greeks, getting the best of both worlds. They built a powerful navy, controlled key trade routes, and made Alexandria the cultural capital of the Greek world. The Ptolemaic dynasty lasted nearly three centuries until Cleopatra VII—yes, that Cleopatra—lost everything to Rome in 30 BCE.

Seleucus got the biggest prize geographically: most of Alexander's Asian conquests, from Syria to Afghanistan. It was massive, multicultural, and a nightmare to defend. The Seleucid Empire was too big to hold together. The eastern provinces, including Bactria, Parthia, and others, gradually broke away. Bactria became an independent Greek kingdom in the middle of nowhere. Parthia turned into Rome's great eastern rival. The Seleucids spent centuries watching their empire shrink, focusing more and more on their core territories in Syria and Mesopotamia. They lasted until the 1st century BCE, when Rome and Parthia carved up what remained.

Macedonia—the homeland—went to the Antigonids, descendants of Antigonus's son Demetrius. It was the smallest of the three major kingdoms, but it was maybe the most prestigious. These were Macedonian kings ruling Macedonia, after all. They controlled Greece (sort of—Greek cities never stopped resisting), commanded the strongest army in Greece, and positioned themselves as protectors of Greek culture. However, they never had the wealth of Egypt or the vast territories of the Seleucids. Rome conquered them in 168 BCE.

Smaller kingdoms sprouted across the former empire like mushrooms after rain. Pergamon in western Asia Minor became wealthy and culturally important. Greek kingdoms existed in places Alexander's conquests had touched, spreading Greek culture thousands of miles from Greece. It was messy, violent, and nothing like the unified empire Alexander had built.

The Wars of the Diadochi proved that Alexander's empire had been held together by his personality, his military genius, and the sheer momentum of conquest. Take Alexander away, and the whole thing fell apart. The generals had personal loyalty to Alexander, not to each other or to the idea of an empire. They'd fought together under Alexander, but that didn't mean they liked each other.

The era of politically dominant and independent city-states was definitively over. The future belonged to kingdoms—massive Greek states ruled by Macedonian dynasties. However, the kingdoms the Diadochi built weren't just fragments of Alexander's empire. They were something new. These massive Greek kingdoms combined Macedonian military power with Persian administrative systems and the resources of conquered territories. They were wealthy, cosmopolitan, and culturally vibrant in ways city-states never were. Greek became the international language from Italy to India. Greek culture mixed with local traditions, creating something neither purely Greek nor purely local but something in between.

The last of the original Diadochi, Seleucus, was assassinated in 281 BCE at the age of seventy-seven while gearing up to invade Macedonia. His death marks the conventional end of the Wars of the Diadochi. By then, the Hellenistic world's structure was set. There were three big kingdoms, a bunch of smaller ones, Greek city-states trying (and failing) to stay independent, and Greek culture everywhere. Alexander had wanted to conquer the world. Instead, he transformed it. It was not the legacy he planned, but it may have lasted longer.

The New Age: Hellenistic Culture and Science

The world Alexander created looked nothing like the Greece his father had conquered. Gone were the cozy city-states where everyone knew everyone else's business. In their place rose massive cosmopolitan cities that would have blown an Athenian's mind. Athens and Sparta? They were still there, but now they were provincial backwaters. The real action had moved east to glittering new capitals like Alexandria, Antioch, and Pergamon—cities so vast they made classical Athens look like a village.

Alexandria became the crown jewel. Alexander founded it in 331 BCE on Egypt's Mediterranean coast, and under the Ptolemies, it exploded into perhaps the greatest city of the ancient world. By the 3rd century BCE, perhaps 300,000 to 500,000 people or more lived there—though such figures are speculative—making it one of the largest cities of the era. Greeks, Egyptians, Jews, Syrians, Persians, and Ethiopians all jammed together in a bustling port city. It had a lighthouse so tall (over three hundred feet) that it became one of the Seven Wonders of the

Ancient World. It had wide streets, a magnificent harbor, and more money flowing through it than anywhere else in the world.

But the Ptolemies wanted more than just wealth. They wanted Alexandria to be the intellectual capital of the world, so they threw money at scholars like modern tech billionaires throw money at startups. They built the Mouseion, a research institute where scholars lived rent-free and got paid to think. Attached to it was the Great Library of Alexandria, which sought to collect every book ever written.

The Great Library's agents were obsessed. They traveled the Mediterranean, buying manuscripts and copying everything they could find. According to later sources, ships docking in Alexandria were supposedly searched for books. Any books were confiscated and copied. The copies were returned to the owners while the originals went to the Library. Whether this policy was consistently enforced or exaggerated in later retellings, the ambition was clear. At its peak, the Great Library reportedly held somewhere between 400,000 and 700,000 scrolls, though such numbers are estimates based on ancient claims that cannot be verified. It would have essentially been everything the ancient world knew, all in one place.

The result was an intellectual boon that wouldn't be matched for over a thousand years.

Euclid showed up in Alexandria around 300 BCE and wrote a math textbook called the *Elements*. It became *the* geometry textbook for the next two thousand years. Every proof and every theorem you learned in geometry class? That's Euclid. The book was still being used in the 1900s.

Then there was Archimedes, the rock star of ancient science. This man from Syracuse figured out volumes of spheres, discovered the principle of buoyancy, and supposedly ran naked through the streets shouting "Eureka!" after realizing he could measure volume by water displacement while taking a bath. He invented war machines so effective that they held off a Roman siege for years. These giant claws grabbed ships and flipped them over. He came close to inventing methods resembling integral calculus eighteen centuries before Isaac Newton. When Roman soldiers finally took Syracuse and a soldier killed Archimedes (despite orders to capture him alive), the Roman general wept. They had just killed the smartest man in the world.

Eratosthenes looked at shadows and figured out the Earth's circumference. He knew the Earth was round—educated Greeks had known that for ages—and he noticed that at noon on the summer solstice, the sun was directly overhead in Syene (modern Aswan) but cast a shadow in Alexandria. He measured the angle, did some geometry, and calculated the Earth's size. Estimates of his accuracy vary depending on which ancient unit of measurement he used, but he was remarkably close to the actual value.

Aristarchus figured out that the Earth goes around the sun, not the other way around. He was absolutely right, although nobody believed him. Most people, including later astronomers, kept insisting the Earth was the center of everything. It took 1,800 years for Copernicus to revive the heliocentric model, though observational confirmation would come later still. Aristarchus was nearly two millennia ahead of his time.

Medicine got weird and fascinating. Herophilus and Erasistratus dissected human bodies in Alexandria, something Greeks hadn't done before due to cultural taboos about desecrating the dead. They traced nerves, identified parts of the brain, and figured out that arteries carried blood (earlier doctors thought they carried air). Later sources, particularly the Christian writer Tertullian and others often considered hostile to pagan practices, claimed they performed vivisection on living criminals. This charge remains debated among scholars and may reflect anti-Alexandrian propaganda. Regardless, their anatomical work advanced the field by centuries.

All this happened because Hellenistic kings decided that funding science made them look good. The Ptolemies didn't care so much about practical applications. They wanted glory and the greatest minds working in their city. So, they paid scholars to do nothing but research and think. It was perhaps the first time in history that governments systematically funded pure research.

Philosophy changed too, but in a different way. In classical Athens, philosophers asked, "How should we organize society?" In the Hellenistic world, that question was pointless. You lived under a king. You couldn't vote. You couldn't change anything. So, philosophers asked a different question: "How do I stay sane in a world I can't control?"

The Stoics, founded by Zeno around 300 BCE, said one should control oneself since one can't control the world. You can't control things whether you're rich or poor, sick or healthy. But you can control how you react to those things. Accept your fate. Do your duty. Don't get worked up about stuff you can't change. It sounds grim, but it was actually liberating. Stop fighting reality and find peace with what is. The philosophy became enormously influential, eventually spreading to Rome. Even emperors became Stoics.

Epicurus went a different direction. He said pleasure is the goal, but he defined pleasure as not suffering. People should live simply. Don't chase wealth or power. Enjoy friendship. Don't fear death because you won't experience it anyway since you'll be dead. Don't fear gods; they exist, but they don't care about you. It was philosophy for people who just wanted to be left alone and live peacefully.

The Cynics said forget all social conventions. Diogenes reportedly lived in a large ceramic jar or barrel (the exact nature of his dwelling is debated and may be somewhat metaphorical), owned nothing, and mocked everyone. When Alexander the Great visited him and asked what he wanted, Diogenes reportedly told him to stop blocking the sun. The Cynics thought civilization made people miserable and advocated dropping out entirely.

Diogenes by Jean-Léon Gérôme (1824–1904).[74]

These philosophies weren't abstract intellectual exercises. They were survival guides for living in a vast, impersonal world where you had no political power and might not even share a language with your neighbors. While classical philosophy had often focused on civic virtue and political organization, Hellenistic philosophy increasingly emphasized personal ethics and individual tranquility in a world of kingdoms and empires.

Greek culture spread everywhere, but it also changed. In Egypt, Greek gods merged with Egyptian ones. In Bactria (modern Afghanistan), Greek kings ruled for over a century, minting coins with Greek on one side and the local script on the other. Art blended styles. The result wasn't purely Greek or purely local but something new and cosmopolitan.

The Winged Nike made during the Hellenistic age.[75]

The Hellenistic age represented Greek culture's widest expansion and most significant transformation. Classical Greek culture was concentrated and tied to small cities. Hellenistic culture was international, diverse, and mixed with everything it touched. It was less purely "Greek" but influenced far more people across a much wider territory. When Rome eventually absorbed the Hellenistic kingdoms, it inherited this sophisticated Greek culture and spread it even further. The Hellenistic synthesis—Greek learning mixed with Mediterranean and Near Eastern ideas—became the foundation for Roman, Byzantine, and Islamic civilizations. Not bad for a bunch of kingdoms built on the ruins of one man's conquered empire.

The Final Curtain: Greek Kingdoms Meet Roman Power

While the Hellenistic kingdoms fought each other and spread Greek culture across the eastern Mediterranean, a new power was rising in the west. Rome started as one Italian city among many, but by the 3rd century BCE, it had conquered the Italian Peninsula. Then it defeated Carthage in brutal wars that gave Rome control of the western Mediterranean. The Romans were good at war, relentless in pursuit of victory, and willing to grind down enemies through sheer persistence. The Hellenistic kingdoms were about to find out what that meant.

Rome's first major clash with a Hellenistic kingdom was Macedonia. Philip V of Macedon made the fatal mistake of allying with Carthage during Rome's war with Hannibal. Rome didn't forget. After defeating Carthage, Rome turned its attention to Macedonia. The Romans presented themselves as liberating Greece from Macedonian domination, which many Greeks initially welcomed, though for Rome, the outcome was political and strategic dominance.

The decisive battle came at Cynoscephalae in 197 BCE. Philip V commanded a Macedonian phalanx, which had dominated Greek warfare for 150 years. The Roman consul Flamininus commanded legions—flexible infantry that could adapt to terrain and circumstances in ways the rigid phalanx couldn't. The battle was close until Roman maniples (subdivisions of the Roman legion) broke through the Macedonian line and attacked from behind. The Macedonian phalanx, formidable in a head-on clash on level ground, proved vulnerable on rough terrain or when its flanks and rear were exposed. Philip lost and had to accept humiliating peace terms.

Rome announced at the Isthmian Games in 196 BCE that it was granting Greek cities their "freedom." Greeks cheered. They didn't yet understand that Roman "freedom" meant doing what Rome wanted. Any city that resisted found out quickly that Roman patience had limits.

Macedonia tried one more time. Perseus, Philip V's son, built up Macedonia's strength and prepared to challenge Rome. The Third Macedonian War ended at the Battle of Pydna in 168 BCE, where Roman legions destroyed another Macedonian phalanx. This time, Rome didn't just defeat Macedonia; it abolished the kingdom entirely, divided it into four republics, and looted the royal treasury. Perseus was paraded through Rome in chains and died in captivity. The Antigonid dynasty was finished.

When the Greek city of Corinth led a rebellion against Roman domination in 146 BCE, Rome's response was brutal. The Roman consul Mummius besieged Corinth, captured it, killed the men, enslaved the women and children, and burned the city to the ground. Then he looted Corinth's art and treasures and shipped them to Rome. The message was clear: Rome's patience with Greek resistance was exhausted. Greece became a Roman province called Achaea. The classical era of sovereign Greek kingdoms had ended. Greek cities continued to exist, but they were under Roman provincial administration.

The Seleucid Empire lasted longer but suffered a slower death. Antiochus III, called "the Great," tried to expand westward into Greece in the early 2nd century BCE. Rome crushed him at the Battle of Magnesia in 190 BCE and imposed a massive war indemnity that crippled Seleucid finances. The empire began to fragment. Judea rebelled and gained independence. The Parthians conquered the eastern provinces. By the 1st century BCE, the Seleucids controlled only Syria. Rome's intervention in 63 BCE, when Pompey arrived to "settle" affairs in the east, significantly curtailed Seleucid power. Over subsequent decades, the empire fragmented and disappeared. The largest of the Hellenistic kingdoms simply dissolved.

Egypt lasted the longest of the three major Hellenistic kingdoms, surviving until 30 BCE. The Ptolemies were smart. They stayed out of Rome's way, paid tribute, and generally kept their heads down. However, Egypt was too wealthy to ignore forever. By the 1st century BCE, Rome was deeply involved in Egyptian politics, propping up friendly Ptolemies and deposing unfriendly ones.

The end came during Rome's civil wars. Cleopatra VII was the last of the Ptolemies and one of the most capable rulers Egypt ever had. She spoke multiple languages, including Egyptian (unusual among the Greek-speaking Ptolemies), understood economics and politics, and knew Egypt's survival depended on backing the right Roman faction.

She allied with Julius Caesar, had a son with him, and survived Caesar's assassination. Then she allied with Mark Antony, one of the three men who divided the Roman world after Caesar's death. Antony and Cleopatra formed a political and romantic partnership that controlled Rome's eastern provinces. They had children together. They dreamed of an eastern empire centered on Egypt that could rival Rome itself.

It didn't work out. Octavian, Caesar's adopted son and the future Emperor Augustus, painted Antony as a Roman traitor who had been seduced by an eastern temptress. The propaganda worked. At the Battle of Actium in 31 BCE, Octavian's fleet defeated Antony and Cleopatra's combined forces. The lovers fled to Egypt. When Octavian's armies approached Alexandria in 30 BCE, Antony committed suicide. Cleopatra tried negotiating with Octavian but realized she'd either be executed or paraded through Rome as a prisoner. She committed suicide, traditionally said to be by snakebite, though ancient sources differ on the details. The exact method remains uncertain.

Octavian annexed Egypt. The last Hellenistic kingdom became a Roman province. The Ptolemaic dynasty, which had ruled Egypt for nearly three centuries, was gone. The age of Hellenistic kingdoms was over.

Rome conquered the Greek world militarily, but culturally, the opposite happened. The Romans admired Greek culture deeply—maybe too deeply. Wealthy Romans hired Greek tutors for their children. Roman artists copied Greek sculptures. Roman architects imitated Greek temples. Roman writers modeled their works on Greek literature. Latin literature essentially began with translations and adaptations of Greek texts.

The Roman poet Horace summed it up best: "Captive Greece took captive her savage conqueror and brought civilization to rustic Latium." Rome conquered Greece with swords, but Greece conquered Rome with culture. Roman emperors spoke Greek, collected Greek art, and patronized Greek intellectuals. The eastern half of the Roman Empire remained Greek-speaking and culturally Greek. When the Western Roman Empire fell, the eastern half—the Byzantine Empire—survived for another thousand years as a Greek Christian empire.

The irony is profound. The Greeks lost their political independence. The kingdoms that Alexander's generals built were absorbed by Rome. Greek city-states became Roman municipalities. Greeks could no longer make war or have an independent foreign policy. But Greek language, literature, philosophy, science, and art became a foundational layer of Roman civilization, interacting and blending with Latin, Near Eastern, Egyptian, and local traditions across the Mediterranean and beyond. Christianity, the religion that would dominate Europe and eventually spread globally, developed in a Greek-speaking environment and used Greek philosophical concepts to articulate its theology.

The age of the great Hellenistic kingdoms ended in 30 BCE with Cleopatra's death. However, ancient Greek cultural influence was just beginning its longest and most successful phase, one that continues to this day. The Greeks lost their kingdoms but won the future.

Conclusion
The Legacy of Ancient Greece

Ancient Greece ended over two thousand years ago. The last Hellenistic kingdom fell in 30 BCE. The city-states that invented democracy, the philosophers who asked fundamental questions about existence, the scientists who calculated the Earth's circumference—they're all long gone. Their cities are ruins. Their books survive only as fragments or copies of copies. Most of what they created has been lost to time.

And yet, ancient Greece is everywhere.

You see it every time you vote, every time you go to a theater, every time you think about ethics or logic or politics. Greek words fill English: democracy, philosophy, theater, politics, history, mathematics, physics, and psychology. We use the Greek alphabet in science and math. We name our sports stadiums and government buildings after Greek temples. We argue about ideas that Socrates, Plato, and Aristotle debated 2,400 years ago.

This isn't nostalgia or coincidence. Ancient Greece shaped the foundations of Western civilization so deeply that we often don't even notice.

Start with democracy. Athens invented the idea that ordinary citizens could govern themselves. The Athenian system was flawed. It excluded women, slaves, and foreigners, and it made terrible decisions driven by emotion and politicking. But the core was revolutionary. Political power doesn't have to flow from kings or gods or military might. It can come from the people. That idea died when Rome conquered Greece. It was forgotten for centuries and then revived during the Enlightenment. Modern democracy isn't a copy of Athens; it's representative rather than direct, includes far more people, and has checks against mob rule. However, the inspiration came from Athens. The American Founding Fathers studied Greek history. They knew about Athens's mistakes and tried to avoid them. Without Athens, modern democracy might never have been imagined.

Or philosophy. Before the Greeks, people explained the world through gods and myths. The Greeks were the first to systematically ask "Why?" and demand logical answers. Thales tried to explain nature through natural causes, not divine intervention. Socrates questioned assumptions and demanded definitions. Plato explored justice, knowledge, and reality through reasoned argument. Aristotle categorized everything from ethics to biology to politics using logic. They created the toolkit of Western philosophy. Every Western philosopher since has been responding to Greek ideas, either building on them or arguing against them. Even if you've never read Plato, you live in a world shaped by the assumption that ideas matter, that logic can reveal truth, and that questioning authority is legitimate. That's from ancient Greece.

Science and mathematics owe a similar debt. Pythagoras discovered mathematical relationships in nature. Euclid systematized geometry in a way that's still taught. Archimedes pioneered methods that anticipated calculus. Eratosthenes measured the Earth. Aristarchus proposed heliocentrism. Hippocrates insisted medicine should be based on observation rather than superstition. These weren't just isolated discoveries. They represented a worldview that nature operates by consistent laws that human reason can understand. That assumption underlies all modern science. When scientists today insist on evidence, demand logical consistency, and test hypotheses, they're following a tradition the Greeks started.

Art and literature carry Greek DNA too. Western drama descends directly from Athens. The plays of Aeschylus, Sophocles, Euripides, and Aristophanes established genres, themes, and structures that playwrights still use. Greek epic poetry influenced Roman literature, which influenced medieval literature, which influenced the Renaissance, which shaped everything since. Greek sculpture's emphasis on a realistic human form set standards that dominated Western art for millennia.

Even when artists rebelled against classical forms, they were rebelling against Greece.

The influence isn't limited to "the West," whatever that means. When Alexander conquered the Persian Empire, Greek culture spread across the Near East and mixed with local traditions. This Hellenistic synthesis became the foundation for Roman civilization. When Rome split, the eastern half—the Byzantine Empire—remained Greek-speaking and preserved Greek learning for a thousand years. When Islam arose, it encountered this Greek heritage in Syria, Egypt, and Persia. Muslim scholars translated Aristotle, Euclid, and Galen into Arabic, studied them, built on them, and preserved what western Europe had largely forgotten. When medieval Europeans rediscovered Greek philosophy and science, they often learned it through Arabic translations. The Renaissance obsession with reviving classical learning meant studying Greek texts. The Enlightenment's emphasis on reason and natural law drew heavily on Greek philosophy. Every major intellectual movement in Europe for two thousand years defined itself partly by its relationship to ancient Greece.

This isn't to say Greece was perfect or that everything good came from Greece. The Greeks were slave owners who excluded women from public life, waged brutal wars, and committed atrocities. Their philosophers justified slavery. Their democracies could be as tyrannical as any dictatorship. They weren't uniquely rational or enlightened. After all, every culture has its thinkers and achievements. China, India, Persia, and many others developed sophisticated philosophies, mathematics, and governance without any Greek influence.

However, Greece's particular achievements—democracy, systematic philosophy, deductive logic, naturalistic science, and realistic art—spread widely and influenced a lot of people. This was partly due to timing and geography. Greece was positioned between the East and the West. It was close enough to older civilizations to learn from them, but independent enough to develop its own traditions. Alexander's conquests spread Greek culture across a huge area, and Hellenistic kings funded scholars to preserve and expand Greek knowledge. Rome conquered Greece militarily but adopted Greek culture enthusiastically and spread it across its empire. Christianity developed in a Greek-speaking environment and used Greek philosophy to explain theology. It was also partly luck; different choices at key moments could have led to very different outcomes.

The point isn't that ancient Greece was perfect or that it deserves all the credit for Western civilization. The point is that understanding ancient Greece helps us understand ourselves. When we debate democracy's strengths and weaknesses, we're continuing arguments Athenians had. When we wonder about justice, knowledge, or the good life, we're asking Socratic questions. When we insist on evidence, we're using Greek tools. When we watch plays exploring human nature through conflict and tragedy, we're experiencing what Athenians experienced 2,500 years ago.

Ancient Greece also reminds us that civilizations rise and fall but ideas endure. The Greek city-states spent centuries fighting each other, exhausted themselves, and were conquered by outsiders. Their political independence ended. But their ideas—preserved in texts, passed down through generations, and translated into dozens of languages—outlived their empires by millennia. The Greeks lost their kingdoms but won the future in a way no Greek could have imagined.

Walking through the ruins of the Parthenon or the Theatre of Dionysus, it's hard not to feel the weight of time. These were real people arguing in the Assembly, watching plays, debating philosophy, fighting wars, loving, dying, and dreaming about the future. Most of them are completely forgotten. But what they created together—their experiments with democracy, their philosophical inquiries, their scientific discoveries, their artistic achievements—echoes through the centuries. Ancient Greece isn't just history. It's part of who we are and how we think. And that makes it worth understanding, not as some distant or irrelevant period, but as surprisingly, uncomfortably, and fascinatingly alive.

Part 3: Ancient Rome for Beginners

The Story of the Roman Empire Simplified for People Who Slept Through History Class

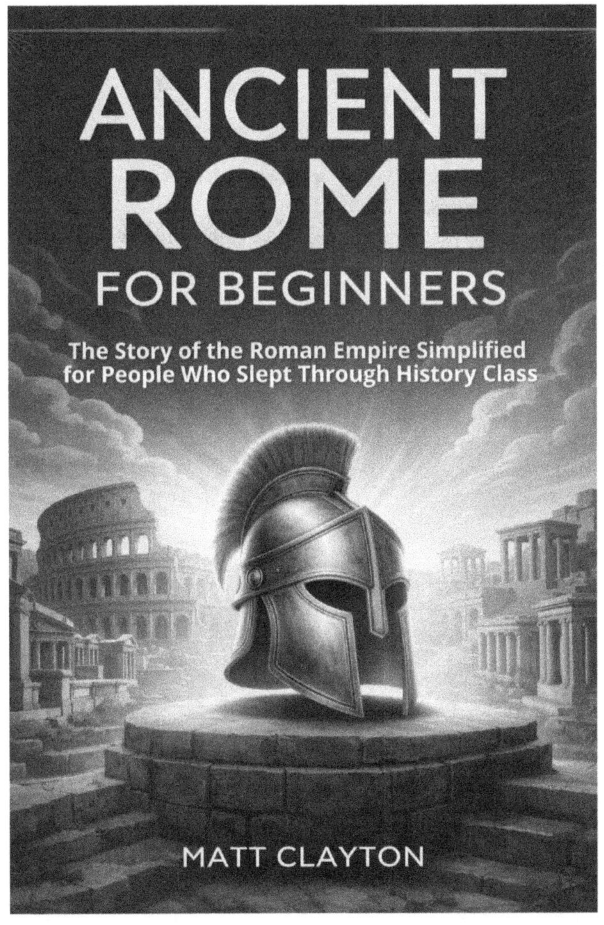

Introduction

You've probably never given much thought to ancient Rome. Maybe you dozed off during that one history class where the teacher droned on about togas and aqueducts. Maybe you watched *Gladiator* and thought, "Cool fight scenes," then moved on with your life. Or maybe you've simply never had a reason to care about a civilization that collapsed over 1,500 years ago.

But here's the thing: Rome never really left.

Right now, as you're reading this, you're surrounded by Roman ghosts. The alphabet on this page? Thank the Romans, who adapted it from the Greeks and Etruscans and spread it across Europe. The language itself—if you're reading in English, French, Spanish, Italian, or Portuguese—is packed with Latin roots. Estimates suggest that roughly 60 percent of English words derive from Latin, either directly or filtered through French after the Norman Conquest. When you say "calculate" or "sincere" or "legal," you're actually speaking a language that would sound familiar to a Roman scholar.

Look around your city. See that government building with the columns and the dome? That's Roman architecture. The US Capitol building is basically a love letter to Roman design. So is the Panthéon in Paris, the British Museum in London, and thousands of other structures across the Western world. For centuries, if you wanted a building to look important and authoritative, you made it look Roman.

The laws that govern your life have Roman DNA, though the degree varies depending on where you live. If you're in a country with a civil law system, like France, Germany, Italy, or most of Latin America, your legal code descends directly from Roman law through the *Corpus Juris Civilis* compiled under Emperor Justinian. If you're in a common-law country like the United States or the United Kingdom, the connection is less direct but still present. The concept that defendants should be presumed innocent, a cornerstone of modern justice, has roots in Roman legal thought, though the modern principle was developed later. Legal terms like "subpoena," "habeas corpus," and "pro bono" are straight-up Latin because our entire legal vocabulary evolved from Roman frameworks.

Your calendar is Roman. July is named after Julius Caesar. August is named after Augustus, Rome's first emperor. The structure you use (12 months, 365 days, with leap years) comes from the Julian calendar reform of 45 BCE, when Caesar fixed Rome's chaotic old calendar that had gotten wildly out of sync with the seasons. Before that reform, Roman priests had to insert extra months whenever they felt like it just to keep things aligned.

Even your entertainment echoes Roman spectacle. The Romans didn't invent the human appetite for watching dramatic conflict and competition, but they perfected it on a massive scale. They packed fifty thousand people into the Colosseum to watch gladiators battle, exotic animals get slaughtered, and criminals get executed in elaborate theatrical productions. They understood that crowds would gather to watch spectacles and violence and that the state could use those gatherings for political purposes. The medium has changed, but the appetite for public competition and drama hasn't.

Christianity, whether you practice it or not, shaped Western civilization in ways that are impossible to untangle from Roman history. Jesus was born in a Roman province and executed by Roman authorities. His followers spread their message along Roman roads, and they were protected (and sometimes persecuted) by Roman law. Christianity was legalized in 313 CE under Constantine and then became the official state religion in 380 under Emperor Theodosius I. When Christianity became part of the empire, it inherited organizational structures, administrative divisions, and political thinking that still shape the Catholic Church today. The Catholic Church's hierarchy, with its pope in Rome and its administrative territories, reflects the Roman world in which it grew up. Even the word "cardinal" comes from the Latin *cardo*, meaning "hinge."

The point is that Rome isn't dead. It's a fossil that turned into the bedrock beneath modern Western civilization. You can't understand how Europe became Europe, how America became America, or how the Western world developed its ideas about government, law, military organization, engineering, and culture without understanding ancient Rome.

But here's what makes Rome truly fascinating. It was a spectacular mess that somehow worked for over a thousand years. This wasn't a civilization that ran smoothly under wise and benevolent rulers. Ancient Rome could be chaotic, brutal, corrupt, innovative, and astonishingly resilient. It was built by fratricide (according to legend), grew through near-constant warfare, survived multiple civil wars, endured insane emperors and plagues, and yet somehow managed to control most of Europe, North Africa, and the Middle East for centuries.

Rome started as a muddy village on the Tiber River—a backwater settlement that no one would have bet on. It grew into a republic where citizens (well, some citizens) had a voice in government. Then it transformed into an empire ruled by emperors who ranged from brilliant administrators to raving lunatics. It built the largest road network the world had ever seen, created concrete that still stands today, and developed military tactics that armies studied for the next two thousand years. It also enslaved millions, destroyed entire civilizations, and committed atrocities that would make modern war criminals blush.

This book is going to take you through the entire story—all 1,200 years of it. We're starting in 753 BCE with the legendary founding of Rome and ending in 476 CE, when the last Western Roman emperor was quietly deposed. We'll cover the rise of the Roman Republic, the Punic Wars against Carthage, the assassination of Julius Caesar, daily life in ancient Rome, and the slow collapse that historians call "the fall of Rome" (though it was more complicated than a simple fall).

Here's the timeline in broad strokes:

753–509 BCE: The Monarchy. Rome is supposedly ruled by seven kings, starting with Romulus (who almost certainly didn't exist as described in legend) and ending with Tarquin the Proud (who might have been a real person, though the stories about him are likely exaggerated). The historical truth is murky. Archaeology tells us Rome existed at this time, but the tales of these early kings blend myth and propaganda. What we do know is that by 509 BCE, Rome had kicked out its last king and developed a permanent hatred of the monarchy.

509-27 BCE: The Republic. Rome develops a complex system of government with elected consuls, a Senate, and citizen assemblies. This is the era of Roman expansion, the Punic Wars, and the rise of powerful generals like Marius, Sulla, Pompey, and Julius Caesar. The Roman Republic ends in civil war and Caesar's assassination.

27 BCE-180 CE: The Early Empire and the Golden Age. Augustus becomes the first emperor while pretending he isn't. Rome enjoys the Pax Romana, two hundred years of relative peace and prosperity. This is when Rome reaches its greatest territorial extent and builds most of the monuments we associate with Rome. It's also when you see some truly insane emperors like Caligula and Nero.

180-284 CE: The Crisis Years. Things start falling apart. The empire faces civil wars, economic collapse, plague, and pressure from outside invaders. In a fifty-year period, Rome has over twenty different emperors, most of whom die violently.

284-476 CE: The Late Empire and the Fall. Diocletian splits the empire into eastern and western halves to make it easier to govern. Constantine legalizes Christianity and moves the capital to Constantinople. Barbarian tribes push into Roman territory. In 476 CE, a Germanic chieftain named Odoacer deposed the last Western Roman emperor, a teenager named Romulus Augustulus, and the Western Roman Empire effectively ended. (The Eastern Empire, later called the Byzantine Empire, continued for another thousand years, but that's a different story.)

This book seeks to explain ancient Rome in a way that makes sense to people who know nothing about it. We're not going to go into obscure debates that only concern academics. We're not going to skip over the interesting parts to focus on dry details about specific laws. And we're definitely not going to assume you remember anything from high school history class.

What we are going to do is tell the story of how a small city on a river became the most powerful empire in the Western world, how it maintained that power for centuries, and why it eventually collapsed. We'll explain how the Roman government worked, how Roman soldiers fought, what daily life was actually like, and why the Romans did some of the bizarre things they did (like watching people get killed for entertainment or worshipping their emperors as gods).

Let's start at the beginning, in that muddy village where legend says two brothers raised by a wolf decided to build a city. One of them ended up dead. The other became Rome's first king. It's a fitting beginning for an empire built on violence, ambition, and an unshakeable belief that Rome was destined to rule the world.

Chapter 1: From Wolf-Milk to Mud Huts

Myth vs. Reality: Romulus, Remus, and the Fratricide That Started It All

Every great civilization needs an origin story, and Rome's is a doozy. According to legend, it all began in 753 BCE with twin brothers, a she-wolf, and a murder.

The story goes like this. A princess named Rhea Silvia was forced to become a Vestal Virgin, which meant she had to remain celibate for at least thirty years. According to the legend, this was to prevent her from having children who might challenge her uncle's throne. But the god Mars had other plans. He seduced (or assaulted, depending on which version you read) Rhea Silvia, and she gave birth to twin boys named Romulus and Remus.

In the traditional account, her uncle ordered the infants thrown into the Tiber River. The servant tasked with this job could not quite bring himself to drown two babies, so he left them in a basket near the riverbank, hoping nature would do the dirty work for him.

Instead, a she-wolf found the twins and nursed them. Yes, the boys grew up on wolf milk. The boys survived and were eventually discovered by a shepherd named Faustulus. They grew up strong and ambitious. When they learned their true heritage, they killed their uncle and decided to found a city of their own.

The she-wolf nursing Remus and Romulus.[76]

This is where things got messy. The brothers could not agree on where to build their city or who would rule it. Romulus wanted Palatine Hill. Remus preferred Aventine Hill. They decided to let the gods choose by watching for birds, a practice called augury that the ancient Romans would use for centuries to make important decisions. In the most common version of the story, Romulus claimed to see twelve vultures while Remus saw only six. In another version, Remus saw his six birds first, but Romulus saw more in total. Either way, the sources agree that a dispute followed, and Romulus declared victory.

Remus, being a sore loser, mocked his brother by jumping over the incomplete city walls, saying, "These walls are pathetic. Anyone could breach them." Romulus responded by killing him on the spot, allegedly declaring, "So perish anyone else who leaps over my walls."

And that's how Rome was founded. According to tradition, Romulus became the first king. He ruled for thirty-seven years before mysteriously vanishing during a thunderstorm and supposedly ascending to become a god.

It's a great story. It's also almost certainly fiction.

Archaeology tells a different tale. The area that would become Rome was inhabited long before 753 BCE. Evidence shows scattered settlements on Rome's hills dating back to at least 1000 BCE. These were not organized cities, just small villages of farmers and shepherds living in simple huts. Around 800 to 750 BCE, these villages started merging into a larger settlement. The famous seven hills of Rome—Palatine, Aventine, Capitoline, Quirinal, Viminal, Esquiline, and Caelian—each had its own communities that gradually unified.

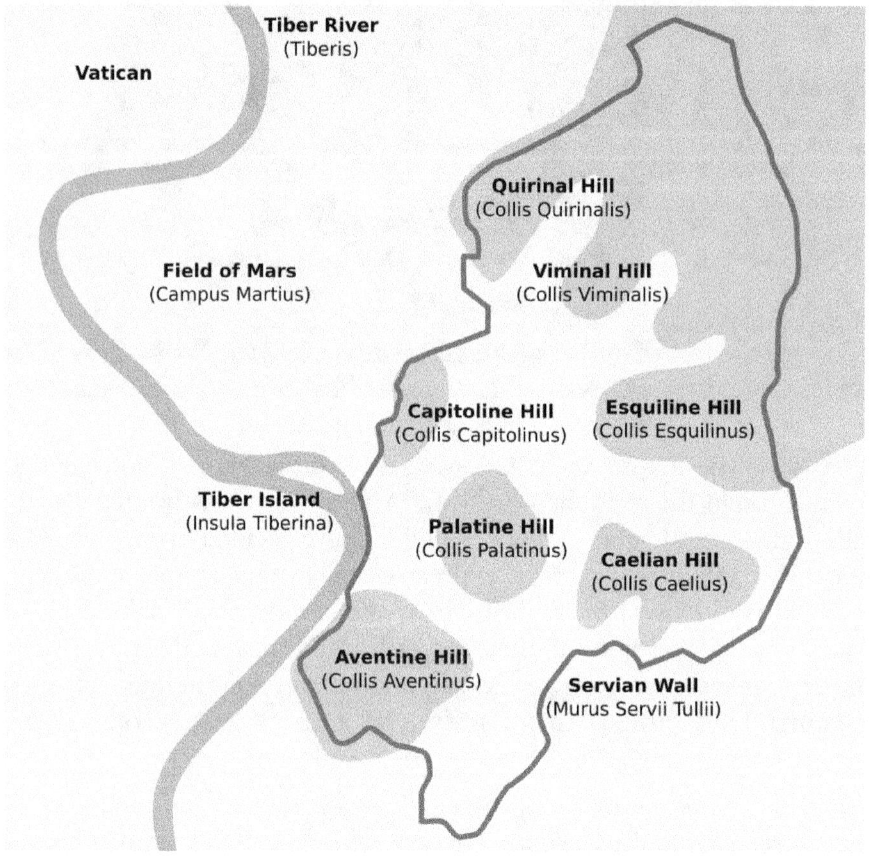

The seven hills of Rome.[77]

The process was likely messy, slow, and boring. There were no divine twins. No she-wolf. Just people deciding that cooperation offered better protection and trade opportunities than staying isolated. The Romans later developed the Romulus story, drawing on Greek models and older Italic traditions to give their city a mythical pedigree that could rival the legendary foundations of Greek cities like Athens or Thebes.

The Romans themselves, at least some of them, likely knew their foundation myth was propaganda. Ancient historians like Livy admitted they could not verify the early stories. Yet they kept telling them anyway because the myths served a purpose. They explained why Rome was special and why Romans had a divine mandate to conquer. The story justified centuries of expansion and war.

So when we talk about Rome's founding, we are really talking about two things: the myth that Romans told themselves and the archaeological reality of a settlement growing on some hills next to a river. Both versions matter. The myth shaped the Roman identity. The reality shaped their circumstances.

What was early Rome actually like? Archaeological excavations on Palatine Hill have uncovered post holes and debris from 8th-century BCE huts, simple oval structures with wattle-and-daub walls and thatched roofs. These were not impressive buildings. A typical hut was maybe ten to fifteen feet across, housing an entire family plus their few possessions. The floor was made of dirt. Cooking happened over an open fire that also provided heat and light. Most Romans were farmers who grew grain, kept a few animals, and hoped nothing went wrong.

The location mattered more than the buildings. Rome sat at one of the most practical crossing points of the Tiber River, about fifteen miles from the sea, with Tiber Island providing natural stepping stones. This made it a natural trade hub where goods moving between Etruria in the north and the Greek colonies in the south had to pass through. The hills provided defense, as it was harder to attack people there than on a flat plain. The river provided water, fish, and transportation. The surrounding land was fertile enough to support farming.

Early Rome survived because of its position and its ability to absorb outsiders. The Romans were never ethnically pure; they were a mix of Latins, Sabines, Etruscans, and whoever else showed up and proved useful. This openness to incorporating foreigners would become one of Rome's greatest strengths. Other cities jealously guarded citizenship. Rome eventually gave it to half the Mediterranean world.

The Seven Kings: How Rome Began as a Monarchy (and Why They Eventually Hated Kings)

According to Roman tradition, Rome was ruled by seven kings between 753 and 509 BCE. The list is suspiciously neat. Exactly seven rulers over exactly 244 years? Most historians think this chronology was tidied up later to make Rome's early history sound more organized than it actually was.

Still, the stories of these kings, even if partially invented, reveal what the ancient Romans believed about their own past.

Romulus (r. 753-716 BCE) was the legendary founder who supposedly established Rome's first institutions. He created the Senate, a council of elders who advised the king. He also solved Rome's woman problem—the new city had plenty of men but few women—by inviting the neighboring Sabines to a festival and then having Roman men abduct the Sabine women. This event, called the Rape of the Sabines, was later depicted in countless paintings and sculptures as if kidnapping your neighbors' daughters was a romantic way to start a civilization. The Sabines naturally declared war, but eventually, the stolen women intervened and negotiated peace. The two peoples merged, doubling Rome's population.

Abduction of a Sabine Woman by Giambologna.[78]

Numa Pompilius (r. 715-673 BCE) was supposedly the complete opposite of Romulus. He was peaceful, religious, and obsessed with proper rituals. He allegedly created Rome's religious calendar, established the Vestal Virgins (priestesses who maintained Rome's sacred flame dedicated to Vesta, the Roman goddess of the hearth and home), and built temples to various gods. If Romulus was the warrior founder, Numa was the priest-king who gave Rome its spiritual structure. He claimed to get advice from a water nymph named Egeria, which was convenient when he needed divine justification for his decisions.

Tullus Hostilius (r. 673-642 BCE) swung back toward warfare. His name literally means "hostile," which tells you something about his reputation. He conquered nearby Alba Longa after a bizarre ritual combat in which three brothers from each side fought to the death (Rome's team won). He allegedly died when Jupiter, the chief Roman god, struck his house with lightning. Ancient Romans interpreted this as divine punishment for performing a religious ritual incorrectly.

Ancus Marcius (r. 642-617 BCE) was supposedly Numa's grandson and tried to balance warfare with religious devotion. He expanded Rome's territory, built the first bridge across the Tiber, and founded the port city of Ostia at the river's mouth, giving Rome access to sea trade. He probably was not a real person, but the bridge and the port certainly existed, so someone built them.

Here is where things get more historically solid. The last three kings were Etruscans, members of a more advanced civilization north of Rome that had a profound influence on Roman culture.

Tarquinius Priscus (r. 616-579 BCE), also called Tarquin the Elder, was supposedly the son of a Greek merchant who moved to Rome and impressed everyone with his wealth and ambition. He gained the kingship through a process involving approval from the Senate and assemblies. This was not a popular election in the modern sense; it was more like acceptance by Rome's leading families. Tarquin the Elder launched major building projects. He started draining the swampy valley between Rome's hills, creating what would become the Forum, Rome's central meeting place. He also began building the Temple of Jupiter Optimus Maximus on Capitoline Hill, which would become Rome's most important religious site.

The Forum of Rome today.[79]

Servius Tullius (r. 578–535 BCE) was credited with organizing Roman society into classes based on wealth and military service. The "Servian constitution" divided citizens into groups according to how much property they owned, which determined what military equipment they could afford and thus what role they would play in the army. Richer citizens formed the cavalry and heavy infantry. Poorer citizens served as light troops. The poorest served as rowers in the navy or did not serve at all. This system of connecting wealth to military obligation would define Roman society for centuries.

Servius also supposedly built Rome's first defensive wall. The Servian Wall that visitors can see today near Rome's Termini Station was actually constructed in the 4th century BCE, after the Gallic sack of 390 BCE, though it might have followed the line of an earlier fortification. Servius expanded the city to include all seven hills and organized it into administrative districts. He was murdered by his son-in-law, Tarquin the Proud, who wanted the throne for himself.

Tarquinius Superbus (r. 535–509 BCE), better known as Tarquin the Proud, was Rome's last king and the villain of the story. According to tradition, he seized power through violence, ruled as a tyrant without consulting the Senate, and generally behaved like a king in a cautionary tale about why monarchy is bad.

The stories about Tarquin emphasize his cruelty and arrogance. He supposedly maintained power through fear and violence, executing political opponents and confiscating their property. His sons were equally terrible. One of them, Sextus Tarquinius, allegedly raped Lucretia, the wife of a Roman nobleman. Lucretia told her husband and father what happened, made them swear to avenge her, and then stabbed herself to death rather than live with the shame.

Her rape and suicide sparked a revolution. A nobleman named Lucius Junius Brutus rallied support, and the Romans expelled Tarquin and his entire family from the city. They swore never to have another king again. The year was 509 BCE.

How much of this is true? Some of it likely is. Tarquin the Proud likely existed, as his name appears in sources outside Rome. The Etruscans probably did rule Rome for a period. The revolution probably happened, though perhaps not as dramatically as the story suggests. However, Lucretia's suicide reads more like a morality play than history, a story Romans told to justify their hatred of kings and to celebrate the virtues of female honor and male vengeance.

The main thing is that Rome transitioned from a monarchy to a republic around 509 BCE, probably through a combination of internal revolts and external pressure from other Latin cities. The Romans later dramatized this transition into a founding myth for their republic, just as they had mythologized their city's original founding.

The Etruscan Influence: The Neighbors Who Shaped Rome

If you want to truly understand early Rome, you need to understand the Etruscans. They were the sophisticated neighbors who profoundly shaped Roman culture in ways that lasted for centuries, yet they remain mysterious because most of their writings have not survived.

The Etruscans lived in Etruria (modern Tuscany) north of Rome. By 800 BCE, while Rome was still a collection of mud huts, Etruscan cities like Veii, Tarquinia, and Caere were thriving urban centers with stone temples, elaborate tombs, sophisticated metalwork, and long-distance trade networks. They dealt in Greek pottery, worked bronze and iron, and had a written language adapted from the Greek alphabet.

Etruscan culture influenced Rome in practical ways. The Romans borrowed Etruscan engineering, learning to drain swamps, build arches, and construct stone foundations for temples. The famous Roman gladiatorial games likely developed from Etruscan funeral rites, though some scholars point to Campanian origins. The purple-bordered toga that Roman magistrates wore was part of the Etruscan fashion. The bundle of rods and axes (called *fasces*) that symbolized Roman authority was an Etruscan symbol of power.

Even the Roman alphabet came through the Etruscans, who had adapted it from Greek colonists in southern Italy. Etruscan religious practices, such as reading omens from bird flight, examining animal entrails to predict the future, and interpreting lightning strikes, became core Roman religious rituals. The Romans never felt confident making major decisions without checking for divine approval, and the Etruscans taught them how.

The Etruscans also likely introduced Greek culture to Rome. Greek colonies dotted southern Italy and Sicily, but Rome had limited direct contact with them early on. The Etruscans, who traded extensively with the Greeks, served as cultural middlemen. Through them, Romans encountered Greek art, mythology, and architecture. Many Roman gods were basically Greek gods with Latin names. Jupiter was Zeus, Venus was Aphrodite, and Neptune was Poseidon. This syncretism probably happened through Etruscan influence.

An Etruscan painting of dancers and musicians.[80]

Politically, the Etruscans might have taught Rome how to organize a city-state. Etruscan cities had kings, councils, and citizen assemblies. They had laws and social hierarchies. Rome's governmental structure during the monarchy period looks suspiciously similar to Etruscan models.

The relationship between the early Romans and the Etruscans was complicated. Sometimes they traded. Sometimes they fought. The three Etruscan kings who ruled Rome showed that Etruscans could gain power in the city, but their eventual expulsion also showed Roman resentment of foreign rule. After the republic was established, Rome spent the next few centuries conquering the Etruscan cities one by one.

By 300 BCE, Etruscan power had been largely broken. By 100 BCE, the Etruscan language was dying out as people adopted Latin. By the time of the Roman Empire, Etruria was just another region of Italy. The Etruscans vanished as a distinct culture, but their influence remained embedded in Roman civilization, including in their DNA.

Modern archaeology has revealed Etruscan cities, tombs filled with elaborate frescoes and grave goods, and enough inscriptions to partially understand their language. However, we cannot read most Etruscan literature because it did not survive. The Romans absorbed Etruscan culture but did not preserve Etruscan writings. What we know about the Etruscans comes largely from their artwork, their tombs, and what the Romans bothered to record about them.

It is one of history's ironies. The people who civilized Rome are now remembered primarily through Roman sources, many of which were written centuries after the Etruscan culture had faded. The teachers became footnotes in the students' story.

The Birth of the Republic: The Scandal That Ended the Monarchy

The transition from monarchy to republic changed everything about how Rome functioned, even if it took time for those changes to fully develop.

When the Romans expelled Tarquin the Proud in 509 BCE, they did not get rid of just one bad king. They abolished the monarchy entirely and created something new: a republic where power was shared, limited, and temporary.

The word "republic" comes from *res publica,* meaning "the public thing" or "the people's affair." The idea was that Rome belonged to its citizens collectively, not to one man. This was radical for its time. Most ancient societies were monarchies or oligarchies. Rome tried something different. The ancient Romans created a system with built-in checks to prevent any individual from accumulating too much power.

Instead of one king, Rome would have two consuls who shared executive power and served for only one year. They could veto each other's decisions, which meant they had to cooperate, or nothing would get done. After their year in office, they returned to being ordinary citizens (though usually very prominent ones). This system prevented anyone from becoming a permanent ruler.

The Senate, which had existed under the kings as an advisory council, gained real power. Senators were former magistrates, usually wealthy landowners with military experience. They controlled foreign policy, public finances, and religious matters. While they could not pass laws on their own, their authority (called *auctoritas*) gave their opinions enormous weight.

The citizen assemblies voted on laws and elected magistrates. There were several different assemblies organized in different ways, and over time, the system became incredibly complicated. However, the basic idea was that Roman citizens had a direct voice in government.

This new system was not a democracy in the modern sense. Power remained concentrated among wealthy families. Poor citizens had less influence than rich ones. Women could not vote. Slaves had no rights at all. But compared to a monarchy, it was revolutionary. Power was distributed and limited. Legal protections developed gradually, most notably with the Twelve Tables around 450 BCE, which codified laws and made them publicly available so that judges could not simply invent rules as they pleased.

The early Roman Republic was chaotic. Tarquin tried multiple times to retake Rome by force, enlisting the help of other Etruscan cities and Lars Porsena, the king of Clusium. Roman legend is full of heroes from this period: Horatius Cocles defending a bridge single-handedly, Mucius Scaevola burning his own hand to show Roman determination, Cincinnatus leaving his plow to save Rome and then returning to his farm afterward. These stories were probably exaggerated, but they reflected real conflicts as Rome fought to preserve its independence.

Rome's survival depended on alliances with other Latin cities. The Latins were a group of related peoples who spoke similar languages, worshiped similar gods, and faced similar threats from the hill tribes around them. Around 493 BCE, Rome joined the Latin League, a defensive alliance of about thirty Latin cities. The treaty, called the Foedus Cassianum after the Roman consul Spurius Cassius who negotiated it, established mutual defense and trade rights. If one city was attacked, the others helped. It was a practical arrangement born of necessity.

But Rome was never content being just a member of the alliance. Over the next century, Rome gradually shifted from partner to leader to overlord. When Latin cities rebelled in 340 BCE during the Latin War, Rome crushed them and dissolved the Latin League. The rebel cities lost their independence. Some were incorporated directly into Rome. Others became Roman allies with obligations to provide troops but had no say in policy. This pattern of alliance, dominance, and absorption became Rome's standard operating procedure for the next several centuries.

The early Roman Republic also faced constant warfare closer to home. The Aequi and Volsci, tribal peoples from the central Italian hills, raided Roman territory almost annually. These were not grand campaigns, just bands of warriors stealing crops, burning farms, and driving off livestock. Rome had to defend itself every fighting season, which meant Roman men spent much of each year in arms. This constant low-level conflict turned Rome into a militarized society where every citizen was expected to serve in the army. Military success was seen as the path to political power.

The republic also faced internal tensions from the start. Two classes of citizens emerged: patricians (wealthy aristocratic families) and plebeians (everyone else). The patricians monopolized political power, holding all the important positions and controlling the Senate. The plebeians, who made up the bulk of the army and the population, had voting rights but limited actual power.

The Romans had replaced a system that concentrated power in one person with a system that distributed power among many. They had traded stability for liberty, certainty for competition. It was messy, inefficient, and prone to deadlock.

The hatred of kingship became foundational to Roman identity. The very word "king" (*rex*) became an insult. Romans tolerated dictators appointed for six-month emergencies and military strongmen who ruled everything but did not hold the title king, but they never accepted the idea of a permanent hereditary monarch. When Julius Caesar flirted with accepting a crown centuries later, it helped get him killed.

This anti-monarchical attitude created a paradox at the heart of the Roman government. Romans wanted strong leadership but feared giving anyone too much power. They needed quick decision-making, but they had to face delays and vetoes. They admired military success but worried about successful generals becoming tyrants. This tension never got resolved. Instead, it created a dynamic political culture where ambition and restraint constantly battled each other.

The Roman Republic's structure also made Rome surprisingly adaptable. When something did not work, Romans could adjust it without overthrowing the entire system. The plebeians could win new rights without destroying the patrician class. New magistracies could be created when needed. The rules were not written in stone; they evolved based on precedent, negotiation, and sometimes mob action. This flexibility let Rome survive crises that might have shattered more rigid systems.

It was also the foundation for everything Rome would become. The republic, with all its internal conflicts and constitutional complications, would last nearly five hundred years. It would conquer Italy, defeat Carthage, and build an empire that stretched from Spain to Syria. The governmental structures created in 509 BCE—the consuls, Senate, and assemblies—would survive even after the Roman Republic died and emperors took control.

But none of that was obvious in 509 BCE. Back then, Rome was just one Latin city among many, distinguished mainly by having recently kicked out its king and invented a new form of government that probably seemed overly complicated to its neighbors.

The mud huts were still there. The population was maybe thirty thousand to forty thousand people total, most of them farmers. Nobody could have predicted that this small city on seven hills would eventually rule the Mediterranean world.

But the Romans had one thing going for them: they were incredibly stubborn. They did not quit. When they lost battles, they raised new armies. When other cities tried to conquer them, they fought back and then conquered those cities instead. When their government did not work, they adjusted it without abandoning the basic structure.

Rome was not founded in a day, despite what Romulus supposedly claimed. It was built gradually, messily, and violently over the centuries. The mud huts eventually became marble temples. The swamp became the Forum Romanum, the center of a world empire. The farmers became the legions that no one could defeat.

But it all started here, in the early republic, when Rome was small, vulnerable, and just beginning to figure out what it wanted to be.

Chapter 2: The Republic: Power to the People (Sort Of)

SPQR Explained: What "The Senate and the People of Rome" Actually Meant

If you've ever seen a Roman eagle standard, a manhole cover in Rome, or a tattoo on someone who really loves ancient history, you've probably seen the letters "SPQR." It stands for *Senatus Populusque Romanus* ("the Senate and the People of Rome").

These four letters summed up the Roman political identity. Power belonged to both the elite ("the Senate") and the citizens ("the People"). It was stamped on official documents, carved into public buildings, and painted on military standards. It appeared on aqueducts, triumphal arches, and even sewer covers. SPQR was Rome's brand, and Romans used it everywhere, not just during the republic but throughout the imperial period as well. During the Roman Empire, emperors' names often appeared alongside SPQR on coins and monuments.

But what did it actually mean in practice?

The phrase suggested a partnership between two groups. "The Senate" represented Rome's aristocratic elite. They were experienced statesmen, former magistrates, and wealthy landowners who advised on policy and controlled public finances. "The People" (*Populus*) represented the citizen body, but this did not mean all residents of Rome. It meant free male citizens. These men voted in assemblies, served in the army, and theoretically held ultimate sovereignty. Women, slaves, freedmen, and foreign residents were not part of the *Populus,* even though they made up most of Rome's actual population.

Notice the word "theoretically." In reality, SPQR was more slogan than substance, at least in the early Roman Republic. The Senate held most of the real power. Senators were not elected; they were appointed by the censors (magistrates who conducted the census and managed public morals) based on prior service as magistrates. Once you became a senator, you usually served for life unless you did something spectacularly disgraceful. The Senate controlled foreign policy, managed state finances, assigned military commands, and directed Rome's religious activities. While the Senate could not technically pass laws or formally veto them (only the assemblies could legislate), the Senate's influence often prevented magistrates from advancing proposals it opposed. Through procedure, religious interpretation, and social pressure, senators could effectively kill legislation without casting a formal veto.

How did the Senate wield this kind of power without formal legal authority? They did so through a combination of prestige, wealth, and social networks. When a magistrate took office, he consulted the Senate before making major decisions. Ignoring senatorial advice was legal but politically suicidal. Senators controlled the patronage networks that determined political careers. They had the wealth to fund elections. They had the social connections to make or break reputations. A young politician who defied the Senate might find himself without support for future campaigns. He would be excluded from profitable governorships or socially ostracized.

Senate membership worked like this. Once you served as quaestor (the entry-level magistracy), you were typically enrolled in the Senate at the next census. The censors could refuse to enroll someone or expel existing senators for moral failings, but this was rare. Most former magistrates remained senators for life. This meant the Senate was a self-perpetuating body of experienced politicians who had proven themselves worthy of high office.

The Senate also controlled Rome's finances through its oversight of the treasury. Want to fund a military campaign? The Senate decided. Need money for public works? The Senate allocated it. Planning to distribute grain to the poor? The Senate had to approve the expenditure. This financial control gave senators enormous leverage over ambitious magistrates who needed resources to achieve their goals.

Senatorial debates followed established customs. The presiding magistrate, usually a consul, would pose a question to the Senate. Experienced senators typically dominated the debate, often speaking at length. Senior ex-consuls and ex-praetors commanded the most attention, while junior senators frequently found themselves waiting for opportunities to speak that might never come. When it came time to vote, senators physically moved to stand with whichever proposal they supported. There were no secret ballots; everyone could see where you stood, literally.

The *Populus*, meanwhile, had voting rights but limited practical power, especially early on. The assemblies could pass laws and elect magistrates, but they could not propose legislation on their own—only magistrates could do that. Tribunes, however, gained increasing legislative power over time, especially after the *Lex Hortensia* in 287 BCE declared that plebiscites (decisions of the plebeian assembly) bound all citizens, not just plebeians. This gave tribunes significant power to propose and pass legislation. Even so, if the Senate opposed something, it could usually find ways to obstruct it. The assemblies were also structured to give more weight to wealthy voters than to poor ones.

So, SPQR represented an ideal more than a reality. Rome claimed to balance aristocratic wisdom with popular sovereignty. The Senate provided expertise and stability. The People provided legitimacy and military manpower. Together, they supposedly governed Rome.

This tension between elite control and popular participation defined Roman politics for centuries. The patricians wanted to preserve their privileges. The plebeians wanted a greater share of power. The Senate wanted authority without accountability. The assemblies wanted influence without chaos. Nobody was entirely happy, which meant everyone had to negotiate, compromise, and occasionally threaten violence to get what they wanted.

Ironically, as plebeians won access to magistracies and entered the Senate, senatorial power actually increased. The expanded Senate became even more dominant in foreign policy and finances, creating an oligarchy that included both patrician and wealthy plebeian families—what historians call the *nobiles*, or nobility.

The fact that the Romans bothered to carve SPQR on everything shows they believed the concept mattered. They did not call themselves "the Senate of Rome" or "the Roman People." They insisted on both.

The Senate could not claim absolute authority without acknowledging the People. The People could not claim total sovereignty without respecting the Senate. The partnership might have been unequal and contested, but it was real enough that both sides had to maintain the fiction.

Over time, as plebeians gained more rights and political power, SPQR became slightly less fictional. However, even at the end of the republic, when populist politicians like Julius Caesar claimed to represent "the People" against "the Senate," both sides still invoked SPQR. It was Rome's political identity, the idea that legitimate government required both aristocratic leadership and popular consent, however you defined those terms.

Patricians vs. Plebeians: The Original Class Struggle

When the Roman Republic began in 509 BCE, Roman society split into two distinct legal classes: patricians and plebeians. This was not about wealth, though patricians were generally richer. It was about birth, legal status, and access to political power.

The patricians were Rome's original aristocratic families. They were the descendants of the senators Romulus supposedly appointed. There were only about a dozen or so patrician clans (*gentes*) in early Rome, including families like the Cornelii, the Fabii, the Claudii, and the Aemilii. These families claimed they alone had the right to hold religious offices, serve as magistrates, and sit in the Senate. They had exclusive knowledge of the law (which was not written down yet) and exclusive access to the gods through special religious rituals. Patricians could not legally marry plebeians until 445 BCE.

Everyone else was a plebeian. This included poor farmers, urban workers, merchants, and even some quite wealthy families who simply were not patrician by birth. Plebeians could vote in assemblies and serve in the army, but they could not hold major political offices or know whether patrician judges were applying laws fairly.

This system was inherently unstable. The patricians needed plebeian soldiers to defend Rome and expand its territory. The plebeians needed patrician leadership and legal protection. But the patricians wanted to hoard political power, and the plebeians increasingly resented being treated as second-class citizens.

The social divide ran deeper than just legal status. Roman society operated on a system of patronage. Wealthy patricians served as *patroni* (patrons) to poorer citizens who became their *clientes* (clients). A patron provided legal protection, financial support, and political advocacy for his clients. In return, clients voted how their patron wanted, showed up to support him in public, and helped enhance his prestige. A wealthy senator might have hundreds of clients who voted as a bloc in assemblies.

This patron-client system reinforced patrician power. Even when plebeians gained voting rights, their votes were often controlled by patrician patrons. Poor citizens depended on wealthy patrons for survival. You could not easily vote against the man who loaned you money, represented you in court, or helped your son get a job. The system was not exactly coercive, but it created obligations that limited political independence.

The result was the Conflict of the Orders, a two-hundred-year struggle that shaped the Roman Republic more than any war or conquest. The conflict began around 494 BCE, just fifteen years after the republic was founded. According to tradition, plebeian soldiers got fed up with fighting wars for patrician commanders while getting no say in government. Many plebeian farmers had fallen into debt. They had been away fighting and could not work their land, so they borrowed money at high interest rates. When they could not repay, creditors could enslave them. Patrician magistrates and judges naturally sided with patrician creditors.

We should note that our sources for these early events, primarily the historian Livy, who wrote around five hundred years after the fact, used literary conventions and dramatic storytelling to reconstruct a period for which they had limited reliable information. We lack contemporary records from the early Roman Republic. The basic outline of a patrician-plebeian conflict is almost certainly real, but specific details like speeches and dramatic scenes follow narrative patterns common to ancient historiography rather than documented historical records.

The plebeians responded with what we would now call a general strike, though the Romans called it a *secessio*. Plebeian soldiers marched out of Rome to the Sacred Mount, a hill a few miles from the city, and refused to come back. They essentially said, "We're done fighting your wars and working your fields until you treat us fairly."

This was a brilliant tactic. Rome faced external threats from neighboring peoples. Without plebeian soldiers, the city was defenseless. The patricians had to negotiate.

The result was a compromise. The plebeians got their own representatives called tribunes of the plebs. Tribunes were sacrosanct, which means they were legally protected by religious law. Anyone who harmed a tribune could be killed on the spot. Tribunes had the power of *intercessio*; they could veto any magistrate's action or any Senate decision. However, this power had a crucial limitation. A tribune had to be personally present to say "veto" (Latin for "I forbid"). He could not leave Rome's city limits, and tradition required that his house door remain open at night so any citizen seeking help could reach him. The plebeians also gained their own assembly, the *Concilium Plebis*, where they could meet and discuss issues without patrician interference.

How the Government Worked: Consuls, Senate, and Assemblies

The Roman government was deliberately complicated. The whole system was designed to prevent any individual from accumulating too much power while still allowing the state to function. It was inefficient and prone to gridlock, but it was also remarkably durable.

Let's start with the magistrates—the elected officials who ran the government.

At the top were the consuls. Two consuls served for one year. They commanded armies, presided over the Senate, enforced laws, and essentially served as heads of state. Each consul could veto the other, which forced them to cooperate or at least negotiate. After their year in office, former consuls usually joined the Senate and often received provincial governorships where they could recoup the money they'd spent on elections and gain military glory.

Below the consuls were praetors, who administered justice. Initially, there was one praetor, but as Rome expanded, more were added. By the late Roman Republic, there were eight praetors handling different courts and provinces. Praetors could also command armies if needed.

Aediles managed Rome's infrastructure, such as roads, public buildings, the water supply, and markets. They also organized public games, which were expensive but great for building popularity if you had political ambitions.

Quaestors handled finances. They managed the treasury, supervised tax collection, and served as financial officers for generals in the field. Serving as quaestor typically qualified a man for Senate membership, though this remained subject to censorial review during the census.

Censors were senior magistrates elected every five years. They conducted the census (counting citizens and assessing their property) and could expel senators for disgraceful behavior. This wasn't just informal social pressure. Censors held formal power called the *regimen morum* (regulation of morals). They could issue a *nota* (mark of ignominy) that stripped a man of his rank, expelled him from the Senate, or removed him from his voting tribe. Censors had enormous authority, though they served only eighteen months and faced political backlash if they wielded their power unfairly.

Tribunes of the plebs represented plebeian interests and could veto magistrates' actions and Senate decisions through their power of *intercessio.* There were ten tribunes, and they served for one year. Tribunes couldn't leave Rome during their term; their power depended on being physically available to intervene when needed.

All these magistracies followed the *cursus honorum* (the "course of honors"), a traditional sequence of offices. You started as quaestor (minimum age thirty), then aedile, then praetor (minimum age thirty-nine), and then consul (minimum age forty-two). You had to wait two years between offices, and you couldn't serve in the same office twice in a row, though this rule was often violated later. The system was supposed to ensure experienced, mature leadership and prevent anyone from dominating politics.

Then there was the Senate. Technically, the Senate was just an advisory body. It couldn't pass laws or command armies directly. However, in practice, it was the most powerful institution in Rome.

Senators were former magistrates. Once you served as quaestor or in a higher position, you entered the Senate for life (unless the censors kicked you out). There were about three hundred senators during most of the Roman Republic. They sat on benches in the Senate House or various temples, debating policy and issuing *senatus consulta*—advisory opinions that magistrates almost always followed.

The Senate controlled foreign policy, declared states of emergency, assigned military commands, and managed public finances. Senators had enormous prestige and informal authority. When the Senate "advised" a consul to take a certain action, that consul usually took it. Defying the Senate was politically dangerous, as you could make powerful enemies who could wreck your career.

Finally, there were the assemblies where citizens voted on laws and elected magistrates. Rome had several different assemblies organized in different ways.

The *Comitia Centuriata* (Centuriate Assembly) voted on declarations of war, elected consuls and praetors, and passed laws. It was organized by wealth. Citizens were divided into groups called centuries based on how much property they owned and what military equipment they could afford.

The *Comitia Tributa* (Tribal Assembly) elected lower magistrates and voted on laws. It was organized by tribes (geographic districts). This was more democratic than the Centuriate Assembly but still gave more weight to property-owning citizens.

The *Concilium Plebis* (Plebeian Council) was the plebeian-only assembly where tribunes were elected and plebiscites were passed. After 287 BCE, its laws became binding for the entire Roman population.

The voting process itself was time-consuming and chaotic. On voting days, citizens gathered at dawn. A magistrate would take the auspices. This means they would check for divine approval by watching birds or examining animal entrails. If the omens were bad, voting was postponed. If the omens were good, voting proceeded. This system could be manipulated strategically. A magistrate opposed to a particular vote could announce he had observed unfavorable omens (*obnuntiatio*), effectively dissolving the assembly before it could vote.

Voting in Roman assemblies wasn't like modern elections. Citizens didn't cast individual ballots that were counted separately. Instead, each century or tribe voted internally and then cast one collective vote. Assemblies met in the Forum or on the Campus Martius, and voting was public. You walked to one side or another to indicate your choice. This made it easy for wealthy patrons to monitor how their clients voted.

The Centuriate Assembly's structure particularly favored the wealthy. Citizens were divided into 193 centuries based on property classes, though the exact numbers and organization varied over time, and our reconstruction relies on later sources. The wealthiest class (those who could afford full cavalry equipment) controlled eighteen centuries. The next wealthiest class (heavy infantry) controlled eighty centuries. Together, these two groups had ninety-eight centuries—a majority. This meant that if the wealthy classes agreed on something, voting stopped before the poorer classes even got to vote. The poorest citizens, grouped into just one century out of 193, almost never had any influence on the outcome.

This system had obvious flaws. Wealthy citizens had disproportionate influence. Voting was public, making intimidation possible. The presiding magistrate controlled the process and could manipulate procedures. Religious officials could declare bad omens to stop votes they didn't like. And since only citizens in Rome could vote (there was no absentee ballot system), farmers from distant regions often couldn't participate because traveling to Rome meant abandoning their farms during the planting or harvest seasons.

The whole system was designed with checks and balances. No individual could dominate the system for long. Power was distributed among multiple institutions with overlapping authorities. Ambitious politicians had to build coalitions, make deals, and compromise.

The downside was that the system worked best when everyone agreed to play by the unwritten rules. When politicians started breaking norms by extending their terms, using violence, or ignoring vetoes, the whole structure became unstable. By the late republic, ambitious generals with loyal armies were able to bypass the traditional system entirely, which is how the Roman Republic eventually died.

But for centuries, this complicated mess of magistrates, senators, and assemblies actually worked. It allowed Rome to conquer Italy, defeat Carthage, and build an empire.

The Citizen-Soldier: Why the Roman Farmer Was the Most Dangerous Man in the Mediterranean

Rome's greatest strength wasn't its government or its laws. It was its soldiers.

Other ancient states had professional armies or hired mercenaries. Rome relied on citizen-soldiers—farmers who fought for part of the year, then returned home to plant crops. This system turned out to be Rome's secret weapon.

Every Roman citizen was liable for military service. By the late Roman Republic, men typically served from age seventeen to their mid-forties. When Rome needed an army, the consuls held a levy. Citizens gathered on Capitoline Hill, and tribunes selected men based on property qualifications and physical fitness. Richer citizens served in the cavalry. Middling property owners formed the heavy infantry. Poorer citizens served as light infantry or support troops. The very poorest, called *proletarii* (those who contributed only children, not property), were usually exempt from the heavy infantry but could be called to serve as rowers in the navy or as auxiliaries during emergencies.

Once selected, soldiers served for a campaign season, usually from spring through fall. During winter, the legions disbanded, and the soldiers went home. If Rome needed them again the following year, they were recalled. A citizen might serve six or seven campaigns over his lifetime, sometimes more during major wars.

Soldiers weren't paid much initially; they received a small stipend and whatever loot they captured. They had to provide their own weapons and armor, which was why military service was tied to property ownership. A heavy infantryman needed a helmet, body armor, a shield, a spear, and a sword. This wasn't cheap.

Nevertheless, the system worked brilliantly for several reasons.

First, citizen-soldiers fought for their own land, families, and city. Mercenaries fought for pay and went home when the money ran out. Roman citizens fought because losing meant their farms could be burned and their families could be enslaved. This gave them motivation that no amount of money could buy.

The connection between land ownership and military service created a vested interest in victory. When Rome conquered new territory, that land could be distributed to citizens who had served in the conquering army, though such distributions were often contested and politically charged. The Gracchi brothers' land reform efforts in the 2nd century BCE would demonstrate just how explosive this issue could become. Still, the possibility that military service might lead to land ownership meant that even poor citizens had economic incentives to support Rome's conquests. Veterans of successful campaigns might receive a small plot of land, turning them into property-owning citizens with even more reason to defend Rome's interests.

Second, Rome could raise new armies incredibly quickly. Other states had limited military manpower. If their professional army were destroyed, they were done. Rome could lose an entire legion and raise another within weeks. As long as Rome had citizens who met the property qualification, it had soldiers. This meant Rome could absorb defeats that would have crushed other states. During the Second Punic War, Rome lost multiple armies to Hannibal—something like fifty thousand to eighty thousand men in just a few battles—yet kept fighting because it could replace those losses.

Rome's Italian allies amplified this advantage. By the 3ʳᵈ century BCE, Rome had bound most of Italy into a network of alliances. Allied cities had to provide troops when Rome demanded them. These allied contingents, called *socii*, often equaled or outnumbered Roman legionaries in any given army. This effectively doubled or tripled Rome's available manpower. When Rome fielded an army of forty thousand men, roughly half were Roman citizens, and half were Italian allies. If that army got destroyed, Rome could raise another Roman legion and demand more allied troops.

Third, the system distributed military experience throughout the population. Many Roman citizens had combat experience. They understood tactics, discipline, and how armies worked. This created a militarized society where military values—courage, discipline, and endurance—were deeply respected. It also meant Rome had a large pool of veterans who could be recalled in emergencies.

Fourth, citizen-soldiers had a stake in Roman politics. Since they risked their lives for Rome, they demanded political rights in return. This was what drove the Conflict of the Orders; plebeians who fought expected political power. The connection between military service and citizenship became fundamental to the Roman identity.

The basic military unit was the legion. By the middle of the Roman Republic, a legion had about 4,200 infantry and 300 cavalry. It was organized into smaller units called maniples, which consisted of about 120 men each. Maniples could move independently, which gave the legion flexibility. Roman soldiers fought in a checkerboard formation. Maniples in the front line covered gaps in the second line, which covered gaps in the third line. This meant Romans could rotate fresh troops into combat while tired ones fell back, maintaining pressure on their enemies. The earlier legion structure was likely less standardized.

It's worth noting that many of our detailed descriptions of Roman training methods come from Vegetius, a military writer from the late 4ᵗʰ century CE—hundreds of years after the Roman Republic fell. While these practices likely had earlier origins, we should be cautious about assuming all soldiers of the Roman Republic trained exactly as later sources describe. That said, the core emphasis on discipline, formation fighting, and practical weapons drill certainly characterized Roman military culture throughout their history.

Roman soldiers were famously disciplined. They trained constantly in weapons drill and formation fighting. They could march twenty miles a day carrying sixty to eighty pounds of gear. They built fortified camps every night when on campaign, even if they only planned to stay one night.

The nightly camp construction was particularly impressive. When a Roman army stopped for the evening, every soldier knew exactly what to do. The army would halt in formation. Scouts would reconnoiter the area and mark out the camp's boundaries. Then, while cavalry and light troops provided security, the heavy infantry would dig a defensive ditch around the entire perimeter, usually about three feet deep and three feet wide. The dirt from the ditch would form a rampart behind it. Sharpened stakes carried by soldiers would be planted on top of the rampart, creating a palisade. Inside, the camp would be laid out in a standardized grid pattern. The commander's tent would be in the center, legion quarters would be in specific blocks, and storage areas would be in designated spots. Every camp looked the same, so soldiers always knew where everything was.

This process took about three hours and required every soldier to work. The result was a fortified position that could withstand attacks and provide security for sleeping troops. Roman armies could march deep into enemy territory and sleep safely every night because they built these fortifications. When the army moved out the next morning, they'd sometimes burn the camp, although they sometimes left it standing; it depended on whether they planned to return.

Recruits practiced with wooden swords heavier than actual weapons, building strength and muscle memory. They trained against wooden posts, learning to thrust rather than slash. The *gladius* was designed for stabbing. It was shorter than most swords, about eighteen to twenty-four inches, with a sharp point. Roman training emphasized repeated thrusting motions at vital points, primarily the throat, abdomen, and groin. Slashing exposes your body to a counterattack. Thrusting from behind a shield is safer and more lethal.

Roman tactics emphasized close combat. The heavy infantry carried a rectangular shield (*scutum*), a short sword (*gladius*), and two javelins (*pila*). They'd throw the javelins at close range to disrupt enemy formations and then charge in with swords.

Roman soldiers also built things. They constructed roads, bridges, siege equipment, and fortifications. Every legionary was part engineer. This made Roman armies incredibly versatile. They could besiege cities, storm fortifications, build supply lines, and fight pitched battles.

The citizen-soldier system did have limits, though. Constant warfare hurt Roman farmers. If you spent months away on campaign every year, your farm suffered. Your family struggled. You fell into debt. By the 2nd century BCE, many small farmers couldn't afford to keep serving. They would lose their land to debt and no longer meet the property qualification.

The problem got worse as Rome's wars moved farther from home. In the early Roman Republic, campaigns were seasonal and local. Romans fought nearby Latin cities, Etruscan towns, or hill tribes. One could march out in spring, fight through summer, and be home by fall harvest. But as Rome expanded into southern Italy, then Sicily, then Spain and Greece, campaigns lasted longer and took soldiers farther from their farms. A campaign in Spain might keep you away for three or four years. Your farm couldn't survive that.

Meanwhile, wealthy landowners prospered. They bought failing farms from indebted soldiers. They used slave labor captured in Rome's wars to work their expanding estates. Large slave-run farms, called *latifundia*, produced more efficiently than small family farms. This created a vicious cycle: wars produced slaves who displaced small farmers, who fell into debt and lost their land, which made them ineligible for military service, which threatened Rome's ability to fight more wars.

For centuries, though, the citizen-soldier system made Rome nearly invincible. Rome could lose battles and bounce back. It could fight multiple wars simultaneously on different fronts. It could grind down opponents through sheer persistence. Hannibal killed over fifty thousand Romans at Cannae in 216 BCE—the worst military defeat in Roman history—yet Rome refused to surrender and eventually won the war.

By the time the Roman Republic entered its imperial phase in the 2nd century BCE, Rome had created one of the most effective military systems the ancient Mediterranean had ever seen. It wasn't the biggest army, as other states could field larger forces. It also wasn't the most sophisticated; Greek armies had better tactical theory. What made Rome unstoppable wasn't size or sophistication. It was endurance, adaptability, and a knack for turning allies into assets. No rival could match that combination.

Rome won wars not because it won every battle but because it never stopped fighting. It could replace losses that would have ended other states, and it bound allies and conquered peoples into its system. Its citizens believed Rome was worth dying for and that military service made them part of something greater than themselves. They were the Senate and People of Rome, carved into monuments and carried on standards. They were SPQR, and they conquered most of the known world.

Chapter 3: The Punic Wars: Rome Meets Its Match

The Rise of Carthage: Rome's First "Superpower" Rival

By 264 BCE, Rome had dominated most of the Italian Peninsula through conquest and alliances. It had spent two centuries conquering its neighbors, absorbing them into alliances, and building a military system that seemed unstoppable. Roman legions had defeated the Samnites, the Etruscans, and even the Greek general Pyrrhus, whose victories were so costly that "Pyrrhic victory" entered the language as a term for winning at an unsustainable price.

Rome was powerful. But it wasn't the most powerful state in the Mediterranean. That distinction belonged to Carthage.

Carthage sat on the coast of North Africa in what's now Tunisia. It was perfectly positioned to control trade across the Mediterranean. Founded around 814 BCE by Phoenician colonists from the city of Tyre in modern Lebanon, Carthage had grown into a commercial empire. While Rome conquered through military force, Carthage dominated through trade, colonies, and naval power.

But Carthage wasn't just a merchant city. The Carthaginians controlled the extraordinarily fertile Bagradas Valley (the modern Medjerda River valley) in Tunisia, which produced massive grain surpluses and supported a substantial agricultural population. Carthaginian expertise in agriculture was so renowned that when Rome eventually conquered Carthage, the Senate ordered the translation of

Mago's agricultural treatise into Latin—one of the few Carthaginian texts Romans bothered to preserve. Carthage's wealth came from a combination of agricultural production, tribute from subject territories, and maritime trade.

The Carthaginian republic (yes, Carthage had a republican government too, with elected officials and a council) controlled ports throughout the western Mediterranean, including Sicily, Sardinia, Corsica, southern Spain, and the North African coast. Carthaginian ships transported grain, metals, wine, olive oil, and luxury goods between these trading posts. The city's military reflected its commercial focus. Carthage relied heavily on hired mercenaries rather than citizen-soldiers for most campaigns, paying professional troops from various ethnic groups to fight its wars. Carthage did maintain elite citizen infantry units, often identified by ancient sources as the "Sacred Band," though modern scholars debate its size, composition, and exact role. These units were generally reserved for defending Carthaginian territory directly and were only deployed in the field during major crises.

The Carthaginian navy was the real power. Carthage fielded hundreds of warships, namely quinqueremes. These were powerful vessels with multiple rowers per oar station rather than five separate decks. They would be crewed by experienced sailors who could outmaneuver most opponents. Roman sources claimed Carthage could field 350 warships at its peak, though this number may be exaggerated. Still, Carthaginian naval dominance in the western Mediterranean was real. They dominated naval power, which meant they dominated trade, which meant they controlled a lot of wealth.

By the 3rd century BCE, Carthage was richer than Rome, more sophisticated, and seemingly more powerful. Carthaginian culture blended Phoenician traditions with Greek influences and African elements. They worshiped gods like Baal Hammon and Tanit. Roman propaganda later accused them of child sacrifice, though modern historians debate whether this actually happened or was just part of Rome's usual tactic of making its enemies look barbaric.

Rome and Carthage had coexisted peacefully for centuries, bound by treaties that divided spheres of influence. Carthage controlled the seas and focused on North Africa, Spain, and the Mediterranean islands. Rome dominated Italy and minded its own business. Neither state threatened the other's core interests.

Then the Mamertines screwed everything up.

The Mamertines were Italian mercenaries who had seized control of Messana (modern Messina) on the northeastern tip of Sicily. When Syracuse, a Greek city-state in Sicily, attacked them, the Mamertines asked Rome for help. This put Rome in an awkward position. The Mamertines were essentially pirates who had stolen a city. Helping them violated Roman principles. But Syracuse was allied with Carthage, and letting Carthage gain control of Messana would give the Carthaginians a foothold just across the narrow strait from Italy; barely two miles of water separated them from Rome's territory.

After much debate, Rome decided to intervene. Roman forces crossed into Sicily in 264 BCE. Carthage responded by sending its own troops. Neither side intended to start a massive war. Both just wanted to protect their interests in Sicily.

They ended up fighting for twenty-three years.

The First Punic War (264–241 BCE) was primarily a naval conflict. Rome started with a serious disadvantage since it barely had a navy. The Romans were land fighters. They'd built a few warships for fighting pirates, but they had nothing comparable to Carthage's fleet. Roman crews initially lacked Carthaginian seamanship and experience with advanced naval tactics.

What the Roman Republic and the Carthaginian Empire looked like at the beginning of the First Punic War.[81]

The war began on land in Sicily, where Rome won initial victories against Carthaginian forces. Roman legions proved superior to Carthaginian mercenaries in infantry combat. However, Carthage controlled the sea, allowing it to supply its forces in Sicily while harassing Roman supply lines. Rome realized it couldn't win the war without challenging Carthaginian naval dominance.

So, the Romans did what they always did when faced with a problem: they studied it, adapted, and persisted.

According to Roman tradition, they captured a beached Carthaginian warship, studied its design, and built a hundred copies in just sixty days. Ancient writers loved this story, but modern historians think it's more legend than fact. The truth was probably messier. Rome had access to expert shipbuilders through its southern Italian allies, especially the Greek cities, which had been building warships for centuries. Rather than copying one boat, Rome likely tapped into this know-how and existing shipyards.

What mattered was the urgency. Rome rushed to build a fleet and trained its crews on land, lining up benches like oars and drilling the timing until their rowers moved as one. They also introduced the *corvus* (Latin for "raven"), a boarding bridge with a spike on the end. In battle, they'd drop it onto an enemy ship to lock the vessels together, turning sea battles into infantry brawls. If they couldn't out-sail the Carthaginians, they'd out-fight them instead.

It worked. Rome won its first major naval battle at Mylae in 260 BCE using the corvus. They won another at Ecnomus in 256 BCE. Ancient historians describe it as involving over 300,000 men total, which would make it the largest naval battle in ancient history, though these figures are likely inflated by sources like Polybius, who tended to emphasize the scale of conflicts.

The corvus gave Rome initial advantages, but it had serious drawbacks. The device was top-heavy, making ships less stable, particularly in rough weather. After Rome lost multiple fleets to storms in 255 and 253 BCE, the corvus disappeared from Roman naval tactics. Rome had to learn actual seamanship rather than relying on a boarding-bridge gimmick.

Rome even attempted to invade North Africa directly, landing an army under the consul Marcus Atilius Regulus. The invasion initially succeeded but ultimately failed when Carthage hired a Spartan mercenary general named Xanthippus, who crushed the Roman force. Regulus was captured, and later Roman legends claimed he was tortured to death, though this story may be propaganda.

Carthage, meanwhile, struggled with the long conflict. Mercenary armies were expensive, and even Carthage's wealth had limits. The Carthaginian government faced internal political disputes about whether to continue the war. Their general in Sicily, Hamilcar Barca, fought brilliantly with limited resources but couldn't force a decisive victory.

Finally, in 241 BCE, Rome scraped together enough money to build one more fleet. This fleet caught the Carthaginian navy near the Aegates Islands and destroyed it. Without naval support, Carthaginian forces in Sicily couldn't be supplied. Carthage sued for peace.

The peace terms were harsh. Carthage had to abandon Sicily entirely, pay Rome 3,200 talents of silver over ten years (an enormous sum), and give up any claim to Sicily's Greek cities. Sicily became Rome's first overseas province. This territory was ruled directly by Rome rather than governed by allies.

Rome had won but barely. The victory cost hundreds of thousands of lives and pushed Rome's resources to their limits. But Carthage had lost, and losing meant humiliation, financial ruin, and the beginning of a hunger for revenge that would explode two decades later when Hamilcar Barca's son decided to finish what his father had started.

That son's name was Hannibal.

Hannibal's Elephants: The Tactical Genius Who Almost Burned Rome to the Ground

Hannibal Barca was probably the most dangerous enemy Rome ever faced. Over a sixteen-year campaign, he invaded Italy and—according to ancient sources—cost Rome well over 100,000 lives. He came closer to destroying Rome than anyone else until the barbarian invasions five centuries later.

He did all this while outnumbered, operating in enemy territory, and never receiving adequate support from his home government. Modern military historians still study his tactics. Napoleon Bonaparte admired him, as did the Duke of Wellington. Hannibal's crossing of the Alps with elephants is legendary, but his real genius was tactical. He understood how to use terrain, psychology, and combined arms to defeat enemies who should have crushed him.

After the First Punic War, Carthage faced a mercenary revolt when it couldn't pay its soldiers. Hamilcar Barca brutally suppressed the revolt, then took his family to Spain, where Carthage still had colonies and silver mines. Hamilcar spent years rebuilding Carthaginian power in Spain, creating a new empire and a new army loyal to his family rather than to the Carthaginian government.

Hamilcar made his son Hannibal swear an oath to hate Rome forever. When Hamilcar died, Hannibal's brother-in-law, Hasdrubal, took command. When Hasdrubal was assassinated, the army elected twenty-six-year-old Hannibal as their general. He was young, brilliant, and absolutely committed to destroying Rome.

The trigger for the Second Punic War (218–201 BCE) was Saguntum, a Spanish city allied with Rome. When Hannibal besieged it in 219 BCE, Rome protested. Hannibal captured and destroyed the city anyway. Rome demanded that Carthage hand over Hannibal, but Carthage refused. War began.

Everyone expected Hannibal to invade Sicily or Sardinia. Instead, he marched overland from Spain to Italy through the Alps, leading to one of history's most daring military maneuvers.

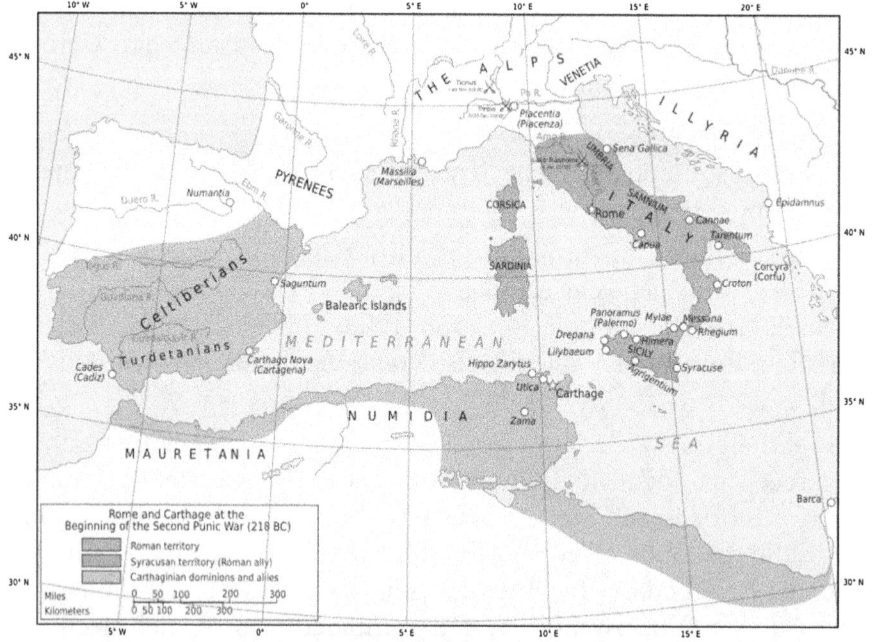

The Roman Republic and Carthage at the beginning of the Second Punic War.[82]

According to ancient estimates, Hannibal began with perhaps around fifty thousand infantry, several thousand cavalry, and a contingent of war elephants. The exact figures are debated, and they decreased significantly during the Alpine crossing. Scholars still argue about which specific Alpine pass Hannibal used. Several routes are possible, and ancient sources don't provide enough detail to be certain. What's clear is that the crossing was brutal. Snow, ice, rockslides, and attacks from hostile mountain tribes killed perhaps a third of his army. Most of the elephants died in the mountains or shortly afterward from the cold.

What made Hannibal's army remarkable wasn't its size but its composition and his ability to hold it together. His troops came from dozens of different peoples and included Iberians from Spain, Numidians from North Africa, Gauls from southern France and northern Italy, Libyans, Greeks, and various other mercenaries. They spoke different languages, worshiped different gods, and had different fighting styles. The Numidian cavalry were light horsemen, fast and mobile. The Spanish infantry were fierce close-combat fighters. The African infantry fought in disciplined formations influenced by Hellenistic tactics. Hannibal had to coordinate all these different groups, keep them supplied, maintain discipline, and prevent ethnic rivalries from tearing his army apart, all while operating in enemy territory with no reliable supply line to Carthage.

He managed it through a combination of personal charisma, shared hardship, and impressive tactical victories that kept his troops confident in his leadership. Hannibal shared the soldiers' hardships. He slept on the ground, wore the same basic gear as his troops, and was always visible during battles. He paid well when he could and distributed plunder fairly. Most importantly, he kept winning, and soldiers follow generals who deliver victories.

Hannibal made it. In autumn 218 BCE, he descended into the Po Valley in northern Italy with an army that, while smaller than what he'd started with, was hardened by the march and ready to fight.

Rome sent an army to stop him. Hannibal destroyed it at the Trebia River, using an ambush and his cavalry superiority to surround and annihilate the Roman force in the river valley.

Rome sent another army. Hannibal ambushed it at Lake Trasimene in 217 BCE, catching the Romans marching along a narrow path between the lake and the hills. Hannibal's troops attacked from the hills, driving the Romans into the lake. Some fifteen thousand Romans died, and the consul Gaius Flaminius was killed in the fighting. It was one of the largest ambushes recorded in ancient warfare.

Rome panicked. Two armies had been destroyed in two years. Hannibal was loose in Italy, and Rome couldn't stop him. The Senate appointed Quintus Fabius Maximus as dictator (an emergency position giving one man complete authority for six months). Fabius adopted a strategy of avoiding direct battle, shadowing Hannibal's army, and harassing his supply lines in the hopes of preventing him from capturing major cities. Romans mocked this cautious approach, calling Fabius "the Delayer." But it worked; it kept Rome from losing another army.

The Roman people, however, wanted victory, not delay. In 216 BCE, they elected two consuls—Gaius Terentius Varro and Lucius Aemilius Paullus—and gave them the largest army Rome had ever fielded: roughly eighty thousand infantry and six thousand cavalry. The Romans would crush Hannibal through sheer numbers.

The armies met at Cannae in southeastern Italy on August 2nd, 216 BCE. What followed was the worst defeat in Roman military history and one of the most studied battles in military education.

Hannibal had about forty thousand infantry and ten thousand cavalry. He was outnumbered nearly two to one. He arranged his infantry in a crescent formation with his weaker Gallic and Spanish troops in the center and his elite African infantry on the flanks. His cavalry was on the wings.

The Romans attacked in their traditional dense formation, pushing forward to break Hannibal's center. The Carthaginian center gave ground, slowly retreating but staying intact. The Roman mass pushed deeper into the crescent, which gradually became a U-shape with Roman troops packed into the center.

Then Hannibal sprang the trap. His cavalry, which had defeated the Roman cavalry on both wings, swept around behind the Roman army. His African infantry on the flanks wheeled inward, attacking the Roman sides. The crescent had become an encirclement with the Romans trapped inside.

The Romans couldn't maneuver. They were packed too tightly, and as the encirclement tightened, the formation became increasingly ineffective. The soldiers in the middle couldn't effectively use their weapons; the press of bodies from all sides limited their ability to fight.

Those in the rear kept pushing forward, not realizing they were forcing their comrades deeper into the killing zone. For hours, Carthaginian soldiers methodically attacked the compressed Roman formation from all sides.

By the end of the day, ancient sources report between fifty thousand and seventy thousand Roman deaths, though exact numbers are debated. The consul Paullus and the eighty senators who had volunteered to serve died. Hannibal's losses were around six thousand men.

According to the historian Livy, Hannibal's cavalry commander Maharbal urged him to march on Rome immediately, allegedly saying, "You know how to win a victory, Hannibal, but you don't know how to use one." Roman historians used dramatic quotes to create a more compelling narrative, so it is very possible these words were never uttered. Nevertheless, Hannibal didn't march on Rome. Modern historians debate why. Maybe Rome's walls were too strong, maybe his army was exhausted, maybe he lacked siege equipment, or maybe he believed Rome would negotiate. We just don't know.

What we do know is that this decision probably cost Carthage the war. Rome didn't surrender. Despite losing three major armies and over 100,000 men, despite several Italian allies defecting to Hannibal, despite Syracuse and Macedon allying with Carthage, Rome refused to negotiate.

Instead, Rome did what it always did. It raised more armies. It changed tactics. And it persisted.

Roman leaders refused to talk peace while Hannibal was still in Italy. They dealt harshly with cowards and deserters, often sending them into the toughest positions rather than letting them go free. To fill the ranks, Rome opened service to men who previously wouldn't have qualified and drew on wealthy citizens to finance the growing war effort.

Rome didn't try to beat Hannibal in a single big battle. Instead, it shadowed him and slowly chipped away at his support. When Hannibal threatened a town, Roman armies rushed in to defend it or cut off his supplies. When he left, they reclaimed territory and punished those who had sided with him. Rome's strategy was patient, and in the end, it wore Hannibal down.

Rome also strangled Hannibal's reinforcements. When his brother Hasdrubal finally crossed the Alps with a second Carthaginian army in 207 BCE, Rome intercepted him at the Metaurus River in northern Italy before he could link up with Hannibal. The Romans destroyed

Hasdrubal's army and killed him. According to Livy, they catapulted his severed head into Hannibal's camp to let him know his brother was dead and no help was coming.

Hannibal spent years roaming Italy, winning tactical victories but unable to force a strategic victory. He couldn't capture Rome or any major Latin city. He couldn't break Rome's alliance system entirely. His supplies dwindled. Reinforcements from Carthage never came in sufficient numbers. The Carthaginian government was divided about supporting him, and Rome's navy controlled the sea lanes.

Rome, meanwhile, opened new fronts. They sent armies to Spain to cut off Carthaginian resources and reinforcements. They invaded North Africa to threaten Carthage itself. They slowly ground down Hannibal's strength through attrition.

Spain became the critical theater. Carthage's Spanish territories provided silver from mines, manpower from Iberian tribes, and a staging ground for reinforcements to Italy. The Barcid family—Hannibal's family—had built their power base there. Hannibal's father, Hamilcar, had conquered much of Spain. His brother-in-law, Hasdrubal the Fair, had founded New Carthage (Cartagena) as a major port and administrative center. When Hannibal left for Italy, he left his younger brother, Hasdrubal Barca, in command of Spain, with orders to hold it and send reinforcements.

Rome sent armies to contest Spain starting in 218 BC. The war there was vicious, with neither side able to gain a decisive advantage initially. In 211 BCE, disaster struck. Both Roman commanders in Spain, Publius Cornelius Scipio and his brother Gnaeus, were killed when their armies were separated and destroyed by superior Carthaginian forces.

This was when the Senate gave command to young Publius Cornelius Scipio. He was only twenty-five; he was technically too young for such a command under Roman law, but desperate times called for flexibility. Scipio knew that Spain wasn't just a sideshow. It was Hannibal's supply line and revenue source. Cut Spain away from Carthage, and Hannibal would wither in Italy.

The war lasted fifteen more years after Cannae. Hannibal remained undefeated in Italy; he was simply too skilled a commander. However, Rome had learned not to fight him on his terms.

Scipio Africanus: The Man Who Learned Hannibal's Tricks and Used Them Against Him

Scipio had learned a hard lesson: Rome couldn't beat Hannibal by doing what Rome had always done. They needed to beat him at his own game.

Scipio didn't act like a typical Roman general. He was young, bold, and willing to break tradition. He trained his troops in new formations and drilled them until they could move quickly and fight as a unit. He studied cavalry tactics—something many Roman commanders ignored—and learned from Hannibal's greatest strength: combining different kinds of troops into one coordinated attack. Infantry, cavalry, speed, and surprise all had to work together. Scipio wasn't just copying Hannibal. He was adapting and getting ready to turn the tables.

In Spain, Scipio captured New Carthage (Cartagena) in a brilliant assault in 209 BCE, seizing Carthage's main Spanish base and cutting off Hannibal's supplies. He defeated multiple Carthaginian armies, driving them out of Spain entirely. He treated captured Spanish tribes honorably, turning many of them against Carthage. By 206 BCE, Rome controlled Spain.

Scipio returned to Rome a hero and pitched a bold plan: take the war to North Africa and force Carthage to call Hannibal back home. The Senate wasn't convinced. Most Romans wanted to get Hannibal out of Italy first. But Scipio had momentum. He was elected consul in 205 BCE and granted special command for the African invasion.

He didn't get much support from the government. But he built and trained his army in Sicily anyway. He drilled them in the fast, flexible tactics he'd studied from Hannibal, especially cavalry maneuvers and coordinated attacks that could break the stiff formations Rome usually relied on.

In 204 BCE, Scipio landed in North Africa with about thirty thousand men. Carthage was caught off guard. For over a decade, the war had been fought in Italy and Spain; now, suddenly, Rome was on their doorstep. Carthage formed an alliance with the Numidian king Syphax, who provided cavalry. Scipio allied with a rival Numidian prince named Masinissa, who brought his own cavalry to the Roman side.

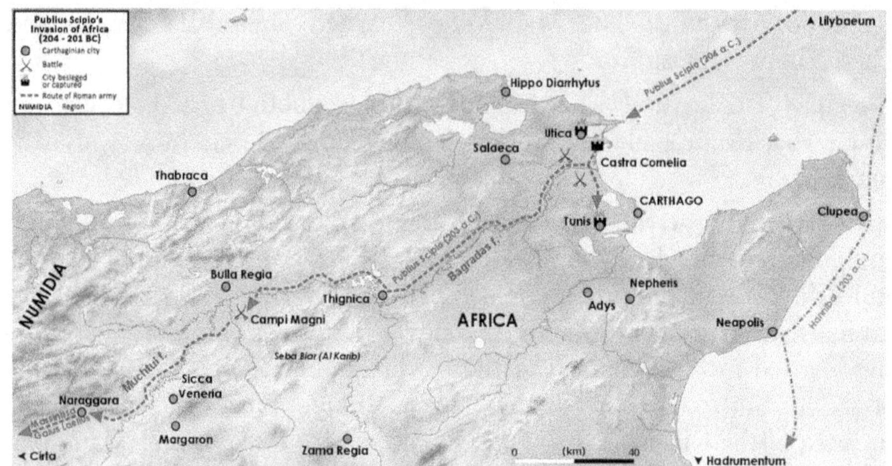

Scipio's campaign in North Africa.[88]

Scipio defeated the Carthaginian-Numidian coalition in several battles. He captured Syphax, besieged Carthaginian cities, and ravaged the countryside. Carthage panicked and recalled Hannibal Barca from Italy after fifteen years.

Hannibal returned to Africa having never lost a major battle in Italy. He still believed he could defeat Rome. But now he would face Scipio—the one Roman general who truly understood him.

The final confrontation came at the Battle of Zama in 202 BCE. The battle pitted two brilliant commanders against each other, both at the peak of their abilities.

According to ancient historians such as Polybius, Hannibal may have had around thirty-six thousand infantry, some cavalry, and a contingent of elephants. Scipio's forces numbered roughly twenty-nine thousand infantry and allied cavalry, primarily Numidian horsemen under Masinissa.

Hannibal planned to use his elephants to break up the Roman formation and then crush them with his veteran infantry from the Italian campaign. Scipio countered by arranging his infantry in columns with gaps between them. When the elephants charged, Roman trumpets and horns frightened many of them. Those elephants that did reach the Roman lines were channeled through the gaps Scipio had created, where skirmishers could attack them from the sides or simply let them pass through harmlessly. The elephant charge, which should have been devastating, achieved little.

The infantry lines clashed. Hannibal's front line of raw recruits gave ground against the disciplined Romans. His second line of Carthaginian citizen-soldiers fought harder but eventually broke. Hannibal kept his third line—his veterans from Italy—in reserve.

Meanwhile, Scipio's cavalry under Masinissa drove off Hannibal's cavalry, just as Hannibal's cavalry had done to the Romans at Cannae. The difference was that Scipio's cavalry returned to the battlefield and attacked Hannibal's veterans from behind.

Scipio had used Hannibal's own tactics against him. The Carthaginian army was surrounded and destroyed. Hannibal himself escaped with a small group of horsemen.

Carthage sued for peace. The terms were devastating. Carthage had to give up Spain and all the Mediterranean islands, surrender its entire navy except ten ships, pay an indemnity that ancient sources report as around ten thousand talents of silver over decades—an enormous sum that would cripple its economy—promise not to wage war outside Africa without Roman permission, and essentially become a Roman client state.

Hannibal advised the Carthaginian Senate to accept the terms. "We fought for empire," he reportedly said, "and we lost. Now we must accept the consequences." Carthage accepted.

Rome had won. Carthage would never again threaten Roman power. Scipio earned the cognomen *Africanus* for his victory and became one of Rome's greatest heroes.

Hannibal remained in Carthage for several years, reforming its government and finances. But his enemies in Carthage accused him of planning a new war with Rome. In 195 BCE, Rome demanded his extradition. Hannibal fled, spending the rest of his life wandering the eastern Mediterranean as a military advisor to various kings. He died around 183 BCE, allegedly by poison to avoid Roman capture. He was around sixty-five years old.

Roman historians claimed he spent his final years bitter and defeated. Or perhaps he simply realized what he'd always known: Rome would never stop, never surrender, and never accept anything less than total victory. He'd come closer to destroying Rome than anyone else would for centuries.

But close wasn't enough.

"Carthage Must Be Destroyed": The Total Annihilation of a Rival

The Second Punic War ended in 201 BCE, but the story of Carthage and Rome wasn't finished. Fifty years of uneasy peace followed, during which Carthage recovered economically. The Carthaginians went back to what they did best: trade. Ancient sources suggest Carthage might have paid off its war indemnity ahead of schedule. The city prospered. By the mid-2nd century BCE, Carthage was once again wealthy, though it was no longer militarily powerful.

During this period, Rome was transforming. The victory over Carthage had made Rome the dominant power in the western Mediterranean. Rome turned its attention eastward, conquering Macedon and Greece, defeating the Seleucid Empire in Asia Minor, and establishing itself as the mediator of Mediterranean politics. Roman wealth increased enormously as tribute, slaves, and trade goods flowed into Italy. However, this wealth was unevenly distributed. It enriched senators and military commanders, while many small farmers who'd fought in the wars lost their land to debt.

Carthage, stripped of its empire and military, focused on agriculture and trade in North Africa. Markets flourished. The population grew. Carthaginian farmers cultivated the fertile lands around the city. Carthaginian merchants traded throughout Africa and the Mediterranean, though now as junior partners to Greek and Italian traders rather than as the dominant commercial power.

This prosperity bothered some Romans. One senator in particular, Marcus Porcius Cato, better known as Cato the Elder, became obsessed with the idea that Carthage posed a threat to Rome.

Cato had served in the Second Punic War. He'd seen what Hannibal could do. He believed that as long as Carthage existed, Rome faced danger. Cato allegedly ended every speech in the Senate, regardless of the topic, with the phrase *Carthago delenda est* ("Carthage must be destroyed").

Ancient sources report that Cato once brought fresh figs from Carthage to the Senate and pointed out how close Carthage was to Rome—just three days by sea—and how fertile and prosperous its territories remained. The implication was clear: Carthage could recover its military power if given time and opportunity.

Other senators thought Cato was paranoid. Carthage had no significant military and couldn't even wage war without Roman permission. It posed no threat. The real danger, they argued, was that Carthage's destruction would remove the external threat that kept Rome unified. As long as Carthage existed, the Romans had a common enemy. Without that enemy, Roman factions might turn on each other.

Both sides were right, though the second group was more right than they knew. Carthage wasn't a military threat, and destroying it would contribute to Rome's internal political collapse.

Rome destroyed Carthage anyway. The push for war came from a coalition of Roman interests. Some senators genuinely feared Carthage. Others saw war as an opportunity for military glory and political advancement. Some were connected to Italian merchants who wanted to eliminate Carthaginian commercial competition. And some Romans simply believed that a great power couldn't leave a former rival alive, even if that rival was now harmless.

Masinissa, Rome's Numidian ally who had helped defeat Hannibal, kept seizing Carthaginian territory. Masinissa was clever. He would provoke border incidents and then appeal to Rome to mediate. Rome consistently ruled in his favor. Over the decades, Carthage lost significant territory because of these seizures. When Carthage complained, Rome told them to accept the decisions. When Carthage tried to defend its borders militarily, Rome accused it of violating the treaty.

Finally, around 151 BCE, Carthage raised an army and attacked Masinissa without Roman permission, technically violating the peace treaty. The attack failed anyway, but Rome now had its excuse.

According to ancient accounts, Rome made increasingly harsh demands that pushed Carthage toward war. First, Rome demanded that Carthage hand over three hundred noble hostages. Carthage complied, desperate to avoid war. Then Rome demanded that Carthage surrender all weapons and armor. Carthage complied, sending thousands of sets of armor and catapults to the Roman army camped outside the city.

Then Rome revealed its final demand. The people had to abandon Carthage entirely, move at least ten miles inland, and build a new city away from the coast.

This was impossible. Carthage's wealth came from maritime trade. Moving inland meant economic death. The Carthaginians realized they'd been set up. Rome wanted war regardless of what Carthage did. The Romans intended to destroy them.

Carthage chose to fight. With no weapons or armor, the Carthaginians improvised. Women cut their hair to make bowstrings. Citizens melted down metal objects to make weapons.

The Third Punic War (149–146 BCE) was a siege, not a campaign. Rome sent an army under the consul Manius Manilius, but the initial Roman efforts were poorly executed. The Romans couldn't break through Carthage's walls or blockade the harbor effectively. The siege dragged on for three years with little progress.

In 147 BCE, Rome sent Scipio Aemilianus, the adopted grandson of Scipio Africanus, to take command. Scipio Aemilianus was a capable general who had served in Spain. He tightened the siege and built a mole (a large, manmade barrier) to block the harbor and starve the city.

By spring 146 BCE, Carthage was out of food. Scipio Aemilianus ordered the final assault. Roman troops breached the walls and fought street by street, house by house. The Carthaginians fought desperately, but they were starving and outnumbered. The battle lasted six days. Roman soldiers set fire to buildings with defenders still inside.

The last Carthaginians retreated to the Temple of Eshmun on Byrsa Hill. Some surrendered. Others, including the wife of the Carthaginian commander Hasdrubal (not the same Hasdrubal who was Hannibal's brother-in-law), threw themselves into the flames rather than surrender. Hasdrubal surrendered to Scipio, reportedly begging for mercy, which Roman sources used to mock him as a coward.

When the fighting ended, Scipio Aemilianus supposedly stood looking at the burning city and wept. According to Polybius, who was present, Scipio quoted Homer. "A day will come when sacred Troy shall perish, and Priam and his people shall be slain." When Polybius asked why he wept, Scipio said he was thinking of Rome and how all empires eventually fall.

Whether this story is true or a later invention is debated. What's certain is that Rome showed no mercy. Ancient sources report that tens of thousands of survivors were sold into slavery. Buildings were torn down. The harbor was destroyed. The site was later reoccupied, so claims that Romans plowed the ground and sowed it with salt to prevent anything from growing are false; this dramatic detail first appeared in 19th-century histories and has no ancient evidence to support it.

The destruction of Carthage was total. A civilization that had existed for nearly seven hundred years, that had controlled Mediterranean trade, that had produced Hannibal and challenged Rome's supremacy, ceased to exist. Only ruins remained.

The Punic Wars were over. Rome had survived Hannibal's invasion through stubborn persistence, adapted its tactics, and ultimately crushed its greatest rival. The victory made Rome master of the western Mediterranean and opened the path to further conquests in Greece, Asia Minor, and beyond.

Chapter 4: The Crack in the Foundation

The Cost of Victory: How Wealth and Slavery Destroyed the Roman Middle Class

Rome won the Punic Wars. It defeated Carthage, conquered Spain, and became the dominant power in the western Mediterranean. Victory brought staggering wealth, as gold, silver, slaves, and tribute poured into Italy. The 2nd century BCE should have been Rome's golden age.

Instead, victory nearly destroyed the Roman Republic.

Here was the problem. Rome got rich, but only some Romans got rich. The wars that made Rome powerful hollowed out the very foundation that had made Rome strong: the farmers who served as citizen-soldiers.

Think about how the system worked. Roman soldiers were citizens who owned property. They were mostly small farmers with five to twenty acres. They grew grain and raised some animals. When Rome needed soldiers, they left their farms to fight. A few months later, they came home, planted crops, and returned to civilian life.

This worked well when wars were short and close to home. Leave in spring, fight through summer, and be back for the fall harvest. Your family could manage while you were gone. But Rome's wars started to change. Campaigns in Spain lasted years. Wars in Greece and Asia Minor kept soldiers away for season after season. The Second Punic War dragged on for nearly two decades.

Long military service destroyed small farmers. Picture it. You're fighting in Spain for three years. Back home, your farm sits unworked. Your wife and children try to keep it going, but plowing and harvesting require a lot of strength. Production drops. The family falls into debt, borrowing money at brutal interest rates just to buy food and seed. When you finally get home—if you get home—you're facing debts you can't possibly repay.

Creditors foreclose. You lose your land. And without land, you can't serve in the army anymore. Rome just lost a soldier. This cycle repeated thousands of times across Italy.

Meanwhile, wealthy Romans were making a killing. Senators and wealthy businessmen (the equestrian class—essentially the business elite just below senators) bought up foreclosed farms. They consolidated small plots into massive estates called *latifundia*. These estates didn't grow grain for local markets. They produced cash crops, such as wine, olive oil, and wool, for export. And they didn't use free labor. They used slaves.

The same wars that destroyed small farmers produced an enormous supply of slaves. When Rome conquered a city, it often enslaved the entire population. By the late 2nd century BCE, Italy's slave population had exploded.

Slaves made economic sense for big landowners. Pay once up front, and then you only have to pay maintenance costs. They didn't have to pay slaves any wages. Slaves couldn't quit. They also couldn't join the army and abandon their work. Large estates using slave labor could produce more efficiently and focus on high-value exports. Rich landowners had money to invest in irrigation, storage, and processing equipment. They had political connections to secure favorable trade arrangements. Small farmers had no chance of competing.

By the 130s BCE, Roman officials conducting the census noticed the problem. The number of citizens who met the property qualification for military service was declining. Fewer citizens owned land. More landless poor crowded into Rome. The wealth gap between the rich and the poor was widening dramatically.

Some senators worried about military manpower. Others worried about social stability. A large population of poor, unemployed citizens was politically dangerous. They could be mobilized by ambitious politicians. They could riot. They needed food subsidies to survive, which strained public finances.

But most wealthy Romans weren't particularly concerned. They were profiting enormously from the existing system. Their estates were productive, and conquered provinces provided new investment opportunities. Why change a system that enriched the people who ran it?

Then, two brothers decided to fix the problem. They came from one of Rome's most prestigious families. Their names were Tiberius and Gaius Gracchus, and their reform efforts would trigger a century of political violence that would eventually destroy the Roman Republic they were trying to save.

The Gracchi Brothers: The First True Populists

Tiberius Sempronius Gracchus was elected tribune of the plebs in 133 BC at the age of thirty. He came from the highest levels of Roman society. His father had been consul twice, and his mother was the daughter of Scipio Africanus, the hero who had defeated Hannibal. Ancient sources describe Tiberius's military service in Spain and Africa favorably. He had every reason to be a defender of the status quo.

Instead, he became a revolutionary.

Tiberius had seen the problem firsthand while traveling through Italy. He'd observed abandoned small farms, huge slave-run estates, and the decline of free citizens working the land. According to ancient sources, he was moved by the plight of displaced farmers and concerned about Rome's military capacity.

As tribune, Tiberius proposed land reform. The proposal was technically simple: enforce an old law that limited how much public land any individual could hold. Rome owned vast territories of *ager publicus* (Latin for "public land"), land conquered from enemies that theoretically belonged to the Roman state. In practice, wealthy Romans had occupied this public land and treated it as their own property, holding far more than the legal limit.

Tiberius's law would reclaim public land held beyond the legal limit and redistribute it to landless citizens in small plots. This would recreate the class of small farmers that Rome's military system required. Citizens would get land. Rome would gain soldiers. The Roman Republic would be saved.

The Senate opposed this. Most senators owned vast tracts of public land or had political connections to those who did. They didn't want to give up land they considered effectively theirs, even if it technically belonged to the state. They argued that Tiberius's proposal violated property rights and set a dangerous precedent by using popular politics to attack the wealthy.

Tiberius responded by taking his proposal directly to the people. He bypassed the Senate and brought his law before the Plebeian Assembly. This was technically legal, as tribunes could propose legislation to the assembly, but it violated an unwritten norm. Traditionally, important legislation was debated in the Senate first, and senators' views were respected even if they were not binding.

Tiberius broke that norm. He appealed to the urban poor and dispossessed farmers, arguing that the Senate was blocking reforms that would help ordinary citizens. Another tribune, Marcus Octavius, tried to veto Tiberius's law. According to ancient accounts, Tiberius responded by having the assembly vote to remove Octavius from office, a move that challenged traditional norms. Tribunes were sacrosanct (legally protected by religious law). Removing one was shocking.

But it worked. The law was passed. A commission was established to survey public lands and redistribute them. Tiberius, his brother Gaius, and his father-in-law, Appius Claudius Pulcher, would manage the process.

The Senate was furious but couldn't legally stop him. But then Tiberius made a fatal mistake: he announced he would run for tribune again. The tribunate was a one-year office. Running for immediate reelection was technically illegal and definitely a violation of tradition. Tiberius argued that his work wasn't finished and that his enemies would prosecute or kill him once he left office.

He was right about the second part.

On election day in 133 BCE, a group of senators and their supporters, led by the pontifex maximus (the highest religious office), Scipio Nasica (a cousin of Tiberius), formed a mob and attacked Tiberius and his followers. They beat Tiberius to death with clubs and wooden benches. Ancient sources report that about three hundred of his supporters were killed. The bodies were thrown into the Tiber River rather than receiving a proper burial.

This was unprecedented. Roman politics had been fierce before. There were insults, threats, and occasional scuffles. But murdering a tribune was something else entirely. By law and religion, tribunes were supposed to be untouchable. Harming one wasn't just illegal; it was sacrilege. Political violence had gone from angry words to outright murder, and the rules that kept Rome's system together suddenly felt breakable.

The Senate justified the murder by claiming Tiberius was trying to make himself king. The accusation was absurd. Tiberius was proposing land redistribution, not claiming royal power, but it served its purpose. Scipio Nasica and his accomplices faced no prosecution. The land commission continued its work, but without Tiberius's driving force, it eventually stalled and was disbanded.

Tiberius's younger brother Gaius observed all this. He was twenty-one when his brother was murdered. He spent the next decade building political support, and in 123 BCE, he was elected tribune. If the Senate thought killing Tiberius would end reform politics, they were wrong. Gaius was more radical, more talented, and more dangerous than his brother had been.

Gaius Gracchus moved fast. First, he revived the land commission and pushed even harder for redistribution. Then he proposed founding new colonies, not just in Italy but overseas, giving poor Romans land and a chance to start over somewhere new.

He also passed a grain law. The state would sell grain at subsidized prices, making food affordable for the poor. Critics called it blatant vote-buying. Supporters said it prevented starvation and mass unrest. Either way, it was the start of Rome's first permanent grain dole—the beginning of the "bread" in "bread and circuses."

Gaius didn't stop there. He took on the court system as well. At the time, senators judged other senators in extortion trials, essentially letting the elite police themselves. Gaius shifted jury duty to the equestrian class, breaking the Senate's grip on the courts and gaining a powerful new base of support.

He went even further than his brother, proposing that Italy's allies be granted full Roman citizenship. These men made up half of Rome's army but had no political rights. It was a bold move, and it made him a lot of enemies.

Gaius was elected tribune for 122 BCE as well; it seems the law prohibiting consecutive terms was being ignored by this point. He dominated Roman politics. The Senate couldn't stop him through legal means, and his legislation passed.

Then the Senate found his weakness: the citizenship proposal. Roman citizens in the lower classes didn't want to share citizenship with Italians. More citizens meant more competition for land, grain subsidies, and jobs. A rival tribune, Marcus Livius Drusus, proposed even more generous land and colonial plans specifically for Roman citizens, not Italians. This split Gaius's coalition, and his citizenship proposal failed.

In 121 BCE, Gaius ran for tribune a third time and lost. Without the tribunate's legal protections, he was vulnerable. The Senate declared a *senatus consultum ultimum* (the "final decree of the Senate" that granted the consuls emergency authority to defend the state by whatever means they deemed necessary). This wasn't a law, but it essentially gave magistrates a shield against prosecution for actions they might take to restore order.

The consul Lucius Opimius raised an armed force and hunted down Gaius and his supporters. Gaius tried to escape across the Tiber but was cornered. He ordered his slave to kill him rather than let him be captured. According to ancient sources, about three thousand of his supporters were killed in the violence. Opimius offered to pay gold for Gaius's head—literally, the head's weight in gold. Someone brought it to him, allegedly with the brain removed and replaced with lead to increase the weight. The Senate rewarded Opimius by allowing him to build a temple to Concord—"harmony"—in the Forum on the site of the massacre. It was supposed to signal reconciliation. Instead, it looked like a monument to bloodshed.

The Gracchi brothers had tried to save the Roman Republic by addressing the economic crisis. They showed that popular tribunes could bypass the Senate by appealing directly to the people. Both were dead, and their reforms were partially rolled back, but the precedent had been set: political disputes could be settled with violence.

Marius and Sulla: When Generals Started Caring More About Their Troops Than the State

The generation after the Gracchi saw the rise of a new type of Roman politician: the military strongman whose power base was his army rather than his political connections.

Gaius Marius was a "new man," someone whose family had never held the consulship before. He came from the equestrian class in the town of Arpinum, not from Rome's aristocratic families. This made him an outsider in a political system dominated by established dynasties.

Marius compensated with his military talent and political ruthlessness.

Marius made his reputation in North Africa fighting a war against Jugurtha, the king of Numidia (modern Algeria). The war had dragged on for years under incompetent commanders. Marius served as legate (similar to a modern general) under Quintus Caecilius Metellus, although he did most of the actual work. He returned to Rome and successfully ran for consul in 107 BCE by claiming that his aristocratic commander was prolonging the war through incompetence.

Attacking a superior officer and running for consul as a new man against senatorial opposition was politically radical. But Marius won by appealing directly to the people, promising to end the war quickly if given command.

Once consul, Marius did something radical: he opened military service to the poorest citizens. Previously, only citizens who owned property could serve. The idea was that property owners had a stake in defending Rome. Marius said forget that. Now, the *capite censi* (literally "head count," the poorest citizens who owned nothing) could join. Rome's army went from a citizen militia to a professional military.

Why would Gaius Marius do this? Rome needed bodies. Wars in Africa and Spain required soldiers, but the pool of property-owning citizens kept shrinking. Marius's reform tapped into thousands of unemployed men desperate for steady pay, three meals a day, and maybe some loot.

The state provided armor, weapons, and shields now. Men no longer had to show up with their own equipment. Soldiers served for years, sometimes decades, developing real professional skills. Roman legions became more effective fighting forces as a result. Veterans formed their own social class. These were career soldiers who saw military service as a job, not a civic duty.

But here's the catch: professional soldiers were loyal to their generals, not to Rome.

Think about it. The state didn't provide pensions. When your service ended, you had nothing. There was no farm to go back to because you never had one to begin with. Your only shot at security was if your general rewarded you with a land grant. So what if your general promised land and the Senate said no? You backed your general. Every time.

Marius won the war against Jugurtha with crucial help from his quaestor, Lucius Cornelius Sulla, who actually captured Jugurtha through diplomacy, something that Marius downplayed and Sulla resented. Then Germanic tribes, the Cimbri and Teutones, invaded from the north, threatening Italy itself. Marius was elected consul five years in a row, from 104 to 100 BCE, breaking the rule that said no one could hold the office twice within ten years. But Rome was scared, and Marius was their war hero.

Marius destroyed the Germanic invaders in two massive battles: Aquae Sextiae in 102 BCE and Vercellae in 101 BCE. He became Rome's savior and most popular general. He used his popularity to push through land grants for his veterans despite senatorial opposition. The precedent was set. Successful generals could demand rewards for their troops and use political pressure or the threat of military force to get them.

But then Marius made a political miscalculation. In 100 BCE, during his sixth consulship, he allied with violent populist politicians Lucius Appuleius Saturninus and Gaius Servilius Glaucia, who used gangs to intimidate opponents and disrupt voting. When their tactics became too extreme, the Senate issued the *senatus consultum ultimum* against them. Marius, as consul, was ordered to suppress his own allies. He did, killing Saturninus and Glaucia, but this destroyed his political base. Marius became isolated. He was too radical for conservatives and seen as too willing to betray allies for populists.

He spent the next decade mostly retired from politics, bitter and waiting for another opportunity to reclaim power. That opportunity came from an unexpected source: a war against Rome's Italian allies.

Rome's Italian allies had been asking for Roman citizenship for decades. They provided half of Rome's soldiers but couldn't vote or hold office. After Gaius Gracchus's citizenship proposal failed in 122 BCE, resentment festered. In 91 BCE, the tribune Marcus Livius Drusus proposed a new citizenship law. When Drusus was assassinated (almost certainly by senatorial opponents), the Italians revolted.

The Social War (91–88 BCE)—named from *socii*, Latin for "allies"— was Rome's most dangerous conflict since Hannibal had invaded. The Italians weren't barbarians or foreigners. They were Latins, Samnites, and other Italic peoples who had fought alongside Rome for centuries. They knew Roman military tactics intimately because they'd served in Roman armies. They created their own confederation, called Italia, with a capital at Corfinium (renamed Italica). They minted their own coins showing an Italian bull goring a Roman wolf, elected their own magistrates, and raised armies using Roman organizational structures.

The Italians weren't trying to destroy Rome. They wanted to be Romans. They wanted citizenship, voting rights, and legal equality. The war was about inclusion, not conquest. However, Rome's initial response was to fight rather than negotiate, viewing the revolt as treason.

The war was brutal and evenly matched. Both sides fought using Roman military tactics. Roman generals like Marius, Sulla, and Pompey Strabo (father of Pompey the Great) led campaigns. Tens of thousands died on both sides.

Rome gradually gained the upper hand militarily but recognized that crushing the revolt outright would be devastating. In 90 BCE, Rome passed the *Lex Julia*, granting citizenship to Italian communities that hadn't revolted or had laid down their arms. In 89 BCE, the *Lex Plautia Papiria* extended citizenship to individuals who registered with Roman authorities within sixty days. These laws essentially gave the Italians what they'd wanted.

The number of Roman citizens jumped from around 400,000 to over a million. The old line between Romans and Italians began to fade. Within a generation, nearly everyone in Italy would simply be Roman.

Then things got worse.

Mithridates VI, King of Pontus (in modern Turkey), invaded Roman territory in Asia Minor and massacred tens of thousands of Roman and Italian civilians. Rome needed to respond with force. The Senate assigned command of the war to the consul Lucius Cornelius Sulla, an aristocratic general from an old patrician family.

A portrait of Sulla on a denarius.[54]

Sulla had been Marius's subordinate in the Jugurthine War, serving as his quaestor. The two men had a complicated relationship. Sulla resented that Marius downplayed his role in capturing Jugurtha. Marius resented Sulla's aristocratic background and rising popularity. Now, in 88 BCE, Sulla had the prestigious eastern command, which Marius wanted.

Marius was in his seventies, but he was still ambitious. He allied with the tribune Publius Sulpicius Rufus, who proposed legislation transferring command of the Mithridatic War from Sulla to Marius. The proposal was blatantly unconstitutional (you couldn't just reassign a consul's command by vote), but it passed through the assembly.

Sulla responded in a way no Roman general had before. He marched on Rome with his army.

Six legions camped outside the city. Sulla told them that Marius was trying to steal their chance for glory and plunder in the east. The soldiers were loyal to Sulla; he was their commander, the man who would reward them with loot from Mithridates's wealthy kingdom. Ancient sources report that many of Sulla's officers refused to march on Rome, but the soldiers followed him.

Sulla's army entered Rome and fought street battles against Marius's supporters. This was civil war—Roman soldiers killing Roman citizens in Rome itself. It had never happened before. Publius Sulpicius Rufus was killed. Marius escaped to Africa. Sulla declared Marius and his supporters enemies of the state, seized their property, and repealed Sulpicius's laws.

Then Sulla made a crucial mistake. He left for the east to fight Mithridates, trusting that his political settlement would hold. It didn't. As soon as Sulla left Italy, Marius returned with an army. The consuls elected for 87 BCE, Gnaeus Octavius and Lucius Cornelius Cinna, split, with Cinna siding with Marius. Civil war broke out again.

Marius and Cinna captured Rome in 87 BCE. They unleashed a reign of terror against Sulla's supporters. Ancient sources describe massacres, proscriptions (official death lists), and the heads of murdered senators displayed in the Forum. Marius was elected consul for the seventh time, but he died in January 86 BCE, barely a month into his term. Cinna continued to control Rome in Sulla's absence.

Sulla spent years in the east defeating Mithridates and restoring Roman control of Greece and Asia Minor. He returned to Italy in 83 BCE with a hardened, loyal army and a determination to destroy his enemies. Young, talented officers flocked to him, including Pompey and Marcus Licinius Crassus. From 83 to 81 BCE, Italy was consumed by civil war as Sulla crushed the Marian faction.

Sulla won. He had himself appointed dictator (an emergency office that granted absolute power for six months). Sulla held this role for three years. He instituted proscriptions on a scale that made Marius's massacres look restrained. Thousands were declared enemies of the state. Their property was confiscated, and they could be killed with impunity. Sulla's supporters enriched themselves by killing proscribed men and seizing their estates.

Sulla used his dictatorial power to reform the Roman Republic. He aimed to restore what he saw as the proper balance of power that had existed before the Gracchi brothers disrupted it. He weakened the tribunate by requiring tribunes to obtain Senate approval before proposing legislation and by making the tribunate a dead-end office; anyone who served as a tribune was barred from holding higher offices.

Sulla doubled the size of the Senate from three hundred to six hundred and packed it with his supporters. He gave the Senate back control of the courts and locked in a strict career ladder for politicians. There were minimum ages, mandatory waiting periods, and no repeating offices. Sulla also settled his veterans across Italy on confiscated land, creating a class of farmer-soldiers loyal to him and to the new order he'd imposed.

In 79 BCE, convinced he had saved the Roman Republic by restoring aristocratic rule, Sulla shocked everyone. He resigned. He gave up power, retired from public life, and died a year later. And not by assassination. He died in bed.

His so-called "reforms" collapsed almost immediately. Sulla had shown that a general with a loyal army could seize Rome, kill his enemies, and rule by force. However, in the decade after his death, Rome would face a different kind of threat, one that exposed the violence and fear upon which the entire Roman system was built.

Spartacus: The Slave Rebellion That Exposed Rome's Greatest Fear

The Third Servile War (Spartacus's famous revolt) wasn't Rome's first major slave rebellion. Sicily had erupted in revolt twice before, from 135 to 132 BCE and from 104 to 100 BCE, when tens of thousands of slaves revolted and seized cities. They held out for years before Rome crushed them. But those rebellions happened on an island, far from Rome itself.

Spartacus's rebellion was different. It happened in Italy.

In 73 BCE, about seventy gladiators escaped from a training school in Capua, south of Rome. Their leader was Spartacus, a Thracian (from modern Bulgaria) who'd been enslaved and forced to fight as a gladiator. The escapees seized weapons from a nearby town, fortified themselves on Mount Vesuvius, and began raiding the surrounding countryside.

Rome sent a small force to crush what looked like a minor disturbance. Spartacus destroyed it. More slaves, agricultural workers, household servants, and anyone who could escape fled to join him. Within months, Spartacus commanded thousands of escaped slaves. Ancient sources claim his army eventually swelled to around seventy thousand.

This scared Rome badly. Slaves made up perhaps a third of Italy's population. If they could organize and fight effectively, they threatened the entire social order. Wealthy Romans who owned large numbers of slaves had reason to worry. The people working their estates knew their routines, had access to tools and weapons, and might flee to join the rebellion.

Rome sent more armies. Spartacus won several major victories, defeating multiple Roman commanders. He wasn't just lucky; he was a capable leader. He equipped his forces with captured Roman weapons and organized them using disciplined tactics. He defeated praetors and even consuls. He marched his army the length of Italy, from south to north, winning engagement after engagement.

Spartacus's goal remains debated. Ancient sources claim he wanted to lead his followers over the Alps and bring them back to their homelands. But when his army reached northern Italy in 72 BCE, they turned back south. Maybe Spartacus lost control of his forces. Maybe his followers wanted to keep plundering Italy. Maybe he never intended to leave. We don't know.

What's clear is that by 71 BCE, Spartacus's army was still in southern Italy, and Rome had finally sent someone competent to deal with them: Marcus Licinius Crassus.

Crassus was Rome's richest man, but he lacked military glory, the one thing Roman politics required for the highest offices. Defeating Spartacus was his chance. The Senate gave him eight legions, over forty thousand soldiers. This time, Rome wasn't taking chances.

Crassus was ruthless. When some of his soldiers fled from battle, he revived the ancient punishment of decimation, in which every tenth man was beaten to death by his fellow soldiers. He wanted his own troops to fear him more than they feared the enemy.

Crassus trapped Spartacus in the toe of Italy, building a wall across the peninsula to contain the slave army. Spartacus broke through and marched north again, but Crassus pursued. In 71 BCE, the armies met in Lucania. The battle was brutal. According to ancient sources, Spartacus tried to fight his way to Crassus himself but was cut down. His body was never identified among the thousands of corpses.

The slave army broke and fled. Roman cavalry hunted down the survivors. Ancient sources report that 6,000 captured slaves were crucified along the Appian Way from Capua to Rome, 120 miles of road, their bodies left hanging as a warning that this was what happened to slaves who rebelled.

Crassus broke the rebellion. But Pompey, returning from Spain, intercepted and killed five thousand fleeing slaves. Pompey then sent dispatches to Rome claiming he'd finished the war, infuriating Crassus, who'd done the actual fighting. Both men wanted consulships. The question of who deserved credit for ending the rebellion became a bitter rivalry that would shape Roman politics for the next decade.

The Spartacus rebellion exposed something Romans didn't like to think about: their entire civilization rested on enslaving millions of people by force. Those people didn't accept their enslavement passively. They would fight for freedom if given the chance. Rome's response was to make the consequences of rebellion so terrifying that slaves would never dare try again.

It worked. For the next several centuries, no slave rebellion in Italy would come close to Spartacus's success. The crucified bodies along the Appian Way made sure of that.

The First Triumvirate: Caesar, Pompey, and Crassus—The Three-Way Tug of War

The generation after Sulla produced three men who would dominate Roman politics and ultimately destroy the Roman Republic: Pompey, Crassus, and Julius Caesar.

Gnaeus Pompeius Magnus, better known as Pompey the Great, earned his reputation at a young age. At twenty-three, he raised legions to support Sulla in the civil war. Sulla called him "the Great" (*Magnus*) sarcastically—the young man was arrogant—but Pompey adopted the nickname seriously. After Sulla's death, Pompey received extraordinary commands to suppress rebellions in Sicily, Africa, and Spain. He defeated the Sertorian rebellion in Spain (though his subordinate actually killed Sertorius). On his return to Italy in 71 BCE, Pompey mopped up the remnants of Spartacus's slave rebellion, which Marcus Licinius Crassus had already defeated, then claimed credit for ending the whole affair.

Marcus Licinius Crassus was Rome's richest man. He made his fortune through political connections, real estate speculation (ancient sources describe him owning a private fire brigade that would negotiate prices while buildings burned), and the purchase of property from proscribed men during Sulla's dictatorship.

In 70 BCE, Pompey and Crassus ran for consul together. They both lacked the constitutional qualifications. Pompey had never held the required lower offices, and both were below the minimum age. They pressured the Senate to waive the requirements. They won the election and used their consulship to undo Sulla's constitutional reforms, restoring the tribunate's powers and opening the courts to equestrians. After their consulship, they became rivals.

Pompey received command of a war against Mediterranean pirates, who were disrupting grain shipments and threatening Rome's food supply. The *Lex Gabinia* in 67 BCE granted Pompey supreme command over the entire Mediterranean and its coasts, with unlimited resources. Pompey cleared the seas of pirates in three months through a massive, coordinated campaign. This achievement greatly enhanced his reputation across Rome.

Then, in 66 BCE, the *Lex Manilia* transferred command of the ongoing war against Mithridates to Pompey. Mithridates VI of Pontus (a kingdom in modern Turkey) had been fighting Rome on and off since 88 BCE, when he'd massacred tens of thousands of Roman and Italian civilians in Asia Minor. Sulla had fought him, and then Lucullus—a capable general who'd been winning steadily for years—commanded the war through the 70s BCE. But Lucullus's troops were exhausted and restive after years of hard campaigning, and Pompey's political allies claimed only Pompey could finish the job.

Pompey defeated Mithridates, who committed suicide to avoid capture. He conquered Syria, reorganized the east, and returned to Italy in 62 BCE as Rome's most successful general, having expanded Roman territory across the eastern Mediterranean.

Pompey expected the Senate to approve his settlements in the east and grant land to his veterans. The Senate, led by Cato the Younger (great-grandson of Cato the Elder), refused. They were not going to let Pompey dictate terms simply because he commanded legions. They blocked his legislation and humiliated him politically.

This drove Pompey to join an alliance with two men who also had grievances against the Senate: Marcus Licinius Crassus and a rising politician named Gaius Julius Caesar.

Julius Caesar came from an ancient patrician family; the Julii claimed descent from the goddess Venus. But they had fallen on hard times. Caesar grew up during the Marian-Sullan civil wars. His aunt Julia was actually married to Marius. His first wife, Cornelia, was the daughter of Cinna (who sided with Marius during the war). When Sulla demanded that Caesar divorce Cornelia, Caesar refused and went into hiding. Sulla's allies pressured him to pardon Caesar, allegedly saying, "You win, but I'm telling you that this boy will destroy everything we've fought for. There are many Mariuses in him."

Caesar climbed the *cursus honorum* through a combination of charm, political skill, and massive debt. He borrowed enormous sums to fund public games, build patronage networks through lavish spending, and create political connections. By 59 BCE, he was deeply in debt to Crassus and needed a lucrative provincial command to restore his finances. He also wanted military glory to match Pompey's.

In 60 BCE, these three men formed a private political alliance known as the First Triumvirate. It was not an official alliance; it was more like an agreement that they would support one another's interests against senatorial opposition. Pompey wanted his eastern settlements ratified and land for his veterans. Crassus wanted tax relief for the equestrian companies with which he was connected. Caesar wanted the consulship for 59 BCE and then a military command.

The alliance worked. Caesar was elected consul for 59 BCE. He pushed through Pompey's legislation by intimidation and violence, ignoring his co-consul Marcus Calpurnius Bibulus, who tried to obstruct him. Caesar then secured command of Cisalpine Gaul (northern Italy) and Transalpine Gaul (southern France) for five years. He commanded four legions. This gave him the military opportunity he needed.

To cement the alliance, Pompey married Caesar's daughter Julia, despite being twenty-three years older than she was. Political marriages were normal in Rome, but ancient sources suggest this one was genuinely affectionate.

Caesar left for Gaul in 58 BCE. Over the next nine years, he would conquer territory roughly the size of modern France and Belgium, build an army of battle-hardened veterans loyal to him personally, and become the most famous general in Rome. He would also become too powerful for the Senate to control.

That story—the Gallic Wars, the civil war, and Caesar's transformation of Rome—would reshape the Roman world forever. But it belongs to the next chapter.

Chapter 5: Julius Caesar: The Man, The Myth, The Knife

The Conquest of Gaul: How Caesar Built His Brand and His Army

Julius Caesar left Rome in 58 BCE as a politician drowning in debt. He came back nine years later as the most famous general in the Mediterranean world, commanding an army of battle-hardened veterans who'd follow him anywhere. The Gallic Wars transformed Caesar from a talented but broke senator into the man who would destroy the Roman Republic.

Caesar's governorship gave him control of Cisalpine Gaul (northern Italy) and Transalpine Gaul (southern France), plus authority over nearby territories. He had four legions and permission to conduct military operations. What he didn't have was a convenient enemy or an obvious war to fight. So Caesar did what Caesar did best: he created his own opportunities.

His first opportunity came immediately. The Helvetii, a Celtic tribe from modern Switzerland, decided to migrate westward across Gaul. They weren't invading Roman territory. They weren't attacking Rome's allies. They just wanted to move. But Caesar claimed their migration threatened Roman interests. What if Germanic tribes filled the vacuum they left? He intercepted the Helvetii with his legions, fought a battle near Bibracte, and forced them home. Caesar's account claims he killed or captured most of the 368,000 Helvetii who'd started the journey. Modern historians think he inflated that number massively, but the point was still made. Caesar was in charge now.

Next came Ariovistus, a Germanic chieftain who'd crossed the Rhine into Gaul with his warriors. Gallic tribes asked Caesar for help, and Caesar was happy to oblige. He fought Ariovistus and drove him back across the Rhine. Caesar spun this as defending Gaul from Germanic invasion. In reality, he was establishing that Rome—meaning Caesar—now ran things in Gaul.

Then Caesar turned to the Belgic tribes in northern Gaul. These were fierce warriors who alarmed him with their military prowess. He campaigned against them, defeating the Nervii in a hard-fought battle in which his legion nearly broke before Caesar personally rallied his troops.

According to Caesar's account, the battle against the Nervii was one of his closest calls. The Nervii waited until Caesar's legions were divided and then launched a surprise attack. They moved so fast that Roman soldiers barely had time to arm themselves. The battle devolved into chaos. One Roman legion was surrounded and being cut to pieces. Caesar's own headquarters was under attack. Roman standards were falling, a catastrophe that would signal complete defeat.

In his *Commentarii de Bello Gallico* (*Commentaries on the Gallic War*), Caesar describes grabbing a shield from a soldier in the rear ranks and pushing forward to the front line, calling out centurions by name and urging the ranks to spread out so they had room to use their swords. Whether this personal intervention happened exactly as Caesar described or was embellished for dramatic effect, the story served its purpose by portraying Caesar as the brave commander who personally turned near-defeat into victory through courage and tactical awareness.

Then the Tenth Legion arrived from the rear and crashed into the Nerviis' flank. The Nervii fought to almost total annihilation, according to ancient sources.

Over the next few years, Caesar systematically brought Gaul under Roman control. He fought the Veneti, a coastal tribe with a powerful navy that controlled trade along the Atlantic coast. The Veneti built heavy vessels with leather sails and high hulls that made them difficult to ram. Caesar had his engineers build Roman ships and adapt grappling hooks on long poles to cut the Veneti's rigging. Without their sails, Veneti ships became helpless, and Roman boarding tactics secured victory. Caesar punished the Veneti harshly. He executed their entire council of elders and sold the rest of the tribe into slavery. The severity was deliberate, a warning to other tribes not to resist.

He crossed the Rhine, constructing a bridge in ten days, according to his account, to raid Germanic territory and demonstrate Roman power. He invaded Britain twice, in 55 and 54 BCE. These expeditions beyond established Roman frontiers led the Romans to describe them as crossing the "Ocean," their term for seas beyond the Mediterranean. The British expeditions achieved little in terms of lasting conquest but generated enormous publicity in Rome, where people were fascinated by reports of this mysterious island at the edge of the known world.

An illustration of the Romans landing in Britain.[85]

The wars weren't easy. Gallic warriors were formidable. They were big, strong, experienced fighters who wielded long swords and shields and favored shock tactics. Celtic culture valued individual martial prowess, and Gallic nobles were raised from birth to be warriors. But the Gauls fought as tribal militias. Each tribe was independent and often feuding with its neighbors. Caesar exploited these divisions ruthlessly, allying with some tribes and keeping Gaul divided and conquerable.

Roman military discipline gave Caesar crucial advantages. His legions could march farther, build faster, and fight in coordinated formations that Gallic war bands couldn't match. Roman engineering allowed Caesar to build camps, bridges, and siege works that amazed his enemies. Roman logistics enabled sustained campaigns that would have exhausted tribal forces. And Caesar himself was a talented commander. He was quick to recognize opportunities, willing to take risks, and skilled at motivating his soldiers.

But the conquest nearly came undone in 52 BCE, when Vercingetorix, a young Gallic nobleman, achieved what no one else had managed: he united most of Gaul against Rome.

Vercingetorix was brilliant. Instead of facing Caesar in pitched battles, where Roman discipline dominated, he used scorched-earth tactics, burning towns and crops to deny Caesar supplies. He employed guerrilla warfare, attacking Roman supply lines and foraging parties. He forced Caesar to chase him across Gaul while Roman soldiers grew hungry and exhausted.

The campaign culminated at Alesia, a fortified Gallic settlement where Vercingetorix concentrated his forces. Caesar besieged it, building eleven miles of fortifications to surround the town. However, a Gallic relief army approached to lift the siege. Caesar claimed the relief force numbered around 250,000 warriors, though modern historians regard this figure as logistically impossible. Regardless of the exact numbers, Caesar faced a substantial force outside Alesia while besieging Vercingetorix inside.

So, Caesar built a second line of fortifications facing outward. His men built fourteen miles of walls, ditches, and defensive positions to protect the Roman army from the relief force. His legions now sat between two enemies, one inside the walls and one outside, with fortifications on both sides.

The battle lasted days. The Gallic relief army attacked Caesar's outer defenses repeatedly. Vercingetorix tried to break out from inside. Caesar's legions fought on both fronts simultaneously. They were exhausted and outnumbered, but they held their positions. The relief army eventually broke and fled. Vercingetorix, seeing no hope of rescue, surrendered to save his people from starvation.

Caesar kept Vercingetorix imprisoned for six years. Ancient sources report that he was then strangled during Caesar's triumph (a victory parade) in 46 BCE.

The Gallic Wars were over. Caesar had conquered territory roughly the size of modern France and Belgium. The cost was staggering. Ancient writers like Plutarch reported Caesar's claims of one million Gauls killed and one million enslaved, though modern historians suggest these figures include combat deaths, massacres, famine caused by scorched-earth tactics and sieges, and displacement rather than direct battlefield casualties alone. Regardless of precise numbers, the wars devastated Gaul's population. Many of those who remained were sold into slavery. Ancient sources report that the wars enriched Caesar personally through plundering Gallic temples, selling captives, and extracting tribute. It made him wealthy enough to pay off his debts and fund future political campaigns.

More importantly, Caesar created an army. Ten legions of veterans had fought with him for nearly a decade. They trusted his leadership, had been rewarded with plunder and bonuses, and expected Caesar to secure land grants when they retired. They would follow him anywhere—even across the Rubicon into Italy against the Senate's authority.

Caesar also created something else. His *Commentarii de Bello Gallico—Commentaries on the Gallic War*—was widely admired by educated Romans for its clear, direct Latin prose and proved highly effective as political communication. Written in the third person (Caesar always referred to himself as "Caesar" rather than "I"), they presented his campaigns as necessary defensive actions taken by a dutiful Roman general protecting Rome's interests. They made Caesar famous not just as a general but as a writer. By the time he crossed the Rubicon, Caesar was arguably the most famous man in Rome.

Crossing the Rubicon: The Point of No Return and the End of the Republic

By 50 BCE, Caesar's enemies in Rome knew they had a problem. Caesar was immensely popular. His *Commentarii* were bestsellers and were being read aloud in the Forum. His military reputation rivaled Pompey's. His wealth was enormous. His army was loyal and battle-hardened. If Caesar returned to Rome with his power intact, he would dominate Roman politics for decades.

The Senate, led by conservatives like Cato the Younger, decided to neutralize Caesar legally. Roman governors lost their authority upon entering Italy. Once Caesar crossed into Italy, he'd be just another citizen, vulnerable to prosecution. The charges might not stick, but the trial would humiliate Caesar and wreck his political career.

Caesar knew this. His solution? Run for consul while still holding his provincial command. He would stay in office continuously. Then, as consul, he would protect himself and reward his veterans with land.

The Senate said no. Caesar had to give up his command, come back as a private citizen, run for consul, and just trust that nobody would prosecute him. Caesar countered that he should be allowed to run without returning to Rome, keeping his command until he could take office. The Senate refused again.

Both sides were playing chicken. The Senate wanted Caesar vulnerable. Caesar wanted guarantees. Neither trusted the other. Both had good reasons not to.

By January 49 BCE, negotiations had collapsed. The Senate passed the *senatus consultum ultimum*, an emergency decree that effectively instructed the consuls to do whatever it took to defend the state. In other words, the consuls had to stop Caesar by force if necessary. The tribunes who supported Caesar, Mark Antony and Quintus Cassius Longinus, fled Rome immediately. They disguised themselves, possibly as slaves, and raced north to Caesar's camp.

Caesar now had his propaganda victory. Tribunes who were supposed to be sacred and untouchable were fleeing Rome? Caesar could present this as persecution, as the Senate driving out the people's representatives. He would march on Rome not as a rebel but as a defender of Roman rights against senatorial tyranny.

On January 10th, 49 BCE, Caesar stood at the Rubicon River, a small stream marking the boundary between his province of Cisalpine Gaul and Italy proper. Roman law strictly forbade generals from bringing armies into Italy without the Senate's permission. Crossing with his legions would be rebellion.

According to ancient sources, Caesar hesitated. He knew that crossing meant civil war. Once across, there was no peaceful solution. If he won, he would be Rome's master. If he lost, he would be executed as a traitor.

Then Caesar said, "Alea iacta est" ("The die is cast"), and crossed with the Thirteenth Legion.

The phrase became immortal. It captured the moment when Caesar chose war over submission, when the Roman Republic's last hope for a peaceful resolution died, and when the course was set toward dictatorship and, eventually, empire. The die was cast. The outcome was now in the hands of fate and force.

Julius Caesar.[86]

Caesar moved fast. He marched south through Italy, not plundering like an invader but presenting himself as a liberator defending the people's rights. Many towns opened their gates without resistance. Caesar's mercy was tactical. He pardoned enemies, spared cities that surrendered, and portrayed himself as reluctant to spill Roman blood. This contrasted sharply with memories of Sulla's brutality, making Caesar appear reasonable.

Pompey and the senatorial forces were unprepared. They had expected Caesar to negotiate or back down. Instead, he moved with shocking speed. Pompey couldn't raise enough troops to defend Italy. On the Senate's advice, he evacuated to Greece, taking his legions and many senators with him. Pompey's strategy was to control the eastern provinces, build an overwhelming force, then invade Italy and crush Caesar with superior numbers.

Caesar entered Rome unopposed in March 49 BCE. He had conquered Italy in sixty days without fighting a major battle. The Senate had fled. Republican institutions continued to function formally, though real political power had shifted decisively to Caesar.

However, the civil war was just beginning. Pompey commanded the east. Senators loyal to the Roman Republic's traditions rallied to his standard. Spain's legions remained uncertain. North Africa was contested. The Mediterranean was split between Caesar's faction and Pompey's coalition. For the next four years, Romans would kill Romans in battles across three continents.

Dictator for Life: Caesar's Reforms and the Ego That Got Him Killed

Caesar spent the years 49 to 45 BCE fighting a civil war on multiple fronts. He defeated Pompey's forces in Spain. He then chased Pompey to Greece and beat him at Pharsalus in 48 BCE.

Pharsalus was the decisive battle of the civil war. Pompey commanded about forty-five thousand infantry and seven thousand cavalry—nearly double Caesar's forces. Pompey's strategy was to use his cavalry superiority to envelop Caesar's right flank and then roll up his entire line. It should have worked. Pompey's cavalry was experienced, his army was larger, and he held the defensive position.

But Caesar anticipated the cavalry attack. He secretly positioned six cohorts (about three thousand men) behind his right wing with orders to target the cavalry specifically. His men were to thrust their javelins upward at the riders' faces rather than throwing them. When Pompey's cavalry charged, these cohorts emerged and attacked with disciplined jabbing motions. The cavalry, unused to infantry aggressively stabbing at their faces, panicked and fled. Caesar's cavalry pursued, then swept around and struck Pompey's infantry from behind.

Pompey's larger army collapsed. Ancient sources report that about fifteen thousand of Pompey's men died, and twenty-four thousand surrendered. Caesar claimed his own casualties were around two hundred, a figure that strains credibility in a battle involving nearly seventy thousand men and likely represents significant underreporting.

Regardless of exact numbers, the battle was very much one-sided. Pompey fled the battlefield, abandoning his army. Caesar's veterans had crushed a much larger force through superior tactics and discipline. Caesar famously commented, "They would have it so," meaning the senatorial faction had forced this battle and suffered the consequences.

Pompey fled to Egypt. The young pharaoh, Ptolemy XIII, had him murdered, probably hoping to score points with Caesar. When Caesar arrived in Alexandria, someone handed him Pompey's head. Caesar supposedly wept. Maybe the tears were real—Pompey had been his son-in-law and ally before becoming his enemy. Maybe they were theater. Either way, they fit Caesar's carefully cultivated image. This merciful victor was saddened by Roman bloodshed.

Caesar spent the winter of 48–47 BCE in Egypt, becoming entangled in Egyptian politics and beginning his famous affair with Cleopatra VII. He backed Cleopatra against her brother Ptolemy in Egypt's civil war. When Caesar left, Cleopatra was in charge, pregnant with Caesar's son, and Egypt was firmly in Rome's—or rather, Caesar's—orbit.

This mattered politically beyond the scandal. Egypt was the richest kingdom in the Mediterranean. It had grain that could feed Rome and gold that made Rome's treasury look pathetic. By making Cleopatra his ally and lover, Caesar controlled Egypt's resources without bothering to ask the Senate. Cleopatra later moved to Rome, living in Caesar's villa across the Tiber. A foreign queen openly living as Caesar's mistress while he was still married horrified conservative Romans. Rumors spread that Caesar planned to marry her, make their son his heir, and maybe even move Rome's capital to Alexandria. This was probably not true, but the rumors fed fears that Caesar wanted to be an eastern-style king, not a Roman magistrate.

Caesar then defeated Pharnaces, King of Pontus, in a brief campaign that produced his famous dispatch, "Veni, vidi, vici" ("I came, I saw, I conquered"). These three words capture Caesar's military genius and his talent for self-promotion.

In 46 BCE, Caesar crushed the remaining senatorial forces in North Africa at Thapsus. In 45 BCE, he destroyed the last resistance at Munda in Spain, where Pompey's sons led a desperate final stand. The civil war was over. Caesar had won. The Senate was cowed. His opponents were dead, exiled, or pardoned and humiliated.

Caesar held multiple dictatorships during these years. They were technically legal emergency positions, but they stretched far beyond their traditional bounds. After Munda, the Senate granted Caesar the dictatorship for ten years. Then, in 44 BCE, they made him *dictator perpetuo*, or dictator for life. This was unprecedented. The dictatorship was supposed to be a six-month emergency office. Making it permanent destroyed the pretense that Caesar's power was temporary.

Caesar used his power to push through massive reforms. Some were genuinely beneficial to Rome. Others enhanced his own authority. All of them reflected Caesar's brilliance, ambition, and dangerous confidence that he knew what Rome needed better than anyone else.

He reformed the calendar, creating what we now call the Julian calendar, with 365 days, 12 months, and leap years. The old Roman calendar had fallen hopelessly out of sync with the seasons because priests manipulated it for political purposes. Caesar fixed it with the help of Greek astronomers. The result was so effective that we still use a version of it today, more than two thousand years later.

Ancient sources report that he expanded the Senate to nine hundred members, packing it with his supporters. This diluted the old senatorial elite's power and ensured Caesar had a compliant Senate. However, it also insulted the aristocracy by elevating men they considered unworthy.

He founded colonies for his veterans and the urban poor. Ancient sources and modern reconstructions suggest he settled perhaps eighty thousand Romans in new communities across the Mediterranean. This relieved pressure on Rome's grain supply and rewarded his soldiers with land.

Caesar also reformed debt laws, helping debtors without completely alienating creditors. He planned massive public works, draining marshes, building a new Forum, and expanding Rome's infrastructure. Some of these projects continued after his death. He granted citizenship more liberally, extending it to communities in Gaul and Spain. This expanded Rome's citizen body and created loyalty to Caesar.

But Caesar also accepted honors that alarmed traditionalists. Ancient sources describe the Senate voting for him to have a golden throne, placing his image on coins (the first living Roman so honored), and renaming the month Quintilis as Julius (our July). They granted him the right to wear a laurel wreath constantly, which conveniently covered his baldness, something Caesar was reportedly vain about. They gave him honors usually reserved for gods, including temples, priests, and religious rituals in his name. Modern scholars debate the timing and political significance of these honors, but it was clear that Caesar was receiving unprecedented recognition.

Caesar accepted all of this. Whether he believed he deserved divine honors or simply couldn't resist the flattery is impossible to know. However, to many Romans, it seemed Caesar wanted to be king or, worse, to be worshiped as a god.

The word "king" (*rex*) was still toxic in Rome. Romans had been taught for five hundred years to hate kings. When someone in a crowd reportedly called Caesar "rex," Caesar immediately replied, "I am Caesar, not rex." When Mark Antony offered Caesar a royal diadem at the Lupercalia festival in February 44 BCE, Caesar publicly refused it twice, for emphasis. Yet the rumors persisted. Why would Antony offer it if Caesar didn't want it? Was Caesar testing public reaction? Was it political theater designed to make him appear humble while preparing the public to accept him as king?

Caesar's veterans loved him. The common people appreciated his generosity and reforms. But senators, even those who had supported him, were becoming increasingly alarmed. Caesar was acting like a monarch. He made decisions unilaterally. He bypassed the Senate. He appointed magistrates rather than allowing elections. He did not consult the great aristocratic families. He treated the Senate like a rubber stamp.

And Caesar was planning to leave Rome again, this time for a massive military expedition against Parthia. He wanted to avenge Crassus's defeat at Carrhae. Caesar would be gone for years campaigning in the east while Rome waited for his return. Such a victory would make Caesar even more powerful, as he would be the conqueror of Rome's only remaining rival.

Some senators decided that Caesar had to die, not for personal reasons—many had been pardoned by him, promoted by him, or enriched by him—but for the republic. They convinced themselves that killing Caesar would allow Rome to return to its traditional government.

They were senators, many from the old aristocracy. They believed in the Roman Republic's values of liberty, shared power, and the rule of law. And they believed that one man, no matter how talented, should not rule Rome. Caesar had destroyed the Roman Republic's system. In their minds, the only way to restore it was to kill him.

The Ides of March: Why His "Friends" Thought They Were Saving Rome by Murdering Him

The conspiracy formed slowly and carefully. Around sixty senators eventually joined, though only a few knew all the details. The ringleaders were Gaius Cassius Longinus and Marcus Junius Brutus.

Recruiting conspirators was a delicate process. Each man had to be absolutely trusted; one informant could expose the entire plot and get everyone executed. The conspirators were recruited primarily from the Senate's ranks, focusing on men who had fought for Pompey or the Republican cause but had been pardoned by Caesar. Many of these men owed their lives to Caesar's clemency, which made their betrayal more shocking but, in their minds, more principled. They were not killing Caesar out of personal hatred but from the belief that he threatened Rome's freedom. The conspirators called themselves the Liberatores (the Liberators).

Cassius was a competent military commander and longtime opponent of Caesar, though he had been pardoned and promoted after the Battle of Pharsalus. Ancient sources portray Cassius's motivations as a complex mix of personal animosity toward Caesar and genuine political conviction. He was driven by envy and ambition, as well as principle.

Brutus was different. He was Caesar's protégé. Ancient sources circulated rumors that he might have been Caesar's illegitimate son since Caesar had an affair with Brutus's mother, Servilia. Caesar favored Brutus, reportedly telling his guards, "Whatever Brutus wants, give it to him. And if he doesn't want it, don't force him." Brutus was descended from Lucius Junius Brutus, the legendary founder of the Roman Republic who expelled Rome's last king. That ancestry gave Brutus enormous symbolic importance. If Brutus joined the conspiracy, it would seem as if the Roman Republic's founder's descendant was saving Rome from a new king.

These men saw themselves as heroes defending Roman liberty against tyranny. They planned to kill Caesar publicly, in front of witnesses, to show they were acting openly for the good of Rome rather than sneaking around like common assassins. The murder would be tyrannicide—the righteous killing of a tyrant—not mere murder.

They chose March 15th (the Ides of March in the Roman calendar) when the Senate would meet in the Theatre of Pompey. Caesar would be in attendance. The conspirators would surround him and strike him down in front of the Senate. Then they would announce that Rome was free and that the Roman Republic had been restored.

In the days before the Ides of March, ancient historians recorded various omens, though whether these were real events or literary devices added later to heighten drama is unclear. A soothsayer supposedly warned Caesar to "beware the Ides of March." Lightning allegedly struck a statue. Sacrificial animals were said to have had no heart. Caesar's wife, Calpurnia, dreamed he was murdered and begged him not to go to the Senate meeting.

On the morning of March 15th, 44 BCE, Caesar almost did not go to the Senate. Calpurnia's dream troubled him. However, Decimus Brutus Albinus, one of the conspirators and one of Caesar's most trusted officers, came to Caesar's house and convinced him that canceling would appear weak. The Senate was waiting to grant Caesar new honors. How would it look if Caesar stayed home because of a bad dream?

So, Caesar went.

As he entered the theater, someone pressed a note into his hand; ancient sources say it listed the conspirators and their plot. Caesar tried to read it but was surrounded by senators eager to greet him. He never read the warning.

Caesar took his seat. The conspirators gathered around him under the pretense of petitioning him. Lucius Tillius Cimber approached first, asking Caesar to recall his exiled brother. When Caesar refused, Cimber grabbed Caesar's toga and pulled it down. This was the signal.

Casca struck first, stabbing Caesar in the neck. The wound was not fatal. Certain ancient accounts, including Suetonius and Plutarch, describe Caesar grabbing Casca's arm and stabbing back with his stylus, the pointed pen Romans used to write on wax tablets.

Then the other conspirators closed in. Twenty-three men stabbed Caesar repeatedly. Ancient sources say Caesar resisted at first, trying to fight off his attackers. But when he saw Brutus with a knife, Caesar allegedly said something. Some sources say he spoke in Greek: "Kai su, teknon?" ("You too, child?"). The famous Latin version, "Et tu, Brute?" comes from Shakespeare, not ancient sources. Whether Caesar said anything at all in his final moments, and if so, what remains uncertain. Eventually, Caesar stopped resisting. He pulled his toga over his head to die with dignity and fell at the base of Pompey's statue. The symbolism was perfect—Caesar died at the feet of his dead rival's memorial.

The conspirators stood there, covered in blood, expecting celebration. They thought the Senate would cheer. They thought the Roman people would praise them as liberators. They thought killing Caesar would restore the Roman Republic.

Instead, there was shocked silence, then panic. Senators fled the theater. The conspirators had no plan beyond the murder itself. They had killed Caesar but had not secured the support of his veterans. They had not prepared for what came next. They ran through the streets waving bloody daggers, shouting that Rome was free. But people hid in their houses. Rome was terrified, not celebrating.

The Liberators had made a catastrophic miscalculation. They thought Caesar was the problem, that removing him would restore the republic. They were wrong. Modern scholars see the Roman Republic's crisis as a structural failure. Sulla had shown that generals with loyal armies could seize Rome. Pompey and Crassus had shown that powerful individuals could bypass the Senate. Caesar had simply made these systemic problems impossible to ignore.

The Roman Republic's collapse stemmed not from one man's power but from the system's inability to withstand the stresses of empire. Rome's government had been designed for a small city-state, not a Mediterranean empire. The concentration of wealth in elite hands, the creation of professional armies loyal to commanders, and the impossibility of representing millions of citizens through assemblies in Rome could not be fixed by murdering Caesar.

Mark Antony, Caesar's ally and co-consul, seized control of Caesar's papers and funds. Caesar's deputy, Marcus Aemilius Lepidus, controlled troops in Rome. The conspirators had no army, no plan, and, within days, no support. Ancient sources such as Appian and Dio describe Caesar's funeral turning into a mob scene as Antony read Caesar's will, which left gardens and money to the Roman people. He also displayed Caesar's bloody toga. The crowd rioted, burned the conspirators' houses, and forced them to flee Rome.

A bust believed to be Mark Antony.[87]

And then there was Caesar's heir. Caesar's will named his eighteen-year-old grandnephew, Gaius Octavius, as his adopted son and heir. This teenager would change everything.

Caesar was dead. But Caesarism—rule by military strongmen claiming to represent the people against an ineffective Senate—would define Rome's future. The conspirators killed the man. They couldn't kill what he represented or reverse what he had revealed: that the Roman Republic couldn't survive as a world empire and that Roman politics would now be settled by armies, not votes.

Chapter 6: Augustus and the Birth of the Empire

Octavian: The Teenager Who Outplayed Everyone and Transformed Rome into an Empire

When Julius Caesar's will was read after his assassination in 44 BCE, it contained a surprise. Caesar had adopted his eighteen-year-old grandnephew, Gaius Octavius, as his son and heir. Most people in Rome had barely heard of this teenager. He was sickly, inexperienced, and came from Rome's elite but not from an established consular dynasty. He had no military experience. He controlled no legions. And he had no political base.

Mark Antony, Caesar's veteran co-consul who controlled Rome, laughed when he heard that this boy was claiming Caesar's inheritance. Cicero, the famous orator and senator, thought he could manipulate the young man, use him against Antony, and then discard him. The assassins who had killed Caesar dismissed Octavian as irrelevant.

They all underestimated him. Gaius Octavius would become Augustus Caesar, Rome's first emperor. He ruled for forty-one years and transformed the Roman state so completely that the republic would never return. He would outlive all his enemies, die peacefully in his bed, and be worshiped as a god. He was perhaps the most successful politician in Roman history—maybe in all of history.

A statue of Augustus.[88]

But in 44 BCE, he was just a teenager who had lost his adoptive father to assassination and was surrounded by powerful men who wanted to use him or destroy him.

Octavian's first move was brilliant. He took Caesar's name. He became Gaius Julius Caesar Octavianus. Names mattered in Rome. Caesar's name carried enormous prestige. Caesar's veterans saw Octavian as Caesar's heir who owed them what Caesar had promised. Caesar's political supporters saw continuity. Caesar's enemies saw a boy pretending to be Caesar, but he was a boy they could not ignore.

Octavian also had money. Caesar left him his personal fortune. Octavian used it expertly, paying bonuses to Caesar's veterans, funding games for the Roman people, and building political support through the time-honored method of strategic generosity.

However, Octavian faced a major obstacle: Mark Antony. Antony had been Caesar's right-hand man. He was a proven military commander and consul in 44 BCE. Antony controlled Rome politically and militarily. He expected to inherit Caesar's political legacy and become the dominant figure in Roman politics.

Antony treated Octavian with contempt, refusing to hand over Caesar's fortune, keeping Octavian waiting for hours during meetings, and publicly mocking him as a boy who owed everything to Caesar's name. This was a mistake. It pushed Octavian directly into an alliance with Antony's enemies.

The Senate, led by Cicero, saw an opportunity. They were terrified of Antony, whom they feared would become another Caesar, a military strongman dominating Rome. But they could not defeat Antony militarily. So, they decided to use Octavian. Cicero delivered speeches (later known as the *Philippics*) attacking Antony and praising Octavian. The Senate granted Octavian military command despite his age and lack of qualifications, hoping he would fight Antony on their behalf.

A fresco by Cesare Maccari depicting Cicero speaking to the Senate.[89]

Octavian accepted. He raised legions from Caesar's veterans, many of whom defected from Antony to serve Caesar's heir. In 43 BCE, Octavian marched north. Two battles were fought against Antony at Mutina (modern Modena). Antony was defeated and fled to Gaul. Both consuls, Aulus Hirtius and Gaius Vibius Pansa, died in the fighting, leaving Octavian in control of their legions. Later propaganda portrayed the nineteen-year-old Octavian as the brilliant commander who defeated Antony. The reality was messier, but the outcome was what mattered.

The Senate was thrilled. They had used Octavian to neutralize Antony. Now they could dispose of the teenager. They passed votes of thanks, denied Octavian the triumph he requested, and tried to strip him of his command. Ancient sources report that Cicero said Octavian should be "praised, honored, and disposed of" (the Latin verb *tollere* meaning both "to raise up" and "to eliminate").

Octavian learned that the Senate's promises were worthless. They would use him and then destroy him, just as they had tried to destroy Caesar. If he wanted to survive, he could not rely on senatorial goodwill.

So, at nineteen years old, Octavian marched on Rome with his legions. He demanded the consulship, backpay for his soldiers, and official recognition. The Senate, staring at armed legions, caved. Octavian became consul in August 43 BCE. He was the youngest consul in Roman history.

Octavian used his consulship to pass the *Lex Pedia*, which declared Caesar's assassins enemies of the state and created special courts to try them. This gave Octavian legal authority to hunt down Brutus, Cassius, and the other conspirators. It also made it clear that Octavian was Caesar's avenger, not the Senate's tool.

But Octavian still faced a problem: Antony. Antony had regrouped in Gaul, gathered legions, and allied with Marcus Aemilius Lepidus, Caesar's former deputy, who commanded troops in Spain and southern Gaul. Together, Antony and Lepidus controlled more military forces than Octavian did. Octavian needed to neutralize them or defeat them.

Instead, he did something unexpected: he allied with them.

The Second Triumvirate: Thirteen Years of Proscriptions, Purges, and Power Politics

In November 43 BCE, Octavian, Antony, and Lepidus met near Bononia (modern Bologna) and formed an alliance. Unlike the First Triumvirate between Caesar, Pompey, and Crassus, which had been a private agreement, the Second Triumvirate was official. The three men had themselves appointed *triumviri rei publicae constituendae* ("three men for restoring the republic") with legal authority for five years. They essentially divided the Roman world among themselves. Antony took Gaul, Lepidus took Spain and southern Gaul, and Octavian took Africa and the islands.

But first, they needed money. They also needed to eliminate their enemies. So, they instituted proscriptions.

The proscriptions of 43–42 BCE were among the most brutal episodes in Roman history. The triumvirs drew up lists of political enemies. These could be senators, equestrians, or anyone who opposed them or whose wealth they wanted. Ancient sources such as Appian report that perhaps three hundred senators and two thousand equestrians were proscribed, though modern historians treat these as estimates rather than precise counts. The exact death toll is unknowable. Being proscribed meant you were declared an enemy of the state. Anyone could kill you and claim a reward. Your property was confiscated. Your family lost its legal protections.

The triumvirs were not killing for ideology. This was political murder for profit. Each triumvir had to sacrifice some of his own allies to satisfy the others' vengeance. Ancient sources describe the negotiations as callous bargaining. Antony wanted Cicero, Lepidus wanted certain senators, and Octavian needed to eliminate potential threats. They traded names like merchants trading goods.

The mechanics of proscription created a reign of terror. Lists were posted in the Forum. Men woke up to discover they were marked for death. Some tried to hide, while others fled. Few succeeded, as the ports were watched, and the roads were patrolled.

Cicero tried to flee Italy. Antony's soldiers caught him at his villa in December 43 BCE. They cut off his head and hands—the hands that had written the *Philippics*—and brought them to Rome. The head and hands were displayed in the Forum, where Cicero had delivered so many speeches.

Thousands died. The proscriptions terrorized Rome and enriched the triumvirs. By late 42 BCE, they had enough wealth to fund their armies and enough fear to prevent opposition.

With Italy secured and their enemies dead or in exile, the triumvirs turned their attention to the conspirators. Brutus and Cassius had fled east after Caesar's assassination and built an army in Greece and Asia Minor. They controlled Rome's eastern provinces and commanded substantial military forces. If Octavian and Antony wanted to secure their power, they needed to destroy them.

In 42 BCE, Octavian and Antony crossed to Greece with their armies. Lepidus stayed in Italy to maintain control. At Philippi in Macedonia, the triumvirs' forces met the armies of Brutus and Cassius in two battles.

The first battle was indecisive. Brutus defeated Octavian's forces on one wing. Ancient sources suggest Octavian was sick and ineffective in battle. He was not present in his camp when it was overrun. But Antony crushed Cassius on the other wing. Cassius, seeing his camp captured and unaware that Brutus had prevailed on the opposite flank, committed suicide.

Three weeks later, Antony forced a second battle. Brutus's army, demoralized by Cassius's death and running low on supplies, fought but was decisively defeated. Brutus fled the battlefield and committed suicide rather than be captured. According to ancient accounts, Octavian treated Brutus's corpse with disrespect, sending the head to Rome to be thrown at the feet of Caesar's statue, though he honored other fallen enemies with a proper burial.

The Roman Republic's last defenders were dead. The triumvirs controlled the Roman world. But now they had to decide how to divide it and who would ultimately rule.

The settlement after Philippi gave Antony the East, the wealthy provinces of Greece, Asia Minor, Syria, and Egypt. Octavian received the West—Italy, Gaul, and Spain—and the difficult task of settling veterans, which required confiscating property and making enemies of displaced Italian landowners. Lepidus was sidelined to Africa, the least important territory. On paper, the division favored Antony. The East was richer, easier to govern, and further from Rome's political chaos. The West faced veteran land settlements, political instability, and the challenge of governing Italy itself.

Octavian's land confiscations triggered an immediate crisis. Italian landowners who lost property to veteran settlements were furious. Antony's brother, Lucius Antonius, and Antony's wife, Fulvia, exploited this anger, rallying opposition against Octavian. In 41 BCE, they raised an army and occupied Rome, claiming to represent Antony's interests and Italian property rights against Octavian's policies.

Octavian besieged them at Perusia (modern Perugia). The siege lasted months. When the city finally surrendered in early 40 BCE, Octavian displayed a ruthlessness he usually concealed behind political theater. Ancient sources report that he executed the city council and perhaps three hundred prominent citizens, allegedly declaring, "They must die" when they pleaded for mercy. He spared Lucius Antonius, Antony's brother, who was too important to kill, but the message was unmistakable. Opposition to Octavian would be crushed.

The Perusine War nearly triggered conflict between Octavian and Antony. However, both men realized that fighting each other would benefit only their enemies. In 40 BCE, they met at Brundisium and renewed their alliance. To seal the agreement, Antony married Octavian's sister Octavia. Antony's previous wife, Fulvia, had conveniently died not long before. The marriage was political, but ancient sources suggest Octavia was respected and dignified, making Antony's later abandonment of her for Cleopatra even more scandalous to Roman sensibilities.

Octavian and Antony faced yet another threat: Sextus Pompey, son of Pompey the Great. Sextus had fled to Sicily after the Battle of Philippi and built a powerful fleet. He controlled Sicily, Sardinia, and Corsica, which were key sources of Rome's grain supply. Sextus also offered refuge to proscribed men and escaped slaves, building a large military force. By blockading grain shipments, he could starve Rome and pressure the triumvirs.

For several years, Sextus functioned as a fourth power in the Roman world. The triumvirs tried bribing him and negotiating with him. Finally, in 39 BCE, they made peace through the Treaty of Misenum, which recognized Sextus's control of the islands in exchange for reopening the grain supply. But the peace did not last.

Between 38 and 36 BCE, Octavian fought a naval war against Sextus. The conflict went badly at first; Octavian lost ships to storms and suffered defeats in battle. However, Agrippa, Octavian's friend and most capable general, built a new fleet and trained crews in a specially constructed harbor. In 36 BCE, Agrippa defeated Sextus's fleet at Naulochus off Sicily. Sextus fled east to Antony's territories, where he was eventually captured and executed.

The defeat of Sextus gave Octavian control of the western Mediterranean and the crucial grain supply. It also provided a pretext to eliminate Lepidus. Lepidus had participated in the Sicilian campaign but later attempted to claim Sicily for himself. Octavian confronted Lepidus with his legions, and Lepidus's soldiers, recognizing which way the wind was blowing, defected to Octavian. Lepidus was forced into retirement and stripped of his triumviral powers, though he was allowed to retain the largely ceremonial position of pontifex maximus until his death in 13 BCE. The Second Triumvirate was now effectively reduced to Octavian and Antony.

But Octavian understood something Antony did not. Controlling Italy meant controlling Rome, and controlling Rome meant controlling the legitimacy that mattered for long-term power. Antony could rule the wealthy East, but Octavian held the symbolic and political heart of the Roman state.

Antony and Cleopatra: The Love Story That Lost an Empire

While Octavian dealt with angry Italian landowners and restive veterans, Antony went east and met Cleopatra VII, queen of Egypt and the former lover of Julius Caesar.

The meeting was political theater. Ancient sources, particularly Plutarch, describe Cleopatra arriving at Tarsus in 41 BCE on a magnificent barge with purple sails, silver oars, and herself dressed as the goddess Venus. It is not known whether the meeting was this dramatic or if later historians embellished it. However, it is clear that Cleopatra needed Roman protection for her throne, and Antony needed Egypt's wealth to fund his eastern campaigns.

They also became lovers. The relationship was genuine. Ancient accounts suggest real affection between them, not just political convenience. Cleopatra was intelligent, educated, charismatic, and one of the few people who could match wits with Antony. Plutarch, who wrote over a century later, claims she spoke multiple languages, including Egyptian. She was politically skilled, having survived court intrigue and civil war to secure her throne. And she had resources, namely Egypt's grain and gold.

Antony and Cleopatra had three children together: twins Alexander Helios and Cleopatra Selene in 40 BCE and Ptolemy Philadelphus in 36 BCE. Antony divided his time between Alexandria and his military campaigns, spending winters in Egypt with Cleopatra and campaigning in the summer.

However, Antony's relationship with Cleopatra created political problems in Rome. Romans hated kings and queens. They particularly hated foreign queens who might influence Roman politics. Memories of Caesar's affair with Cleopatra (she had lived in Rome during Caesar's lifetime) fed fears that Antony was being seduced by Eastern luxury and abandoning Roman values.

Octavian exploited these fears brilliantly. He couldn't openly attack Antony—they were still technically allies, though the alliance was fraying—but he could attack Cleopatra. Octavian's propaganda machine portrayed Cleopatra as a dangerous foreign seductress who had enslaved Antony, turned him against Rome, and aimed to make herself queen of the Roman Empire. Ancient sources suggest that Octavian spread rumors that Antony was constantly drunk, had "gone native" and adopted Egyptian customs, and planned to move Rome's capital to Alexandria.

These charges had some basis in reality. Antony did spend significant time in Egypt. He did have children with Cleopatra. He participated in Egyptian ceremonies and adopted some Eastern customs. In 34 BCE, Antony held a ceremony in Alexandria known as the "Donations of Alexandria," during which he distributed eastern territories to Cleopatra and their children. He declared Cleopatra "Queen of Kings" and Caesarion—Cleopatra's son by Julius Caesar—"King of Kings." He gave Alexander Helios territories in the East, Cleopatra Selene territories in North Africa, and Ptolemy Philadelphus territories in Syria.

Romans were outraged. Antony was giving away Roman territories, or at least territories Rome claimed, to an Egyptian queen and her children. He was treating Caesarion as Caesar's legitimate heir, which challenged Octavian's position as Caesar's adopted son and heir. He was conducting himself like an Eastern monarch rather than a Roman magistrate.

Octavian seized the opportunity. He claimed Antony had abandoned Rome and Roman values. He broke into the Temple of the Vestal Virgins in Rome, where Roman wills were stored, and seized Antony's will—a sacrilegious act that showed Octavian's ruthlessness. Octavian claimed the will proved Antony wanted to be buried in Alexandria with Cleopatra rather than in Rome. He also supposedly wanted to make Caesarion Caesar's heir and planned to make Cleopatra queen of Rome. Whether the will actually said these things or whether Octavian fabricated parts of it is debated by modern scholars, but the political effect was devastating.

The Senate, dominated by Octavian's supporters, stripped Antony of his powers and declared war, not on Antony, but on Cleopatra. This was clever. Octavian avoided declaring civil war on a Roman citizen. Instead, Rome was defending itself against a foreign queen who threatened Roman independence. Antony was merely the unfortunate Roman general who had been seduced and corrupted by this dangerous foreign woman.

It was propaganda, but it was effective propaganda. By 32 BCE, Octavian had successfully painted the coming conflict not as a civil war between Romans but as a patriotic defense of Rome against foreign conquest.

The Battle of Actium: The Shortest "Battle" That Changed History

In 31 BCE, the forces of Octavian and Antony finally met. Ancient sources provide varying estimates, but Antony and Cleopatra appear to have gathered substantial forces in Greece, perhaps around five hundred ships and seventy-five thousand infantry. Octavian commanded similar forces, led by his general Marcus Vipsanius Agrippa, one of the most competent military commanders in Roman history and Octavian's closest friend and ally.

The two fleets met near Actium on the western coast of Greece on September 2nd, 31 BCE. What happened next is one of the most debated events in Roman history because the ancient accounts contradict each other and are colored by pro-Octavian propaganda.

The traditional narrative, found in sources like Plutarch, says Antony's fleet was larger but became trapped in the Gulf of Actium by Agrippa's blockade. Antony's crews were sick, supplies were running low, and desertion was increasing. When battle came, Antony's fleet tried to break through the blockade. During the fighting, Cleopatra's squadron—perhaps sixty ships—suddenly hoisted sails and fled south toward Egypt. Antony, seeing Cleopatra flee, abandoned his fleet and followed her with a few ships. His fleet was left leaderless and surrendered or was destroyed. Antony's army surrendered shortly afterward.

The pro-Octavian interpretation was that Antony was so besotted with Cleopatra that he abandoned his army and fleet to follow his lover. This was the ultimate proof that he had been corrupted by foreign seduction and was unfit to lead the Romans.

Modern historians have questioned this narrative. Some suggest Actium was not a great naval battle but a strategic retreat that went wrong.

Antony's position was untenable. Perhaps he planned to break out with his best ships, escape to Egypt, and regroup.

If so, the plan failed. Most of Antony's fleet did not break through, and his army surrendered. Antony and Cleopatra reached Egypt, but without an army or fleet, they were finished.

Octavian spent several months securing the eastern provinces and Antony's former territories. He moved slowly and deliberately, letting Antony's remaining support collapse. By the time Octavian reached Egypt in 30 BCE, Antony and Cleopatra's position was hopeless.

Ancient sources describe their final days with dramatic flair. Antony supposedly heard false rumors that Cleopatra was dead and stabbed himself, only to learn she was alive. He asked to be carried to her monument to die in her arms. Cleopatra, captured by Octavian's forces and held under guard, allegedly killed herself with an asp, a poisonous snake, rather than be paraded through Rome in Octavian's triumph. Modern scholars debate whether the snake story is true or a legend, but Cleopatra definitely died in Egypt. Octavian claimed Egypt as his personal property rather than a Roman province.

Octavian had Caesarion, Cleopatra's son by Julius Caesar, executed. Octavian could not allow a potential rival who claimed to be Caesar's biological son to survive. Cleopatra's other children were spared and raised in Rome by Octavian's sister Octavia, who had been married to Antony before he left her for Cleopatra.

The civil wars were over. Octavian stood alone. No armies opposed him. No rivals remained. The Roman world was his to reshape.

The Principate: How to Become Emperor Without Calling Yourself King

Octavian returned to Rome in 29 BCE. He celebrated three triumphs for his victories. The Senate voted him honors. He was the undisputed master of the Roman state. However, he faced a crucial question: what to do with his power?

Octavian had learned from Caesar's mistakes. Caesar had accumulated power openly, accepted honors that suggested monarchy, and was assassinated by senators who claimed to be defending the Roman Republic. Octavian understood that Romans hated kings and loved the republic, or at least the idea of the republic. If Octavian wanted to rule without being assassinated, he needed to rule without appearing to be a king.

In 27 BCE, he appeared before the Senate and announced that he was restoring the republic. He resigned all his extraordinary powers and returned control of the provinces to the Senate. Octavian presented himself as a loyal citizen who had saved Rome from civil war and now wished to retire to private life, content that the republic was restored.

The Senate, dominated by Octavian's supporters and allies, reacted as Octavian knew it would. The senators begged him not to retire. They insisted Rome needed his leadership. They voted him honors and powers: the name "Augustus" (meaning "revered" or "majestic"), control of the most important provinces (those with significant military forces), supreme command of the army (*imperium*), and the authority of a tribune (including sacrosanctity and veto power).

This was the foundation of the Principate, the system of government that would last for centuries. On the surface, it looked as though the Roman Republic still existed. The Senate still met. Magistrates were still elected. Laws were still passed. But beneath the surface, Augustus controlled everything that mattered: the army, the wealthy provinces, and the grain supply that fed Rome.

Augustus called himself *princeps,* meaning "first citizen." He was not a king. Not a dictator. Just the first among equals in the Roman state. This was fiction, but it was carefully maintained fiction. Augustus was careful to respect the Senate, at least publicly. He consulted it on important matters. He allowed it to govern some provinces and treated senior senators with respect. He lived relatively modestly compared to Hellenistic monarchs, in a large but not palace-like house on Palatine Hill.

But Augustus's power was absolute. He controlled the provinces with legions. These provinces generated most of Rome's revenue and contained most of Rome's military force. The Senate controlled peaceful, urbanized provinces such as Greece and Asia Minor that had no legions. Augustus appointed the governors of his provinces directly. He could override the Senate when necessary. His word was effectively law.

Augustus also revolutionized the Roman administration. He created a professional civil service, using talented men from the equestrian class to administer finances, the grain supply, and imperial provinces. He reformed the army, reducing it to approximately 28 legions (around 150,000 men) of professional soldiers who served long-term enlistments and received land grants upon retirement. He established the Praetorian

Guard, elite troops stationed in Italy, ostensibly to protect the emperor but also to enforce his power in Rome. He expanded the road network, postal system, and administrative infrastructure that made governing the empire possible.

He reformed taxation, creating regular census records and a systematic collection system. He established a treasury separate from the Senate's treasury to manage imperial funds. He founded colonies for veterans throughout the empire, spreading Roman culture and creating loyal communities. He beautified Rome with temples, forums, and public buildings, famously claiming that he "found Rome a city of brick and left it a city of marble."

Augustus also launched an ambitious program of social and moral reform, attempting to restore what he presented as traditional Roman values. In 18 and 17 BCE, he passed legislation to encourage marriage and childbearing among the upper classes. The Julian Laws penalized unmarried men and childless couples by restricting their inheritance rights while rewarding families with three or more children with legal privileges. He promoted marriage by making divorce more difficult and adultery a criminal offense; previously, it had been a private family matter.

These laws were deeply unpopular with the Roman elite, who resented state interference in private life. The laws were regularly evaded and eventually modified. Ironically, Augustus's own family provided the most scandalous violation. His daughter, Julia, was caught in an adultery scandal in 2 BCE. Augustus was forced by his own laws to exile his daughter to a barren island.

Augustus also revived the traditional Roman religion, which had been neglected during the civil wars. According to his own *Res Gestae*, a record of his achievements that he had inscribed throughout the empire, he rebuilt eighty-two temples in Rome. He revived ancient priesthoods and rituals that had fallen into disuse and promoted traditional festivals and ceremonies.

This religious revival served political purposes. By positioning himself as the restorer of tradition and piety, Augustus presented his rule as a return to Rome's glorious past rather than a revolutionary break with it. He also created a new religious dimension to imperial power: the cult of Augustus.

In the provinces, particularly the Greek East, ruler worship was traditional. Hellenistic kings had been worshiped as gods for centuries. Augustus carefully managed this practice. He discouraged worship of himself as a god in Italy during his lifetime, as that was too close to kingship for Roman sensibilities. However, he encouraged worship of Roma and the Divine Julius (the deified Caesar) alongside his *genius* (his divine spirit or guardian). In the Eastern provinces, he allowed temples to be built for "Rome and Augustus," positioning himself as Rome's representative rather than claiming personal divinity.

After his death, the Senate declared him divine—*Divus Augustus*—and established an official cult with priests and temples. His successors would follow this pattern. Emperors were mortal men during their lifetime but could be declared gods after death, if the Senate approved. This helped legitimize the emperor's power.

Augustus also addressed the crucial problem of succession. He had no sons, only a daughter, Julia. Roman law and custom had no clear way for transferring power because, officially, Rome was still a republic and Augustus was just another magistrate. But unofficially, Augustus needed to build a dynasty.

His succession planning became a decades-long tragedy of premature deaths and dashed hopes. Augustus first groomed his nephew Marcellus (the son of his sister Octavia) by marrying him to Julia in 25 BCE, when Marcellus was about seventeen, and Julia was fourteen. However, Marcellus died of illness in 23 BCE at age nineteen or twenty. Augustus then married Julia to his closest friend and general, Marcus Agrippa, in 21 BCE. Agrippa was much older than Julia, but the match was political. Julia and Agrippa had five children, including two sons, Gaius and Lucius Caesar.

Augustus adopted Gaius and Lucius as his own sons in 17 BCE, making them his heirs. He advanced them rapidly through political honors and military commands, grooming them to succeed him. Roman hopes for a smooth succession centered on these young princes. But tragedy struck again. Lucius died in 2 CE at age nineteen, possibly of illness. Gaius died in 4 CE at age twenty-three from wounds received while fighting in Armenia.

With both designated heirs dead, Augustus turned to his stepson, Tiberius. Tiberius was from Livia's first marriage to Tiberius Claudius Nero. He was capable, experienced, and had proven himself in military campaigns in Pannonia and Germany. But Augustus had previously treated him as second-tier; Tiberius was a useful commander but not heir material. In 12 BCE, Augustus forced Tiberius to divorce his beloved wife, Vipsania (Agrippa's daughter from his first marriage), to marry Julia, Augustus's daughter and Agrippa's widow. This was a loveless political marriage. Ancient sources suggest Julia and Tiberius loathed each other.

Julia's behavior became increasingly scandalous. Ancient sources, particularly Suetonius, describe her conducting affairs openly, even reportedly using the Forum itself. Whether the stories were true or exaggerated by hostile sources, Julia's behavior violated Augustus's own moral legislation. In 2 BCE, Augustus was forced to acknowledge his daughter's adultery. He exiled Julia to the island of Pandateria, forbade her wine and luxuries, and refused to see her again. Several of her alleged lovers were executed or exiled.

The scandal was devastating to Augustus and politically damaging to his image as a moral reformer. But it also removed complications from the succession process. With Julia exiled and disgraced, Tiberius was clearly Augustus's heir.

Augustus adopted Tiberius in 4 CE, along with his last surviving grandson, Agrippa Postumus (Julia's youngest son with Agrippa). Agrippa Postumus proved difficult; ancient sources describe him as coarse and possibly mentally unstable. Augustus eventually exiled him in 7 CE. When Augustus died in 14 CE, Agrippa Postumus was quietly executed, removing any potential rival to Tiberius. Some ancient sources and modern scholars have speculated about Livia's role in the convenient deaths and exiles of Augustus's preferred heirs, though evidence for such involvement remains circumstantial and debated.

Tiberius succeeded Augustus smoothly despite his tragic path to power. The Principate would continue. Augustus had established a system flexible enough to survive succession crises and transfer power across generations.

The Pax Romana: What Peace Meant in an Empire Built on Conquest

One of Augustus's greatest achievements—and most effective propaganda claims—was bringing peace after a century of civil wars. The *Pax Romana* (Roman Peace) became synonymous with Augustus's reign. But what did this "peace" actually mean?

For Romans in Italy, peace was real. No armies marched through Italian cities. No proscriptions terrorized the elite. No rival warlords fought for supremacy. Trade flourished. Roads were safe. The grain supply was secure. After generations of civil war, Italians experienced genuine stability. Augustus had ended the cycle of Roman killing Roman that had consumed the republic.

However, the Pax Romana was not universal peace. Rome's borders expanded under Augustus through continuous military campaigns. In the north, Roman armies conquered the Alpine regions, pushing Rome's frontier to the Danube River. Generals such as Tiberius and Drusus (Augustus's stepsons) campaigned for years in Pannonia, Raetia, and Germania, subduing tribes and establishing Roman control. These were not defensive wars; they were wars of conquest aimed at expanding Roman territory and glorifying Augustus through military victories.

The conquest of Germania proved particularly costly. From 12 to 9 BCE, Drusus campaigned successfully east of the Rhine, penetrating deep into Germanic territory. After Drusus died from injuries in 9 BCE, other commanders continued the expansion. By 9 CE, the Romans believed that Germania up to the Elbe River had been pacified and could be organized as a Roman province.

Then disaster struck. In 9 CE, the Germanic chieftain Arminius, who had served in Roman auxiliaries and held Roman citizenship, turned against Rome. He ambushed three Roman legions under the command of Publius Quinctilius Varus in the Teutoburg Forest. Over three days of fighting in terrible terrain during a rainstorm, Germanic warriors destroyed the legions almost completely. Ancient sources suggest perhaps fifteen thousand to twenty thousand Roman soldiers died. Varus committed suicide.

When Augustus received news of the disaster, he was devastated. For months afterward, he allegedly banged his head against doors, crying, "Quinctili Vare, legiones redde!"—"Quintilius Varus, give me back my legions!" The defeat traumatized Augustus in his final years. Rome never again seriously attempted to conquer Germania beyond the Rhine. The disaster at the Teutoburg Forest essentially fixed Rome's northern frontier for centuries.

In the East, Augustus pursued a different strategy. Rather than costly conquests, he established client kingdoms. These were nominally independent states ruled by friendly kings who accepted Roman supremacy. Judea, Armenia, and other eastern territories were governed through this system, giving Rome control without the expense of direct administration. When client kings proved unreliable, Rome intervened or annexed territories, but it preferred indirect rule.

In Egypt, Augustus took a unique approach. He treated Egypt as his personal property rather than a normal Roman province. Senators were forbidden from entering Egypt without Augustus's permission. He appointed equestrians rather than senators to govern Egypt. Egypt's enormous wealth belonged to Augustus personally, not the Roman state, which gave Augustus financial independence from the Senate and ensured that no rival could seize Egypt's resources.

For conquered peoples, the Pax Romana meant enforced peace. Roman legions stationed throughout the provinces maintained order. Revolts were crushed brutally. Tribes that resisted were enslaved or massacred. Roman governors extracted taxes, requisitioned supplies, and demanded military conscription from subject peoples. The benefits of Roman rule, including roads, aqueducts, legal systems, and urban development, came with costs like taxation, conscription, loss of independence, and Roman cultural dominance.

However, for many provincials, Roman rule offered advantages compared to previous alternatives. Roman law was more predictable than that of arbitrary local rulers. Roman citizenship brought legal protections and economic opportunities. Roman military presence suppressed banditry and tribal warfare. Roman infrastructure connected provinces to larger trade networks. Cities prospered under Roman administration. The Romanization of the provinces would ultimately create a unified Mediterranean civilization that lasted for centuries.

The Julio-Claudians: When "Mad" Emperors Proved the System Worked

Augustus died in 14 CE. The question everyone had was whether the system could survive without him. The next hundred years would answer that question. The Julio-Claudian dynasty—five emperors connected by blood or adoption to Julius Caesar and Augustus—would include competent administrators, cautious rulers, and, according to ancient sources, at least two emperors who were genuinely insane. Yet the empire not only survived; it also prospered. This proved that Augustus had built something more durable than personal rule. He had created an imperial system.

Tiberius (r. 14–37 CE): The Reluctant Emperor

Tiberius succeeded Augustus at age fifty-five after a long military career. Ancient sources, particularly Tacitus and Suetonius, paint Tiberius as gloomy, suspicious, and increasingly tyrannical. But the historical reality was more complex. Tiberius was a capable administrator who upheld Augustus's policies, maintained peace in the provinces, and managed finances responsibly. The treasury was fuller when he died than when he took power, which is still a rare achievement for any ruler.

Tiberius's problem was political theater. Augustus had been a master performer, playing the modest first citizen while wielding absolute power. Tiberius was competent but awkward. He was uncomfortable with the Senate's flattery and ill-suited to the social aspects of ruling. He reportedly hated giving games and public spectacles that the Romans expected. His relationship with the Senate was tense. He expected senators to debate and advise, but they had learned under Augustus to defer to imperial wishes.

The most notorious aspect of Tiberius's reign was the rise of Sejanus, the Praetorian prefect who became Tiberius's chief minister. Ancient sources accuse Sejanus of manipulating Tiberius, conducting treason trials to eliminate rivals, and plotting to seize power. Whether Sejanus was truly a villain or Tacitus exaggerated his role is debated. What is clear is that when Tiberius finally turned against Sejanus in 31 CE, he had him executed along with his supporters, family members, and even his children.

In 26 CE, Tiberius retired to Capri, an island off southern Italy. He never returned to Rome. Instead, he governed the empire through correspondence for the last eleven years of his reign. While Rome remained administratively stable during this period, ancient sources describe increasing paranoia and reliance on informers, leading to heightened purges and treason trials. These sources also include scandalous stories. Tacitus and Suetonius describe debauched parties and perverse acts. Modern historians note that regardless of Tiberius's personal behavior or increasing isolation, the empire's administration continued to function, though whether this represents effective governance or was merely momentum from Augustus's reign remains debated.

Caligula (r. 37–41 CE): Four Years of Increasing Madness

When Tiberius died in 37 CE, the Romans rejoiced. His successor was Gaius Caesar, known as Caligula ("Little Boots," a nickname from his childhood in military camps). Caligula was the son of Germanicus, a beloved general, and a great-grandson of Augustus. Romans had high hopes.

Those hopes lasted about seven months. According to ancient sources, Caligula began his reign with sensible policies, moderate behavior, and popularity. Then he fell seriously ill. When he recovered, ancient historians claim he was a different person. He was paranoid, cruel, and possibly insane.

What followed, if ancient sources are to be believed, was one of the strangest reigns in Roman history. Caligula declared himself a living god and built temples for his own worship. He reportedly had conversations with statues of Jupiter. He planned to make his horse Incitatus a consul, though this might have been a mockery of the Senate rather than genuine madness. He executed senators and equestrians on a whim. Ancient sources claim he slept with his sisters, particularly Drusilla. When Drusilla died in 38 CE, he forced the Senate to declare her a goddess. He spent enormous sums on bizarre projects, exhausting Tiberius's carefully managed treasury. Caligula humiliated the Senate by forcing senators to run alongside his chariot. He led a military "campaign" to Germany and Gaul that achieved nothing, then had his troops collect seashells from the beach as "spoils of conquering the Ocean."

Modern historians debate how much of this is true. Ancient sources such as Suetonius and Cassius Dio wrote decades later from the perspective of the senatorial class—the very people Caligula oppressed. The sources contradict each other on specific events. Many of Caligula's alleged acts of "madness" are now seen as deliberate political theater or calculated insults to the Senate that were later recast as insanity. Some actions might have been provocations meant to test the limits of imperial power and humiliate senators who had collaborated in his family's destruction under Tiberius.

But several facts are clear. Caligula became increasingly autocratic, rejecting Augustus's fiction of being merely "first citizen." He emphasized his absolute power and divine status. He executed senators he suspected of disloyalty. He depleted the treasury. After less than four years as emperor, the Praetorian Guard assassinated him in 41 CE, becoming the first Roman emperor murdered by his own troops.

Claudius (r. 41–54 CE): The Unlikely Emperor Who Conquered Britain

After Caligula's assassination, the Praetorian Guard found Claudius hiding behind a curtain in the palace. Claudius was Caligula's uncle. He was a fifty-year-old man with physical disabilities. Ancient sources describe a limp, a stutter, and involuntary movements that Romans interpreted as signs of stupidity. The imperial family had kept him out of politics, considering him an embarrassment.

The Praetorians decided to make him emperor anyway, possibly because he was the only adult male Julian left alive, and they wanted someone controllable. They were wrong about the controllable part.

Claudius proved to be an excellent administrator. He was educated; he had written histories and studied under scholars during his years of political exclusion. He expanded the imperial bureaucracy, using freedmen (former slaves) as ministers to manage finances, correspondence, and petitions. This professionalized the imperial administration but offended senatorial sensibilities. Freed slaves wielding power over senators was humiliating to the aristocracy.

Claudius's greatest achievement was the conquest of Britain. In 43 CE, he launched a full-scale invasion with four legions. Previous Roman expeditions to Britain, such as Julius Caesar's raids, had achieved little. Claudius's invasion was a systematic conquest. Roman forces defeated British tribes, captured the stronghold of Camulodunum (modern Colchester), and established Roman control over southern Britain. Claudius personally visited Britain for sixteen days to accept the surrender of British chiefs.

Claudius also extended Roman citizenship more liberally, incorporated Gallic nobles into the Senate, and built infrastructure, including new harbors and aqueducts. Ancient sources credit him with generally sound governance, though they also portray him as being dominated by his wives and freedmen.

His personal life was messier. Claudius's fourth wife was his niece Agrippina the Younger (daughter of Germanicus and sister of Caligula). Agrippina was described as ambitious and ruthless. She persuaded Claudius to adopt her son Nero and make him heir instead of Claudius's own son, Britannicus. In 54 CE, Claudius died; ancient sources claim Agrippina poisoned him with mushrooms. Whether this is true or

Claudius died naturally is unknown, but Agrippina's son Nero became emperor at age sixteen.

Nero (r. 54–68 CE): The Artist Emperor Who Burned Rome (Allegedly)

Nero was guided by capable advisors, the philosopher Seneca and the Praetorian Prefect Burrus. For the first five years, Nero's government was competent. Ancient sources call this period the *Quinquennium Neronis*—Nero's five good years.

But Nero wanted to be an artist, not an administrator. He was passionate about music, poetry, theater, and chariot racing. He wanted to perform publicly, which Romans considered inappropriate for someone of his status. Entertainment was for professionals and slaves, not emperors. Nero did not care. He performed in theaters, sang at public events, and raced chariots. To elite Romans, this was humiliating. To common people, Nero was popular. He sponsored games and entertainment and seemed more accessible than distant, aristocratic emperors.

Nero's reign grew darker as he consolidated power. In 59 CE, he arranged his mother's murder. In 62 CE, Burrus died, and Seneca retired, removing stabilizing influences. Nero married Poppaea Sabina after divorcing his first wife, Octavia (Claudius's daughter), whom he then had executed on false adultery charges.

Then, in 64 CE, came the Great Fire of Rome. The fire burned for six days, destroying large portions of the city. Romans needed someone to blame. Ancient sources written by senatorial historians hostile to Nero claim he started the fire, that he wanted to clear space for a massive palace complex called the Domus Aurea ("Golden House"). Whether Nero was actually responsible is unknown and heavily debated by modern scholars. What is documented is that Nero accused Christians—then a small, unpopular sect—of arson to deflect blame. The historian Tacitus, writing about fifty years later, describes brutal persecutions. Christians were burned alive as torches, torn apart by dogs, and crucified. The extent of these persecutions is debated, but this episode marks the first major Roman persecution of Christians.

Nero built his Golden House on cleared land in central Rome. It was a massive palace complex with artificial lakes, pavilions, and, supposedly, a hundred-foot statue of Nero as the sun god. The extravagance shocked Romans.

In 65 CE, senators and officers plotted to assassinate Nero (known as the Pisonian conspiracy). The plot was discovered. Nero executed dozens of conspirators and forced many prominent Romans to commit suicide, including Seneca. This reign of terror destroyed what remained of Nero's support among the elite.

By 68 CE, provincial governors were in revolt. The governor of Hispania, Galba, marched on Rome with his legions. The Praetorian Guard defected to Galba. The Senate declared Nero an enemy of the state. Nero fled Rome and committed suicide, allegedly saying, "What an artist dies in me!" as he prepared to kill himself. Nero's death ended the Julio-Claudian dynasty.

The dynasty's collapse triggered a brief civil war known as the Year of the Four Emperors. Within a year, Vespasian, a capable general from a non-aristocratic family, established a new dynasty and restored order. The empire endured.

A bust of Vespasian.[90]

Chapter 7: Bread, Circuses, and Bathhouses: What It Was Actually Like to Live in the Roman Empire

History books love emperors, generals, and battles. But most Romans never commanded an army, never saw the emperor, and spent their lives working, eating, gossiping, and trying to survive in crowded cities or on rural farms. So, what was life actually like for regular people in the Roman Empire?

Let's find out by following a typical day for someone living in Rome during the empire's peak—say, around 150 CE, under Emperor Antoninus Pius. Rome had about a million residents, making it the largest city in the ancient world. Most people were not wealthy senators or merchants. They were the urban poor and working class, living in apartment buildings and scraping by on whatever work they could find.

A Day in the Life: Living in a Roman Insula

You wake up in your *insula*, a multistory apartment building, the ancient Roman equivalent of a modern apartment complex. However, this is nothing like a nice modern apartment.

Your apartment is on the fifth floor. That's not ideal. The higher you live, the cheaper the rent, but it was also more dangerous. *Insulae* in Rome were thrown up quickly and cheaply, often exceeding height limits. Your building sways in strong winds. The wooden floors creak ominously. You have heard stories of entire buildings collapsing, killing everyone inside. It happens often enough that you try not to think about it.

Your apartment is one room; it is maybe two hundred to three hundred square feet for an entire family. There is no kitchen, no bathroom, and no running water. There is definitely no plumbing. The walls are thin wood and plaster, so you can hear everything your neighbors do. The ceiling is low. The single window faces a narrow alley, so not much light gets in. During the summer, it is unbearably hot. During winter, it is freezing, and you huddle around a small brazier that fills the room with smoke since there is no chimney.

You sleep on a simple wooden bed frame with a straw mattress. Your furniture consists of a small table, a couple of stools, and maybe a chest for storing clothes and valuables. That is it. You are fortunate to have that much. Many poorer Romans sleep on the floor.

The first thing you notice when you wake up is the noise. Rome never sleeps. All night, you have been hearing wagons rumbling through the streets—delivery carts that are only allowed in the city after dark to reduce daytime congestion. You have heard people shouting, singing, and fighting. You have heard your neighbors arguing, making love, and dealing with crying babies. The building itself creaks and groans. And now, as dawn approaches, the noise increases as the city wakes.

You need to urinate. This is a problem. There is no toilet in your apartment. You have a chamber pot, which you empty into a large jar. When the jar is full, you are supposed to carry it down five flights of stairs and dump it into the public sewer. But that is annoying, and the stairs are dark and dangerous. So, like many Romans, you sometimes just throw it out the window into the street. There are laws against this—people have been fined when falling waste injures pedestrians—but it happens often enough that walking Rome's streets at night is genuinely dangerous.

There is no water in your apartment either. On the fifth floor, you must carry water up from the ground floor or from a public fountain in the street. Lower floors of some insulae have access to cisterns or basic plumbing, but you are too high up. Every day, someone in your family makes multiple trips up and down five flights of stairs carrying heavy water containers. This is exhausting and time-consuming. Wealthy Romans have running water piped directly to their houses. You do not.

For breakfast, you eat bread soaked in watered wine or water, perhaps with some chickpeas or lentils if you have them. Bread is the staple of the Roman diet. Legumes, like lentils, chickpeas, and beans, provide the primary protein for the urban poor. The government provides a free grain dole (*annona*) to eligible Roman citizens. About 200,000 people receive free grain monthly, though eligibility requirements mean that not all poor Romans qualify. This is not charity; it is politics. Emperors learned long ago that keeping the urban poor fed prevents riots. The term "bread and circuses" refers to giving the masses food and entertainment so that they will stay peaceful.

If you are not eligible for the grain dole, you must buy your food. Bread from a bakery costs a few *asses* (small bronze coins). You might also buy olives, garlic, onions, or legumes from a street vendor or the market. If you are doing well, perhaps you will buy some cheese. Meat is expensive and rare. You may eat it a few times a month, usually pork or chicken.

You do not cook at home because there is no kitchen and because open flames in wooden buildings are disasters waiting to happen. Rome experiences fires frequently. Small fires occur regularly, and major conflagrations such as the Great Fire of 64 CE under Nero, which destroyed huge portions of the city, demonstrate the catastrophic potential. Your landlord has forbidden cooking fires in the apartments, though some people do it anyway and hope they do not burn the building down.

So, you eat food from street vendors or from taverns called *popinae*. These are everywhere in Rome (archaeological evidence suggests there were thousands of food establishments throughout the city). You can buy hot porridge, stews, grilled meats, bread, vegetables, and wine. It is essentially Roman fast food. It is not fancy, but it is cheap and convenient.

You head out for work. Perhaps you work at the docks unloading ships, at a construction site hauling materials, or in a warehouse organizing goods. You are paid daily, usually a few sesterces (larger bronze coins). This is enough to cover food, rent, and little else. You have no job security. If you are injured or sick and cannot work, you do not get paid. If there is no work available today, you do not eat today.

Or perhaps you are a shopkeeper, a craftsman, or part of a trade guild. If so, you are doing somewhat better. You have a more stable income and a higher social status. But you still live in an insula and still deal with the same noise, dirt, and fire risks. Even middle-class Romans lived in apartments, not houses. Only the wealthy owned private *domus*, houses with courtyards, multiple rooms, gardens, and private water supplies.

Rome's streets are crowded, noisy, and honestly kind of disgusting. The streets are narrow; many are only ten to fifteen feet wide. Buildings loom on both sides, blocking out the sun. The streets are paved with stone, which helps, but they are covered in filth. There is animal dung from horses, donkeys, and dogs. There is human waste thrown from windows. There is rotting garbage and puddles of unidentifiable liquids. You walk carefully, watching where you step.

The streets are packed with people: slaves running errands, merchants hawking goods, beggars asking for coins, prostitutes soliciting customers, performers entertaining crowds, and pickpockets looking for marks. Street vendors sell everything, from bread, fruit, vegetables, and wine to cooked food, cheap goods, and trinkets. The noise is overwhelming. People are shouting, haggling, arguing, and laughing. Animals bleat and bray. Wagons squeak, and hammers pound in workshops.

Rome is a sensory overload. It smells of smoke, human and animal waste, rotting garbage, perfumes and incense from shops and temples, food cooking, and leather tanning. It is loud and crowded beyond anything most modern cities experience. And it is exciting, vibrant, and alive in a way that makes rural life seem boring.

After a morning of work, you are hungry and tired. It is midday, so it is time for the most important part of a Roman's day: the baths.

The Baths: More Than Just Washing—The Social Hub of the Empire

If you want to understand Roman culture, you need to understand the baths. Bathing was not just about getting clean. It was the social center of Roman life. It was where people relaxed, exercised, gossiped, conducted business, and spent hours every afternoon.

Rome had hundreds of baths. There were small private baths run by individuals or companies that charged a small entry fee, perhaps a *quadrans*, the smallest coin, about a quarter of an *as*. Then there were the massive imperial baths. These were gigantic complexes built by emperors and opened to the public for either free or for a small fee. The Baths of Trajan, completed in 109 CE, and the older Baths of Agrippa could accommodate hundreds or even thousands of bathers. These were more than just bathhouses; they were also massive recreational complexes with gardens, libraries, meeting rooms, exercise areas, and more.

You would pay your entrance fee (or enter for free if it is a public day) and check your clothes in the changing room. Theft was common, so attendants watched your clothes, though you might still bribe an attendant or have a slave guard your possessions. Romans bathed naked, which was not considered immodest but normal and practical.

The bathing process followed a specific routine. You started in the *palaestra*, an exercise courtyard. Here, people engaged in various physical activities like wrestling, ball games, weightlifting, and running. Romans valued physical fitness and believed exercise was essential to health. You might spend thirty minutes to an hour working up a good sweat.

Then you moved inside to begin bathing. First was the *tepidarium*, a warm room that helped your body adjust to the heat. This was like a warm-up, a transitional space between the cool outside and the hot baths. You might spend ten to fifteen minutes here, chatting with friends and letting your body acclimate.

Next came the *caldarium*, the hot room. This was where you really start to sweat. The room was heated by a hypocaust, an underfloor heating system in which hot air from furnaces circulated beneath the floor and through spaces in the walls. The floor was literally hot enough that Romans wore wooden sandals to avoid burning their feet. There was a hot-water pool where they could soak. After fifteen to twenty minutes, you would be thoroughly heated and sweating.

Now came the actual cleaning. Romans did not use soap; they used olive oil. You or a slave rubbed your body with oil, then scraped it off with a curved metal tool called a *strigil*. The oil pulled the dirt and dead skin from your body. It was surprisingly effective.

Then you moved to the *frigidarium*, the cold room. This had a cold-water pool. It was often unheated and quite bracing. After being overheated in the caldarium, plunging into cold water was shocking but invigorating. Romans believed the contrast in temperature was healthy. You might spend only a few minutes here before exiting.

Finally, you dried off, got dressed, and perhaps relaxed in one of the bath's gardens or sitting rooms.

However, the bathing itself was almost secondary to the social experience. The baths were where Romans of all classes mingled. A poor laborer might bathe next to a wealthy merchant. Slaves attended their masters. Baths typically had separate hours or separate facilities for men and women, though mixed bathing occurred in some places, often scandalizing more conservative Romans.

People conducted business at the baths. Lawyers met clients. Merchants negotiated deals. Politicians canvassed for support. The baths were where Romans networked, exchanged information, and built relationships. There is no modern equivalent. Imagine if the gym, the coffee shop, the spa, the library, and the town square all existed in one place, and everyone in the city went there every afternoon.

You also heard all the city's gossip at the baths: who was sleeping with whom, which senator was in political trouble, what the emperor had done recently, which businesses were thriving or failing, which neighborhoods were dangerous, and what new laws were being proposed. Information flowed through the baths like water through the pools.

The baths had other amenities too. There were often libraries where educated Romans could read. There were massage rooms where you could pay for a rubdown. There were snack bars where you could buy food and wine. There were hair removal services, as Romans valued hairless bodies and used various painful methods to achieve this. There were vendors selling oils, perfumes, and grooming supplies.

You might spend two to four hours at the baths. This was not considered wasteful or lazy. This was normal. In a society without television, the internet, or most forms of modern entertainment, the baths were the primary recreational activity for millions of Romans throughout the empire.

After the baths, you might head to dinner, or you might decide to do what hundreds of thousands of Romans did several times a year: attend the games.

The Colosseum: The Logistics of Blood Sport and Why Romans Loved It

The Colosseum is Rome's most famous building. Completed in 80 CE under Emperor Titus, it could hold between fifty thousand and eighty thousand spectators. It is an engineering marvel. It is 159 feet tall, 620 feet long, built from travertine stone and concrete, and has a complex system of corridors, staircases, trapdoors, and underground chambers.

The Colosseum.[91]

But let's talk about what happened inside: the games.

Roman games included several types of spectacles. There were theatrical performances, athletic competitions, and public executions. But what Romans really loved were gladiatorial combat and animal hunts.

Let's say you are attending the games on a festival day. Entry is free; emperors sponsor the games as a gift to the Roman people. You arrive early because getting a good seat requires showing up hours before the games begin. Your seating is determined by social class. Senators sit in the front rows, close to the action. Equestrians sit behind them. Regular citizens sit in the middle tiers. Women, slaves, and the poorest Romans sit in the highest sections, far from the arena floor. Your social status is literally visible in where you sit.

The seating system is actually quite sophisticated. Each entrance is numbered, and your section is marked. You enter through one of the eighty ground-level arches, climb stairs to your level, and find your seat. The architects designed it so efficiently that the entire Colosseum could be evacuated in minutes if necessary. Modern stadiums still use similar principles.

The games typically begin in the morning with animal hunts (*venationes*). The arena floor is set up to resemble a landscape with artificial trees, rocks, and painted backdrops. Then the animals are released. You might see lions, bears, elephants, leopards, crocodiles, ostriches, bulls, or other exotic creatures. Professional hunters called *venatores* fight and kill the animals while the crowd cheers.

These animal hunts were spectacular and expensive. Ancient sources claim that nine thousand animals were killed during the Colosseum's inaugural games over one hundred days. Modern historians view this figure as a likely exaggeration, though the actual scale was still enormous. Animals were imported from Africa, Asia, and throughout the empire. Lions, elephants, and other exotic beasts were costly and difficult to transport. The logistics of moving large numbers of animals to Rome and keeping them alive in underground holding facilities beneath the Colosseum would have been a massive undertaking.

Modern people often find these animal hunts disturbing; killing animals for entertainment seems cruel and wasteful. Romans saw it differently. Wild animals represented untamed nature, chaos, and danger. Killing them demonstrated Roman power over nature and the empire's wild fringes.

At midday, there is a break for executions. Condemned criminals are brought into the arena and killed in various ways. Some are beheaded or crucified. Others are killed by animals, thrown to lions or bears, or tied to stakes while wild animals tear them apart. Sometimes the executions are staged as reenactments of myths. For instance, a criminal may be dressed as Icarus and dropped from a height, someone dressed as Orpheus may be torn apart by bears, or a criminal playing Hercules may be burned alive on a pyre.

This is the part of the games that is hardest for modern people to understand. Romans watched human beings as they were tortured and killed while treating it as entertainment. Romans believed criminals deserved harsh punishment. The people being executed had been convicted of serious crimes like murder, treason, armed robbery, and arson. In Roman thinking, they forfeited their humanity through their crimes. Making their deaths public and dramatic served as deterrence and retribution. It was also a display of the emperor's power to punish lawbreakers.

The main event would come in the afternoon: gladiatorial combat.

Gladiators came from various backgrounds. Many were enslaved prisoners of war or condemned criminals forced to fight. However, a significant number were free volunteers who signed contracts to become gladiators for a period of years. Why would free men volunteer for such a dangerous profession? They did it for money and fame.

Successful gladiators could become wealthy. They received prize money for victories, gifts from wealthy patrons, and the benefits of celebrity status. Famous gladiators' images appeared on oil lamps, pottery, and graffiti throughout the empire, not through commercial contracts like modern athlete endorsements but because fans wanted to display their favorite fighters. The most famous gladiators were celebrities comparable to modern athletes or movie stars. Free men might volunteer because they were poor and desperate, seeking glory, or simply because they enjoyed combat.

A mosaic of gladiators in combat.[92]

Gladiators trained in specialized schools (*ludi*) run by managers (*lanistae*). They trained in different fighting styles, each with distinctive weapons and armor. A *murmillo* wore a helmet with a fish crest and carried a short sword and a large rectangular shield. A *retiarius* had no helmet, carried a net and trident, and relied on speed and agility. A *thraex* used a small round shield and a curved sword. A *hoplomachus* was heavily armored, wielding a spear and a small shield.

Gladiatorial combat was more complex than "fight to the death." Matches were usually between gladiators of different styles, like a *murmillo* versus a *retiarius*, for example. The contrasting styles created interesting tactical matchups. The fights were real, dangerous, and sometimes fatal.

When you watch the gladiatorial match on the festival day, you see skilled fighters using real weapons in genuine combat. Blood is spilled. Injuries occur. But the goal is not always to kill. The goal is to win by forcing your opponent to surrender or by incapacitating them. If a gladiator is wounded or outmatched, he can appeal to the crowd for mercy by raising a finger.

Then comes the famous moment. The crowd and the sponsor of the games—often the emperor, if present—decide the loser's fate. The crowd expresses its opinion with gestures (though today we are not actually sure whether a thumbs-up meant life or death in Roman times; the sources are ambiguous). The sponsor makes the final decision, deciding the loser should live.

If the loser fought well, showed bravery, and pleased the crowd, he was usually spared. Killing gladiators was expensive. Gladiators required significant investment in training, feeding, and housing. Sponsors did not want to waste money killing gladiators unnecessarily. Most gladiators survived their fights. Studies of gladiator graves suggest mortality rates of around 10 to 20 percent per bout; the fights were still dangerous, but they did not lead to the guaranteed death sentence many imagine.

If the sponsor signaled for death, the winner delivered a killing blow. The loser was expected to accept death bravely without resistance or pleading—that was part of the gladiatorial code. Arena attendants dressed as Charon, the ferryman of the dead, would come out, confirm death by striking the body with a hammer, and drag the corpse away through the "Gate of Death." Fresh sand was spread over the blood, and the next match began.

Why did the Romans love this? Well, it was undeniably exciting. There was real danger, real skill, and unpredictable outcomes. It was a display of Roman virtues, including courage, discipline, skill in arms, and acceptance of fate. Gladiators who fought bravely embodied the Roman ideal of *virtus*—manly courage and excellence. Even though gladiators were legally *infames* (disgraced people), they were admired for their fighting ability.

The games also reinforced Roman identity and values. They displayed Roman power and wealth; only Rome could afford such spectacular entertainment. They demonstrated Roman control over life and death. They reminded Romans of their military heritage. Gladiatorial combat actually originated as funeral rites honoring dead warriors. And they provided a release for aggression and bloodlust in a controlled, legal setting.

For you, sitting in the stands, it is an afternoon of entertainment unlike anything else in the ancient world. You cheer for your favorite gladiators, boo the ones you dislike, eat snacks bought from vendors, chat with fellow spectators, and feel part of something larger. You are participating in a shared cultural experience with tens of thousands of other Romans. For a few hours, social hierarchies matter less. Rich and poor cheer together. You are all Romans, enjoying the gifts of the emperor, celebrating Roman culture, and bonding through shared bloodlust.

By late afternoon, the games end. You file out through the efficient exit system, return to your daily life, and look forward to the next games. If you are lucky, there will be another spectacle in a few weeks. And there is always tomorrow, when you can return to the baths and relive the day's excitement with fellow Romans.

But before we leave the subject of Roman daily life, we need to address the foundations that made it all possible: religion.

Roman Religion: Why You're Praying to a Hundred Different Gods

Roman religion was everywhere in daily life, but it worked completely differently from modern religions.

Romans did not care so much what a person believed. They cared more about what a person did. There was no sacred text to study. No unified theology to debate. No creed to recite. What mattered was performing the correct rituals at the correct times. Sacrifice to the gods properly, and they would be favorable. Neglect the rituals, and the gods grew angry. And when the gods were angry, bad things happened to everyone.

Romans thought of religion as a kind of contract. You gave offerings to the gods, and the gods gave you benefits. This principle was called *do ut des*—"I give so that you may give." You sacrificed a sheep to Mars before battle. Mars got the sheep, and you expected a victory. If you lost, perhaps you had not sacrificed enough. Perhaps you had performed the ritual incorrectly. Perhaps you had offended Mars somehow.

Roman religion was also communal, not personal. It was not about an individual relationship with the divine or personal salvation. It was about maintaining the *pax deorum*—the peace with the gods that kept Rome prosperous. Religious rituals were public civic events. Priests were government officials. Temples were state institutions. Religion was a patriotic duty.

The Roman pantheon was crowded. At the top sat the Capitoline Triad: Jupiter (king of the gods), Juno (his wife, goddess of marriage), and Minerva (goddess of wisdom and war). Romans borrowed these gods from the Greeks. Jupiter was essentially Zeus under a Roman name, Juno was Hera, and Minerva was Athena.

There were dozens more gods: Mars for war, Venus for love, Apollo for prophecy and healing, Diana for hunting, Neptune for the sea, Mercury for commerce, Ceres for agriculture, and Bacchus for wine and intoxication. There were also countless minor deities and spirits. Every home had household guardians—Lares and Penates—who protected the family. Every river, grove, and crossroads had its own spirit.

Still, the Roman religion was remarkably tolerant. When the Romans conquered new territories, they did not suppress local religions. They absorbed them. The Germanic god Wotan became associated with Mercury. The Celtic goddess Sulis in Britain became Sulis Minerva. The Egyptian Isis and the Persian Mithras became popular in Rome. One more god was no problem—unless that religion threatened the social order.

The Romans persecuted Christians and Jews. It was not about worshiping an additional god; the Romans were comfortable with that. The problem was that Christians and Jews refused to participate in civic rituals and imperial cult worship. To Romans, that refusal was unpatriotic and dangerous.

This led to the imperial cult: the worship of emperors.

After Augustus died, the Senate declared him a god. Temples were built to worship *Divus Augustus*. This was not metaphorical. Romans believed Augustus had become divine after death. Later emperors could also be deified if the Senate judged them worthy.

The imperial cult went beyond worshiping dead emperors. Throughout the empire, especially in the eastern provinces where ruler worship had long been traditional, people built temples to the living emperor's *genius* (guardian spirit) or to Roma, the personification of Rome, together with the emperor. The imperial cult was more prominent and elaborate in the Greek-speaking East than in Rome itself. Making offerings at these temples and swearing oaths by the emperor's *genius* functioned as loyalty tests. They proved you were a faithful subject.

For most Romans, worshiping the emperor was not controversial. You were already worshiping dozens of gods; one more posed no problem. It was patriotic rather than religious in the modern sense. You honored Rome's power and success by honoring its leader.

For Christians and Jews, however, the imperial cult was an impossible demand. Their belief in one God forbade worshiping anyone else. Refusing to make offerings to the emperor's *genius* could be interpreted as treason, as it was evidence of disloyalty to Roman authority.

Even so, the reality of Christian persecution was more complex than simply refusing to worship the emperor. Persecutions varied enormously by time, place, and circumstance. Sometimes Christians were targeted for refusing civic rituals. Often, they were scapegoated for disasters because their refusal to honor traditional gods was believed to anger those gods and bring divine punishment on the community. Local officials might persecute Christians to appease crowds demanding action after a crisis, even without direct imperial orders. Some emperors actively persecuted Christians. Others ignored them, and still others protected them. Persecution was sporadic and inconsistent rather than a systematic, empire-wide policy until much later.

For you, a regular Roman, religion means daily offerings to household gods, attending festivals throughout the year, perhaps consulting an oracle or priest for divine guidance, and participating in civic rituals. You might also be initiated into one of the mystery cults, which promise personal salvation and secret knowledge. These cults offer something the traditional Roman religion does not: hope for a good afterlife and a personal relationship with the divine.

Traditional Roman religion offers no clear afterlife. The dead go to a shadowy underworld, where they exist as weak shades. There is no heaven, no reward for virtue, and no eternal punishment for sin. This was why mystery cults—and eventually Christianity—became so appealing. They promised something better than existing forever as a powerless ghost in the darkness.

For most of your life, however, Roman religion is about duty to the gods, to your family, and to your community. You make offerings, attend festivals, and hope the gods remain favorable. And so far, they have been. Rome is the largest and most powerful empire in the world. The gods must be pleased.

Legions, Laws, and Concrete: The Three Pillars of Roman Power

We have talked about daily life, entertainment, and religion. But what made Rome an empire that dominated the known world for centuries? Three things: a superior military system, a sophisticated legal framework, and engineering that made the impossible routine.

The Roman Legion: Why Rome's Army Dominated for Centuries

The Roman legion was one of the most successful military organizations in history. Around the 2nd century CE, roughly twenty-five to thirty legions controlled everything from Britain to Mesopotamia, from the Rhine to the Sahara. That was about 150,000 to 180,000 legionaries, plus an equal or larger number of auxiliary troops. It was not a huge army by modern standards, but it was devastatingly effective.

Why? Four reasons: training, discipline, equipment, and engineering.

A legion had about five thousand to six thousand men organized into smaller units commanded by centurions, professional officers who'd risen through the ranks. These centurions were the backbone of the legion. They trained the troops, enforced discipline, and led in battle. They also carried staffs and beat soldiers who screwed up.

Legionaries were all Roman citizens who served twenty to twenty-five years. They got regular pay, land grants when they retired, and citizenship for their children. This created a professional, disciplined force with long-term loyalty to Rome and often to their commanding general, which caused major problems during civil wars.

Training was brutal. Legionaries drilled constantly in formations, weapons handling, and camp construction. They marched twenty to thirty miles a day, carrying sixty to eighty pounds of equipment. New recruits spent months learning to fight in tight formation, follow commands instantly, and maintain discipline when people were trying to kill them.

Equipment was standardized. Segmented plate armor or chain mail provided protection. A large rectangular shield covered most of the body. A short stabbing sword (*gladius*) was designed for close combat. Two javelins (*pila*) had iron shanks that bent on impact. They couldn't be thrown back, and they sometimes pinned enemy shields together.

Tactics emphasized coordination over individual heroics. Legionaries fought in tight formations. They threw javelins to disrupt enemy lines, then advanced with shields and swords, fighting in ranks where discipline beat bravery. The famous "turtle" formation (*testudo*) had soldiers overlapping shields to create a mobile fortress that could approach walls under arrow fire.

Here was the part that amazed other armies: legions built a fortified camp every single night. After marching all day, they dug ditches, built earthwork walls, and constructed a defensible camp. Barbarian armies slept in the open. Romans slept behind fortifications.

Engineering was central to Roman military success. Legionaries built roads, bridges, siege equipment, and fortifications. They were soldiers and engineers. When Caesar besieged Alesia, his legions built double walls—one to trap the Gauls inside and one to keep the relief army outside. When Trajan campaigned in Dacia, his legions built a massive bridge across the Danube. Roman military engineering made operations possible that other armies couldn't even imagine.

Discipline was legendary and brutal. Deserters were executed. Cowardice by a unit could result in decimation; every tenth man would be selected by lot and beaten to death by his fellow soldiers. This was rare, but it demonstrated Rome's absolute commitment to discipline.

This combination of professional troops, superior training, standardized equipment, engineering capability, and brutal discipline made the Roman legion nearly unbeatable. Rome lost battles occasionally, but Rome almost always won wars.

Roman Law: Why Modern Legal Systems Still Use Roman Ideas

Law was one of Rome's most lasting legacies. Modern legal systems throughout Europe, Latin America, and much of the world have been based on Roman legal principles developed over centuries.

What made Roman law revolutionary? The Romans had written laws that everyone could see. You could actually know what the law required.

This was far fairer than systems based on unwritten customs or whatever the ruler felt like that day.

There were also established courts, rules for trials, evidence requirements, and rights for the accused. It wasn't perfect. Trials could be biased, corruption existed, and slaves were tortured for testimony, but there was a system rather than arbitrary justice.

Rome developed jurists, legal experts who studied, interpreted, and wrote about law. Their opinions carried weight and helped develop legal principles. Famous jurists like Gaius and Ulpian wrote treatises that became authoritative.

Roman law had sophisticated rules about property, contracts, inheritance, and obligations. This provided predictability for business and allowed complex commercial relationships. The *Corpus Juris Civilis*, compiled under Byzantine Emperor Justinian in the 6th century CE, preserved Roman legal writings and formed the basis for many modern legal systems. Roman principles, such as "the burden of proof lies with the accuser," influenced modern law.

Of course, Roman law wasn't perfect by modern standards. Slavery was legal and protected. Women had limited rights. Torture was used on slaves. Punishments were brutal. People could be crucified, burned alive, or thrown to wild animals. The law treated people differently based on status.

Still, Roman law provided a framework for resolving disputes, protecting property, and maintaining order across a vast empire. It allowed people in Britain, Egypt, Spain, and Syria to conduct business and resolve disputes under common legal principles. This was essential to Rome's economy and political stability.

Engineering Marvels: How Rome Built an Empire That's Still Standing

Roman engineering is visible everywhere, even today, two thousand years later. Roman roads served as foundations for modern highways. Roman aqueducts still stand. Some Roman concrete is more durable than modern concrete.

Rome built over 250,000 miles of roads throughout the empire. Major roads like the Appian Way were built in layers with large stones, gravel, and paving stones. They were designed for drainage and durability. Roman roads were straight whenever possible, running directly toward destinations. They included bridges, tunnels, and cut through hills.

Milestones marked distances. Way stations provided shelter and supplies.

The Appian Way.[98]

The saying "all roads lead to Rome" was pretty much true. You could travel from Rome to Britain or Egypt while staying on Roman roads nearly the entire way. This road network connected cities, facilitated trade, sped military movements, and integrated the empire.

Aqueducts brought water from miles away. Rome needed massive amounts of water for drinking, baths, fountains, and sewers. The city eventually had eleven major aqueducts bringing water from sources up to fifty miles away. These used gravity flow, maintaining a steady downward grade over dozens of miles. Where valleys required it, massive arched bridges carried the water. The Pont du Gard in France stood 160 feet tall. Many Roman aqueducts still function today.

The Pont du Gard in France.[94]

Clean water was crucial to public health. Roman cities were healthier than medieval cities, partly because of reliable water and sewer systems.

Roman concrete was revolutionary. Made from volcanic ash, lime, and aggregate, it could be poured into forms and even set underwater. The Pantheon in Rome has the world's largest unreinforced concrete dome; it is 142 feet across. It was completed around 125 CE and is still standing and still waterproof.

Roman concrete used *pozzolana*, volcanic ash from near Naples, which reacted with lime to create an incredibly strong material. Some Roman marine concrete actually got stronger over time as seawater reacted with the volcanic ash, creating new minerals that reinforced the structure. Roman harbor installations have lasted two thousand years underwater.

Roman architecture combined Greek aesthetics with engineering innovation. The arch, the vault, and the dome allowed the Romans to build larger, more complex structures than anyone before. Amphitheaters, bath complexes, temples, and aqueducts all used these innovations.

Romans developed concrete faced with brick or stone, allowing them to build quickly on a massive scale. The Colosseum, the Baths of Caracalla, and countless other structures demonstrate Roman architectural ambition and engineering skill.

Slavery: The Foundation Nobody Talks About

We need to address the uncomfortable truth. All of this—the legions, the roads, the aqueducts, the games, the prosperity—was built on slavery.

Rome was a slave society. Scholars estimated that during the height of the Roman Republic following major conquests, perhaps 30 to 40 percent of Italy's population were slaves. By the mid-2nd century CE—a period of relative stability—the proportion was likely closer to 20 to 30 percent. In the city of Rome itself, the proportion of slaves remained substantial. Throughout the empire, millions of people were enslaved.

Slaves came from multiple sources. They could be prisoners of war (the largest source), children born to slave mothers, people sold by their parents, kidnapped victims, and people enslaved as punishment for crimes. Roman conquests during the Roman Republic and early empire flooded Italy with slaves. When Rome conquered Carthage, tens of thousands were enslaved. Caesar claimed in his *Commentaries* to have enslaved a million people during his Gallic campaigns—a figure modern historians see as typical military exaggeration, though the actual numbers were still substantial.

Slaves did everything. They worked on the large estates (*latifundia*), which produced grain, wine, and olive oil. They worked in mines and quarries under brutal conditions. Mining was essentially a death sentence, and slaves were worked to death in mines throughout the empire. They worked in workshops producing goods. They also worked as domestic servants in wealthy households, cooking, cleaning, and caring for children.

Some slaves held skilled positions. They could work as teachers, doctors, accountants, and secretaries. Imperial slaves—those owned by the emperor—could hold important administrative posts. Some skilled slaves accumulated money and eventually bought their freedom.

Slavery in Rome was not based on race. Slaves came from all ethnicities and regions. It was based on legal status. A Gaul could be enslaved by Romans, and a Roman could be enslaved by pirates or foreign enemies. Anyone could become a slave through bad luck.

However, this did not make Roman slavery less brutal. Slaves had no legal rights. Masters could punish them however they wanted, including execution. Sexual exploitation of slaves was common and legal. Slaves could not legally marry, and their children were property. They could be sold at any time, separating families. The threat of being sold to the mines or forced to fight as gladiators kept slaves compliant.

Manumission (freeing slaves) was common in Rome compared to some other slave societies. Masters freed slaves for various reasons. It could be a reward for loyal service because the slave bought their freedom or through provisions in the master's will. Freed slaves (*liberti*) became Roman citizens, though with some limitations. Their children were full citizens, which created social mobility that was unavailable in many societies, but it did not make slavery acceptable.

Rome's prosperity depended on slave labor. The grain that fed the city came from estates worked by slaves. The mines that produced silver for coins and metals for weapons used slave labor. The construction projects that beautified cities used slave labor. The workshops that produced goods used slave labor. Roman citizens enjoyed leisure time partly because slaves did much of the work.

When you walked through Rome, enjoying the entertainment, the baths, and the public buildings, you were seeing a civilization built by enslaved people. This was an uncomfortable truth, but it was essential to understanding Rome. The glory, the achievements, the culture—it was all interconnected with the exploitation of millions of enslaved human beings.

Chapter 8: The Five Good Emperors and the Empire's Peak

If you had to pick one century to live in the Roman Empire, most historians would tell you to pick the 2nd century CE. This was Rome's golden age. The empire was at its height, the economy was humming along, cities flourished, and the Mediterranean world experienced unprecedented peace and stability. Was it Rome's absolute peak? Historians argue about that. However, the 2nd century CE represented one of humanity's most successful experiments in running a massive empire.

What made this century so special? Five emperors in a row were actually competent and chosen through a system that worked—adoptive succession. Instead of passing power to their biological sons (who might be idiots), these emperors adopted talented men and made them heirs. It was Rome's approach to picking leaders based on merit.

These five emperors were Nerva, Trajan, Hadrian, Antoninus Pius, and Marcus Aurelius. Later historians called them the "Five Good Emperors." Marcus Aurelius broke the system by passing power to his biological son, Commodus, who was not a good ruler. And the golden age ended.

Let's see how it all worked and why it couldn't last.

The Adoptive Succession: When Rome Figured Out How to Pick Good Emperors

The year 96 CE was messy. Emperor Domitian, the last of the Flavian dynasty, which had ruled since 69 CE, was assassinated by members of his own household. Domitian had become increasingly paranoid and tyrannical, conducting treason trials and executing senators he suspected of disloyalty. His murder was a palace coup, and Rome faced the familiar question of who would be emperor next.

The conspirators chose Nerva, an elderly, respected senator with no military background and no children. He was sixty-six years old. Nerva was a safe, transitional figure who wouldn't threaten anyone and wasn't expected to reign for many years.

However, Nerva faced an immediate problem. The Praetorian Guard was angry that Domitian had been murdered without their approval, and they wanted revenge. Nerva was politically isolated and militarily weak. He needed the support of the legions, and he needed an heir who could command respect from the military.

So, in 97 CE, Nerva did something that established a pattern for the next century. He adopted Marcus Ulpius Traianus (Trajan) as his son and designated heir. Trajan was a successful general commanding legions in Germania, a Roman from a Spanish family, and popular with the troops. When Nerva died in 98 CE after reigning only sixteen months, Trajan succeeded him peacefully. The legions and the Senate accepted him. The transition was smooth.

This established the principle of the emperor choosing the best man available as his successor and adopting him. The heir would be trained in government and military command, proving his abilities before taking power. When the emperor died, the adopted son would succeed without a civil war or dispute.

It sounded simple, but it was revolutionary. This wasn't a formal system or constitutional law. It depended entirely on emperors making wise choices and on lucky circumstances, particularly the lack of biological heirs who might claim precedence. But when it worked, Rome had a way to ensure competent leadership. And for nearly a century, the stars aligned, and emperors chose well.

Trajan (r. 98–117 CE): The Empire Reaches Its Greatest Extent

Trajan came from a Roman family in Hispania (Spain). This signaled an important shift: the empire was becoming genuinely multi-ethnic, with leadership coming from the provinces, not just old Roman families in Italy.

Ancient sources described Trajan as the ideal emperor. He was militarily successful, brave, respectful toward the Senate, and generous with public spending. The Senate later decreed that each new emperor should be wished to be "luckier than Augustus and better than Trajan," making Trajan the standard for imperial excellence.

Trajan was best known for his military campaigns. Between 101 and 106 CE, he fought two wars against Dacia (roughly modern Romania), a wealthy kingdom north of the Danube that had previously defeated Roman armies. The Dacian Wars were brutal, large-scale campaigns involving multiple legions fighting in difficult terrain.

The wars were documented in extraordinary detail on Trajan's Column in Rome, which was completed in 113 CE. This 125-foot-tall marble column depicted the campaigns in a continuous spiral frieze with over 2,500 figures—soldiers marching, building fortifications, fighting battles, besieging cities, and accepting surrender. It is one of our best sources for how Roman armies actually looked and operated.

The Dacian Wars ended with a complete Roman victory. The Dacian king Decebalus committed suicide rather than be captured. Dacia became a Roman province, and its gold mines filled Rome's treasury. Ancient sources claimed Trajan brought back enormous quantities of gold. This wealth funded massive building projects in Rome and throughout the empire.

Trajan used the Dacian gold to transform Rome. He built Trajan's Forum in Rome, the largest and most elaborate of the imperial forums. This massive complex included a basilica (the Basilica Ulpia), two libraries (one for Latin texts and one for Greek), a monumental column, and Trajan's Market—a multi-story commercial complex that is sometimes called the world's first shopping mall, though it was more complex than that, including administrative offices and storage facilities.

Trajan's Market today.[95]

Trajan's Forum was architectural propaganda. It celebrated his military victories while demonstrating Rome's wealth and sophistication. The Basilica Ulpia was the largest basilica in Rome, with enormous granite columns imported from Egypt. The libraries housed Rome's greatest collection of scrolls and codices. The whole complex was faced with marble and decorated with sculptures and reliefs showing Roman superiority over barbarians.

But Trajan did not just build in Rome. Throughout the empire, he funded infrastructure projects: roads connecting provinces, bridges spanning rivers that had hindered commerce, harbors improving maritime trade, and aqueducts bringing water to growing cities. In Alcántara, Spain, a bridge he built in 106 CE still stands and carries traffic today.

Trajan also enhanced social welfare in Italy through the *alimenta* program—a system in which the imperial treasury loaned money to farmers at low interest rates. The interest payments funded stipends for poor children. This was not charity in the modern sense but a program to ensure Italy's agricultural productivity while supporting the freeborn population.

Ancient sources also praised Trajan for his accessible, modest personal style despite his absolute power. Pliny the Younger, who served under Trajan, described an emperor who consulted the Senate respectfully, who did not surround himself with excessive luxury, and who was approachable to ordinary citizens. Whether this reflected reality or was propaganda is debatable, but it showed the ideal against which Romans measured emperors.

But Trajan's ambitions were not satisfied with Dacia. Between 113 and 117 CE, he launched a war against the Parthian Empire in the east. Rome and Parthia had fought on and off for over a century, with neither side achieving a decisive victory. Trajan wanted to succeed where others had failed and conquer Mesopotamia.

The Parthian War started well. Roman forces conquered Armenia, then advanced into Mesopotamia, capturing Ctesiphon, the Parthian capital. Trajan reached the Persian Gulf, the farthest east any Roman emperor had campaigned. In 116 CE, the Roman Empire reached its maximum territorial extent, stretching from Scotland to Mesopotamia, from the Atlantic to the Persian Gulf.

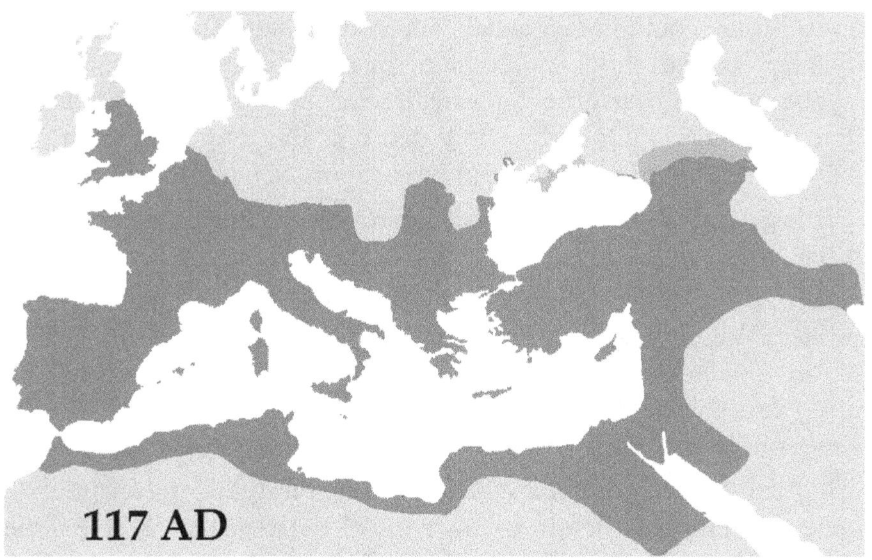

The greatest extent of the Roman Empire.[96]

But of course, conquering territory was different from holding it. The newly conquered regions revolted almost immediately. Jewish populations in Cyprus, Egypt, and Cyrenaica (eastern part of Libya) rebelled in what is known as the Kitos War or the Diaspora Revolt (115–117 CE). Whether these uprisings were coordinated responses to Trajan's Mesopotamian campaign or separate revolts with different local causes has been debated by historians, but they stretched Roman forces dangerously thin. Trajan had to send legions to suppress these uprisings while trying to hold Mesopotamia.

Then Trajan's health failed. He fell seriously ill in 117 CE, possibly from a stroke. He began withdrawing from Mesopotamia, recognizing that Rome could not hold these eastern conquests. Trajan died in August 117 CE in Cilicia (southern Turkey) on the journey back to Rome. He was sixty-three years old.

Before dying, Trajan allegedly adopted Hadrian, his cousin and ward, as his successor. It is possible that Hadrian's wife, Plotina, forged the document, as the announcement came very close to Trajan's death. Hadrian commanded legions in Syria, and the army supported him, so the Senate quickly confirmed him as emperor.

Hadrian immediately abandoned most of Trajan's conquests. Mesopotamia was given up, and Armenia became a client kingdom again. The empire returned to roughly the borders it had held before Trajan's eastern wars. Modern historians interpreted this as strategic realism. Rome could not sustainably defend and govern these territories. Whether Hadrian understood something Trajan had not, whether circumstances had changed, or whether the two emperors simply had different strategic philosophies was debated, the effect was clear. The empire contracted to what Hadrian saw as more defensible frontiers.

Hadrian (r. 117–138 CE): The Emperor Who Built Walls and Loved Greece

Hadrian was almost the opposite of Trajan in temperament and priorities. Where Trajan was a soldier who loved campaigning, Hadrian was an intellectual who loved Greek culture, architecture, and philosophy. Where Trajan expanded the empire aggressively, Hadrian focused on consolidating and defending what Rome already held.

Hadrian spent more than half his reign traveling throughout the empire. No emperor before or since traveled as extensively. He visited nearly every province, inspecting fortifications, meeting with local officials, settling disputes, and overseeing construction projects. Ancient sources suggested he traveled approximately eleven years out of his twenty-one-year reign—an extraordinary amount of time away from Rome.

These journeys were not tourism. Hadrian was inspecting and strengthening the empire's frontiers. He believed Rome had reached its natural limits and that future policy should focus on defending borders, not expanding them. This was a fundamental shift from centuries of Roman expansion.

The most famous result of this defensive policy was Hadrian's Wall in Britain, which was built between 122 and 128 CE. This massive stone fortification stretched seventy-three miles across northern Britain, from coast to coast, marking the northernmost frontier of the empire. The wall was about fifteen to twenty feet tall, with a deep ditch on the northern side, milecastles (small forts) every Roman mile, and larger forts at intervals. Thousands of soldiers garrisoned the wall, controlling movement between Roman Britain and the unconquered lands to the north.

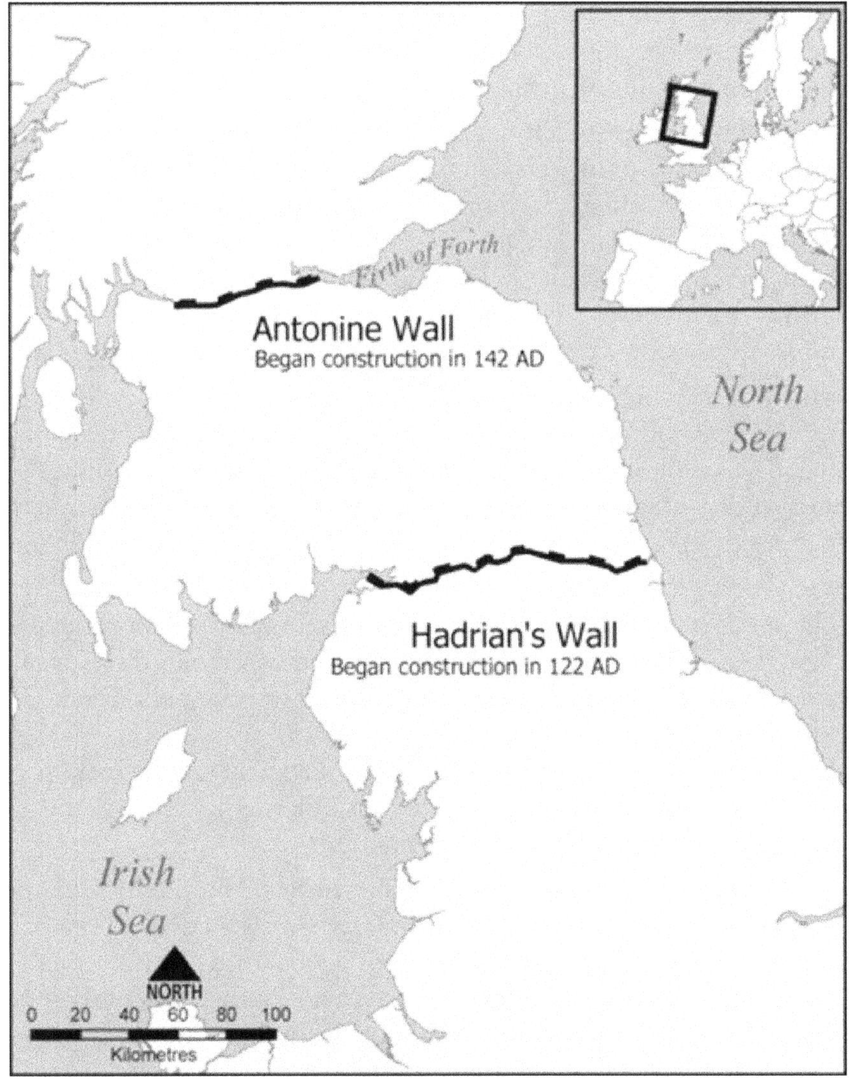

Map of Hadrian's Wall and the Antonine Wall.[97]

Hadrian's Wall was not primarily a military barrier in the sense of stopping armies, as a determined force could eventually overcome it. Its purposes were to control and monitor movement across the frontier, collect customs duties on trade, project Roman power into unconquered territories, and provide a clear, dramatic boundary between Roman civilization and the barbarian lands beyond.

Hadrian built similar frontier fortifications elsewhere. In Germania, he constructed a wooden palisade and earthwork barrier called the Limes Germanicus, defining the frontier between the Rhine and the Danube. In North Africa, he built defensive works in the Sahara. Throughout the empire, he strengthened border fortifications and improved military infrastructure.

But Hadrian was equally famous for his cultural projects. He was deeply philhellenic—a lover of Greek culture—to the point that he wore a Greek-style beard, which was unusual for Romans, who were traditionally clean-shaven (the beard might also have concealed skin blemishes, according to ancient sources). He commissioned magnificent buildings throughout the empire, especially in Athens and Rome.

Hadrian also reformed imperial administration. He regularized the bureaucracy, creating a professional civil service staffed by equestrians rather than relying on senatorial aristocrats or freedmen. He codified Roman law, commissioning the jurist Salvius Julianus to compile the Praetor's Edict—the body of case law that governed Roman legal practice. This became the foundation for later legal codes and influenced European law for centuries.

These reforms made the empire more efficient and less dependent on the emperor. Provinces were governed more systematically. Taxation became more predictable. Legal procedures were standardized. This might seem like boring bureaucratic stuff, but it was crucial to managing an empire of fifty to sixty million people spread across three continents. Hadrian understood that one man could not run everything and that institutions needed to function independently.

In Athens, Hadrian completed the enormous Temple of Olympian Zeus, which had been under construction for over six hundred years. He built libraries, aqueducts, and other public buildings. The Athenians honored him as a new founder of their city. Hadrian saw himself as a patron of Greek culture and a protector of classical civilization.

In Rome, Hadrian built his most famous monument, the Pantheon. The original Pantheon had been built by Agrippa in the 20s BCE but had burned down. Hadrian rebuilt it completely between 118 and 128 CE, creating one of the most extraordinary buildings in history. The Pantheon's dome—142 feet in diameter—is the largest unreinforced concrete dome in the world. It is still standing today, nearly 1,900 years later. It is one of the best-preserved Roman buildings and is still used as a church.

The Pantheon's dome.[98]

Hadrian also built an enormous villa complex at Tivoli, just outside Rome. Hadrian's Villa was a vast estate covering about 250 acres, with palaces, temples, theaters, libraries, bathhouses, and gardens designed to recreate famous buildings and landscapes from throughout the empire, especially from Greece and Egypt. It was Hadrian's personal retreat, where he could surround himself with beauty and culture.

However, Hadrian's reign was not all peaceful construction. In 132 CE, Judaea erupted in revolt—the Bar Kokhba Revolt, named after its leader, Simon bar Kokhba, who claimed to be the messiah. The causes included religious tensions, economic grievances, and Hadrian's plan to build a Roman colony on the site of Jerusalem with a temple to Jupiter on the Temple Mount.

The revolt was massive and well organized. Jewish forces controlled much of Judaea for three years. Rome sent multiple legions and some of its best generals. The fighting was brutal. The ancient historian Cassius Dio claimed that 580,000 Jews were killed and 50 Judean fortified towns and 985 villages were destroyed. Modern historians view these figures as likely exaggerated or symbolic of the scale of destruction rather than precise counts, but they still indicate enormous casualties and devastation.

Rome won, but at a terrible cost. Entire legions were lost. The province of Judaea was devastated. After the revolt, Hadrian expelled Jews from Jerusalem, which he rebuilt as a Roman colony called Aelia Capitolina. The province was renamed Syria Palaestina, deliberately erasing the name Judaea. The Jewish population was decimated, and the religious and cultural center of Judaism was destroyed. It would take until the 20ᵗʰ century for Jews to regain political sovereignty in their ancestral homeland.

Hadrian's personal life was also marked by tragedy. He had no children with his wife, Sabina. Their marriage was reportedly cold and unhappy. But Hadrian had a passionate relationship with a young Greek man named Antinous. In 130 CE, while traveling in Egypt, Antinous drowned in the Nile River. The circumstances were mysterious; ancient sources suggested suicide, accident, or even ritual sacrifice. Hadrian was devastated.

He had Antinous declared a god and established a cult in his honor. Cities throughout the empire built temples to Antinous. Hundreds of statues were created—more than survive of any other private individual from antiquity. Hadrian founded a city at the site of Antinous's death called Antinoopolis.

Hadrian's later years were difficult. He suffered from poor health and became increasingly suspicious and cruel. He executed several senators and officials, alienating the Senate. When choosing his successor, he adopted Antoninus in 138 CE with the condition that Antoninus would adopt two younger men: Marcus Aurelius (Hadrian's great-nephew) and Lucius Verus. Hadrian was planning succession two generations ahead.

Hadrian died in July 138 CE at the age of sixty-two. He was ill and reportedly in great pain. Ancient sources suggested he begged his servants to kill him to end his suffering, but they refused. He composed a famous short poem just before his death:

"Little soul, wandering, gentle,

Guest and companion of the body,

To what places will you now go,

Pale, stiff, naked,

Unable to play as you used to?"

It was a poignant meditation on mortality from a man who had seen more of the world than perhaps any other person in antiquity.

Antoninus Pius (r. 138–161 CE): The Peaceful Emperor

Antoninus Pius is the least famous of the Five Good Emperors, probably because his reign was peaceful and relatively uneventful. After the dramatic building projects of Trajan and Hadrian and the constant travel and frontier wars, Antoninus's reign seems almost boring. But boring is good when you're ruling an empire.

Antoninus was fifty-one when he became emperor and ruled for twenty-three years—one of the longest reigns in Roman history. Ancient sources describe him as conscientious, moderate, and respectful of the Senate. He was given the title "Pius" (dutiful or devoted) because of his efforts to ensure Hadrian's deification. The Senate had been reluctant because Hadrian had executed senators in his final years, but Antoninus insisted on honoring his adoptive father.

Unlike Hadrian, Antoninus didn't travel. He spent his entire reign in Italy, mostly in Rome or at imperial villas. He was essentially a peacetime administrator, managing the empire efficiently without dramatic initiatives.

The empire prospered under Antoninus, though some frontier areas faced persistent pressures even during this relatively peaceful period. Overall, trade flourished in the empire's core regions. Cities grew. The frontiers remained mostly peaceful, with only minor campaigns, the most significant being the construction of the Antonine Wall in Scotland around 142 CE. This pushed the Roman frontier north of Hadrian's Wall. However, the Antonine Wall was abandoned within twenty years, and the frontier returned to Hadrian's Wall, suggesting the northern expansion wasn't sustainable.

Antoninus managed imperial finances conservatively. He didn't undertake massive building projects like his predecessors. He lowered taxes when possible and left a full treasury to his successors. His reign demonstrated that Rome could function peacefully and prosperously under competent administration.

Marcus Aurelius, Antoninus's adopted son, spent these years being trained for power. He held consular positions, learned government administration, and studied philosophy with the best teachers in Rome. When Antoninus died peacefully in 161 CE at the age of seventy-four, Marcus was prepared to rule. The succession was smooth, as the adoptive system intended.

Marcus Aurelius (r. 161–180 CE): The Philosopher King Who Spent His Life at War

Marcus Aurelius is probably the most famous of the Five Good Emperors today, largely because his personal philosophical writings, the *Meditations*, survived and became one of the most influential works of Stoic philosophy. He's the ideal of the "philosopher king" that Plato described. Marcus Aurelius was a ruler who loved wisdom, sought virtue, and governed with justice.

The irony is that Marcus Aurelius spent almost his entire reign at war. The philosopher who wanted to live a life of contemplation and virtue spent nearly twenty years on military campaigns on the frontiers, fighting enemies who threatened the empire's survival.

Marcus made an unusual decision immediately after becoming emperor. He shared power with his adoptive brother, Lucius Verus, making him co-emperor. This was unprecedented. Rome had never had two equal emperors ruling simultaneously (Hadrian's proposal of this was more theoretical). Marcus and Lucius ruled together from 161 to 169 CE, until Lucius died.

Almost immediately after their accession, Rome faced crises on multiple frontiers. In the east, the Parthian Empire invaded Armenia and Syria in 161 CE, defeating Roman forces and threatening Rome's eastern provinces. Lucius Verus was sent east with reinforcements. The war lasted until 166 CE, with Roman forces eventually defeating Parthia. However, Roman soldiers returning from the east brought back something more dangerous than Parthian soldiers: a plague.

The Antonine Plague, which began in 165, was likely smallpox or measles. It devastated the empire for over a decade, killing millions. Ancient sources describe cities emptied of inhabitants and mass funeral pyres. The historian Cassius Dio and the physician Galen both describe the plague's symptoms and devastating impact. Estimates suggest the plague killed anywhere from five to ten million people, which was perhaps a tenth of the empire's population.

The plague's effects went beyond immediate deaths. Agricultural production declined as farmers died, leading to food shortages. Tax revenues fell as populations shrank, straining imperial finances. Trade networks were disrupted as merchants and ship crews died. The Roman army was so depleted that Marcus had to recruit gladiators and even bandits to fill the ranks, showing how desperate the manpower situation had become. Some historians argue that the Antonine Plague marked the beginning of Rome's decline, weakening the empire's demographic and economic foundations as external pressures increased.

While the empire was weakening from the plague, Germanic tribes along the Rhine and Danube frontiers saw an opportunity. The Marcomannic Wars began in 166 CE and would continue for most of Marcus's reign. Germanic and Sarmatian tribes crossed the Danube in massive numbers. They were not just raiding. They were migrating and seeking land to settle.

In 167, Germanic tribes invaded Italy itself for the first time in over 250 years, reaching Aquileia in northeastern Italy. This was a shocking violation of Italy's sanctity. Italy was supposed to be safe, far from barbarian threats. Marcus rushed north with legions to repel the invasion.

The Marcomannic Wars were a grinding series of campaigns along the Danube frontier. Marcus spent years living in military camps, commanding armies in the field, negotiating with tribal leaders, and trying to stabilize a frontier that seemed constantly on the verge of collapse. These were not glorious conquests like Trajan's Dacian Wars. These were defensive wars of survival aimed at preventing barbarian tribes from overrunning Roman provinces.

During these long campaigns on the Danube, Marcus wrote his *Meditations*, personal philosophical reflections in Greek. The *Meditations* are remarkable for their Stoic philosophy (a school of thought emphasizing virtue, self-control, and accepting what you cannot change) and their humility. Marcus reminds himself constantly to be virtuous, to accept fate, to not be corrupted by power, to serve others, and to remember his own mortality.

Here are some of the more famous passages:

"You have power over your mind—not outside events. Realize this, and you will find strength."

"Waste no more time arguing about what a good man should be. Be one."

"When you arise in the morning, think of what a precious privilege it is to be alive—to breathe, to think, to enjoy, to love."

"The impediment to action advances action. What stands in the way becomes the way."

These are the thoughts of a man who had absolute power but saw it as a burden. He wanted to be wise and good despite being emperor and was fighting wars he didn't want while longing for philosophical contemplation. The *Meditations* reveal a deeply human figure struggling with duty, mortality, and the gap between ideals and reality.

Lucius Verus died in 169 CE, possibly from the plague. Marcus continued ruling alone. The wars dragged on. By the late 170s, Marcus had achieved some success. The Germanic tribes were defeated, and the frontier seemed temporarily stable. Some ancient sources suggest Marcus Aurelius planned to annex territories beyond the Danube, creating a new province of Marcomannia.

However, in 180, Marcus Aurelius fell ill and died at the age of fifty-eight in a military camp at Vindobona (modern Vienna) while still on campaign. He had spent nearly his entire reign at war, never achieving the peace he desired. His death is often seen as the end of the Pax Romana, the long peace that had characterized the 2nd century, though peace and prosperity continued in many regions. What's clear is that after 180, the empire faced increasing military pressures, political instability, and economic challenges that the rulers of the 2nd century had largely avoided.

This was because Marcus passed power to his biological son, Commodus. Marcus had no real choice. Commodus was his only surviving son, and passing over him would have risked civil war. But Commodus was not chosen for ability. He was heir by birth, and he would prove disastrously unfit for power.

Commodus (r. 180–192 CE): When the System Broke

Commodus became emperor at age eighteen. Unlike the previous emperors, who had been trained in government and military command for years before taking power, Commodus was young, inexperienced, and had spent his life as an imperial prince with few serious responsibilities.

Ancient sources describe Commodus as lazy, cruel, and obsessed with gladiatorial combat. He reportedly fought in the arena himself. He dressed as a gladiator, killing animals and fighting carefully arranged matches against opponents who were ordered not to harm him. He saw himself as Hercules reborn and had statues made depicting him dressed as the hero, with a lion's skin and club.

This was scandalous. Emperors were supposed to be dignified and serious. They might attend the games, but they didn't perform in them. Gladiators were *infames*—legally disgraced people. For an emperor to fight as a gladiator humiliated the imperial office and horrified the senatorial class.

Commodus also renamed Rome itself "Colonia Commodiana" (the Colony of Commodus). He renamed the months of the year after his own titles. He wanted the Senate renamed "Commodian Senate." This megalomania went beyond normal imperial self-aggrandizement into what ancient sources portrayed as insanity.

However, we must note that ancient sources on Commodus are heavily biased. They were written by senators who hated him and had every reason to portray him in the worst possible light. Modern historians debate whether Commodus was genuinely unstable or whether some of his actions were provocative attacks on senatorial privilege. By fighting as a gladiator, Commodus was rejecting the Senate's values and appealing to the common people, who loved gladiatorial combat. This might have been calculated political theater rather than madness. The truth likely lies somewhere between the characterization of a mad tyrant and a strategic ruler. Commodus appears to have been both impulsive and calculating, both cruel and crowd-pleasing.

Regardless of his motivations, Commodus's reign was disastrous for governance. He delegated the actual administration to praetorian prefects and favorites who became corrupt and abusive. He executed senators he suspected of disloyalty. He debased the currency to fund his lavish lifestyle and games. The government that had functioned smoothly under the Five Good Emperors began to break down.

In 192, conspirators, including Commodus's mistress Marcia and the Praetorian prefect, planned his assassination. They tried to poison him, but he vomited up the poison. So, they sent a wrestler named Narcissus to strangle him in his bath. Commodus was thirty-one years old; he died after twelve years of increasingly erratic rule.

His death triggered a civil war. Multiple generals proclaimed themselves emperor. The Year of the Five Emperors (193 CE) saw rapid turnover until Septimius Severus emerged victorious in 197, establishing a new dynasty. The golden age was over.

From peaks, there's only one direction to go.

A bust of Septimius Severus.[99]

Chapter 9: The Third-Century Crisis: Fifty Years of Chaos That Nearly Destroyed Rome

The assassination of Commodus in 192 didn't restore the golden age. Instead, it triggered a civil war. Multiple generals proclaimed themselves emperor. Armies fought each other across the empire. After a year of chaos, Septimius Severus emerged victorious in 197, establishing the Severan dynasty. The Severans ruled for about forty years, maintaining some stability, though their reigns were marked by military campaigns, increased taxation, and growing reliance on the army.

In 235, when the last Severan emperor was murdered by his own troops, something broke. The next fifty years—from 235 to 284—saw the Roman Empire nearly collapse. This period is called the Crisis of the Third Century, and it was one of the worst sustained catastrophes in Roman history. The empire faced simultaneous military invasions, economic collapse, devastating plagues, political chaos, and the near-total breakdown of central authority.

Ancient sources from this period are fragmentary and confusing, which makes sense. When your civilization is falling apart, keeping detailed historical records isn't the priority. But we can piece together what happened. What we know is that a disaster came terrifyingly close to ending the Roman Empire forever.

The Barracks Emperors: When Soldiers Decided Who Ruled Rome

The fundamental problem was simple: the Roman army had learned it could make emperors and unmake them.

When Maximinus Thrax became emperor in 235 after his soldiers murdered Severus Alexander, he set a precedent. Maximinus wasn't a senator. He wasn't from a noble family. He wasn't even Italian; ancient sources describe him as a Thracian (from roughly modern Bulgaria) of low birth. He was supposedly a former shepherd who joined the army and rose through the ranks. His elevation showed that military force alone could create an emperor.

This broke what little remained of the adoptive system's principle that emperors should be chosen for ability and legitimacy. Now, any general with enough loyal troops could proclaim himself emperor. And many did.

Between 235 and 284, ancient sources record that somewhere between fifty and seventy men claimed the title of emperor. This figure includes all regional usurpers and generals proclaimed by single military units; the number of emperors widely accepted by large factions or the Senate was closer to twenty or thirty. Regardless of the exact count, the turnover was extraordinary. Most reigned for less than a year. Many were murdered by their own soldiers. A few died in battle against foreign enemies. Almost none died peacefully.

These emperors are sometimes called the "Barracks emperors" because they were made by soldiers in military camps, not through any legitimate succession process. The pattern was depressingly predictable:

1. An emperor leads troops on campaign.
2. The campaign goes badly, the emperor doesn't pay his soldiers enough, or the troops just get bored.
3. Soldiers murder the emperor and proclaim their general as the new emperor.
4. Other armies hear about this and proclaim their own generals as emperor.
5. Civil war breaks out as rival claimants fight for supremacy.
6. Eventually, someone wins and becomes emperor.
7. Within months or years, the cycle repeats.

This sounds almost comical in its absurdity, but the consequences were catastrophic. Every civil war meant Roman armies were fighting each other instead of defending frontiers. Every murdered emperor meant disrupted administration and broken treaties. Every new claimant needed money to pay his troops, so taxation increased, and the currency was debased. The empire was consuming itself.

Some examples show just how chaotic it became:

Gordian I and Gordian II (238 CE): This father and son duo were proclaimed co-emperors in Africa. They reigned for twenty-two days before both of them died. Gordian II was killed in battle, and Gordian I committed suicide when he heard the news.

Pupienus and Balbinus (238 CE): The Senate appointed these two as co-emperors to oppose Maximinus Thrax. They reigned for ninety-nine days before the Praetorian Guard murdered them both.

Philip the Arab (244–249 CE): He was a relatively successful emperor who celebrated Rome's one-thousandth anniversary in 248 CE with massive games. He was murdered by his own troops the following year.

Decius (249–251 CE): He launched the first empire-wide persecution of Christians, trying to restore the traditional Roman religion and unity. He was killed fighting Goths at the Battle of Abritus, making him the first Roman emperor killed in battle by foreign enemies in centuries.

Valerian (253–260 CE): He was captured by the Sasanian Persian Empire in 260 CE; he was allegedly used as a footstool by the Persian king. Valerian was the only Roman emperor ever captured alive by a foreign enemy. He died in captivity, a humiliation Rome had never experienced before.

Gallienus (253–268 CE): He ruled for fifteen years, making this one of the longest reigns of the period. He was murdered by his own officers during a siege.

The rapid turnover created chaos. New emperors couldn't learn the job before being killed. Policies changed constantly. Nobody could plan for the long term when the government might collapse next month. The empire lost any coherent direction.

The Frontiers Collapse: When Everyone Attacked at Once

While Romans were killing each other, Rome's enemies noticed the chaos and attacked.

The northern frontiers—the Rhine and Danube regions that had held for centuries—collapsed. Germanic tribes poured across the rivers in massive numbers. These weren't just raids anymore. Entire peoples were migrating, seeking land and plunder, and pushing into Roman territory.

The Alemanni invaded Italy in 259 CE in a raid that reached the Milan area before being defeated. Germanic tribes raided Gaul repeatedly, devastating cities and the countryside. The Goths crossed the Lower Danube, invaded the Balkans, and even launched naval raids into the Aegean Sea. Athens was sacked by a Germanic tribe in 267. The unthinkable was happening—Athens, the cultural heart of the classical world, was being pillaged by barbarians.

In the east, the situation was even worse. The Sasanian Empire, a new, aggressive Persian dynasty that had overthrown the Parthians, proved far more formidable than the Parthians had been. The Sasanians were militarily sophisticated, ideologically motivated (they promoted Zoroastrianism as the state religion), and determined to reconquer territories they considered rightfully Persian.

Between 241 and 272, the Sasanians repeatedly invaded Roman territory. They captured and sacked cities, took prisoners, and extracted tribute. The capture of Valerian in 260 was a spectacular Sasanian success. Persian armies under King Shapur I captured Antioch (one of Rome's largest cities) and raided deep into Roman territory. Roman forces were stretched so thin that defending one frontier meant abandoning another.

Then the empire fragmented into semi-independent polities.

In 260, the western provinces—Gaul, Britain, and Spain—broke away and formed the Gallic Empire under Postumus, a general who had been defending the Rhine frontier. Postumus wasn't trying to conquer Rome or reject Roman identity; he claimed to be protecting the western provinces since the central government couldn't. He maintained Roman institutions and framed his rule as temporary until Rome could recover. The Gallic Empire had its own emperors, armies, and administration. It lasted until 274.

Around the same time, the city of Palmyra in Syria became effectively independent under Queen Zenobia. Palmyra was a wealthy trading city that had been a Roman ally. When Rome couldn't defend the east, Palmyra's forces stepped into the power vacuum, conquering Egypt around 270, along with Syria and parts of Asia Minor, creating the Palmyrene Empire. Zenobia styled herself as a Roman empress and claimed to be protecting Roman territories from Persian invasion. She was not rejecting Rome but filling the void Rome had left.

By 270, the "Roman Empire" consisted of three competing polities: the central empire ruled from Rome, the Gallic Empire in the west, and the Palmyrene Empire in the east. Rome controlled only Italy, the Balkans, and North Africa. The empire that had dominated the Mediterranean for centuries had fragmented into competing states. Complete collapse seemed imminent.

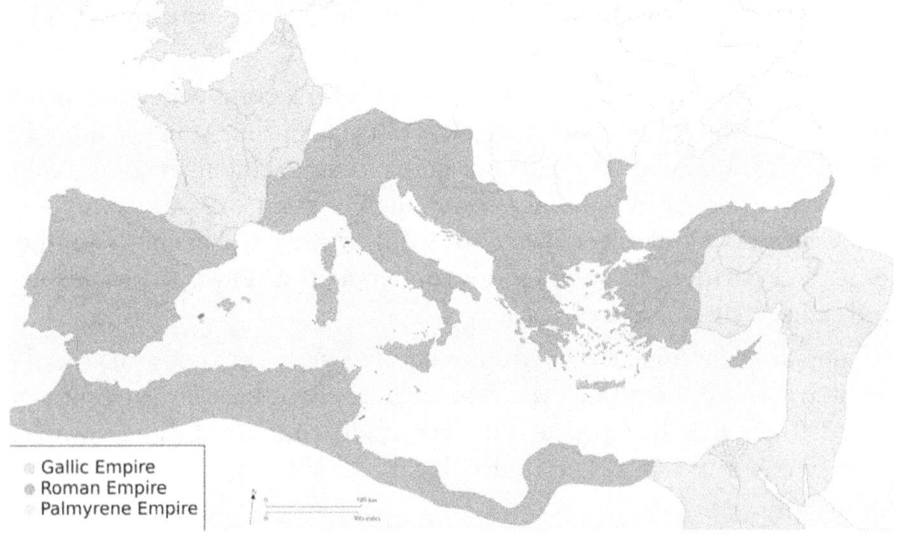

The Roman Empire, the Gallic Empire, and the Palmyrene Empire.[100]

The Economy Collapses: When Money Stopped Being Money

The economic crisis worsened the military disaster. The empire's financial system, which had been relatively stable for centuries, completely broke down.

The core problem was that the emperors needed money to pay their armies, but the empire's tax base was shrinking as provinces were devastated by war and plague. The solution the emperors adopted was to debase the currency—reduce the precious-metal content of coins while maintaining the same face value.

Roman silver coins (*denarii*) had historically contained about 95 percent silver. By the 230s, this had dropped to about 50 percent. By the 260s, the silver content had dropped to 5 percent. By the 270s, what had once been silver coins were basically bronze coins with a thin silver wash. You could rub the silver coating off with your fingers.

This caused catastrophic inflation. When merchants realized coins contained almost no precious metal, they raised prices—a lot. Ancient sources and surviving data suggest that prices increased perhaps 1,000 percent or more over the 3rd century.

Imagine you're a Roman trying to buy bread in 260 CE. The baker won't accept coins at face value because everyone knows they're worthless. You need to bring huge quantities of debased coins to buy basic necessities. A loaf of bread that cost one denarius in 200 CE might cost many times that amount in 270. And the baker might refuse coins entirely, demanding payment in grain or goods.

The government tried to address this by issuing coins with even higher face values, which just made inflation worse. Ancient sources describe soldiers refusing debased coins and demanding payment in goods, gold, or land instead. Army mutinies sometimes erupted over worthless pay. Tax collectors couldn't collect taxes in worthless currency, so they demanded payment in grain, goods, or services—a return to payment in kind rather than monetized taxation.

Long-distance trade declined dramatically. Why ship goods across the Mediterranean if the money you'll be paid in is worthless by the time you arrive? Cities that had prospered from trade contracted. The complex urban economy simplified into local subsistence agriculture and production.

Government spending collapsed. The emperors couldn't afford to maintain roads, aqueducts, or public buildings. The infrastructure that had taken centuries to build deteriorated in decades. Cities that couldn't maintain their water supplies or grain imports shrank significantly. Some smaller settlements were abandoned entirely as people fled to larger, more defensible urban centers or to rural estates. The urban landscape was transforming, with cities building defensive walls (like Rome's Aurelian Walls) and prioritizing survival over prosperity.

Wealthy people who had invested in property, businesses, and trade saw their fortunes collapse. The middle classes were wiped out. The poor, who had little to lose, became even more desperate. Social mobility disappeared. The Roman world was becoming poorer, simpler, and more desperate.

The Plague Returns: When Disease Compounded Disaster

As if military invasions and economic collapse weren't enough, plague struck repeatedly during the 3rd century.

We don't know exactly what disease it was, although it was likely smallpox, measles, or possibly both in successive waves. Ancient sources describe symptoms consistent with these diseases, such as fever, pustules, blindness, and death. The Plague of Cyprian, named after a bishop who described it, ravaged the empire from approximately 249 to 262 CE. Cities reported thousands of deaths daily at its peak.

The plague killed indiscriminately. Rich and poor, soldiers and civilians, young and old—all died. The population declined significantly, though exact figures are unknown. Some estimates suggest the plague killed 20 to 30 percent of the empire's population over the course of the 3rd century, though this is highly speculative.

The demographic impact was catastrophic. Farmers died, leading to abandoned farmland and reduced food production. Artisans died, disrupting the production of goods. Soldiers died, weakening the army at the worst possible time. Tax collectors couldn't collect from the dead, further reducing imperial revenue.

The psychological impact was equally severe. Living through repeated plague outbreaks while watching your civilization collapse creates despair. Ancient sources describe cities emptied of inhabitants, bodies lying unburied in streets, and survivors fleeing to the countryside. The traditional religion seemed powerless. It was clear that the gods weren't protecting Rome. This created a spiritual crisis that made people receptive to new religious movements promising salvation and meaning in a chaotic world.

The Soldier-Emperors Save Rome (Temporarily)

Yet somehow, the empire survived. Between 268 and 284, a series of tough, competent military commanders, mostly from Illyria (roughly the Balkans), stabilized the situation and began the recovery process. These "Illyrian emperors" or "soldier-emperors" weren't cultured, educated aristocrats. They were hardened military professionals who spent their reigns fighting on the frontiers.

Claudius II took power in 268 CE and immediately faced a massive Gothic invasion. At the Battle of Naissus in 269, Roman forces slaughtered tens of thousands of Goths. Claudius earned the title "Gothicus" for this triumph. However, the plague killed him in 270 after only two years as emperor.

His successor, Aurelian, was perhaps the most significant emperor of the crisis period. A brilliant general and ruthless pragmatist, Aurelian understood that Rome couldn't hold everything. In 271, he made the painful decision to abandon Dacia, the province Trajan had conquered 165 years earlier. The Danube would be the frontier again. This strategic withdrawal shortened the defensive line and freed up troops for more critical fronts.

Then Aurelian set about reunifying the empire. In 272, he marched east against Palmyra. Queen Zenobia's forces fought hard, but Roman discipline and Aurelian's tactical skill won out. Palmyra fell. Zenobia was captured and brought to Rome in triumph, paraded through the streets in golden chains. Aurelian later granted her a villa and pension rather than executing her. The eastern provinces were Roman again.

In 274, Aurelian turned west and defeated the Gallic Empire. After fourteen years of fragmentation, the Roman Empire was whole again under one emperor. Contemporaries called Aurelian "Restorer of the World" (*Restitutor Orbis*).

Aurelian also did something that would have been unthinkable two centuries earlier: he built walls around Rome. The Aurelian Walls were twelve miles long, twenty feet high, and still stand today. They were designed to protect the eternal city from barbarian invasions that might reach Italy itself. The fact that Rome needed walls showed how much had changed. Aurelian also reformed the currency, issuing new coins with higher precious metal content. He couldn't fully fix the inflation, but he stabilized it.

A section of the Aurelian Walls today.[101]

In 275, officers murdered Aurelian based on a forged document suggesting he planned to execute them. It seems even successful emperors couldn't escape the cycle of military violence.

Probus continued Aurelian's work when he took power in 276. He defeated Germanic tribes, repelled Sasanian incursions, and secured the frontiers. He attempted to restore discipline in the army by making soldiers help with civilian construction projects, which included building roads, draining marshes, and planting vineyards. The troops resented doing non-military labor. In 282, they murdered him.

The next emperor, Carus, campaigned successfully against the Sasanians and reached the Persian capital, Ctesiphon. Then, in 283, he died mysteriously. He might have been struck by lightning or murdered. His sons, Carinus and Numerian, divided the empire between them. Numerian died in 284; he was possibly murdered. Carinus was defeated and killed in battle by Diocles, an obscure Dalmatian general who proclaimed himself emperor and took the name Diocletian.

These soldier-emperors had accomplished something remarkable. They had beaten back invasions, reunified the empire, and restored some order. However, they had only treated the symptoms, not the causes. How could one emperor defend frontiers stretching thousands of miles? How could the government function when emperors kept being murdered? How could the economy recover when currency was worthless and trade had collapsed?

The empire needed fundamental reform. And Diocletian would provide it.

Diocletian's Solution: Dividing the Empire to Save It

Diocletian reigned from 284 to 305 CE. He was a brilliant administrator who understood that the empire's problems required systemic solutions, not just military force.

His most radical innovation was the Tetrarchy, the "rule of four." In 286, Diocletian appointed Maximian as co-emperor, with both holding the title Augustus, and divided the empire administratively. Diocletian ruled the East from Nicomedia in Asia Minor. Maximian ruled the West from Milan. They were not splitting the empire permanently; they were colleagues sharing power.

Then, in 293, Diocletian created the Tetrarchy. Each Augustus appointed a junior emperor called a Caesar, who governed part of his territory and would eventually succeed him. Diocletian appointed

Galerius as his Caesar in the East. Maximian appointed Constantius Chlorus as his Caesar in the West. Four emperors now ruled cooperatively, each responsible for defending part of the empire's frontiers.

This solved several problems at once. Militarily, four emperors meant four mobile courts and four field armies. When the Germanic tribes threatened the Rhine, Constantius could respond immediately. When the Persians invaded Syria, Galerius handled it. The empire could now defend multiple frontiers simultaneously instead of rushing one emperor back and forth.

The Caesars were the designated heirs. They were trained in government and military command for years before taking power. When the Augusti retired (or died), the Caesars would become the Augusti and appoint new Caesars. This created a structured succession plan that avoided civil wars, at least in theory.

Administratively, the empire was divided into four prefectures, twelve dioceses, and about one hundred provinces. This created smaller, more manageable units. Provincial governors had less power to rebel since they commanded fewer resources and governed smaller territories. Civil and military authority were separated; governors couldn't use troops for rebellion, and military commanders (*duces*) had no civil authority. This reduced the risk of provincial officials accumulating enough power to proclaim themselves emperor.

Diocletian also reformed taxation. He established regular censuses to assess property and population. He created standardized tax assessments based on land productivity and resources, and he imposed new taxes on commerce and professions. These reforms were harsh since taxation increased significantly, but they were predictable and systematic, allowing the government to budget and plan.

He reformed the currency, issuing new coins with a higher precious metal content. He tried to fix prices through the Edict on Maximum Prices in 301, which set legal maximum prices for hundreds of goods and services. Like most price controls, this didn't work well—people evaded it through black markets—but it showed Diocletian's ambition to restore economic order.

He reformed the army, increasing its size to perhaps 400,000 to 600,000 men and reorganizing it into mobile field armies and permanent frontier garrisons. The field armies could respond quickly to invasions while frontier garrisons held defensive positions.

Diocletian also changed the nature of imperial power. He abandoned the Augustan fiction of being "first citizen" and embraced open autocracy. He styled himself *dominus et deus* ("lord and god"). He surrounded himself with elaborate Persian-style court ceremonies. Subjects prostrated themselves before him. He wore purple silk and jeweled crowns. The emperor was now explicitly an absolute monarch, not a magistrate.

This wasn't megalomania; it was strategic. By emphasizing the emperor's sacred status and surrounding him with ceremony, Diocletian made imperial power seem beyond ordinary reach. You don't casually murder someone who was semi-divine.

Diocletian's reforms worked, as the empire stabilized. But in 305, Diocletian did something unprecedented: he voluntarily retired. He forced Maximian to retire as well. Both Augusti stepped down on the same day. The Caesars became Augusti, new Caesars were appointed, and the Tetrarchy's succession plan was activated.

But it immediately collapsed. Within a year, multiple claimants were fighting for power. The Caesars weren't willing to wait their turn. Biological sons of emperors demanded power.

One of those sons was Constantine. His father Constantius Chlorus had been one of Diocletian's Caesars, governing Britain and Gaul. When Constantius died in 306 at York in Britain, his troops proclaimed Constantine emperor. But so did several other generals and their armies. By 312, there were six men claiming to be emperor. The Tetrarchy's elegant succession mechanism had failed.

Constantine spent the next few years fighting rivals for control. In 312, he marched on Rome to confront Maxentius, who controlled Italy. The two armies met at the Milvian Bridge outside Rome on October 28th, 312. According to Christian sources written later, Constantine had a vision before the battle. It was either a cross of light in the sky or a dream in which Christ told him to mark his soldiers' shields with a Christian symbol. Constantine won the battle decisively. Maxentius drowned while fleeing across the bridge.

Constantine attributed his victory to the Christian God. This would change everything.

The Rise of Christianity: From Persecution to Imperial Religion

Christianity had been growing steadily throughout the empire for three centuries. Despite periodic persecutions, despite being illegal, and despite being despised by many traditional Romans, Christianity spread. By 300 CE, Christians were perhaps 10 percent of the empire's population. They were still a minority, but their numbers were growing.

Why did Christianity grow during Rome's worst crisis? Well, Christianity promised salvation and eternal life to all believers regardless of social status. In a world where everything seemed to be collapsing, this hope was attractive. The traditional Roman religion offered no clear afterlife, no promise of justice, and no explanation for suffering. Christianity offered all of these.

Christian churches provided social networks, charity, and mutual support. When plague struck, Christians cared for the sick—even non-Christians—while many pagans fled their sick relatives. Nursing sick people improved survival rates, so Christian communities often had lower mortality rates than pagan communities during epidemics. When the economic crisis made people desperate, churches provided food, financial assistance to the poor, and support for widows and orphans. Christian communities functioned as mutual aid societies at a time when traditional civic institutions were failing. This charity converted people as much as theology did; when a Christian community feeds you during a famine, you notice.

Christianity explained suffering as temporary, as a test of faith, and as part of God's plan. It gave cosmic meaning to the chaos. The world might be ending, but Christians believed a new, better world would follow, either after death in heaven or after Christ's return to establish God's kingdom on earth. This hope made present suffering bearable. Traditional Roman religion had no good explanation for why the gods would allow the empire to suffer such catastrophes.

Diocletian saw Christianity as a threat. In 303, he launched the Great Persecution, the last and most systematic attempt to destroy Christianity. Churches were destroyed, scriptures burned, and Christians were required to sacrifice to traditional gods or face execution. The persecution lasted about ten years and varied in intensity by region.

The persecution failed. Christianity was too widespread, too organized, and too resilient. Galerius, one of the tetrarchs, issued an edict of toleration in 311 on his deathbed, effectively admitting defeat. Christianity had survived Rome's worst.

Constantine changed everything. After his victory at the Milvian Bridge in 312, which he attributed to the Christian God, Constantine openly embraced Christianity. In 313, he and Licinius (another claimant to imperial power) issued the Edict of Milan, which legalized Christianity and restored confiscated property to churches.

Constantine didn't just tolerate Christianity; he actively promoted it. He funded church construction, including the original St. Peter's Basilica in Rome. He gave Christian clergy tax exemptions and legal privileges. He made Sunday a day of rest. He got involved in theological disputes, convening the Council of Nicaea in 325 to resolve the Arian controversy about Christ's nature.

Why did Constantine embrace Christianity? The sources, which were mostly written by Christian bishops who admired him, say he had a genuine conversion experience. Modern historians debate whether it was sincere religious belief, political calculation (recognizing Christianity's growing power), or both. What's clear is that Constantine's conversion transformed Christianity's status. When the emperor converted to Christianity, the religion became fashionable and politically advantageous. Conversions increased dramatically.

By 380, Emperor Theodosius I made Christianity the official state religion with the Edict of Thessalonica. Pagan worship was increasingly restricted and eventually banned. The empire that had persecuted Christians for centuries became a Christian empire within eighty years.

This religious transformation was as significant as any political or military development. Christianity would shape medieval and modern Europe. The alliance between the Christian Church and the Roman state would define Western civilization for over a thousand years. Constantine's conversion changed the course of history.

The empire survived the Crisis of the Third Century. The reforms of Diocletian and Constantine created a system that worked well enough. The Eastern Roman Empire, which we call the Byzantine Empire today, would continue for another eleven centuries. Even the Western Roman Empire had nearly two more centuries before its final collapse in 476.

Rome had faced its worst crisis and survived. The question was, for how long?

Chapter 10: The Long Goodbye: How Rome Fell So Slowly You Could Barely Tell It Was Happening

The Roman Empire didn't fall with a dramatic bang. It didn't collapse overnight. Instead, it experienced what might be the slowest, most gradual decline in history. This process was so slow that people living through it might not have realized they were watching the end of an era.

Here's the thing that confuses people about Rome's "fall": the Roman Empire didn't actually fall in many of the ways we usually think. The Eastern Roman Empire—what we call the Byzantine Empire, though they always called themselves Romans—survived for another thousand years after the traditional "fall" date of 476 CE. Constantinople, the Eastern capital, didn't fall until 1453 when the Ottoman Turks conquered it. That's over a millennium of continuous Roman government, law, and culture.

What fell in the 5th century was the Western Roman Empire, the Latin-speaking half centered in Italy. But even that "fall" was more like a slow transformation than a sudden collapse. Germanic kingdoms gradually replaced Roman administration. Roman institutions persisted under barbarian kings. Latin evolved into Romance languages. Roman law continued. Christianity, which Rome had adopted, spread to the barbarians.

So the "fall of Rome" is really the story of how the unified Mediterranean empire became medieval kingdoms in the West and the Byzantine Empire in the East. It was a messy, complicated process that took centuries and didn't feel like the end of the world to most people living through it.

Let's see how it happened.

Constantine and Constantinople: Moving the Capital East

We left off with Constantine reunifying the empire in 324 after defeating all his rivals in civil wars that followed the collapse of Diocletian's Tetrarchy. Constantine now ruled alone over the entire Roman Empire.

One of Constantine's most consequential decisions was to found a new capital. Rome still mattered symbolically—it was Rome, after all, the Eternal City, home to the Senate and centuries of tradition. But strategically, Rome's location was terrible. It was far from the frontiers where armies fought Persians and Germanic tribes. It was dominated by pagan aristocratic families who resisted Constantine's Christian innovations. The Senate, though politically weak, still represented traditional republican values and the pagan religion that Constantine wanted to move past. Rome was the past; Constantine wanted to build the future.

So in 324, after defeating his last rival, Licinius, Constantine decided to build a new capital on the site of Byzantium, an ancient Greek city on the Bosphorus Strait where Europe meets Asia. The location was perfect. It controlled the strait connecting the Mediterranean to the Black Sea, which was crucial for grain shipments. It was near the wealthy Eastern provinces, the empire's economic powerhouse. It was close to both the Persian and Danube frontiers. And it was highly defensible, as it was surrounded by water on three sides, making it nearly impregnable.

Constantine poured enormous resources into building his new capital. He constructed massive defensive walls that would be expanded in the 5th century into the Theodosian Walls. These triple walls made Constantinople the most heavily fortified city in the world. He built a hippodrome for chariot racing that could seat perhaps 100,000 spectators. Chariot racing was the most popular sport in the Byzantine Empire, and the hippodrome would be the center of political life for centuries. He constructed forums, monumental columns, aqueducts to bring fresh water, palaces for the emperor and government, public baths, and libraries.

And churches. Lots of churches. This would be a Christian capital, the New Rome, deliberately free from associations with paganism and pagan temples. Constantine founded the Church of the Holy Apostles, where he would eventually be buried alongside relics of the apostles, positioning himself as the thirteenth apostle. He founded the original Hagia Sophia (Holy Wisdom), though the famous building that stands today was built two centuries later under Justinian. Constantinople would have hundreds of churches, monasteries, and Christian institutions, making it visibly and unmistakably a Christian city.

Constantine encouraged migration by offering generous incentives. Free grain distributions modeled on Rome's *annona* ensured that poor citizens could eat. Building programs created jobs for craftsmen, laborers, and architects. Constantine established a Senate in Constantinople to rival Rome's, though initially it had lower status. Its members were called *clari* (distinguished), while Rome's senators were *clarissimi* (most distinguished). Within a generation, Constantinople was rivaling Rome in population, perhaps reaching 300,000 to 400,000 residents by mid-century.

The city was formally dedicated on May 11th, 330, as Constantinople (Constantine's City). The founding of Constantinople had profound consequences. It marked a shift in the empire's center of gravity from West to East. The Eastern provinces were wealthier, more urbanized, and more economically dynamic than the West. By moving the capital east, Constantine was acknowledging that the future of the empire was in the East.

Constantine continued promoting Christianity. He funded churches throughout the empire, including the Church of the Holy Sepulchre in Jerusalem (built over what Christians believed was Jesus's tomb) and the original St. Peter's Basilica in Rome. But Constantine didn't abolish paganism. Pagan temples remained open. The traditional religion was still legal and widely practiced. Constantine walked a careful line, promoting Christianity without alienating the empire's pagan majority. This approach allowed Christianity to grow without triggering a religious civil war.

Constantine died in 337, having been baptized on his deathbed (a common practice since baptism washed away sins, and many people wanted to die freshly purified). He had reunified the empire, stabilized the frontiers, promoted Christianity, and founded a new capital that would outlast Rome itself. His sons—Constantine II, Constantius II, and

Constans—inherited the empire and promptly started fighting each other because Roman politics never stayed peaceful for long.

The next fifty years saw the usual pattern of civil wars, usurpations, and brief reigns. However, two developments were particularly significant.

In 361, Constantine's nephew, Julian the Apostate, became emperor and tried to reverse Christianization. Julian was a devoted pagan who wanted to restore the traditional religion. He withdrew Christian privileges, promoted pagan worship, and tried to revive paganism intellectually and culturally. But Julian died in 363 after reigning for only two years; he was killed during a campaign against Persia. His pagan revival died with him, showing that Christianity's growth was irreversible.

The emperor who made Christianity official was Theodosius I. In 380, Theodosius issued the Edict of Thessalonica, declaring that all subjects must follow the Nicene Christian faith. This made Christianity the official state religion. Theodosius went further, banning pagan worship, closing temples, and suppressing pagan practices. By the 390s, being pagan was illegal. The Roman Empire was now officially Christian.

When Theodosius died in 395, he divided the empire between his sons. Arcadius got the East, and Honorius got the West. This division was meant to be administrative, not permanent; both were theoretically part of one empire. But in practice, the division became permanent. The Eastern and Western Roman Empires would develop separately, face different challenges, and have dramatically different fates.

The Barbarian Invasions: Why They Were Moving In

The term "barbarian invasions" is somewhat misleading. What happened in the 4th and 5th centuries was a complex mix of mass migration (entire peoples moving with families and possessions), military conquest (armed groups seizing territory), and political coercion (using military threats to extract land grants).

Why were these people groups migrating? Northern Europe might have experienced cooler, wetter conditions in the 4th and 5th centuries that made agriculture harder, creating food shortages and pressure for farmable land, though other factors were probably more important. Germanic populations had been growing for centuries. More people meant more land was needed to settle, and the territories beyond Rome's frontiers were filling up. At the same time, Germanic societies were becoming more organized. Successful war leaders were creating tribal confederations, such as the Goths, Alemanni, and Franks, which could mobilize larger forces and undertake ambitious migrations.

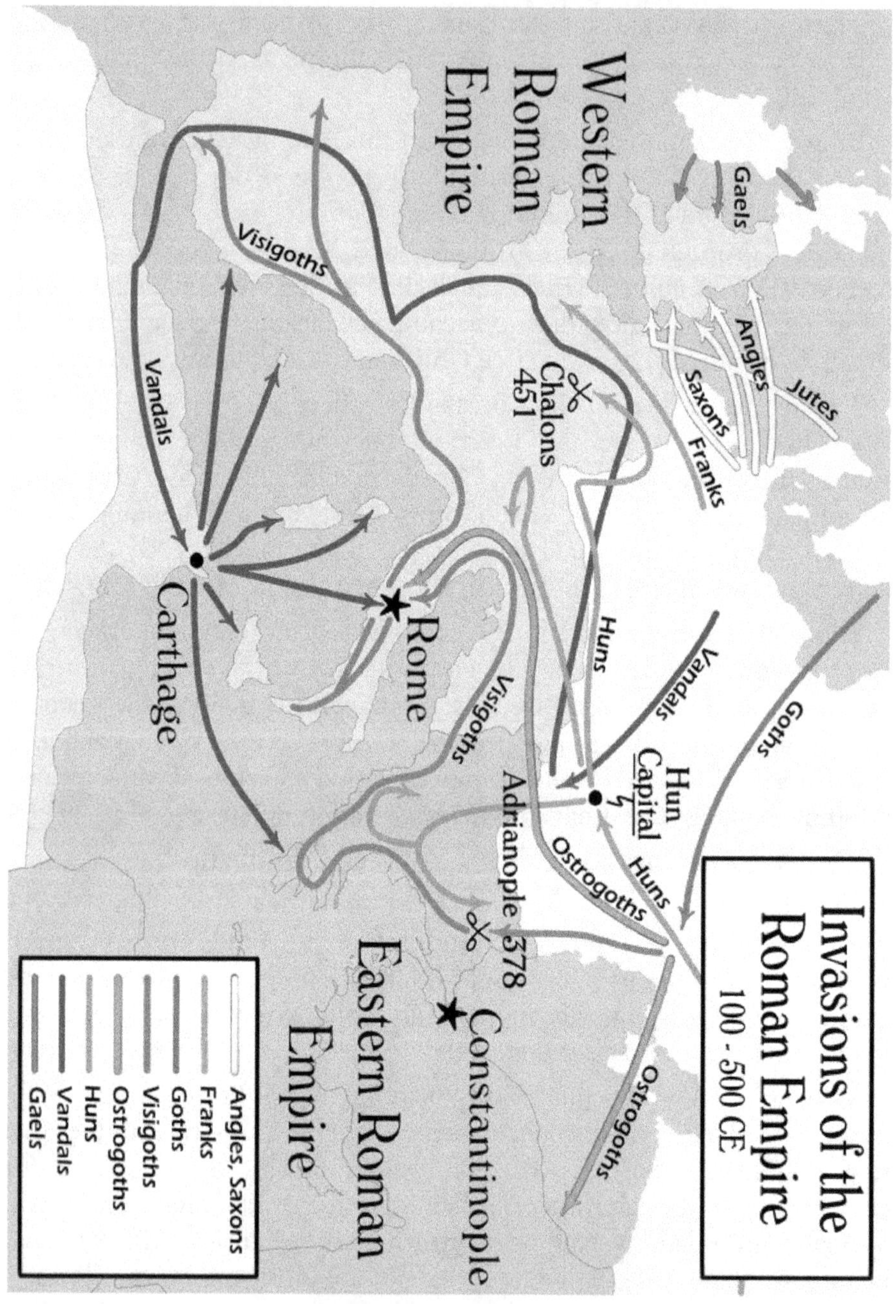

Invasions of the Roman Empire.[102]

Rome's weakness was obvious. The Crisis of the Third Century had shown that Rome could be defeated. Germanic tribes knew that Rome was vulnerable and that the empire's wealth was attractive. Why live in Germania's forests when you could settle in Gaul with its cities, roads, and villas?

However, the immediate trigger was the Huns.

The Huns were a nomadic confederation from the Eurasian Steppe who swept into Europe in the 370s CE. They were formidable warriors. These skilled horsemen used composite bows from horseback with devastating effect. Roman sources describe them as living on horseback and eating raw meat, things that were utterly alien to Roman culture. Modern historians realize these descriptions were stereotypes and exaggerated, but the Huns were certainly militarily effective. They conquered or displaced Germanic tribes in their path, creating a domino effect. Tribes along the Danube and in Ukraine suddenly needed to move—and quickly.

The Huns weren't trying to conquer Rome initially. They were pushing westward, conquering and incorporating Germanic tribes into their confederation, extracting tribute, and building what would become a nomadic empire under Attila in the 440s. But their movement displaced everyone else. Germanic tribes that had been Rome's neighbors for centuries suddenly became desperate refugees seeking safety within Roman borders.

The result was that multiple Germanic peoples appeared at Rome's frontiers in the late 4th and 5th centuries, asking for asylum, demanding land, or simply forcing their way across. The empire faced an unprecedented challenge: how to manage the mass migration of armed populations while defending against other threats.

The Goths provide the clearest example. In 376, a large group of Goths appeared at the Danube frontier asking for asylum. Ancient sources suggest there were perhaps 200,000 people. They were fleeing the Huns and wanted to settle peacefully in Roman territory. Emperor Valens agreed, seeing an opportunity to gain taxpayers and soldiers.

But Roman officials exploited and mistreated the Gothic refugees. They were charged exorbitant prices for food. Their weapons were supposed to be confiscated, although they often weren't. They were settled in inadequate areas. The Goths grew desperate and angry.

In 378, the Goths rebelled. Emperor Valens marched from Constantinople with an army to suppress them. The two forces met at Adrianople (modern Edirne in Turkey) on August 9th, 378 CE.

The Battle of Adrianople was a catastrophe for Rome. Valens's army was destroyed—perhaps two-thirds were killed, possibly twenty thousand men. Valens himself died in the battle, though accounts vary about how.

This was shocking. Roman armies had lost battles before, but this was different. The Goths weren't trying to raid and leave; they were settled in Roman territory and had destroyed an imperial army. The empire couldn't expel or control them. The Goths were now a permanent presence inside the empire, a semi-autonomous people who acknowledged Roman authority nominally but acted independently.

Theodosius I eventually made peace with the Goths in 382, granting them lands in the Balkans in exchange for military service. This seemed like a solution, but it created a precedent. Barbarian peoples could settle inside the empire, maintain their own leadership and identity, and provide soldiers rather than being assimilated into Roman culture.

Over the next decades, more Germanic peoples entered the empire: Vandals, Burgundians, Alans, and Suevi, among others. Some entered peacefully as *foederati* (federated allies), settling in specific areas and providing troops in exchange for land. Others entered violently, fighting Roman armies and carving out territories.

The Western Empire was becoming a patchwork of barbarian-settled regions nominally under Roman authority but practically autonomous. Roman emperors increasingly relied on barbarian generals and troops. Many top military positions were held by men of Germanic origin. The line between "Roman" and "barbarian" was blurring.

410 CE: The Sack of Rome—When the Unthinkable Happened

Then came the psychological shock that told everyone the empire was dying: Rome was sacked.

The Visigoths (Western Goths) had settled in the Balkans after 382, providing soldiers for Rome. But they were mistreated, underpaid, and exploited by Roman officials. Their leader, Alaric, demanded better treatment, fair pay, and a proper place in the Roman hierarchy. When the Western Roman government refused, Alaric marched his army into Italy.

The Western Emperor Honorius had moved the capital from Rome to Ravenna, a city on Italy's northeast coast surrounded by marshes. It was easier to defend than Rome. Honorius stayed safe in Ravenna while Alaric besieged Rome three times between 408 and 410.

The third siege succeeded. On August 24th, 410, Alaric's forces entered Rome. What followed was three days of looting, destruction, and violence. However, it was relatively restrained by ancient standards. Alaric was a Christian and ordered his troops not to harm people seeking refuge in churches or to burn the city. Most of Rome's population survived. Still, the symbolism was devastating.

The Sack of Rome in 410 by the Vandals by Joseph-Noël Sylvestre.[108]

Rome hadn't been captured by foreign enemies in eight hundred years, not since the Gauls had sacked it in 390 BCE. Rome was supposed to be eternal and protected by the gods. If Rome could fall, nothing was safe.

The psychological impact was profound. Saint Jerome, writing from Bethlehem, said, "The city which had taken the whole world was itself taken." Saint Augustine began writing *The City of God* partly to address the question. If Rome was Christian and protected by God, why did God allow Rome to be sacked?

The sack didn't destroy Rome or end the empire. Alaric withdrew from Rome after three days; he didn't want to rule it, just to pressure the imperial government. He died later that year. The Western Roman Empire continued. Life went on.

The Long Decline: How the West Slowly Stopped Being Roman

After 410 CE, the Western Empire entered a slow decline. It wasn't dramatic. There was no final catastrophic battle. Instead, the empire gradually lost control over its territories as Germanic kingdoms established themselves on former Roman lands.

Real power in the Western Empire increasingly belonged to military strongmen, usually of Germanic origin. Flavius Aetius, a Roman general, defended what remained of the empire in the 430s and 440s, defeating Attila the Hun's invasion of Gaul in 451 at the Battle of the Catalaunian Plains (with help from Gothic and Frankish allies). But Aetius was murdered in 454 by Emperor Valentinian III, who was then murdered in 455 by Aetius's supporters. The cycle of violence and instability continued.

The Western emperors became increasingly irrelevant. They were proclaimed by military strongmen, recognized or ignored by Constantinople, and held little actual power. Real authority belonged to Germanic generals who commanded the armies, such as Ricimer, Gundobad, and Odoacer.

These Germanic kingdoms didn't destroy the Roman civilization. They tried to preserve it. Germanic kings wanted to rule as Romans did, using Roman law, administration, and legitimacy. They saw themselves as part of the Roman world, not destroyers of it.

In Britain, Roman legions withdrew around 410 to defend more critical areas, particularly Gaul and Italy. Britain was left to defend itself against raiders from Ireland, Scotland, and Germania. The Romano-

British population tried to maintain Roman civilization, but without imperial support, Roman institutions gradually collapsed. Within decades, Anglo-Saxon invaders from northern Germany and Denmark were conquering and settling Britain. Unlike other Germanic groups, the Anglo-Saxons largely displaced Romano-British culture rather than assimilating into it. Roman cities were abandoned, villa estates fell into ruin, and Latin ceased to be spoken except by the clergy. By 450, Britain was transitioning from Roman to Anglo-Saxon, though Romano-British culture persisted in Wales, Cornwall, and other western areas. The memory of Roman Britain would later inspire the Arthurian legends—stories of a lost golden age when Britain was civilized and unified.

The situation in Gaul was very different. The Visigoths settled in southwestern Gaul (modern Aquitaine and southern France) after leaving Italy in 412 CE, establishing a kingdom centered in Toulouse. The Burgundians settled in southeastern Gaul (roughly modern Burgundy). The Franks gradually conquered northern Gaul from their base in what's now Belgium and northern France. These Germanic kingdoms maintained Roman structures. Visigothic kings issued laws in Latin based on Roman legal principles; for example, the Visigothic Code combined Germanic customs with Roman law. They employed Roman administrators who knew how to collect taxes and run the government. They preserved cities, though these were not as large as they had been. Latin remained the language of government, law, and religion, though Germanic languages were spoken by the ruling elite.

The Frankish Kingdom under the Merovingian dynasty would prove especially successful. When Clovis, King of the Franks, converted to Catholic Christianity (rather than Arian Christianity that most Germanic tribes practiced) around 496, he gained the support of the Roman Catholic Church and the Gallo-Roman population. The Franks would eventually unite most of Gaul under their rule, preserving Roman law, Latin language, and Christian culture while adding Germanic elements. Frankish Gaul would evolve into medieval France; the name "France" derives from "Franks."

The Visigoths moved from Gaul to Spain in the 470s after being pushed out by the Franks. They established a kingdom centered in Toledo that would last until the Muslim conquest in 711. The Visigothic Kingdom of Spain was highly Romanized. Laws were based on Roman codes, administration followed Roman models, the population remained largely Latin-speaking, and the kings saw themselves as successors to

Roman authority. The Visigoths were a small minority ruling a larger Roman population, so assimilation to Roman culture was a necessity.

In North Africa, the Vandals, led by King Gaiseric, crossed from Spain to North Africa in 429. By 439, they had captured Carthage, one of the empire's most important cities and the center of North Africa's agricultural production. The loss of Africa was economically catastrophic for the Western Empire, as Italy depended heavily on African grain. Without African grain shipments, feeding Italy became a problem that the Western government couldn't solve.

The Vandals established a maritime kingdom based on Carthage's naval power. They built a fleet and raided throughout the Mediterranean. In 455, a Vandal fleet sailed to Rome and sacked it more thoroughly than Alaric's Visigoths had in 410, though still without massive slaughter. The Vandals ruled North Africa using Roman administrative systems, collected taxes as Romans had, and maintained the agricultural estates that produced grain and olive oil.

Italy itself remained nominally under Western Roman control until 476, but real power lay with Germanic generals who commanded the armies. Odoacer, who deposed the last Western emperor, governed Italy as "King of Italy" using entirely Roman systems. He maintained the Senate, Roman law, tax collection, and administration. For the Roman population of Italy, Odoacer's rule didn't feel dramatically different from having a weak Roman emperor, which was what they'd had for decades anyway.

In 493, the Ostrogoths (Eastern Goths) under Theodoric conquered Italy. Theodoric ruled as king of Italy from 493 to 526, and his reign was remarkably successful. He preserved Roman institutions, employed Roman senators in government, patronized Roman culture, and saw himself as continuing the Roman imperial tradition. Theodoric's court at Ravenna patronized scholars, preserved Latin literature, and maintained classical education. The Roman population viewed Theodoric as a legitimate ruler, and his kingdom was stable and prosperous.

By 500 CE, the Western Roman Empire no longer existed as a political entity. However, former Roman territories were ruled by Germanic kingdoms that preserved Roman law, the Latin language, Christianity, and much of Roman civilization.

476 CE: The End That Wasn't Really an End

In 475 CE, a general named Orestes made his young son emperor. The boy's name was Romulus Augustulus, ironically named after Rome's legendary founder, Romulus, and its first emperor, Augustus. He was between twelve and sixteen years old.

Romulus Augustulus had no real power. He was a puppet emperor installed by his father. He ruled from Ravenna, not Rome. He controlled barely any territory beyond Italy. He was emperor in name only.

In 476, Germanic soldiers in Italy demanded land. When Orestes refused, the soldiers mutinied. They proclaimed their commander, Odoacer, as king. Odoacer's forces captured Ravenna, and Orestes was executed. Romulus Augustulus was deposed.

But Odoacer didn't proclaim himself emperor. He didn't need to. Instead, he sent the imperial regalia—the crown, purple robes, and other symbols of the imperial office—to Constantinople. He informed Emperor Zeno that the West didn't need its own emperor. The Eastern emperor could rule the whole empire in theory. Odoacer would govern Italy as his representative, holding the title "King of Italy."

Zeno accepted this arrangement, though he also recognized Julius Nepos (a previous Western emperor living in exile) as the legitimate Western emperor. When Nepos died in 480, Zeno didn't appoint a replacement. The Western Roman Empire had ended, not through dramatic conquest but through administrative adjustment.

This is why 476 CE is traditionally marked as the "fall of Rome." The last Western emperor had been deposed. The Western imperial office ceased to exist. However, nothing dramatic happened on the ground. The city of Rome continued to stand.

For most people in Italy, daily life didn't change. They had a king instead of an emperor, but he governed through existing institutions. They still paid taxes, still went to church, and still spoke Latin. Rome had "fallen," but most Romans barely noticed.

What Caused the Fall? (Every Historian Has a Theory)

Historians have been arguing about why Rome fell for over 1,500 years. Edward Gibbon's *The Decline and Fall of the Roman Empire* (1776-1789) blamed Christianity for sapping Roman military virtue. Other theories have blamed:

- Barbarian invasions
- Economic decline
- Moral decay
- Government corruption
- Military weakness
- Division of the empire
- Loss of civic virtue
- Climate change
- Plague
- Currency debasement
- Overextension
- Bad emperors
- Christianity (for weakening traditional values)
- Paganism (for angering the Christian God)

Modern historians believe the fall was caused by many interacting factors rather than one single thing.

Economically, the Western Roman Empire was weaker than the East. It had fewer wealthy cities, less developed trade, and a more vulnerable tax base. When territories were lost to Germanic kingdoms, tax revenue collapsed. The government couldn't afford to pay soldiers. Unpaid soldiers became unreliable or rebelled.

Militarily, the army became increasingly composed of barbarian foederati whose loyalty lay with their tribal leaders, not with Rome. When conflicts arose, these troops often fought for barbarian interests rather than Roman ones. The empire depended on barbarians to defend against other barbarians, which was an unstable situation.

Politically, the Western government lacked legitimacy and effectiveness. Emperors were frequently children controlled by generals. Real power belonged to military strongmen. The government couldn't command loyalty or enforce its will. Political fragmentation was severe.

Demographically, plague and warfare had reduced the empire's population. Fewer people meant fewer taxpayers and fewer potential soldiers. Some regions never recovered their pre-crisis populations.

Geopolitically, the West faced greater external pressure than the East. Germanic migrations affected the Rhine and Danube frontiers, the West's borders. The East faced Persian threats but managed them better and could use diplomacy and gold to deflect barbarian pressure toward the West.

Some historians argue we shouldn't call it a "fall" at all. The Western Empire transformed into Germanic kingdoms that preserved Roman law, Christianity, the Latin language (evolving into Romance languages), and many Roman institutions. Roman civilization didn't end; it evolved into medieval European civilization.

The truth is, Rome probably fell because empires fall. All political structures are temporary. Rome lasted longer than most—over one thousand years from the republic to the fall of the West and over two thousand years if you count the Byzantine Empire. That's an extraordinary run. What's remarkable isn't that Rome fell, but that it lasted so long.

The Byzantine Survivor: Why the East Lived On

While the West fragmented into Germanic kingdoms, the Eastern Roman Empire thrived. Why?

The East was simply wealthier. Cities like Constantinople, Alexandria, Antioch, and Ephesus were major economic centers. Trade routes connected the East to Asia, bringing in spices, silk, and luxury goods. Tax revenues were higher and more reliable. Geography helped too; Constantinople was nearly impregnable, surrounded by water with massive land walls. The Danube frontier was shorter and easier to defend than the Rhine-Danube line the West had to protect.

Eastern emperors were masterful diplomats. They played barbarian tribes against each other, paid to redirect barbarian attacks toward the West, and used marriage alliances, religious conversion, and political manipulation to manage threats without always fighting. The Eastern government remained functional in ways the West's didn't. It could collect taxes, pay soldiers, maintain infrastructure, and enforce laws. The bureaucracy worked. This sounds basic, but it's important—states survive when their governments can govern.

The Eastern army remained professional, well paid, and loyal. It could defend frontiers, suppress rebellions, and respond to crises. Unlike the West, the East didn't rely heavily on barbarian foederati whose loyalty was questionable. The East was also more culturally unified.

Greek was the common language of administration, commerce, and culture, though many local languages persisted. Orthodox Christianity provided religious unity and cultural identity. There was a sense of shared identity as Romans (*Romaioi* in Greek), even as the empire became increasingly Greek in language and culture while preserving Roman political and legal traditions.

The Byzantine Empire would face enormous challenges over the next millennium, but it would repeatedly demonstrate remarkable resilience. Emperor Justinian I (r. 527–565 CE) temporarily reconquered much of the former Western Empire. His general Belisarius defeated the Vandals in North Africa (533–534 CE) and conquered the Ostrogothic Kingdom in Italy (535–554 CE), though the Italian conquest was devastating and took twenty years of brutal warfare. Justinian's forces also reconquered parts of southern Spain.

For a brief period, the Mediterranean was Roman again. But Justinian's reconquests were expensive and temporary. The empire couldn't hold these western territories permanently. After Justinian's death, the Lombards invaded Italy in 568, conquering much of it and leaving Byzantium with only scattered holdings. The effort to reconquer the West had stretched Byzantine resources dangerously thin.

Justinian's more lasting achievement was codifying Roman law. The *Corpus Juris Civilis* (Body of Civil Law) systematized centuries of Roman legal tradition. It remains the foundation of civil-law systems throughout Europe and Latin America today. Justinian also built the magnificent Hagia Sophia in Constantinople, an architectural marvel with its massive dome that seemed to float on light. It stood as Christendom's greatest church for nine hundred years.

In the 6th and 7th centuries, Byzantium fought endless wars with the Sasanian Persian Empire. These conflicts drained both empires' resources in wars of attrition that neither could definitively win. The Byzantine-Persian Wars reached their climax between 602 and 628 CE, when the Persians conquered Syria, Palestine, Egypt, and parts of Anatolia. These devastating losses seemed to herald Byzantium's end. But Emperor Heraclius (r. 610–641 CE) fought back, defeated the Persians, and recovered the lost territories by 628.

Both Byzantium and Persia were exhausted by their long wars. Then a new force emerged: Islam. Arab armies erupted from Arabia in the 630s, conquering with stunning speed. By 650, the Arabs had conquered Syria,

Palestine, Egypt, Mesopotamia, and Persia. The Byzantine Empire lost its wealthiest provinces. The loss of Egypt was particularly devastating economically. But Byzantium survived. Constantinople's walls held against multiple Arab sieges, most famously in 678 CE and 718. Byzantine forces used Greek fire, an incendiary weapon whose exact composition remains unknown, to destroy Arab fleets. The empire contracted to Anatolia, the Balkans, and scattered holdings, but the core survived and eventually stabilized.

Under the Macedonian dynasty in the 9th through 11th centuries, Byzantium experienced a cultural and military revival. Byzantine forces reconquered territories from the Arabs. The economy recovered. Constantinople became one of the world's greatest cities. It had perhaps 400,000 inhabitants and was wealthy, sophisticated, and a center of trade between Asia and Europe. Byzantine culture flourished. This was Byzantium's golden age. It was Christianity's strongest defender and Mediterranean civilization's greatest power.

Byzantium's decline came not from Muslims but from fellow Christians. The Fourth Crusade, intended to fight Muslims in Egypt, instead attacked Constantinople in 1204. Crusaders sacked the city, massacring civilians, looting treasures, and destroying irreplaceable manuscripts and art. They established the Latin Empire of Constantinople while Byzantine refugees established competing states. Byzantine forces recaptured Constantinople in 1261 under Michael VIII Palaiologos, but the empire was shattered. It never recovered its former strength. Over the next two centuries, the Ottoman Turks conquered Byzantine territories piece by piece.

By the 1450s, the Byzantine Empire consisted of little more than Constantinople and its immediate surroundings. Sultan Mehmed II of the Ottoman Empire besieged Constantinople in April 1453 with a huge army and massive cannons capable of breaching the ancient walls. After nearly two months, on May 29th, 1453, Ottoman forces breached the walls and took the city. Emperor Constantine XI died fighting in the streets. The Byzantine Empire ended.

The Byzantine Empire had lasted over one thousand years from Constantine's founding of Constantinople to its fall to the Ottomans. During that millennium, it preserved Roman law, Greek philosophy, and Christian theology. It served as a buffer protecting Europe from successive waves of invaders. It spread classical learning to medieval Europe and the Islamic world. When Constantinople fell, Byzantine scholars fled to Italy, bringing manuscripts and knowledge that helped spark the Renaissance.

The Byzantine Empire was the Roman Empire. Its citizens called themselves Romans (*Romaioi* in Greek). Its emperors claimed to be the legitimate successors of Augustus. Its laws were based on Justinian's codification of Roman law. When it finally fell in 1453, the Roman Empire truly ended.

Conclusion:
The Eternal City

We started this journey in 753 BCE, with Romulus drawing a plow around Palatine Hill. We watched Rome grow from a village into a republic, transform into an empire ruling lands from Britain to Mesopotamia, survive catastrophic crises, and finally—slowly, messily— transform into the medieval world.

Did Rome fall? Yes and no.

The Western Empire collapsed in the 5th century CE. The Eastern Empire survived another thousand years, until 1453. But Rome's legacy never died.

What Rome Left Behind

Modern legal systems throughout Europe, Latin America, and much of the world are based on Roman law. Concepts like contracts, property rights, legal procedure, and civil law all trace back to Rome. Latin did not die; it evolved into French, Spanish, Italian, Portuguese, and Romanian. English, though Germanic, borrowed thousands of Latin words. Latin still appears in legal, medical, and scientific terminology.

The religion Rome adopted shaped Western civilization for nearly two thousand years. The organizational structure of the Catholic Church mirrors that of the Roman imperial administration. The alliance between church and state that Constantine forged influenced medieval and modern politics. Roman roads still serve as foundations for modern highways. Roman engineering principles—the arch, the vault, and concrete—influenced architecture for centuries. Aqueducts, bridges, and buildings that the Romans built still stand.

The idea of a universal empire ruling diverse peoples under a common law endured long after Rome's political power faded. The Holy Roman Empire, the Russian concept of a "Third Rome," and even modern global powers have been compared to Rome. Roman writers, such as Cicero, Virgil, Ovid, Seneca, and Marcus Aurelius, shaped Western literature and thought. Renaissance humanists looked to Rome for models of eloquence and virtue. Enlightenment thinkers drew on Roman republican ideals. Rome pioneered the idea that citizenship was a legal status with defined rights and obligations, separate from ethnicity or birthplace; this revolutionary concept influenced modern ideas of citizenship and democracy.

When we say "Western civilization," what we mostly refer to is Roman civilization that has been transformed through the centuries.

What We Can Learn from Rome's Rise and Fall

Rome lasted over a thousand years, from the Roman Republic's establishment to the Western Empire's end—or more than two thousand years if Byzantium is included. By any measure, that was extraordinary. What made Rome successful, and what finally brought it down?

Rome's success came from pragmatism over ideology. Rome adapted constantly, borrowing from Greeks, Etruscans, and Carthaginians. It granted citizenship to former enemies and assimilated conquered peoples rather than merely exploiting them. Flexibility kept Rome relevant as circumstances changed.

Rome survived bad emperors when its institutions—the army, the bureaucracy, and the legal system—functioned independently. Good systems can withstand poor leadership, at least temporarily. Roads, aqueducts, and ports were not just engineering feats; they made an empire possible. Moving armies, goods, and ideas quickly created economic and political integration.

But Rome's failures are equally instructive. Rome conquered more territory than it could sustainably govern or defend. The frontiers became indefensible, resources were stretched too thin, and size became a liability. The gap between the rich and the poor destroyed the republic. When wealth was concentrated in a few hands, when the middle class disappeared, and when the masses depended on handouts, stability collapsed. Economic inequality bred political instability.

When Rome relied on barbarian soldiers to defend against barbarians, when generals became kingmakers, and when armies murdered emperors for better pay, military force replaced legitimacy. Once violence became the path to power, violence became constant. When governments inflated currency to pay their bills, they destroyed economic trust. Rome's 3rd-century hyperinflation devastated the economy and took generations to recover.

These are not just ancient problems. Modern societies face similar questions. How do you govern complex, diverse populations? How do you balance security and freedom? How do you prevent inequality from destroying political stability? How do you maintain institutions when individuals seek power? How do you know when you have overextended?

Rome had no easy answers. Neither do we.

The Final Word

Rome was brutal and brilliant, generous and cruel, sophisticated and savage. It was built on slavery and conquest, but also on law and engineering. It gave us philosophy, gladiatorial combat, aqueducts, and crucifixions.

Rome was never one thing. It was a republic and an empire, pagan and Christian, Italian and multicultural. It conquered through violence and won loyalty through citizenship. It collapsed in the West and endured in the East, or perhaps it simply transformed into something new.

Understanding Rome means understanding contradiction—how the same civilization produced both *Meditations* and bloodsports, both sophisticated law and casual brutality.

But most importantly, understanding Rome means understanding that we are still shaped by it. Our institutions, our languages, our laws, and our cities are all Roman inheritances. When we struggle with how to govern diverse populations, balance security and freedom, or create lasting institutions, we face the same challenges Rome faced.

Rome taught us that empires are temporary but that ideas endure. Rome's political power ended long ago, but Roman law, language, architecture, and political concepts still shape the world. What matters is not how long power lasts, but what it leaves behind.

Rome's story is not just about the past. It is about us.

Here's another book by Matt Clayton that you might like

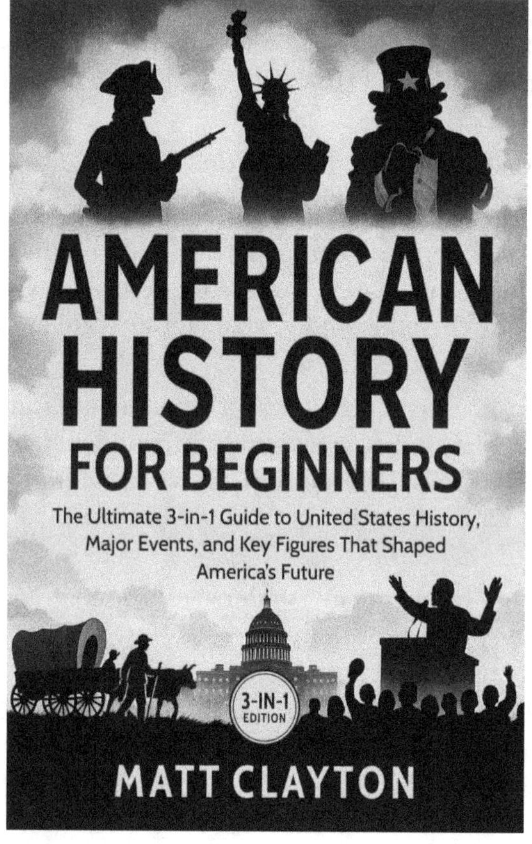

Free Bonus from Captivating History
(Available for a Limited time)

Hi History Lovers!

Now you have a chance to join our exclusive history list so you can get your first history ebook for free as well as discounts and a potential to get more history books for free!

Simply visit the link below to join.

Or, Scan the QR code!

captivatinghistory.com/ebook

Also, make sure to follow us on Facebook, X, and YouTube by searching for Captivating History.

References

Part 1: Ancient Egypt for Beginners

Assmann, Jan. *Death and Salvation in Ancient Egypt. Translated by David Lorton.* Ithaca: Cornell University Press, 2005.

Bard, Kathryn A. *An Introduction to the Archaeology of Ancient Egypt. 2nd ed.* Oxford: Wiley-Blackwell, 2015.

Cline, Eric H., and David O'Connor, eds. *Thutmose III: A New Biography.* Ann Arbor: University of Michigan Press, 2006.

Grajetzki, Wolfram. *The Middle Kingdom of Ancient Egypt: History, Archaeology and Society.* London: Duckworth, 2006.

Hornung, Erik. *Akhenaten and the Religion of Light. Translated by David Lorton.* Ithaca: Cornell University Press, 1999.

Ikram, Salima. *Death and Burial in Ancient Egypt.* London: Longman, 2003.

Kitchen, Kenneth A. *Pharaoh Triumphant: The Life and Times of Ramesses II, King of Egypt.* Warminster: Aris & Phillips, 1982.

Kemp, Barry J. *Ancient Egypt: Anatomy of a Civilization.* 3rd ed. London: Routledge, 2018.

Lehner, Mark. *The Complete Pyramids.* London: Thames & Hudson, 1997.

Midant-Reynes, Béatrix. *The Prehistory of Egypt: From the First Egyptians to the First Pharaohs.* Translated by Ian Shaw. Oxford: Blackwell Publishers, 2000.

Moran, William L., ed. *The Amarna Letters.* Baltimore: Johns Hopkins University Press, 1992.

Morkot, Robert G. *The Black Pharaohs: Egypt's Nubian Rulers.* London: Rubicon Press, 2000.

Morris, Ellen. *The Architecture of Imperialism: Military Bases and the Evolution of Foreign Policy in Egypt's New Kingdom.* Leiden: Brill, 2005.

O'Connor, David, and Eric H. Cline, eds. *Amenhotep III: Perspectives on His Reign.* Ann Arbor: University of Michigan Press, 1998.

Parkinson, R. B. *The Tale of Sinuhe and Other Ancient Egyptian Poems, 1940–1640 BC.* Oxford: Oxford University Press, 1997.

Quirke, Stephen. *The Administration of Egypt in the Late Middle Kingdom.* New Malden: SIA Publishing, 1990.

Shaw, Ian, ed. *The Oxford History of Ancient Egypt.* Oxford: Oxford University Press, 2000.

Taylor, John H. *Death and the Afterlife in Ancient Egypt.* London: British Museum Press, 2001.

Wilkinson, Richard H. *The Complete Gods and Goddesses of Ancient Egypt.* London: Thames & Hudson, 2003.

Wilkinson, Toby A. H. *Early Dynastic Egypt.* London: Routledge, 1999.

Part 2: Ancient Greece for Beginners

Cartledge, Paul. *Ancient Greek Political Thought in Practice.* Cambridge: Cambridge University Press, 2009.

Cartledge, Paul. *The Greeks: A Portrait of Self and Others.* 2nd ed. Oxford: Oxford University Press, 2002.

Dickinson, Oliver. *The Aegean Bronze Age.* Cambridge: Cambridge University Press, 1994.

Dickinson, Oliver. *The Aegean from Bronze Age to Iron Age.* London: Routledge, 2006.

Martin, Thomas R. *Ancient Greece: From Prehistoric to Hellenistic Times.* 2nd ed. New Haven: Yale University Press, 2013.

Morris, Ian, and Barry B. Powell, eds. *A New Companion to Homer.* Leiden: Brill, 1997.

Osborne, Robin. *Greece in the Making, 1200–479 BC.* 2nd ed. London: Routledge, 2009.

Pomeroy, Sarah B., Stanley M. Burstein, Walter Donlan, and Jennifer Tolbert Roberts. *Ancient Greece: A Political, Social, and Cultural History.* 3rd ed. New York: Oxford University Press, 2012.

Strauss, Barry. *The Battle of Salamis: The Naval Encounter That Saved Greece—and Western Civilization.* New York: Simon & Schuster, 2004.

Lazenby, J. F. *The Defence of Greece, 490–479 B.C.* Warminster: Aris & Phillips, 1993.

Part 3: Ancient Rome for Beginners

Beard, Mary. *SPQR: A History of Ancient Rome.* New York: Liveright Publishing, 2015.

Caesar, Julius. *The Gallic War.* Translated by Carolyn Hammond. Oxford: Oxford University Press, 1996.

Cornell, T. J. *The Beginnings of Rome: Italy and Rome from the Bronze Age to the Punic Wars (c. 1000–264 BC).* London: Routledge, 1995.

Eck, Werner. *The Age of Augustus.* 2nd ed. Translated by Deborah Lucas Schneider. Oxford: Blackwell, 2007.

Everitt, Anthony. *Augustus: The Life of Rome's First Emperor.* New York: Random House, 2006.

Forsythe, Gary. *A Critical History of Early Rome: From Prehistory to the First Punic War.* Berkeley: University of California Press, 2005.

Garnsey, Peter, and Richard Saller. *The Roman Empire: Economy, Society and Culture.* 2nd ed. Oakland: University of California Press, 2014.

Gelzer, Matthias. *Caesar: Politician and Statesman.* Translated by Peter Needham. Cambridge, MA: Harvard University Press, 1968.

Goldsworthy, Adrian. *Augustus: First Emperor of Rome.* New Haven: Yale University Press, 2014.

Goldsworthy, Adrian. *Caesar: Life of a Colossus.* New Haven: Yale University Press, 2006.

Goldsworthy, Adrian. *The Complete Roman Army.* London: Thames & Hudson, 2003.

Goldsworthy, Adrian. *The Punic Wars.* London: Cassell, 2000.

Gruen, Erich S. "The Making of the Principate." In *The Cambridge Ancient History,* vol. 10, 2nd ed., 70–96. Cambridge: Cambridge University Press, 1996.

Halsall, Guy. *Barbarian Migrations and the Roman West, 376–568.* Cambridge: Cambridge University Press, 2007.

Heather, Peter. *The Fall of the Roman Empire: A New History of Rome and the Barbarians.* Oxford: Oxford University Press, 2006.

Hoyos, Dexter. *Mastering the West: Rome and Carthage at War.* Oxford: Oxford University Press, 2015.

Kulikowski, Michael. *Imperial Tragedy: From Constantine's Empire to the Destruction of Roman Italy, AD 363–568.* London: Profile Books, 2019.

Lancel, Serge. *Carthage: A History.* Translated by Antonia Nevill. Oxford: Blackwell, 1995.

Lazenby, J. F. *Hannibal's War: A Military History of the Second Punic War.* Norman: University of Oklahoma Press, 1998.

Livy. *The Early History of Rome (Books I–V of The History of Rome from Its Foundation)*. Translated by Aubrey de Sélincourt. London: Penguin Classics, 2002.

Livy. *The War with Hannibal (Books XXI–XXX of The History of Rome from Its Foundation)*. Translated by Aubrey de Sélincourt. London: Penguin Classics, 1972.

Meier, Christian. *Caesar: A Biography*. Translated by David McLintock. New York: Basic Books, 1995.

Millar, Fergus. *The Roman Republic in Political Thought*. Hanover, NH: University Press of New England, 2002.

Mitchell, Stephen. *A History of the Later Roman Empire, AD 284–641*. 2nd ed. Oxford: Wiley-Blackwell, 2015.

Osgood, Josiah. *Caesar's Legacy: Civil War and the Emergence of the Roman Empire*. Cambridge: Cambridge University Press, 2006.

Plutarch. *Life of Caesar*. In *Fall of the Roman Republic*. Translated by Rex Warner. London: Penguin Classics, 1972.

Polybius. *The Histories*. Translated by Robin Waterfield. Oxford: Oxford University Press, 2010.

Scullard, H. H. *Scipio Africanus: Soldier and Politician*. Ithaca, NY: Cornell University Press, 1970.

Smith, Christopher. *Early Rome and Latium: Economy and Society c. 1000 to 500 BC*. Oxford: Clarendon Press, 1996.

Southern, Pat. *Augustus*. 2nd ed. London: Routledge, 2014.

Strauss, Barry. *The Death of Caesar: The Story of History's Most Famous Assassination*. New York: Simon & Schuster, 2015.

Suetonius. *The Twelve Caesars*. Translated by Robert Graves. London: Penguin Classics, 2007.

Syme, Ronald. *The Roman Revolution*. Oxford: Oxford University Press, 1939.

Ward-Perkins, Bryan. *The Fall of Rome and the End of Civilization*. Oxford: Oxford University Press, 2005.

Wickham, Chris. *The Inheritance of Rome: Illuminating the Dark Ages, 400–1000*. New York: Penguin, 2009.

Image Sources

1   Jeff Dahl, CC BY-SA 4.0 <https://creativecommons.org/licenses/by-sa/4.0>, via Wikimedia Commons, https://commons.wikimedia.org /wiki/File:Ancient_Egypt_map-en.svg

2   H.Seldon, CC BY-SA 3.0 <http://creativecommons.org/licenses/by-sa/3.0/>, via Wikimedia Commons, https://commons.wikimedia.org/wiki/File:NaqadaI.svg

3   Metropolitan Museum of Art, CC0, via Wikimedia Commons, https://commons.wikimedia.org/wiki/File:Jar,_Late_Naqada_II,_3500-3300_BCE,_Egypt.jpg

4   Charles J. Sharp, CC BY-SA 3.0 <https://creativecommons.org/licenses/by-sa/3.0>, via Wikimedia Commons, https://commons.wikimedia.org/wiki/File:Saqqara_pyramid_ver_2.jpg

5   Ivrienen at English Wikipedia, CC BY 3.0 <https://creativecommons.org/licenses/by/3.0>, via Wikimedia Commons, https://commons.wikimedia.org/wiki/File:Snefru%27s_Bent_Pyramid_in_Dahshur.jpg

6   Olaf Tausch, CC BY 3.0 <https://creativecommons.org/licenses/by/3.0>, via Wikimedia Commons, https://commons.wikimedia.org/wiki/File:Rote_Pyramide_(Dahschur)_04.jpg

7   KennyOMG, CC BY-SA 4.0 <https://creativecommons.org/licenses/by-sa/4.0>, via Wikimedia Commons, https://commons.wikimedia.org/wiki/File:Pyramids_of_the_Giza_Necropolis.jpg

8   British Museum, CC BY-SA 3.0 <http://creativecommons.org/licenses/by-sa/3.0/>, via Wikimedia Commons, https://commons.wikimedia.org/wiki/File:ThreeStatuesOfSesotrisIII-RightProfiles-BritishMuseum-August19-08.jpg

9   https://www.metmuseum.org/art/collection/search/545728

10 Tim Evanson from Cleveland Heights, Ohio, USA, CC BY-SA 2.0
<https://creativecommons.org/licenses/by-sa/2.0>, via Wikimedia Commons,
https://commons.wikimedia.org/wiki/File:Ring_scarab_-_Pharaoh_exhibit_-
_Cleveland_Museum_of_Art_(cropped).jpg

11 https://commons.wikimedia.org/wiki/File:Sequenre_tao.JPG

12 Metropolitan Museum of Art, CC0, via Wikimedia Commons,
https://commons.wikimedia.org/wiki/File:Seated_Statue_of_Hatshepsut_MET_Hats
hepsut2012.jpg

13 Unknown author, CC BY-SA 2.5 <https://creativecommons.org/licenses/by-sa/2.5>,
via Wikimedia Commons, https://commons.wikimedia.org/wiki/File:Pa-
rehu,_the_Prince_of_Punt,_his_wife_and_his_two_sons,_and_a_daughter._(1902)_
-_TIMEA.jpg

14 Diego Delso, CC BY-SA 4.0 <https://creativecommons.org/licenses/by-sa/4.0>, via
Wikimedia Commons, https://commons.wikimedia.org/wiki/File:
Templo_funerario_de_Hatshepsut,_Luxor,_Egipto,_2022-04-03,_DD_13.jpg

15 https://commons.wikimedia.org/wiki/File:Thutmosis_III-2.jpg

16 Olaf Tausch, CC BY 3.0 <https://creativecommons.org/licenses/by/3.0>, via
Wikimedia Commons, https://commons.wikimedia.org/wiki/File:Kom_el-
Hettan_24.jpg

17 https://commons.wikimedia.org/wiki/File:Egyptian_-
_Commemorative_Scarab_of_Amenhotep_III_-_Walters_42206_-_Bottom.jpg

18 This file is licensed under the Creative Commons Attribution-Share Alike 2.5
Generic license, https://creativecommons.org/licenses/by-sa/2.5/deed.en.
https://commons.wikimedia.org/wiki/File:GD-EG-Caire-Mus%C3%A9e061.JPG

19 Osama Shukir Muhammed Amin FRCP(Glasg), CC BY-SA 4.0
<https://creativecommons.org/licenses/by-sa/4.0>, via Wikimedia Commons,
https://commons.wikimedia.org/wiki/File:Alabaster_sunken_relief_depicting_Akhen
aten,_Nefertiti,_and_daughter_Meritaten._Early_Aten_cartouches_on_king%27s_ar
m_and_chest._From_Amarna,_Egypt._18th_Dynasty._The_Petrie_Museum_of_Eg
yptian_Archaeology,_London.jpg

20 Neoclassicism Enthusiast, CC BY-SA 4.0 <https://creativecommons.org/licenses/by-
sa/4.0>, via Wikimedia Commons,
https://commons.wikimedia.org/wiki/File:Relief_depicting_Akhenaton_and_Nefertit
i_with_three_of_their_daughters_under_the_rays_of_Aton_01_(cropped).jpg

21 https://commons.wikimedia.org/wiki/File:CairoEgMuseumTaaMaskMostly
Photographed.jpg

22 https://commons.wikimedia.org/wiki/File:Anuk.PNG

23 Museo Egizio In Turin (IT), CC0, via Wikimedia Commons,
https://commons.wikimedia.org/wiki/File:Statue_of_king_Horemheb_with_the_god
_Amun.png

24 Philip Pikart, CC BY-SA 3.0 <https://creativecommons.org/licenses/by-sa/3.0>, via Wikimedia Commons, https://commons.wikimedia.org/wiki/File: Nofretete_Neues_Museum.jpg

25 Forever Egypt, CC BY-SA 4.0 <https://creativecommons.org/licenses/by-sa/4.0>, via Wikimedia Commons, https://commons.wikimedia.org/wiki/File: Temple_of_Sethi_I_03,_egypt_forever.jpg

26 Carole Raddato from Frankfurt, Germany, CC BY-SA 2.0 <https://creativecommons.org/licenses/by-sa/2.0>, via Wikimedia Commons, https://commons.wikimedia.org/wiki/File:KV17,_the_tomb_of_Pharaoh_Seti_I_of_ the_Nineteenth_Dynasty,_Valley_of_the_Kings,_Egypt_(49846343021).jpg

27 This file is licensed under the Creative Commons Attribution-Share Alike 3.0 Unported license, https://creativecommons.org/licenses/by-sa/3.0/deed.en. https://commons.wikimedia.org/wiki/File:Egypt_Abou_Simbel6.jpg

28 Roland Unger, CC BY-SA 3.0 <https://creativecommons.org/licenses/by-sa/3.0>, via Wikimedia Commons, https://commons.wikimedia.org/wiki/File: RamesseumPM10.jpg

29 youssef_alam, CC BY 3.0 <https://creativecommons.org/licenses/by/3.0>, via Wikimedia Commons, https://commons.wikimedia.org/wiki/File: Ramsis,_Aswan_Governorate,_Egypt_-_panoramio.jpg

30 https://commons.wikimedia.org/wiki/File:Abusimbel.jpg

31 Marc Ryckaert, CC BY-SA 4.0 <https://creativecommons.org/licenses/by-sa/4.0>, via Wikimedia Commons, https://commons.wikimedia.org/wiki/File: Karnak_Hypostyle_Hall_R05.jpg

32 Onceinawhile, CC BY-SA 4.0 <https://creativecommons.org/licenses/by-sa/4.0>, via Wikimedia Commons, https://commons.wikimedia.org/wiki/File: Tomb_of_Nefertari_2022_84.jpg

33 https://commons.wikimedia.org/wiki/File:Medinet_Habu_Ramses_III._ Tempel_Nordostwand_Abzeichnung_01.jpg

34 Original map: LommesAddition of Kushite heartland पाटलिपुत्र (talk) Source: National Geographic 2019, CC BY-SA 4.0 <https://creativecommons.org/licenses/by-sa/4.0>, via Wikimedia Commons, https://commons.wikimedia.org/wiki/File:Kushite_heartland_and_Kushite_Empire_ of_the_25th_dynasty_circa_700_BCE.jpg

35 https://commons.wikimedia.org/wiki/File:Taharqa,_Louvre_Museum.jpg

36 Photograph by Rama, Wikimedia Commons, Cc-by-sa-2.0-fr, CC BY-SA 2.0 FR <https://creativecommons.org/licenses/by-sa/2.0/fr/deed.en>, via Wikimedia Commons, https://commons.wikimedia.org/wiki/File:Head_of_Nectanebo_II- MBA_Lyon_H1701-IMG_0204.jpg

37 https://commons.wikimedia.org/wiki/File:Philip_Galle_- _Lighthouse_of_Alexandria_(Pharos_of_Alexandria)_-_1572.jpg

38 https://commons.wikimedia.org/wiki/File:Cleopatra_and_Caesar_by_Jean-Leon-Gerome.jpg

39 https://commons.wikimedia.org/wiki/File:Jean-Baptiste_Regnault_-_Death_of_Cleopatra_-_Google_Art_Project.jpg

40 https://commons.wikimedia.org/wiki/File:Kleopatra-VII.-Altes-Museum-Berlin1.jpg

41 Jeff Dahl, CC BY-SA 4.0 <https://creativecommons.org/licenses/by-sa/4.0>, via Wikimedia Commons, https://commons.wikimedia.org/wiki/File:Eye_of_Horus_bw.svg

42 Amice M.Calverley, Alan Gardiner, 1935, CC BY-SA 4.0 <https://creativecommons.org/licenses/by-sa/4.0>, via Wikimedia Commons, https://commons.wikimedia.org/wiki/File:Sethos2-Disrobing-Amen-Re.jpg

43 https://commons.wikimedia.org/wiki/File:27.1_Iaru.tif

44 Jon Bodsworth, Copyrighted free use, via Wikimedia Commons, https://commons.wikimedia.org/wiki/File:Mastaba-faraoun-3.jpg

45 Nikola Smolenski, CC BY-SA 3.0 RS <https://creativecommons.org/licenses/by-sa/3.0/rs/deed.en>, via Wikimedia Commons, https://commons.wikimedia.org/wiki/File:Valley_of_the_Kings_panorama.jpg

46 Diego Delso, CC BY-SA 4.0 <https://creativecommons.org/licenses/by-sa/4.0>, via Wikimedia Commons, https://commons.wikimedia.org/wiki/File:Deir_el-Medina,_Luxor,_Egipto,_2022-04-03,_DD_18.jpg

47 Bernard Gagnon, CC BY-SA 3.0 <https://creativecommons.org/licenses/by-sa/3.0>, via Wikimedia Commons, https://commons.wikimedia.org/wiki/File:Knossos_-_North_Portico_02.jpg

48 https://commons.wikimedia.org/wiki/File:Knossos_bull_leaping_fresco.jpg

49 User:Alexikoua, User:Panthera tigris tigris, TL User:Reedside, CC BY-SA 3.0 <https://creativecommons.org/licenses/by-sa/3.0>, via Wikimedia Commons, https://commons.wikimedia.org/wiki/File:Mycenaean_World_en.png

50 Joyofmuseums, CC BY-SA 4.0 <https://creativecommons.org/licenses/by-sa/4.0>, via Wikimedia Commons, https://commons.wikimedia.org/wiki/File:Lion_Gate_-_Mycenae_by_Joy_of_Museums.jpg

51 https://commons.wikimedia.org/wiki/File:Athens_%E2%80%94_Mask_of_Agamemnon.jpg

52 https://commons.wikimedia.org/wiki/File:Homer_British_Museum.jpg

53 https://commons.wikimedia.org/wiki/File:Apollon_Tempel_im_antiken_Korinth.jpg

54 Oblomov2, CC0, via Wikimedia Commons, https://commons.wikimedia.org/wiki/File:Vix_crater_hoplite_circa_500_BCE.jpg

55 Dipa1965, CC BY-SA 4.0 <https://creativecommons.org/licenses/by-sa/4.0>, via Wikimedia Commons, https://commons.wikimedia.org/wiki/File:Greek_Colonization_Archaic_Period.svg

56 Sailko, CC BY-SA 3.0 <https://creativecommons.org/licenses/by-sa/3.0>, via Wikimedia Commons, https://commons.wikimedia.org/wiki/File: Ignoto,_c.d._solone,_replica_del_90_dc_ca_da_orig._greco_del_110_ac._ca,_6143. JPG

57 User:Bibi Saint-Pol, CC BY-SA 3.0 <http://creativecommons.org/licenses/by-sa/3.0/>, via Wikimedia Commons, https://commons.wikimedia.org/wiki/File:Map_Greco-Persian_Wars-en.svg

58 https://commons.wikimedia.org/wiki/File:L%C3%A9onidas_aux_Thermopyles_-_Jacques-Louis_David_-_Mus%C3%A9e_du_Louvre_Peintures_INV_ 3690_;_L_3711.jpg

59 https://commons.wikimedia.org/wiki/File:Battle_of_Thermopylae_ and_movements_to_Salamis,_480_BC.gif

60 https://commons.wikimedia.org/wiki/File:Battle_of_salamis.png

61 https://commons.wikimedia.org/wiki/File:Spartans_at_Plataea.jpg

62 https://commons.wikimedia.org/wiki/File:Pericles_Pio-Clementino_Inv269_n2.jpg

63 Steve Swayne, CC BY 2.0 <https://creativecommons.org/licenses/by/2.0>, via Wikimedia Commons, https://commons.wikimedia.org/wiki/File: The_Parthenon_in_Athens.jpg

64 No machine-readable author provided. MatthiasKabel assumed (based on copyright claims)., CC BY-SA 3.0 <http://creativecommons.org/licenses/by-sa/3.0/>, via Wikimedia Commons, https://commons.wikimedia.org/wiki/File: Roman_bronze_copy_of_Myron%E2%80%99s_Discobolos,_2nd_century_CE_(Gl yptothek_Munich).jpg

65 Niko Kitsakis, CC BY 4.0 <https://creativecommons.org/licenses/by/4.0>, via Wikimedia Commons, https://commons.wikimedia.org/wiki/File: Varvakeion_Athena.jpg

66 No machine-readable author provided. Harrieta171 assumed (based on copyright claims)., CC BY-SA 3.0 <http://creativecommons.org/licenses/by-sa/3.0/>, via Wikimedia Commons, https://commons.wikimedia.org/wiki/File: Ath%C3%A8nes_Acropole_Caryatides.JPG

67 I, Abu America, CC BY-SA 3.0 <http://creativecommons.org/licenses/by-sa/3.0/>, via Wikimedia Commons, https://commons.wikimedia.org/wiki/File: Greece_alliances_431bc.jpg

68 https://commons.wikimedia.org/wiki/File:Herma_Demosthenes_ Glyptothek_Munich_292.jpg

69 https://commons.wikimedia.org/wiki/File:Pelopennesian_War,_ Walls_Protecting_the_City,_431_B.C..JPG

70 https://commons.wikimedia.org/wiki/File:Makedonische_phalanx.png

71 https://commons.wikimedia.org/wiki/File:Alexander_and_Bucephalus_-_Battle_of_Issus_mosaic_-_Museo_Archeologico_Nazionale_-_Naples_BW.jpg

72 Generic Mapping Tools, CC BY-SA 3.0 <http://creativecommons.org/licenses/by-sa/3.0/>, via Wikimedia Commons, https://commons.wikimedia.org/wiki/File:MacedonEmpire.jpg

73 Diadochen1.png: Captain_BloodDiadochi IT.svg: Luigi Chiesa (talk) This vector image includes elements that have been taken or adapted from this file: Battle icon gladii.svg.derivative work: Homo lupustranslator: Manlleus (ca), CC BY-SA 3.0 <https://creativecommons.org/licenses/by-sa/3.0>, via Wikimedia Commons, https://commons.wikimedia.org/wiki/File:Diadochi_LA.svg

74 https://commons.wikimedia.org/wiki/File:Jean-L%C3%A9on_G%C3%A9r%C3%B4me_-_Diogenes_-_Walters_37131.jpg

75 https://commons.wikimedia.org/wiki/File:Nike_of_Samothrake_Louvre_Ma2369_n4.jpg

76 Capitoline Museums, CC0, via Wikimedia Commons, https://commons.wikimedia.org/wiki/File:Lupa_Capitolina,_Rome.jpg

77 Renata3, CC BY-SA 4.0 <https://creativecommons.org/licenses/by-sa/4.0>, via Wikimedia Commons, https://commons.wikimedia.org/wiki/File:Seven_Hills_of_Rome.svg

78 Abduction of a Sabine Woman (1579–1583), by Giambologna, https://commons.wikimedia.org/wiki/File:Giambologna_sabine.jpg

79 BeBo86, CC BY-SA 3.0 <https://creativecommons.org/licenses/by-sa/3.0>, via Wikimedia Commons, https://commons.wikimedia.org/wiki/File:Forum_romanum_6k_(5760x2097).jpg

80 https://commons.wikimedia.org/wiki/File:Danseurs_et_musiciens,_tombe_des_l%C3%A9opards.jpg

81 Harrias, CC BY-SA 4.0 <https://creativecommons.org/licenses/by-sa/4.0>, via Wikimedia Commons, https://commons.wikimedia.org/wiki/File:First_Punic_War_264_BC_v3.png

82 William Robert Shepherd, CC BY-SA 4.0 <https://creativecommons.org/licenses/by-sa/4.0>, via Wikimedia Commons, https://commons.wikimedia.org/wiki/File:Map_of_Rome_and_Carthage_at_the_start_of_the_Second_Punic_War_Modified.svg

83 Harrias, CC BY 3.0 <https://creativecommons.org/licenses/by/3.0>, via Wikimedia Commons, https://commons.wikimedia.org/wiki/File:Publius_Scipio%27s_Invasion_of_Africa,_204%E2%80%93201_BC.png

84 Classical Numismatic Group, Inc. http://www.cngcoins.com, CC BY-SA 2.5 <https://creativecommons.org/licenses/by-sa/2.5>, via Wikimedia Commons, https://commons.wikimedia.org/wiki/File:Q._Pompeius_Rufus,_denarius,_54_BC,_RRC_434-1_(Sulla_only).jpg

85 https://commons.wikimedia.org/wiki/File:Landing_of_the_Romans_on_the__Coast_of_Kent.jpg

86 https://commons.wikimedia.org/wiki/File:Retrato_de_Julio_C%C3%A9sar_(
26724093101)_(cropped).jpg

87 Bust: unknown ancient Roman artist of the 1st century AD; photo: unknown
photographer., CC BY-SA 4.0 <https://creativecommons.org/licenses/by-sa/4.0>, via
Wikimedia Commons, https://commons.wikimedia.org/wiki/File:
Marble_bust_of_Mark_Antony_(Vatican_Museums).jpg

88 Vatican Museums, CC BY-SA 4.0 <https://creativecommons.org/licenses/by-sa/4.0>,
via Wikimedia Commons, https://commons.wikimedia.org/wiki/File:
Augustus_of_Prima_Porta_(inv._2290).jpg

89 https://commons.wikimedia.org/wiki/File:Cicero_Denounces_Catiline_
in_the_Roman_Senate_by_Cesare_Maccari.png

90 Carole Raddato from FRANKFURT, Germany, CC BY-SA 2.0
<https://creativecommons.org/licenses/by-sa/2.0>, via Wikimedia Commons,
https://commons.wikimedia.org/wiki/File:Vespasian,_from_Naples,_c._AD_70,_Ny
_Carlsberg_Glyptotek,_Copenhagen_(13646730625).jpg

91 FeaturedPics, CC BY-SA 4.0 <https://creativecommons.org/licenses/by-sa/4.0>, via
Wikimedia Commons, https://commons.wikimedia.org/wiki/File:
Colosseo_2020.jpg

92 TimeTravelRome, CC BY 2.0 <https://creativecommons.org/licenses/by/2.0>, via
Wikimedia Commons, https://commons.wikimedia.org/wiki/File:
Nennig_Roman_Villa_and_Mosaics_-_51134391753.jpg

93 https://commons.wikimedia.org/wiki/File:Appia_antica_2-7-05_048.jpg

94 Roberto Ferrari, CC BY-SA 2.0 <https://creativecommons.org/licenses/by-sa/2.0>,
via Wikimedia Commons, https://commons.wikimedia.org/wiki/File:
Pont_du_Gard_3.jpg

95 https://commons.wikimedia.org/wiki/File:Mercati_di_Traiano,_2013.jpg

96 Tataryn77, CC BY-SA 3.0 <https://creativecommons.org/licenses/by-sa/3.0>, via
Wikimedia Commons, https://commons.wikimedia.org/wiki/File:
RomanEmpireTrajan117AD.png

97 NormanEinstein. This file is licensed under the Creative Commons Attribution-
Share Alike 3.0 Unported license, https://creativecommons.org/licenses/by-
sa/3.0/deed.en, https://commons.wikimedia.org/wiki/File:Hadrians_Wall_map.png

98 Mohammad Reza Domiri Ganji, CC BY-SA 4.0
<https://creativecommons.org/licenses/by-sa/4.0>, via Wikimedia Commons,
https://commons.wikimedia.org/wiki/File:Rome-Pantheon.jpg

99 Capitoline Museums, CC BY 2.0 <https://creativecommons.org/licenses/by/2.0>, via
Wikimedia Commons,
https://commons.wikimedia.org/wiki/File:Septimius_Severus_busto-
Musei_Capitolini.jpg

100 Blank map of South Europe and North Africa.svg: historicair 23:27, 8 August 2007 (UTC), CC BY-SA 2.5 <https://creativecommons.org/licenses/by-sa/2.5>, via Wikimedia Commons, https://commons.wikimedia.org/wiki/File: Map_of_Ancient_Rome_271_AD.svg

101 https://commons.wikimedia.org/wiki/File:Celio_- _le_mura_tra_porta_san_Sebastiano_e_porta_Ardeatina_1974.JPG

102 User:MapMaster, CC BY-SA 2.5 <https://creativecommons.org/licenses/by-sa/2.5>, via Wikimedia Commons, https://commons.wikimedia.org/wiki/File:Invasions_of _the_Roman_Empire_1.png

103 https://commons.wikimedia.org/wiki/File:Sack_of_Rome_by_the_ Visigoths_on_24_August_410_by_JN_Sylvestre_1890.jpg